Hands-on Software Architecture

Soo Dong Kim • Mira Kim

Hands-on Software Architecture

Unified Architecture Process

Soo Dong Kim
School of Software
Soongsil University (Seoul, Korea)
Seoul, Korea (Republic of)

Mira Kim
Department of Computer Science
California State University - Fullerton
Fullerton, CA, USA

ISBN 978-3-032-01183-1 ISBN 978-3-032-01184-8 (eBook)
https://doi.org/10.1007/978-3-032-01184-8

This Springer imprint is published by the registered company Springer Nature Switzerland AG
The registered company address is: Gewerbestrasse 11, 6330 Cham, Switzerland

Preface

Welcome to a comprehensive and methodical journey into the understanding, design, documentation, and validation of software system architectures. This book introduces an integrated and in-depth methodology for designing software architecture, developed to address the inherent challenges and complexities of modern software systems.

It aims to provide readers with a structured foundation in software architecture, reinforced by a systematic design process and practical guidelines. By combining theoretical foundations with practical guidance, this book equips both students and practitioners to confidently design architectures that address functional and non-functional requirements.

Software Architecture

Software architecture defines the high-level structure of a software system, including its components, their interactions, behaviors, and the principles that guide its design and evolution. It serves as a strategic blueprint for system development and evolution, ensuring adherence to specified quality attributes and alignment with business objectives.

Software architecture plays a pivotal role in the development of complex systems. It is widely recognized as one of the most critical, sophisticated, and overarching design artifacts in software development—especially in the context of large-scale or high-assurance systems.

Challenges in Software Architecture Design

Designing software architecture for modern systems presents substantial technical challenges, driven by the following key factors:

- **Extensive and Fragmented Knowledge Base**
  The field of software architecture encompasses an expansive and complex body of knowledge, characterized by numerous technology elements and intricate interdependencies. Acquiring the essential technical expertise for designing software architecture is a challenging endeavor.

- **Limited Resources for Industrial Systems Architecture**
  Industrial software systems are characterized by high functional complexity and stringent quality requirements. While existing literature provides valuable insights, it offers limited coverage of systematic design processes and detailed design guidelines suited to the unique challenges of industrial software development.
- **Limited Availability of Best Practices**
  Best practices in software architecture consist of proven design and validation methods effective in specific system contexts. They reflect the collective expertise of seasoned practitioners and offer reusable, pragmatic guidance. However, comprehensive and empirically validated practices tailored to architectural design remain scarce.

As a result, software architecture is frequently designed in an ad hoc manner, relying predominantly on experiential heuristics with similar systems.

Our Approach to Addressing Challenges

To overcome these challenges, this book presents an integrated approach that combines methodological rigor with practical engagement. By uniting structured process models with direct experiential learning, it offers a balanced pathway for effectively designing software architecture in complex system environments.

This integrated approach is realized through two complementary dimensions:

- **Methodological approach**: *Software Architecture Methodology* refers to a systematic process comprising principles, practices, and techniques that guide the design of software architecture. By applying the methodology, high-level architecture designs can be produced efficiently while minimizing efforts.
- **Hands-on approach**: The *Hands-on Approach* emphasizes practical, experiential, and action-oriented engagement. It involves direct interaction with design tasks, templates, examples, and tools, fostering deeper understanding and enabling the effective application of architectural principles in real-world scenarios.

Unified Architecture Process

Central to this book is the *Unified Architecture Process*, a comprehensive methodology that synthesizes methodological rigor with hands-on applicability. It introduces a process model that encapsulates the full lifecycle of architecture design, supported by step-by-step instructions for each phase and activity.

This process has been developed and refined over nearly two decades through the authors' sustained academic research and its practical application in industrial settings. It has been taught to software engineers and project managers in leading IT organizations and successfully applied to the design of complex enterprise-scale systems.

The process framework is hierarchically structured into three tiers: *Activities*, *Steps*, and *Tasks*.

- **Activity**
  An activity in the process denotes a major phase within the architecture design process, each aligned with a specific design objective. The six activities defined within the process are shown below.

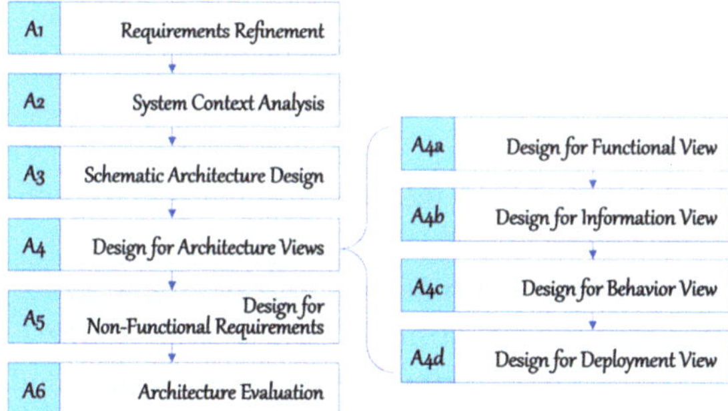

  - **A1. Requirements Refinement**
    This activity is to refine stakeholder and system-level requirements to form a solid foundation for architectural decisions.
  - **A2. System Context Analysis**
    This activity is to analyze the external environment, interfaces, and operational context of the system.
  - **A3. Schematic Architecture Design**
    This activity is to design a high-level structure and identify key architectural components and their interactions.
  - **A4. Design for Architecture Views**
    This activity is to design the architectural representations of four distinct system views and is further decomposed into four sub-activities, labeled A4a through A4d.
  - **A5. Design for Non-Functional Requirements**
    This activity is to design the architecture to address the system's non-functional requirements, such as performance, scalability, reliability, and security.
  - **A6. Architecture Evaluation**
    This activity is to evaluate the architectural design against functional requirements and quality criteria to ensure its adequacy, consistency, and feasibility.
- **Step**
  A step within an activity represents a structured unit of work that specifies the procedures necessary to achieve the intended outcome of that activity.
- **Task**
  A task within a step denotes the most fine-grained unit of work, detailing specific design actions or decisions required to complete the step.

Organization of the Book

This book is structured into three main parts.

- **Part I. Overview of Software Architecture**
  This part introduces the foundational principles of software architecture and presents an overview of the Unified Architecture Process, which serves as the central methodological framework of the book.
  - **Chapter 1. Introduction to Software Architecture**
    This chapter offers a comprehensive introduction to software architecture, tracing its evolution over time, defining core concepts, and specifying key elements of software architecture. It further explores the challenges associated with architectural design and examines the critical role of software architects.
  - **Chapter 2. Introduction to Unified Architecture Process**
    This chapter introduces the *Unified Architecture Process*—a comprehensive methodology for designing software architecture—and outlines guidelines for adapting the process to the specific characteristics and requirements of a target system.
- **Part II. Guidelines for Unified Architecture Process**
  This part presents the Unified Architecture Process methodology through detailed guidelines for executing its activities, steps, and tasks. It provides technical rationales, sequential procedures, design templates, examples, and checklists to support deep understanding and effective application. Each chapter in this part corresponds to a specific activity defined in the Unified Architecture Process. Accordingly, chapter titles are aligned with the activity names specified in the process.
  - **Chapter 3. Activity A1. Requirements Refinement**
  - **Chapter 4. Activity A2. System Context Analysis**
  - **Chapter 5. Activity A3. Schematic Architecture Design**
  - **Chapter 6. Activity A4a. Design for Functional View**
  - **Chapter 7. Activity A4b. Design for Information View**
  - **Chapter 8. Activity A4c. Design for Behavior View**
  - **Chapter 9. Activity A4d. Design for Deployment View**
  - **Chapter 10. Activity A5. Design for Non-Functional Requirements**
  - **Chapter 11. Activity A6. Architecture Evaluation**

Each chapter in this part is further structured into sections that correspond to the steps defined for that activity. For example, *Activity A1. Requirements Refinement* comprises three steps; accordingly, Chap. 3 addressing this activity is organized into three corresponding sections:

- **3.1 Step 1. Identify Stakeholders**
- **3.2 Step 2. Refine Functional Requirements**
- **3.3 Step 3. Refine Non-Functional Requirements**
- **Checklist**

Each chapter in Part II includes a comprehensive checklist comprising items that capture the critical design aspects of the activity and reflect established best practices. These checklists serve as validation tools for assessing the outcomes of the activity and ensuring alignment with design objectives.

- **Exercise Problems**
  Each chapter in Part II includes a set of exercise problems intended to reinforce the reader's understanding of the concepts, principles, design process, and methods presented. These problems are designed to assess comprehension of architectural design principles, promote deeper insight into architectural thinking, and facilitate the practical application of design methods.
- **Part III. Resources for Software Architecture Design**
  This part provides two categories of essential and practical resources to support software architecture design.
  - **Chapter 12. Catalog of Architecture Styles**
    This chapter presents a comprehensive catalog of more than 30 representative software architecture styles. Each style is described with an overview, structural characteristics, collaboration model, and key advantages and disadvantages. Architecture styles serve as foundational building blocks for schematic architectural design.
  - **Chapter 13. Architecture Evaluation Methods**
    This chapter presents a comprehensive overview of software architecture evaluation methods. Each evaluation method is described with an overview, applicable contexts, procedural steps, and illustrative examples. Architecture Evaluation is an essential activity for verifying and validating design decisions prior to system implementation.

In addition to the three main parts, the book includes two appendices:

- **Appendix A. Quick Reference for Unified Architecture Process**
  This appendix provides a concise reference guide to the Unified Architecture Process, summarizing its phases and associated activities to promote consistent and systematic architectural practices.
- **Appendix B. SRS for Case Study System**
  This appendix presents a complete Software Requirements Specification (SRS) for a case study system—*Car Rental Management System*—demonstrating the practical application of the Unified Architecture Process as discussed throughout the book.

Intended Readers

This book is primarily intended as a resource for diverse groups of IT professionals and students engaged in computer science, software engineering, and related disciplines.

- **Software Engineers**
  Software engineers will gain practical knowledge of architectural design principles and methods. By engaging with the architectural foundations presented in this book, they can enhance their ability to design well-structured, maintainable, and scalable software

systems. The book also deepens their understanding of the rationale behind architectural decisions and their implications for downstream development activities.

- **Software Architects**
  Software architects will directly benefit from a methodical framework for architectural modeling, evaluation, and documentation. The book provides a well-defined process and supporting methods for defining schematic architecture, constructing architectural views, and designing for specified non-functional requirements. It also enhances their ability to produce architecture descriptions that align with business objectives and stakeholder needs in a cost-effective manner through the application of the proposed methodology.
- **Project Managers**
  Project managers will benefit from the book's insights into the role of software architecture in project planning, cost estimation, risk management, and team coordination. Understanding architectural structure and complexity allows managers to make better-informed decisions regarding resource allocation, technical debt, and lifecycle management.
- **Students**
  Students at the undergraduate and graduate levels will find the book an accessible yet rigorous introduction to the principles and practices of software architecture. Through a blend of theoretical foundations, methodological guidelines, and real-world case studies, students will develop architectural thinking and acquire the skills needed to participate in or lead the architectural design of complex software systems.

How to Utilize the Book

This book can be utilized in various ways to support learning, design, and reference needs in the field of software architecture:

- **As a Learning Resource**
  The book serves as a comprehensive instructional resource for students and professionals seeking to understand the foundational principles, processes, and practices of software architecture. It is well suited for use in academic courses, industry training programs, certification programs for software architects, and independent study.
- **As a Methodology Guidebook**
  This book presents a comprehensive and structured methodology—the *Unified Architecture Process*. Practitioners, including software architects, senior developers, and technical leads, can apply this process to guide architectural development in real-world projects. Each design activity is accompanied by a checklist to support the verification and validation of architectural artifacts. Additionally, the methodology provides standardized templates for documenting architectural designs, ensuring consistency, completeness, and traceability throughout the architecture development lifecycle.

- **As an Architecture Reference**
  This book provides a comprehensive catalog of representative architecture styles, serving as a practical resource for software architects in selecting, tailoring, and integrating suitable architecture styles for a given system. In addition, it presents a thorough overview of essential architecture evaluation methods, enabling the systematic assessment of architectural decisions and design alternatives. Together, these resources support informed architectural design and facilitate evidence-based decision-making throughout the architecture development process.

Supplementary Materials (on Web Site)

A companion Web site provides a range of supplementary resources designed to support and extend the learning experience beyond the contents of the book. These materials are intended to facilitate both instructional use and practical application in professional settings.

The online resources include:

- **Templates for Architecture Description**
  A structured set of templates for documenting architectural designs is available on the companion Web site. Each template is closely aligned with the design activities, steps, and tasks defined in the *Unified Architecture Process*. These templates support effective process application, promote consistency and clarity in architectural documentation, and encourage cost-efficient design practices. Ultimately, they contribute to the development of high-quality architectural solutions.
- **Case Studies of Architecture Design**
  A collection of realistic case studies is available on the companion Web site to demonstrate the application of the *Unified Architecture Process* across a variety of software systems. These case studies span diverse domains, including enterprise systems, mobile applications, embedded systems, cloud platforms, autonomous systems, machine learning–based systems, and medical diagnosis systems. They serve as a valuable learning resource by illustrating the end-to-end architecture design process in context, highlighting domain-specific challenges, and showcasing effective solutions.
- **Quick Reference Charts of the Unified Architecture Process**
  These charts provide a concise visual summary of the activities, steps, tasks, and corresponding artifacts defined in the *Unified Architecture Process*. Designed to support quick recall and facilitate efficient process navigation, they serve as practical aids for both learning and applying the process in real-world architectural design.
- **Errata**
  A regularly updated list of corrections to errors identified in the book, ensuring continued accuracy and reliability for all readers.

All supplementary resources are available on the companion Web site:
https://www.handsonse.org.

In Closing

This book presents a comprehensive and systematically organized framework for software architecture design. It is intended to serve as a trusted companion for both professional practice and academic growth. Whether the reader is a software engineer, architect, project manager, or student, the concepts, principles, and methodologies introduced in these chapters are structured to provide the knowledge and confidence needed to design high-quality software systems—systems that not only meet demanding functional requirements but also address critical non-functional concerns.

Readers are encouraged to explore, apply, and continuously refine the methodologies presented herein as they architect the complex software systems of the future. As the field of software architecture evolves, we hope this book will remain a reliable foundation—supporting lifelong learning, sparking innovation, and fostering disciplined engineering practice.

Seoul, Republic of Korea — Soo Dong Kim
Fullerton, CA, USA — Mira Kim

Competing Interests
The authors have no competing interests to declare that are relevant to the content of this manuscript.

Contents

List of Figures

List of Tables

Part I

Overview of Software Architecture

Introduction to Software Architecture 1

Objective of the Chapter
The objective of this chapter is to establish a core understanding of software architecture and its significance in the development of complex systems. It defines the scope and characteristics of software architecture, introduces its evolution as a multidisciplinary engineering discipline, and highlights its role in bridging technical and stakeholder concerns. The chapter explores key elements of architectural design, including schematic architecture, architectural views, and non-functional requirements. It also examines the challenges faced in architectural design and clarifies the responsibilities of software architects, thereby promoting a systematic, architecture-driven approach across the software development lifecycle.

1.1 What Is Software Architecture?

Software architecture refers to the fundamental design of a software system's structure and its key properties. It defines the system's components, their relationships, and the mechanisms of their interaction to fulfill specified objectives.

Building Architecture
Historically, architecture has been associated with the design, planning, and construction of physical structures such as buildings, bridges, and infrastructure. Rooted in disciplines such as civil engineering and construction, it is an art, a science, and an engineering discipline [1].

Architecture has evolved over thousands of years in parallel with human societies, technologies, and cultural values. It began with primitive shelters constructed from readily

S. D. Kim, M. Kim, *Hands-on Software Architecture*,
https://doi.org/10.1007/978-3-032-01184-8_1

available materials such as wood, stone, and animal skins. As civilizations progressed, architectural practices advanced accordingly. Architects have long balanced aesthetics, functionality, material limitations, and environmental conditions—principles that continue to guide innovation in modern structures ranging from skyscrapers to smart cities.

The design of building architecture encompasses not only structural aspects but also quality attributes such as aesthetics, functionality, sustainability, and the integration of environmental and cultural contexts. These factors ensure that a building is structurally sound while also fulfilling the needs of its occupants and harmonizing with its surroundings [2, 3].

Transition to Software Architecture

In the digital era, the concept of *architecture* extends beyond the physical domain and finds critical application in software development. Just as physical structures rely on careful planning, detailed blueprints, and sound design principles, software systems require a well-defined architecture to meet both functional and quality requirements.

Software architecture serves as the blueprint for complex software systems, defining their structure, components, and interactions. A well-designed architecture not only ensures that the system operates as intended but also facilitates scalability, adaptability to future changes, and resilience to evolving challenges [4].

1.1.1 Definitions of Software Architecture

The concept of software architecture is interpreted across diverse scopes and levels of abstraction, resulting in a variety of definitions. This section reviews representative definitions from both academic literature and standards to establish a comprehensive understanding. Based on this analysis, a practical definition of software architecture is formulated to align with prevailing engineering practices and the demands of modern industrial systems.

Definitions in Literature

Various definitions of software architecture have emerged in the literature, reflecting both common themes and diverse viewpoints. To provide conceptual clarity, these definitions are categorized according to their characteristics, key perspectives, and areas of emphasis:

- **Definitions as fundamental structure of software systems**
  These definitions characterize software architecture as the fundamental structure of a software system, encompassing its components, their interactions, and the design principles that shape their structure and evolution [4–6].
- **Definitions emphasizing architecture styles**
  From this perspective, software architecture is defined in terms of the application of architectural styles to organize components and their interactions [7–9]. By leveraging

reusable design solutions, architecture ensures that systems are scalable, maintainable, and adaptable.

- **Definitions emphasizing architectural process**
  These definitions characterize software architecture as the result of key design decisions that define the structure and organization of a system [10, 11]. It encompasses well-established design processes and guidelines for involving stakeholders, identifying constraints, defining system structures, and designing components and behaviors.
- **Definitions focusing on fulfillment of functional and quality requirements**
  In these definitions, software architecture is described as the structured design of a system that integrates both functional and non-functional requirements [3, 11, 12]. It involves modeling components and their interactions to meet functional needs and applying various techniques to address non-functional requirements.

Definitions in Standards

In standards, definitions of software architecture are formalized to ensure a consistent understanding across industries and application domains. The following are key definitions provided by major standards bodies:

- **ISO/IEC/IEEE 42010:2011 (Systems and Software Engineering—Architecture Description)** [13]
  This standard defines software architecture as the fundamental organization of a system, expressed through its components, their interrelationships, and their interactions with the environment, as well as the principles governing its design and evolution. It highlights that software architecture encompasses both the structure of components and their interactions while also stressing the importance of the guiding principles that shape the system's long-term evolution. This standard supersedes IEEE 1471-2000.
- **ISO/IEC 12207:2008 (Systems and Software Engineering—Software Lifecycle Processes)** [14]
  This standard defines software architecture as a set of structures essential for reasoning about the system, consisting of software elements, their relationships, and the properties of both. It emphasizes that software architecture provides a foundation for understanding and analyzing system behavior by clearly defining the elements, their interconnections, and the properties they exhibit.
- **TOGAF (The Open Group Architecture Framework)** [15]
  TOGAF is recognized as an industry framework, rather than a formal international standard, yet it is widely adopted across industries for enterprise architecture practices. The framework defines software architecture as a detailed description of the system's components, their interactions, and the principles guiding their design and evolution. It emphasizes the importance of a well-structured, consistent approach to managing and understanding architecture.

All three—ISO/IEC/IEEE 42010:2011, ISO/IEC 12207:2008, and TOGAF—focus on defining and managing system architecture. They emphasize the organization of components, their interactions, and the principles guiding system design and evolution.

The main differences lie in scope and formality. ISO/IEC/IEEE 42010:2011 focuses specifically on architectural descriptions. ISO/IEC 12207:2008 addresses the entire software lifecycle, with architecture as one aspect. TOGAF is a broader enterprise architecture framework that spans software, business, information, and technology domains.

Definition from Industrial Perspective

The definition of software architecture in this book is grounded in the specific demands of industrial software systems and the need for practical, implementable design solutions. Such systems are typically large-scale and complex, with stringent non-functional requirements. As a result, architectural complexity is inherently high, and producing designs that are both effective and implementable presents a significant engineering challenge.

The following presents the definition of software architecture.

> Software architecture is the design of a system's structure, architectural views, and architectural tactics aimed at fulfilling both functional and non-functional requirements. It provides a comprehensive and detailed design blueprint that serves as the foundation for system implementation.

This definition highlights three essential aspects of software architecture: *structural design*, *architectural views*, and *architectural tactics*. Structural design refers to the schematic organization of system components and their interactions. Architectural views provide multiple perspectives to address stakeholder concerns and manage system complexity. Architectural tactics are design strategies employed to address specific non-functional requirements.

The key components of this definition are illustrated in Fig. 1.1.

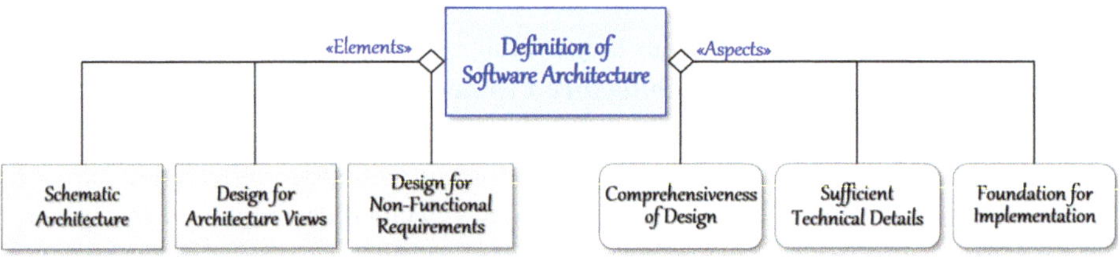

Fig. 1.1 Key Components of Software Architecture Definition

The figure illustrates the key elements of software architecture on the left and the primary aspects of its definition on the right. The first sentence of the definition specifies three key elements of software architecture design:

- **Schematic Architecture**: refers to the structural layout of the system, including the arrangement of tiers, layers, and their interrelationships
- **Design for Architectural Views**: involves design decisions for multiple architectural views, such as the functional view, information view, behavior view, and deployment view
- **Design for Non-Functional Requirements**: entails the application of architectural tactics aimed at effectively addressing non-functional requirements

The second sentence of the definition highlights the key aspects of software architecture:

- **Comprehensiveness of Design**: refers to the extent to which architectural design addresses all critical aspects of the system, ensuring that both functional and non-functional requirements are met
- **Sufficient Technical Details**: indicates that architectural design provides enough technical specificity—including components, interfaces, persistence, control flow, deployment, and quality strategies
- **Foundation for Implementation**: emphasizes that software architecture serves as the essential groundwork for system implementation by encapsulating all critical design decisions required to realize the system effectively

1.1.2 Multidisciplinary Engineering Discipline

Software architecture is the comprehensive design of a system's structural layout, constituent components, runtime behavior, and the strategies employed to fulfill quality requirements. Designing software architecture is inherently complex, involving the careful planning of structure, modular components, interfaces, inter-component interactions, integration with external systems and services, and technical approaches to address non-functional attributes such as reliability, efficiency, scalability, and maintainability.

In this regard, designing software architecture is akin to filmmaking or orchestral composition, where diverse elements must be harmonized to form a cohesive and functional whole. These endeavors, like software architecture, operate within an interdisciplinary context and are considerably more demanding than creating single-disciplinary artifacts such as essays, paintings, or solo performances.

Designing robust software architecture requires a comprehensive understanding application of multiple underlying technologies, as illustrated in Fig. 1.2.

Fig. 1.2 Key Technologies of Software Architecture Design

The figure categorizes the key technologies supporting software architecture design into three groups. The left group encompasses foundational software engineering disciplines that support systematic development and quality assurance. The right group includes technologies intrinsic to software architecture design, such as architectural patterns, documentation, and evaluation. The bottom group comprises object-oriented technologies that facilitate modularization, abstraction, and systematic modeling.

Software architecture has evolved substantially over time, shaped by advances in computing paradigms, software technologies, and development methodologies. This evolution can be characterized by distinct eras, each marked by shifts in computing platforms, computational models, architectural patterns, and system design principles, as illustrated in Fig. 1.2.

Object-Oriented Analysis and Design (OOAD) Versus Architecture Design
OOAD is a structured methodology grounded in object-oriented principles and has become the de facto standard for developing industrial software systems—particularly with the adoption of the Unified Modeling Language (UML) as an ISO standard [16]. In contrast, software architecture is a comprehensive design discipline that defines a system's high-level structure, components, interfaces, object persistence, and runtime behavior while incorporating architectural tactics to address non-functional requirements.

Software architecture is often discussed in conjunction with OOAD methods, as architectural design extensively utilizes OOAD to model and represent components, their relationships, and interactions. A key distinction between the two lies in the types of requirements they address, as illustrated in Fig. 1.3.

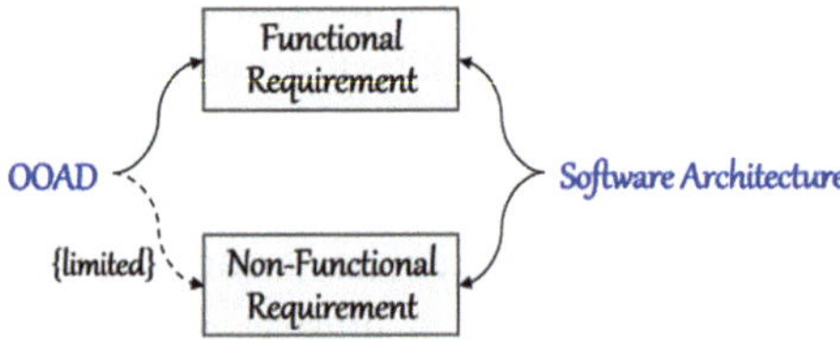

Fig. 1.3 Requirements Addressed by OOAD and Software Architecture

As shown in the figure, OOAD primarily focuses on fulfilling functional requirements, ensuring that the system performs its intended operations. In contrast, software architecture addresses both functional and non-functional requirements, ensuring not only that the system functions correctly but also that it satisfies key quality attributes such as performance, scalability, and security.

1.1.3 Evolution of Software Architecture

Software architecture has evolved significantly over time, reflecting advancements in computing paradigms, software technologies, and development methodologies. This evolution can be summarized by eras characterized by shifts in computing devices, computational models, architectural patterns, and system design principles, as shown in Fig. 1.4.

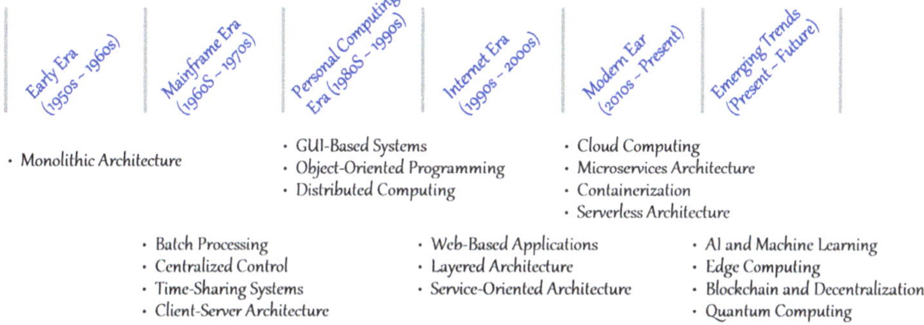

Fig. 1.4 Evolution of Software Architecture Across Computing Eras

Early Era (1950s–1960s)
The concept of software architecture emerged during this period, with systems typically characterized by monolithic structures. In monolithic architecture, the entire application was implemented as a single, large program running on mainframes. While this approach was simple and straightforward to develop, it often resulted in tightly coupled systems that were difficult to modify, scale, and maintain.

Mainframe Era (1960s–1970s)
The mainframe era was characterized by centralized computing systems, where a single mainframe managed all processing and data management tasks. Software architecture during this period emphasized the efficient utilization of centralized resources, prioritizing control and security—often at the cost of flexibility and scalability.

The key architectural features associated to centralized computing include the following:

- **Batch Processing**
  Software systems during this era were primarily designed for batch processing, in which large volumes of data were processed in bulk, typically during off-peak hours. Given the limited computing power, architectural focus centered on efficiency and resource optimization through sequential task execution.
- **Centralized Control**
  Mainframe systems were highly centralized, with the mainframe serving as the core for both processing and data management. This centralized control provided strong security and efficient resource allocation but introduced performance bottlenecks as computational demand increased.
- **Time-Sharing Systems**
  To increase the utility of expensive mainframe resources, time-sharing systems were introduced, allowing multiple users to access and share computing power concurrently. This enabled interactive computing, making systems more responsive to user needs and expanding the scope of mainframe usage.
- **Client-Server Architecture**
  The concept of client-server computing emerged, introducing a separation between client systems that handled user interaction and centralized servers responsible for data processing and storage. This architecture improved resource management by distributing responsibilities across distinct components of the system.

Personal Computing Era (1980s–1990s)
The rise of personal computers in the 1980s significantly reshaped software architecture. The availability of affordable desktop machines shifted software development toward systems emphasizing usability, interactivity, and increasingly sophisticated computational models. This era laid the foundation for modern software architecture by introducing new programming paradigms, enhancing user experience, and promoting distributed computing models—trends that continued to evolve throughout the 1990s.

The key architectural features associated with personal computing include the following:

- **GUI-Based Systems**
  The emergence of personal computers and graphical user interfaces (GUIs) shifted architectural focus toward enhancing user experience. Systems became more intuitive and interactive, emphasizing usability and responsiveness. Software architectures evolved to support event-driven models, enabling user interaction through interface components such as windows, buttons, and menus.
- **Object-Oriented Programming (OOP)**
  OOP emerged as a dominant programming paradigm during this era, introducing key concepts such as objects, encapsulation, inheritance, and polymorphism. These

principles profoundly influenced software architecture by promoting modularity, reusability, and structured design. With the adoption of languages like C++ and Java, OOP encouraged developers to design systems as collections of interacting components with well-defined responsibilities.

- **Distributed Computing**
  Advances in personal computing and networking technologies, coupled with increasing scalability demands, fostered the widespread adoption of distributed computing. Unlike monolithic systems, distributed architectures enabled components to run on separate machines, improving resource utilization, load balancing, and fault tolerance. This approach enhanced overall system performance and reliability while supporting more complex, interconnected applications.

Internet Era (1990s–2000s)
The explosion of the Internet in the 1990s marked a major shift in software architecture, transitioning from stand-alone applications to Web-based platforms. This era was defined by the rapid growth of online services, global connectivity, and increasing demands for scalability and modularity to support large-scale user interactions. Architectural priorities during the Internet Era shifted toward ensuring performance, availability, and extensibility to support the demands of globally distributed, Web-based systems.

The key architectural features associated to the Internet Era include the following:

- **Web-Based Applications**
  The rise of the Internet transformed software development by shifting the focus to Web-based applications accessed through browsers, eliminating the need for local installation. This transition enabled broader distribution and accessibility, allowing users to interact with applications from any location with an internet connection. Web applications also simplified updates and maintenance, as changes could be deployed server side without user intervention, improving efficiency and user experience.
- **Layered Architecture**
  To manage the growing complexity of Web applications, layered architecture became a widely adopted design model. It organizes software into distinct layers, each responsible for a specific concern. This separation enhances modularity, maintainability, and scalability, facilitating easier system evolution. A common variant is the Model-View-Controller (MVC) architecture, which separates an application into three components—model, view, and controller—to support clearer structure and more efficient management of complex enterprise systems [17].
- **Service-Oriented Architecture (SOA)**
  SOA introduced a modular approach by decomposing systems into loosely coupled, reusable services that communicate via standardized protocols such as SOAP and REST. This architecture enables independent development and deployment of system components, promoting flexibility and ease of integration. SOA is particularly beneficial in large-scale enterprise environments where diverse systems must interoperate reliably.

Modern Era (2010s–Present)

The modern era of software architecture is defined by the rise of cloud-native development, microservices, automation, and agile deployment practices. As global-scale applications and complex infrastructures have become standard, architectural approaches have evolved to emphasize scalability, flexibility, and operational efficiency.

The key architectural features associated to the Modern Era include the following:

- **Cloud Computing**
  Cloud computing has redefined software architecture by enabling applications to scale dynamically based on demand. Platforms such as Amazon Web Services, Google Cloud, and Microsoft Azure provide on-demand infrastructure, eliminating the need for large upfront hardware investments.
- **Microservices Architecture**
  Microservices architecture decomposes monolithic applications into smaller, independently deployable services, each focused on a specific business capability. This approach enhances scalability, flexibility, and fault isolation, as each service can be developed, deployed, and scaled autonomously.
- **Containerization**
  Container technologies like Docker and orchestration tools like Kubernetes have revolutionized application deployment and management. Containers provide lightweight, portable environments that ensure consistency across development, testing, and production. This enhances deployment efficiency, scalability, and reliability while streamlining infrastructure management.

Emerging Trends (Present to Future)

As software architecture continues to evolve, several cutting-edge technologies and design paradigms are shaping the future of architectural styles and practices. These trends are redefining how systems are structured, deployed, and operated—driving the development of more efficient, intelligent, and adaptable solutions.

The following represent key emerging architectural trends shaping the future of software systems:

- **Serverless Architecture**
  Serverless computing is an emerging cloud-native paradigm in which developers focus solely on implementing application logic, while infrastructure provisioning, scaling, and management are handled by the cloud provider. In serverless platforms, code is executed in response to events, eliminating the need to manage servers directly. This model simplifies deployment and enables automatic scaling based on demand, making it suitable for event-driven and micro-task-oriented workloads.
- **Edge Computing**
  Edge computing relocates computation and data storage closer to data sources, reducing latency and improving responsiveness for time-sensitive applications such as IoT,

autonomous vehicles, and smart infrastructure. By processing data locally, edge architectures minimize reliance on centralized cloud resources, improving performance, bandwidth efficiency, and data privacy. This decentralized approach supports real-time decision-making and enhances system reliability in distributed environments.

- **Artificial Intelligence (AI) and Machine Learning (ML)**
  AI and ML are increasingly integrated into software architecture, driving innovation across major application domains. In particular, generative AI models—such as large language models (LLMs)—have introduced new architectural requirements related to prompt engineering, contextual memory management, interaction flow design, and inference optimization. These intelligent systems also introduce architectural challenges that go beyond traditional software, including support for data collection, model training, performance optimization, deployment workflows, and real-time inference management.
- **Quantum Computing**
  While still in its early stages of development, quantum computing has the potential to transform software architecture by addressing problems beyond the reach of classical systems. Leveraging qubits and quantum parallelism, it promises breakthroughs in cryptography, optimization, simulation, and machine learning.

These technologies vary in their levels of maturity and adoption—while some, such as AI/ML and edge computing, are already influencing mainstream architectural practices, others like quantum computing and serverless architecture remain emergent and are still evolving toward broader applicability.

1.1.4 Parallels Between Building and Software Architecture

Software architecture shares important parallels with building architecture, especially in terms of design intent and the core elements that constitute the overall architectural structure.

Shared Purpose of Building and Software Architecture

The purpose of building architecture is to design a functional and aesthetically optimized structure that fulfills the needs of its occupants while satisfying critical quality requirements such as safety, durability, energy efficiency, and environmental sustainability. It serves as the foundational blueprint for guiding the physical construction of the building.

Similarly, the purpose of software architecture is to design the entire system to meet both functional and non-functional requirements defined by stakeholders. It provides the foundational structure for guiding system implementation.

Thus, both building architecture and software architecture share two primary objectives: (1) to satisfy stakeholder-defined functional and non-functional requirements and (2) to serve as the guiding framework for construction or implementation.

Core Elements of Building and Software Architecture

Both building architecture and software architecture comprise three core elements: schematic architecture, architectural view design, and strategies for satisfying quality requirements.

- **Schematic Layout**

  In building architecture, the architecture *blueprint* defines the schematic layout of the structure. It specifies the spatial arrangement, dimensions, and relationships among various structural components, ensuring compliance with functional, aesthetic, and regulatory requirements.

  Similarly, in software architecture, the *architecture description* defines the schematic structure of the system using subsystems, tiers, layers, partitions, and their interconnections. It establishes the system's high-level organization and interactions among components.

  Examples of schematic layouts in both building and software architectures are illustrated in Fig. 1.5.

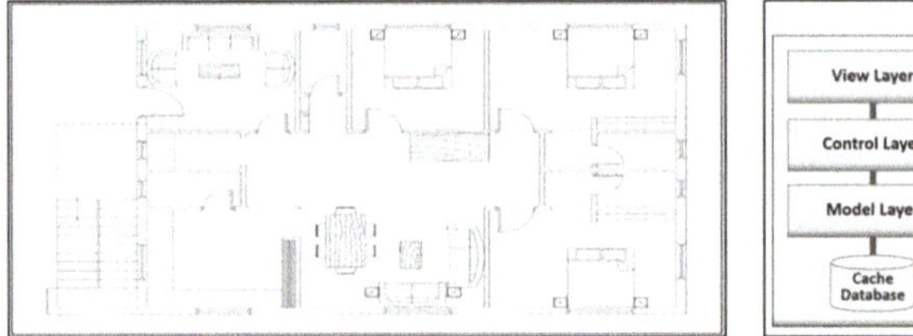

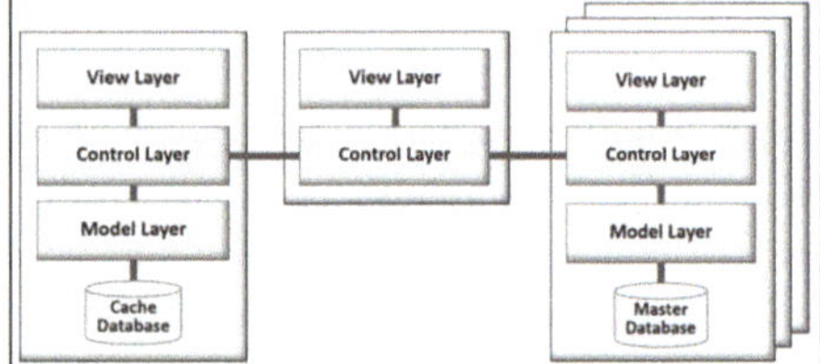

Fig. 1.5 Schematic Layouts of Building and Software Architecture

- **Design for Architecture Views**

  Building architecture is designed to incorporate multiple architectural views, such as the site plan, landscape view, bird's-eye view, 3D view, elevation view, floor plan, roof plan, section view, HVAC view, air circulation view, fire safety plan, electrical systems view, and plumbing layout.

  Examples of building architecture views are shown in Fig. 1.6.

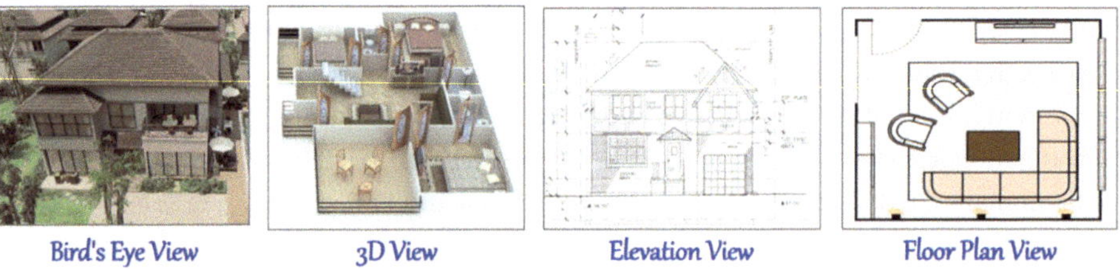

Fig. 1.6 Architecture Views of Buildings

Designing building architecture with multiple views offers several benefits, including focusing on a single view at a time to reduce errors and enhance precision.
Similarly, software architecture is designed to encompass multiple architectural views, including the functional view, information view, behavior view, deployment view, and development view. Designing software architecture using these views offers several advantages, such as managing complexity and improving the clarity of design decisions. Examples of software architecture views are shown in Fig. 1.7.

Fig. 1.7 Architecture Views of Software Systems

The figure presents a use case diagram for the functional view, a class diagram for the information view, and an activity diagram for the behavior view.

- **Strategies for Quality Requirements**
  In building architecture, the design process typically begins with the schematic layout and architectural views, followed by efforts to ensure compliance with key quality requirements. These include safety, accessibility, energy efficiency, aesthetic appeal, space utilization, structural resilience, and environmental sustainability.
- Similarly, software architecture begins with defining the system structure and corresponding architectural views and then progresses to address non-functional requirements. Architecture tactics are employed to align the system with stakeholder expectations and to ensure its long-term adaptability and sustainability.
  In both domains, the architectural design is ultimately refined and finalized through activities focused on fulfilling quality—i.e., non-functional—requirements.

In summary, building architecture and software architecture share common design purposes and key architectural elements, as outlined in Table 1.1.

Lessons Drawn from Building Architecture

Building architecture has evolved over thousands of years, shaped by diverse styles, techniques, and cultural influences. As a result, its principles and methodologies are significantly more mature than those of software architecture, which has developed only in recent decades.

Table 1.1 Commonalities Between Building Architecture and Software Architecture

Criteria	Sub-criteria	Building Architecture	Software Architecture
Purposes	Fulfillment of both functional and quality requirements	✓	✓
	Serving as the foundational basis for construction or implementation	✓	✓
Key Elements	Design of schematic architectural structures	✓	✓
	Design for Multiple Architecture Views	✓	✓
	Design for Non-Functional Requirements	✓	✓

Accordingly, key principles derived from building architecture can be applied to the structural and methodological design of software architecture, as outlined below.

- **Comprehensiveness of Building Architecture Design**
  A building architecture design is considered complete and ready for construction only when it encompasses all essential elements—such as the schematic layout, multiple architectural views, and provisions for key quality requirements. Omission of any of these elements renders the blueprint inadequate for guiding construction.
  Likewise, software architecture must be comprehensive, incorporating all critical architectural elements. Without such completeness, the design cannot effectively fulfill specified requirements or serve as a reliable foundation for system implementation.
- **Construction-Level Details of Building Architecture Design**
  A building architecture design is in depth, providing the necessary sufficient details to effectively guide construction. It includes detailed design decisions such as dimensions, materials, component types, structural connections, quality standards, electrical outlet placement, load calculations, and installation methods. Omission of such details can lead to serious consequences, including construction errors, delays, increased costs, compromised quality, safety risks, and regulatory non-compliance.
  In contrast, software architecture has traditionally been viewed as a high-level representation of system structure, often lacking detailed technical specifications. However, contemporary practices increasingly emphasize the inclusion of in-depth technical details due to their practical value in ensuring system correctness, maintainability, and implementation alignment [18–20].
- **Rigorous Validation of Building Architecture Design**
  Because building construction strictly adheres to the blueprint, rigorous validation of the architectural design is essential before execution. This process—often performed by an independent third party—ensures objectivity and compliance with applicable standards and regulations. Validation involves a detailed review of all architectural elements, including dimensions, materials, structural soundness, and adherence to local codes. It also verifies that the design satisfies both functional and quality requirements, such as energy efficiency, durability, and sustainability.

Software architecture design is seldom subjected to rigorous or systematic validation; instead, it is often evaluated informally through scenario-based techniques or in an ad hoc manner. Moreover, validation is typically performed by the architect and their immediate team, in contrast to building architecture, where blueprints are commonly reviewed by independent third parties. As a result, design flaws in software architecture may go unnoticed, potentially leading to operational issues and system failures.

These observations highlight several key lessons for software architecture design: the need for comprehensive and in-depth architectural specifications, the importance of explicitly addressing quality requirements, and the value of independent and systematic validation

1.1.5 Architecture Description

The term *architecture description* is defined by the ISO standard [13] as "a work product used to express the architecture of a system." It refers to a structured collection of documents that describe the architecture in terms of its structure, functionality, and behavior.

Elements of Architecture Description

The key elements of an architecture description are defined in the ISO/IEC/IEEE 42010 standard. According to the standard, an architecture description consists of a structured collection of artifacts, including one or more architecture views, where each view conforms to exactly one viewpoint. A viewpoint frames one or more concerns held by stakeholders.

Although standardized templates for writing architecture descriptions are not strictly prescribed, the contents of a well-engineered architecture description—consistent with recognized software engineering documentation practices and aligned with the ISO/IEC/IEEE 42010 standard—should include the following key elements:

- **Introduction**
  States the purpose, scope, intended audience, and structure of the architecture description
- **Overview of the Target System**
  Describes the system's primary objectives, functionality, quality requirements, operational context, and boundaries within its environment
- **Design of Schematic Architecture**
  Provides a high-level structural representation of the system, including major components, their roles, and interactions
- **Design for Architecture Views**
  Provides architectural design for multiple architectural views including functional, information, behavior, and deployment views

- **Design for Non-Functional Requirements**
  Describes how the architecture supports key quality attributes, often through the application of architectural tactic
- **Architectural Rationale and Stakeholder Alignment**
  Documents critical architectural decisions, including design alternatives, trade-offs, and the rationale behind them, identifies key stakeholders and their concerns, and explains how these concerns are addressed in the architectural design
- **Glossary of Terms**
  Defines domain-specific terminology, acronyms, and abbreviations used throughout the architecture description to ensure clarity and consistency
- **References**
  Cites external documents, architectural frameworks, standards, and specifications that inform or support the architecture design
- **Appendices**
  Provides supplementary information such as detailed architectural models, interface definitions, deployment diagrams, and other supporting artifacts

Quality of Architecture Description

The quality of an architecture description is not explicitly defined in architecture-related standards such as ISO/IEC/IEEE 42010; however, ensuring the production of a high-quality architecture description is essential for effective communication, evaluation, and governance throughout the system lifecycle.

The quality of an architecture description should be determined by the following seven critical criteria—each beginning with the letter 'C':

- **Completeness of design**
  The architecture description should comprehensively address all essential aspects of the system, including the schematic structure, components, connectors, interactions, and architectural tactics for satisfying non-functional requirements.
- **Correctness of design**
  The architecture description must accurately represent the intended system structure and behavior. All specified components, interactions, and constraints should correctly reflect the system requirements and operational context. Errors in logic, misrepresentations, or omissions can compromise the reliability of the resulting system.
- **Conciseness of design**
  While being comprehensive, the architecture description should remain concise—avoiding unnecessary elaboration or repetition. For instance, algorithm descriptions should highlight key steps without detailing code-level implementations.
- **Conformance to stakeholder needs**
  The architecture description must reflect the concerns and requirements of all identified stakeholders, typically documented in the Software Requirements Specification (SRS).

- **Conformance to standards**
  The architecture description should align with well-established industry standards and best practices. For example, AUTOSAR (AUTomotive Open System ARchitecture) is an international standard that promotes scalability, interchangeability, and reusability of software components across vehicle platforms. Adhering to such standards provides significant benefits, particularly for OEMs and suppliers.
- **Consistency of design**
  All elements of the architecture description must be internally consistent, with no contradictions across views or models. Diagrams and textual descriptions should be aligned to ensure architectural coherence.
- **Constructability of design**
  The design must be practically realizable, considering the available technologies, resources, and constraints. Highly theoretical models based solely on formalism may lack applicability in typical development environments.

1.2 Elements of Software Architecture

Software architecture fundamentally consists of three core elements, as illustrated in Fig. 1.8.

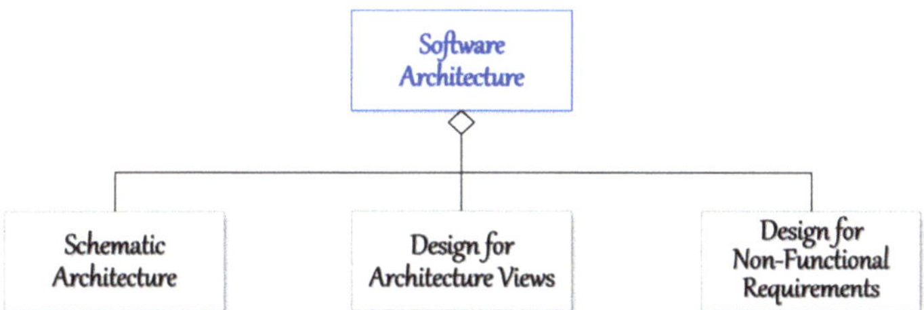

Fig. 1.8 Elements of Software Architecture

1.2.1 Design of Schematic Architecture

Schematic Architecture refers to the structured, visual representation of a system's stable and enduring structural layout. It defines the primary architectural elements—such as tiers, layers, and partitions—along with their respective roles and the relationships among them.

Serving as the core structural framework of the system, the schematic architecture provides a stable foundation upon which subsequent architectural decisions are made. It guides the organization of the system and supports consistent reasoning about component placement, responsibilities, and interactions.

About Architecture Styles

An architecture style is a high-level, reusable design framework that defines the structural organization and behavioral coordination of a software system. It establishes a set of design principles and constraints for arranging system components, specifying their interactions, and guiding the overall system configuration. Common examples include client-server, layered, model-view-controller (MVC), pipe-and-filter, publish-subscribe, and microservices. A comprehensive catalog of widely recognized architecture styles is presented in Chapter 12.

Architecture styles serve a purpose similar to that of design patterns: both provide formalized, reusable solutions to recurring design problems. However, their scope and level of abstraction differ. Design patterns typically address micro-level concerns, offering solutions for specific component-level interactions. In contrast, architecture styles operate at the macro level, structuring the entire system. For example, the Adapter design pattern enables compatibility between incompatible interfaces by acting as a bridge. In contrast, the Client-Server Architecture Style defines the system in terms of two primary tiers: a client tier that requests services and a server tier that provides them.

Schematic Architecture Design Using Architecture Styles

Schematic architecture is designed by selecting architecture styles that align with the structural requirements and constraints of the target system. These styles are then integrated to form a cohesive architectural design, as illustrated in Fig. 1.9.

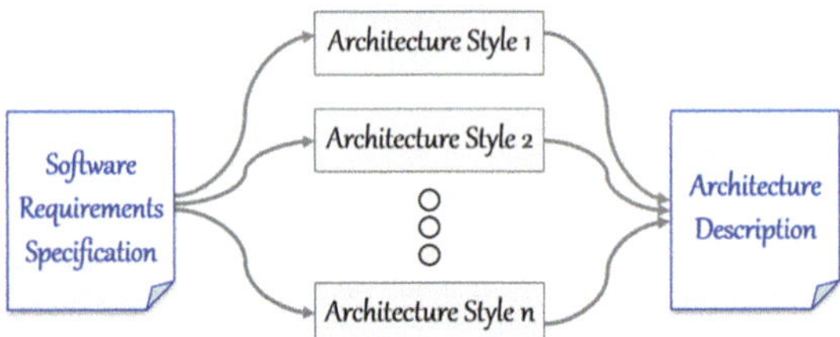

Fig. 1.9 Schematic Architecture Derived from Architecture Styles

This figure illustrates how schematic architecture is derived by identifying and applying appropriate architecture styles. Once selected, the styles are integrated to construct the overall architectural description. Therefore, knowledge and proficiency in architecture styles are essential for software architects, as they help select suitable structures, address system constraints, and create architectures that meet quality goals and stakeholder needs.

1.2.2 Design for Architectural Views

An architecture view represents the software architecture from a specific perspective, each emphasizing a distinct aspect of the system—such as functionality, data persistence, runtime behavior, or deployment configuration. Designing architecture through multiple views helps reduce complexity by allowing architects to focus on one concern at a time. This makes it easier to manage complex systems and ensures that each view is clear, well structured, and fit for its purpose.

Architecture Views in the ISO/IEC/IEEE 42010

The ISO/IEC/IEEE 42010 standard defines the key concepts of architecture view and architecture viewpoint. A *view* is a representation of a system, or a part of it, that reflects a related set of stakeholder concerns. In contrast, a *viewpoint* is a specification that defines how a view is constructed and used—it provides the conventions, notations, and modeling rules necessary to create views that effectively address specific concerns.

Notably, the standard does not prescribe specific views to be used. Instead, it offers a framework for structuring architecture views in a way that ensures stakeholder concerns are systematically addressed.

Architecture Views in Literature

To better understand commonly adopted architectural views, well-established view categories from the literature are summarized.

- **Rozanski and Woods** [11]
  This book introduces several architectural views, each aimed at addressing specific stakeholder concerns. The Functional View focuses on the system's functional elements and how they deliver the required behavior. The Information View describes how data is stored, managed, and processed within the system. The Concurrency View explains the system's handling of concurrent activities, including processes, threads, and synchronization mechanisms. The Development View represents the static structure of the system from the developers' perspective, including modules, components, and layers. The Deployment View captures the physical configuration of the system, detailing how software components are mapped onto hardware and network infrastructure. Finally, the Operational View addresses the system's runtime management, including aspects of operation, monitoring, and maintenance.
- **Clements, Bachmann, et al.** [21]
  This book introduces several architectural views designed to systematically document software architectures. The **Module View** captures the system's static structure by representing modules and their relationships. The **Component and Connector View** describes the system's dynamic behavior by illustrating how components interact and communicate at runtime. The **Allocation View** maps software elements to physical resources, such as hardware platforms or organizational units. The **Deployment View** focuses on how the system is distributed across the physical infrastructure. Lastly, the **Use Case View** demonstrates how the architecture supports specific functional requirements through representative scenarios.

- **Kruchten** [22]
  This journal article introduces the 4+1 view model as a framework for describing software architectures from multiple perspectives. The Logical View addresses the system's functional requirements by representing key abstractions and object models. The Development View captures the organization of the software into modules and layers from the developer's perspective. The Process View focuses on the system's runtime behavior, including aspects such as concurrency, inter-process communication, and scheduling. The Physical View maps software components onto the underlying hardware, describing how the system is distributed across the physical infrastructure. Finally, the Use Case View illustrates how the architecture supports specific functional requirements through real-world scenarios, helping validate the design by demonstrating interactions between components and ensuring alignment with stakeholder needs.

Although different sources may use varying terminologies to classify architecture views, there is substantial commonality in the underlying types and purposes of these views.

Architecture Views in Unified Architecture Process

This book presents a comprehensive introduction to the Unified Architecture Process—a dedicated software methodology designed to support the efficient and cost-effective development of high-quality software architectures. The seven architectural views defined in the Unified Architecture Process are illustrated in Fig. 1.10.

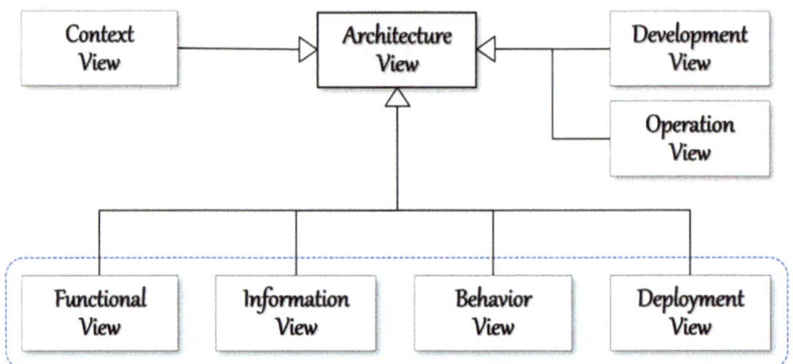

Fig. 1.10 Architecture Views in Unified Architecture Process

Among the views depicted in the figure, the four views highlighted—*Functional View*, *Information View*, *Behavior View*, and *Deployment View*—are regarded as essential for a broad range of software projects. The remaining three views—*Context View*, *Development View*, and *Operation View*—may be selectively applied based on the project's specific needs, scale, and complexity.

- **Context View**
  The context view provides a high-level perspective of the system in relation to its external environment and is typically the starting point of architectural design. It illustrates how the system interacts with external entities—such as users, services, and other systems—while clarifying its responsibilities, interfaces, and environmental constraints.
- **Functional View**
  The functional view concentrates on the system's functional capabilities, addressing the design of functional components, their interfaces, interactions, and responsibilities. Serving as the foundation for other architectural views, this view is central to the realization of the system's core functionality.
- **Information View**
  The information view focuses on the definition, organization, and manipulation of persistent data within the system. It specifies the structure of datasets, data access mechanisms, and the interactions between data and functional components.
- **Behavior View**
  The behavior view captures the dynamic aspects of the system, modeling how components interact and evolve over time in response to events, inputs, and system states. It provides insight into runtime interactions, control flows, and the sequencing of operations.
- **Deployment View**
  The deployment view addresses the mapping of software components to the physical infrastructure. It defines how components are distributed across hardware nodes and focuses on deployment configurations, inter-node communication, system scalability, fault tolerance, and performance.
- **Development View**
  The development view focuses on the internal organization of the system from a software construction perspective. It includes the module structure, source code organization, component reuse, and development dependencies.
- **Operation View**
  The operation view emphasizes the system's behavior in a production environment. It addresses concerns related to monitoring, logging, fault detection, recovery, maintenance, and system administration. This view ensures that the system can be effectively operated and sustained throughout its lifecycle, supporting reliability, security, and maintainability.

This set of seven views is broadly applicable to a wide range of software systems; however, additional views may be defined and incorporated based on the specific characteristics of the target system.

1.2.3 Design for Non-Functional Requirements

A Software Requirements Specification typically encompasses both functional requirements and non-functional requirements (NFRs). While functional requirements define what the system should do, NFRs specify the quality attributes the system must exhibit as well as any applicable constraints.

Architectural design must address both categories of requirements. Architecting the system with explicit consideration of NFRs not only enhances quality-in-use but also contributes to overall product competitiveness by ensuring the system is robust, efficient, and sustainable in its operational context.

Architecture Tactics for NFRs

Architecture Tactic refers to a design strategy, method, or technique employed to effectively address and fulfill a specific NFR. While the spectrum of architecture tactics is broad, they are commonly categorized into the following groups:

- **Software Design Principles**—foundational guidelines for designing software that enhance design quality such as modularity, extensibility, modifiability, reliability, and reusability
- **Object-Oriented Paradigms**—concepts such as encapsulation, inheritance, and polymorphism used to improve modularity, reusability, and scalability
- **Design Patterns**—proven solutions to recurring design problems that promote architectural consistency and flexibility
- **Algorithms**—computational strategies that enhance performance, scalability, or accuracy in specific system functions
- **Machine Learning Models**—predictive or adaptive techniques used to optimize system behavior and enable intelligent functionalities
- **Reusable Assets**—pre-built components, including open-source libraries and SDKs, that reduce development effort and improve reliability
- **Services**—modular services such as cloud services or microservices that support scalability, elasticity, and fault isolation.
- **Software Frameworks and Platforms**—integrated development environments and runtime systems that provide reusable infrastructure and enforce architectural conventions
- **Computing Paradigms**—architectural approaches like functional programming, reactive programming, or quantum computing that influence system design and behavior
- **Emerging IT Trends**—industry practices such as DevOps, CI/CD pipelines, and blockchain that support automation, traceability, and operational efficiency
- **Operational Guidelines**—best practices for deployment, monitoring, logging, and fault management that ensure reliability and maintainability in production environments

The body of knowledge on architecture tactics is substantially broad, encompassing a wide range of strategies and techniques across different domains and technologies. As it is impractical for architects to master all tactics in advance, a more effective approach is to perform on-demand exploration and selection of tactics tailored to the specific non-functional requirement at hand. This just-in-time strategy supports practical and context-sensitive architectural decision-making.

1.3 Challenges in Software Architecture Design

Designing software architecture presents significant technical challenges due to various contributing factors. Common challenges include the following:

- **Comprehending requirements**
  Eliciting and thoroughly understanding both functional and non-functional requirements of the target system is a fundamental challenge. Inadequate comprehension of these requirements may lead to an architecture that does not fully satisfy its intended objectives.
- **Aligning stakeholder concerns**
  Stakeholders are the primary sources for eliciting and validating system requirements. However, they often have differing perspectives and priorities, which makes aligning their concerns and achieving a unified architectural vision particularly challenging.
- **Handling system complexity**
  Modern software systems are inherently complex, comprising multiple modules deployed across various tiers and layers that must interoperate seamlessly. Furthermore, integration with external systems, services, and libraries adds additional layers of complexity.
  Engineering a robust architecture to manage this complexity is a demanding task. In particular, addressing a large set of technically demanding non-functional requirements (NFRs) presents significant challenges in architectural design.
- **Applying multidisciplinary technologies**
  Contemporary software systems typically involve the application of multiple technologies from diverse disciplines, each with its own design principles, methodologies, tools, and best practices. Integrating these technologies is often challenging due to their complementary roles and potential conflicts in assumptions, interfaces, or operational constraints.
- **Documenting architecture description**
  Software architecture entails a complex design that integrates multiple elements, making the resulting architecture description both intricate and comprehensive. Developing an architecture description that ensures correctness, precision, sufficiency, and consistency—while remaining understandable to both stakeholders and developers—is a technically demanding task.

Approaches to Remedy the Challenges

The challenges and complexities involved in software architecture design have led to the development of various approaches and techniques aimed at effectively addressing them. The following are key strategies recommended for overcoming these challenges:

- **Establishing core competency in software architecture foundations**
  Software architecture design requires the application of various foundational methods and techniques, as outlined above. A deep understanding of the underlying theories, methods, and best practices enables architects to build a solid foundation for making informed design decisions and addressing the challenges encountered throughout the design process.
- **Developing practical skills for architecture design**
  Beyond foundational knowledge, acquiring practical skills is essential for effective software architecture design. These skills are cultivated through hands-on experience in real-world projects, where architects learn to evaluate trade-offs, apply architectural tactics, and implement solutions that satisfy both functional and non-functional requirements.
- **Adopting a methodological approach to architecture design**
  A well-defined design methodology offers a structured process, along with supporting methods, guidelines, and best practices that guide architects throughout the design lifecycle. By following a systematic approach, architects can more effectively manage complexity, ensure alignment with both functional and non-functional requirements, and reduce the risk of architectural defects or inefficiencies.

1.4 Roles of Software Architects

A software architect is a senior-level technical expert responsible for designing a system architecture that defines the overall structure, captures key design decisions across multiple architectural views, and incorporates strategies to meet both functional and non-functional requirements. The roles of software architects can be broadly categorized into two key areas—communication and technical leadership—as illustrated in Fig. 1.11.

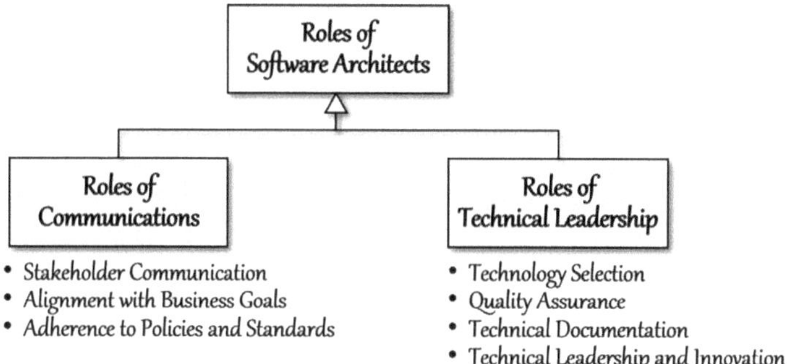

Fig. 1.11 Roles of Software Architects

Software architects play communication roles that involve facilitating effective interaction with stakeholders, aligning architectural decisions with business goals, and ensuring compliance with organizational policies and standards. In this capacity, architects act as key communicators who translate stakeholder concerns, business objectives, and technical constraints into architectural solutions that are both strategically aligned and technically feasible.

In parallel, software architects also fulfill technical leadership roles, which encompass selecting appropriate technologies, ensuring architectural quality, producing technical documentation, and fostering innovation. These responsibilities position architects as technical visionaries and decision-makers who guide engineering teams, manage complexity, and ensure that the architecture remains robust, scalable, and maintainable throughout the system's lifecycle.

Introduction to Unified Architecture Process

2

Objective of the Chapter

The objective of this chapter is to introduce the Unified Architecture Process (UAP), a structured methodology for designing software architecture that addresses both functional and non-functional requirements. It presents the foundational concepts of UAP, including its process model and supporting instructions, and explains its methodological approach to architecture design. The chapter also provides guidance on tailoring the process to the specific characteristics and requirements of the target system and emphasizes the practical benefits of applying UAP to achieve scalable, maintainable, and cost-effective architectural solutions.

2.1 What Is Unified Architecture Process?

The Unified Architecture Process is a comprehensive, production-ready methodology tailored to support the cost-effective development of high-quality software architecture. It provides a structured framework encompassing all essential architectural design activities, along with step-by-step guidance for their execution.

Motivation for Unified Architecture Process

The Unified Architecture Process was conceived to address several recurring challenges and questions frequently raised by software designers and architects:

- How can software architecture be designed systematically, akin to a cookbook offering step-by-step guidance?
- Where can one find concrete, detailed guidelines for executing each architectural design activity?

S. D. Kim, M. Kim, *Hands-on Software Architecture*,
https://doi.org/10.1007/978-3-032-01184-8_2

- How can architects effectively design for non-functional requirements, which are often intricate and difficult to formalize?
- What strategies enable effective architectural design even for large-scale or highly complex systems?
- Is there a well-established template or standardized format for documenting architecture descriptions with minimal effort and maximal clarity?

To respond to these questions, the Unified Architecture Process was devised with the following key strategies:

- **Systematic Design Process of Software Architecture**
  The Unified Architecture Process provides a well-structured process model that organizes architectural design into a sequence of activities, each with clearly defined procedural steps.
- **Acquisition of Detailed Design Guidelines**
  For each design activity, the process delivers detailed, implementation-level guidelines and includes validation checklists to ensure design completeness and correctness.
- **Architecture Design for Addressing Non-Functional Requirements**
  The process defines a dedicated design activity—*A5. Design for Non-Functional Requirements*—that provides focused guidance for effectively addressing critical quality attributes such as performance, security, and modifiability.
- **Design for Complex Software Systems**
  The process is specifically tailored to support the development of software architectures for complex, large-scale systems. It provides structured methodologies and best practices for managing architectural complexity.
- **Adoption of a Standardized Architecture Description Template**
  The Unified Architecture Process provides a standardized architecture description template that is fully aligned with its process model to support efficient and consistent documentation.

Evolution of Unified Architecture Process

The Unified Architecture Process is the result of over two decades of academic research in software engineering, combined with extensive practical experience from the design of large-scale systems across government and industry. As such, it is both theoretically robust and grounded in well-established software engineering principles and practices.

The process has been applied to a wide range of real-world systems, including management information systems, enterprise systems, cloud service platforms, mobile applications, embedded systems, real-time systems, autonomous systems, machine learning applications, and platform software. Its continued refinement is driven by insights gained from these industrial applications.

Contributors to the design and evolution of the Unified Architecture Process include software architects and senior developers from major IT corporations as well as faculty members in Computer Science. Iterative feedback and insights gained from their project experiences have played a pivotal role in shaping and continuously advancing the methodology.

Underlying Technologies of Unified Architecture Process

The Unified Architecture Process is grounded in a range of foundational technologies, each offering unique and valuable features that contribute to the creation of high-quality software architectures. Collectively, these technologies enhance the effectiveness and precision of the architectural design process.

The core technologies underlying the Unified Architecture Process are illustrated in Fig. 2.1.

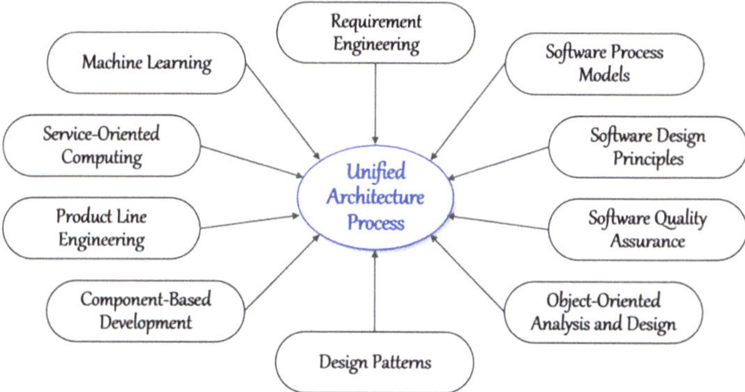

Fig. 2.1 Underlying Technologies of Unified Architecture Process

- **Requirement Engineering**
  Requirements Engineering systematically captures and manages functional and non-functional requirements to ensure alignment with stakeholder needs and system goals. It forms the foundation for effective architectural design and guides the requirements refinement phase in the Unified Architecture Process.
- **Software Process Models**
  Software Process Models define structured phases for software development, enabling systematic planning, design, implementation, testing, and maintenance. The Unified Architecture Process integrates these standard phases and incorporates iterative and incremental development principles.

- **Software Design Principles**
  Software Design Principles are foundational guidelines that promote clarity, correctness, adaptability, and maintainability in software systems. They serve to ensure that software architecture is robust, efficient, scalable, and responsive to evolving requirements. The design methods employed in the Unified Architecture Process are grounded in several key design principles including the following:
  - **Abstraction**
    Abstraction focuses on simplifying complexity by extracting only the essential features of a system or component while omitting less important details.
  - **Modularity**
    Modularity is a fundamental design principle that structures a system into self-contained modules, each responsible for a specific functionality, thereby facilitating development, testing, maintenance, and scalability. It is typically assessed using two key metrics: cohesion and coupling.
  - **Separation of Concerns**
    Separation of concerns (SoC) is a design principle that divides a system into distinct parts, each addressing a specific concern. This enhances maintainability, readability, and scalability by allowing changes in one part without affecting others, enabling developers to focus on individual concerns independently.
  - **SOLID Principles**
    SOLID principles provide essential guidelines for designing maintainable, extensible, and scalable software systems. They include the single responsibility, open/closed, Liskov substitution, interface segregation, and dependency inversion principles.
- **Software Quality Assurance**
  Software Quality Assurance (SQA) is a systematic framework that ensures software meets defined requirements and quality standards throughout the development lifecycle. The Unified Architecture Process incorporates SQA principles into its architectural viewpoints and tactics to address and fulfill quality requirements effectively.
- **Object-Oriented Analysis and Design**
  Object-Oriented Analysis and Design (OOAD) is a methodology for analyzing and designing systems using object-oriented constructs. Its results are typically represented through Unified Modeling Language (UML) Diagrams [16]. The Unified Architecture Process extensively applies OOAD methods to define and structure its architectural design guidelines.
- **Design Patterns**
  Design Patterns are reusable solutions to common design problems within specific contexts. They are typically categorized into creational, structural, and behavioral patterns [23]. The Unified Architecture Process incorporates design patterns extensively in the definition of architectural viewpoints and tactics, particularly for addressing non-functional requirements.

- **Component-Based Development**
  Component-Based Development (CBD) is an approach that focuses on building software systems from reusable, self-contained components. The Unified Architecture Process applies CBD principles in its methods for designing components, defining interfaces, and specifying inter-component relationships.
- **Product Line Engineering**
  Product Line Engineering (PLE) is a software engineering approach aimed at developing a family of related products from a shared set of core assets. The Unified Architecture Process leverages PLE, along with the open-closed principle, to define components that are generic, customizable, and extensible across different product variants.
- **Service-Oriented Computing**
  Service-Oriented Computing (SOC) is a computing paradigm centered on designing and managing software systems using services as fundamental building blocks. The Unified Architecture Process adopts SOC principles to define methods for developing loosely coupled service components and invoking their functionalities, including microservices.
- **Machine Learning**
  Machine Learning (ML) is a branch of artificial intelligence that enables systems to learn from data, recognize patterns, and make decisions with minimal human input. The Unified Architecture Process incorporates ML as a tactical approach to address the intelligence requirements of systems and their components.

This set of underlying technologies in the Unified Architecture Process supports the design of software architectures that conform to specified requirements and enables the development of high-quality software systems.

2.2 Methodological Approach to Architecture Design

General Definition of Methodology

A *methodology* is a structured collection of principles, procedures, methods, and rules formulated to accomplish a specific task or address a defined problem. It establishes a coherent framework that outlines the processes, techniques, and tools essential to a particular activity. The concept of methodology is widely adopted across diverse disciplines, including research, science, engineering, and business, to ensure systematic and repeatable practices.

- **Methodology for Cooking**
  In the culinary domain, a cookbook serves as a methodological guide that compiles recipes and procedural instructions for preparing various dishes. It details the end-to-end process of food preparation, often including visual aids such as photographs or illustrations of completed meals.

- **Methodology in Education**
  In education, methodologies such as the Montessori method, Bloom's taxonomy, and inquiry-based learning offer structured frameworks for instruction. For example, the Montessori method emphasizes self-directed learning and hands-on exploration. These approaches guide curriculum design, teaching strategies, assessment, and feedback to align with learning objectives.
- **Methodology for Sports**
  In sports, training methodologies enhance performance, skill development, and physical conditioning through structured approaches such as periodization, tactical periodization, and the Game Sense Method. Periodization divides training into cycles to balance intensity, recovery, and progression. In professional golf academies, a comprehensive methodology integrates technical skills, physical and mental conditioning, on-course practice, competition, and career development.
- **Methodology in Research**
  In academic and scientific research, methodology refers to the systematic approach used to conduct research. It includes the research design, data collection methods, data analysis techniques, and guidelines for ensuring validity and reliability of results. A rigorous methodology ensures transparency, reproducibility, and alignment with the research questions and objectives, thereby enhancing the credibility and generalizability of findings.
- **Methodology in Software Engineering**
  In software engineering, a methodology defines a systematic process for software development, specifying phases, best practices, and artifacts required to manage the software project lifecycle. For example, the Unified Process (UP) adopts an iterative and incremental development model structured into inception, elaboration, construction, and transition phases, enabling adaptability to evolving requirements. DevOps integrates development and operations teams, promoting collaboration, automation, and continuous integration/delivery (CI/CD) to accelerate deployment while enhancing reliability and responsiveness.

Regardless of the domain, a well-defined methodology encompasses both a structured process and its corresponding instructions. The process outlines a sequence of activities aimed at achieving a specific objective or solving a defined problem, while the instructions offer detailed guidance for executing each step. Together, they are grounded in a comprehensive knowledge base that integrates proven principles, established methods, and best practices relevant to the field.

Methodological Approach to Software Architecture
Designing a robust software architecture presents significant technical challenges. Without a structured approach, architecture design efforts may lead to defects, incomplete or sub-optimal solutions, non-compliance with requirements, excessive complexity in documentation, and increased development overhead.

An effective means of addressing these challenges is the adoption of a well-defined methodology tailored to architectural design. The benefits of methodological rigor—such as consistency, traceability, and quality assurance—are particularly impactful in the context of software architecture, especially when designing complex industrial systems with stringent requirements.

Given the relatively recent emergence of software architecture as a distinct discipline, the field still lacks a wide range of mature, comprehensive methodologies. The *Unified Architecture Process* was developed to address this gap, offering a systematic and scalable methodology specifically designed to handle architectural complexity and to satisfy demanding non-functional requirements.

2.3 Elements of Unified Architecture Process

The Unified Architecture Process comprises a process model and a set of detailed instructions for executing architecture design activities.

2.3.1 Process Model

The process model of the Unified Architecture Process is organized into three hierarchical work units, *Activity*, *Step*, and *Task*, as illustrated in Fig. 2.2.

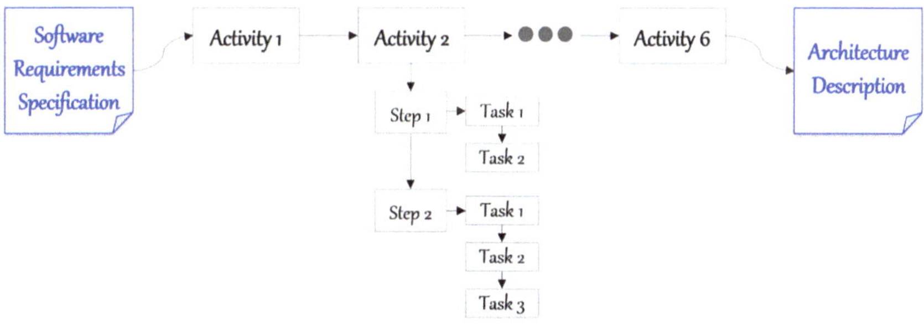

Fig. 2.2 Work Units in Unified Architecture Process

- **Activity**
  An *Activity* is a high-level unit of work that corresponds to a major phase of the architecture design process. Each activity defines a cohesive set of objectives and comprises multiple steps.
- **Step**
  A *Step* is a structured subunit within an activity. It specifies a procedure or set of actions required to advance the activity. Each step comprises a sequence of tasks that collectively fulfill its objective.

- **Task**
  A *Task* is the most granular unit of work. It denotes concrete actions or operations that must be executed to complete a step.

This hierarchical structure ensures that the process remains both systematic and manageable, supporting step-by-step progression through the architectural design phases.

Activities in Unified Architecture Process

The Unified Architecture Process is structured as a sequence of six major design activities, as shown in Fig. 2.3.

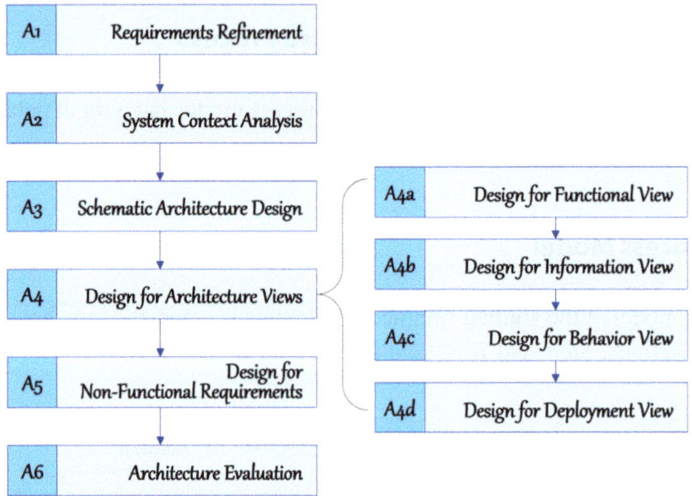

Fig. 2.3 Activities in Unified Architecture Process

Each activity addresses a distinct phase in the architectural design process, progressing from Requirements Refinement to Architecture Evaluation. Notably, *Activity A4: Design for Architecture Views* is further decomposed into four sub-activities, each dedicated to designing a specific architectural view: functional, information, behavior, and deployment.

- **Activity A1. Requirements Refinement**
  This activity focuses on refining the initial requirements provided by stakeholders. These initial requirements often contain deficiencies that, if left unaddressed, may lead to defects in subsequent design models. Therefore, requirements should be thoroughly refined prior to making any architectural decisions.
  The steps comprising this activity are shown in Fig. 2.4.

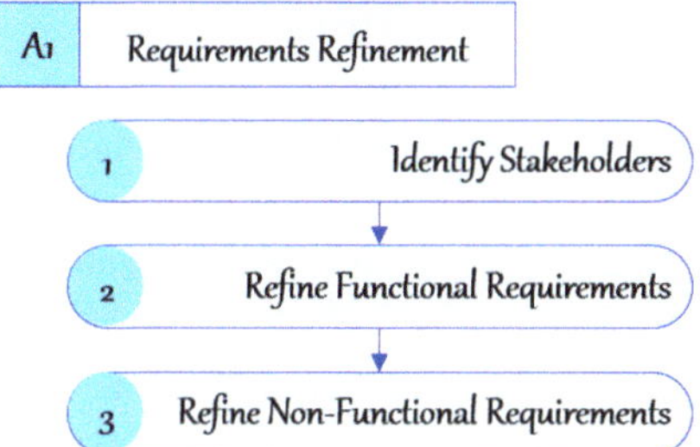

Fig. 2.4 Steps in Activity A1. Requirements Refinement

Step 1 is to identify the system's stakeholders, enabling architects to initiate communication and begin refining the requirements. Step 2 is to identify and address deficiencies in the functional requirements using established requirements engineering principles. Step 3 is to refine non-functional requirements by collecting architectural concerns from stakeholders, detecting gaps or inconsistencies, and applying appropriate engineering practices.

- **Activity A2. System Context Analysis**
  This activity aims to construct a context model for the system by analyzing the refined requirements. In software architecture, a context model provides a high-level view of the system's boundaries, functionality, data, and behavior. This activity is especially critical for architects who have limited familiarity with the target system, as the context model helps clarify its scope, features, and interactions.
  The steps comprising this activity are shown in Fig. 2.5.

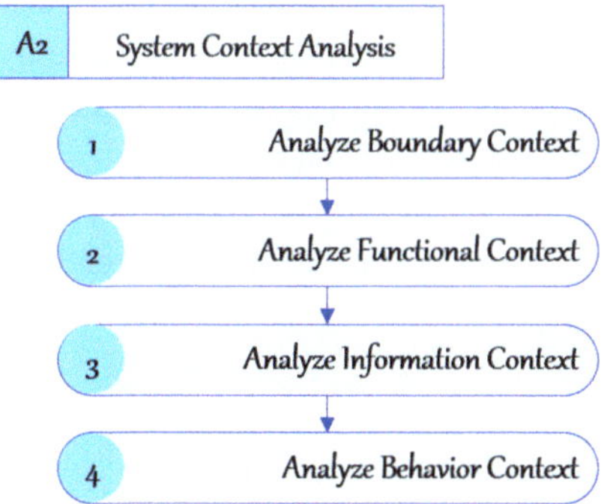

Fig. 2.5 Steps in Activity A2. System Context Analysis

Step 1 is to analyze the system's boundary context, providing a high-level overview of the system and its interacting elements. Step 2 is to examine the functional context by identifying key functions and representing them through use cases. Step 3 is to analyze the information context by specifying persistent datasets and their relationships. Step 4 is to analyze the behavior context, defining the system's runtime control flow.

- **Activity A3. Schematic Architecture Design**
  This activity involves designing the schematic architecture of a target system by integrating appropriate architecture styles. Schematic Architecture refers to the structured and visual representation of a system's stable and enduring layout, typically defined by structural elements such as tiers, layers, components, and the interrelationships among them.
  The steps comprising this activity are shown in Fig. 2.6.

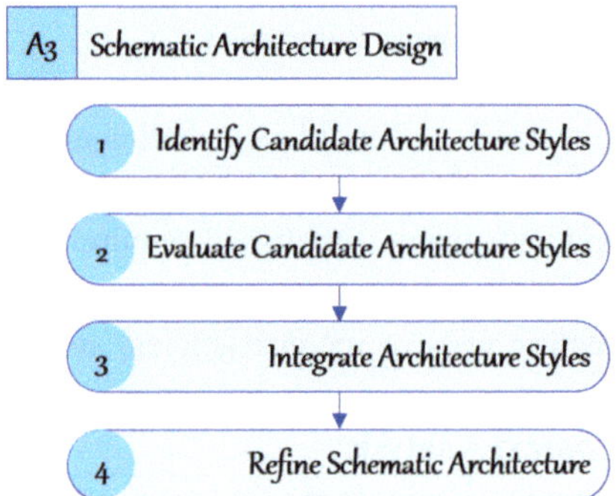

Fig. 2.6 Steps in Activity A3. Schematic Architecture Design

  Step 1 is to identify candidate architecture styles by analyzing the structural characteristics of the target system and determining styles suitable for its schematic architecture. Step 2 is to evaluate the applicability of these styles based on their contextual suitability, strengths, and limitations. Step 3 is to integrate the selected styles into the system's schematic architecture. Step 4 is to refine the architecture by elaborating on structural elements and interaction paths to ensure coherence and completeness.
- **Activity A4. Design for Architecture Views**
  This activity focuses on designing the architecture from multiple architectural perspectives, recognizing that architecture design inherently involves distinct views. Accordingly, this activity is subdivided into the following view-specific design activities:
  - **Activity 4a. Design for Functional View**
  - **Activity 4b. Design for Information View**
  - **Activity 4c. Design for Behavior View**
  - **Activity 4d. Design for Deployment View**
- **Activity A4a. Design for Functional View**
  This activity involves designing the architecture for the functional view, which focuses on modeling the system's functionality by defining functional components and interfaces and allocating them within the schematic architecture.

The steps comprising this activity are shown in Fig. 2.7.

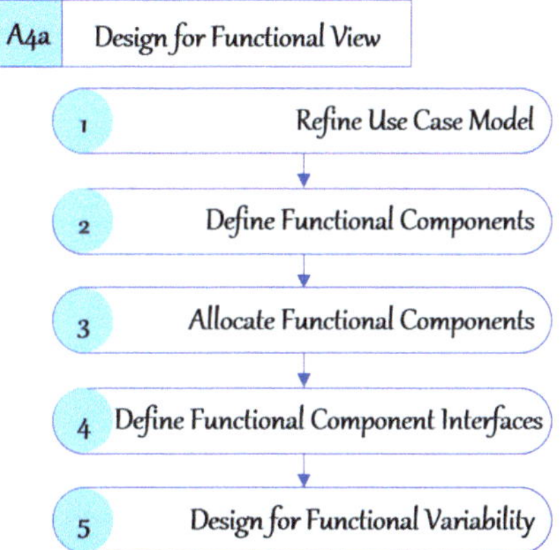

Fig. 2.7 Steps in Activity A4a. Design for Functional View

Step 1 is to refine the context-level use case model by adding detail and precision to actors, use cases, and their relationships, thereby establishing a solid foundation for functional view design. Step 2 is to identify the functional components of the target system based on the refined use case model, where each component encapsulates a cohesive unit of functionality. Step 3 is to allocate these functional components to appropriate locations within the schematic architecture. Step 4 is to define the interfaces of each functional component, specifying the protocols for external interaction. Step 5 is to design for functional variability within components by applying the open-closed principle, thereby supporting customizability at designated variation points.

- **Activity A4b. Design for Information View**
  This activity focuses on designing the architecture for the information view, which primarily addresses persistent datasets, data components, their relationships, and the allocation of these components within the schematic architecture.
  The steps comprising this activity are shown in Fig. 2.8.

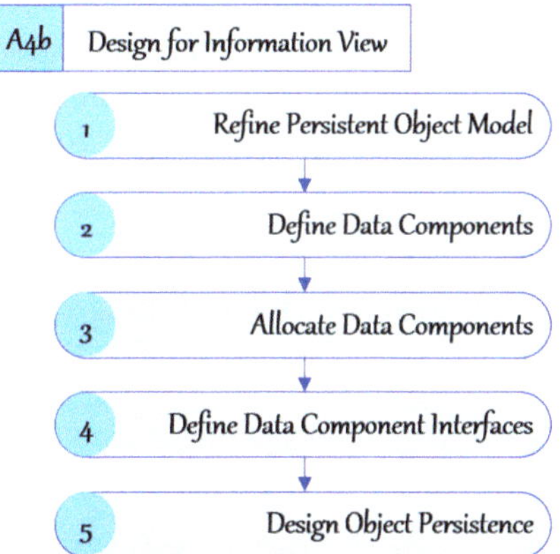

Fig. 2.8 Steps in Activity A4b. Design for Information View

Step 1 is to refine the context-level object model, typically represented as a class diagram, by adding detail and improving precision regarding persistent classes, their attributes, and relationships. Step 2 is to define data components by grouping closely related classes into self-contained units that represent cohesive datasets. Step 3 is to allocate these data components to their designated placeholders within the schematic architecture. Step 4 is to specify the interfaces of data components. Step 5 is to design object persistence for the data components, typically leveraging database management systems or cloud-based storage solutions.

- **Activity A4c. Design for Behavior View**
  This activity focuses on designing the architecture for the behavior view, which primarily addresses the system's runtime behavior and the detailed control flows of complex functional elements.
  The steps comprising this activity are shown in Fig. 2.9.

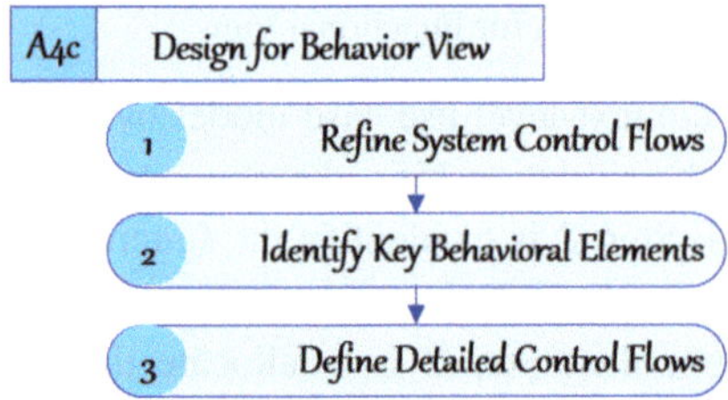

Fig. 2.9 Steps in Activity A4c. Design for Behavior View

Step 1 is to refine the system control flows by analyzing the system's runtime behavior and ensuring that the control flows are clearly defined. Step 2 focuses on identifying key behavioral elements, such as components or actions that exhibit complex runtime behavior. Step 3 is to design detailed control flows for selected elements using appropriate modeling schemes.

- **Activity A4d. Design for Deployment View**
  This activity focuses on designing the architecture for the deployment view, which primarily addresses the configuration of computing nodes, execution environments, network connectivity, and the allocation of software artifacts to these nodes.
  The steps comprising this activity are shown in Fig. 2.10.

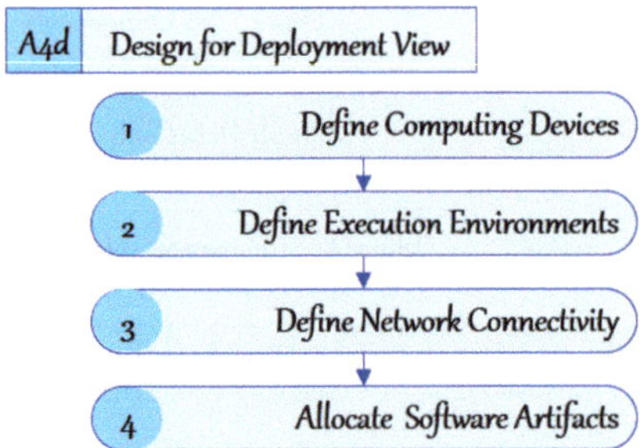

Fig. 2.10 Steps in Activity A4d. Design for Deployment View

Step 1 is to specify the computing devices required for the target system—hardware nodes capable of executing software artifacts. Step 2 is to define the execution environments, including system software such as operating systems, platforms, frameworks, or middleware that provide runtime support for applications. Step 3 is to establish the network connectivity among computing nodes, ensuring the necessary communication infrastructure for distributed interactions. Step 4 is to deploy software artifacts onto the designated computing nodes and execution environments.

- **Activity A5. Design for Non-Functional Requirements**
  This activity focuses on performing architecture design for specified NFRs. It aims to enhance view-based architecture design by incorporating architectural tactics that systematically address the target system's non-functional concerns.
  The steps comprising this activity are shown in Fig. 2.11.

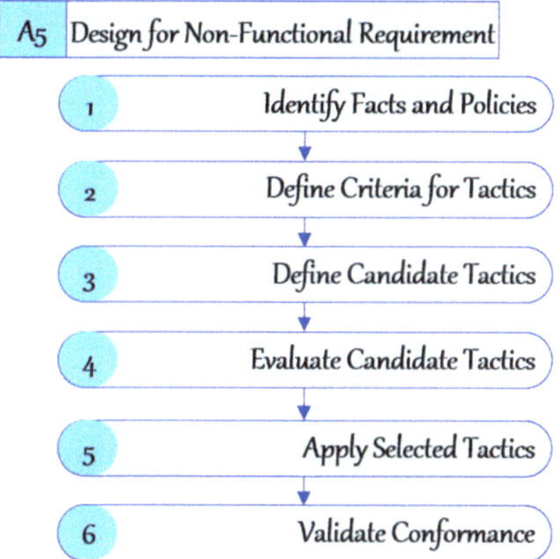

Fig. 2.11 Steps in Activity A5. Design for Non-Functional Requirements

Step 1 is to explore each non-functional requirement and refine it in terms of underlying facts and policies. Step 2 is to define criteria for deriving architectural tactics based on the refined requirement, ensuring alignment with identified facts and policies. Step 3 is to propose candidate architectural tactics that meet these criteria, with each tactic described in sufficient technical detail. Step 4 is to evaluate the effectiveness and feasibility of the candidate tactics, selecting a subset through cost-benefit analysis. Step 5 is to analyze the impact of the selected tactics on the architectural views and integrate them into the overall design to ensure that both functional and non-functional requirements are addressed. Step 6 is to validate that the resulting architecture satisfies all system requirements.

- **Activity A6. Architecture Evaluation**
  This activity focuses on evaluating the architecture design of the target system. Software Architecture Evaluation is a systematic and structured process for assessing the quality and overall suitability of the design. By identifying design flaws—such as risks, inconsistencies, and potential drawbacks—this process enables proactive refinement of the architecture prior to implementation.

The steps comprising this activity are shown in Fig. 2.12.

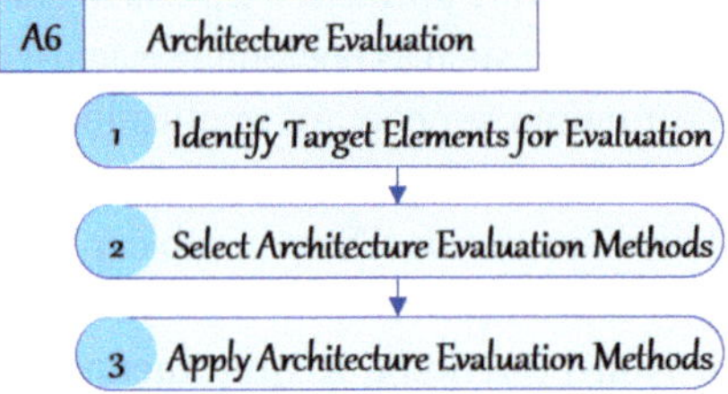

Fig. 2.12 Steps in Activity A6. Architecture Evaluation

Step 1 involves selecting specific elements of the architecture design that require evaluation, such as architecture styles, schematic architecture, view-specific design, component allocation, and deployment design. Step 2 is to determine the most suitable evaluation methods for the selected elements based on their nature and content. Step 3 is to apply the selected architecture evaluation methods on the target design elements.

Process Chart of Unified Architecture Process

The process chart illustrates the sequence of activities and their corresponding steps within the Unified Architecture Process, as shown in Fig. 2.13.

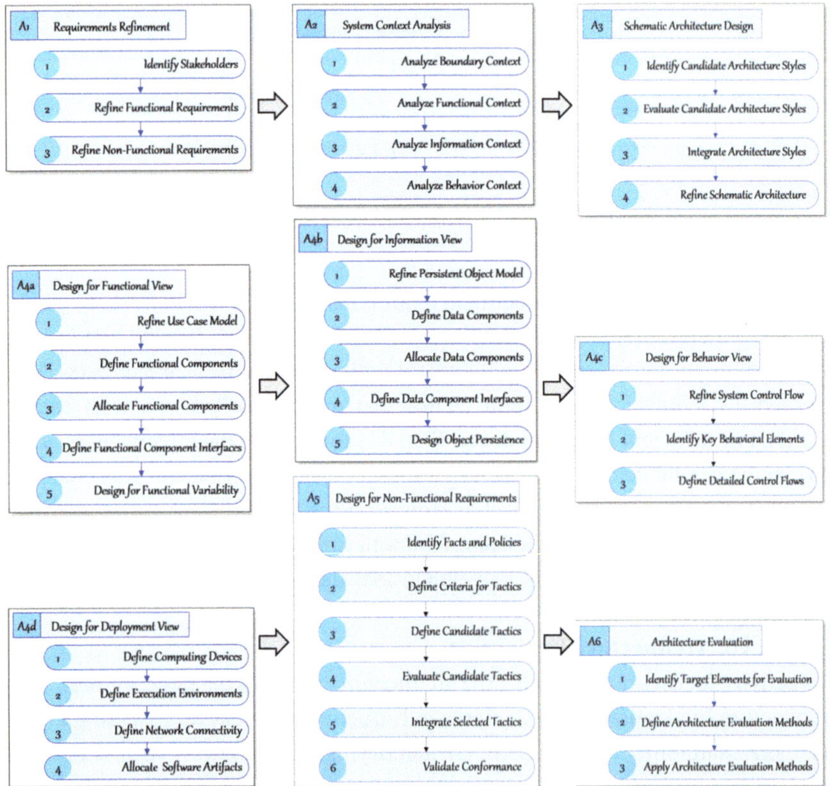

Fig. 2.13 Chart of the Unified Architecture Process

This chart provides a quick reference for understanding the overall workflow of the Unified Architecture Process, highlighting the sequence of activities, their interdependencies, and the detailed steps involved in designing and evaluating software architecture.

Architecture Description Template

The Unified Architecture Process provides a structured template that closely aligns with its methodological framework, enabling architects to document design decisions consistently and effectively. The template is organized to reflect the process's defined activities, steps, and tasks, thereby ensuring traceability and coherence throughout the architectural development lifecycle. Each chapter of the template corresponds to a specific activity, allowing for the systematic documentation of architectural artifacts, design rationale, and resulting outcomes in a standardized format. By mapping directly to the process framework, the template reinforces methodological rigor and enhances communication among stakeholders.

The template, along with detailed usage guidelines, can be downloaded from the companion Web site at https://handson-se.com. The site also offers additional supplementary resources to support the application of the Unified Architecture Process.

2.3.2 Instructions

In the Unified Architecture Process, each activity is composed of a series of steps, and each step is further decomposed into a sequence of tasks. Each step is accompanied by a specific instruction that provides detailed methods, best practices, and illustrative examples to ensure the step is performed correctly, consistently, and effectively.

Criteria for Instruction Development

Instructions in the Unified Architecture Process are developed according to the following criteria:

- **Logical sequencing of tasks**
  To manage the complexity of architectural design, each step in the Unified Architecture Process is decomposed into a series of logically ordered, fine-grained tasks. This aligns with the divide-and-conquer principle, enabling architects to handle design objectives in manageable, focused units while ensuring that tasks are executed systematically and efficiently.
- **Specificity**
  Instructions in the Unified Architecture Process are written with detailed precision to ensure clarity and eliminate ambiguity. By providing figures, diagrams, tables, and examples alongside textual guidance, the process supports accurate interpretation and execution of each design task, thereby enhancing architectural quality.

- **Consistency**
  The Unified Architecture Process maintains consistency in terminology, notation, and methodology across all activities, steps, and tasks. This uniformity improves understanding, reduces the likelihood of errors, and supports collaborative work, ultimately reinforcing alignment with the system's architectural goals.

2.4 Tailoring Unified Architecture Process to Target System

The Unified Architecture Process defines a comprehensive set of design activities; however, not all activities are necessary for every project. Depending on the system's specific requirements and project context, certain activities may be excluded.

To facilitate tailoring the process model to a target system, apply the following criteria to determine which activities may be omitted.

- **Criteria for Omitting A1. Requirement Refinement**
  This activity may be omitted under the following conditions:
  - The system requirements are well defined, and the architects possess a comprehensive and in-depth understanding of them.
  - The project scope is limited, and the requirements are simple, unambiguous, and low in complexity.
  - The requirements have been thoroughly validated or reviewed in prior projects, eliminating the need for additional refinement.
- **Criteria for Discarding A2. System Context Analysis**
  This activity can be omitted under the following conditions:
  - The system context closely mirrors that of previous projects, and architects possess a deep understanding of those contexts.
  - The architecture is reused from a prior implementation in which the system context was already well defined.
  - The system's functionality and its interactions with external entities are simple and clearly understood, making separate context analysis unnecessary.
- **Criteria for Discarding A3. Schematic Architecture Design**
  This activity can be omitted under the following conditions:
  - The architecture was thoroughly defined in a previous phase or project, and no substantial changes to the system structure are necessary.
  - The system is small and straightforward, with minimal complexity, making a schematic architecture design unnecessary overhead.
  - The interaction and structure of components, tiers, and layers are already clear and well understood, removing the need for a separate schematic design effort.

- **Criteria for Discarding A4a. Design for Functional View**
  This activity can be omitted under the following conditions:
  – The system's functional components were previously defined in an earlier project or system, and the functional architecture has already been thoroughly designed and validated.
  – The system's functionality is simple or narrowly scoped, making additional functional design unnecessary and offering limited added value.
- **Criteria for Discarding A4b. Design for Information View**
  This activity can be omitted under the following conditions:
  – The system's persistent datasets have already been clearly defined and validated in a previous project, requiring no additional design effort.
  – The data requirements are minimal or straightforward, making further design of the information view of limited value.
- **Criteria for Discarding A4c. Design for Behavior View**
  This activity can be omitted under the following conditions:
  – The system's runtime behavior and control flows were thoroughly defined and validated in a prior project, requiring no additional behavioral design.
  – The behavioral logic is simple or narrowly scoped, making further design for the behavior view of limited value.
  – An existing behavior model or behavioral architecture from a similar project is being reused, and the behavior view has already been successfully designed and validated.
- **Criteria for Discarding A4d. Design for Deployment View**
  This activity can be omitted under the following conditions:
  – The deployment architecture has already been clearly defined and validated in a previous project, requiring no additional design effort.
  – The deployment environment is simple or standardized, offering little benefit from further design of the deployment view.
- **Criteria for Discarding A5. Design for Non-Functional Requirement**
  This activity can be omitted under the following conditions:
  – The system's non-functional requirements were thoroughly addressed and validated in a prior project, requiring no further design effort.
  – The non-functional requirements are minimal or straightforward, and additional design work would offer limited architectural benefit.
  – An architecture from a similar project is being reused, where the non-functional requirements were effectively addressed and no substantial modifications are needed.
- **Criteria for Discarding A6. Architecture Evaluation**
  This activity can be omitted under the following conditions:
  – The architecture was thoroughly evaluated and validated in a previous project or phase, and no significant modifications have been introduced that would require reevaluation.
  – The system architecture is simple or based on well-established patterns with minimal risk, making formal evaluation unnecessary.

Process Tailoring Example #1

Consider tailoring the Unified Architecture Process for project A.

- **Project Scope and System Characteristics**

  The project A focuses on developing an enhanced version of a cloud-based system serving a global user base. Although the requirements have been clearly defined and validated in previous projects, stakeholders seek to optimize the system structure and improve quality attributes such as availability and scalability.

  The lead architect, having participated in the earlier version's development, possesses deep knowledge of the existing system design.
- **Tailored Process Model**
  - **Activity A1: Requirement Refinement—Discarded**

    This activity may be omitted, as the system's requirements have been thoroughly validated in previous projects and remain largely unchanged.
  - **Activity A2: System Context Analysis—Discarded**

    This activity can be omitted, as the architect possesses in-depth knowledge of the system context from their involvement in the previous version.
  - **Activity A3: Schematic Architecture Design—Applied**

    This activity should be retained to optimize the system architecture and address new deployment environment requirements.
  - **Activities A4a–A4d: View-Based Design—Applied**

    All view-based design activities should be performed, as the schematic architecture will be refined. These views are essential for enhancing overall system quality.
  - **Activity A5: Design for Non-Functional Requirements—Applied**

    This activity is necessary to meet stakeholder expectations regarding improved quality attributes, particularly service availability and scalability.
  - **Activity A6: Architecture Evaluation—Applied**

    This activity should be conducted to ensure the revised architecture satisfies updated requirements and performs effectively in the new deployment environment.

Accordingly, the tailored process for Project A is illustrated in Fig. 2.14.

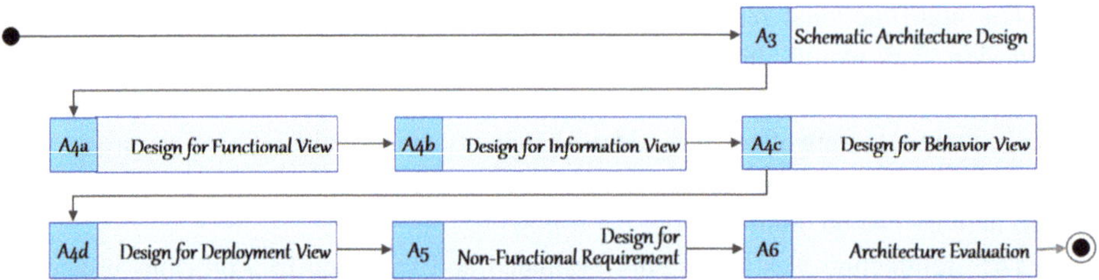

Fig. 2.14 Example of Process Tailoring for Project A

Process Tailoring Example #2

Consider tailoring the Unified Architecture Process for project B.

- **Project Scope and System Characteristics**
  The project B involves developing embedded software for an Adaptive Cruise Control (ACC) system in automobiles, enabling intelligent and safe cruise control through the integration of deep learning models. While the architects and developers are relatively new to machine learning, they can leverage reference architectures for ACC systems available within the AUTOSAR community to guide system structure and deployment design.

  The development team is responsible for designing and implementing deep learning models for object detection and classification near the vehicle, as well as integrating these models into the system architecture.
- **Tailored Process Model**
  - **Activity A1: Requirement Refinement—Applied**
    This activity should be performed to ensure the new features are thoroughly understood and well documented, with particular attention to their integration with existing platform functionality.
  - **Activity A2: System Context Analysis—Applied**
    This activity should be applied to confirm that the new features interact appropriately with external systems, such as third-party payment processors and shipping services already integrated into the platform.
  - **Activity A3: Schematic Architecture Design—Discarded**
    This activity may be omitted, as the existing architecture has been validated and remains stable. The new features do not introduce structural changes requiring a redesign of the schematic architecture.
  - **Activities A4a–A4c: View-Based Design—Applied**
    These activities should be applied to support the integration of deep learning models.

    A4a (*Functional View*) ensures proper design and integration of components related to machine learning, object detection, and control logic.

    A4b (*Information View*) is necessary for managing persistent data and session-related structures.

    A4c (*Behavior View*) captures runtime behavior and control flows, ensuring the system responds correctly based on model predictions and control inputs.
  - **Activity A4d: Deployment View—Discarded**
    This activity can be omitted, as the schematic architecture is unchanged and the existing deployment architecture remains applicable and well understood within the AUTOSAR community.

- **Activity A5: Design for Non-Functional Requirements—Applied**
  This activity is essential to address key non-functional concerns introduced by the integration of deep learning models:
  Performance and efficiency: Ensures real-time operation despite added computational load
  Scalability: Supports consistent performance across vehicle models and configurations
  Safety and reliability: Maintains compliance with automotive safety standards
  Latency: Ensures low-latency responses required for safe operation in real-time systems
- **Activity A6: Architecture Evaluation—Applied**
  This activity should be conducted to verify that the updated system continues to meet both functional and non-functional requirements and performs reliably within the existing architectural framework.
- Accordingly, the tailored process for Project B is illustrated in Fig. 2.15.

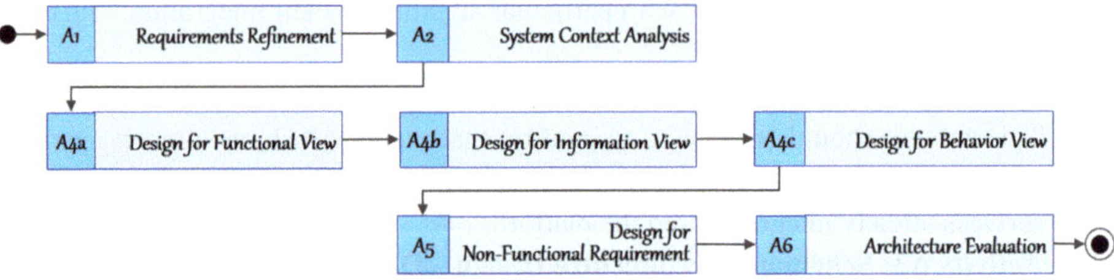

Fig. 2.15 Example of Process Tailoring for Project B

2.5 Benefits of Unified Architecture Process

The Unified Architecture Process offers several advantages when applied to software architecture design, as outlined below.

- **Benefits with the Process Model**
  The Unified Architecture Process provides a structured process model that organizes architectural design into a logical sequence of activities, steps, and tasks. This decomposition facilitates the management of complex design phases, improves clarity, and enhances execution efficiency. The model is also highly adaptable, allowing tailoring to meet the specific requirements of diverse systems and projects.
- **Benefits with Instructions**
  The Unified Architecture Process includes detailed design instructions for each step within every activity. These guidelines incorporate practical examples, diagrams, and best practices, ensuring thorough coverage of implementation specifics. Additionally, embedded checklists help validate design decisions, promoting accuracy and alignment with project objectives.

- **Benefits with Templates**
  The Unified Architecture Process offers a standardized template for documenting architecture at various levels of granularity. This template, aligned with the process model, promotes consistency and completeness in documentation.
- **Addressing Non-Functional Requirements**
  Through Activity A5 (*Design for Non-Functional Requirements*), the Unified Architecture Process provides explicit guidance for addressing critical non-functional concerns such as performance, scalability, and reliability. This dedicated activity ensures that non-functional aspects are treated as first-class design concerns throughout the architecture process.
- **Managing Design Complexity**
  The Unified Architecture Process is well suited for designing complex, large-scale systems. It incorporates established reasoning paradigms—including abstraction, generalization, specialization, divide and conquer, separation of concerns, traceability, and adaptability—to systematically manage complexity. Its structured methodology ensures scalability, maintainability, and robustness in architectural design.
- **Enhancing Design Productivity**
  UAP improves productivity and cost-efficiency by offering a clear, step-by-step roadmap that guides architects through each phase of the design process. By minimizing rework, reducing decision-making overhead, and embedding reusable best practices, the process accelerates development. Standardized tools, templates, and diagrams further streamline communication and facilitate effective collaboration across teams.

Part II

Guidelines for Unified Architecture Process

Activity A1. Requirements Refinement 3

Objective of the Chapter
The objective of this chapter is to provide guidelines for refining system requirements as a foundation for architectural design. It covers the identification of stakeholders, the analysis and enhancement of functional requirements, and the elicitation and refinement of non-functional requirements. These guidelines enable architects to ensure that the system requirements are complete, precise, and aligned with both stakeholder expectations and architectural design objectives.

Introducing Activity A1. Requirements Refinement
This activity is to analyze the initial requirements, identify deficiencies, and refine them. Initial requirements frequently exhibit flaws that may propagate defects into subsequent design models [24, 25]. Therefore, it is essential to conduct a thorough refinement process to resolve these deficiencies before advancing to architectural decision-making.

Common Types of Deficiencies in Software Requirements Specification (SRS)
While SRSs may exhibit a range of deficiencies, six common types are frequently observed, as illustrated in Fig. 3.1.
In the figure, the cloud shape represents the true requirements, while the rectangle symbolizes the initial SRS provided by stakeholders. The partial overlap between the two shapes illustrates that some true requirements are missing from the SRS and that some documented requirements may not accurately represent the actual needs.

S. D. Kim, M. Kim, *Hands-on Software Architecture*,
https://doi.org/10.1007/978-3-032-01184-8_3

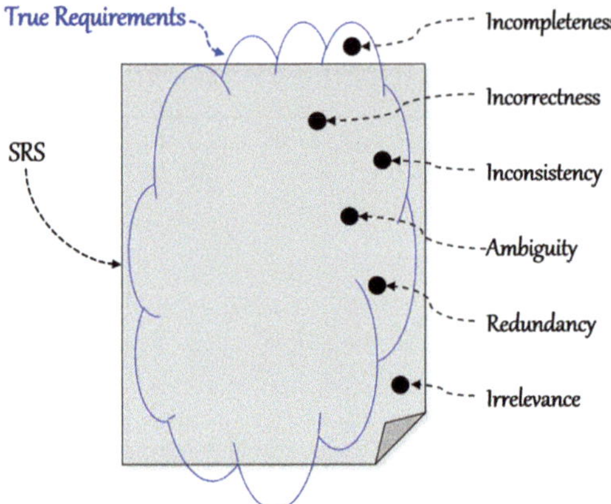

Fig. 3.1 Common deficiencies in software requirements specification

The common types of deficiencies depicted in the figure are briefly outlined.

- **Incompleteness**
  Incompleteness refers to the omission of essential information or specifications needed to construct the intended system. This deficiency can result in missing features or functionalities expected by stakeholders.
- **Incorrectness**
  Incorrectness refers to the inclusion of inaccurate or erroneous information. This may cause the system to perform unintended operations or yield incorrect outcomes.
- **Inconsistency**
  Inconsistency arises when requirements conflict with one another. This can lead to confusion, misinterpretation, and complications during system development.
- **Ambiguity**
  Ambiguity refers to vague or imprecise statements that allow multiple interpretations. This can result in misunderstandings, misaligned stakeholder expectations, and design flaws.
- **Redundancy**
  Redundancy involves the repetition of information within the SRS. This can create confusion, increase the likelihood of inconsistencies, and reduce overall efficiency in development.
- **Irrelevance**
  Irrelevance pertains to the inclusion of information that does not contribute to system requirements. This can clutter the specification and obscure critical requirements during the design process.

Steps in A1. Requirements Refinement

The refinement of system requirements can be systematically carried out through a sequence of steps, as shown in Fig. 3.2.

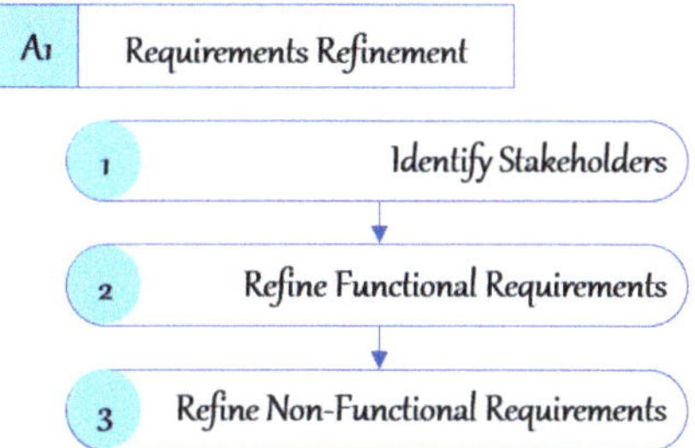

Fig. 3.2 Steps in A1. Requirements Refinement

- **Step 1. Identify Stakeholders**
  This step is to identify the stakeholders of the system. Architects then engage with them to initiate the refinement of requirements.
- **Step 2. Refine Functional Requirements**
  This step is to identify deficiencies in the functional requirements and address them using established requirements engineering principles.
- **Step 3. Refine Non-Functional Requirements**
  This step is to elicit architectural concerns from stakeholders, identify deficiencies in the non-functional requirements, and refine them using requirements engineering principles.

3.1 Step 1. Identify Stakeholders

This step is to identify the stakeholders of the target system. A stakeholder refers to any person, group, or organization involved in the project who holds an interest in the system being developed. Each stakeholder possesses unique concerns and expectations regarding the system. By identifying and engaging stakeholders, architects can make more informed and comprehensive design decisions, thereby ensuring that the architecture aligns with stakeholders' expectations.

3.1.1 Task 1. Locate Stakeholder Groups

This task is to identify the stakeholder groups associated with the target system. Since each system development project has its own set of stakeholder groups, architects must identify the key groups that can provide insights, express concerns, and specify requirements related to the system.

Different software projects involve varying stakeholder groups, but the typical stakeholder groups for software systems are as follows:

- **End-User**: An individual who directly uses or interacts with the system
- **Customer**: An individual or entity that commissions and funds the system, expecting specific outcomes
- **Project manager**: An individual who oversees the project timeline, resources, and budget, ensuring alignment with stakeholder expectations
- **Developer**: An individual or team responsible for designing, implementing, and testing the system
- **Quality assurance specialist**: An individual responsible for verifying that the system meets specified quality standards and identifying potential issues prior to deployment
- **Operator**: An individual who operates, manages, or maintains the deployed system
- **Supplier and vendor**: An entity that provides components, software, or services required for the system
- **Regulator**: An authority that imposes rules, standards, or guidelines with which the system must comply
- **Owner/investor**: An individual or entity with financial or strategic interests in the system

Example

Consider a *Car Rental Management System*, for which the SRS is provided in Appendix B. The system offers a comprehensive set of functionalities designed to streamline operations for car rental companies. Key functionalities include user profile management, car inventory management, reservation management, checkout procedures, and return processes.

Based on the system requirements, several stakeholder groups can be identified, including the following:

- **Customer**: An individual or entity renting vehicles, who interacts with the system to make reservations, manage rentals, and perform transactions
- **Rental center staff**: Employees responsible for day-to-day operations at rental centers, including vehicle checkouts, returns, inventory management, and customer assistance
- **Headquarters staff**: Personnel based at the central office who oversee and coordinate activities across rental locations, ensuring consistent service quality and operational efficiency
- **Finance team**: Individuals responsible for setting rental pricing, analyzing profitability, and managing financial transactions across rental operations, including cost optimization and revenue generation

- **Insurance provider**: External parties offering insurance options to customers, such as full coverage or damage waivers, and verifying personal insurance during the rental checkout process
- **Fleet manager**: An individual who oversees the rental car inventory; manages acquisitions, reallocations, and retirements of vehicles; and ensures optimal inventory levels based on demand
- **Developer**: The individual or team responsible for designing, implementing, testing, and maintaining the Car Rental Management System software
- **Transportation lawyer**: A legal advisor who ensures that the system and its operations comply with transportation laws and regulations and assists in handling legal issues related to rentals and accidents

3.1.2 Task 2. Create Stakeholder Profiles

This task is to identify specific individuals within each stakeholder group and to create profiles for them. A stakeholder profile includes information such as the stakeholder's identification, contact details, and availability.

A template for creating stakeholder profiles is provided in Table 3.1.

Table 3.1 Stakeholder Profile Template

Stakeholder Group	Representative	Contact Information	Availability
...	...	...	...

- **Stakeholder Group**
  Identifies the name of the stakeholder group
- **Representative**
  Specifies the name and affiliation of the individual or entity representing the stakeholder group
- **Contact Information**
  Provides essential contact details, including affiliation, title, phone number, and email address
- **Availability**
  Indicates the stakeholder's general availability for communication (e.g., specific days or time windows), supporting effective scheduling and coordination

Architects can use stakeholder profiles to establish clear, timely, and effective communication with stakeholders throughout the project.

Example
The stakeholder profile table for the Car Rental Management System is presented in Table 3.2.

Table 3.2 Stakeholder Profile for Car Rental Management System

Stakeholder Group	Representative	Contact Information	Availability
Customer	Linda Johnson New York City, NY	(555) 555-0100 name1@example.com	9:00 a.m.–5:00 p.m., Mon–Wed Phone or Online
Customer	James Brown Chicago, IL	(555) 555-0200 name2@example.com	2:00 p.m.–5:00 p.m., Wed—Fri, Phone or Online
Rental Center Staff	Susan Taylor Los Angeles, CA	(555) 555-0300 name3@example.com	9:00 a.m.–noon, Mon–Fri, Office Visits
Headquarters Staff	David Harris Los Angeles, CA	(555) 555-0400 name4@example.com	9:00 a.m.–3:00 p.m., Tue and Wed, Office Visits
…	…	…	…

As illustrated in the table, a stakeholder group may have multiple representatives. Stakeholder availability varies depending on time constraints and preferred methods of communication. Architects can use stakeholder profiles to schedule meetings, conduct interviews, and gather detailed requirements from relevant participants. These profiles also support traceability by documenting who contributed specific inputs or approvals.

3.2 Step 2. Refine Functional Requirements

This step is to refine the system's functional requirements by applying principles and techniques from requirements engineering. Requirements engineering is a discipline concerned with the systematic elicitation, analysis, specification, validation, and management of both functional and non-functional requirements of a software system [26, 27]. It involves engaging stakeholders to gather requirements, analyzing them for consistency and completeness, specifying them in a clear and unambiguous manner, and validating them to ensure they align with user needs and business objectives.

Requirement Engineering Techniques
Requirements engineering techniques are structured approaches used to identify, elicit, analyze, document, and manage system requirements. They aim to clarify what a system should do and how it should perform, ensuring alignment between the final product and

stakeholder expectations as well as project goals. These techniques promote effective communication, consensus building, and prioritization among stakeholders. By reducing ambiguity and improving shared understanding, they help ensure that the resulting system is both technically feasible and valuable to its users.

Various requirements engineering techniques have been proposed [27, 28], and commonly applied techniques are summarized below.

- **Interviews**
  Conduct structured or semi-structured discussions with stakeholders to gather detailed information about their needs, goals, and constraints.
- **Workshops**
  Facilitate collaborative sessions where stakeholders jointly elicit, discuss, and refine requirements—often leading to consensus and clearer understanding.
- **Brainstorming**
  Encourage creative sessions to generate ideas and reveal potential requirements that may not surface through more formal methods.
- **Storyboarding and Scenarios**
  Use visual aids or narrative descriptions to depict specific interactions or user experiences, helping stakeholders better articulate their expectations.
- **Surveys and Questionnaires**
  Use structured instruments to collect data from a broad set of stakeholders, enabling quantitative analysis and a broader understanding of stakeholder perspectives.
- **Job Shadowing**
  Observe users in their actual work environment to identify implicit needs and understand workflows that may not be verbally expressed.
- **Requirements Modeling with Diagrams**
  Utilize visual models to represent system functionality, data flow, and other components to support communication and validation.
- **Use Case Analysis**
  Develop detailed descriptions of system interactions from a user's perspective to define functional requirements and user scenarios.
- **Document Analysis**
  Examine existing artifacts such as specifications, standards, or business rules to extract established requirements and constraints.
- **Prototyping**
  Construct early models or prototypes of the system to visualize and validate requirements in collaboration with stakeholders, especially when requirements are ambiguous.
- **Requirements Prioritization**
  Rank requirements based on importance, urgency, and stakeholder value. Prioritization helps focus efforts on critical features while considering constraints in time, budget, and resources.

3.2.1 Task 1. Identify Deficiencies in Functional Requirements

This task is to identify deficiencies in the functional requirements documented in the initial SRS. Each requirement should be systematically reviewed using the following approaches:

- Apply requirements engineering techniques to examine each functional requirement from multiple perspectives.
- Adopt a critical and analytical mindset to proactively examine each functional requirement, aiming to detect potential issues such as ambiguity, incompleteness, inconsistency, redundancy, irrelevance, and unverifiability that could impair the quality of design and implementation.
- Leverage established taxonomies and best practices to systematically recognize and categorize common deficiency types frequently encountered in functional requirements.

To facilitate tracking and reference, assign a unique identifier to each identified deficiency. A recommended format is FR-DEF-01, FR-DEF-02, and so on, where:

- **FR** denotes Functional Requirement
- **DEF** indicates a Deficiency
- **01** is a sequential number corresponding to each issue identified

This naming convention enables consistent tracking and efficient cross-referencing of deficiencies throughout the refinement process.

3.2.2 Task 2. Resolve Deficiencies in Functional Requirements

This task is to resolve the deficiencies identified in the functional requirements. Begin by formulating specific clarifying questions related to each deficient item. Engage in focused communication with relevant stakeholders to obtain explanations, confirm assumptions, and gather additional insights.

Based on the information acquired, refine the requirement accordingly, and document each refinement. Maintaining a clear record of refinements is essential for traceability, accountability, and preserving the rationale behind changes. Refinements may be documented using either a tabular format or a structured text format, depending on the project's documentation standards.

SRS Refinement Table

The refinements of functional requirements can be systematically documented using an SRS Refinement Table, as shown in Table 3.3.

Table 3.3 SRS Refinement Table

Deficiency ID	Deficiency	Location
Original Context		
Questioning		
Refined Context		

Fill out the table using the following guidelines:

- **Deficiency ID**: Assign a unique identifier to each deficiency for tracking purposes. Use the prefix "FR" for functional requirements and "NFR" for non-functional requirements. For example, *FR-DEF-01*.
- **Deficiency (Type)**: Indicate the type of deficiency, such as *Incompleteness*, *Inconsistency*, *Incorrectness*, *Ambiguity*, *Redundancy*, or *Irrelevance*.
- **Location**: Specify where the deficiency occurs within the requirements document. This is typically a functional requirement number or the relevant section in the SRS.
- **Original Context**: Provide the original form of the requirement that contains the deficiency. This can be a direct copy or a concise summary highlighting the problematic portion.
- **Questioning**: Pose specific questions that aim to clarify or resolve the deficiency. These questions guide stakeholder communication and help uncover missing or incorrect information.
- **Refined Context**: Present the revised version of the requirement after the deficiency has been addressed. The refinement should be clear, accurate, complete, and aligned with stakeholder expectations and project objectives.

Example

The SRS for the Car Rental Management System reveals several potential deficiencies in the functional requirements. Table 3.4 presents a refinement for deficiency FR.DEF.01, which relates to the incompleteness of the Inventory Management functionality. The missing aspects of this requirement are clarified through targeted inquiries made by the architect.

Table 3.4 SRS Refinement Table for FR.DEF.01

Deficiency ID	FR.DEF.01	Deficiency	Incomplete	Location	Inventory management
Original Context	"Vehicles are reallocated among rental centers as needed, optimizing availability across locations"				
Questioning	Should the decision for relocating cars be made by staff members or by the system?				
Refined Context	The system should monitor inventory levels at rental centers, evaluate additional relevant factors, and autonomously generate relocation orders as necessary				

Two representative deficiencies are illustrated in Tables 3.4 and 3.5.

Table 3.5 presents a refinement for deficiency FR.DEF.02, which pertains to the ambiguity of the In-Rental Management functionality. The ambiguous aspects of this requirement are resolved through clarification questions and further analysis by the architect.

Table 3.5 SRS Refinement Table for FR.DEF.02

Deficiency ID	FR.DEF.02	**Deficiency**	Ambiguity	**Location**	In-Rental Management
Original Context	"In the event of a car accident involving a rental vehicle, the company provides essential support to assist the customer in managing and resolving the situation"				
Questioning	Is this essential support provided by staff members, or is it facilitated through the system? Specifically, what functionalities should the system offer to deliver this service effectively?				
Refined Context	Essential support in the event of a car accident should be realized through a collaborative effort between the system and staff members. The system should provide immediate functionalities such as notifying the company about the accident, capturing accident details, and generating an incident report. Staff members play a critical role in delivering personalized assistance once the initial information has been collected by the system				

3.3 Step 3. Refine Non-Functional Requirements

This step is to refine the system's non-functional requirements by applying the principles and techniques of requirements engineering.

3.3.1 Task 1. Acquire Architectural Concerns

This task is to obtain architectural concerns from stakeholders and derive non-functional requirements (NFRs) from those concerns. Architectural concerns represent high-level requirements, expectations, or constraints from stakeholders that influence the architecture of the target system, encompassing both quality attributes and design restrictions. Architects analyze these architectural concerns and map them to specific NFR items.

The relationship between architectural concerns and NFRs is illustrated in Fig. 3.3.

Fig. 3.3 Mapping Between Architectural Concerns and NFRs

An architectural concern may map to zero or more NFR items, whereas each NFR item must be associated with at least one architectural concern. However, not all architectural concerns need to be formalized as NFRs because some concerns may be insignificant, less relevant to the system's objectives, or adequately addressed through architectural decisions without undergoing a formal engineering process.

Example

The architectural concerns regarding the Car Rental Management System are identified as follows:

- **Concern 1: Usability (from customers)**
  The system should provide an intuitive, user-friendly interface that enhances understandability and learnability, ensuring high operability for end-users.
- **Concern 2: Security (from headquarters staff)**
  The system should protect sensitive data from unauthorized access and breaches by maintaining robust security protocols.
- **Concern 3: Maintainability (from maintenance team)**
  The system should be easy to maintain and update, supported by a well-documented design and a clearly annotated codebase.
- **Concern 4: Auditability (from transportation lawyers)**
  The system should log critical transactions in a traceable format to facilitate efficient audit processes.

The initial SRS for the Car Rental Management System specified three NFRs:

- **NFR #1. Enhancing the Profitability of the Car Rental Business**
- **NFR #2. Providing a Wide Range of Applicability**
- **NFR #3. Ensuring High Availability of the Headquarters Server**

Through a careful analysis of the architectural concerns, two additional NFRs were identified, as described below.

- **Concern 1: Usability**
  Usability, while essential, is often treated as a general design guideline rather than formalized as a stringent non-functional requirement.
- **Concern 2: Security → NFR #4. High Security**
  Security is a critical requirement for the target system, which handles sensitive data including customer profiles, inventory, rental transactions, and accounting information. By mapping it to an NFR, the system design ensures rigorous compliance with security protocols, addressing both organizational policies and legal obligations.

- **Concern 3: Maintainability**
  Maintainability, although important for the development and maintenance teams, is generally managed as a quality attribute within standard development practices. Furthermore, the Car Rental Management System is not anticipated to undergo frequent or significant architectural changes.
- **Concern 4: Auditability → NFR #5. High Auditability**
  Auditability is essential for ensuring legal and regulatory compliance, particularly in industries where operational traceability is mandatory. Formalizing this concern as an NFR ensures that the system meets strict audit requirements, thereby promoting accountability and transparency.

This example illustrates how architectural concerns collected from stakeholders can be systematically analyzed to determine whether they should be formalized as non-functional requirements. By carefully evaluating the significance and impact of each concern, architects ensure that the system's architecture appropriately addresses critical quality attributes while maintaining a practical and balanced requirements specification.

3.3.2 Task 2. Identify Deficiencies in Non-Functional Requirements

This task is to identify deficiencies in the non-functional requirements (NFRs) documented in the initial SRS. Each NFR should be systematically reviewed using approaches similar to those applied for functional requirements:

- Apply requirements engineering techniques to assess each non-functional requirement from multiple perspectives, including clarity, feasibility, and testability.
- Adopt a critical and analytical mindset to proactively identify potential deficiencies such as ambiguity, incompleteness, inconsistency, redundancy, irrelevance, unverifiability, or conflict with functional requirements.
- Leverage established taxonomies and best practices to systematically recognize and categorize common deficiency types frequently encountered in non-functional requirements.

To facilitate tracking and reference, assign a unique identifier to each identified deficiency. A recommended format is NFR.DEF.01, NFR.DEF.02, and so on, where:

- **NFR** denotes Non-Functional Requirement
- **DEF** indicates a Deficiency
- **01** is a sequential number corresponding to each issue identified

This naming convention enables consistent tracking and efficient cross-referencing of deficiencies throughout the refinement process.

3.3.3 Task 3. Resolve Deficiencies in Non-Functional Requirements

This task is to resolve the deficiencies identified in the NFRs. Begin by formulating specific clarifying questions related to each deficient item. Engage in focused communication with relevant stakeholders to obtain explanations, validate assumptions, and gather additional insights regarding quality attributes, constraints, or external standards.

Based on the information acquired, refine the NFR accordingly, and document each refinement. Maintaining a clear and detailed record of refinements is essential for traceability, accountability, and preserving the rationale behind changes. Refinements may be documented using either a tabular format or a structured text format, depending on the project's documentation standards.

Example

The SRS for the Car Rental Management System reveals several potential deficiencies in the non-functional requirements. Table 3.6 presents a refinement for deficiency NFR.DEF.01, which relates to the ambiguity of the NFR #1, *High Profitability of Car Rental Business*.

Table 3.7 presents a refinement for deficiency NFR.DEF.02, which relates to the incompleteness of the NFR #2, *Providing Wide Range of Applicability*.

Table 3.6 SRS Refinement Table for NFR.DEF.01

Deficiency ID	NFR.DEF.01	**Deficiency**	Ambiguity	**Location**	NFR #1 of Profitability
Original Context	"For example, rental fee pricing is a key strategy for maximizing revenue while staying competitive for customers. This involves a multifaceted approach that considers several criteria"				
Questioning	What are the key criteria to consider when determining rental fee pricing?				
Refined Context	The pricing criteria are not fixed; rather, each company and rental center may establish and apply its own optimal set of criteria by referencing commonly used factors. Common factors include demand and seasonality, vehicle type and class, rental duration, location-based influences, market competitiveness, operating costs, customer segment preferences, vehicle age and condition, optional add-on services, and the application of dynamic pricing algorithms to adjust rates in real time				

Table 3.7 SRS Refinement Table for NFR.DEF.02

Deficiency ID	NFR.DEF.02	**Deficiency**	Incomplete	**Location**	NFR #2 of Applicability
Original Context	"The missing aspects of this functionality are clarified through inquiries made by the architect"				
Questioning	What are the essential common and variable features that should be considered?				
Refined Context	The system's common and variable features have not been explicitly defined. Therefore, these features should be systematically identified and modeled by the development team during the system development process				

Revising SRS with Refinements

After addressing all identified deficiencies, the initial SRS should be updated to incorporate the corresponding refinements.

3.4 Checklist for A1: Requirements Refinement

The following checklist items can be used to validate the refinement of system development requirements.

3.4.1 Checklist for Step 1: Identify Stakeholders

- Have all potential stakeholder groups been accurately identified based on the given SRS?
- Have stakeholder groups also been identified through diverse sources such as user interviews, current system analysis, document review, and domain expertise?
- Are stakeholder groups appropriately categorized according to their roles, influence, and relevance to the system?
- Have appropriate representatives been identified for each stakeholder group, and are they willing to share their concerns and requirements regarding the target system?
- Is there a comprehensive plan in place for maintaining regular and on-demand communication to ensure ongoing engagement with all stakeholders?

3.4.2 Checklist for Step 2: Refine Functional Requirements

- Have the functional requirements been thoroughly reviewed to ensure they are free from common deficiencies, including incompleteness, inaccuracy, inconsistency, ambiguity, redundancy, and irrelevance?
- Have stakeholders reviewed and validated each refined functional requirement?
- Are the refined functional requirements consistent with one another, without conflicts or contradictions?
- Is each refined requirement technically and practically feasible given the current resources and project constraints?
- Can each refined requirement be traced back to its original source, such as stakeholder needs or higher-level system requirements?
- Has the SRS been systematically updated to incorporate all functional refinements?

3.4.3 Checklist for Step 3: Refine Non-Functional Requirements

- Have all architectural concerns related to non-functional requirements been thoroughly identified and documented?
- Have new non-functional requirements been accurately derived from the identified architectural concerns?
- Have the non-functional requirements been thoroughly reviewed to ensure they are free from common deficiencies, including incompleteness, inaccuracy, inconsistency, ambiguity, redundancy, and irrelevance?
- Have stakeholders reviewed and validated each refined non-functional requirement?
- Is each non-functional requirement technically feasible given the system's current constraints and operational environment?
- Is there clear traceability from each non-functional requirement to its originating architectural concern or stakeholder expectation?
- Has the SRS been systematically updated to incorporate all non-functional refinements?

3.5 Exercise Problems

1. **Amplification of Requirement Defect**
   Explain how a defect introduced during the requirements phase can be amplified in later phases of the development lifecycle. Select a specific type of requirement defect—such as ambiguity, incompleteness, or incorrectness—and explain how this defect propagates and escalates through system design, implementation, testing, and deployment. Provide a concrete example that supports and illustrates your explanation.
2. **Distinction Between Functional and Non-Functional Requirements**
   A software requirements specification typically includes both functional and non-functional requirements. Explain the key distinctions between these two types of requirements. Additionally, discuss how functional and non-functional requirements are related within the context of system development.
3. **Deficiency Types in Software Requirements Specification**
   Identify and describe the common types of deficiencies that may occur in a software requirements specification. For each deficiency type, illustrate with a concrete example derived from either a real-world or hypothetical software project.
4. **Significance of Early Stakeholder Identification**
   Analyze the importance of identifying stakeholders at the early stages of the software architecture process. Discuss how early stakeholder involvement enhances the accuracy, completeness, and clarity of the captured requirements.

5. **Classification of Stakeholder Groups and Their Roles**
   Enumerate and characterize the primary stakeholder groups typically engaged in software system development. Explain the unique roles, perspectives, and contributions of each group.
6. **Techniques for Eliciting and Refining Requirements**
   Describe at least three techniques commonly used in requirements engineering—such as interviews and brainstorming. For each technique, explain how it facilitates the discovery of hidden, implicit, or unclear requirements.
7. **Use of Structured Identifiers in Requirements Refinement**
   Explain the value of employing a structured identifier format (e.g., FR.DEF.01) to track requirement deficiencies. Discuss how such identifiers enhance traceability, promote clarity, and improve documentation throughout the refinement process.
8. **Requirement Refinement Table for Payment Processing in e-Commerce Systems**
   Construct a refinement table entry for a functional requirement related to payment processing in an e-Commerce System. Identify a specific deficiency, formulate appropriate clarifying questions, and present a revised version of the requirement that resolves the identified issue.
9. **Derivation of Non-Functional Requirements from Architectural Concerns**
   Describe the process of deriving NFRs from broader architectural concerns. Illustrate your explanation with an example in which a specific stakeholder concern is systematically translated into a clearly defined NFR.

Activity A2. System Context Analysis

4

Objective of the Chapter

The objective of this chapter is to provide guidelines for analyzing the system context to establish a clear understanding of the system's boundaries and interactions. It covers the analysis of boundary context, functional context, information context, and behavior context. These guidelines enable architects to identify external actors, connected systems, persistent data dependencies, and control flow interactions, thereby ensuring that the architectural design is properly grounded in its operational environment.

Introducing Activity A2. System Context Analysis

This activity is to construct a system context model, which serves as a high-level representation of the system's boundaries, key functionalities, datasets, and behavioral interactions. A system context provides a high-level understanding of the target system by depicting its boundaries, core functionalities, persistent data, and runtime behaviors.

The system context is not a design model; rather, it functions as a foundational reference that informs detailed design decisions in subsequent development stages. Constructing a system context model is particularly valuable when dealing with complex systems or when architects have limited prior knowledge or experience within the system's domain.

The types of system context models can vary across projects; however, common context types typically include the following:

- **Boundary Context**

  The boundary context defines the scope and external interfaces of the system, establishing clear boundaries that distinguish internal components from external elements. It specifies system nodes, elements at the system boundary, essential datasets to be stored, and their interactions. Boundary elements may include users, external systems, and connected hardware devices.

S. D. Kim, M. Kim, *Hands-on Software Architecture*,
https://doi.org/10.1007/978-3-032-01184-8_4

- **Functional Context**
  The functional context defines the specific functionalities provided by the target system, including its interactions with users, external systems, and hardware devices. Understanding the functional context enables stakeholders to gain a comprehensive view of the system's operational capabilities, supported tasks, and external interactions.
- **Information Context**
  The information context specifies the persistent datasets managed by the system and the relationships among them. In object-oriented development, persistent datasets are typically modeled as persistent object classes.
- **Behavior Context**
  The behavior context defines the overall runtime behavior of the system by capturing valid control flows and activity sequences. While the functional context emphasizes *what* the system can do, the behavior context emphasizes *how* the system operates dynamically during runtime.
- **Other Types of System Context**
  Although the boundary, functional, information, and behavior contexts are typically sufficient to capture most system contexts, certain systems may exhibit unique characteristics that necessitate additional context types.
  For example, a *presentation context* may be valuable for systems with extensive user interaction, such as online games, focusing on user interface design, user experience, and interaction patterns. Similarly, a *deployment context* becomes essential for platform-as-a-service (PaaS) systems. This context captures deployment architectures, infrastructure requirements, scalability considerations, and system administration aspects.

Steps in A2. System Context Analysis

The analysis of system context can be systematically performed with a sequence of steps, as shown in Fig. 4.1.

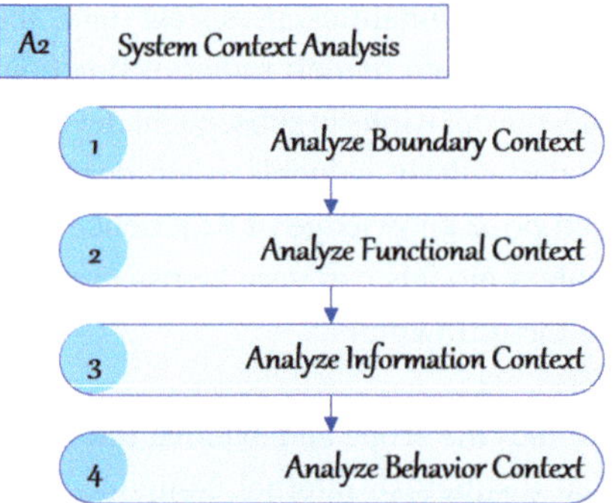

Fig. 4.1 Steps in A2. System Context Analysis

- **Step 1. Analyze Boundary Context**
  This step is to analyze the boundary context of the system by identifying computing nodes, users, external systems, connected devices, and persistent datasets located at the system boundary.
- **Step 2. Analyze Functional Context**
  This step is to analyze the functional context by identifying use cases and the corresponding actors that invoke these use cases.
- **Step 3. Analyze Information Context**
  This step is to analyze the information context by specifying the persistent datasets managed by the system and defining the relationships among them.
- **Step 4. Analyze Behavior Context**
  This step is to analyze the behavior context by specifying the runtime control flows and valid activity sequences within the target system.

4.1 Step 1. Analyze Boundary Context

Data Flow diagram (DFD) includes a partitioning mechanism that allows for decomposing a process into smaller, more granular processes at lower levels. However, to represent the boundary context, only the level 0 DFD—also known as the context diagram—is sufficient, as it provides a high-level overview of the system's interactions with external entities.

This diagram consists of four main elements as illustrated in Fig. 4.2.

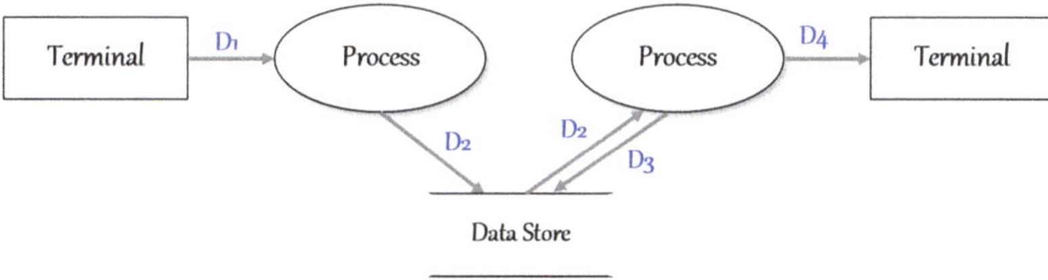

Fig. 4.2 Elements of Data Flow Diagram

- **Process**
  This element represents the transformation of input data into output data within the system, symbolizing an operation or function that processes data.
- **Terminal**
  This element represents external entities, such as users or external systems, that interact with the system, either providing input data to the system or receiving output from it.

- **Data Store**
  This element represents a storage location within the system where data is persistently maintained for future retrieval or processing.
- **Data Flow**
  This element represents the movement of data between processes, terminals, and data stores, illustrating how information travels throughout the system. A data flow can be defined between a terminal and a process, between two processes, or between a process and a data store.

Elements of a DFD are effectively used to represent the elements of a boundary context. A System or subsystem is mapped to a *Process* in the DFD. External Elements in the Boundary are mapped to *Terminals* in the DFD. Persistent Data is mapped to a *Data Store* in the DFD. Finally, Information Flow is mapped to a *Data Flow* in the DFD.

4.1.1 Task 1. Represent System Tiers as Processes

This task is to identify the system tiers of the target system and represent them as processes. In a Level 0 DFD, each process symbolizes a physical system tier, which may correspond to the entire system or a specific subsystem.

- **For a Single-Tier System**
  In a system operating on a single node, the DFD consists of a single process that encapsulates the entire system's functionality.
- **For a Multi-Tier System**
  In a system distributed across multiple tiers, the DFD includes multiple processes, each representing a distinct tier or subsystem.

Example
In the Car Rental Management System, the SRS specifies distinct system tiers, each corresponding to a specific process in the DFD, as illustrated in Fig. 4.3.

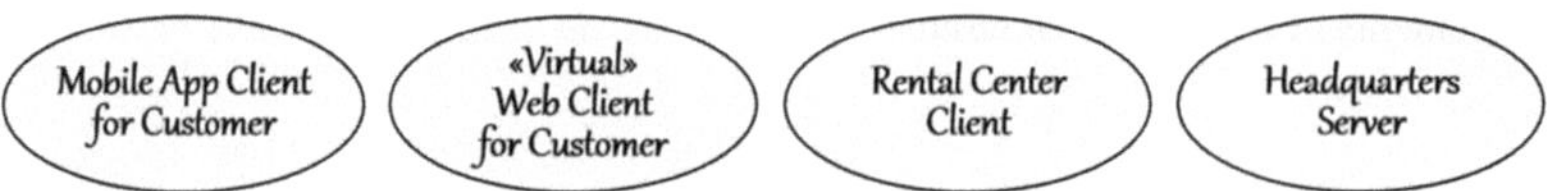

Fig. 4.3 DFD Processes of Car Rental Management System

- **Process of Mobile App Client (for Customer)**
  This process represents the mobile app that provides customers with limited functionalities such as making reservations and retrieving rental contracts.

- **Process of Web Client (for Customer)**
  This process represents a Web-based interface that offers customers functionalities similar to those available in the Mobile App Client. Unlike traditional client applications, the Web Client is specified as a virtual node because customers access its functionalities through Web browsers without installing any software components.
- **Process of Rental Center Client**
  This process represents the client system used by rental center staff, offering core functionalities essential for daily operations.
- **Process of Headquarters Server**
  This process represents the Headquarters system delivering server-side functionalities to its client applications.

4.1.2 Task 2. Represent Boundary Elements as Terminals

This task is to model the boundary elements of a system and represent them as terminals in a DFD. Boundary elements are external entities that interact with the system but exist outside its boundary. These include users, external systems, and connected hardware devices. In a DFD, a *Terminal* represents a boundary element that either provides input to the system or consumes output from it.

Types of Terminals in DFD

- **User**
  A system typically interacts with users who either provide input to the system or consume output from it. These users are represented as terminals.
- **External System**
  A system may interact with external systems that supply data to it or process data from it. These external systems are represented as terminals.
- **Hardware Device**
  A system may interface with connected hardware devices that exchange data with it. These devices are represented as terminals only if they either supply data to the system or consume data from it.
  Examples of hardware devices that qualify as terminals include sensors, actuators, IoT devices, barcode scanners, and printers. Conversely, hardware devices such as cooling fans, power supplies, and similar non-interactive components are not represented as terminals.

Example

The SRS of Car Rental Management System specifies or implies various types of terminals, as shown in Fig. 4.4.

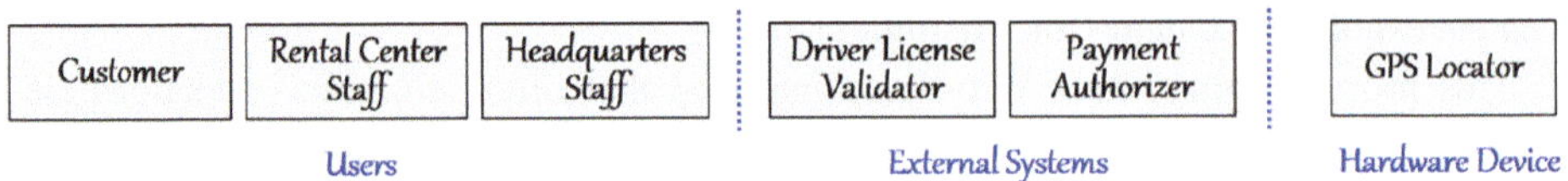

Fig. 4.4 DFD Terminals of Car Rental Management System

- **Terminals of Users**
  The system engages with three types of users: Customers, Rental Center Staff, and Headquarters Staff.
- **Terminals of External Systems**
  The system interfaces with two external systems: the Driver License Validator, which verifies customers' driver licenses, and the Payment Authorizer, which authorizes payments.
- **Terminal of Hardware Device**
  The system interfaces with a GPS Locator, a hardware device preinstalled in rental vehicles, which provides real-time geographical location data to the system.

4.1.3 Task 3. Represent Persistent Data as Data Stores

This task is to identify the persistent datasets managed by the target system and represent them as data stores. In a DFD, a *Data Store* represents a persistent dataset that the system accesses and manipulates. It is typically depicted using a double-lined symbol. A Data Store in a DFD may correspond to various forms of storage, such as a file, a database table, or a main memory buffer.

Persistent datasets can be identified by analyzing the data manipulated by system functionalities, as each function typically operates on specific data. Architects are advised to determine these datasets by posing the question: "What dataset is manipulated by each system function?"

Example

By analyzing the datasets associated with the core functions outlined in the SRS of the Car Rental Management System, the system's persistent datasets can be identified as shown in Fig. 4.5.

The data stores shown in the diagram model the persistent information of the system, categorized into customer-related datasets (Customer, Staff, Rental Center), vehicle-related datasets (Car Model, Car Item, Fee and Rate), transaction-related datasets (Reservation, Rental, Payment, Return Car Service), and operational support datasets (In-Rental Incident, Maintenance).

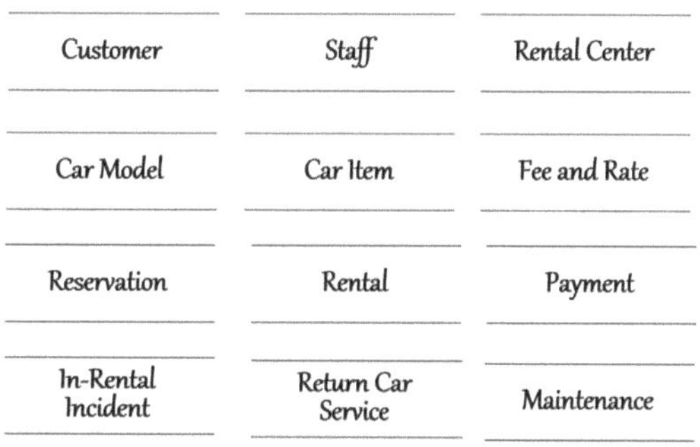

Customer	Staff	Rental Center
Car Model	Car Item	Fee and Rate
Reservation	Rental	Payment
In-Rental Incident	Return Car Service	Maintenance

Fig. 4.5 DFD Data Stores of DFD for Car Rental Management System

4.1.4 Task 4. Represent Information Flows as Data Flows

This task is to identify data flows among processes, terminals, and data stores. Each data flow is represented by a directed arrow with an accompanying textual label. Since data flows are typically not fully specified in the SRS, architects must infer and define them by considering the following questions:

- What input does each terminal provide, and which process receives and processes this input?
- What output does each process generate, and which terminal consumes this output?
- In which data store is the output from a process saved?
- From which data store does a process retrieve the data it requires?
- What data items are exchanged between two interacting processes?

After identifying the data flows, they should be represented as directed arrows with corresponding textual labels. However, when illustrating the system boundary, it is acceptable to omit the textual labels (i.e., the names of data items) for simplicity.

Example

For the Car Rental Management System, several data flows have been identified. The completed Level 0 DFD, which incorporates all four elements—processes, terminals, data stores, and data flows—is presented in Fig. 4.6.

This DFD for the Car Rental Management System incorporates all four element types: processes, terminals, data stores, and data flows. The *Headquarters Server* manages the system's master repository, which explains why all data stores are connected to the *Headquarters Server* process. In contrast, the *Rental Center Client* node handles only a subset of the full dataset within its local database, enabling it to process data independently.

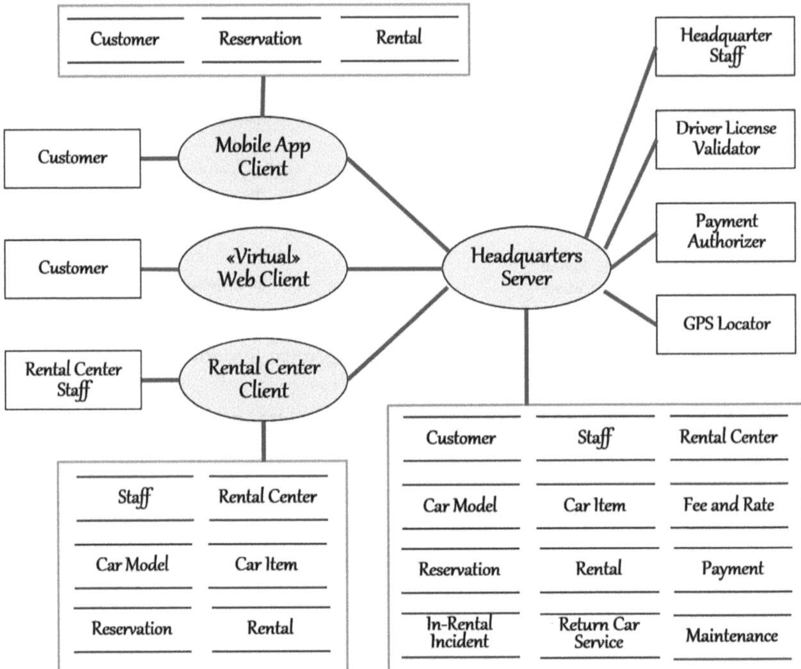

Fig. 4.6 Boundary Context of Car Rental Management System

4.2 Step 2. Analyze Functional Context

This step is to analyze the functional context of the target system and represent it using a use case diagram. The functional context is defined by the collection of functions offered by the system and the actors who interact with these functions. It focuses solely on the functionality the system provides, without addressing the associated datasets or the system's runtime control flows.

The functional context is effectively represented by a use case diagram, which depicts actors, use cases, and the relationships between them, as shown in Fig. 4.7.

The diagram illustrates the elements of a use case diagram, including actors, use cases, and their relationships. Actors initiate interactions with use cases, while use cases may be related through *include* and *extend* relationships. An *include* relationship indicates that a use case explicitly incorporates the behavior of another use case, whereas an *extend* relationship represents optional behavior that is conditionally inserted into the base use case.

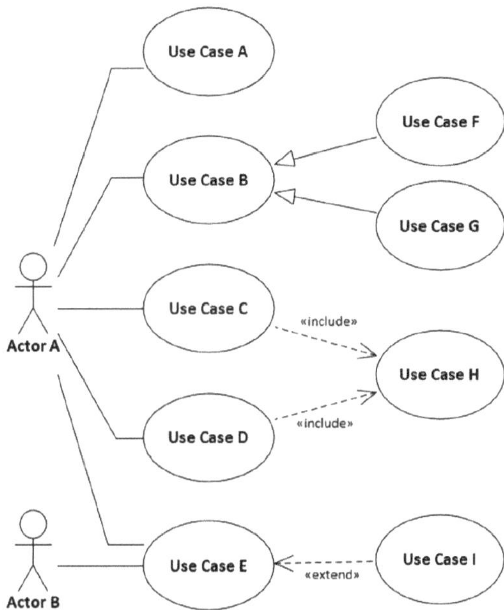

Fig. 4.7 Elements of Use Case Diagram

4.2.1 Task 1. Define Actors

This task is to identify the actors interacting with the target system. In a use case diagram, an actor represents a specific role fulfilled by an entity that engages with the system. Actors may include human users, external systems, hardware devices, or software agents. A software agent actor, often referred to as a daemon process, is an autonomous entity that operates in the background, independently invoking relevant use cases.

Active Actors and Passive Actors

Actors can be classified as active actors or passive actors. An active actor initiates interactions with the system, typically triggering use cases by sending requests or commands. In contrast, a passive actor does not initiate interactions; rather, it is engaged by the system as part of a process or operation. Passive actors respond to the system's actions or receive outputs but do not independently trigger use cases.

Example

The SRS of the Car Rental Management System specifies or implies various actors, as shown in Fig. 4.8.

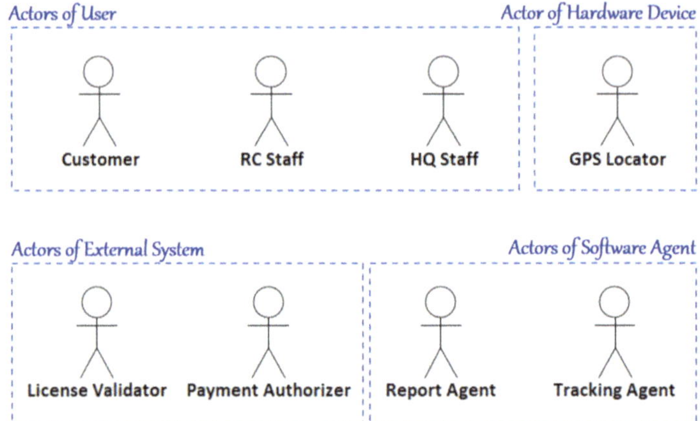

Fig. 4.8 Actors in Car Rental Management System

This system includes all four types of actors.

- **Actors of Users**
  The system interacts with three types of users—*Customer*, *RC Staff*, and *HQ Staff*—all of which are modeled as active actors.
- **Actors of Hardware Devices**
  The system interacts with the *GPS Locator*, which transmits the location of rental vehicles through cellular networks. Hence, it is modeled as a hardware device actor.
- **Actors of External Systems**
  The system interacts with two external systems: the *Driver License Validator*, which validates customers' driver licenses, and the *Payment Authorizer*, which authorizes payments. These are modeled as external system actors.
- **Actors of Software Agents**
  Software agents are not explicitly specified in the SRS. However, architects can enhance the system design by incorporating software agents to enable more efficient operations. This system includes two software agents: the *Report Agent*, which generates periodic business reports, and the *Tracking Agent*, which monitors the location of rental vehicles.

4.2.2 Task 2. Define Use Cases

This task is to analyze the functionality provided by the target system and represent it through use cases. Each use case encapsulates a specific and cohesive function of the system. An effective approach to defining use cases is to first identify the functional groups within the system and then derive specific use cases for each group.

Identifying Functional Groups

A functional group represents a distinct category of system functionality, allowing the system's functionality to be organized as a collection of functional groups. The functional requirements in the SRS are typically organized into a set of functional categories. For example, the SRS of the Car Rental Management System includes categories such as Customer Profile Management, Staff Profile Management, Inventory Management, Reservation Management, and Checkout Management. These functional categories largely serve as candidate functional groups.

The names of the functional groups can either be identical to or closely resemble the functional category names. Each functional group is assigned a unique prefix to facilitate the easy identification, organization, and referencing of use cases associated with it. The prefix is typically formed by taking the first letter of each word in the functional group name. For example, *Customer Profile Management* may be abbreviated as *CP*.

For example, the functional groups for the Car Rental Management System are derived from the functional categories outlined in the SRS, as shown below:

- Customer Profile Management (CP)
- Staff Profile Management (SP)
- Rental Center Profile Registration (RP)
- Inventory Management (IM)
- Rental Rate Management (RR)
- Reservation Management (RS)
- Checkout Management (CH)
- In-Rental Management (IR)
- Return Management (RE)
- Car Maintenance (CM)
- Report Generation (RP)

Defining Use Cases

Use cases are identified for each functional group, with a unique identifier assigned to each. Use case names are expressed in verb form to clearly convey specific functionalities. Each identifier consists of the functional group prefix followed by a sequential number.

Use cases for each functional group can be effectively identified by thoroughly analyzing the functionalities described in the SRS. Since the SRS may not fully specify all relevant use cases, architects should supplement their analysis by leveraging domain knowledge and applying appropriate analysis techniques to identify additional use cases.

For example, some of the use cases for the Car Rental Management System are shown in Fig. 4.9.

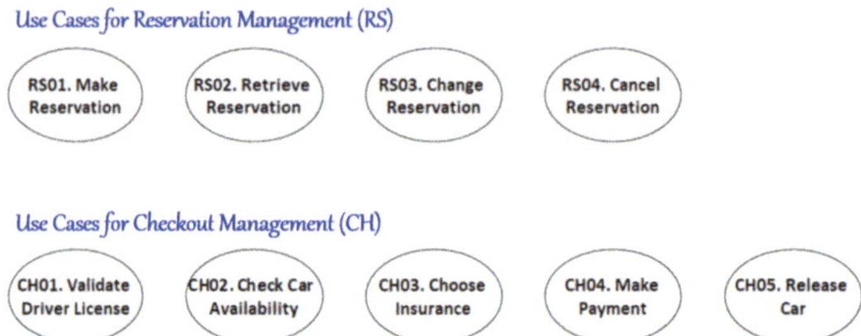

Fig. 4.9 Use Cases Organized by Functional Areas

The diagram shows the use cases for two functional groups: *Reservation Management* (*RS*) and *Checkout Management* (*CH*). Each use case represents a distinct functionality within its corresponding functional group.

4.2.3 Task 3. Define Relationships in Use Case Diagram

This task is to define the relationships within the use case diagram, including relationships among actors, between actors and use cases, and among the use cases themselves. Properly defining these relationships is essential to accurately represent the interactions and dependencies within the system.

Types of Relationships in Use Case Diagram

Use Case Diagram defines several types of relationships, including invocation, generalization, include, and extend, as illustrated in Fig. 4.10.

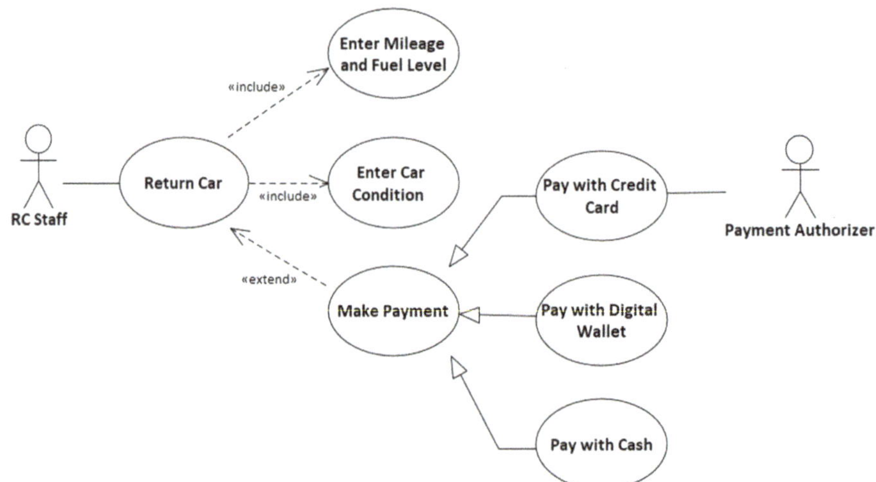

Fig. 4.10 Types of Relationships in Use Case Diagram

- **Invocation Relationship**
  An invocation relationship represents an interaction between an actor and a use case. In a use case diagram, an active actor initiates or invokes a use case, whereas a passive actor is invoked by a use case. This relationship is typically depicted by a solid line connecting the actor to the use case. In some cases, a directed arrow may be used to explicitly indicate the direction of invocation, showing which entity initiates or receives the interaction.
  The *RC Staff* (an active actor) invokes the *Return Car* use case, while the *Payment Authorizer* (a passive actor) is invoked by the *Pay with Credit Card* use case. This distinction helps clarify the roles of different actors in interacting with various functionalities within the system.
- **Generalization Relationship**
  The generalization relationship in a use case diagram represents a relationship where a more general element abstracts and encompasses more specific elements.
  - **Generalization Between Actors**
    A generalization relationship can exist between actors, involving a base actor and one or more derived actors. A derived actor inherits the ability to invoke all the use cases accessible to the base actor. For example, in a system, *Customer* can be defined as a base actor and *VIP Customer* as a derived actor. As a result, the *VIP Customer* actor inherits access to all use cases available to the *Customer* actor, along with any additional use cases specific to *VIP Customer.*
  - **Generalization Between Use Cases**
    A generalization relationship can also exist between use cases, involving a generalized (base) use case and one or more specialized use cases. The generalized use case represents a generic functionality, which is further specialized by its derived use cases.
    In the figure, the *Make Payment* use case acts as a generalized base use case, with its functionality refined by three specialized use cases: *Pay with Credit Card*, *Pay with Digital Wallet*, and *Pay in Cash.*
- **Include Relationship**
  The include relationship in a use case diagram defines a connection between a base use case and an included use case. When the base use case is executed, it always invokes the included use case as a mandatory part of its behavior. The include relationship is typically applied in two primary contexts:
  - **Include Relationship for Decomposing Functionality**
    The *include* relationship can be applied to decompose the functionality of a coarse-grained use case by factoring out specific and distinguishable functional segments into separate included use cases. This facilitates coordination of the overall workflow and enhances modularity.

For example, in Fig. 4.10, invoking the base use case *Return Car* always triggers its two included use cases, *Enter Mileage and Fuel Level* and *Enter Car Condition*. This ensures that, as part of the return process, the system consistently collects mileage, fuel level, and vehicle condition—thereby ensuring these steps are systematically executed.

- **Include Relationship for Encapsulating Shared Functionality**
  The *include* relationship can be applied to encapsulate shared functionality into a reusable included use case that may be invoked by multiple base use cases. This promotes modularity and reduces redundancy within the model.
  For example, in the Car Rental Management System, the use case *Make Rental Payment* for processing an initial rental payment and the use case *Make Additional Payment* for handling a late return payment both invoke the shared functionality encapsulated in the included use case *Make Payment*.

• **Extend Relationship**
The *extend* relationship in a use case diagram defines a connection between a base use case and an extended use case. When the base use case is invoked, the extended use case may optionally be triggered, depending on specific conditions. This relationship is used to represent optional functionality that is executed only under certain circumstances.

For example, in the figure, invoking the base use case *Return Car* may or may not trigger the extended use case *Make Payment*. The extended use case is invoked only if the rental car is returned later than the scheduled return date, thereby requiring an additional payment.

Example

The use case diagram illustrating the functional context of the Car Rental Management System is presented in Fig. 4.11.

This use case diagram provides a high-level overview of the functionality of the Car Rental Management System, illustrating the actors, use cases, and their relationships.

Note that this context-level use case diagram is not intended to provide a comprehensive or precise representation of the system's entire functionality. Instead, it is designed to convey a high-level understanding of the system's functionality. This diagram is further refined with additional details and corrections during the design for functional view.

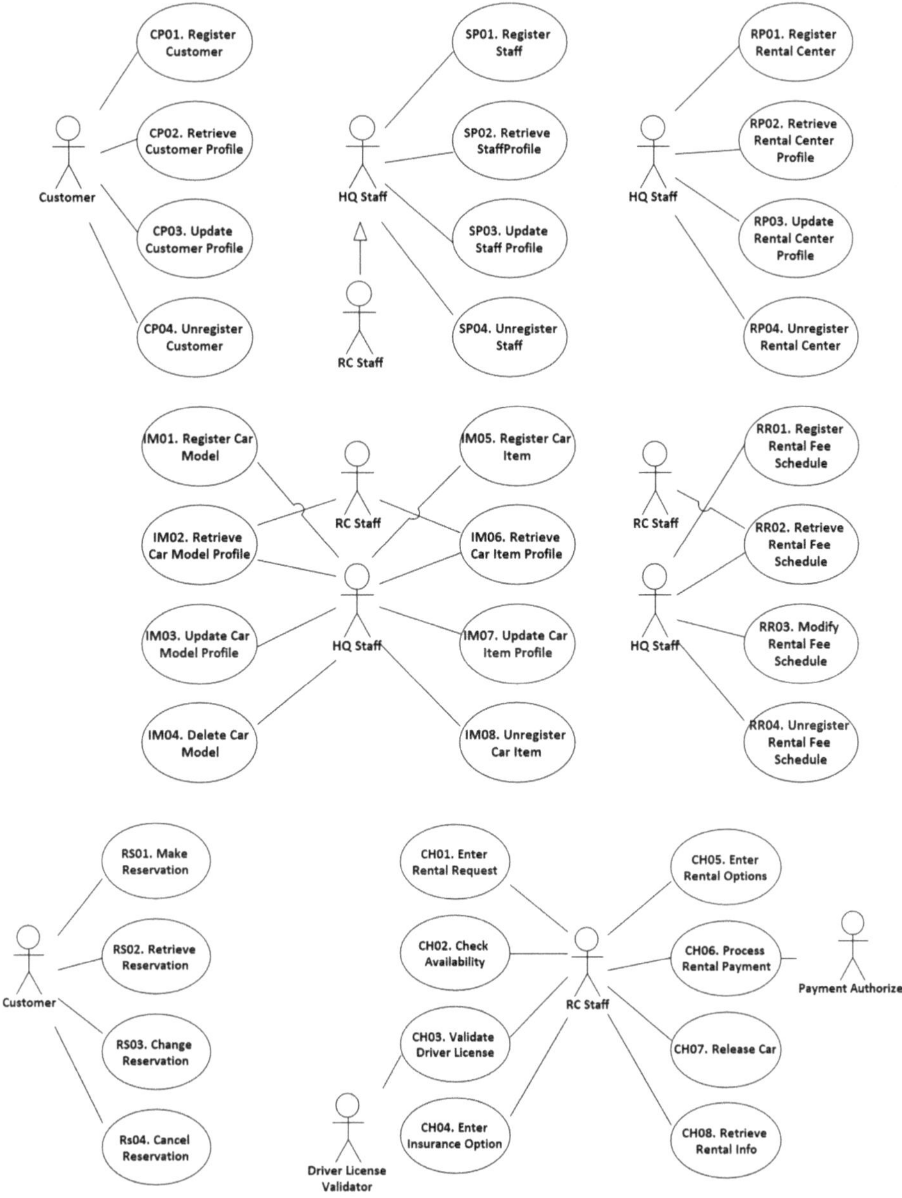

Fig. 4.11 Functional Context of Car Rental Management System

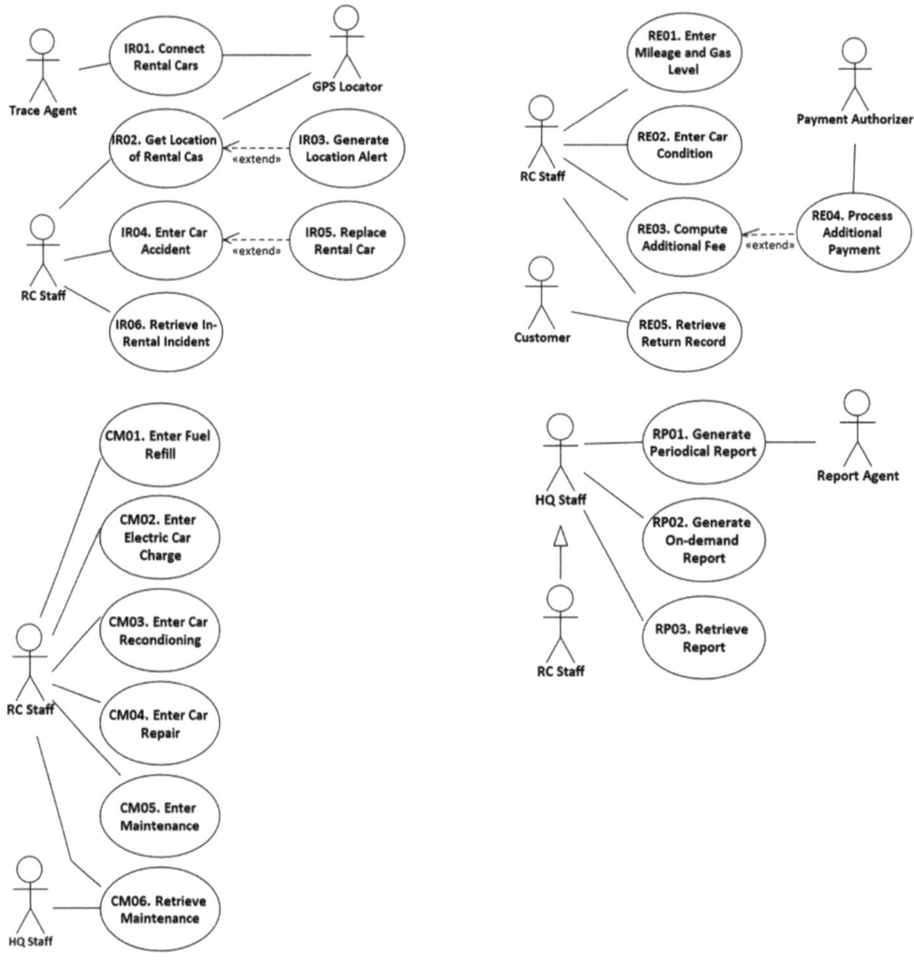

Fig. 4.11 (continued)

4.3 Step 3. Analyze Information Context

This step is to analyze the information context of the target system and represent it using a class diagram. Persistent data refers to data that remains stored and accessible beyond the execution lifecycle of individual processes or transactions. Such data is typically maintained in storage systems, such as databases, and supports consistent retrieval and modification across different sessions.

The information context is effectively represented by a class diagram, which defines classes and their relationships. The key elements of a class diagram are illustrated in Fig. 4.12.

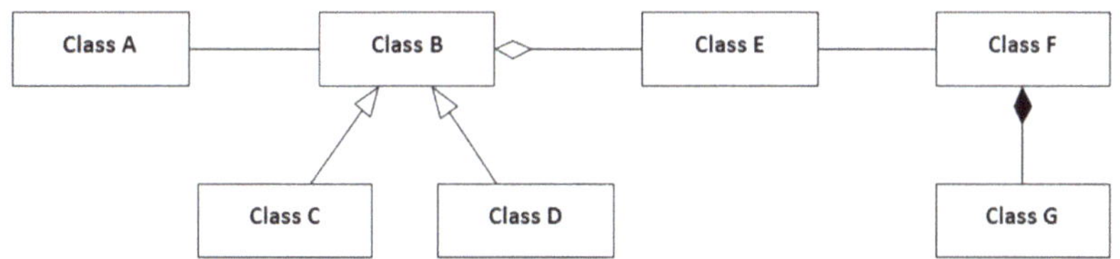

Fig. 4.12 Classes and Relationships in Class Diagram

This class diagram presents seven classes, labeled A through G, interconnected by various relationships. An association relationship is established between Class A and Class B, while inheritance relationships connect Class B with Class C and Class D. An aggregation relationship links the composite Class B to its part Class E, whereas a composition relationship connects the composite Class F to its part Class G.

4.3.1 Task 1. Define Persistent Data as Classes

This task is to identify the persistent datasets managed by the system and represent them as persistent object classes.

Physical Object Classes vs. Logical Object Classes

Persistent object classes are categorized as either physical object classes or logical object classes. A physical object class represents a tangible entity that exists in the real world, such as a *Customer*, *Vehicle*, or *Product*. These classes are typically used to model entities with a concrete presence that are directly referenced within the system's domain.

In contrast, a logical object class represents an abstract data entity that does not correspond to a physical object but is essential for supporting system functionality. Examples include classes that manage transactions, sessions, or configuration settings. Logical object classes are often used to encapsulate business rules, session data, or operational metadata necessary for the system's processes.

For the Car Rental Management System, representative physical and logical classes are illustrated in Fig. 4.13.

Fig. 4.13 Physical and Logical Object Classes

In the figure, the three physical object classes represent tangible, real-world entities directly managed by the Car Rental Management System. In contrast, the three logical object classes represent the outcomes of business transactions and do not correspond to physical entities.

Identifying Persistent Object Classes

The primary source for identifying persistent object classes is the system's functionalities, as each function provides its intended service by manipulating specific data. Nearly every function within the system is therefore associated with data manipulation.

Based on this observation, persistent data can be more precisely identified by examining the data processed within each use case. For example, the *Register Customer* use case creates new customer data, *Update Customer Profile* modifies existing customer data, *Make Reservation* generates new reservation data, and *Retrieve Rental Information* accesses relevant rental data. Subsequently, the manipulated data can be mapped to corresponding persistent object classes.

The relationships among software artifacts involved in inferring persistent object classes are illustrated in Fig. 4.14.

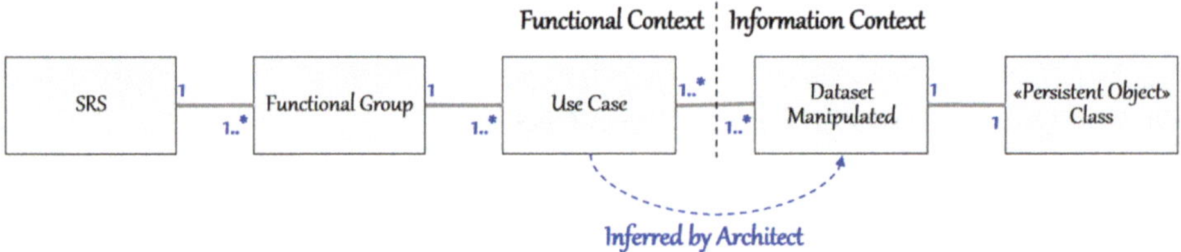

Fig. 4.14 Inferring Persistent Object Classes

This figure illustrates the process of inferring persistent object classes by defining relationships among various software artifacts. The SRS is linked to one or more functional groups, each containing multiple use cases. Each use case delivers its intended functionality by manipulating a specific dataset, which is then mapped to a corresponding persistent object class.

For example, the Car Rental Management System includes a functional group for *Reservation Management* containing multiple use cases. By analyzing these use cases, the data they manipulate can be inferred and subsequently mapped to a persistent object class named *Reservation*.

Identifying Session-Related Logical Classes

A session is a structured record of system usage or user activities. Session information stores essential data for future analysis, auditing, analytics, or reporting. To support these purposes, many modern system designs incorporate session-related classes.

Session-related classes are categorized as logical object classes, as they capture the outcomes of activities and events over time. They are often associated with relevant physical or logical classes, establishing links that reflect their role in representing interactions within the system.

Sessions can be categorized into types such as system sessions, user sessions, and business transaction sessions. A system session records activities and events from system start-up to shutdown. A user session logs activities performed by a user from login to logout. A business transaction session captures the details of a single transaction, such as *Make Deposit*, *Withdraw Money*, or *Transfer Funds* in banking systems.

For example, in the Car Rental Management System, the logical classes *Reservation* and *Rental* serve as session classes. As another example, consider a healthcare management system. Medical treatment for a patient typically involves managing symptoms, conducting diagnostic tests, prescribing medications, and, in some cases, performing surgical procedures. Because medical treatment constitutes a fundamental operational unit in the hospital domain, the logical class *Treatment* should be modeled as a session class.

4.3.2 Task 2. Define Relationships Between Classes

This task is to establish relationships among the identified classes. In a class diagram, five types of relationships are commonly used: dependency, association, aggregation, composition, and inheritance.

Dependency

A dependency relationship represents a connection between two classes in which one class depends on the other in some capacity. It conveys a temporary, contextual, or weak association between classes and is depicted as a dashed arrow pointing from the dependent class to the supplier class. Dependency relationships are often omitted from class diagrams to maintain clarity and emphasize stronger relationships.

Association

An association relationship represents a stable and structural connection between classes. It establishes links between instances of one class and instances of another, enabling interactions between the connected instances. Association is the most common and fundamental relationship type in a class diagram and is represented by a solid line connecting the associated classes.

An example of an association relationship in the Car Rental Management System is illustrated in Fig. 4.15.

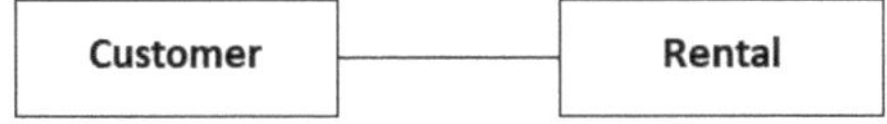

Fig. 4.15 Association Relationships Between Classes

The association between the *Customer* and *Rental* classes establishes a persistent connection between their instances. An instance of the Customer class can be linked to an instance of the Rental class and vice versa.

Aggregation

An aggregation relationship represents a *part-of* or *has-a* association, indicating that one class contains instances of other classes as its parts or components. In this relationship, one class functions as the "whole," while the other class represents a "part" of that whole. Aggregation is visually depicted by a hollow diamond shape on the side of the whole class.

An example of an aggregation relationship for a Graphic Editing Application is illustrated in Fig. 4.16.

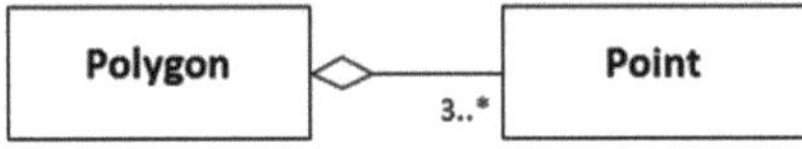

Fig. 4.16 Aggregation Relationship Between Classes

The aggregation relationship indicates that an instance of the *Polygon* class is composed of three or more instances of the *Point* class. The *Polygon* class serves as the whole, while the *Point* class represents its component parts.

Composition

A composition relationship is a stronger form of aggregation in which the lifetime of the part objects is intrinsically tied to the lifetime of the whole object. When the whole object is destroyed, its part objects are also automatically destroyed. Composition is visually depicted by a filled diamond shape on the side of the whole class.

An example of a composition relationship for a Graphic Editing Application is illustrated in Fig. 4.17.

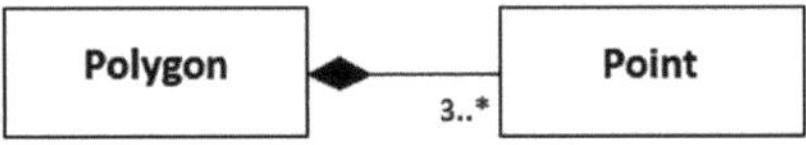

Fig. 4.17 Composition Relationship Between Classes

The composition relationship indicates that a *Polygon* object is composed of *Point* objects, with the lifetime of the *Point* objects tied to that of the *Polygon* object. When the *Polygon* object is destroyed, its associated *Point* objects are also destroyed.

Inheritance

An inheritance relationship represents a generalization between a general class, known as the *superclass*, and a more specific class, known as the *subclass*. This relationship enables the subclass to inherit the attributes, methods, and relationships defined in its superclass, promoting reusability and supporting a hierarchical organization of classes.

The inheritance relationship is often interpreted as an "IS-A" relationship between a superclass and its subclasses. It implies that a subclass is a specialized version of its superclass, inheriting the superclass's features while potentially adding its own unique attributes and methods.

An example of an inheritance relationship for the Car Rental Management System is shown in Fig. 4.18.

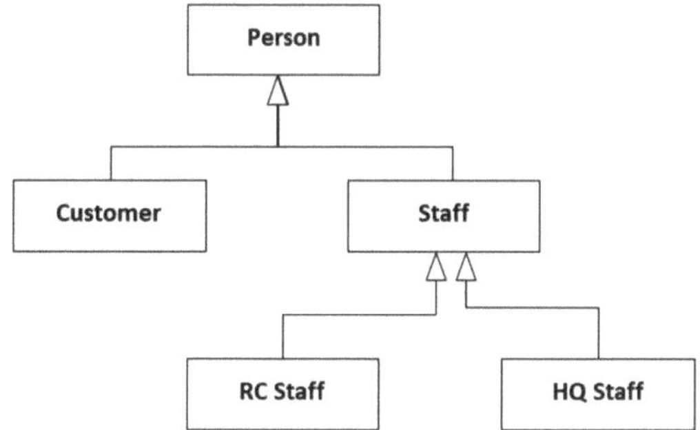

Fig. 4.18 Inheritance Relationship Between Classes

The superclass *Person* serves as a generalization for its subclasses *Customer* and *Staff*. The *Staff* class further generalizes its own subclasses, *RC Staff* and *HQ Staff*. Through inheritance, each subclass inherits attributes, operations, and relationships from its respective superclass while extending its functionality with additional features specific to the subclass.

4.3.3 Task 3. Define Cardinality on Relationships

This task is to define cardinalities in relationships. Cardinality specifies the number of instances of one class that can be associated with instances of another class through a given relationship. It establishes the multiplicity of objects participating in the relationship, indicating how many instances of each class can be linked together.

Cardinality is represented using numbers, ranges, or specific symbols to indicate the multiplicity of a relationship. The most commonly used symbols to denote cardinality are as follows:

- "**1**" indicates a cardinality of exactly one instance.
- "**0..1**" represents an optional cardinality, allowing for zero or one instance.
- "**0..***" denotes a cardinality of zero or more instances.
- "**1..***" signifies a cardinality of one or more instances.

- "**m..n**" denotes a cardinality range, a minimum of *m* and a maximum of *n* instances.

Figure 4.19 shows the cardinalities of relationships among classes.

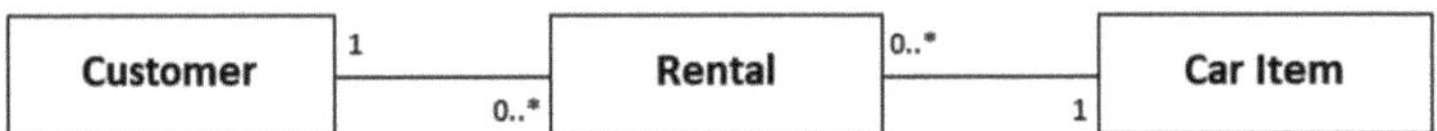

Fig. 4.19 Cardinality of Relationships in Car Rental Management System

The *Customer* class has an association relationship with the *Rental* class. An instance of *Customer* can be associated with zero or more instances of *Rental*, while each instance of *Rental* is associated with exactly one instance of *Customer*.

Similarly, the cardinalities in the association relationship between *Rental* and *Car Item* specify the multiplicities of participating objects: an instance of *Rental* can be associated with zero or more instances of *Car Item*, and each *Car Item* is associated with exactly one instance of *Rental*.

Completing the Class Diagram for Information Context

At this stage, the information context of the system is finalized by integrating the identified classes, relationships, and cardinalities into the class diagram. The completed class diagram provides a comprehensive representation of the system's persistent data entities and their interrelationships.

The class diagram illustrating the information context of the Car Rental Management System is presented in Fig. 4.20.

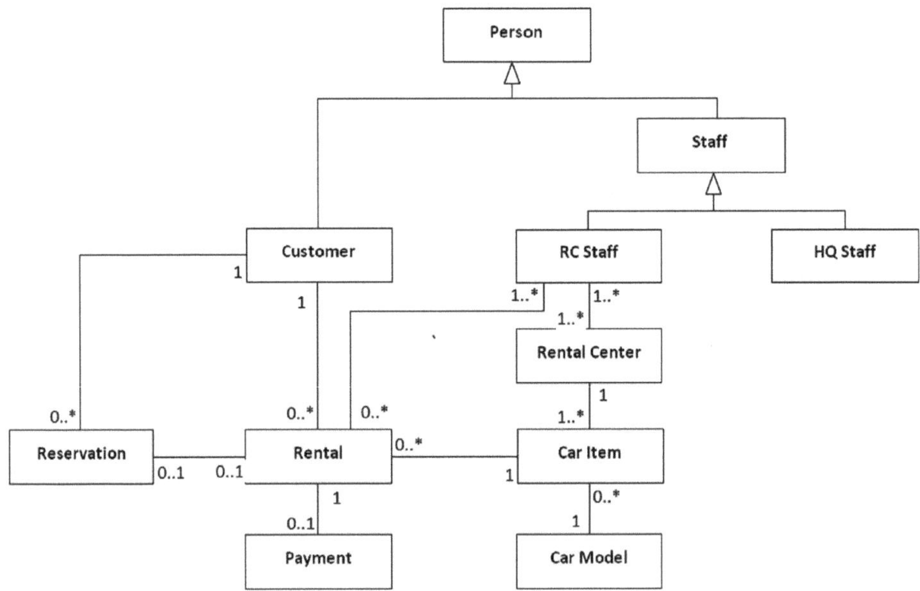

Fig. 4.20 Information Context of Car Rental Management System

This class diagram represents the essential persistent datasets as classes, along with the relationships among them. It provides a high-level overview of the persistent data managed by the Car Rental Management System.

Note that this context-level class diagram is not intended to provide a complete or detailed representation of the system's information structure. Rather, it is designed to convey a high-level understanding of the system's persistent datasets. This diagram is subsequently refined with additional details and corrections during the design of the information view.

4.4 Step 4. Analyze Behavior Context

This step is to analyze the behavioral context of the target system and represent it using an activity diagram. The behavioral context provides a high-level overview of the system's overall control flow, illustrating the sequence of execution during runtime.

Typically, a system's overall control flow is implemented within a main method or function, such as the main() function in C or C++, the main() method of a class in Java, or the if __name__ == "__main__" block in Python.

Activity Diagram for Behavior Context

The behavior context of a system can be effectively modeled using an activity diagram in UML, which provides a comprehensive set of constructs for representing system behavior. Key elements of an activity diagram are shown in Fig. 4.21.

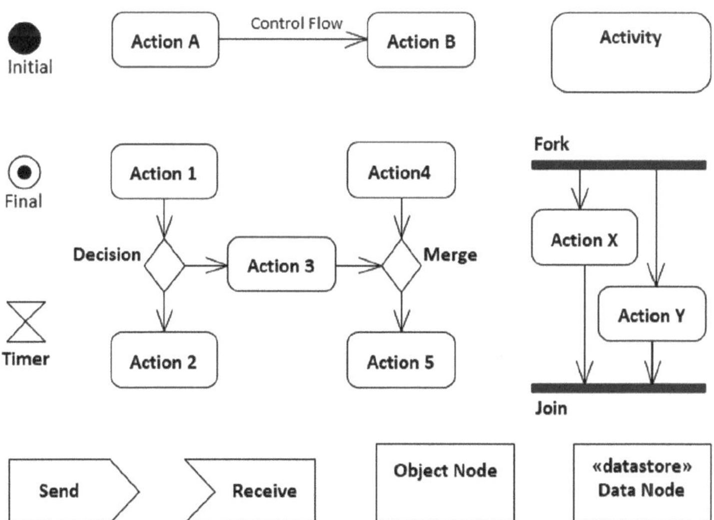

Fig. 4.21 Key Elements of Activity Diagram

- **Action**
  An action represents a single, atomic operation within the system. It must either complete entirely or abort without partial execution. An action signifies a specific, indivisible task performed as part of the system's behavior.
- **Activity**
  An activity represents a coherent and self-contained unit of work comprising multiple actions. It encapsulates a collection of actions to provide a broader representation of the system's behavior.
- **Initial Node**
  An initial node marks the starting point of the control flow in an activity diagram. It indicates where the execution of an activity begins.
- **Final Node**
  A final node signifies the termination of an activity or a system process. It represents the end point of the control flow within the diagram.
- **Control Flow**
  A control flow defines the sequence in which actions and activities are executed. It visually represents the progression of steps during the execution process.
- **Decision Node**
  A decision node represents a point where the control flow diverges into multiple alternative paths based on specified conditions. It models decision-making logic within the system or an activity.
- **Merge Node**
  A merge node represents the convergence of multiple alternative control flows back into a single path. It is typically paired with a decision node to model branching and merging in the control flow.
- **Fork and Join Nodes**
  Fork and join nodes represent parallelism and synchronization within the control flow. A fork node splits a single control flow into multiple concurrent paths, enabling parallel execution of actions or activities. A join node synchronizes multiple concurrent control flows, merging them into a single path and ensuring that all parallel paths have completed before continuing.
- **Partition**
  A partition, also known as a swimlane, groups related actions or activities based on an organizational entity, such as a subsystem, component, or object. Partitions organize activities to enhance clarity and provide a structured view of system behavior.
- **Event**
  An event represents an occurrence or trigger that initiates a change in the system's behavior or alters the control flow. Events may be external, such as user input or incoming messages, or internal, such as timer expirations or state changes.
- **Timer**
  A timer models a time-based event or condition. It specifies that a particular action or activity is triggered after a specified duration or at a specific point in time. Timers are used to model time-dependent behaviors and impose timing constraints on system activities.

4.4.1 Task 1. Allocate Functional Groups onto Tiers

This task is to assign the functional groups of a system across multiple tiers within a tiered architecture. It aims to distribute the system's functional components optimally across these tiers, ensuring that each tier handles specific aspects of the overall functionality. This allocation is crucial for ensuring that each tier operates independently with maximal efficiency while supporting robust communication and coordination between tiers.

The allocation of functional groups can be specified using a table, as illustrated in Table 4.1.

Table 4.1 Functional Group Allocation Table

	Tiers		
Functional Groups	Tier #1	Tier #2	Tier #3
Functional Group #1	✓		
Functional Group #2		✓	✓
Functional Group #3	✓	✓	
…	…	…	….

Each functional group is assigned to one or more tiers within the system. When a functional group spans multiple tiers, its functionality may exhibit subtle differences across these tiers, reflecting the specific role and capabilities of each tier.

Example

In the Car Rental Management System, the boundary context specifies four tiers. However, the *Web Client tier* is designated as a virtual node. Therefore, the system's functional groups are allocated across the three physical tiers, as shown in Table 4.2.

Table 4.2 Functional Group Allocation for Car Rental Management System

	Tiers		
Functional Groups	Mobile Client	Rental Center Client	Headquarters Server
Customer Profile Management	✓		✓ (Read-only)
Staff Profile Management		✓	✓
Rental Center Profile Registration		✓ (Read-only)	✓
Inventory Management		✓ (Read-only)	✓
Rental Rate Management		✓ (Read-only)	✓
Reservation Management	✓	✓ (Read-only)	✓ (Read-only)
Checkout Management	✓ (Read-only)	✓	✓ (Read-only)
In-Rental Management		✓	✓ (Read-only)
Return Management	✓ (Read-only)	✓	✓ (Read-only)
Car Maintenance		✓	✓ (Read-only)
Report Generation		✓	✓

Each tier is allocated its respective functional groups. Within a tier, some functional groups are designated as *Read-only*, indicating that the tier exclusively handles read operations for those groups.

- **Functionality of Headquarters Server Tier**
  The Headquarters Server tier provides an extensive range of functionalities, offering essential services to client applications and handling computation-intensive operations.
- **Functionality of Rental Center Client Tier**
  The Rental Center Client tier provides functionalities related to operations performed at rental centers, such as check-out and return procedures.
- **Functionality of Mobile Client Tier**
  The Mobile Client tier provides functionalities available to customers, including registering customer profiles, making reservations, and retrieving rental information.

4.4.2 Task 2. Define Invocation Patterns

This task is to identify the most suitable invocation patterns for each functional group within each tier. Defining the overall system control flow is often challenging, as the SRS typically does not explicitly specify the system's runtime behavior. An effective approach to addressing this challenge is to apply invocation patterns and define the behavioral context based on the identified patterns.

Common Invocation Patterns

An invocation pattern represents a reusable control flow commonly employed in system behavior modeling. Each pattern is characterized by a specific sequence of actions and is tailored to achieve a distinct type of system behavior. Invocation patterns are represented using activity diagrams.

Commonly used patterns are shown in Fig. 4.22.

- **Sequential Invocation**
  The sequential invocation pattern is employed when a system must execute actions or activities in a strict sequence without any branching. While a sequential invocation can constitute part of a system's main process, it frequently appears within other invocation patterns, such as the closed loop pattern or parallel invocation.
- **Explicit Invocation**
  The explicit invocation pattern is applied when a user selects an action from a predefined set of options. In this pattern, the system presents a menu of options; the user selects an option, and the system executes the corresponding action. The selected functionality is executed synchronously—while one option is active, all other options remain unavailable until the current action completes.

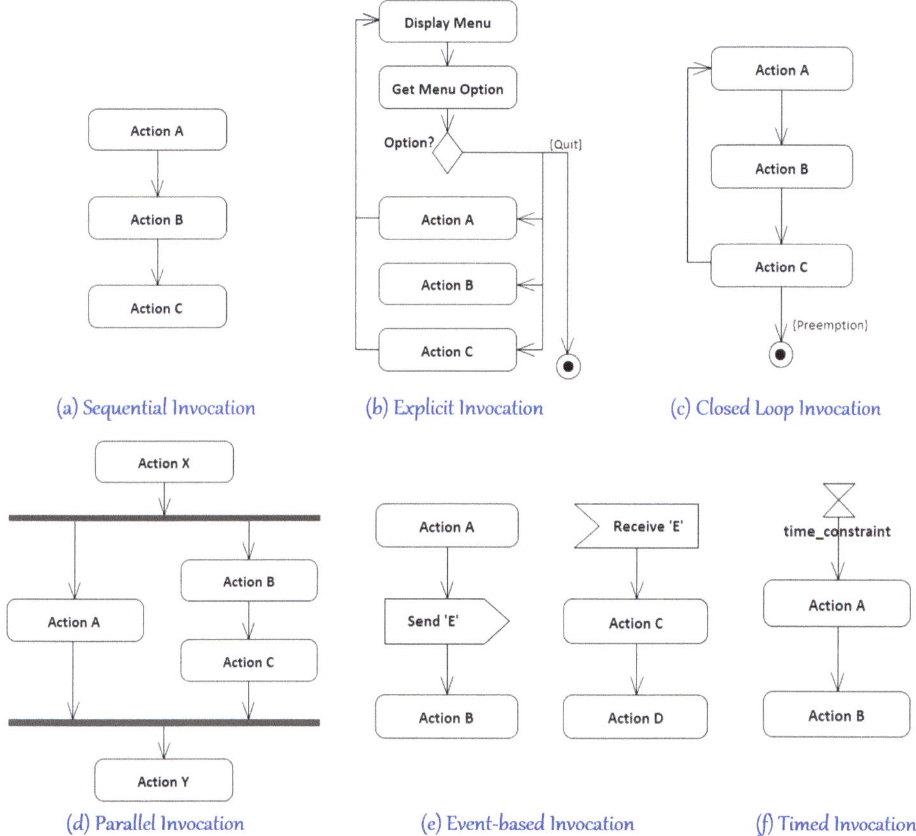

Fig. 4.22 Invocation Patterns for Modeling System Behavior

- **Closed Loop Invocation**
  The closed loop invocation pattern is used when a system needs to repeatedly execute specific functionality without interruption. This pattern is often applied in the development of embedded systems that require self-managing capabilities. For example, autonomous vehicles operate with limited driver intervention, functioning instead in a self-managed manner. The closed loop invocation pattern can effectively model this behavior. Functionality governed by a closed loop invocation can be terminated or paused through preemption or interruption mechanisms.
- **Parallel Invocation**
  The parallel invocation pattern is used when a system must execute multiple threads of control simultaneously. Each thread operates independently, and upon completion, all threads converge at a synchronization point. To ensure the integrity of parallel processing, it is crucial that each thread initiated at the fork point has a corresponding thread at the join point.

- **Event-Based Invocation**
  The event-based invocation pattern is used when a system executes specific functionality in response to incoming events. In this pattern, the system comprises event emitters and event handlers; when an event occurs, it triggers the associated event handler. Event emitters and handlers are designed as separate entities, such as distinct threads, processes, or tiers, enabling asynchronous operation. Events may be exchanged within a single tier or across multiple tiers, facilitating flexible and distributed event-driven processing.
  - **Intra-tier Event**
    An intra-tier event is generated and processed within the same tier. This type of event transmission is typically implemented through message broadcasting schemes, allowing components within the tier to receive and process events locally.
  - **Inter-tier Event**
    An inter-tier event is generated in one tier and processed in another. This type of event transmission is typically achieved using inter-tier messaging schemes, enabling communication and coordination across different system layers or components.
- **Timed Invocation**
  The timed invocation pattern is used when a system needs to execute functionality at defined time intervals or within specific time constraints. Common types of timed invocation include the following:
  - **Invocation at Fixed Intervals**
    The target functionality is invoked at predefined intervals, such as daily at 5:00 p.m., every Friday, or at the end of each month.
  - **Invocation Within a Time Period**
    The target functionality is triggered within a specified time window, such as between 8:00 a.m. and 8:10 a.m. or only during weekends.
  - **Invocation After Time Elapse**
    The target functionality is invoked following a specified delay, such as "30 min later" or "before sunset."

  Additional time constraints can be flexibly defined to meet specific system requirements.

Example
The Car Rental Management System is organized into several functional groups, as detailed in the functional context. Each functional group is configured with one or more appropriate invocation patterns.

An essential macro-level design decision for system behavior is determining parallelism among functional groups, specifically identifying which functional groups can operate concurrently. In the Car Rental Management System, the following functional groups are designed to operate in parallel:

- Checkout Management
- Rental Incident Management
- Return Management

- Post-return Maintenance
- Business Report Generation

These functional groups are represented as distinct, independent threads within a fork-join construct in the activity diagram.

After identifying the functional groups with parallel invocation, appropriate invocation patterns are assigned to each functional group. The designated invocation patterns for the system are summarized in Table 4.3.

Table 4.3 Invocation Pattern Table for Car Rental Management System

Tiers / Functional Components	Mobile Client	Rental Center Client	Headquarters Server
Customer Profile Management	Explicit	Explicit (Read)	Explicit (Read)
Staff Profile Management		Explicit	Explicit
Rental Center Profile Registration		Explicit (Read)	Explicit
Inventory Management		Explicit	Explicit
Rental Rate Management		Explicit (Read)	Explicit
Reservation Management	Explicit	Explicit (Read)	Explicit (Read)
Checkout Management	Explicit (Read)	Explicit	Explicit (Read)
In-Rental Management		Explicit, C-Loop, Event	Explicit (Read)
Return Management	Explicit (Read)	Explicit	Explicit (Read)
Car Maintenance		Explicit	Explicit (Read)
Report Generation		Explicit	Explicit, C-Loop, Timer

In the table, each functional group is defined with one or more invocation patterns.

- **Functional Groups of the Mobile Client Tier**
  This tier is assigned functional groups that employ explicit invocation patterns. Customers using this tier can manage their profiles and handle reservations. They have read-only access to information related to checkouts and returns.
- **Functional Groups of the Rental Center Client Tier**
  This tier is assigned the full set of functional groups and manages core rental-related functionalities such as *Checkout Management*, *In-Rental Management*, and *Return Management*. The functional group *In-Rental Management* is configured with multiple invocation patterns, including closed-loop and event-based invocations. As a result, this functionality operates in a continuous loop, with certain actions triggered by specific events.
- **Functional Groups of the Headquarters Server Tier**
  This tier is assigned the full set of functional groups but has read-only access to core rental-related functionalities. This configuration allows the server tier to directly manage corporate-level inventory management and rental fee management while being limited to retrieving rental-related data.

4.4.3 Task 3. Define Context-level System Control Flow

This task is to define the context-level control flow of the system by creating an activity diagram for each tier. The activity diagram can be effectively constructed by leveraging the invocation patterns assigned to the functional groups.

Procedure for Defining System Control Flow with Activity Diagram
The system's overall control flow can be systematically specified using an activity diagram by following the sequence below:

1. **Define Initial and Final Nodes**
   Establish a starting node and one or more final nodes to represent the initiation and termination points of the control flow.
2. **Define Initialization Behavior**
   Specify the initialization behavior at the beginning of the activity diagram, as most software systems require setup procedures at the start of the main process. Examples of initialization behaviors include loading the initial user interface, establishing network connections, connecting to hardware devices, accessing external services, and setting system attributes.
3. **Define Parallel Processing Behavior at the Macro Level**
   Establish a fork-join construct to model parallelism and create multiple threads for functional groups that employ parallel invocation patterns.
4. **Define the Control Flow for Each Functional Group**
   Establish the control flow for each functional group by referencing the use cases associated with that group. The control flow should incorporate the invocation patterns defined for each functional group.
5. **Define Clean-up Behavior**
   Specify the clean-up behavior at the conclusion of the activity, as software systems typically require finalization tasks upon completing the main process. Examples of clean-up tasks include displaying session closure messages, disconnecting network connections, terminating connections to hardware devices, closing access to external services, and saving persistent information to external storage.

Example
The boundary context of the Car Rental Management System encompasses three physical tiers, each requiring a corresponding activity diagram to illustrate its control flow. The activity diagram for each tier can be constructed based on the invocation patterns assigned to the functional groups.

For example, the activity diagram for the Rental Center Client tier is illustrated in Fig. 4.23.

- **Defining the Initialization Behavior**
  Following the initial node, the system performs a login procedure as part of the initialization process.

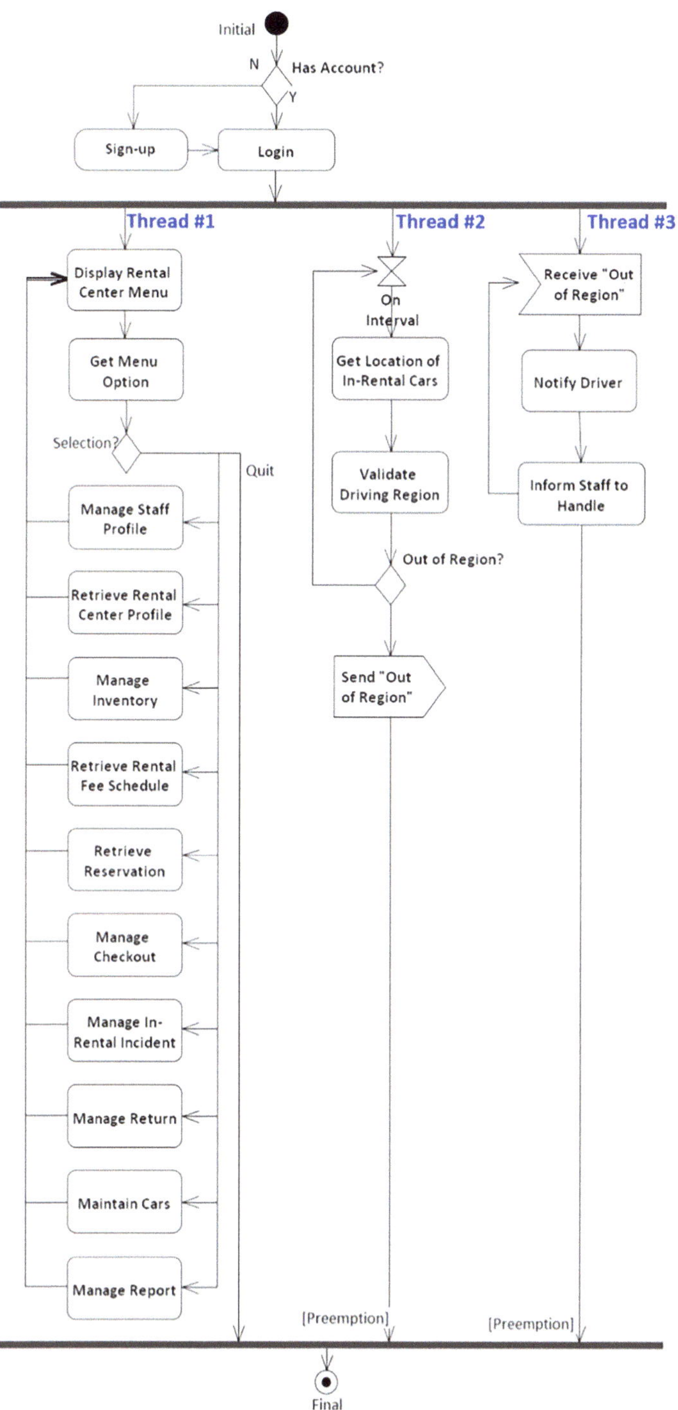

Fig. 4.23 Behavior Context of Rental Center Client Tier

- **Defining Parallel Processing Behavior**
  After the login, the system initiates three parallel threads using a fork-join construct.
  - **Thread #1: Explicit Invocation**
    This thread presents a menu of functional groups employing explicit invocation patterns to the rental center staff. The user selects an option, which is then explicitly invoked based on their choice.
    In a UML Activity Diagram, a rounded rectangle represents either an action or an activity. In this thread, rounded rectangles labeled with names starting with "Manage"—such as *Manage Staff Profile* and *Manage Inventory*—indicate activities whose behaviors are further refined into sets of nested actions.
  - **Thread #2: Closed Loop with Timer**
    This thread operates as a closed loop governed by a timer, repeatedly performing operations such as retrieving the locations of active rental cars, validating their driving regions, and sending alerts if rental cars are detected outside the permitted areas.
  - **Thread #3: Closed Loop with Events**
    This thread manages the detection of an "Out of Region" anomaly. Upon detecting such an event, the system responds by notifying the rental driver and alerting a staff member to take appropriate corrective actions.

As demonstrated in this example, the activity diagram effectively models the overall control flow of the Rental Center Client tier.

Note that this context-level activity diagram is not intended to provide a complete or detailed specification of the system's dynamic behavior. Rather, it is designed to convey a high-level understanding of the major control flows within a system tier. This diagram is subsequently refined with additional details and corrections during the design of the behavior view.

4.5 Checklist for A2: System Context Analysis

The following checklist items can be used to validate the system context analysis.

4.5.1 Checklist for Step 1: Analyze Boundary Context

For Processes

- Does the DFD depict processes that correspond to the specified or implied system nodes (e.g., tiers) as defined in the SRS?
- Does each system node represented in the DFD demonstrate a high degree of independence, being self-contained and capable of independent deployment and maintenance from other nodes?
- Is the communication overhead between system nodes over the network minimized? If not, are strategies established to mitigate this overhead?

For Terminals

- Does the DFD include terminals representing all defined user types?
- Does the DFD include terminals for all connected hardware devices, including sensors and actuators?
- Does the DFD include terminals representing all interacting external systems, including cloud services and microservices?

For Data Stores

- Does the DFD identify and specify data stores for all relevant persistent data managed by each tier associated with a process?
- Does each data store represent persistent data elements rather than transient data elements?
- If a data store is redundantly specified across multiple processes, does this redundancy provide significant benefits, such as enhanced data availability, without incurring unjustifiable costs or risks?

For Data Flows

- Is each data flow specified with one or more data items being transferred?
- Are data flows specified only between valid components, such as terminals and processes, processes and data stores, or between processes?
- Does the DFD avoid invalid data flows, such as flows between two terminals, between two data stores, or between a terminal and a data store?

4.5.2 Checklist for Step 2: Analyze Functional Context

For Functional Groups

- Do the defined functional groups correspond to the functional categories outlined in the SRS?
- If the functional groups do not fully align with the SRS, do they represent a logical and valid refinement of the specified categories?
- Is each functional group mutually exclusive, ensuring no functional overlap or redundancy among groups?

For Actors

- Does the use case diagram include all relevant active actors?
- Does the use case diagram include all relevant passive actors?
- Does the use case diagram include all relevant actors representing users?
- Does the use case diagram include all relevant actors representing hardware devices interacting with the system?
- Does the use case diagram include all relevant actors representing external systems or services interacting with the system?

- Does the use case diagram include all relevant software agent actors responsible for enabling automatic or autonomous control?

For Use Cases

- Does the complete set of use cases capture the full functionality of the target system, ensuring no functionality is omitted?
- Does the use case diagram include use cases for CRUD (Create, Read, Update, Delete) operations covering the manipulation of persistent data elements?
- Beyond CRUD operations, does the use case diagram include intrinsic system use cases critical to the system's core functionality?
- Does each use case include a unique use case ID and a meaningful name, following a structured naming convention (e.g., a prefix representing the functional group such as "CP" for Customer Profile Management)?
- Are the granularities of the use cases consistent and appropriately detailed across the model?
- Are the use cases functionally unique and mutually exclusive, avoiding redundancy or overlap?

For Invocation Relationships

- Does each active actor (e.g., user, customer) appropriately invoke relevant use cases?
- Is each passive actor (e.g., external system, microservice) appropriately invoked by one or more use cases?
- Are direct interactions between actors excluded from the use case diagram, ensuring that actor-to-actor interactions external to the system boundary are not represented within the system's use case model?

For Generalization, "include", and "extend" Relationships

- Is generalization the only permitted relationship between actors?
- Is a generalized base use case properly specialized into multiple derived use cases where appropriate?
- Does the base use case always invoke its included use case as specified by the "include" relationship?
- Does the base use case optionally invoke its extended use case under defined conditions, as specified by the "extend" relationship?
- Is the "include" relationship correctly applied to represent the inclusion of sub-functionality within broader functionality, without specifying control flow or invocation order among use cases?

4.5.3 Checklist for Step 3: Analyze Information Context

For Persistent Object Classes

- Does each class in the class diagram correspond to a persistent data entity manipulated by the system, with transient or temporary datasets excluded from the information context?
- Is the granularity of each class logically defined, adhering to the principles of data cohesiveness and single responsibility?

For Physical and Logical Object Classes

- Does the class diagram capture all relevant physical object classes, such as *Customer* and *CarItem* in a Car Rental Management System?
- Does the diagram include all relevant logical object classes, such as conceptual entities like *Reservation* and *Rental*?
- Does the diagram include logical object classes that represent session-related information, including user sessions, system-intrinsic sessions, and system-level sessions?

For Relationships

- Does the class diagram specify relationships between classes, including association, aggregation, composition, and inheritance, while appropriately omitting dependency relationships?
- For associations between two classes (A and B), does each instance of class A maintain permanent links or dependencies with instances of class B, and vice versa, where necessary?
- For aggregation relationships, are instances of the whole object created with their part objects, ensuring that the whole cannot exist without its parts?
- For composition relationships, are part objects created with the whole object and deleted when the whole object is deleted, ensuring that part objects share the lifetime of the whole?
- In inheritance relationships, is the ISA or AKO relationship correctly maintained between the superclass and subclass, ensuring that the subclass is properly defined as a subtype of the superclass?

For Cardinalities

- Are valid cardinalities specified for every relationship, excluding inheritance?
- Where applicable, is the cardinality of 1 replaced with 0..1 to allow for optional links?
- When a relationship between two classes involves multiple occurrences on both sides, is the use of an association class considered and applied appropriately?

4.5.4 Checklist for Step 4: Analyze Behavior Context

Number of Activity Diagrams

- Is the number of activity diagrams equal to the number of tiers in the system, excluding virtual nodes?
- Is each activity diagram clearly associated with a specific system tier, representing its behavioral control flow independently?

Partitioning of Functionality Across Tiers

- Is each functional group appropriately allocated to one or more tiers, reflecting the system's functional decomposition?
- Is each tier assigned specific and relevant functional groups, avoiding unnecessary duplication or omission of responsibilities?

Consistency with Functional Context

- Do the actions and activities represented in the activity diagrams correspond directly to the use cases defined in the use case diagrams?
- Are there any use cases in the functional context that are not reflected in the behavior context?
- Are there any actions or activities in the activity diagrams that do not have corresponding use cases, indicating potential inconsistencies or undocumented functionality?

For Invocation Patterns

- Is each functional group mapped to one or more appropriate invocation patterns (e.g., explicit invocation, time-triggered invocation, event-triggered invocation)?
- Is the Parallel Invocation pattern correctly applied to functional groups that are designed to execute concurrently?

Constructing the Activity Diagram

- Is the number of outgoing threads at each fork node equal to the number of incoming threads at the corresponding join node, ensuring proper thread synchronization?
- Are parallel threads designed to operate independently, avoiding unintended interactions and ensuring true parallel execution?
- Is a "Receive Event" action defined for every "Send Event" action, ensuring complete event-based communication modeling?
- Are interactions between tiers explicitly defined using appropriate communication schemes, such as event-based or message-driven mechanisms?
- For closed-loop control flows, is termination properly defined through a preemption mechanism, ensuring that loops can be safely interrupted based on specified conditions?

4.6 Exercise Problems

4.6.1 Exercise Problems for Boundary Context Analysis

1. **Boundary Context Representation Across System Tiers**
For a software system deployed across mobile, Web, and backend tiers, describe how each tier can be modeled as a distinct process in a boundary context model. Explain the role and responsibility of each tier.
2. **Level 0 DFD as Boundary Context**
Level 0 DFD is the highest level of a DFD that provides a broad overview of the entire system, showing the system as a single process with its interactions with external entities and major data flows. Justify why a Level 0 DFD is adequate for representing the boundary context of a target system.
3. **Modeling External Entities in a Healthcare Appointment System**
Identify the key external entities that interact with a Healthcare Appointment System, including patients, physicians, healthcare administrators, and insurance service providers. Specify the types of data exchanged, and characterize the nature of each interaction with the system.
4. **Identifying Terminals in Smart Home Automation Systems**
Identify at least three IoT devices that serve as data sources or sinks in a Smart Home Automation System. Explain the role of each device as a data source or data sink, and describe how it should be represented as a terminal in a Level 0 DFD.
5. **Comparison of User-Type and External System-Type Terminals**
Identify the user-type terminals and external system-type terminals in the context of an e-commerce platform. Explain how these two categories of terminals differ in terms of their roles, responsibilities, and modes of interaction with the system.
6. **Construct a Boundary Context for a Ride-Sharing System**
Draw a Level 0 DFD representing the boundary context of a Ride-Sharing System. Identify major processes, terminals, data stores, and data flows. Explain the rationale behind your modeling decisions.
7. **Construct a Boundary Context for a Hotel Reservation System**
Draw a Level 0 DFD representing the boundary context of a Hotel Reservation System. Identify major processes such as room booking, cancellation, and billing, along with terminals, data stores, and data flows. Explain the rationale behind your modeling decisions.
8. **Construct a Boundary Context for a Food Delivery System**
Draw a Level 0 DFD representing the boundary context of a Food Delivery System. Identify major processes such as order placement, order dispatching, delivery tracking, and payment processing, along with terminals, data stores, and data flows. Explain the rationale behind your modeling decisions.

9. **Construct a Boundary Context for an Adaptive Cruise Control (ACC) System**
Draw a Level 0 DFD representing the boundary context of an Adaptive Cruise Control System. Identify major processes such as speed monitoring, obstacle detection, distance calculation, and cruise control adjustment, along with hardware-based external entities (e.g., radar sensors, vehicle control unit, and brake actuators), relevant data stores, and data flows.

4.6.2 Exercise Problems for Functional Context Analysis

10. **Active Actors and Passive Actors**
Actors in a use case diagram can be classified as either active or passive, depending on the nature of their interaction with the system. Explain the difference between active and passive actors using a concrete example derived from either a real-world or hypothetical software system.
11. **Agent-Type Actors**
An agent-type actor is a software component, such as a daemon process, that autonomously interacts with the system to perform delegated tasks, operating without direct human intervention. Explain the key difference between conventional actors (e.g., human users or external systems) and agent-type actors using a concrete example derived from an Adaptive Cruise Control (ACC) System.
12. **Modeling Include and Extent Relationships**
In a Library Management System, when a user borrows a book, the system must always verify the user's membership status and may optionally calculate a fine if the book is overdue. Draw a use case diagram representing these use cases and their relationships.
Explain why the *membership verification* should be modeled using an "include" relationship and the *fine calculation* should be modeled using an "extend" relationship, based on their mandatory and optional nature, respectively.
13. **Impacts of Functional Context Defect**
Functional context defects in a use case diagram can propagate and negatively impact subsequent development phases. Select one defect type—such as an invalid actor, a missing use case, or an incorrect relationship—and explain how this defect could escalate through the system design, implementation, testing, and deployment stages. Provide a concrete example to illustrate the defect's potential consequences.
14. **Comprehending the Functional Context from a Use Case Diagram**
Suppose a use case diagram capturing the functional context of a system is available. Explain how the functional context can be interpreted from the diagram. Specifically, describe how each element—such as actors, use cases, and their relationships—contributes to understanding the system's overall functionality, patterns of user interaction, and the organization of related functional groups.

15. **Construct a Functional Context for a Ride-Sharing System**
Draw a use case diagram representing the functional context of a Ride-Sharing System. Identify relevant actors, group use cases according to functional categories, and depict the relationships among use cases within the system. Provide a rationale for your modeling decisions.
16. **Construct a Functional Context for a Hotel Reservation System**
Draw a use case diagram representing the functional context of a Hotel Reservation System. Identify relevant actors, group use cases according to functional categories, and depict the relationships among use cases within the system. Provide a rationale for your modeling decisions.
17. **Construct a Functional Context for a Food Delivery System**
Draw a use case diagram representing the functional context of a Food Delivery System. Identify relevant actors, group use cases according to functional categories, and depict the relationships among use cases within the system. Provide a rationale for your modeling decisions.
18. **Construct a Functional Context for an Adaptive Cruise Control (ACC) System**
Draw a use case diagram representing the functional context of an Adaptive Cruise Control (ACC) System. Identify relevant actors including hardware-type actors, group use cases according to functional categories, and depict the relationships among use cases within the system. Provide a rationale for your modeling decisions.

4.6.3 Exercise Problems for Information Context Analysis

19. **Essence of Logical Object Classes**
A logical object class represents abstract data entities that do not directly correspond to tangible entities, while a physical object class represents concrete implementations of these entities in the real world. Explain why identifying logical object classes is essential for understanding the information context of a system. Provide a specific example from a real-world or hypothetical software system to illustrate this concept.
20. **Session-Related Classes**
A session represents a comprehensive record of user activities or system usage within a specific timeframe. A session-related class captures the data pertinent to a specific session type. Explain the role of session-related classes, using a specific example from a Food Delivery System to illustrate this concept.
21. **Difference Between Association and Link Relationships**
Discuss how association relationships model links between objects. Using a Hotel Reservation System as an example, explain the association relationship between two classes, *User* and *Reservation*, and describe the link relationships between instances of these classes.

22. **Impact of Cardinality in Relationship Modeling**
Explain the importance of defining cardinality in relationships within class diagrams. Illustrate this concept with examples of one-to-one, one-to-many, and many-to-many relationships using a Hotel Reservation System.
23. **Aggregation vs. Composition Relationships**
Consider two classes, *Family* and *Member* in a Family Registration System, where a specific family consists of one or more members. Determine whether the relationship between these classes should be modeled as an aggregation or a composition as shown below. Justify your choice.

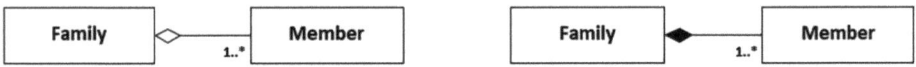

24. **Interpreting Aggregation and Composition Relationships**
Consider two classes, *Triangle* and *Point*, where a *Triangle* instance consists of three *Point* instances. This relationship can be modeled either as aggregation or composition.
Given the class diagram below, interpret the meaning of each model in terms of object ownership, lifecycle dependency, and reusability of Point instances.

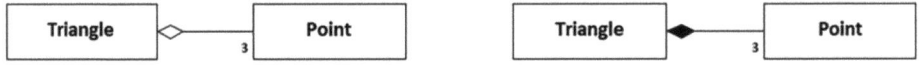

25. **Modeling an Inheritance Hierarchy for Product Types in e-Commerce Systems**
An e-Commerce platform offers a wide variety of products, including books, electronics, and clothing. Furthermore, books are available in different formats—eBook, printed book, and audiobook—each with format-specific variations. Design an inheritance hierarchy that models this product structure.
26. **Comprehending the Information Context from a Class Diagram**
Suppose a class diagram capturing the information context of a system is given. Explain how this context can be interpreted from the diagram. Specifically, describe how each element—such as classes, relationships, and their cardinalities—contributes to understanding the system's persistent data structures, entity associations, and overall data organization.
27. **Construct an Information Context for a Ride-Sharing System**
Draw a class diagram representing the information context of a Ride-Sharing System. Identify relevant classes, relationships, and cardinalities. Attributes and methods may be omitted, as the focus is on capturing the information context of the system. Provide a rationale for your modeling decisions.
28. **Construct an Information Context for a Hotel Reservation System**
Draw a class diagram representing the information context of a Hotel Reservation System. Identify relevant classes, relationships, and cardinalities. Attributes and methods may be omitted, as the focus is on capturing the information context of the system. Provide a rationale for your modeling decisions.

29. **Construct an Information Context for a Food Delivery System**
Draw a class diagram representing the information context of a Food Delivery System. Identify relevant classes, relationships, and cardinalities. Attributes and methods may be omitted, as the focus is on capturing the information context of the system. Provide a rationale for your modeling decisions.
30. **Construct an Information Context for an Adaptive Cruise Control (ACC) System**
Draw a class diagram representing the information context of an Adaptive Cruise Control (ACC) System. Identify relevant classes, relationships, and cardinalities. Attributes and methods may be omitted, as the focus is on capturing the information context of the system. Provide a rationale for your modeling decisions.

4.6.4 Exercise Problems for Behavior Context Analysis

31. **Use of Multiple Activity Diagrams in Multi-Tiered Systems**
In systems composed of multiple system nodes (i.e., tiers), it is often necessary to construct a distinct activity diagram for each node. Explain why it is necessary to create multiple activity diagrams in such systems.
32. **Consistency Between Functional Context and Behavior Context**
The functional context and behavior context capture distinct yet complementary aspects of a system. While the functional context defines the system's functional units and their responsibilities, the behavior context models the dynamic execution of those functions. Explain the rationale behind the design principle that the behavior context should be constructed to maintain consistency with the functional context.
33. **Modeling Interactions Between Subsystems in Activity Diagrams**
In activity diagrams, actions and activities are used to represent the invocation of corresponding functions within a subsystem. However, complex systems often consist of multiple subsystems that interact with one another through various communication mechanisms. Explain how inter-subsystem interactions can be effectively represented in activity diagrams.
34. **Fork-Join Construct for Parallel Processing**
The Fork-Join construct in an activity diagram is used to model parallel processing behavior. A Fork node splits the control flow into multiple parallel threads, while a corresponding Join node synchronizes these threads. A key design principle requires that the number of parallel threads originating from the Fork must match the number of threads converging at the Join. Explain the rationale behind this design principle.
35. **Essence of Invocation Patterns**
Describe the concept of invocation patterns used for modeling system behavior, and explain how it helps model common runtime control flows. Give examples of sequential, explicit, closed-loop, and event-based invocation patterns.
36. **Invocation Patterns in Autonomous Systems**
In autonomous systems—such as self-driving vehicles—the closed-loop invocation pattern is predominantly employed, while the explicit invocation pattern is used less frequently. Explain the rationale behind this design observation.

37. **Applying Timed Invocation Pattern**
    Explain how the timed invocation pattern can be applied to model the behavior of a medical monitoring system that performs periodic checks on patient data and triggers real-time alerts when anomalies are detected.
38. **Comprehending the Behavior Context from an Activity Diagram**
    Suppose an activity diagram capturing the behavior context of a system is given. Explain how this context can be interpreted from the diagram. Specifically, describe how each element—such as action, activity, control flow, fork-join, and event—contributes to understanding the system's runtime behavior.
39. **Construct a Behavior Context for a Ride-Sharing System**
    Construct an activity diagram that represents the behavior context of a Ride-Sharing System by applying invocation patterns. Identify key actions, activities, and control flows that reflect the dynamic behavior of the system. Clearly illustrate how invocation patterns structure the sequencing and coordination of behaviors. Provide a rationale for your modeling decisions.
40. **Construct a Behavior Context for a Hotel Reservation System**
    Construct an activity diagram representing the behavior context of a Hotel Reservation System, using appropriate invocation patterns and providing modeling rationale.
41. **Construct a Behavior Context for a Food Delivery System**
    Construct an activity diagram representing the behavior context of a Food Delivery System, using appropriate invocation patterns and providing modeling rationale.
42. **Construct a Behavior Context for an Adaptive Cruise Control (ACC) System**
    Construct an activity diagram representing the behavior context of an Adaptive Cruise Control System, applying closed-loop and event-based invocation patterns. Provide a rationale for your modeling decisions.

Activity A3. Schematic Architecture Design

5

Objective of the Chapter

The objective of this chapter is to present a systematic approach for designing schematic architecture. It emphasizes the identification, evaluation, integration, and refinement of suitable architecture styles to construct a cohesive architectural design for the target system. Key steps in schematic architecture design include evaluating candidate architecture styles, selecting appropriate styles for the target system, and integrating them into a unified schematic architecture. Through guided refinement, this chapter aims to support architects in developing a final schematic architecture that is comprehensive, adaptable, and aligned with the specific requirements of the target system.

Introducing Activity A3. Schematic Architecture Design

This activity is to design the schematic architecture of the target system by identifying and integrating appropriate architecture styles. Schematic architecture provides a visual representation of the system's topological layout, defined by structural elements such as tiers, layers, partitions, and components.

Schematic architecture is characterized by the following key aspects:

- **Structural Stability**

  Schematic architecture establishes a stable foundation for making subsequent architectural decisions, including the design of architectural views and the refinement of non-functional requirements. This stability helps maintain alignment with the overall architectural vision as the system evolves.

S. D. Kim, M. Kim, *Hands-on Software Architecture*,
https://doi.org/10.1007/978-3-032-01184-8_5

- **Placeholders for Components and Elements**
  Schematic architecture defines placeholders for components and other structural elements, which are further refined and specified during the design of architectural views. These placeholders guide the placement and interaction of components, ensuring coherence in the system layout.
- **Integration of Architecture Styles**
  Schematic architecture often incorporates specific architecture styles, reflected in the system's structural organization. This integration provides a cohesive structural pattern that supports both functional and technical requirements.

Architecture Styles for Designing Schematic Architecture

Schematic architecture can be effectively designed by leveraging architecture styles, which provide reusable design patterns and best practices tailored to specific system contexts. These patterns and practices typically define a structural layout, key components, and interactions among components, forming a solid foundation for schematic architecture design.

The primary benefits of using architecture styles in schematic architecture design include minimizing design effort and ensuring the development of high-quality, reliable architecture. By adopting established patterns, architects can avoid designing from scratch and instead rely on proven solutions, thereby streamlining the design process. Architecture styles also bring well-documented best practices and guidelines validated through prior implementations, enhancing the effectiveness and robustness of schematic architecture.

However, a schematic architecture based on an architecture style should not be regarded as a complete or final architecture. Each system presents unique requirements and constraints that must be addressed. Therefore, customizing a schematic architecture derived from architecture styles is often necessary to optimize it for the specific system context.

Steps in A3. Schematic Architecture Design

The design of schematic architecture can be systematically designed with the sequence of steps shown in Fig. 5.1.

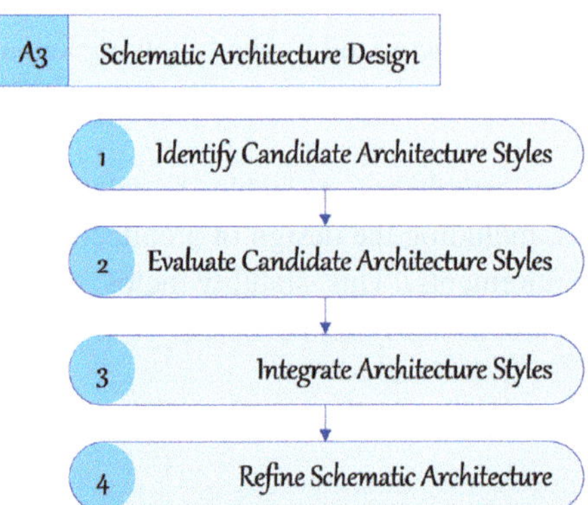

Fig. 5.1 Steps in A3. Schematic Architecture Design

- **Step 1. Identify Candidate Architecture Styles**
  This step is to analyze the structural characteristics of the target system and identifies candidate architecture styles that are suitable for designing its schematic architecture.
- **Step 2. Evaluate Candidate Architecture Styles**
  This step is to assess the suitability of each candidate architecture style by examining its applicable contexts, advantages, and limitations.
- **Step 3. Integrate Architecture Styles**
  This step is to integrate the selected architecture styles into a coherent schematic architecture for the target system.
- **Step 4. Refine Schematic Architecture**
  This step is to refine the schematic architecture by specifying its structural elements in greater detail and defining clear interaction paths among these elements.

5.1 Step 1. Identify Candidate Architecture Styles

This step is to identify architecture styles suitable for designing the schematic architecture. It requires analyzing the intrinsic characteristics of the target system and selecting architecture styles that are best aligned with those characteristics.

5.1.1 Task 1. Observe Structural Characteristics

This task is to identify the structural properties and constraints of the target system that are relevant to its architectural design. These observations establish a foundational basis for selecting appropriate architecture styles, which will guide the design of the schematic architecture.

Observing Structural Properties

- **Observing Structural Requirements in the SRS**
  Observe the structural requirements specified explicitly or implied in the SRS. These requirements often describe a layout organized around structural elements such as tiers, layers, partitions, components, devices, external systems, and services.
- **Acquiring Structural Concerns from Stakeholders**
  While the SRS typically captures the majority of structural requirements, additional structural concerns may exist that are not explicitly documented. Architects should engage with stakeholders to actively uncover any additional structural concerns or constraints that extend beyond the SRS.

- **Observing Non-Functional Requirements Affecting Structural Layout**
  Architects should review the NFRs to identify aspects that may influence the schematic architecture. Although NFRs do not typically prescribe a specific architectural scheme, certain requirements may suggest structural approaches. For instance, a high availability requirement for a cloud service system may imply the need for a load-balanced architecture with server replication to ensure reliability, stability, and scalability.

Observing System Constraints

- **Observe the Structural Constraints from Functionality**
  Analyze the complexity of system functionality, considering factors such as intensive data manipulation, high computational demands, and extensive interactions with users or external systems. Based on this analysis, architects should identify specific structural constraints—such as the need for parallel processing, data caching, or load-balancing mechanisms—that must be incorporated into the schematic architecture to support efficient system operation.
- **Observe Structural Constraints from Behavior**
  Analyze system behavioral characteristics, including data streaming between components, event-driven invocations, closed-loop processes, and timed invocations. Based on this analysis, architects should identify structural constraints—such as the need for asynchronous messaging queues, event-driven components, or distributed coordination mechanisms—that should be embedded in the schematic architecture to support the intended system behavior.

5.1.2 Task 2. Determine Inherent Types of the System

This task is to identify the inherent types of the target system to facilitate the selection of appropriate architecture styles. Selecting candidate architecture styles from among more than 30 available options is often non-trivial. A practical approach to streamline this process is to first determine the inherent types of the system, which serves to narrow down the applicable architecture styles and guide their selection.

Types of Software Systems
Although no universally accepted taxonomy of software system types exists, several classifications are commonly referenced in the literature and widely adopted in industry practices. The following provides a summary of some frequently cited system types.

- **Data Flow Systems**
  This type of system is characterized by an architectural configuration that incorporates multiple components dedicated to data manipulation. Data flow systems are designed to facilitate the movement of large volumes of data among components. Each component is responsible for executing specific manipulations on datasets and subsequently transmitting the modified data to downstream components in the process.

The general structure of data flow systems is illustrated Fig. 5.2.

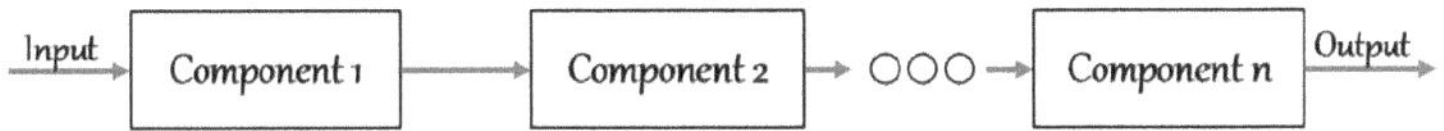

Fig. 5.2 General Structure of Data Flow Systems

As an example, consider a conventional compiler for a programming language, which integrates various data manipulation components. Initially, a tokenizer component processes the source code (e.g., a C program), breaking it down into individual tokens and passing them forward. Next, a parser component reads this token stream and organizes it into an internal structure, such as an abstract syntax tree. Following this, the linker component combines the parsed object codes with necessary libraries, managing external dependencies. Finally, the code generator component produces an executable file, completing the compilation process. Hence, compilers are classified as a type of data flow system.

The following architecture styles are commonly applied in the design of data flow systems.

– Batch Sequential Architecture Style
– Pipe-and-Filter Architecture Style

- **Data Sharing Systems**

This type of system is characterized by a structural layout designed to efficiently manage and store large volumes of data, enabling multiple applications to access and utilize the data as needed. Data is written to and read from a central repository, eliminating the need for direct data transmission between applications.

The general structure of data sharing systems is shown in Fig. 5.3.

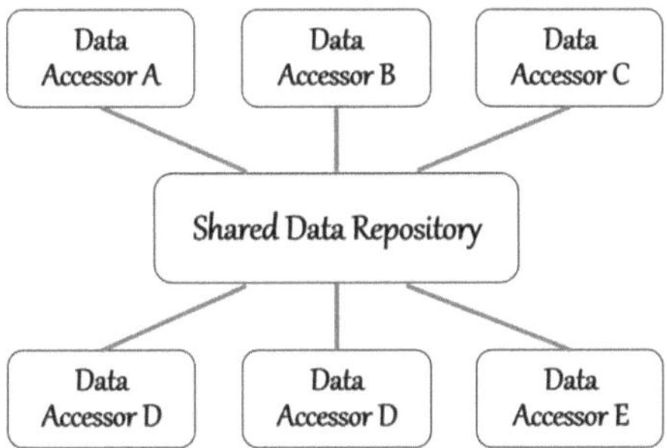

Fig. 5.3 General Structure of Data Sharing Systems

For example, banking systems typically comprise multiple sub-systems, such as *Deposit Management System*, *Loan Processing Systems*, *Foreign Exchange System*, and *Credit Card Processing System*. These sub-systems frequently share access to customer account information and transaction data via the central repository, ensuring consistency and availability of data across the system. Hence, banking systems are classified as a type of data sharing system.

The following architecture styles are commonly applied in the design of data sharing systems.

- Shared Repository Architecture Style
- Active Repository Architecture Style
- Blackboard Architecture Style

- **Layered Systems**

  This type of system is characterized by a structural layout that organizes the system as a series of hierarchical layers, where each layer provides a defined set of functionalities and services to the layer directly above it. Layers are arranged hierarchically, with the topmost layer typically representing the user interface and the lowest layer representing the foundational infrastructure.

  The general structure of layered systems is shown in Fig. 5.4.

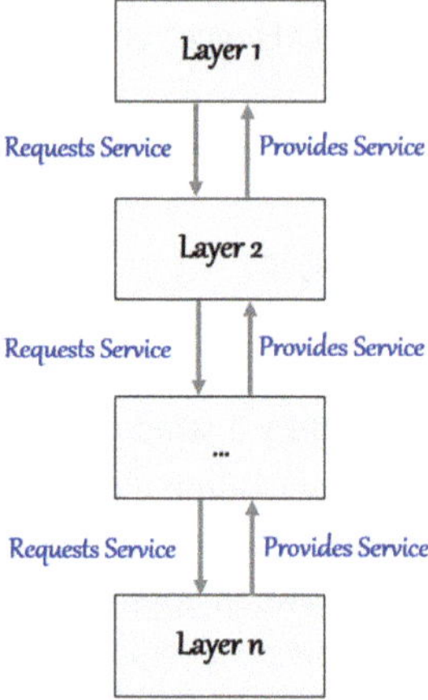

Fig. 5.4 General Structure of Layered Systems

In layered systems, each layer interacts only with the layer directly above or below it, promoting loose coupling and allowing changes to be made within one layer without significantly impacting others.

The following architecture styles are commonly applied in the design of layered systems.

- Layered Architecture Style
- Model-View-Controller (MVC) Architecture Style
- Variation of MVC Style

- **Tiered Systems**

  This type of system is characterized by a structural layout that employs multiple tiers, where each tier represents a distinct physical computer system. Each tier is responsible for a specific large-scale functionality within the system and interacts with other tiers to achieve the overall system objectives.

A tiered system typically consists of two or more tiers, which can be arranged various topological layouts, as shown in Fig. 5.5.

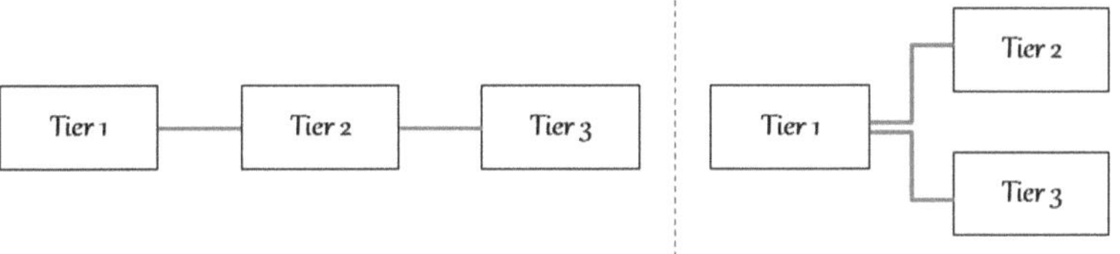

Fig. 5.5 General Structure of Tiered Systems

Enterprise systems are commonly structured with multiple tiers to achieve targeted functionality and enhance scalability. For example, banking systems utilize multiple tiers to handle distinct functionalities, as illustrated in Fig. 5.6.

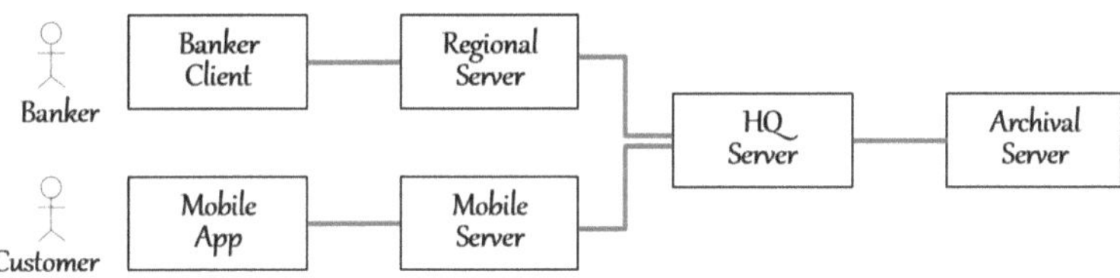

Fig. 5.6 Banking System with Multiple Tiers

Each tier is dedicated to a specific functionality within the system. Bankers use a *Banker Client* tier connected to a *Regional Server* tier, while customers access services via a *Mobile App* tier that connects to a *Mobile Server* tier. Both the regional and mobile server tiers communicate with a central *HQ Server* tier, which coordinates high-level data management and operations. Additionally, the *HQ Server* tier connects to an *Archival Server* tier for long-term storage and historical data management, supporting data archiving and retrieval.

This tiered structure ensures efficient distribution of workload, allowing specialized tiers to handle specific tasks while maintaining centralized control and secure data storage. The design promotes scalability, security, and streamlined access for users with different roles and requirements.

The following architecture styles are commonly applied in the design of tiered systems.

- Client-Server Architecture Style
- N-Tier Architecture Style
- Peer-to-Peer Architecture Style

- **Load-Balancing Systems**
  This type of system is characterized by a structural layout comprising multiple servers and a load balancer that distributes computational workloads evenly across the servers. This configuration enhances overall system performance and reliability by preventing any single server from becoming overloaded with requests and by providing redundancy to handle server failures.
  Load-balancing systems can be configured in two primary ways: using replicated servers or dedicated servers.
  - **Load-Balancing with Replicated Servers**
    A load-balancing system can be configured with a set of replicated servers, where each server is an instance of the same server configuration. The general structure of a load-balancing system with replicated servers is illustrated in Fig. 5.7

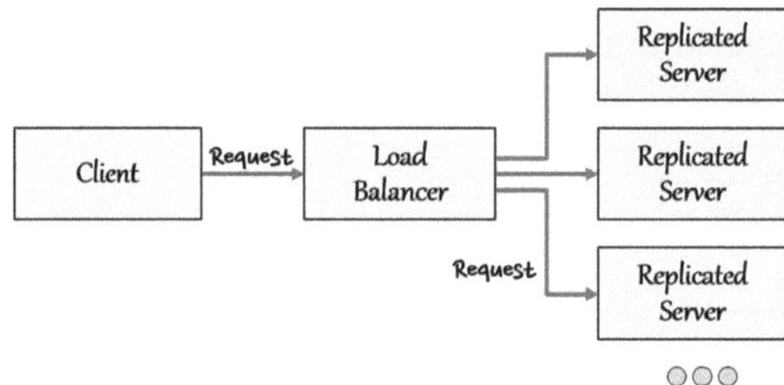

Fig. 5.7 Structure of Load-Balancing Systems with Replicated Servers

In the figure, a client sends requests to a load balancer, which distributes them evenly across multiple replicated servers to ensure a balanced workload. This setup enhances system performance and reliability by preventing any single server from becoming overloaded.
For example, a cloud service system is often configured with numerous replicated cloud servers distributed across different geographic regions to ensure high availability and reliability. Additionally, multiple load balancers are deployed in each region to distribute workloads effectively across the replicated servers.
The following architecture styles are commonly applied in the design of load-balancing systems with replicated servers.
  - Broker Architecture Style
  - Dispatcher Architecture Style
  - Using Dedicated Servers

  - **Load-Balancing with Dedicated Servers**
    A load-balancing system can be configured with a set of dedicated servers, where each server provides a specific functionality. The general structure of load-balancing systems with dedicated servers is shown in Fig. 5.8.

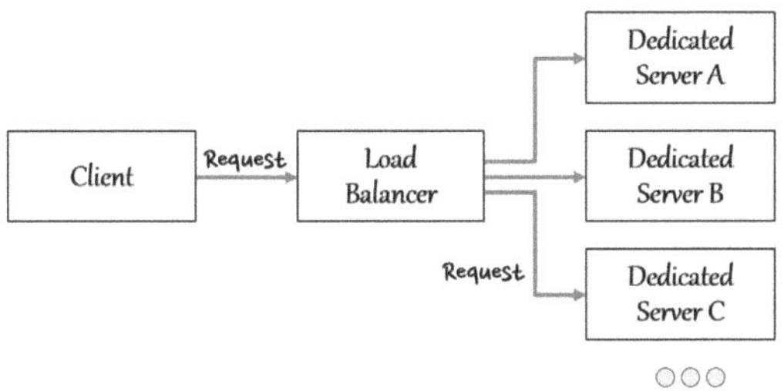

Fig. 5.8 Structure of Load-Balancing Systems with Dedicated Servers

In the figure, a client sends requests to a load balancer. The load balancer partitions each request into multiple tasks and orchestrates their execution across dedicated servers. Each task is routed to the appropriate dedicated server, and the load balancer then synthesizes the results from the participating servers to complete the client's request.

For example, large-scale Platform-as-a-Service (PaaS) configurations often involve multiple dedicated servers, each responsible for providing a specific, well-defined service to ensure comprehensive system functionality. In this setup, the load balancer directs tasks to the appropriate servers based on the specific functionality required by each request.

The following architecture styles are commonly applied in the design of load-balancing systems with dedicated servers.

Master-Slave Architecture Style

Edge Computing Architecture Style

- **Event-Based Systems**

  This type of system is characterized by a structural layout in which the control flow is largely determined by events. Events in an event-driven system can originate from various sources, including user interactions, hardware devices, software agents, or other software components.

  The general structure of event-based systems is shown in Fig. 5.9.

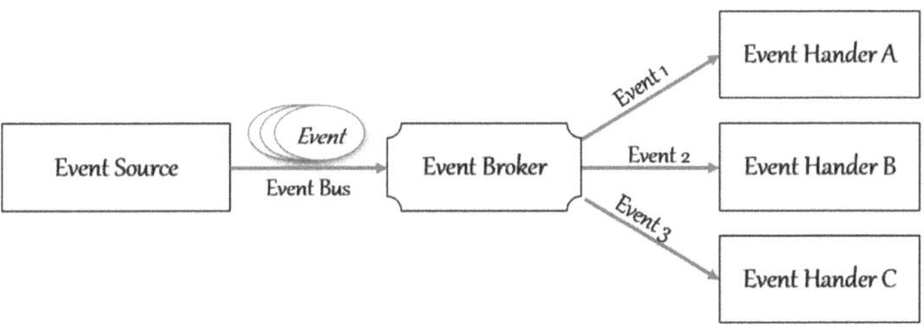

Fig. 5.9 Structure of Event-Based Systems

In the figure, an *Event Source* generates events and sends them to an *Event Broker* via an *Event Bus*. The *Event Broker* acts as a central hub, managing the flow of events and routing them to the appropriate *Event Handlers* based on the type of event. An *Event Handler* is an entity that handles a specific type of event and executes the necessary logic associated with the received event.
The following architecture styles are commonly applied in the design of event-based systems.
- Event-Driven Architecture Style
- Publish-Subscriber Architecture Style
- Sensor Controller Actuator Architecture Style

- **Service-Based Systems**
This type of system is characterized by a structural layout in which the system utilizes external services to fulfill specific parts of its overall functionality. These external services can include cloud services, microservices, or other stand-alone services, each contributing a defined function to the system.
The general structure of a service-based system is shown in Fig. 5.10.

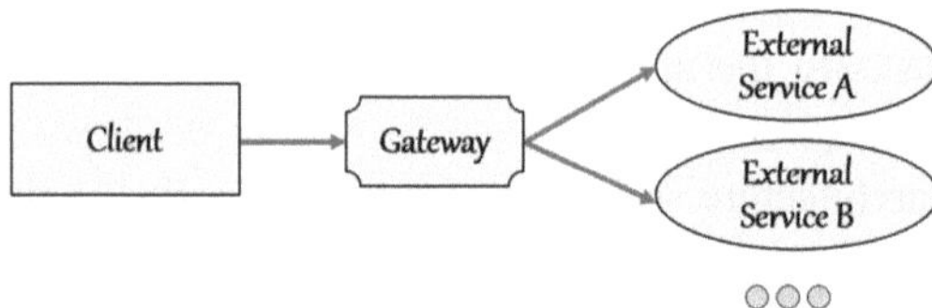

Fig. 5.10 Structure of Service-Based Systems

In the figure, a *Client* interacts with external services through a *Gateway*. The *Gateway* acts as an intermediary, directing the client's requests to the appropriate external services, such as *External Service A* and *External Service B*.
This setup enables the client to access multiple external services seamlessly through a single access point, ensuring that requests are properly routed based on the required functionality. The *Gateway* simplifies client interactions and manages communication with various services, thereby enhancing system modularity and scalability.
The following architecture styles are commonly applied in the design of service-based systems.
- Microservice Architecture Style
- Service-Oriented Architecture (SOA) Style

- **Adaptive Systems**
This type of system is characterized by its ability to modify its behavior and configuration in response to changes in the environment or user requirements. Adaptive systems are designed to be flexible and adjustable, enabling them to respond effectively to varying conditions and maintain optimal performance. An adaptive system is typically

structured with both fixed and variable elements. Fixed elements represent stable system features that remain constant over time, whereas variable elements represent components or features that can be dynamically adjusted based on changing environmental conditions.

Adaptive systems have applications across diverse domains, including personalized recommendation systems, intelligent assistants, smart home automation, dynamic resource allocation in cloud computing, and medical treatment recommendation systems.

Adaptive systems can be effectively developed using open-closed design schemes, allowing for flexible modification without altering the core structure. The general structure of adaptive systems utilizing plug-in components is shown in Fig. 5.11.

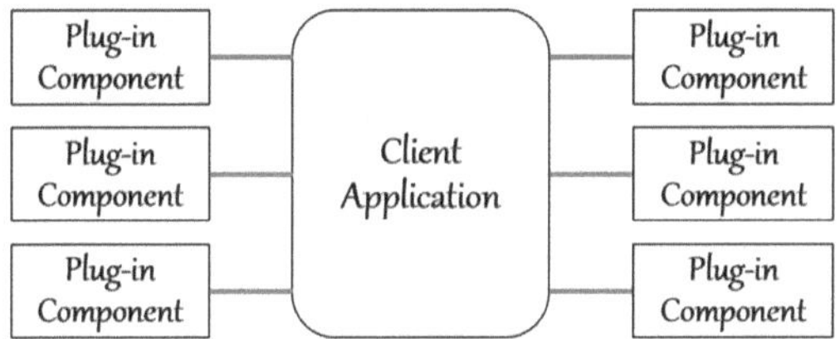

Fig. 5.11 Structure of Adaptive Systems with Plug-in Components

In the figure, a *Client Application* is configured to dynamically accept externally implemented plug-in components. Each plug-in component adheres to a specified interface required by the client application, ensuring seamless integration. The client application is designed to interact with these plug-in components, allowing it to extend or modify its functionality as needed without altering its core structure.

Eclipse is an open-source integrated development environment that exemplifies the characteristics of adaptive systems. Through its plug-in architecture, it offers a modular and extensible platform, enabling developers to enhance and customize their environments by installing additional plug-ins and extensions to meet specific requirements.

The following architecture styles are commonly applied in the design of adaptive systems.

- Microkernel Architecture Style
- Blackboard Architecture Style

The system types outlined above are not exhaustive, and various other types of systems exist. Architects are encouraged to explore additional system types that may be more appropriate for addressing the specific needs and characteristics of the target system.

It is also important to recognize that a target system may exhibit characteristics of multiple system types. Architects should identify all relevant system types associated with the target system and select appropriate architecture styles based on these identified types to ensure a comprehensive and effective design.

Example

For the Car Rental Management System, the following system types can well be identified:

- **Tiered System**
  The system's SRS defines a tiered structure consisting of a mobile application and a Web-based client for customers, a client application for rental center staff, and a central server that manages the master database and provides functionalities to both client applications.
- **Layered System**
  Each tier in the system can be configured with a hierarchy of layers: a user interface layer, a business logic coordination layer, and a data management layer responsible for handling persistent rental data.
- **Load-Balancing System**
  Service requests from customers and rental center staff are managed by the central headquarters server. Given the potential for high load during peak periods, along with the critical need for high reliability and availability, the system exhibits key characteristics of a load-balancing architecture.

5.1.3 Task 3. Determine Candidate Architecture Styles

This task is to determine the most suitable architecture styles for the identified system types. The objective is to derive candidate architecture styles that best align with the requirements and characteristics of the target system types.

The architecture styles suitable for each system type are summarized in Table 5.1. Note that the architecture styles listed in the table are not exhaustive; other applicable architecture styles may also exist for each system type.

Using this table, the most appropriate architecture style for each of the previously identified system types is selected, as illustrated in Fig. 5.12.

This figure illustrates the process of selecting candidate architecture styles for different system types based on the SRS. Starting with three system types (*System Type 1*, *System Type 2*, and *System Type 3*), each is associated with a set of applicable architecture styles that could satisfy its requirements. For each system type, one architecture style is highlighted as the *Candidate Architecture Style*, selected based on additional suitability criteria.

For example, the Car Rental Management System comprises three distinct system types: Tiered, Layered, and Load Balancing. An appropriate architecture style is selected for each system type as follows:

- **N-Tier Architecture Style** for the Tiered System Type
- **Model-View-Controller (MVC) Architecture Style** for the Layered System Type
- **Dispatcher Architecture Style** for the Load-Balancing System Type

Table 5.1 Architecture Styles for System Types

System Types	Architecture Styles
Tiered System	N-Tier Architecture Style
	Client-Server Architecture Style
	Peer-to-Peer Architecture Style
Layered System	Layered Architecture Style
	Model-View-Controller (MVC) Architecture Style
	Variations of MVC Style (such as MVP and MVVM)
Load-Balancing System	Broker Architecture Style
	Dispatcher Architecture Style
	Master-Slave Architecture Style
	Edge-Computing Architecture Style
Service-Based System	Microservice Architecture Style
	Service-Oriented Architecture (SOA) Style
Data Flow System	Batch Sequential Architecture Style
	Pipe-and-Filter Architecture Style
Data Sharing System	Shared Repository Architecture Style
	Active Repository Architecture Style
	Blackboard Architecture Style (with Data)
Event-Based System	Event-Driven Architecture Style
	Publish-Subscriber Architecture Style
	Sensor Controller Actuator Architecture Style
Adaptive System	Microkernel Architecture Style
	Blackboard Architecture Style (with Program)

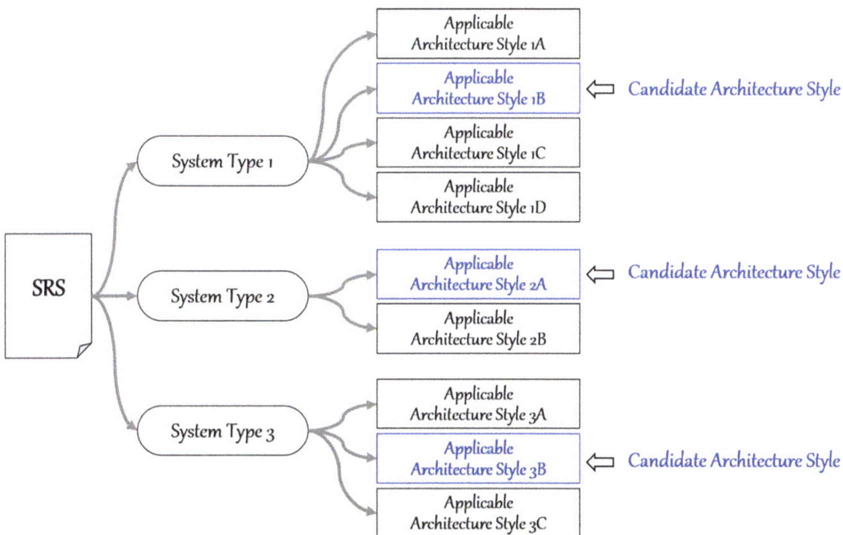

Fig. 5.12 Deriving Candidate Architecture Styles Based on System Types

5.2 Step 2. Evaluate Candidate Architecture Styles

This step is to evaluate candidate architecture styles to determine their suitability for the target system. The evaluation criteria include examining the applicable situations, benefits, and drawbacks associated with each style.

- **Evaluating Applicable Situations**
  Each architecture style is suited to specific situations, which define the contexts in which it can be effectively applied. This criterion involves assessing whether the characteristics of the target system align with the applicable situations of each candidate architecture style.
- **Evaluating Benefits of Each Style**
  Each architecture style offers distinct advantages for systems that implement it. This criterion focuses on evaluating how the target system can leverage the strengths provided by each candidate style.
- **Evaluating Drawbacks of Each Style**
  Architecture styles often exhibit inherent drawbacks or limitations. This criterion assesses how the target system might address, tolerate, or mitigate the potential drawbacks associated with each candidate style.

By applying these evaluation criteria, the selection of architecture styles that are best suited for the target system can be finalized with greater confidence and justification.

5.2.1 Task 1. Evaluate Applicable Situations

This task is to validate whether the target system aligns with the applicable situations defined by each candidate architecture style. It involves creating a table that lists the applicable situations for each style, the corresponding situations within the target system, and the degree of alignment between them.

The evaluation of applicable situations for each candidate architecture style can be summarized as shown in Table 5.2.

Table 5.2 Evaluating Applicable Situations of Style

Applicable Situations of Style	Alignment	Corresponding Situations

The *Applicable Situations* column lists the relevant situations for the candidate architecture style. The *Corresponding Situations* column describes the related situations within the target system. The *Alignment* column specifies the degree of alignment between the applicable situations and the corresponding situations, categorized into three levels:

- **O** for high alignment
- **Δ** for partial alignment
- **X** for no alignment

A high number of **O** symbols in the table indicates strong alignment with the applicable situations. Conversely, a large number of **X** symbols suggests minimal or no alignment. A predominance of **Δ** symbols indicates partial alignment, warranting further in-depth investigation into applicability. Other combinations of these three symbols should be interpreted based on the specific evaluation context and criteria.

Example

One candidate architecture style for the Car Rental Management System is the *Dispatcher Architecture Style*. Table 5.3 provides an evaluation of the applicable situations for this style.

Table 5.3 Evaluating Applicable Situations of Dispatcher Architecture Style

Applicable Situations of Style	Alignment	Corresponding Situations
High QoS on Server The server system must deliver a high level of QoS, which includes reliability, scalability, and availability	**O**	**High QoS Requirement** The server in the target system, CRMS, is essential for delivering core functionality to both rental centers and customers. Therefore, it must maintain a high level of QoS, including reliability, scalability, and availability
Handling Evolving Invocation Load The system's invocation load is expected to vary over time. The system should be able to adapt effectively to these changes, ensuring consistent and smooth operation	**O**	**Dynamic Invocation Load Handling** Invocation loads from rental center client nodes and mobile applications vary significantly, ranging from idle periods to peak usage. The system must be designed to effectively manage these dynamically changing invocation loads
Dynamic Allocation of Server Due to fluctuations in QoS resulting from varying invocation loads and environmental conditions, the system should be capable of dynamically allocating high-QoS servers to meet client node requests	**O**	**Dynamic Server Allocation** The QoS provided by servers in CRMS can fluctuate due to various operational factors. Consequently, the system should have the capability to dynamically allocate high-QoS servers in response to client requests

(continued)

Table 5.3 (continued)

Applicable Situations of Style	Alignment	Corresponding Situations
Low overhead of intermediary agent The runtime overhead introduced by any intermediary agent between client and server nodes must be minimized to ensure efficiency	**O**	**Minimized overhead of intermediary agent** Increased runtime overhead from the intermediary agent can degrade overall system performance. To mitigate this, CRMS must be designed to minimize the overhead associated with the intermediary agent
Cost justification of server replication The expense associated with server replication should be justified by the enhancements it brings to QoS	**O**	**Justification for server replication costs** The cost of deploying replicated servers in CRMS is justified due to the substantial improvements in QoS it brings, enhancing reliability and service availability

The table presents the applicable situations for the Dispatcher Architecture Style, each compared against the corresponding situation in the target system. All five situations demonstrate a high degree of alignment with their counterparts in the target system.

5.2.2 Task 2. Evaluate Benefits

This task is to assess whether the target system can effectively leverage the benefits provided by the candidate architecture style. It involves creating a table that lists the benefits of the style, the corresponding advantages for the target system, and the degree of alignment between them.

The evaluation of benefit applicability for the candidate architecture style can be summarized as shown in Table 5.4.

Table 5.4 Evaluating Benefits of Style

Benefits of Style	Alignment	Corresponding Benefits

The *Benefits of Style* column lists the benefits provided by the candidate architecture style. The *Corresponding Benefits* column describes the advantages the target system gains from these benefits. The *Alignment* column indicates the degree of alignment between them, categorized into three levels:

- **O** for high benefits
- **Δ** for partial benefits
- **X** for no benefits

A high number of **O** symbols in the table indicates a strong alignment with the benefits. Conversely, a high number of **X** symbols suggests minimal or no alignment. A predominance of **Δ** symbols indicates partial alignment, warranting further investigation into applicability. Other combinations of the three symbols should be interpreted based on the specific evaluation context and criteria.

Example

Next, the benefits provided by the Dispatcher Architecture Style for the target system are evaluated. This evaluation is summarized in Table 5.5.

Table 5.5 Evaluating Benefits of Dispatcher Architecture Style

Benefits of Style	Alignment	Corresponding Benefits
Increased QoS on Server Load balancing through replicated servers ensures high QoS, enhancing system performance, scalability, reliability, and availability. Multiple servers operating in parallel maintain consistent performance. In case of server failure, overall system performance remains unaffected, ensuring uninterrupted operation	O	**High QoS in CRMS** Load balancing with replicated servers in CRMS ensures high QoS in terms of performance, scalability, reliability, and availability, providing significant advantages to CRMS
Minimal Overhead of Intermediary Agent Using a dispatcher as an intermediary reduces overhead compared to a broker, as the dispatcher identifies a high-QoS server for the client, allowing direct interaction with the assigned server	O	**Efficient Performance in CRMS** In CRMS, the dispatcher efficiently manages high invocation loads from rental centers and customer mobile apps. Minimizing dispatcher overhead is essential to maintain high system performance

The table outlines two key benefits of the Dispatcher Architecture Style, comparing each benefit with its corresponding advantage in the target system. Both benefits demonstrate a high degree of alignment with their respective advantages in the Car Rental Management System.

5.2.3 Task 3. Evaluate Drawbacks

This task is to assess whether the target system can effectively manage and mitigate the drawbacks associated with the candidate architecture style. It involves creating a table that lists the drawbacks of the style, describes the corresponding mitigation strategies implemented in the target system, and evaluates the degree of successful remediation for each drawback.

The evaluation of mitigation strategies for addressing the drawbacks of the candidate architecture style is summarized as shown in Table 5.6.

Table 5.6 Evaluating Drawbacks of Style

Drawbacks of Style	Alignment	Mitigation Strategies

The *Drawbacks of Style* column lists the potential drawbacks associated with the candidate architecture style. The *Mitigation Strategies* column describes how the target system addresses these drawbacks. The Alignment column indicates the degree of success in mitigating each drawback, categorized into three levels:

- **O** for high success in mitigating drawbacks
- **Δ** for partial success in mitigating drawbacks
- **X** for no success in mitigating drawbacks

A high number of **O** symbols in the table indicates a strong degree of successful remediation for the drawbacks. Conversely, a high number of **X** symbols suggests minimal or no remediation. A predominance of **Δ** symbols indicates partial remediation, warranting further in-depth investigation into applicability. Other combinations of these three symbols should be interpreted based on the specific evaluation context and criteria.

Example

Consider evaluating how the drawbacks of the Dispatcher Architecture Style can be mitigated in the target system. This evaluation is summarized in a table, as shown in Table 5.7.

Table 5.7 Evaluating Drawbacks of Dispatcher Architecture Style

Drawbacks of Style	Alignment	Mitigation Strategies
Failure of Dispatcher The dispatcher is a critical component, creating a potential single point of failure that could impact the system's overall reliability	O	**Active-Redundancy Implementation** To address this risk, the target system, CRMS, implements an Active-Redundancy tactic for the dispatcher, reducing the likelihood of failure. The cost of this tactic is relatively low
Cost for Replicating Servers Operating a set of replicated servers incurs high costs, including both initial deployment and ongoing operational expenses	O	**Justification of Replication Costs** The high cost of server replication is justified by the substantial benefits in QoS, making this architecture style essential for reliability and availability in CRMS

The table presents two major drawbacks of the Dispatcher Architecture Style along with their corresponding mitigation strategies in the target system. Both drawbacks are successfully mitigated through their respective mitigation strategies, ensuring they will not have a significant negative impact on the target system.

5.2.4 Task 4. Determine Applicability

This task determines the suitability of each candidate architecture style by consolidating the results of evaluations regarding applicability, benefits, and drawbacks.

Considering Average Alignment Scores

The decision regarding applicability is primarily based on the alignment scores observed in the three evaluation tables: Applicable Situations, Benefits, and Drawbacks.

- **High Degree of Applicability**
  If the average alignment level for applicable situations of a candidate architecture style is high, the style is considered for final implementation in the schematic architecture of the target system, provided the average alignment levels for benefits and drawbacks are also favorable.
- **Medium Degree of Applicability**
  If the average alignment level for applicable situations is medium, the style may be considered for inclusion in the schematic architecture, but only if the alignment levels for benefits and mitigating drawbacks are significantly high.
- **Low Degree of Applicability**
  If the average alignment level for applicable situations is low, the style should not be considered for inclusion in the schematic architecture, regardless of the alignment levels for benefits and mitigating drawbacks.

For the Dispatcher Architecture Style applied to the Car Rental Management System, all three evaluation criteria—applicable situations, benefits, and drawbacks—indicate a high level of compatibility. Therefore, this candidate architecture style is deemed suitable for incorporation into the schematic architecture of the target system.

Considering Relevant Weights on Evaluation Items

Another factor to consider when determining applicability is the relative weight assigned to evaluation items within each criterion, such as Applicable Situations, Benefits, or Drawbacks of the architecture style. Each evaluation criterion typically comprises several items, with some designated as primary and others as secondary.

Assigning appropriate weights to these items ensures that critical factors receive greater emphasis in the decision-making process, leading to a more balanced and accurate assessment of each architecture style's suitability. This weighting approach enables architects to prioritize the most relevant aspects of each style, thereby aligning the final selection more closely with system requirements and goals.

5.3 Step 3. Integrate Architecture Styles

This step is to incorporate the selected architecture styles into the schematic architecture of the target system. Each architecture style contributes its unique structure and structural elements. The integration process focuses on unifying the structural aspects of the selected architecture styles into a cohesive and fully articulated schematic architecture, as illustrated in Fig. 5.13.

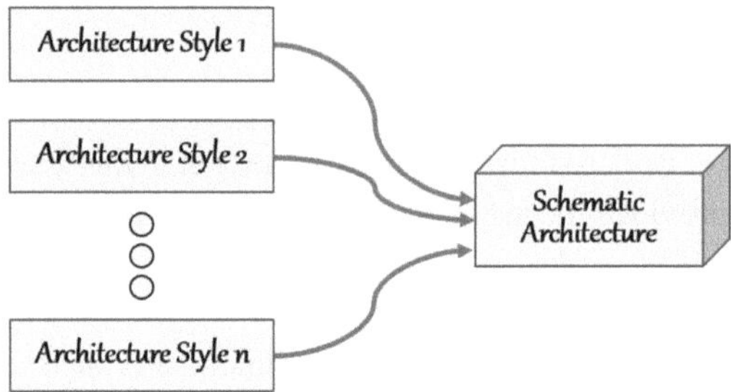

Fig. 5.13 Integration of Architecture Styles into Schematic Architecture

Instantiating Each Architecture Style

Before integrating the selected styles, each architecture style must first be instantiated for the target system by applying the following procedure:

- **Customize Structural Layout of Each Style**
  Begin by replicating the fundamental structure of each architecture style, including its components and connectors. Customize this structure as necessary to align with the specific requirements and characteristics of the target system. Customization may involve creating multiple instances of structural elements, defining necessary connectors among elements, and modifying the topological layout while ensuring that the intended structural properties of the style remain unchanged.
  For example, consider the *Pipe-and-Filter* style. Begin by replicating its basic structure, which consists of pipes and filters. Next, tailor the layout by instantiating multiple pipes based on the number of required data manipulation components. Define filters between the pipes to correspond with the necessary data transfer paths.
- **Define Meaningful Names for Structural Elements**
  Assign descriptive names to the structural elements within the architecture style, reflecting the context of the target system. These names should clearly represent the purpose and functionality of each element, enhancing clarity and relevance within the specific application domain.

Principle of Integrating Architecture Styles

Each architecture style addresses specific aspects of the system; therefore, all selected styles must be seamlessly integrated to form a cohesive and functional system architecture or schematic architecture. The key principle in integrating two different architecture styles is to identify structural elements in both styles that fulfill similar roles. Although these elements may have different names, their functions are aligned across the two styles.

Note that the mapping of structural elements between two architecture styles may not always be one to one; a structural element in one style may correspond to multiple elements in another. For example, in the integration of the Shared Repository and MVC architecture styles, an analysis of their structural layouts and components reveals two pairs of corresponding elements:

- The “Shared Repository” element in the Shared Repository Style corresponds to the “Database” elements in the MVC architecture style.
- The “Application” element in Shared Repository Architecture Style corresponds to the “group of View, Control and Model” element.

These mappings, along with the integrated architecture, are illustrated in Fig. 5.14.

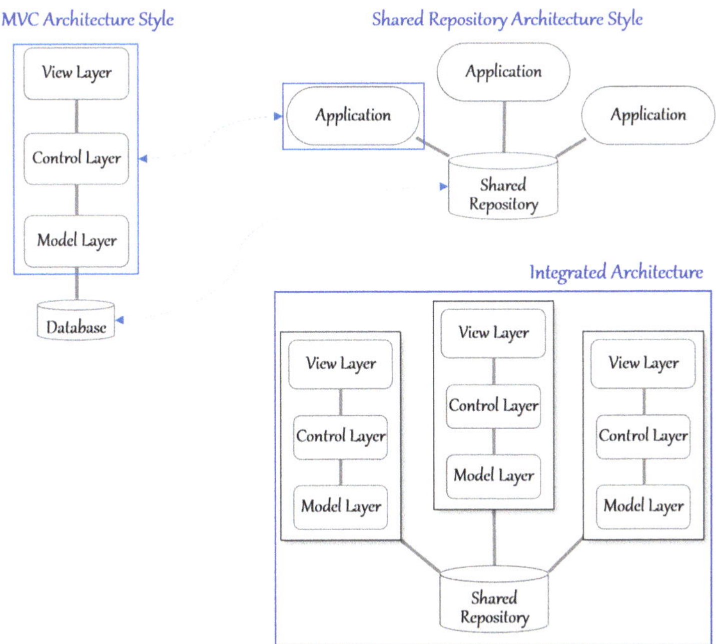

Fig. 5.14 Integration of Shared Repository with MVC Architecture Styles

Order of Integrating Architecture Styles

The integration of architecture styles follows a specific order based on their layout coverage. The process begins by merging architecture styles that have the highest layout coverage, followed by those with progressively lower layout coverage.

The recommended sequence for integrating architecture styles is as follows:

- Architecture Styles with Tiers
- Architecture Styles with Services
- Architecture Styles with Layers
- Architecture Styles with Behavior Patterns
- Architecture Styles with Variability
- Other Architecture Styles

This order ensures a structured and seamless integration process, starting with foundational, broad-scoped styles and progressing toward more specialized or adaptive styles.

5.3.1 Task 1. Integrate Architecture Styles with Tiers

This task is to integrate architecture styles that are organized based on tiered structures. Tiered architecture styles provide the most extensive layout coverage among architecture styles; therefore, they are integrated before others.

For example, the layout coverage of the Client-Server Architecture Style spans the entire system, partitioning it into two tiers: the Client tier and the Server tier. Architecture styles in this category include:

- Client-Server Architecture Style
- N-Tier Architecture Style
- Peer-to-Peer Architecture Style

In addition, load-balancing architecture styles may also fall into this category. These styles organize the system into a client tier, an intermediary agent tier, and a replicated or dedicated Server tier. Note that these styles can be applied to either the whole system or a subsystem. Architecture styles in this category include:

- Broker Architecture Style
- Dispatcher Architecture Style
- Master-Slave Architecture Style
- Edge Computing Architecture Style

Example
Consider designing the schematic architecture for the Car Rental Management System. The SRS specifies multiple tiers within the system; therefore, the N-Tier Architecture Style is appropriate.

Multiple options exist for instantiating this architecture style, as illustrated in Fig. 5.15.

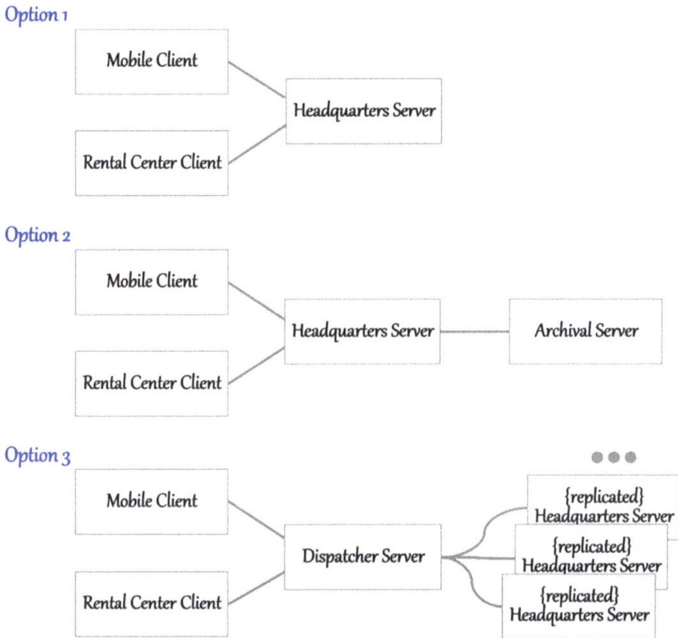

Fig. 5.15 Options for Applying N-Tier Style to Car Rental Management System

- **Option (1): Applying Three Tiers**
  The SRS specifies three distinct system nodes. Accordingly, this option defines the *Mobile Client* for customers, the *Rental Center Client* for rental center staff, and the *Headquarters Server*, which maintains the master repository and provides rental-related functionality to both client systems.
  This option maintains a high level of consistency with the structural requirements of the SRS.
- **Option (2): Applying Four Tiers**
  Building on the three tiers from Option 1, this option introduces an additional tier dedicated to data archiving. The *Archival Server* tier is responsible for securely storing essential business datasets, ensuring data security and recoverability.

- **Option (3): Adding Dispatcher Tier**
  This option addresses the requirements for high availability, reliability, and performance of the *Headquarters Server*. In this configuration, a load-balancing approach is implemented by applying the Dispatcher Architecture Style to the Headquarters Server.
- **Other Options**
  In addition to the three options discussed, several other approaches for applying the N-Tier Architecture Style are possible, as outlined below:
  - **Applying Both Archival Server Tier and Dispatcher Tier**
    This option combines the use of both the Archival Server Tier and the Dispatcher Tier to enhance the system's data management and load-balancing capabilities.
  - **Applying Three Tiers with Active Redundancy**
    Active redundancy is a high-availability architecture in which multiple identical instances of a system operate simultaneously, each processing real workloads. This approach ensures continuous availability, allowing the system to function seamlessly even if one instance fails.
  - **Applying Three Tiers with Passive Redundancy**
    Passive redundancy is an architecture in which one system actively handles all workloads while one or more identical backup systems remain idle but ready to take over upon failure of the primary system. This approach ensures high availability with less complexity and typically incurs lower costs compared to active redundancy.
  - **Applying Three Tiers with Cold Spare Redundancy**
    Cold spare redundancy is a minimal high-availability approach in which backup systems remain completely powered off until needed. While this option offers the lowest ongoing operational costs, it also results in the longest recovery time, as the backup system must undergo full start-up and data restoration when activated.

Architects should select the most appropriate option for applying the N-tier architecture to effectively satisfy the system requirements.

5.3.2 Task 2. Integrate Architecture Styles with Services

This task is to integrate architecture styles that leverage external services provided over a network. These services are typically deployed and managed by third-party providers, allowing application systems to invoke them to support specific functionalities.

Architecture styles in this category include:

- Microservice Architecture Style
- Cloud Service in the form of Component-as-a-Service (CaaS)
- Service-Oriented Architecture (SOA) Style

All these architecture styles share a common objective of enabling modular, network-based service integration. All promote loose coupling and scalability through the use of independently managed components. However, Microservices focus on fine-grained, autonomously deployable services, CaaS emphasizes the consumption of externally hosted software components, and SOA formalizes service interaction through standards such as WS-BPEL, SOAP, WSDL, and UDDI to ensure interoperability across heterogeneous systems.

Example

Consider an *Audio Diary Mobile App* designed to capture a user's spoken diary entries, convert them into text, analyze the semantic content, and store the entries on a central server. An effective strategy for developing this app is to utilize two types of external services:

- **Speech-to-Text (STT) Service**
  STT (Speech-to-Text) is an automated process that converts spoken words into written text by analyzing audio input. A reliable STT capability is critical for this mobile app and can be achieved by integrating a high-quality STT microservice, such as Amazon Transcribe, Google Cloud Speech-to-Text, or Microsoft Azure Speech Services.
- **Sentiment Analysis Service**
  Sentiment Analysis is an automated process that applies natural language processing techniques to determine the emotional tone or attitude expressed in text. This capability is essential for developing the app and can be realized by integrating a sentiment analysis service, such as Amazon Comprehend, Google Cloud Natural Language API, IBM Watson Natural Language Understanding, or Microsoft Azure Text Analytics.

The architecture of integrating these two microservices is shown in Fig. 5.16.

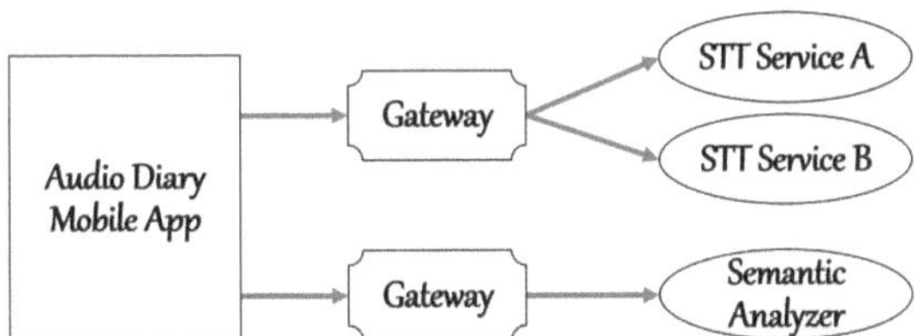

Fig. 5.16 Integrating STT and Sentiment Analysis Microservices for Audio Diary App

In the figure, *Gateway* handles interface adaptation, dynamic routing, and load balancing between the mobile app and external microservices, selecting the most appropriate service based on runtime conditions. This architecture specifies two distinct STT microservice providers, labeled STT Service A and STT Service B, with the Gateway dynamically selecting the appropriate STT service according to the runtime environment and conditions.

5.3.3 Task 3. Integrate Architecture Styles with Layers

This task is to integrate architecture styles that adopt a layered approach. In layered systems, the architecture is divided into distinct vertical layers, each serving a specific role within the system. Each layer addresses a particular aspect of functionality, facilitating a modular and organized approach to system design and development.

The architecture styles in this category include:

- Layered Architecture Style
- MVC (Model-View-Controller) Architecture Style
- Variations of MVC Architecture Style such as:
  - Model-View-Presenter (MVP) Style
  - Model-View-ViewModel (MVVM) Style
  - Model-View-Presenter-ViewModel (MVPVM) Style
  - Hierarchical Model-View-Controller (HMVC) Style
  - Model View Adapter (MVA) Style

When applying the Layered Architecture Style, architects should determine the appropriate number of layers and define the specific responsibilities of each layer. These layers should be organized into a vertical hierarchy following the virtual machine principle, where each layer interacts only with its immediate neighboring layers, thereby promoting modularity and separation of concerns.

In the case of the MVC pattern and its variations, the layers and roles are predefined. However, architects may need to refine the layer names to make them more intuitive and reflective of their specific functions within the target system.

Example

Consider applying the MVC Architecture Style to the Car Rental Management System, assuming architecture with four tiers, as shown in Fig. 5.17.

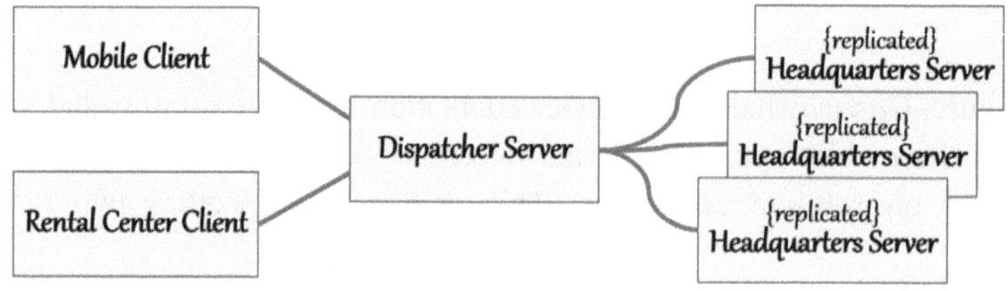

Fig. 5.17 Tiers in Car Rental Management System

Among the tiers, the *Mobile Client*, *Rental Center Client*, and *Headquarters Server* tiers can be effectively configured using the MVC Architecture Style, as each of these tiers benefits from the clear separation of concerns provided by MVC. This approach enables distinct handling of presentation with a view layer, processing of core business logic with a controller layer, and data management with a model layer.

The architecture of applying the MVC Architecture Style on these tiers is shown in Fig. 5.18.

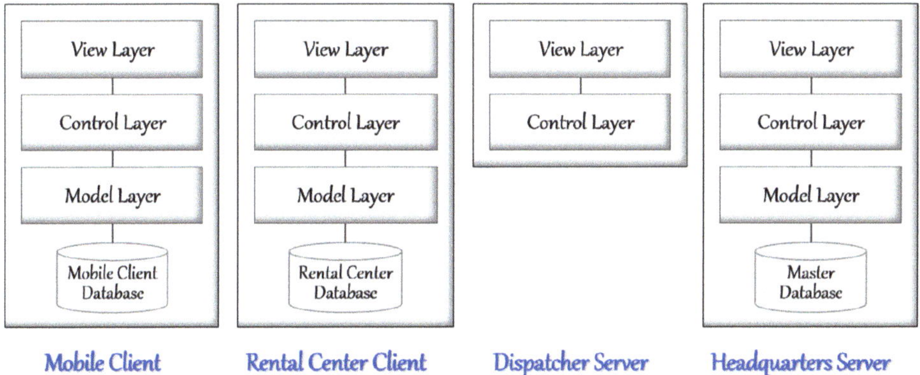

Fig. 5.18 MVC Style Applied to Car Rental Management System

Note that the Dispatcher Server tier is configured with only a view layer and a control layer, indicating that it is not intended to manage persistent datasets and, therefore, does not require a model layer.

5.3.4 Task 4. Integrate Architecture Styles with Behavior

This task is to integrate architecture styles that define specific behaviors, such as invocation or interaction paradigms. These styles establish clear patterns for how components interact with or invoke one another.

Architecture styles focused on specific interactions do not alter the overall structure of the schematic architecture; instead, they primarily refine the design of a specific structural element, typically the control layer. By introducing defined interaction patterns and mechanisms, these styles enhance and optimize the functionality of the control layer while preserving the integrity of the existing schematic architecture.

Example

Consider applying the *Pipe-and-Filter* Architecture Style, which defines a specific approach for transmitting datasets between data manipulation components, known as streaming. This style comprises two types of elements: *filters*, which function as data manipulation components, and *pipes*, which serve as data streaming, as illustrated in Fig. 5.19.

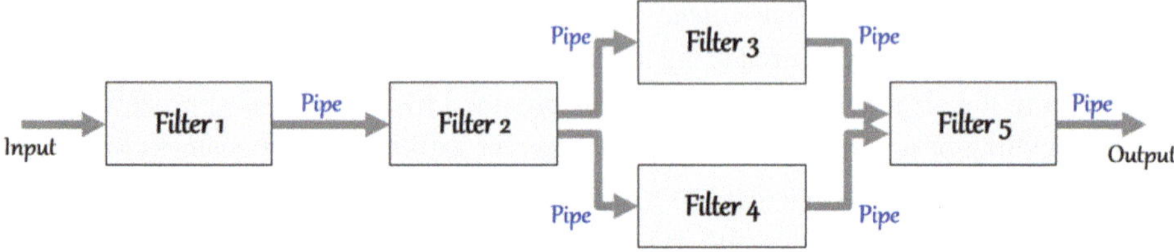

Fig. 5.19 Elements of Pipe-and-Filter Architecture Style

This style establishes specific rules for data flow and transformation within the system using pipes, i.e., data streaming. Additionally, it supports parallel processing across filters, enhancing efficiency and scalability.

The architecture styles in this category include the following:

- Batch Sequential Architecture Style
- Pipe-and-Filter Architecture Style
- Event-Driven Architecture Style
- Publish-and-Subscriber Architecture Style

Example

Consider integrating the *Event-Driven Architecture Style* with the *MVC Architecture Style*. The Event-Driven Architecture Style defines a specific invocation pattern: executing designated functionality in response to predefined types of events. In the MVC structure, the Control Layer is responsible for receiving user requests and executing the necessary functionality. Therefore, the event-driven invocation pattern is well suited for application within the Control Layer of the MVC

The integrated architecture of these two styles is shown in Fig. 5.20.

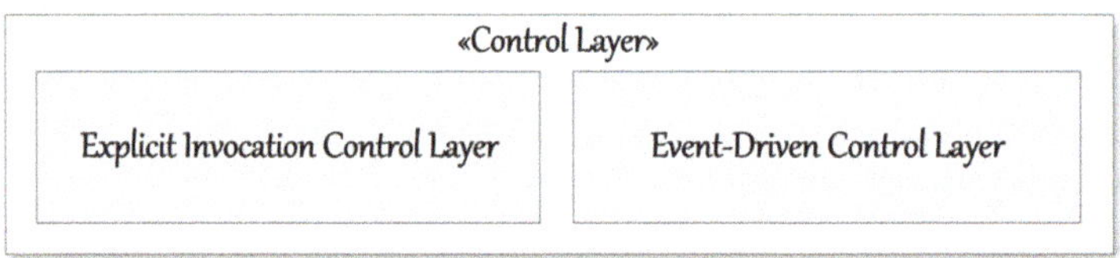

Fig. 5.20 Integration of Event-Driven Architecture Style Within the Control Layer

Note that the Control Layer in the MVC architecture is divided into two sublayers. The *Explicit Invocation Control Layer* hosts functional components that use explicit invocation, while the *Event-Driven Control Layer* accommodates functional components that operate based on event-driven invocation. This design accounts for cases where not all functional components in the Control Layer are invoked by events; some components are explicitly invoked through user actions.

5.3.5 Task 5. Integrate Architecture Styles with Adaptability

This task is to integrate architecture styles that enhance the adaptability of the target system. Adaptability is the ability of a system to adjust its behavior, structure, or components in response to changing requirements, environments, or usage conditions. This capability ensures that the system remains functional, efficient, and relevant over time, even as external demands or internal configurations evolve.

Adaptive systems are typically designed with a combination of fixed and variable features, enabling flexibility and responsiveness to evolving requirements. Adaptability is particularly critical for systems with variable components, such as system-level software (e.g., operating systems, middleware, platform software) and cloud services, where dynamic adjustments are necessary to maintain performance and relevance under changing conditions.

The architecture styles in this category include:

- Microkernel Architecture Style
- Microservice Architecture Style
- Blackboard Architecture Style

Each style in this category defines a structural layout with placeholders to accommodate the system's fixed (common) and flexible (variable) elements. In addition, each style includes a scheme for binding specific variants to designated variation points. Therefore, all placeholders and binding schemes for these variants should be integrated into the schematic architecture to support adaptability.

Example

Consider integrating the *Microkernel Architecture Style* with the *MVC Architecture Style*. The Microkernel style promotes architectural adaptability through a plug-in scheme, where components implementing specified interfaces can be added to extend functionality. This approach allows for flexibility and extensibility by enabling the integration of externally developed components, known as plug-ins. In the MVC structure, the Control Layer handles user requests, making it suitable for applying an event-driven invocation pattern within the Control Layer of the MVC architecture.

The integrated architecture of these two styles is shown in Fig. 5.21.

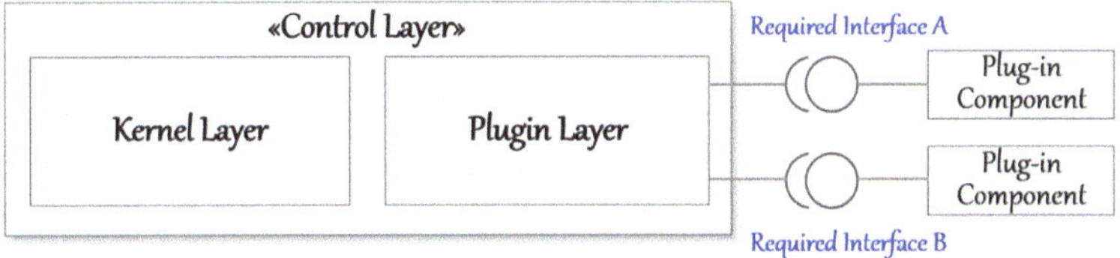

Fig. 5.21 Integration of Microkernel Architecture Style Within the Control Layer

Note that the Control Layer in the MVC architecture is divided into two sub-layers: *Kernel Layer* and *Plugin-Layer*.

- **Kernel Layer**
  This layer hosts functional components that provide the system's common and fixed functionality. Its design follows a *Closed Design* approach, consistent with the Open/Closed Principle, ensuring that core functionality remains stable and unmodifiable without altering the kernel.
- **Plug-In Layer**
  This layer accommodates plug-in components that implement the interfaces specified within it. The interfaces in this layer allow for various implementations (i.e., plug-ins) to adapt to different environmental conditions. Consequently, the Plug-In Layer follows an *Open Design* approach under the Open/Closed Principle to enable flexibility and extensibility.
  UML provides a specific interface type, called a *Required Interface*, to support this type of variability management. In UML, a *Provided Interface* represents the functionality a component offers to other components, while a *Required Interface* defines the functionality that a component depends on or requires from other components. It specifies the set of methods that must be implemented by plug-in object classes to fulfill these dependencies. Hence, UML *Required Interfaces* can be effectively utilized to define the interfaces in the Plug-In Layer.

5.3.6 Task 6. Integrate Remaining Architecture Styles

This task is to integrate any architecture styles that have not yet been incorporated into the schematic architecture. Since no exhaustive taxonomy of architecture styles exists, certain styles may fall outside the previously defined categories. In such cases, the components and connectors of these additional architecture styles should be integrated into the existing schematic architecture to ensure overall cohesion and compatibility.

Schematic Architecture of Car Rental Management System
For this system, three architecture styles were selected, the N-Tier Architecture Style, the MVC Architecture Style, and the Dispatcher Architecture Style, as described earlier. The integration of these styles forms the schematic architecture of the system, as illustrated in Fig. 5.22.

As shown in the figure, the application of the N-Tier Architecture Style defines four tiers within the system. The implementation of the MVC Architecture Style establishes three layers—View, Control, and Model—within each tier. Additionally, the application of the Dispatcher Architecture Style introduces a Dispatcher Server, which facilitates communication between the client nodes and the server node.

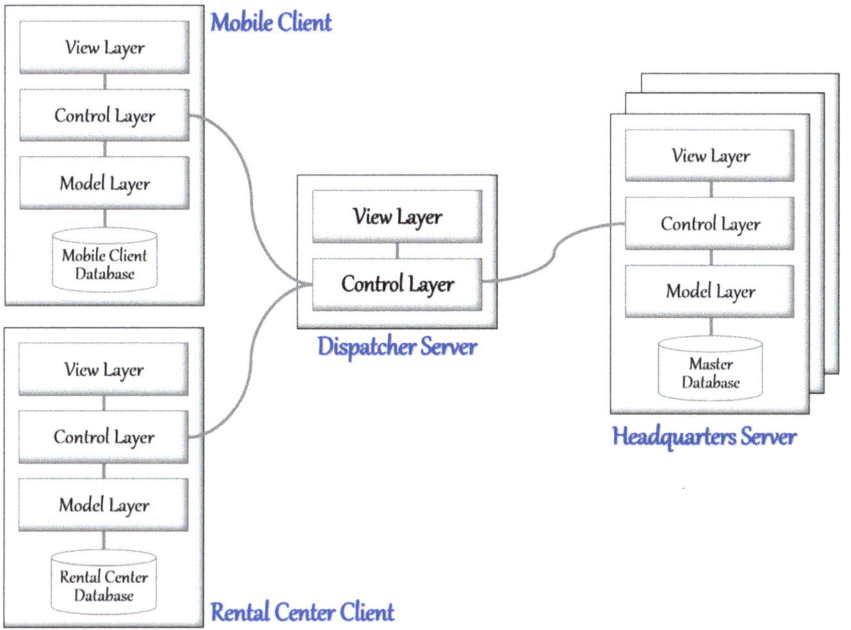

Fig. 5.22 Schematic Architecure of Car Rental Management System

5.4 Step 4. Refine Schematic Architecture

This step is to refine the schematic architecture by making additions and modifications to ensure that it fully satisfies the requirements of the target system. Although applying appropriate architecture styles defines a substantial portion of the schematic architecture, the resulting structure may not completely meet all the system's structural requirements and characteristics. Therefore, it is necessary to carefully examine the schematic architecture, identify required modifications, determine any additional components and connectors that must be incorporated, and implement the necessary changes and additions.

In practice, the schematic architecture is often finalized through a series of refinements throughout the design process, as illustrated in Fig. 5.23.

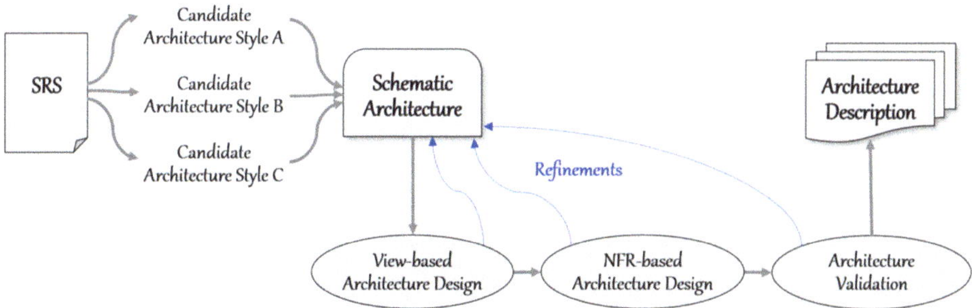

Fig. 5.23 Refinements to Schematic Architecture

This figure illustrates the incremental development process of a schematic architecture. Starting from the SRS, suitable architecture styles are selected and integrated into an initial schematic architecture, which is then refined through View-based and NFR-based Architecture Design processes. Architecture refinement occurs in two forms: refinement of structural elements and refinement of connectors.

5.4.1 Task 1. Refining Structural Elements

This task is to refine the structural elements of the schematic architecture by examining the current design and iteratively improving it. Structural elements include constructs such as tiers, layers, partitions within layers, and external services.

Refinements are performed by adding, modifying, or removing structural elements as needed. Examples of such refinements include:

- Adding a new tier dedicated to archiving persistent datasets
- Dividing the control layer into two layers—a high-level service layer and a lower-level infrastructure layer—to enhance maintainability
- Adding a console view layer for logging and monitoring system performance, enabling real-time issue diagnosis, and improving observability and operational resilience
- Incorporating a new required service within the Plug-In Layer to utilize a newly identified microservice
- Integrating a security layer to manage authentication and authorization, thereby strengthening the system's overall security posture

5.4.2 Task 2. Refining Connectors

This task is to refine the connectors within the schematic architecture by examining the existing design and iteratively improving it. Connectors define the interaction paths between structural elements and are characterized by attributes such as relationship type, cardinality, direction of reference, and interaction scheme.

Refinements to structural elements typically necessitate corresponding refinements to the connectors associated with those elements. Examples of connector refinements include:

- Adding a connector between two tiers
- Adding a new pipe between a source filter and a target filter
- Adding a side channel to enable direct interaction between two non-adjacent layers
- Removing a connector between two components that no longer need to interact, thereby simplifying the architecture and reducing coupling

While it is generally recommended to preserve the interaction paths defined by an architecture style, refinements may involve adding new connectors, modifying existing ones, or, in exceptional cases, deliberately disabling certain paths for specific reasons. In such cases, it is essential to thoroughly review the modified schematic architecture to ensure its validity and assess the potential impact of deviating from the established architecture style.

Consider an example of connector refinement in the schematic architecture of the Car Rental Management System. In this architecture, a substantial volume of rental-related data is transferred between the Rental Center Client tier and the Headquarters Server tier. By default, this data flows along the path: *Control Layer of the Client → Control Layer of the Server → Model Layer of the Server*. However, this default data flow path may degrade runtime performance, even for simple update operations, as all data must pass through the Server's Control Layer.

To address this performance limitation, a new connector can be introduced to enable direct interaction between the Client's Control Layer and the Server's Model Layer, as shown in Fig. 5.24.

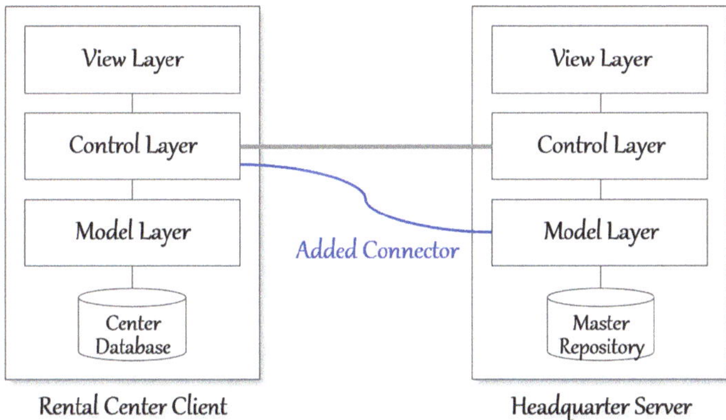

Fig. 5.24 Refining Schematic Architecure with New Connector

The addition of this new connector can help alleviate the data transmission bottleneck and improve the runtime performance.

5.5 Checklist for A3: Schematic Architecture Design

The following checklist items can be used to validate the schematic architecture design.

5.5.1 Checklist for Step 1: Identify Candidate Architecture Styles

- Does the architect consider the structural layout and constraints explicitly specified in the SRS when deriving candidate architecture styles, ensuring alignment with system goals?
- Does the architect also consider structural layouts and constraints implied by non-functional requirements in the SRS, such as scalability, availability, or security?
- Is the set of inherent system types (e.g., distributed system, interactive system) identified accurately and comprehensively to guide style selection?
- Is the set of candidate architecture styles complete, without redundant overlaps, structural conflicts, or other complications that could affect design clarity?

5.5.2 Checklist for Step 2: Evaluate Candidate Architecture Styles

- Are all essential evaluation items for the criterion *Applicable Situations of Style* thoroughly included and appropriately considered when assessing suitability?
- Are all corresponding applicable situations specific to the target system clearly identified and reflected in the evaluation process?
- Are all essential evaluation items for the criterion *Benefits of Style* properly included to capture the strengths each style offers to the system?
- Are the benefits specific to the target system fully considered to ensure the style selections maximize system advantages?
- Are all essential evaluation items for the criterion *Drawbacks of Style* carefully included to identify potential risks or limitations?
- Are mitigation strategies for the identified drawbacks defined clearly and practically to minimize risks without undermining system performance?
- Is the decision on style applicability made systematically by considering both the average alignment scores across criteria and the relative importance (weights) assigned to each evaluation item?

5.5.3 Checklist for Step 3: Integrate Architecture Styles

- Does the instantiation of each selected architecture style include all required structural elements, ensuring completeness of design?
- Are the names assigned to instantiated structural elements clear, consistent, and relevant to their roles within the target system?
- Is the resulting schematic architecture free from structural redundancies, conflicts, or ambiguities that could impair system integrity?

- Does the integration of selected architecture styles follow the recommended sequential order to avoid conflicts and dependency issues?
- Are the interactions and dependencies between integrated architecture styles explicitly defined, minimizing the potential for misinterpretation or design errors?
- Does the integration maintain a clear separation of concerns, ensuring that each style addresses its intended functionality without unintended overlap with others?

5.5.4 Checklist for Step 4: Refine Schematic Architecture

- Do the refined structural elements continue to align with both the functional and non-functional system requirements identified in the SRS?
- Do the refined connectors properly reflect the updated relationships among structural elements after refinements are made?
- Are the newly added connectors justified by measurable benefits, and do they avoid introducing significant additional costs, risks, or unnecessary complexity?
- If any refinements introduce conflicts or inconsistencies, are these issues promptly identified, addressed, and corrected to maintain architectural integrity?

5.6 Exercise Problems

1. **Applying Architecture Styles to Design Schematic Architecture**
   Explain why the design of schematic architecture can be effectively guided by the selection and integration of appropriate architecture styles. Specify the roles that the selected architecture styles play in shaping the structural organization, interaction patterns, and component allocation within the schematic architecture.
2. **Determining System Types**
   An effective approach to identifying candidate architecture styles for a target system is to first determine the inherent system types it embodies and then select appropriate architecture style for each system type. Determine the system types for an e-commerce system in which the system provider maintains a cluster of servers to ensure reliability, availability, and scalability. Customers interact with the system through mobile applications or Web browsers to browse products, place orders, and complete payments. Additionally, the system integrates with external services, including product suppliers, delivery providers, and payment processing firms.
3. **Determining Candidate Architecture Styles for an e-Commerce System**
   Based on the system types identified for the e-commerce system, determine a set of candidate architecture styles to be integrated into the schematic architecture. Provide a rationale for your selection.

4. **Determining Candidate Architecture Styles for a Story Generation System**
   A Story Generation System is a cloud-based application designed to produce diverse forms of narrative content based on user preferences. This system leverages various generative AI models, including large language models (LLMs) for text generation, diffusion-based models for image generation, and animation synthesis models for dynamic visual storytelling. Given the heterogeneous nature of these models and the need for seamless orchestration, the system must be architected to support reliability, availability, and scalability. Propose candidate architecture styles for this system, and justify your selection.
5. **Evaluating Microservice Architecture Style**
   The Audio Diary Application supports functionalities such as recording voice diaries, converting speech to text, reading text aloud, and analyzing semantic or sentimental information using AI. These core functionalities are naturally decomposable into discrete services—such as Speech-to-Text, Text-to-Speech, and Semantic Analysis—making the system a strong candidate for the Microservice Architecture Style.
   Evaluate the appropriateness of applying this architecture style to the target system by referring to the evaluation tables, which outline the applicable situations, benefits, and drawbacks of the Microservice Architecture Style.
6. **Applying Layered Architecture Style**
   The Layered Architecture Style organizes the system as an ordered sequence of layers, where each layer acts as a virtual machine for the layer above. Propose design guidelines for (1) determining the appropriate number of layers for a given system and (2) defining the role and responsibilities of each layer.
7. **MVC Architecture Style and Its Variations**
   The MVC Architecture Style structures a system into three layers—Model, View, and Controller—each with distinct responsibilities. Select three architecture styles that are variations of MVC. Then, compare the original MVC architecture with the selected variations in terms of structural organization and interaction patterns among layers.
8. **Comparing Batch Sequential and Pipe-and-Filter Architecture Styles**
   Both the Batch Sequential and Pipe-and-Filter Architecture Styles are widely used in the design of data flow systems. Identify and explain the key similarities and differences between these two architecture styles in terms of structure, data processing behavior, and execution characteristics.
9. **Comparing Shared Repository and Active Repository Architecture Styles**
   Both the Shared Repository and Active Repository Architecture Styles are employed in the design of data-sharing systems. Describe the key differences between these two architecture styles in terms of their structure and control mechanisms. Additionally, specify the extra design task required when implementing the Active Repository Style.
10. **Applying N-Tier Architecture Style**
    The N-Tier Architecture Style organizes a system as a set of distributed system nodes, or tiers, where each tier is responsible for a specific category of system functionality and is deployed independently. Propose design guidelines for (1) determining the appropriate number of tiers for a given system and (2) defining the role and responsibilities of each tier.

11. **Broker Architecture Style vs. Dispatcher Architecture Style**
    Both the Broker and Dispatcher Architecture Styles are widely used in the design of load-balancing systems. Identify and explain the key similarities and differences between these two architecture styles in terms of structural organization, control flow, and communication mechanisms. In your comparison, consider aspects such as server allocation schemes, the degree of dependency on specific servers, and how client-service interactions are managed.
12. **Essence of Edge Computing Architecture Style**
    The Edge Computing Architecture Style shifts data processing and computation closer to data sources or end-user devices, rather than relying solely on centralized cloud servers. This architecture is particularly beneficial for latency-sensitive, bandwidth-constrained, or context-aware applications.
    Describe the structural characteristics and deployment model of the Edge Computing Architecture Style. Then, analyze its advantages and limitations compared to cloud-centric architectures with respect to latency, scalability, data privacy, and resource management.
13. **Essence of Publish Subscriber Architecture Style**
    Pulling is a data-fetching scheme in which a client explicitly requests data and receives it synchronously. Pushing is a scheme where relevant data is automatically delivered to registered subscribers as it becomes available.
    The Publish-Subscribe Architecture Style represents an alternative interaction model, characterized by a register-notify-fetch pattern, where subscribers are notified of new data and may fetch it as needed. Compare the Publish-Subscribe Architecture Style with the Pulling and Pushing schemes in terms of data flow control, decoupling between producers and consumers, scalability, and responsiveness.
14. **Essence of Microservice Architecture Style**
    The Microservice Architecture Style has emerged as a prominent approach with the increasing availability and adoption of microservices. Compare the concept of a microservice with the notion of a service in Service-Oriented Architecture (SOA) and Cloud Services. Highlight the similarities and differences in terms of granularity, autonomy, deployment, and communication models.
15. **Serverless Architecture Style**
    The term Serverless Architecture Style can be misleading, as it suggests the absence of servers. In reality, this style relies on servers managed by third-party providers. Describe the structural characteristics of this architecture style, and explain the collaboration model between the application components and the underlying server infrastructure.

Activity A4a. Design for Functional View 6

Objective of the Chapter
The objective of this chapter is to provide guidelines for designing the functional view of a software system. It covers the refinement of the context-level use case model, the identification of functional components, the allocation of these components to functionality placeholders within a schematic architecture, the design of component interfaces, and the design of functional variability through the identification of variation points and the definition of valid variants. Together, these guidelines enable architects to construct a functional architecture that is coherent, modular, and aligned with both system requirements and architectural principles.

Introducing Activity A4a. Design for Functional View
This activity is to design the architecture from the functional view of a target system. The functional view focuses on modeling system functionality by identifying functional components, defining their responsibilities and interfaces, and designing these components while accounting for potential functional variability.

The architectural design established through this view serves as a foundation for the development of other architectural views, offering a structured and comprehensive understanding of the system's functional aspects.

Steps in A4a. Functional View Design
The functional view design can be systematically achieved through a sequence of steps, as shown in Fig. 6.1.

- **Step 1. Refine Use Case Model**
  This step is to refine the context-level *Use Case Diagram* by elaborating actors, use cases, and their relationships with greater precision. The refined use case model establishes the foundation for subsequent functional view design.

S. D. Kim, M. Kim, *Hands-on Software Architecture*,
https://doi.org/10.1007/978-3-032-01184-8_6

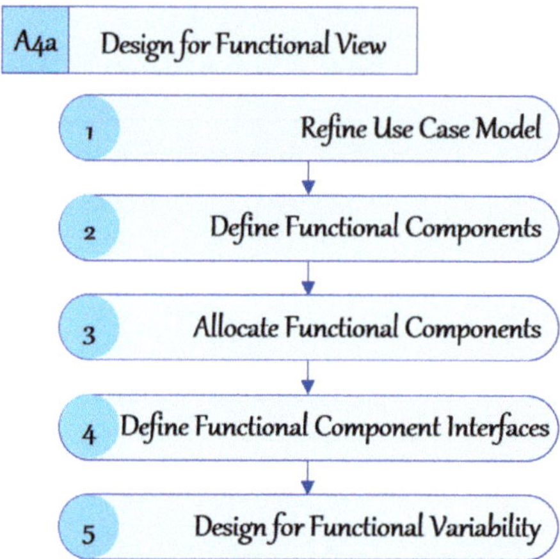

Fig. 6.1 Steps in A4a. Functional View Design

- **Step 2. Define Functional Components**
  This step is to identify the functional components of the target system based on the refined use case model. A functional component is a cohesive, self-contained unit that encapsulates specific system functionality.
- **Step 3. Allocate Functional Components**
  This step is to allocate the functional components to corresponding functionality placeholders within the schematic architecture. A functionality placeholder is a structural element designed to accommodate components that provide specific system functionalities.
- **Step 4. Define Functional Component Interfaces**
  This step is to specify the interfaces of the functional components. The interface of a functional component is a public protocol used to access its functionality, defined as a set of method signatures and semantic descriptions.
- **Step 5. Design for Functional Variability**
  This step is to identify variation points within functional components and apply open-closed design principles. Designing for variability enhances the genericity, modifiability, and extensibility of the components, enabling systematic customization.

6.1 Step 1. Refine Use Case Model

This step is to refine the context-level use case diagram by adding additional details and enhancing the precision of actors, use cases, and their relationships. This step also involves writing detailed descriptions for use cases that encompass complex functionality.

6.1.1 Task 1. Refine Functional Groups

This task is to refine the functional groups initially identified in the context model to enhance the understanding of the system's functionality. The primary criteria for refining functional groups are as follows:

- **Single Responsibility Principle**
  This criterion ensures that each functional group represents a single, cohesive, and independent functionality within the system. If a functional group encompasses multiple functionalities, it should be decomposed into separate, independent groups. Conversely, if a specific functionality is fragmented across multiple groups, they should be consolidated into a single, unified functional group.
- **Dataset Sharing**
  Typically, use cases within a functional group manipulate the same dataset. If a functional group contains use cases that operate on different datasets, it should be divided into multiple independent groups aligned with dataset boundaries.
- **Low Coupling**
  Functional groups should maintain minimal dependencies among one another. If two functional groups exhibit high interdependency, they should be considered for consolidation into a single group to minimize coupling and improve cohesion.

Example

For the Car Rental Management System, the context-level functional groups remain unchanged except for the addition of a new functional group named "Payment Management," as listed below:

- Customer Profile Management (CP)
- Staff Profile Management (SP)
- Rental Center Profile Registration (RP)
- Inventory Management (IM)
- Rental Rate Management (RR)
- Reservation Management (RS)
- Checkout Management (CH)
- In-Rental Management (IR)
- Return Management (RE)
- Car Maintenance (CM)
- Report Generation (RP)
- Payment Management (PM)

The new functional group, "Payment Management," provides functionalities for processing rental-related payments, retrieving payment records, and canceling payments. This functionality is utilized by two other functional groups: "Checkout Management" and

"Return Management." The addition of the Payment Management group is necessary to streamline and centralize payment-related operations within a single cohesive functional group.

6.1.2 Task 2. Refine Actors

This task is to refine the actors in the use case diagram by applying the following guidelines.

Refining Active Actors

Active actors are those that initiate or interact with use cases, typically representing user-type actors. For example, in the Car Rental Management System, the actor "Customer" is an active actor who initiates use cases such as *Register Customer* and *Make Reservation.*

Active actors are classified as either *primary* or *secondary* based on the extent of their access to use cases.

- **Primary Active Actor**

  A primary active actor has access to the majority, if not all, of the use cases within a functional group. For instance, the actor *Customer* can access all six use cases within the *Customer Profile Management* functional group, as illustrated in Fig. 6.2.

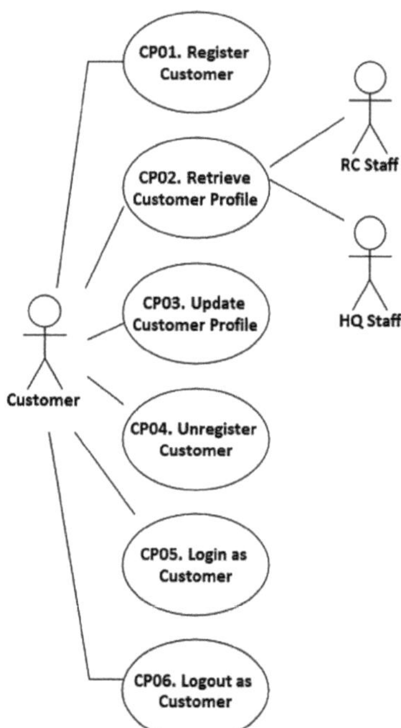

Fig. 6.2 Primary and Secondary Active Actors

- **Secondary Active Actor**
  A secondary active actor has access to a limited subset of use cases within a functional group.
  This type of actor typically has permissions for specific, restricted use cases, such as "read-only" functionalities.
  For example, the *RC Staff* and *HQ Staff* are secondary actors who have access only to the single use case *CP02: Retrieve Customer Profile*, as shown in Fig. 6.2. These actors are limited to read-only access to customer profile information.

Refining Passive Actors

Passive actors do not initiate or trigger use cases themselves; instead, they respond to service requests initiated by active actors, processing each request and returning outputs if applicable. External systems and hardware devices commonly function as passive actors within use cases.

In the Car Rental Management System, the *RC Staff* is an active actor who initiates the use case *Ch03. Validate Driver License*, while the *Driver License Validator* is a passive actor invoked by this use case, as illustrated in Fig. 6.3.

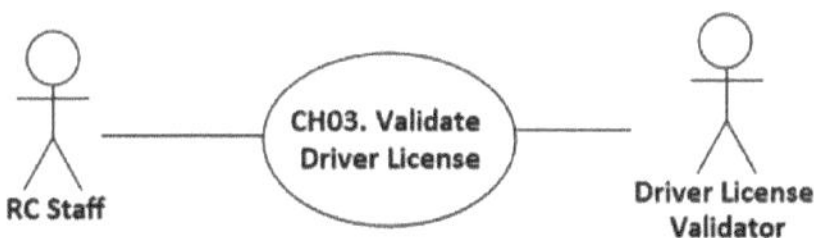

Fig. 6.3 Active Actor and Passive Actor

This passive actor provides a validation service for the customer's driver's license in response to requests from the use case.

Refining Actors of Software Agent type

A software agent-type actor is an object or a component that operates autonomously in the background, invoking relevant use cases without direct user intervention. These actors are essential for enabling functionality that operates independently, supporting background operations that do not require real-time human interaction. Autonomous software systems often utilize software agent–type actors to facilitate closed-loop operations, allowing the system to function independently.

Software agent–type actors can be effectively used to model autonomous agents in various Agentic AI systems. These actors represent autonomous entities capable of independently initiating actions, interacting with other system components, and making decisions based on internal objectives or environmental conditions. In modern implementations, frameworks such as *LangChain* and *LangGraph* provide structured approaches for developing such agents.

LangChain agents autonomously select and execute tools to achieve goals based on reasoning chains, while LangGraph extends this paradigm by modeling agent interactions and decision flows as dynamic computational graphs. By leveraging these frameworks, Agentic AI systems can simulate intelligent, goal-directed behaviors and facilitate closed-loop operations without requiring continuous human intervention.

Software agent–type actors can be effectively used to model autonomous agents in various Agentic AI system.

In the Car Rental Management System, the *Report Agent* is a software agent-type actor that autonomously invokes the use case *RP02. Generate Periodical Report* to produce periodic reports, as illustrated in Fig. 6.4.

Fig. 6.4 Actor of Software Agent Type

The refined list of actors for the Car Rental Management System is summarized below:

- **Actors of User type**: User, RC Staff, HQ Staff
- **Actors of Hardware Device type**: GPS Locator
- **Actors of External System type**: Driver License Validator, Payment Authorizer
- **Actors of Software Agent type**: Tracking Agent, Report Agent

Mapping Actors to Functional Groups

An effective method for deriving and validating actors is to map the identified actors to the system's functional groups. This approach ensures that each functional group is properly associated with its relevant actors, facilitating comprehensive coverage and alignment across the system's functionality.

The mapping of actors to their corresponding functional groups is typically presented in tabular form. For example, the actors identified for the Car Rental Management System are mapped to their respective functional groups, as shown in Table 6.1.

In the *Checkout Management* functional group, the primary actor, *RC Staff*, has full access to all checkout-related functionalities. In contrast, the secondary actors, *HQ Staff* and *Customer*, are granted access only to read-only functionalities. Additionally, this functional group includes a passive actor, the *Driver License Validator*, which is responsible for validating customers' driver licenses.

Table 6.1 Allocation of Actors to Functional Groups

Actors / Functional Groups	Active Actors: Primary	Active Actors: Secondary	Passive Actors
Customer Profile Management	Customer	RC Staff, HQ Staff	
Staff Profile Management	RC Staff, HQ Staff		
Rental Center Profile Registration	RC Staff, HQ Staff		
Inventory Management	HQ Staff	RC Staff	
Rental Rate Management	HQ Staff	RC Staff, Customer	
Reservation Management	Customer	RC Staff	
Checkout Management	RC Staff	HQ Staff, Customer	Driver License Validator
In-Rental Management	Trace Agent, RC Staff	HQ Staff	GPS Locator
Return Management	RC Staff	HQ Staff, Customer	
Car Maintenance	RC Staff	HQ Staff	
Report Generation	RC Staff, HQ Staff	Report Agent	
Payment Management	"Checkout" & "Return"	RC Staff	Payment Authorizer

6.1.3 Task 3. Refine Use Cases

This task is to refine the use cases in the context-level use case diagram by applying the following guidelines. Each functional group represents a cohesive unit of functionality and operates on a specific dataset. This dataset is typically subject to four standard data manipulation operations: Create, Retrieve, Update, and Delete (CRUD).

By applying CRUD operations to the dataset, the use cases associated with the functional group can be systematically derived, as illustrated in Fig. 6.5.

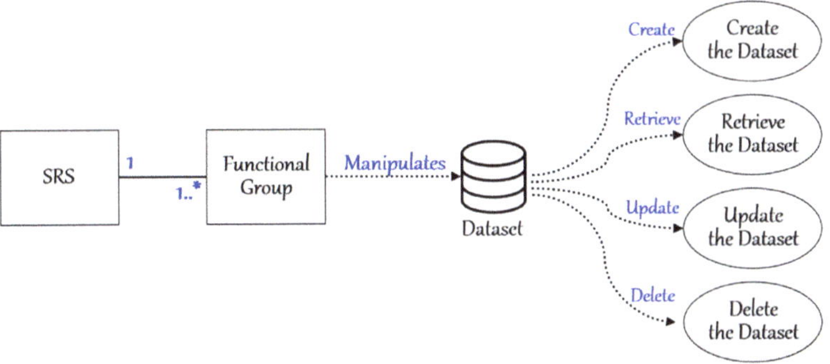

Fig. 6.5 Derivation of Use Cases Based on CRUD operations

The figure illustrates a structured approach in which functional groups are derived from the SRS, each functional group manages a specific dataset, and the corresponding use cases are systematically derived by applying CRUD operations to the dataset.

For example, the Reservation Management functional group manages the Reservation dataset. By applying CRUD operations to this dataset, the following use cases are derived: *Make Reservation*, *Retrieve Reservation*, *Change Reservation*, and *Cancel Reservation*.

6.1.4 Task 4. Refine Relationships

This task is to refine the relationships in the context-level use case diagram by defining new relationships, adjusting existing ones, or removing those that are inappropriate or redundant.

Refining Generalization Relationships

Generalization refinement focuses on organizing common and variant behaviors into hierarchical relationships.

- **Refining Generalization Between Actors**
  Examine actors that have access to a common set of use cases and introduce a generalization relationship between them with careful justification. Ensure that each derived (specialized) actor inherits the ability to invoke all use cases associated with the base (generalized) actor. This refinement results in a more concise and modular use case model.
- **Refining Generalization Between Use Cases**
  Examine the use cases to identify overlapping behaviors that can be abstracted into a base use case. Ensure that each specialized use case provides a specific realization of the common behavior defined in the base use case.
  For example, the Car Rental Management System supports multiple payment methods that share the fundamental functionality of processing a payment. Abstract this shared functionality into a base use case, such as *Make Payment*. Then, define specialized use cases—such as *Pay with Credit Card*, *Pay with Digital Wallet*, and *Pay with Cash*—to represent the distinct procedures associated with each payment method.

Refining Include Relationships

Include relationship refinement involves refining the relationships in two cases:

- **Refining Include Relationship for Decomposing Functionality**
  Identify specific, distinguishable functional segments within a coarse-grained use case and factor them into separate included use cases. This refinement supports modularization and clarifies the internal structure of the base use case.

For example, the base use case *Return Car* can be decomposed into included use cases such as *Enter Mileage and Fuel Level* and *Enter Car Condition*, both of which are systematically triggered as part of the car return process.

- **Refining Include Relationship for Encapsulating Shared Functionality**
  Identify common sequences or subprocesses embedded in multiple use cases and factor them into separate included use cases. Ensure that when the base use case is executed, it always triggers the included use case as a mandatory part of its functionality.
  For example, the two use cases *CH09. Make Rental Payment* and *RE05. Make Additional Payment* both invoke the shared functionality encapsulated in the included use case *PM01. Make Payment*, as shown in Fig. 6.6.

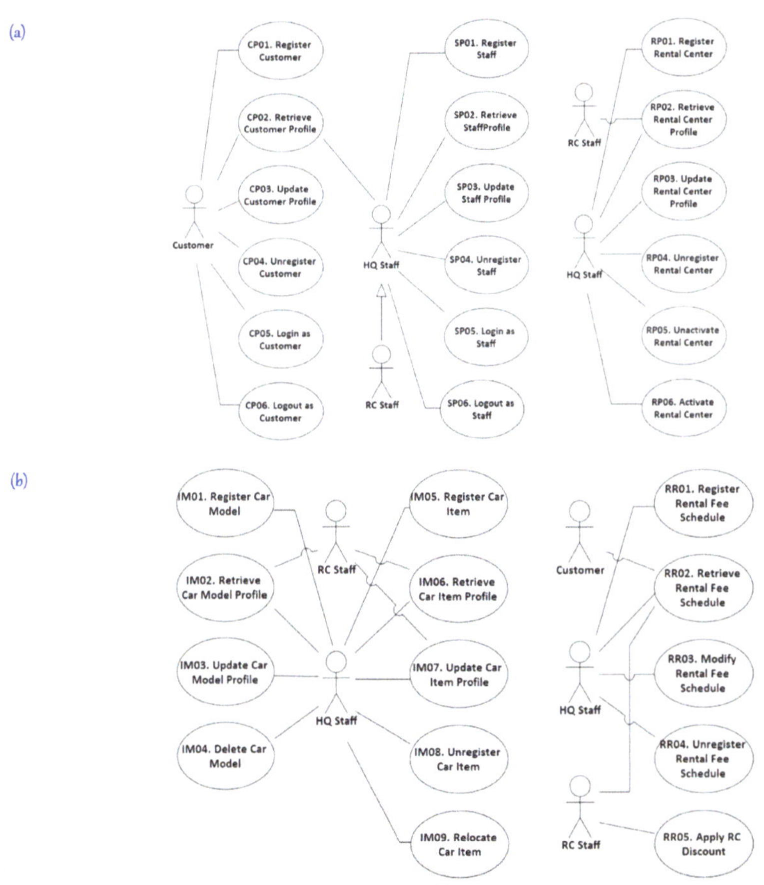

Fig. 6.6 Refined Use Case Diagram of Car Rental Management System

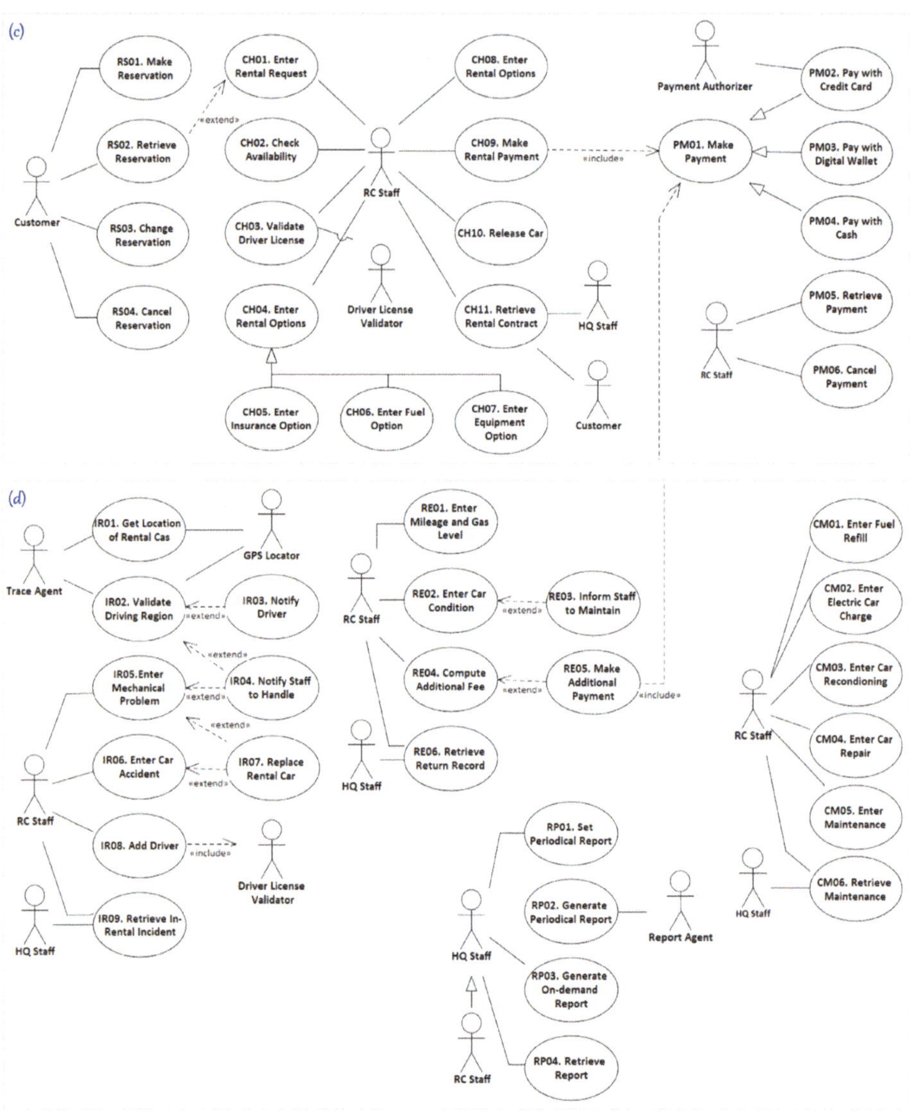

Fig. 6.6 (continued)

Refining Extend Relationships

Refining an *extend* relationship involves restructuring the use case model to modularize optional or conditional behaviors more clearly and systematically.

- **Refining Conditional or Optional Behavior**
  Review existing use cases to identify behaviors that occur only under certain conditions. Refine the model by isolating such behavior into extension use cases, thereby enhancing clarity and flexibility.

For example, in the Car Rental Management System, the use case *IR06. Enter Car Accident* may conditionally invoke the extended use case *IR07. Replace Rental Car*, depending on the severity and circumstances of the reported accident.

- **Refining Extension Conditions**
  Ensure that each extend relationship is accompanied by clearly specified conditions that determine when the extension is triggered.
  For example, the condition for triggering the extended use case *IR07. Replace Rental Car* may be that the reported damage renders the vehicle inoperable. In UML, such conditions should be expressed as Boolean guard conditions enclosed in square brackets—for instance, [vehicle is not drivable].

Constructing the Refined Use Case Diagram

Construct the refined use case diagram by incorporating the revised actors, use cases, and relationships resulting from the refinement process. The refined use case diagram for the Car Rental Management System is shown in Fig. 6.6.

Figure 6.6a presents use cases categorized under the functional groups of Customer Profile Management (CP), Staff Profile Management (SP), and Rental Center Profile Registration (RP). Fig. 6.6b presents use cases categorized under Inventory Management (IM) and Rental Rate Management (RR). Fig. 6.6c presents use cases categorized under Reservation Management (RS), Checkout Management (CH), and Payment Management (PM). Fig. 6.6d presents use cases categorized under In-Rental Management (IR), Return Management (RE), Car Maintenance (CM), and Report Generation (RP).

This use case diagram demonstrates a significant level of refinement compared to the context-level use case diagram, with greater detail in actors, use cases, and relationships. Table 6.2 compares the number of use cases in the context-level diagram with those in the refined diagram, highlighting an increase in use cases in the refined version.

Table 6.2 Comparison of Use Case Counts Before and After Refinement

Functional Groups	Context-Level Use Case Diagram	Refined Use Case Diagram
Customer Profile Management	4	6
Staff Profile Management	4	6
Rental Center Profile Registration	4	6
Inventory Management	8	9
Rental Rate Management	5	5
Reservation Management	4	4
Checkout Management	8	11
Payment Management	*n/a*	7
In-Rental Management	6	9
Car Maintenance	6	6
Return Management	5	6
Report Generation	3	4
Total # of Use Cases	**57**	**79**

The table indicates that the number of use cases has increased from 57 to 79, which has consequently led to an increase in their relationships as well.

6.1.5 Task 5. Write Use Case Descriptions

This task is to identify and document use cases that exhibit high complexity, critical functionality, or strong user interaction. Not all use cases require detailed descriptions; it is recommended to focus on those that significantly influence system behavior or user experience and would benefit from the elaboration of scenarios.

A *use case description* is a structured narrative that specifies the dynamic behavior of a use case. It typically includes preconditions, postconditions, the main scenario, alternative flows, and exception scenarios. This comprehensive specification clarifies how the system interacts with various actors and handles control flow, ensuring that all possible outcomes and interactions are clearly defined. Use case descriptions serve as a critical reference for stakeholders, supporting shared understanding and guiding accurate system implementation.

Elements of Use Case Description

A comprehensive use case description consists of the following key elements:

[1] **Use Case Name**

This is the title of the use case, often accompanied by a unique use case ID for reference and tracking.

[2] **Brief Description**

A concise summary of the use case's primary goal and intent. Common phrasings include "This use case provides…," "This use case is to…," "This use case allows the user to…," or "This use case enables the user to…."

[3] **Actors**

The actors that interact with the system during the execution of the use case.

[4] **Precondition**

The conditions or constraints that must hold true before the use case can be initiated. Example: For a "Login" use case, a precondition might be: "The user must be registered in the system."

[5] **Postcondition**

The expected outcomes or resulting states of the system after the use case completes, including both successful and failure outcomes.

Example: A "Process Order" use case may result in a confirmed order (success) or an "order failure due to payment error" (failure).

[6] **Related Use Cases**

Use cases that are functionally or logically connected to the current use case. These may share actors, invoke common behavior, or be part of a sequential process. Identifying related use cases helps contextualize the broader system behavior.

[7] **Workflow**
A detailed specification of the interaction sequence between the actors and the system. The workflow typically includes the following components:
- **Main Flow**
The primary sequence of interactions that lead to the successful completion of the use case.
Example: In a "Login" use case, the user enters valid credentials and gains access to the system.
- **Alternative Flow**
Variants of the main flow that achieve the same goal through different conditions or choices. Note that alternative flows still result in successful completion of the use case.
Example: Logging in via a third-party provider instead of using traditional credentials.
- **Error Flow**
Sequences that describe how the system responds to error conditions or failures. Note that error flows do not lead to successful completion of the use case but are essential for defining system robustness.
Example: In a "Make Payment" use case, an error flow may handle scenarios where the payment is declined, prompting the user to retry or select a different payment method.

Incorporating all three flow types—main, alternative, and error—ensures the use case description addresses the full range of execution scenarios. This structure improves the completeness, resilience, and communicability of the use case documentation.

The workflow specification is regarded as the most essential element of a use case description, as it presents a comprehensive and detailed depiction of the use case's functionality. It also serves as a foundational resource for designing the system's control flows—i.e., the behavioral aspects—using sequence diagrams, activity diagrams, and state machine diagrams.

The use case workflow can be represented either as a structured textual narrative or in tabular format.

Representing Workflow Using Textual Description

A textual description of a use case workflow provides a narrative representation of the interaction sequence, detailing user actions, system responses, and internal processing logic.

This format offers flexibility in capturing complex behaviors, including conditional paths and decision points.

- **Specifying Main Flow**
  The primary flow of events can be documented as a series of clearly numbered steps that outline the standard interaction between the actor and the system. This sequential format provides a straightforward, step-by-step depiction of the typical execution scenario.
  - Step 1. …
  - Step 2. …
- **Using Conditional Steps**
  To account for alternative or error flows within the main sequence, conditional logic can be embedded using annotations or branching notations. Conditions that trigger deviations from the main flow are typically indicated in parentheses or introduced as nested sub-steps.
  This approach allows the main flow to remain concise while still referencing the points at which alternative or exceptional behavior may occur.

For example, consider the *Checkout Car* use case in the Car Rental Management System. This use case represents a relatively complex and critical workflow, making it essential to provide a detailed and structured description. The corresponding textual specification is presented below.

- **Use Case Name**: Checkout Car
- **Brief Description**
  This use case facilitates the successful rental of a car to a customer, ensuring that all necessary conditions—such as a valid driver's license, payment authorization, and car availability—are met.
- **Actors**
  - *Primary Actor*: Rental Staff
  - *Secondary Actors*: Payment Authorization System, Driver's License Validation System
- **Precondition**
  The customer either has an existing reservation or arrives as a walk-in, and a car must be available for checkout—either the reserved vehicle or an accessible alternative model.
- **Postcondition**
  If the checkout is successful, the car is rented to the customer, and the rental information is recorded in the system. If the checkout fails, the transaction is aborted, the customer is notified, and no rental information is recorded.
- **Main Flow**
  - The customer approaches the Rental Staff with an existing reservation.
  - If the customer is a walk-in, proceed to Alternative Flow A1.
  - The system verifies the customer's driver's license using the Driver's License Validation System.

  - If the license is invalid, proceed to Error Flow E1.
  - The system confirms the availability of the reserved or requested car.
  - If the reserved car is unavailable, proceed to Alternative Flow A2.
  - The Rental Staff presents available insurance options to the customer (e.g., collision damage waiver, personal accident insurance).
  - The customer selects a payment method and submits payment.
  - The Payment System processes the payment.
  - If the payment fails, proceed to Error Flow E2.
  - Upon successful payment, the system generates a rental agreement and updates the car status to be rented.
  - The Rental Staff provides the customer with the keys and rental documentation.
- **Alternative Flow A1: Walk-In Customer**
  - For a walk-in customer, the Rental Staff checks available cars in the system.
  - The system displays available car options, and the Rental Staff presents them to the customer.
  - If the customer selects a car model, the checkout process is initiated.
  - If the customer does not accept any available car, proceed to Error Flow E3.
  - Return to step 3 in the Main Flow.
- **Alternative Flow A2: Unavailable Reserved Car**
  - If the reserved car is unavailable, the system notifies the Rental Staff.
  - The Rental Staff presents the customer with alternative car models.
  - The customer selects a model, and the system updates the reservation.
  - Return to step 4 in the Main Flow.
- **Error Flow E1: Invalid Driver's License**
  - If license verification fails, the system notifies the Rental Staff.
  - The system displays: "Checkout Aborted: Invalid Driver's License."
  - The use case terminates unsuccessfully unless a valid license is provided.
- **Error Flow E2: Payment Failure**
  - If payment fails, the system notifies the Rental Staff.
  - The system displays: "Checkout Aborted: Payment Failure."
  - If an alternative payment method is provided, return to step 5 in the Main Flow.
- **Error Flow E3: No Available Car Accepted**
  - If the customer declines all available car models, the system displays: "Checkout Aborted: Car Not Available."
  - The use case terminates unsuccessfully.

Representing Workflow using Tabular Format

The workflow of a use case can be effectively represented using a structured table format. This approach provides a clear and organized depiction of each step, facilitating easier comprehension of the sequence of actions and associated conditions.

For example, the *Checkout Car* use case can be described in tabular form as follows.

- **Main Flow**

RC Staff	System
Initiates car rental request	
	Collects Driver License information
	Validates the Driver License. If not validated, branch to Error Flow E1
Provides reservation details or indicates 'Walk-in'	
	Prompts for reservation information
	For "Walk-in," branch to Alternative Flow A1
	Confirms car availability. If car is unavailable, branches to Alternative Flow A2
Presents available insurance options to the customer	
Customer selects payment method	
	Processes payment via the Payment System
	If payment fails, branches to Error Flow E2
	Generates a rental agreement
	Updates car status to "rented"
Provides customer with the keys and rental documentation	

- **Alternative Flow A1: Walk-In Customer**

RC Staff	System
Checks for available cars	
	Presents available car options to the Rental Agent
Offers car options to the customer	
If customer selects a car model, initiates checkout	
If customer does not accept any available car model, branches to Error Flow E3	
	Returns to step 3 in the Main Flow

- **Alternative Flow A2: Unavailable Reserved Car**

RC Staff	System
Receives notification of unavailable reserved car	Notifies Rental Agent of unavailability
Presents list of alternative car models to the customer	
Customer selects an alternative car model	
	Updates the reservation with the selected car model
	Returns to step 4 in the Main Flow

- **Error Flow E1: Invalid Driver's License**

RC Staff	System
Receives notification of invalid driver's license	Notifies Rental Agent of the driver's license issue
	Prints message: "Checkout Aborted: Invalid Driver's License"
	Ends use case unsuccessfully if a valid license cannot be presented

- **Error Flow E2: Payment Failure**

RC Staff	System
Receives notification of payment failure	Notifies Rental Agent of the payment error
	Prints message: "Checkout Aborted: Payment Failure"
	Returns to step 5 in the Main Flow if an alternate payment method is provided

- **Error Flow E3: No Available Car Accepted**

RC Staff	System
Receives notification that customer did not accept any available car model	
	Prints message: "Checkout Aborted: Car Not Available"
	Ends use case unsuccessfully

6.2 Step 2. Define Functional Components

This step is to define the functional components of a target system.

6.2.1 Task 1. Define Functional Components from Use Case Diagram

This task is to identify functional components by organizing related use cases into cohesive groups. A *functional component* is defined as a cohesive software module that provides a set of closely related functions.

Identifying these components can be intuitive and efficient by analyzing the use cases associated with each functional group. As previously explained, use cases are typically categorized by functional groups through the application of CRUD operations. Consequently, each set of related use cases often forms the foundation for a corresponding functional component.

In general, functional components align with predefined functional groups, as each group is characterized by a well-defined set of related use cases. Thus, each functional group within the system is likely to map directly to a distinct functional component. Although the mapping is typically one to one, a detailed examination of the use cases may reveal more complex relationships—such as one-to-many or many-to-one mappings—between functional groups and components.

For instance, consider the *Reservation Management* functional group in the Car Rental Management System. This group comprises four use cases that support reservation-related services. These use cases can be grouped into a single functional component named *Reservation Manager*, as illustrated in Fig. 6.7.

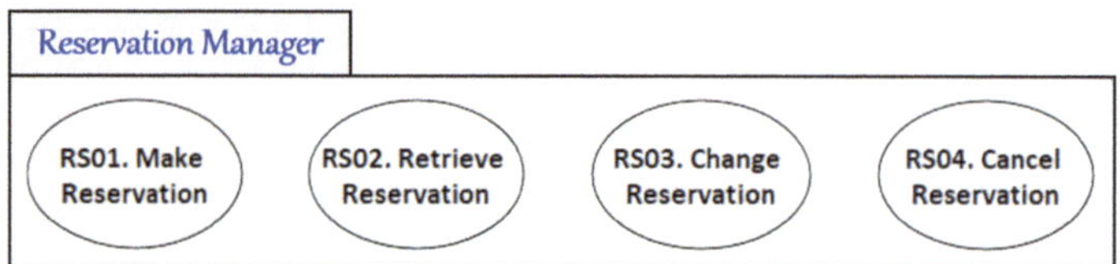

Fig. 6.7 Derivation of Functional Component from Related Use Cases

The resulting component, *Reservation Manager*, aligns closely with the functional group *Reservation Management*, illustrating a clear one-to-one correspondence.

Example

Consider the definition of functional components for the Car Rental Management System. Figure 6.7 illustrates how related use cases are grouped into a corresponding functional component within the system (Fig. 6.8).

The functional components derived from the use case diagram can be summarized in the UML Component Diagram shown in Fig. 6.9.

Once the functional components are identified, each is briefly described to provide an overview of its purpose and functionality.

- **Customer Profile Manager**
  Manages the profiles of customers who use the system to rent cars
- **Staff Profile Manager**
  Manages the profiles of staff members involved in rental operations
- **Rental Center Profile Manager**
  Manages the profiles of rental centers where car rental and return activities take place
- **Inventory Manager**
  Oversees the inventory of rental cars, including the management of car models and individual rental units

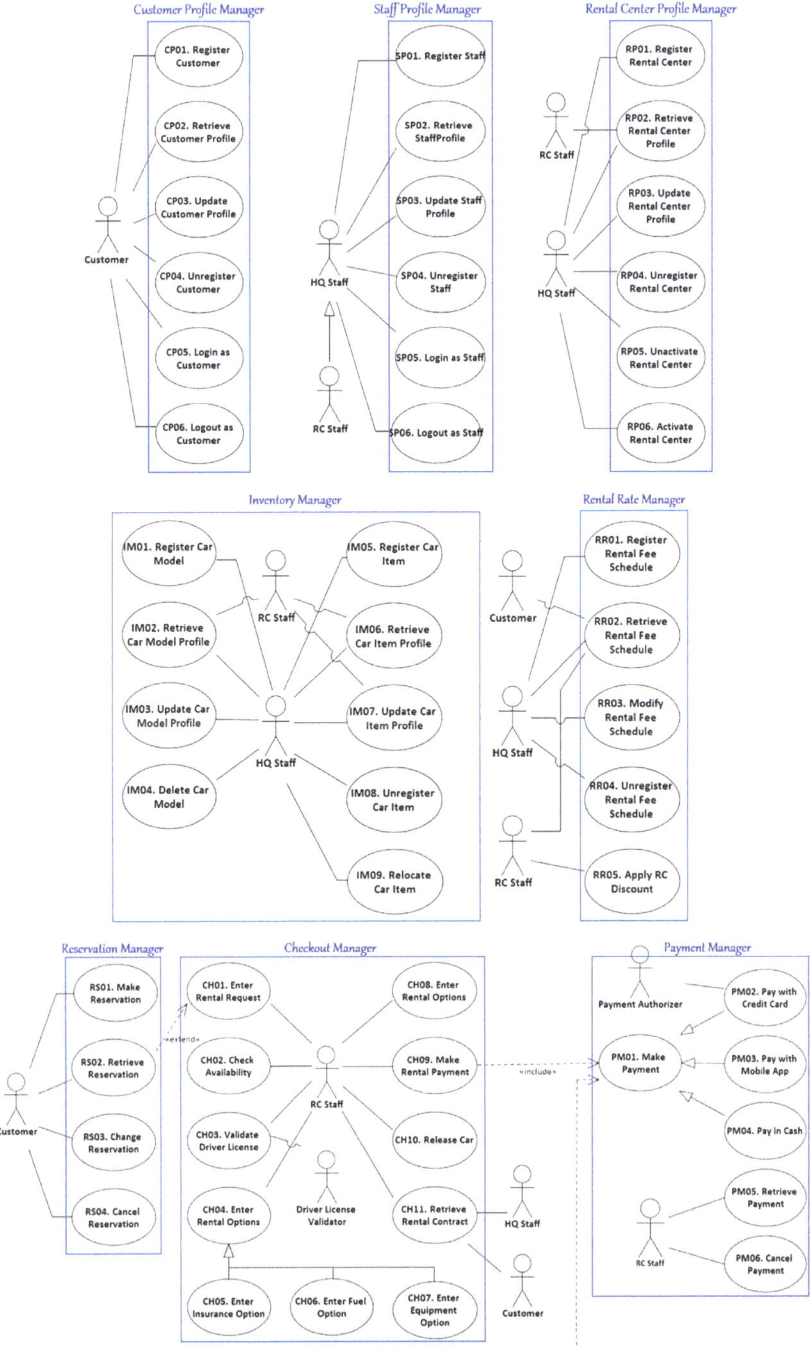

Fig. 6.8 Functional Components of Car Rental Management System

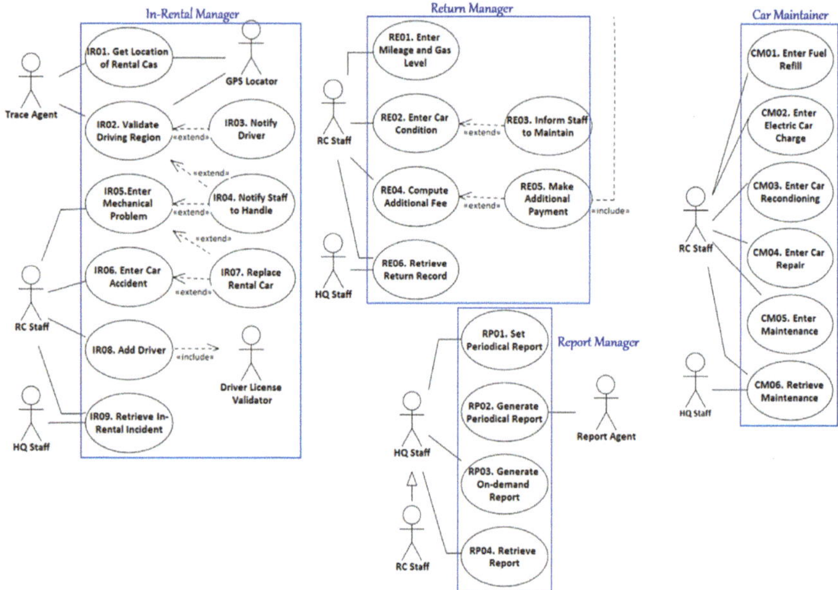

Fig. 6.8 (continued)

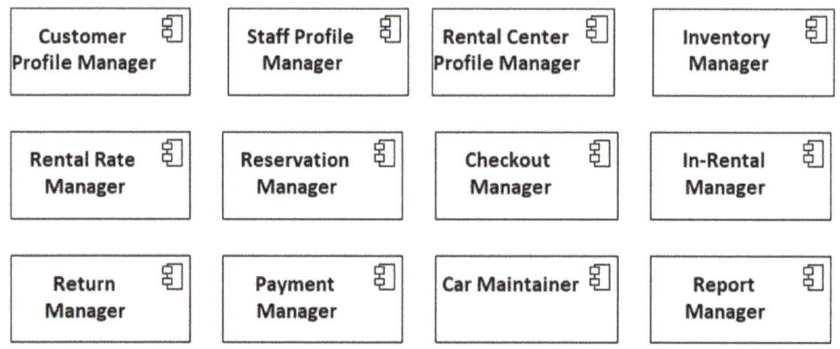

Fig. 6.9 Functional Components in UML Component Diagram

- **Rental Rate Manager**
  Manages the standard rental fee schedules applied across all rental centers, including the application of location-specific discounts
- **Reservation Manager**
  Handles the management of car rental reservations
- **Checkout Manager**
  Manages operations related to the car rental checkout process
- **In-Rental Manager**
  Oversees activities during active rental periods, including car tracking, mechanical issue reporting, and accident handling

- **Return Manager**
  Manages operations related to the return of rental cars
- **Payment Manager**
  Facilitates various types of payment transactions
- **Car Maintainer**
  Tracks and manages maintenance activities for rental cars
- **Report Manager**
  Manages the generation of business reports, including periodic operational summaries
  Note that there are 12 functional components, while only 11 functional groups exist. This discrepancy arises because the use cases involving payment operations have been consolidated into a dedicated functional component, *Payment Manager*. This consolidation is essential because both the *Checkout Manager* and *Return Manager* invoke payment-related functionality. By centralizing these functions within the *Payment Manager* component, the system ensures consistent and efficient handling of payment operations across use cases.

6.2.2 Task 2. Define Functional Components from Architecture Styles

This task is to define functional components based on the selected architecture style. Each architecture style is characterized by a unique set of components, relationships, and interactions.

Some architecture styles necessitate specific functional components to support their core features and runtime behaviors.

However, not all architecture styles require additional functional components. For example, the *Layered Architecture Style* can typically be implemented without introducing extra functionality. In contrast, the *Dispatcher Architecture Style* requires a component to evaluate the Quality of Service (QoS) of replicated servers, as well as a component to dispatch the selected server to the requesting client. Similarly, the *Microservice Architecture Style* often requires a functional component to manage API Gateway operations.

The two functional components required to support the *Dispatcher Architecture Style* are illustrated in Fig. 6.10.

Fig. 6.10 Functional Components for Dispatcher Architecture Style

The *QoS Evaluator* component is responsible for assessing the quality of service (QoS) of replicated servers. The *Server Allocator* component selects a server with high QoS and dispatches it to the client for further interaction.

6.2.3 Task 3. Define Interface Components

This task is to identify the interface components of the target system. An interface component defines a set of public methods without providing their underlying implementations. These methods specify the interactions and data exchanges available to other system components or external entities, thereby establishing a standardized communication structure throughout the system.

Interface in Software Engineering

The concept of an *interface component* is widely recognized across software engineering standards, modeling tools, and design principles. It serves as a foundational construct for defining standardized interactions while decoupling implementation details.

- **Interface in SOLID Principles**
  In the SOLID design principles, the role of interfaces is most prominently emphasized in the *Interface Segregation Principle*, which states: "Clients should not be forced to depend on interfaces they do not use." This principle encourages the design of small, specific interfaces rather than large, monolithic ones.
- **Interface in Object-Oriented Design**
  In object-oriented design, an interface defines a *contract* that specifies a set of behaviors a class must provide, without prescribing how those behaviors should be implemented. This separation between specification and implementation promotes polymorphism, enabling multiple classes to implement the same interface in diverse ways.
- **Interface in UML**
  In UML, interfaces are explicitly represented using the «interface» keyword, distinguishing them from concrete classes. A UML interface specifies a collection of operations that must be implemented by conforming classes or components. By abstracting behavior from implementation, UML interfaces facilitate loose coupling and standardized communication across components, supporting modularity, interoperability, and reusability.
- **Design Pattern: Separating Interface from Implementation**
  Separating the interface from the implementation is a key principle in many design patterns. This approach reduces direct dependencies between components, making the system more flexible and easier to maintain. By defining what a component should do (the interface) without specifying how it does it (the implementation), changes can be made to one part of the system without requiring changes to others.
- **Interface in Programming Languages**
- Interfaces are supported either explicitly or implicitly in various object-oriented programming languages.
  - **Java**
    Java provides explicit syntax with the *interface* keyword, which defines a set of method signatures without providing the underlying implementations.

- **C++**
  In C++, interfaces are typically implemented using pure virtual classes. A pure virtual class is a class that contains at least one pure virtual function (a function declared with "= 0"), making it abstract and uninstantiable.
- **Python**
  Python lacks a native interface construct but provides *Abstract Base Classes* (*ABCs*) through the *abc* module. ABCs allow the definition of abstract methods that must be implemented by any subclass, thereby emulating the behavior of interfaces and enforcing behavioral contracts.

Situations for Defining Interface Components

Interface components should be defined as part of the architectural design process in the following situations:

- **To Standardize Communication Between Components**
  An interface component is essential when multiple components must interact consistently. It provides a unified set of accessible operations, ensuring standardized communication across the system and facilitating modular integration.
- **To Separate Specification from Implementation**
  Interfaces support the definition of behavior independently of its implementation. This separation enhances system flexibility, allowing implementations to be modified, replaced, or extended without impacting dependent components. It promotes maintainability and architectural adaptability.
- **To Enable Multiple Implementations**
  Interfaces enable the system to support multiple interchangeable implementations of a given functionality. This fosters flexibility in choosing or switching implementations at runtime or design time without altering the consuming components.
- **To Promote Reusability Across the System**
  Interfaces promote reusability by enabling various system components to interact with a common abstraction, regardless of the specific implementation. This reduces duplication and enhances extensibility across the architecture.

Defining interface components in these situations strengthens the overall architecture by fostering modularity, enabling flexibility, and aligning the design with established software engineering principles.

Example of Hardware Abstract Layer (HAL)

A HAL is a widely adopted design scheme that defines interface components to standardize interactions between software and hardware. By abstracting hardware-specific details, HAL provides a consistent interface for software to access and control various hardware functionalities.

For example, consider a Smart Home Platform that uses networked devices to manage the home environment, enhancing convenience, safety, and energy efficiency. Key features include remote monitoring, appliance control, and management of lighting and thermostats. To support seamless integration of diverse hardware components, the platform incorporates a Hardware Abstraction Layer (HAL), which defines unified interfaces for various device types, as illustrated in Fig. 6.11.

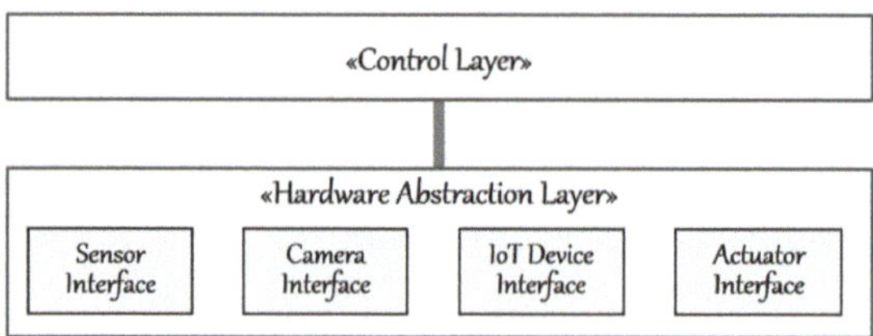

Fig. 6.11 Interface Components of HAL in Smart Home Platform

In the figure showing layers of the Smart Home Platform, the top is the *Control Layer*, which orchestrates the system's operations and interacts with hardware through the *Hardware Abstraction Layer* (*HAL*). The HAL defines four distinct interface components—Sensor Interface, Camera Interface, IoT Device Interface, and Actuator Interface—each responsible for abstracting and managing communication with a specific category of hardware devices. This layered design enables consistent and modular integration of heterogeneous devices, promoting scalability, maintainability, and interoperability within the platform.

Each interface within the HAL can be further specialized to support specific hardware types. For example, the *Sensor Interface* can be refined to accommodate a range of sensor types used in the Smart Home Platform, as illustrated in Fig. 6.12.

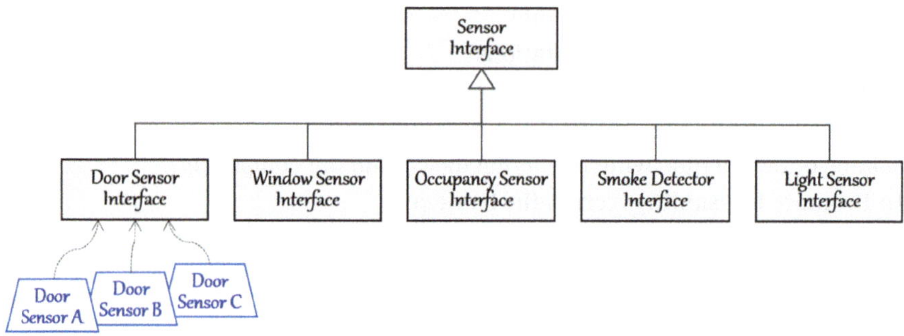

Fig. 6.12 Specializing Sensor Interface for Different Sensor Types

The *Sensor Interface* within the *HAL* is structured to support a diverse set of sensor types through dedicated sub-interfaces, such as those for *Door Sensors*, *Window Sensors*, *Occupancy Sensors*, *Smoke Detectors*, and *Light Sensors*.

Each sub-interface can then be implemented by specific sensor models or devices. For example, as shown in the figure, *Door Sensor A*, *Door Sensor B*, and *Door Sensor C* all implement the *Door Sensor* Interface, enabling standardized interaction while accommodating device-specific behaviors.

6.3 Step 3. Allocate Functional Components

This step is to allocate functional components to their corresponding placeholders within the schematic architecture. A *functional placeholder* refers to a designated architectural location intended to host components that provide specific system functionalities. This allocation ensures that each component is correctly positioned to fulfill its functional role within the overall architecture.

6.3.1 Task 1. Assign Functional Components onto Tiers

This task is to assign each functional component to one or more tiers within the schematic architecture. The allocation of functional components can be visualized using a tabular representation, as illustrated in Table 6.3.

Table 6.3 Functional Component Allocation Table

Tiers / Components	Tier 1	Tier 2	Tier 3
Functional Component 1	✓		
Functional Component 2		✓	
Functional Component 3		✓	✓
Functional Component 4	✓		✓
…			

In the table, both *Functional Component 1* and *Functional Component 2* are assigned to a single tier, indicating that their functionality is confined to that specific tier. In contrast, *Functional Components 3* and *4* are distributed across two tiers, although their roles may vary between tiers.

Example

Consider the allocation of functional components in the Car Rental Management System, whose schematic architecture consists of four physical nodes. Taking into account the roles of these four tiers and the specific functionalities of each component, their allocations to the appropriate tiers are summarized in Table 6.4.

Each functional component is allocated to at least one tier. When a component is distributed across multiple tiers, the functionality it provides may vary by tier. For example, the *Reservation Manager* component spans three tiers: the *Mobile Client* tier offers full CRUD capabilities for managing reservations, whereas the *Rental Center Client* and *Headquarters Server* tiers are limited to read-only access.

Note that components derived from the Dispatcher Architecture Style—namely, *QoS Evaluator* and *Server Allocator*—are exclusively deployed on the *Dispatcher Server* node.

Table 6.4 Functional Component Allocation for Car Rental Management System

Functional Components \ Tiers	Mobile Client	Rental Center Client	Dispatcher Server	Headquarters Server
Customer Profile Manager	✓	✓		✓ (Read)
Staff Profile Manager		✓		✓
Rental Center Profile Manager		✓		✓
Inventory Manager		✓		✓
Rental Rate Manager		✓ (Read)		✓
Reservation Manager	✓	✓ (Read)		✓ (Read)
Checkout Manager	✓ (Read)	✓		✓ (Read)
In-Rental Manager		✓		✓
Return Manager	✓ (Read)	✓		✓ (Read)
Payment Manager		✓		✓
Car Maintainer		✓		✓ (Read)
Report Manager		✓		✓
QoS Evaluator			✓	
Server Allocator			✓	

6.3.2 Task 2. Identify Functionality Placeholders

This task is to identify functionality placeholders within a schematic architecture. A functionality placeholder serves as a container for accommodating functional components and is typically located within layers or partitions of a layer.

To identify functionality placeholders, analyze the roles and responsibilities assigned to each layer or partition. Functionality placeholders are commonly positioned at locations where essential interactions or data manipulations are required to support system operations, acting as containers for the functional components within each tier.

Example

Consider the identification of functionality placeholders in the schematic architecture of the Car Rental Management System. Fig. 6.13 illustrates the functionality placeholders across its four tiers.

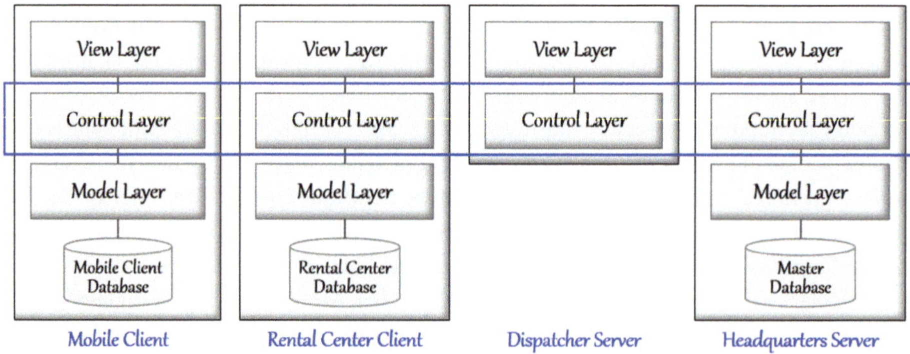

Fig. 6.13 Functionality Placeholders in the Car Rental Management System

Each tier of this schematic architecture includes a *Control Layer* that serves as a functionality placeholder, accommodating specific functional components.

6.3.3 Task 3. Allocate Functional Components onto Placeholders

This task is to allocate the functional components to their designated functionality placeholders. This is achieved by assigning the components to the identified placeholders for each tier, based on the functional component placements presented in the Functional Component Allocation.

Example

For example, the allocation of functional components for the Car Rental Management System is performed according to Table 6.4, and the result is shown in Fig. 6.14.

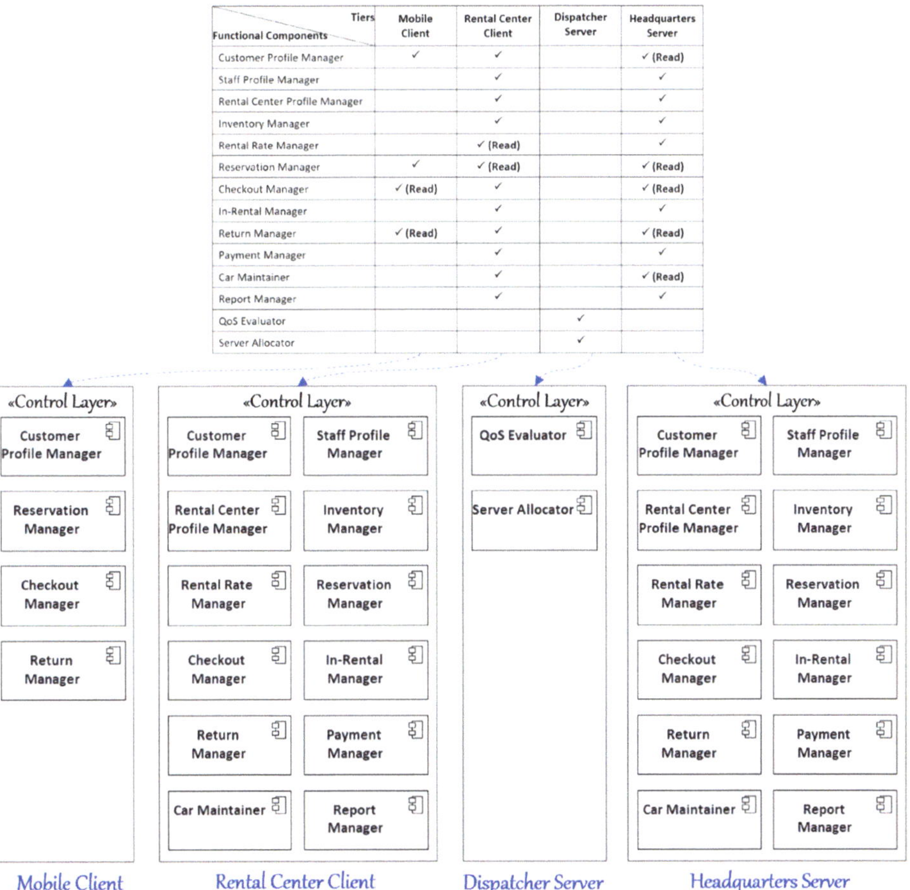

Functional Components \ Tiers	Mobile Client	Rental Center Client	Dispatcher Server	Headquarters Server
Customer Profile Manager	✓	✓		✓ (Read)
Staff Profile Manager		✓		✓
Rental Center Profile Manager		✓		✓
Inventory Manager		✓		✓
Rental Rate Manager		✓ (Read)		✓
Reservation Manager	✓	✓ (Read)		✓ (Read)
Checkout Manager	✓ (Read)	✓		✓ (Read)
In-Rental Manager		✓		✓
Return Manager	✓ (Read)	✓		✓ (Read)
Payment Manager		✓		✓
Car Maintainer		✓		✓ (Read)
Report Manager		✓		✓
QoS Evaluator			✓	
Server Allocator			✓	

Fig. 6.14 Allocation of Functional Components to Functionality Placeholders

The functional components for each tier, as specified in the table, are mapped onto the functionality placeholders within that tier. With this allocation, the schematic architecture becomes more complete and operational.

6.4 Step 4. Define Functional Component Interfaces

This step is to define the interfaces of functional components. An *interface* refers to a contract or protocol that specifies how other components can interact with a given functional component. In essence, it is a public protocol that exposes the component's functionality through a defined set of method signatures accompanied by their semantic descriptions.

Establishing well-defined interfaces is essential for several reasons, including improved clarity and understandability, encapsulation of internal logic, enhanced interoperability, reduction of integration errors, improved maintainability, and adherence to standards. A well-defined interface facilitates reliable and efficient interaction among system components.

6.4.1 Task 1. Select Target Functional Components

This task is to identify the functional components that require a precise definition of their interfaces. Not all components need their interfaces to be explicitly defined by architects; instead, those with specific characteristics are selected for detailed interface specification.

Select the functional components with the following characteristics, and define their interfaces.

- **Components with Complex Functionality**
  Components that exhibit complex functionality typically perform multiple, multifaceted operations and support diverse use cases involving intricate logic and workflows. Due to this complexity, such components generally require interfaces with numerous methods and a substantial number of well-defined parameters.
- **Components Requiring Interface Stability**
  Components requiring stable interfaces must maintain consistent interactions with other internal or external system components over time. Well-defined, stable interfaces ensure long-term compatibility, reduce maintenance overhead, and support reliable integration—making them essential for systems that depend on consistent, unchanging access points.

Blackbox Components and Whitebox Components

Regarding component interfaces, components can be categorized as either *blackbox* or *whitebox*, based on their visibility. These represent two distinct approaches to the accessibility of a software component's internal structure and behavior.

- **Blackbox Component**

  A *blackbox* component is one whose internal structure, design, and implementation details are entirely hidden from external clients. Interaction with the component is restricted to its defined inputs and outputs, without any visibility into its internal workings.

  This concealment promotes modularity by decoupling the component's implementation from other system parts. It also enhances usability, as the component can be used without requiring knowledge of its internal mechanisms. Furthermore, it improves maintainability and extensibility, allowing internal changes without affecting dependent systems, as long as the input-output behavior remains consistent.

  Examples of blackbox components include proprietary software libraries or APIs, where source code and design details are inaccessible.

- **Whitebox Component**

  A *whitebox* component is one whose internal structure, design, and implementation details are fully visible and accessible to external clients. This transparency enables developers to inspect and understand the component's internal behavior, allowing for direct modification and optimization as needed.

  Whitebox components are typically used in contexts where a deep understanding of the component is essential, such as in customized software environments or systems that require tight integration. Their openness supports debugging and testing by providing access to internal variables, methods, and logic, thereby facilitating performance tuning and issue resolution.

  Examples of whitebox components include open-source software, where source code is accessible, allowing developers to adapt and enhance the component to meet specific project requirements.

Component interfaces are typically specified using either *Component Diagrams* or *Package Diagrams* in UML. These diagrams provide distinct notations and structural views for representing component organization and interface exposure. The UML notations for components and packages are illustrated in Fig. 6.15.

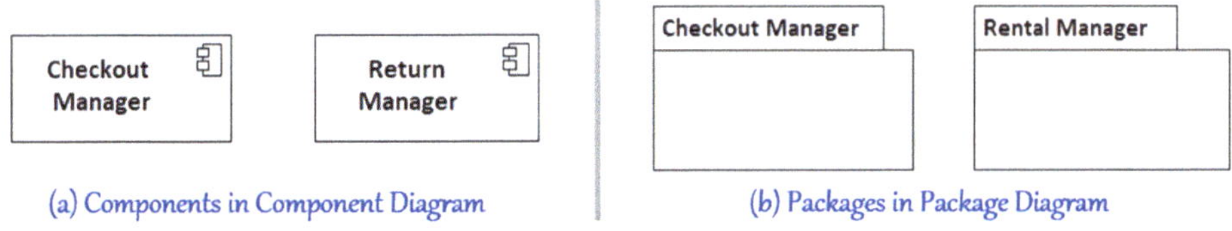

Fig. 6.15 Components and Packages in UML

A solid understanding of these diagram types is essential, as they offer structural perspectives that clarify component organization, interface visibility, and inter-component dependencies.

Specifying Blackbox Components Using Component Diagram

Component Diagram is primarily used to model the high-level structure of a system by illustrating its software components, their provided and required interfaces, and the dependencies among them. This diagram represents components as blackbox form, meaning that only the external interfaces are visible, while internal implementation details are hidden.

A Component Diagram provides two distinct types of interfaces:

- **Provided Interface**
  A *Provided Interface* is represented by a small circle (commonly called a "lollipop") attached to the boundary of a component. It denotes the services or functionalities that the component offers to other components. This interface specifies the operations or methods accessible to external clients.
- **Required Interface**
  A *Required Interface* is depicted as a small half-circle (often referred to as a "socket") on the component boundary. It indicates the services or functionalities that the component needs from other components to operate correctly. Required interfaces make a component's dependencies explicit, supporting clear contract definitions between interacting components.

Specifying White Components Using Package Diagram

Package Diagram is primarily used to organize the logical structure of a system by grouping related elements into packages and illustrating dependencies among them. This diagram presents components in *whitebox* form, where the internal elements of each package—such as classes or components—are visible and accessible.

Unlike Component Diagrams, Package Diagrams do not incorporate the concept of interfaces. Their primary purpose is to structure and relate system elements, not to define external contracts. Since packages inherently allow access to internal elements, specifying provided or required interfaces is generally unnecessary.

6.4.2 Task 2. Define Provided Interfaces

This task is to define the provided interface for each functional component. The *Provided Interface* of Component Diagram represents the set of services that a component offers to other components. In the context of component modeling, the term *interface* typically refers to the provided interface and is often used interchangeably with the word "interface."

The *Provided Interface* is denoted using the lollipop notation as shown in Fig. 6.16.

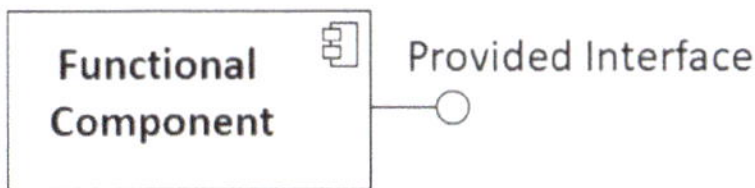

Fig. 6.16 Provided Interface in UML

Deriving Provided Interfaces from Use Case Diagram

An interface of a functional component primarily consists of public methods, though it may also include private methods.

- **Deriving Public Methods**

  Public methods of an interface are identified based on invocation relationships between actors and the use cases they initiate. For each use case invoked by an actor, define one or more corresponding public methods, as illustrated in Fig. 6.17.

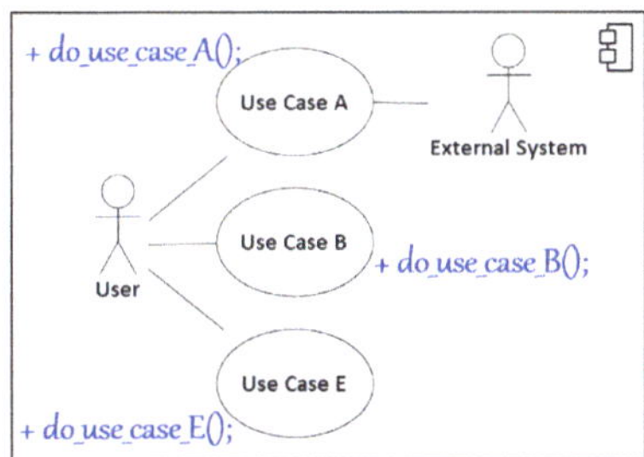

Fig. 6.17 Public Methods Derived from Invocation Relationships

In the figure, the actor User invokes three use cases, and the public methods are derived from these use cases. For example, the public method *do_use_case_A()* is derived from the *Use Case A*.

- **Deriving Private Interfaces**

  Private methods are identified by analyzing the relationships among use cases, such as generalization, inclusion, and extension. These methods are designated as *private* because they are intended solely for internal use within the functional component. This promotes encapsulation and prevents direct access by external actors or components. An example of deriving private methods is shown in Fig. 6.18.

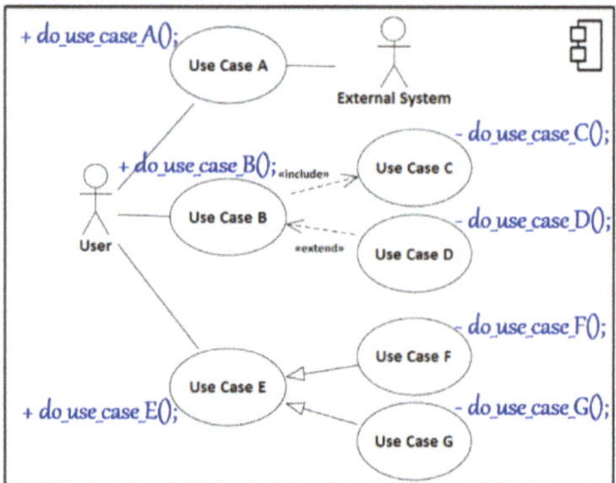

Fig. 6.18 Private Methods Derived from Relationships Between Use Cases

This figure includes use cases with *include*, *extend*, and *generalization* relationships. It illustrates how these relationships are applied to derive private methods from related use cases. For example, the private method *do_use_case_C()* is derived from the included use case *Use Case C*, which is referenced by *Use Case B*. Thus, *Use Case B* invokes *Use Case C* through this private method.

Deriving Multiple Methods from a Single Use Case

A single use case within a functional component may lead to the derivation of multiple methods, each accommodating a different invocation pattern. These methods are typically distinguished by variations in their parameter lists.

For example, consider the *Reservation Manager* component of the Car Rental Management System, which encompasses four use cases, as illustrated in Fig. 6.19.

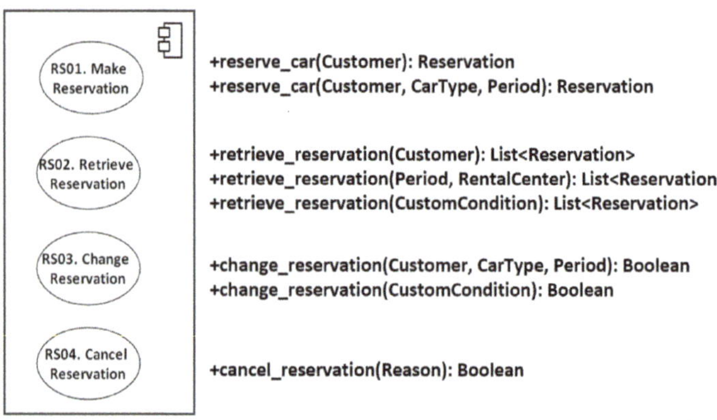

Fig. 6.19 Multiple Methods from Single Use Case

This figure illustrates how certain use cases result in a single method, while others lead to multiple method variants. For instance, the use case *RS01. Make Reservation* gives rise to two methods with different parameter configurations, whereas *RS04. Cancel Reservation* corresponds to a single derived method.

Specifying Methods in an Interface

Each method in an interface is defined by its method signature and a corresponding semantic description.

- **Method Signature**

  The method signature specifies the method's name, visibility, input parameters, return type, and, optionally, exceptions it may raise. In UML, the standard format for representing a method signature is as follows:

  <visibility> <name>(<parameter list>): <return type> {<property list>}
- Visibility indicates the method's accessibility to other components or classes. UML defines four visibility modifiers:
  - `+ for public`
  - `- for private`
  - `# for protected`
  - `~ for package`

  Name of the method is an identifier that describes its purpose or functionality. *Parameter List* specifies the input values required by the method. Each parameter is defined with its name and type, formatted as <name>: <type>. Multiple parameters are separated by commas and are enclosed within parentheses.

  Return Type indicates the type of value the method will return after execution. It is specified after a colon (:) following the parameter list. If a method does not return a value, this is omitted or specified as void in some contexts.

  Property List provides additional information about the method's behavior or attributes. Enclosed within curly braces, it can include keywords like *static*, *query*, or *ordered.*

  For example, consider a method designed to compute the area of a rectangle. Its signature can be defined as follows:

  + calculateArea(length: Double, width: Double): Double

- **Semantic Description**

  The semantic description of a method clearly explains the method's purpose, behavior, and any relevant constraints or conditions. It is essential for ensuring accurate implementation and usage, especially for interfaces requiring formal and precise definitions.
- A complete semantic description typically includes the following elements:
  - **Purpose**: A brief statement of what the method is intended to accomplish
  - **Behavior**: A detailed explanation of the method's logic and the steps performed during execution

- **Input Constraints**: Any conditions applied to input values, such as valid ranges, formats, or data types
- **Preconditions**: Required states or conditions that must be true before the method can be invoked
- **Postconditions**: Conditions guaranteed to be true after successful method execution
- **Output Description**: An explanation of the returned result, including its type and semantic meaning
- **Exception**: Potential anomalies or errors that might occur during execution
- **Side Effects**: Any changes to system state or external resources caused by the method's execution, if applicable

6.4.3 Task 3. Define Required Interfaces

This task is to define the required interface for each functional component that depends on services provided by other components. A *required interface* specifies the services or functionalities that a component needs from external components to function correctly. In contrast, a *provided interface* defines the services that the component offers to others. Required interfaces are primarily introduced to support enhanced customizability and extensibility, particularly for variable or optional features within a functional component.

In UML, a *Required Interface* is represented by a half-circle or "socket" symbol connected to the component, as illustrated in Fig. 6.20. This figure shows a functional component along with its associated *Required Interface* and *Provided Interface*.

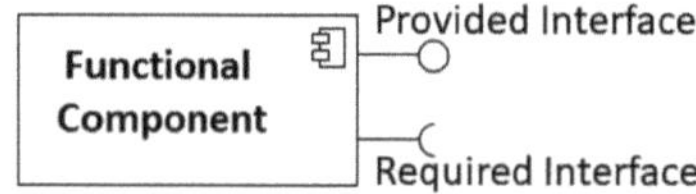

Fig. 6.20 Required Interface in UML

Situations for Defining Required Interfaces

Required Interfaces are particularly useful in software architecture design when variability exists within a functional component, and each variation point can be resolved by external (plug-in) components that implement the required interface.

Common scenarios for utilizing required interfaces include the following:

- **Runtime Binding for Variation Points**

  Define a required interface when a component includes a variation point that must be resolved with different implementations, dynamically bound at runtime. For instance, a logging component may support various storage mechanisms (e.g., file based, database, or cloud based). A required interface specifying common logging methods allows flexible binding to the appropriate storage mechanism at runtime.

- **Supporting Dynamic System Behavior**
  Define a required interface when a component must dynamically discover and invoke services at runtime. This approach enables flexible binding and late composition of system behavior. For example, in a plug-in framework, plug-ins declare required interfaces to communicate with the host system, enabling dynamic service discovery and interaction at runtime.
- **Integration with External or Internal Services**
  Define a required interface when a component depends on services provided by either external systems or other internal components. This abstraction promotes modularity, loose coupling, and flexibility, enabling seamless substitution or upgrade of service providers without impacting the core logic of the dependent component.
  For example, a weather application may define a required interface such as *WeatherService*, with methods like *getCurrentWeather()* and *getForecast()*. Any weather service implementation that conforms to this interface can be used interchangeably.
- **Ensuring Backward Compatibility**
  Define a required interface when a system must support both legacy and new components while maintaining backward compatibility. A consistent interface contract allows newer implementations to coexist with existing ones, enabling system evolution without disrupting established functionality.

Guidelines for Defining Required Interface

Required interfaces of functional components can be systematically defined by following the procedure below.

[1] **Identify Variation Points**
Identify variation points within a functional component that need to be resolved using external services. A *variation point* is a specific location within the component that represents a variable feature or functionality requiring external realization.
Example: In a payment processing component, the ability to support multiple payment methods—such as credit cards, digital wallets, or cryptocurrencies—can be considered a variation point.

[2] **Define Required Interfaces for Variation Points**
Define a required interface that specifies a unified set of methods to invoke the functionalities associated with the identified variation point. This interface acts as a contract between the component and the external services or components responsible for resolving the variation.
Example: For a payment processing component, a required interface named *iPaymentService* may define the following methods:

processPayment(amount: Double, currency: String)
validatePaymentDetails(details: PaymentDetails)

[3] **Define Setter Methods to Accept External Implementations**
Define setter methods within the component's Provided Interface to enable dynamic binding and interaction with external service variants that conform to the required interface.
Example: A setter method such as *setPaymentService(service: iPaymentService)* can be defined in the provided interface of the payment component. This allows dynamic configuration of any payment service implementation that conforms to *iPaymentService*.

[4] **Implement the Required Interface**
Implement the required interface in multiple ways, with each implementation addressing the specific functionality of a particular variant. The number of implementations corresponds to the number of supported variants for the defined variation point.

[5] **Bind External Implementations**
Instantiate a plug-in object for each implementation, and bind it to the component using a designated setter method. This enables the component to dynamically integrate external services that conform to the required interface.
In UML, the binding between a required interface and its implementation is represented using an *Assembly Connector*, as shown in Fig. 6.21.

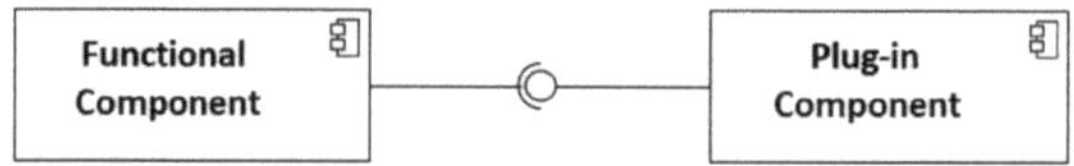

Fig. 6.21 Assembly Connector in UML

The figure shows how an *Assembly Connector* links a functional component's required interface to a plug-in component's provided interface. This indicates that the plug-in supplies the service needed by the functional component.

Example

Consider a functional component, *Range Finder*, which measures the distance between the user and a target in a specified unit of measurement. This component can be applied in various embedded systems that detect proximity, such as robotic navigation systems, automotive parking sensors, drone altimeters, or handheld measuring tools.

The provided interface of *RangeFinder* is illustrated in Fig. 6.22.

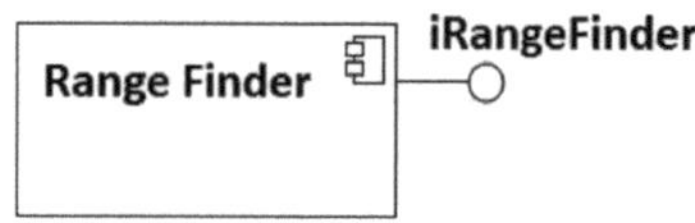

Fig. 6.22 Provided Interface of RangeFinder Component

The methods for *iRangeFinder*, can be defined as follows:

```
+ measureDistance(): double
+ measureDistanceAtAngle(angle: double): double
+ setMeasurementUnit(unit: String): void
+ getMeasurementUnit(): String
+ calibrateSensor(): void
+ getSensorStatus(): String
```

Now, apply the procedure to define the required interface, and bind plug-in objects to the *RangeFinder* component.

- **Applying [1] Identify Variation Points**
  The core functionality of the *Range Finder* depends on a proximity sensor, which measures the distance to a target by emitting signals and calculating the time taken for the signal to return. However, proximity sensors vary widely in their underlying technology—such as ultrasonic, infrared, laser, or radar-based—and in their performance characteristics.
  Moreover, even sensors of the same type may require different drivers due to manufacturer-specific implementations. This diversity introduces a variation point in the design of the *RangeFinder* component.
- **Applying [2] Define Required Interfaces for Variation Points**
  To resolve the variation point for proximity sensors, a required interface named *iProximitySensor* is defined, as shown in Fig. 6.23.

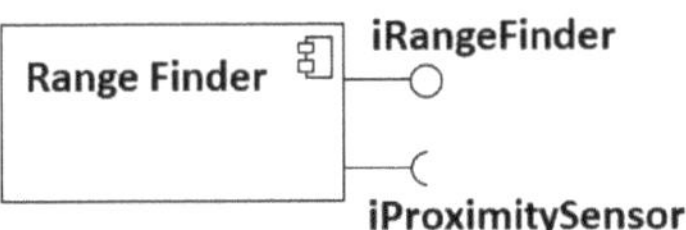

Fig. 6.23 Required Interface of RangeFinder Component

The figure illustrates the *RangeFinder* component, which includes both a provided interface (*iRangeFinder*) and a required interface (*iProximitySensor*). The required interface serves as a contract between the *RangeFinder* and external proximity sensor implementations, allowing the component to remain adaptable and modular.
The methods of the provided interface, *iProximitySensor*, are defined based on common functionality shared across various proximity sensor types:

```
+ initializeSensor(): void
+ readDistance(): double
+ calibrateSensor(): void
+ getSensorType(): String
+ getSensorStatus(): String
+ resetSensor(): void
```

- **Applying [3] Define Setter Methods to Accept External Implementations**
  In addition to defining the required interface, it is essential to include a setter method within the *Provided Interface* of the component to enable dynamic binding of plug-in objects. This method should not be placed in the *Required Interface*, which only declares the services needed but does not manage their integration.
  The *Provided Interface* reflects the full capabilities of the component, including its ability to configure and incorporate external implementations. In contrast, the *Required Interface* simply defines the expected services.
  The signature of the setter method can be defined as follows:
  ```
  + setProximitySensor(sensor: iProximitySensor): void
  ```
  This method enables the dynamic binding of a plug-in object that implements the IProximitySensor interface, allowing the system to support a range of proximity sensor technologies in a flexible and modular manner.
- **Applying [4] Implement the Required Interface**
  This is to implement the required interface to support various types and manufacturers of proximity sensor devices. Each sensor model must provide its own implementation of the required interface, typically using a vendor-supplied device driver to ensure proper functionality and compatibility.
  Java code examples of implementing this required interface for an ultrasonic sensor and a laser sensor are shown below:
  ```
  public class UltrasonicSensor implements iProximitySensor {
  ...
  }
  public class LaserSensor implements iProximitySensor {
  ...
  }
  ```
- **Applying [5] Bind External Implementations**
  This step involves instantiating objects from multiple implementations of the required interface, `IProximitySensor`, resulting in several plug-in objects. An appropriate plug-in object is then selected and passed to the setter method `setProximitySensor()` for dynamic binding.
  The following Java examples demonstrate how to instantiate and bind plug-in objects to the required interface:
  ```
  iProximitySensor ultrasonicSensor = new UltrasonicSensor();
  rangeFinder.setProximitySensor(ultrasonicSensor);
  iProximitySensor laserSensor = new LaserSensor();
  rangeFinder.setProximitySensor(laserSensor);
  ```
  The binding relationship between a component and its plug-in object can be represented using the *Assembly* connector in UML, as illustrated in Fig. 6.24.

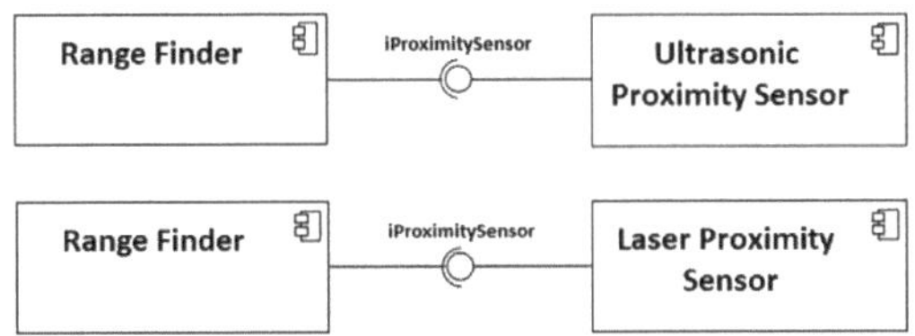

Fig. 6.24 Assembly Between RangeFinder and Its Plug-in Objects

6.5 Step 5. Design for Functional Variability

This step focuses on modeling the variability embedded in functional components and designing them to support flexible configurations. Such configurations address both static and dynamic functional demands while maintaining system consistency and integrity.

Designing functional components with variability in mind offers significant benefits, including enhanced adaptability, improved reusability, and the capacity to efficiently accommodate evolving requirements. Conversely, omitting variability considerations may reduce adaptability, constrain reusability, and increase the cost of accommodating future changes. Therefore, designing for variability is essential for developing scalable, maintainable, and reusable components that can effectively address diverse and evolving system needs.

Variability in the Real World

The concept of variability is widespread and enduring, observable in many physical products. Embracing variability enhances the ability to perform tasks, explore alternatives, and use tools more effectively.

Consider the case of hair dryers. Although their core function is to emit warm air for drying hair, different models exhibit variability in key features, such as:

- Voltage: may support 110 volts, 220 volts, or both
- Air temperature: may offer cool, warm, or hot settings
- Airflow speed: may range from low to medium to high

When a hair dryer supports these variations—allowing users to choose among multiple options—it achieves broader usability and marketability. In contrast, a hair dryer limited to a fixed voltage, temperature, and airflow setting significantly restricts its applicability. This limitation parallels the challenges faced by rigid software solutions, which often struggle to meet diverse user needs effectively.

Variability in Software

In software systems, variability refers to the capacity of a system to be customized, extended, or configured to meet specific contexts or requirements. Variability modeling offers a systematic approach for capturing and managing the inherent variability in software architecture. It is therefore a foundational practice for developing adaptable and flexible systems.

Software systems with a high degree of variability include operating systems, middleware, platforms, and frameworks. Their variability arises from the wide range of use cases and operational environments they must support, necessitating adaptable system behavior and structure.

In particular, variability often appears in functional components, where components must be configured, extended, or adapted to suit different requirements. The design goal is to ensure that such components are both reusable and adaptable, enabling them to address diverse conditions without requiring a full redesign.

For example, consider the functional component *Payment Manager* in a Car Rental Management System. Variability arises in the modes of payment—such as credit card, digital wallet, cash, or cryptocurrency. To manage this variability, a variation point can be established within the component. Each payment method represents a valid variant, and the *Payment Manager* should be designed to integrate these variants through a unified, well-defined interface.

6.5.1 Task 1. Identify Variation Points and Variants

This task is to identify the inherent variability within functional components and explicitly define it through variation points and their corresponding variants. Variability modeling has been extensively applied in software engineering to develop systems that are adaptable, reusable, and configurable. A comprehensive discussion of software variability, including variation points and their respective variants, is provided in [29, 30].

Variation Point

A *variation point* in a functional component refers to a specific location where variability is introduced. It may appear in different aspects, such as the overall control flow, specific logic within the control structure, component interfaces, persistent datasets, or external services invoked by the component.

For instance, several functional components of the Car Rental Management System exhibit variability, as illustrated below:

- **Component: Checkout Manager**
  Variation Point: Insurance options offered for car rentals
- **Component: Payment Manager**
  Variation Point: Supported payment methods (as discussed earlier)
- **Component: Inventory Manager**
  Variation Point: Algorithms employed for relocating cars
- **Component: In-Rental Manager**
  Variation Point: Mechanisms for notifying staff to handle "Out of Region" anomalies

Identifying all essential variation points within a functional component is a prerequisite for designing the component to ensure high adaptability, applicability, and customizability.

Variant

A *variant* refers to a valid value or object that can be bound to its corresponding variation point. The variability of a variation point is defined by its set of associated variants. The set of variants may be binary, consist of multiple predefined options, or be open ended to accommodate future or unforeseen possibilities.

The relationships among functional components, variation points, and variants are illustrated in Fig. 6.25.

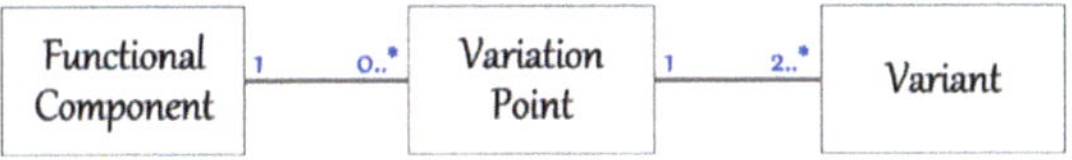

Fig. 6.25 Variation Point and Its Variants

A functional component may be associated with zero or more variation points. Each variation point must be linked to at least two variants, underscoring that a variation point always represents a choice among multiple alternatives.

For example, consider the functional components that exhibit variability within the Car Rental Management System. The variation points, scopes of variants, and specific variants are summarized in the *Variability Modeling Table*, as shown in Table 6.5.

Table 6.5 Variability Modeling Table for Car Rental Management System

Functional Component	Variation Point	Variant Scope	Variants
Checkout Manager	Insurance Options	Open-Ended	Collision Damage Waiver, Supplemental Liability, Personal Accident Insurance, and Unknown
Payment Manager	Payment Methods	Selection	Credit Card, Digital Wallet, Cash, and Cryptocurrency
Inventory Manager	Car Relocation Algorithm	Open-Ended	Historical Usage Pattern Analysis, Demand Forecasting, Zone Balancing Algorithm, and Unknown
In-Rental Manager	Anomaly Notification Methods	Selection	SMS Message, Phone Call, Email, and In-App Notification

In variability modeling, an *Open-Ended* scope refers to a variation point with a flexible set of variants that can be extended over time, allowing new options to be added as needed. In contrast, a *Selection* scope restricts the variation point to a predefined set of alternatives, enabling the system to choose among fixed, known options during configuration or execution.

For instance, the Checkout Manager includes an *open-ended* variation point for insurance options, accommodating not only existing alternatives such as collision damage waiver and supplemental liability but also allowing for the incorporation of unforeseen insurance types in the future. In contrast, the Payment Manager features a *selection-based* variation point for supported payment methods, offering a fixed set of predefined choices, including credit cards, digital wallets, and cryptocurrencies.

6.5.2 Task 2. Design Adaptation Schemes for Variability

This task is to design effective adaptation schemes to address the identified variability within each functional component. Adaptation schemes are structured strategies or design approaches that enable functional components to accommodate valid variants at their variation points, either statically at compile time or dynamically at runtime.

These schemes are fundamentally grounded in the *Open-Closed Principle* (*OCP*), which advocates designing components that are open for extension—allowing new variants to be introduced—yet closed for modification, thereby preserving the stability and integrity of existing functionality.

Open-Closed Principle (OCP)

OCP is a fundamental design principle in software engineering, asserting that software entities—such as classes, modules, and functions—should be open for extension but closed to modification [31, 32]. It is a foundational concept in object-oriented software design and design patterns, promoting the development of robust, adaptable systems [23, 32].

The essential tenets of OCP are as follows:

- **Open for Extension**
  Components should be designed to allow their functionality to be extended to support new requirements or enhancements without altering their existing structure.
- **Closed for Modification**
  Components should be structured such that their core implementation remains stable and unchanged, ensuring the preservation of existing behavior while still supporting external extensions.

The benefits of applying OCP in software design are well recognized across a wide range of software engineering methodologies and implementation technologies. Notably, OCP has played a pivotal role in the development of numerous design patterns [23].

Adaptation Schemes Aligned with the Open-Closed Principle

A wide range of adaptation schemes have been developed based on the Open-Closed Principle (OCP). These schemes provide structured strategies for accommodating variability without modifying existing code. Representative adaptation schemes include the following:

- **Parameterization**
  This scheme defines configurable parameters that enable dynamic adjustments to component behavior without altering the core design.
- **Inheritance and Polymorphism**
  This scheme leverages object-oriented principles to extend or override behaviors in derived classes while preserving the stability of base classes. Mechanisms such as method overriding, object substitution, and dynamic binding facilitate runtime adaptation of variants.
- **Design Patterns**
  This scheme utilizes established design patterns to encapsulate variability and promote reusable, adaptable designs. Design patterns clearly delineate the open extension points from the closed implementation parts, thereby supporting intuitive and effective adaptation of variants.
- **Required Interfaces and Plug-in Objects**
  This scheme defines explicit interfaces for variation points and integrates plug-in objects as variants. These plug-ins can be added without modifying existing code. A detailed example of this scheme is presented in Sect. 6.4.3.
- **Event-Driven Invocation**
  This scheme separates variation points from their corresponding variants through the use of events. Event emitters define the variation points, while event listeners act as the variants by dynamically responding with specific behaviors. This separation enables integration or replacement of variants without modifying the core design.
- **Configuration Management**
  This scheme employs external configuration files to manage variation at runtime. By isolating configuration logic from application logic, the system can flexibly adapt behavior and functionality based on context-specific parameters, settings, or rules defined in configuration files.
- **Dynamic Configuration and Invocation of External Services**
  This scheme dynamically selects and invokes external services—such as microservices—based on runtime conditions, user input, or service-level metrics. These services provide concrete implementations of variants, while the variation points remain in the main application logic.
- **Aspect-Oriented Programming (AOP)**
  This scheme addresses cross-cutting concerns by defining variation points in the core logic and implementing corresponding variants as modular aspects. This approach supports separation of concerns for behaviors like logging, security, or monitoring, allowing aspects to be independently managed and integrated.

Example

Consider the functional component *Payment Manager* in the Car Rental Management System.

- **Interface of Payment Manager**

  The interface of this component comprises a set of methods for processing payments and handling refunds. The key methods are defined as follows:

  + makePayment(details: PaymentDetails, amount: Decimal, currency: String): PaymentResult
  + getPaymentStatus(transactionId: String): PaymentStatus
  + processRefund(transactionId: String, amount: Decimal): RefundResult
  + getRefundStatus(refundId: String): RefundStatus

  The *makePayment()* method initiates a payment transaction using the specified payment details, amount, and currency. The *getPaymentStatus()* method retrieves the current status of a transaction using the transaction ID. The *processRefund()* method initiates a refund for a given transaction ID and amount. The *getRefundStatus()* method obtains the status of a refund request using the refund ID. Collectively, these methods enable comprehensive management of payment and refund operations within the Payment Manager component.

- **Variation Point in Payment Manager**

  Based on the system's functional requirements, variability is observed in the payment methods employed by this component. Specifically, a variation point exists for Payment Methods, as described in Table 6.5. This variation point includes four defined variants: Credit Card, Digital Wallet, Cash, and Cryptocurrency.

- **Apply Strategy Design Pattern to Manage Variability**

  Strategy Pattern is a behavioral design pattern that facilitates dynamic selection of an algorithm at runtime by defining a family of interchangeable algorithms, each encapsulated in a separate class. The pattern introduces a variation point through a common strategy interface, with each variant implemented as a concrete strategy.

  The design of the *Payment Manager*, applying the Strategy Pattern, is illustrated in Fig. 6.26.

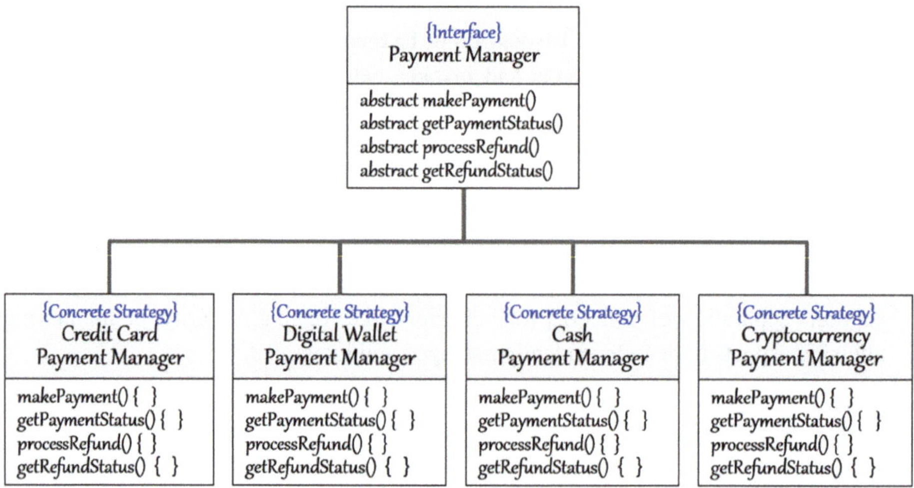

Fig. 6.26 Strategy Pattern Realizing Variation Point on makePayment() Method

In the figure, the *Payment Manager* interface defines a set of abstract methods for handling payment and refund operations. Each of the four concrete strategy classes implements this interface, providing variant-specific behavior corresponding to a particular payment method. Each concrete class instance can be substituted for the *Payment Manager* interface, enabling dynamic binding to the appropriate payment method implementation at runtime. This structure enables dynamic selection and integration of a payment method variant at runtime. By encapsulating each predefined variant as a separate strategy, the design adheres to the Open-Closed Principle.

6.6 Checklist for A4a: Functional View Design

The following checklist items can be used to validate the design for functional view.

6.6.1 Checklist for Step 1: Refine Use Case Model

- Have the functional groups been refined to adhere to the Single Responsibility Principle by encapsulating a single, cohesive functionality?
- Have all use cases within each functional group been comprehensively identified using a CRUD-based identification method?
- Have all actors been accurately identified based on the specified system requirements?
- Have software agent–type actors been considered to enable autonomous invocation of use cases?
- Have all actors been clearly classified into active and passive roles, with active actors further distinguished as primary or secondary?
- Have all actor–use case relationships been precisely defined and clearly mapped, taking into account both the roles of actors and the services provided by the use cases?
- Have generalization, inclusion, and extension relationships among use cases been thoroughly refined to ensure alignment with their intended purposes, as prescribed by UML guidelines?
- Are detailed use case descriptions provided for complex or critical use cases?
- Have alternate flows and error flows been appropriately addressed in the use case descriptions?

6.6.2 Checklist for Step 2: Define Functional Components

- Have all functional groups been accurately mapped to their corresponding functional components, maintaining a one-to-one mapping unless special cases are explicitly justified?
- Have architecture style–specific components been properly identified and incorporated, where applicable? Certain architecture styles require dedicated components to support their distinctive structural or behavioral characteristics.

- Have all essential interface-centric components been identified to abstract interactions and establish clear service contracts?
- Are the scope and boundaries of each functional component clearly delineated?
- Do the defined functional components exhibit high internal cohesion and low coupling with other components?
- Are component names consistently expressed in noun form and aligned with the established naming convention?
- Has a UML Component Diagram been provided to visually represent the defined functional components?

6.6.3 Checklist for Step 3: Allocate Functional Components

- Have all functionality placeholders been clearly identified within the schematic architecture?
  Each placeholder should represent a distinct functional responsibility.
- Have functional components been allocated to appropriate tiers based on their functionality, including considerations for components spanning multiple tiers?
- Have read-only and full-access roles been clearly differentiated for components in common tiers, as specified in the Functional Component Allocation Table?
- Has the schematic architecture been fully populated with functional components, aligned with the functional placeholders and the Functional Component Allocation Table?
- Have architecture style–specific component placement rules been applied when allocating components to tiers? Confirm that the allocation respects constraints imposed by the chosen architecture style.
- Has the allocation ensured balanced distribution of responsibilities across tiers to prevent overload or underutilization? Evaluate whether the computational and functional load is reasonably balanced. This supports scalability, maintainability, and system responsiveness.

6.6.4 Checklist for Step 4: Define Functional Component Interfaces

- Have functional components requiring interface definitions been correctly identified, excluding small, low-complexity, or secondary components where interfaces are unnecessary?
- Are provided interfaces clearly defined with well-structured public methods that expose the services offered by the component?
- Have public methods in the provided interface been identified based on the use cases assigned to the component? Ensure that the interface methods are traceable to specific use case behaviors.

- Are required interfaces defined for components that depend on external variants, such as plug-in objects? Required interfaces should abstract the external functionality needed by the component.
- Have setter methods been defined to bind external implementations (e.g., plug-ins) at runtime or configuration time? These enable flexible and decoupled integration of variants.
- Are method signatures complete and compliant with UML conventions, including visibility, parameters, and return types?

6.6.5 Checklist for Step 5: Design for Functional Variability

- Has variability within each functional component been modeled using well-defined variation points and their corresponding variants?
- Have all variation points within the component been thoroughly identified and clearly documented?
- Have all valid variants been clearly defined for each variation point?
  Each variant should be explicitly described, reflecting meaningful differences in behavior or configuration.
- Is the scope of variants for each variation point clearly classified as Binary, Selection, or Open Ended?
- Have UML assembly connectors been correctly used to represent the binding between variation points and their corresponding variants? Use UML conventions to visually depict how components are configured or extended with specific variants.
- Do the selected adaptation schemes conform to the Open-Closed Principle (OCP)?

6.7 Exercise Problems

1. **Refinement of a Context-Level Use Case Diagram**
   Refining the context-level use case diagram is a crucial step in the functional view design of software systems. It clarifies system boundaries and improves the granularity of user interactions. Describe specific types of refinements that can be applied to the functional context.
2. **Refining the Context-Level Use Case Diagram for a Food Delivery System**
   Refine the use case diagram representing the functional context of a Food Delivery System. Identify deficiencies in the initial diagram and revise it accordingly. Then, compare the refined (view-level) diagram with the context-level diagram by listing all changes made.

3. **Writing a Use Case Description for the "Checkout Car" Use Case**
   Write a complete use case description for the *Checkout Car* use case in the Car Rental Management System. Include preconditions, postconditions, main flow, alternative flows, and error flows, using the tabular format described in Sect. 6.1.5.
4. **Alignment of Functional Components with Functional Groups**
   Functional components are generally aligned with predefined functional groups through a one-to-one mapping. Discuss scenarios in which one-to-many or many-to-one mappings may occur between functional groups and functional components, and explain how such mappings affect component design.
5. **Identifying Functional Components for a Food Delivery System**
   Based on the refined Use Case Diagram of the Food Delivery System, identify the corresponding functional components. Represent them using a UML Component Diagram and evaluate the degree of alignment between functional groups and components.
6. **Identifying Interface Components for an Adaptive Cruise Control (ACC) System**
   Interface components define public methods without providing implementation. Identify interface components, such as those in the Hardware Abstraction Layer (HAL), for an Adaptive Cruise Control System. Explain their role in supporting platform independence and modular design.
7. **Functionality Placeholders in Architecture Styles**
   Architecture styles often define functionality placeholders—designated positions intended to host functional components. Identify and describe functionality placeholders for the following architecture styles: Pipe-and-Filter, Layered, Model-View-Controller (MVC), Event-Driven, and Publisher-Subscriber.
8. **Allocation of Functional Components in a Multi-Tier Architecture**
   Under what circumstances should a functional component be distributed across multiple tiers in a schematic architecture? Describe the impact of such distribution on functionality and accessibility. Provide a concrete example of a component allocated across tiers.
9. **Guidelines for Choosing Whitebox or Blackbox Components**
   Whitebox components expose internal structure and logic, while blackbox components conceal them. Present specific design guidelines for deciding between whitebox and blackbox components in different contexts.
10. **Provided and Required Interfaces for Components**
    UML allows components to declare provided and required interfaces. Describe when each interface type should be used, and illustrate with concrete examples from real-world or domain-specific systems.
11. **Defining a Provided Interface for the Checkout Manager Component**
    Define the provided interface for the Checkout Manager component in the Car Rental Management System. Derive its method signatures from the associated use cases, and provide detailed semantic descriptions for each method.

12. **Designing the Alert Manager with Functional Variability**
    The *Alert Manager* component in a Hospital Monitoring System must support multiple alert delivery mechanisms (e.g., audible alarm, nurse station notification, doctor's mobile app alert). Identify the relevant variation point(s) and corresponding variants. Then, design the component to support dynamic selection of alert mechanisms at runtime.
13. **Using a Required Interface as an Adaptation Scheme**
    A *required interface* can serve as an adaptation mechanism for managing variability. Propose a design procedure that includes identifying variation points, defining a required interface, implementing concrete variants, and binding them dynamically using a setter method.
14. **Open-Closed Principle (OCP) Schemes for Variability**
    The OCP enables extensible yet stable component design. Explain why OCP-based schemes are effective for managing functional variability, and provide an example of applying a relevant design pattern, such as Strategy or Plug-in, in component design.

7 Activity A4b. Design for Information View

Objective of the Chapter
The objective of this chapter is to provide guidelines for designing the information view of a software system. It covers the refinement of the persistent object model, the definition of data components based on semantic cohesion, the allocation of these components to appropriate data placeholders within the architecture, the specification of data component interfaces, and the design of object persistence mechanisms. Together, these guidelines enable architects to construct a robust information architecture that ensures data consistency, facilitates modular data management, and supports reliable data storage and retrieval in alignment with system requirements.

Introducing Activity A4b. Design for Information View
This activity is to design the architecture of the information view for a target system. The information view in software architecture primarily addresses the identification of persistent datasets, the specification of their relationships, and the mapping of these datasets to persistent storage mechanisms.

The architectural design for the information view provides a structured framework for managing and persisting data, defining how it is modeled, stored, accessed, and maintained to ensure consistency, scalability, and efficiency. Accordingly, the primary objective of the information view is to manage persistent datasets—typically represented as persistent object classes and their interrelationships. In addition, this view entails allocating data components to the schematic architecture and designing them to ensure robust and reliable data persistence.

S. D. Kim, M. Kim, *Hands-on Software Architecture*,
https://doi.org/10.1007/978-3-032-01184-8_7

Steps in A4b. Information View Design

The design for information view can be systematically performed with a sequence of steps, as shown Fig. 7.1.

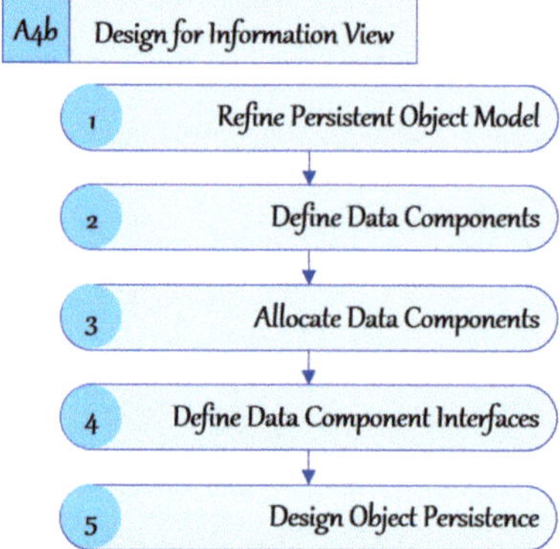

Fig. 7.1 Steps in A4b. Information View Design

- **Step 1. Refine Persistent Object Model**
  This step is to refine the context-level object model, typically represented as a class diagram, by incorporating detailed specifications of persistent classes, persistent attributes, and their relationships. The refinement aims to enhance precision and completeness.
- **Step 2. Define Data Components**
  This step is to identify data components by grouping semantically cohesive classes. A data component is a self-contained architectural unit that encapsulates a set of interrelated datasets serving specific functional roles within the system.
- **Step 3. Allocate Data Components**
  This step is to map the identified data components to corresponding data placeholders within the schematic architecture. A data placeholder is a structural element defined to accommodate components responsible for managing distinct and cohesive datasets.
- **Step 4. Define Data Component Interfaces**
  This step is to specify the interfaces of each data component. A data component interface provides public access to its persistent datasets through a well-defined set of method signatures and accompanying semantic descriptions.
- **Step 5. Design Object Persistence**
  This step is to design the mechanisms for permanent storage of persistent objects. This typically involves selecting appropriate database management systems (DBMS) or cloud-based storage solutions that support efficient and reliable data storage and retrieval.

7.1 Step 1. Refine Persistent Object Model

This step is to develop a well-defined persistent object model by refining and elaborating the context-level object model. Specifically, the class diagram is enhanced to incorporate detailed definitions of persistent classes, their attributes, and relationships.

7.1.1 Task 1. Refine Persistent Object Classes

This task is to refine the persistent object classes in the context-level class diagram. By leveraging the insights obtained from the schematic architecture and the functional view, architects gain a more comprehensive understanding of the system's structure and behavior. Based on this understanding, the persistent object classes are refined to clarify their types and roles within the system.

Typical refinements to persistent object classes include the following:

- **Adding Missing Classes**
  If a persistent dataset in the system is not yet represented, a corresponding class should be introduced. Each persistent dataset must be mapped to one or more classes to ensure complete and accurate representation.
- **Removing Unnecessary Classes**
  Any class that does not correspond to a persistent dataset should be removed. This includes classes that represent non-persistent elements such as subsystems, functional components, databases, or user interface elements.
- **Modifying Existing Classes**
  Existing classes may require modification to better reflect their intended role in data persistence. This includes renaming classes for clarity, redefining attributes to align with data semantics, and updating relationships to accurately represent associations among datasets.

Refinement with Logical Classes

The class diagram for information view design may include both *physical* and *logical* classes that represent datasets requiring persistence within the system. *Physical classes* are typically straightforward to identify. In contrast, *logical classes*, which correspond to abstract datasets derived from system requirements, may not be immediately apparent. It is therefore important to identify all relevant logical datasets that require persistence and explicitly model them as logical classes in the class diagram.

For example, in the Car Rental Management System, the following are representative logical persistent classes:

- **Reservation**: Represents the persistent data associated with car rental reservations made by customers
- **Rental**: Captures the results of completed car rental processes, including vehicle assignment and usage records
- **Payment**: Represents the financial transactions associated with rental payments, including payment methods and amounts

Refinement with Session Classes

As a type of logical class, a *session class* records tasks or activities that occur within a defined time period. When a system is required to capture and retain such information for purposes such as analysis, reporting, or historical reference, a session class should be defined. Session classes—such as activity logs—are persistent and are categorized as logical classes due to their role in capturing temporally scoped behavior.

For example, in the Car Rental Management System, *Reservation* and *Rental* serve as session-type logical classes. In a Healthcare Management System, *Treatment*—which encompasses symptoms, diagnostic tests, prescriptions, and surgical procedures—serves as a core session class.

A session class typically maintains associations with physical classes and, in some cases, other logical classes to identify entities relevant to each session instance. For example, the session class *Treatment* establishes relationships with several entities, as shown in Fig. 7.2.

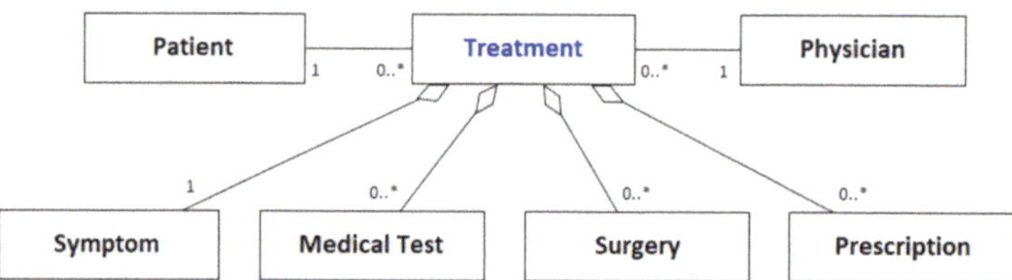

Fig. 7.2 Refinement with Session Class

In the figure, the session class *Treatment* acts as the central aggregator that composes various elements involved in a medical treatment session. It maintains associations with both *Patient* and *Physician*, and it aggregates multiple logical classes—*Symptom*, *Medical Test*, *Surgery*, and *Prescription.*

By maintaining the *Treatment* session class, the system can systematically capture and manage the full scope of a medical session, including the patient involved, the attending physician, observed symptoms, conducted medical tests, performed surgeries, and issued prescriptions. This enables comprehensive tracking of treatment histories, supports clinical decision-making, facilitates reporting and analysis, and ensures data consistency across related medical entities.

Refinement with Association Classes

An *association class* in a class diagram is a specialized class that represents an association relationship between two or more classes. It is used when the association itself requires additional attributes, operations, or behavior that cannot be directly represented by the related classes alone.

Association classes should be identified and refined by analyzing relationships among classes to determine whether any supplemental information or behavior needs to be encapsulated within the association.

For example, consider a system designed to track employment histories within a community. The initial class diagram can be refined by introducing an association class to more accurately model the relationship between the primary classes. This refinement is illustrated in Fig. 7.3.

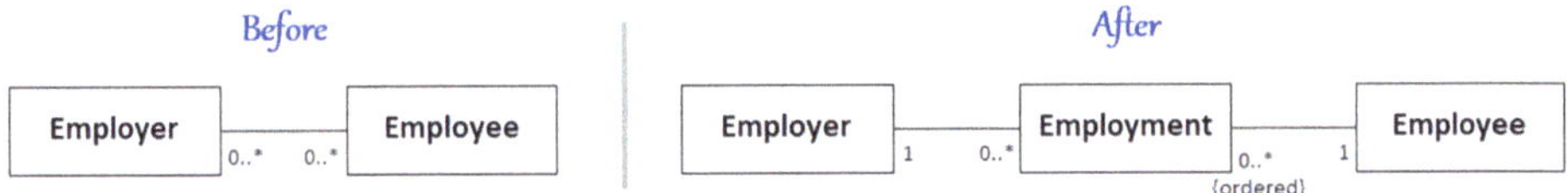

Fig. 7.3 Refinement with Association Class

The figure demonstrates how the original class diagram (left) is enhanced by incorporating an association class (right), allowing the relationship between *Employer* and *Employee* to be more explicitly represented through the *Employment* class.

The initial class diagram models a direct many-to-many association between *Employer* and *Employee*, allowing multiple relationships on both sides. While it captures the basic linkage, it cannot represent employment-specific details like job roles or dates. It also incorrectly permits concurrent employments, which may be unrealistic.

The refined class diagram introduces an *Employment* association class to represent the relationship with additional attributes and behaviors. The multiplicities are adjusted to reflect that an employer can have multiple employment relationships with employees and vice versa. Additionally, the *{ordered}* constraint is added to organize an employee's employment records in a specific sequence, such as by date.

Refinement with Technology-Related Classes

A *technology-related class* is a specialized logical class designed to represent and manage information pertaining to the technologies employed within a system. In systems that integrate diverse technologies, it is often necessary to track such information within session contexts for purposes such as usage monitoring, auditing, or future reference.

For example, in a system that incorporates machine learning capabilities, it may be necessary to store metadata related to trained and deployed models. To support this need, architects can define a class such as *Machine Learning Model* to systematically organize and manage model-specific information.

By defining technology-related classes, a system can ensure effective tracking and referencing of technology-specific artifacts, thereby enhancing maintainability, traceability, and support for advanced analytics.

7.1.2 Task 2. Refine Relationships Between Classes

This task is to refine the relationships among classes, including the specification of their cardinalities. Relationships play a critical role in defining object dependencies and establishing communication paths for message invocation between objects. Therefore, refining relationships is as essential as refining the classes themselves, ensuring that the resulting class diagram accurately represents the structural and behavioral aspects of the system.

Refinement of Association Relationship

An *association relationship* is a connection between two classes that represents a persistent link between their respective instances. When an instance of one class maintains a persistent reference to an instance of another class, it is appropriate to define an association relationship between them.

This persistent link is stored in permanent storage, enabling future retrieval and navigation. It ensures that object relationships are preserved across system sessions and can be accessed when needed.

Examples of association relationships are shown in Fig. 7.4.

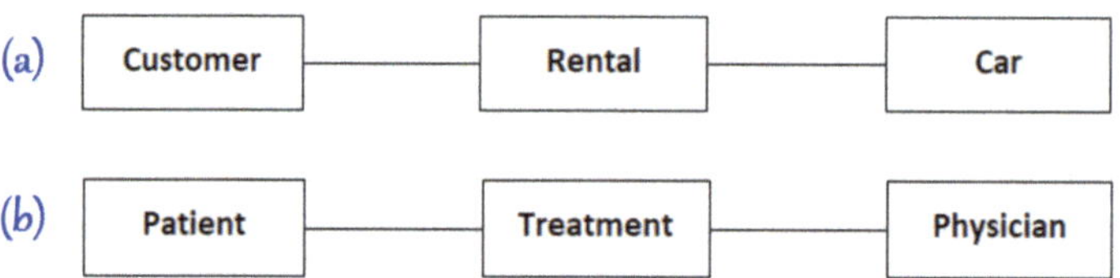

Fig. 7.4 Example of Association Relationship

In the figure (a), the *Rental* class maintains persistent associations with both *Customer* and *Car*, representing the entities involved in each rental transaction. In the figure (b), the *Treatment* class is associated with *Patient* and *Physician*, capturing the participants in a medical session. These associations reflect persistent links that must be retained across system sessions for accurate tracking and retrieval.

To refine association relationships, architects should begin by observing the dependencies between classes that are *persistent* rather than *transient*. Persistent dependencies indicate lasting links that must be maintained across system sessions, making them suitable candidates for association relationships. Architects should then examine the purpose and semantics of each connection, clarify the directionality of the relationship, and determine appropriate multiplicities.

Refinement of Aggregation Relationship

An *aggregation relationship* is a form of association in which one class represents the "whole" and the other represents the "part." If an instance of the *whole* class is composed of one or more instances of the *part* class, and those parts can exist independently, it is appropriate to define an aggregation relationship.

For example, in a University Registration System, students register for courses at the beginning of each semester. An aggregation relationship exists between the *Registration* class and the *Course* class, as shown in Fig. 7.5.

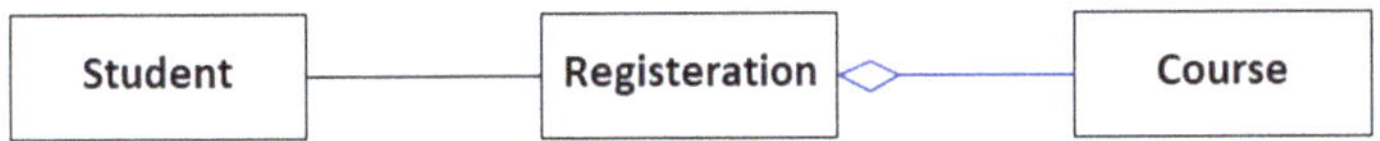

Fig. 7.5 Example of Aggregation Relationship

In the figure, the *Student* class is associated with the *Registration* class, and the *Registration* class aggregates instances of the *Course* class. The *Registration* class serves as the *whole*, while the *Course* class acts as the *part*. The aggregation relationship implies that a *Registration* cannot exist meaningfully without referencing at least one *Course*, though each *Course* can exist independently.

To refine aggregation relationships, architects should begin by identifying *whole-part* structures where one object logically consists of other independent objects. This involves confirming that the part objects can exist outside the context of the whole and that the relationship reflects logical grouping rather than ownership. Next, the cardinalities and role names of each end should be specified to clarify the expected structure and semantics.

Refinement of Composition Relationship

A *composition relationship* is a strong form of association in which one class owns another as part of its internal structure. If an instance of the "whole" class is composed of one or more instances of the "part" class, and the deletion of the whole implies the automatic deletion of its parts, then a composition relationship should be established between them.

For example, a composition relationship exists between the *Car* class and the *Engine* class, as shown in Fig. 7.6.

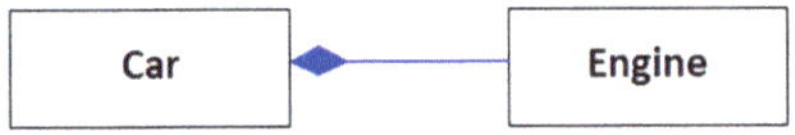

Fig. 7.6 Example of Composition Relationship

When an instance of *Car* is discarded, its associated *Engine* instance must also be deleted—demonstrating *cascading deletions*. This relationship enforces an implementation in which the constructor of the *Car* class must create and assign an *Engine* object at instantiation. Similarly, the destructor of the *Car* class must ensure that the associated *Engine* instance is properly destroyed when the *Car* instance is removed.

To refine composition relationships, architects should identify tightly coupled *whole-part* structures in which the part object cannot exist independently of the whole. It is essential to confirm that the part is created and destroyed exclusively through the lifecycle of the whole. Additionally, cardinalities, role names, and ownership semantics should be explicitly defined to clarify object containment and responsibility.

Refinement of Generalization and Specialization Relationships

A *generalization relationship* is a conceptual abstraction in which a base class (superclass) encapsulates the shared characteristics—such as attributes and behaviors—of its derived classes (subclasses). A *specialization relationship* is the counterpart of generalization, where a derived class inherits from a base class and introduces more specific attributes or behaviors.

Generalization and specialization relationships establish an *IS-A* relationship between the base class and its derived classes. The *IS-A* term implies that the derived class represents a specialized form of the base class.

For example, generalization and specialization relationships can be used to model personnel within the Car Rental Management System, as shown in Fig. 7.7.

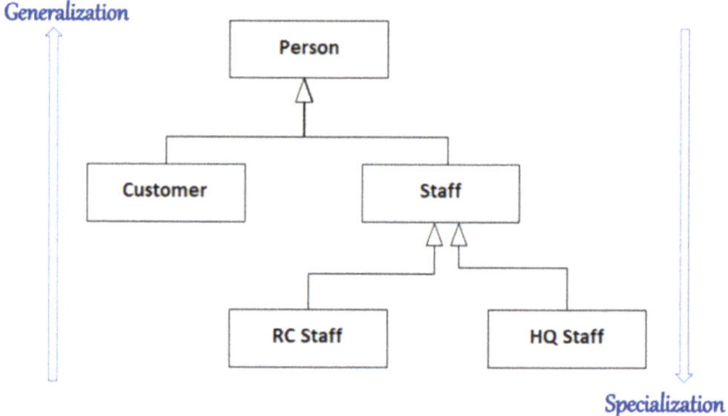

Fig. 7.7 Example of Generalization and Specialization Relationships

In the figure, the *Person* class is generalized into two specialized subclasses: *Customer* and *Staff*. The *Staff* class is further specialized into *RC Staff* and *HQ Staff*, representing role-specific staff members. This hierarchical structure demonstrates how generalization captures shared features in a base class, while specialization defines more specific roles with additional characteristics, supporting abstraction, reuse, and clear organizational modeling. This bidirectional view underscores the flexibility of generalization and specialization relationships in modeling hierarchical structures and supporting reuse through abstraction.

To refine generalization and specialization relationships, architects should begin by identifying classes that share common attributes and behaviors, which can be abstracted into a generalized superclass. It is essential to ensure that each subclass represents a true specialization of the base class, adhering to the IS-A principle—that is, each subclass must logically be "a kind of" the superclass. Care must be taken to avoid arbitrary or forced generalization; only stable and conceptually meaningful features should be factored out into the superclass. Additionally, architects should verify that subclass instances can be safely substituted for superclass instances without violating expected behavior, thus preserving semantic consistency and supporting polymorphism.

Refinement of Cardinalities on Relationships

Cardinality defines the number of instances from one class that can be associated with instances of another class in a relationship. It specifies multiplicity constraints that must be satisfied for each occurrence of the relationship. When the initial cardinalities do not accurately reflect the system's requirements or intended behavior, they must be refined to ensure correctness and alignment with domain semantics.

If the specified cardinalities are too broad, overly restrictive, or inconsistent with business rules, they should be updated accordingly. Refining cardinalities improves the precision of the model and ensures that each relationship reflects realistic usage scenarios.

An example of refining cardinalities in the association relationships of the Car Rental Management System is shown in Fig. 7.8.

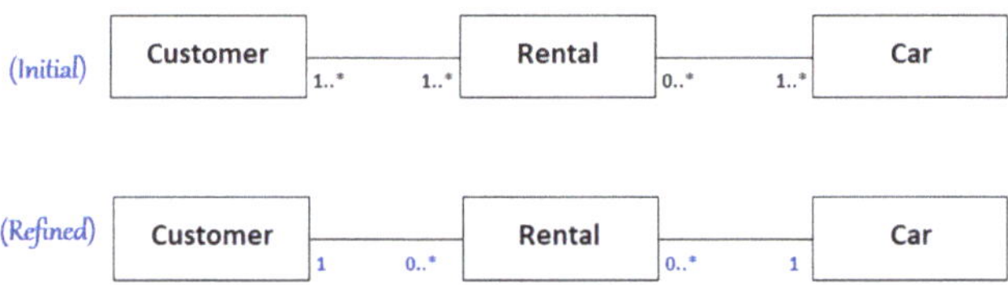

Fig. 7.8 Refining Cardinalities of Relationships

In the initial model, the cardinalities are overly broad and ambiguous—for instance, allowing a rental to be associated with multiple cars or requiring every customer to have at least one rental. In the refined model, the cardinalities are adjusted to better reflect realistic system constraints: each *Customer* must be linked to one or more *Rental* instances, while each *Rental* involves exactly one *Car*. These refinements help ensure that the class diagram enforce valid configurations and align more accurately with the domain's operational rules.

To refine cardinalities in class relationships, architects should begin by analyzing the real-world constraints and usage scenarios that govern how instances of classes interact. It is essential to determine whether each relationship represents optional or mandatory participation and whether it involves one-to-one, one-to-many, or many-to-many associations. Ambiguous or overly permissive cardinalities—such as unconstrained many-to-many relationships—should be revised to reflect more precise system behavior. Refinements should also eliminate logical inconsistencies, such as requiring a minimum number of related objects when some may be optional. When refining, consider business rules, data integrity, and lifecycle dependencies to ensure the model supports valid configurations without overconstraining flexibility.

Refinement with Design Patterns

Design patterns offer well-established solutions to recurring design problems by encapsulating best practices into reusable templates. Each pattern defines a structural configuration within a class diagram, specifying key participant classes, their relationships, and patterns of collaboration.

Design patterns are generally categorized into three types: creational, structural, and behavioral [23]. Among these, *structural design patterns* are particularly valuable for refining class diagrams, as they provide rigorously defined architectures tailored to common structural challenges. For instance, the *Composite* pattern is well suited for modeling hierarchical systems—such as tree structures—where individual components and their subcomponents must be treated uniformly.

Incorporating structural design patterns into class diagram refinement offers significant benefits, including improved modularity, clearer management of complex associations, increased design reusability, and a more explicit separation of concerns. Furthermore, the refined class diagram inherits the robustness, flexibility, and proven design integrity inherent in the applied pattern, resulting in a more maintainable and extensible architecture.

The class diagram can be refined by identifying and applying the unique structural features and design properties encapsulated in each structural pattern, as outlined below.

- **Adapter Pattern** enables the integration of incompatible interfaces by introducing an adapter class that allows them to work together seamlessly.
- **Bridge Pattern** decouples an abstraction from its implementation, allowing both to evolve independently.
- **Composite Pattern** models part-whole hierarchies recursively, enabling clients to treat individual objects and compositions uniformly.
- **Decorator Pattern** allows responsibilities to be dynamically added to an object without modifying its core code, supporting flexibility and reusability.
- **Facade Pattern** provides a simplified interface to a complex subsystem, reducing coupling and improving ease of use.
- **Flyweight Pattern** minimizes memory usage by sharing common parts of the object state across multiple instances.
- **Proxy Pattern** introduces a surrogate or placeholder that controls access to another object and optionally adds extra behavior such as lazy initialization or access control.

For example, consider a *Graphic Editing Application* that supports the creation of complex graphics composed of smaller graphic elements. The *Composite* pattern can be applied to model the recursive aggregation of figure objects, allowing individual shapes and composite figures to be treated uniformly, as shown in Fig. 7.9.

In the figure, the abstract class *Figure* serves as the common supertype for all graphic elements. It is specialized into *Leaf Figure* and *Compound Figure*. The *Leaf Figure* subclass is further specialized into concrete shapes such as *Line*, *Circle*, and *Rectangle*, each representing atomic graphic elements. The *Compound Figure* class models composite elements that aggregate multiple *Figure* instances through a recursive composition relationship labeled *Children*. This structure enables both simple and composite figures to be

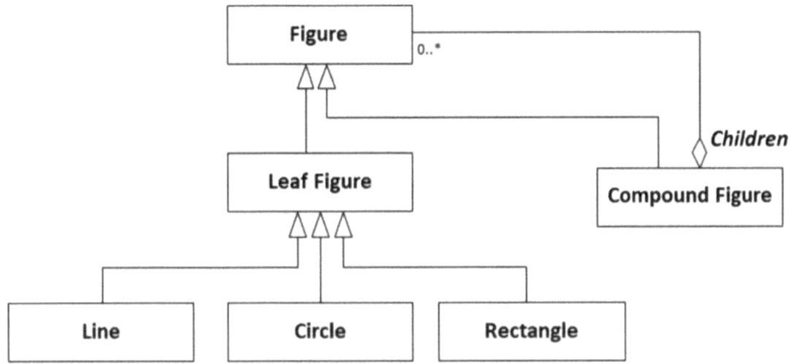

Fig. 7.9 Composite Pattern Applied to Graphic Editing Application

treated uniformly, supporting recursive composition and consistent operations across all figure types.

Refined Object Model for Car Rental Management System

The refined context-level class diagram for the Car Rental Management System is shown in Fig. 7.10.

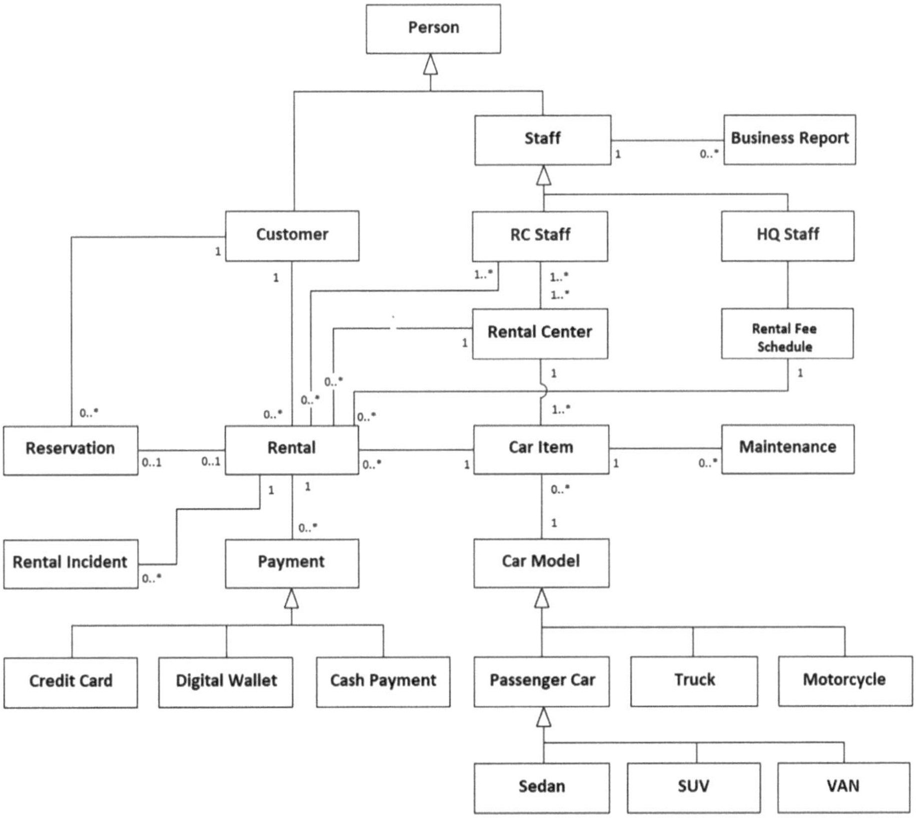

Fig. 7.10 Refined Class Diagram for Car Rental Management System

This class diagram illustrates several enhancements to classes, their relationships, and the cardinalities of those relationships, as summarized below.

- **Adding Business Report class**
  This class is introduced to store metadata related to generated business reports, improving the efficiency of retrieving and managing report data.
- **Adding *Rental Fee Schedule* class**
  This class is defined to manage rental fee schedules for different car models across various rental locations. These schedules are determined by headquarters staff, represented as instances of the *HQ Staff* class.
- **Adding *Maintenance* class**
  This class captures information related to the maintenance of rental cars. The data can be used for various analytics purposes, including maintenance schedules, associated fees, and service time tracking.
- **Adding *Rental Incident* class**
  A rental incident refers to any unexpected event or issue occurring during a rental period—such as accidents, theft, or damage. This class is defined to capture information about such incidents to support reporting and analysis.
- **Refining cardinality between *Rental* and *Payment* classes**
  In the original diagram, the cardinality on the side of the *Payment* class was 0..1, indicating that each rental could be associated with at most one payment. However, to accommodate scenarios involving multiple payment methods—such as a combination of credit card and cash—the cardinality has been updated to 0..*.
- **Specializing *Payment* class**
  The Payment class is specialized into three subclasses: Credit Card Payment, Digital Wallet Payment, and Cash Payment. Each subclass defines payment-specific attributes and methods.
- **Specializing *Car Model* class**
  The *Car Model* class is specialized into three subclasses representing distinct categories: *Passenger Car*, *Truck*, and *Motorcycle*. Furthermore, the *Passenger Car* class is refined into *Sedan*, *SUV*, and *VAN* subclasses.
  Note that the context-level class diagram shown in Fig. 4.20 includes 11 persistent object classes, whereas the refined class diagram at the information view level comprises 24 classes, reflecting a substantial refinement of the class structure. Consequently, the relationships in the diagram have also been refined to accommodate and accurately represent the expanded set of classes.

7.1.3 Task 3. Define Persistent Attributes

This task is to define the essential persistent attributes for the classes in the class diagram. Persistent attributes represent the data elements whose values must be stored in permanent storage. Architects are not required to identify all possible attributes within a class. Instead, the focus is on specifying only those attributes essential for persistence, ensuring that critical data elements are not overlooked during implementation.

For example, the persistent attributes for the *Rental* class are defined as shown in Fig. 7.11

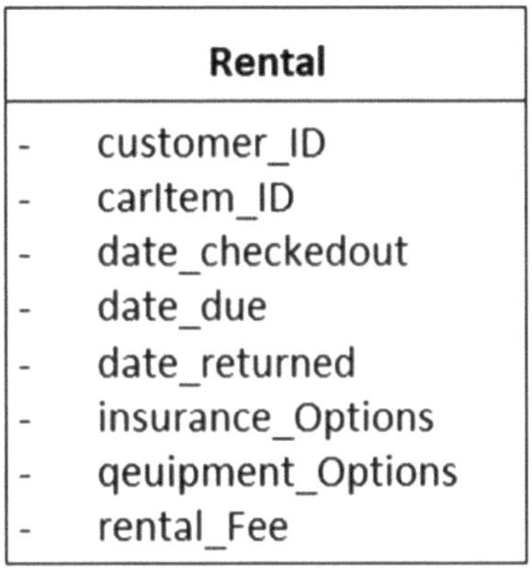

Rental
- customer_ID
- carItem_ID
- date_checkedout
- date_due
- date_returned
- insurance_Options
- qeuipment_Options
- rental_Fee

Fig. 7.11 Defining Attributes for Rental class

The attributes defined in the class represent essential data elements that must be stored persistently to support core rental operations.

7.2 Step 2. Define Data Components

This step involves deriving data components from the refined class diagram. A *data component* is a cohesive unit composed of closely related classes that are grouped based on their interrelationships.

The number of data components is typically smaller than the total number of classes in the class diagram. Each data component represents a cohesive data module that encapsulates and hides its internal class structure.

Grouping related classes into data components and manipulating datasets through these components provides several benefits, including the following:

- **Improved Modularity**
  Encapsulating related classes into a single cohesive unit simplifies the overall design and improves maintainability
- **Encapsulation of Complexity**
  Hiding the internal class structure within a data component reduces system complexity and promotes cleaner, more maintainable interfaces
- **Enhanced Reusability**
  Data components can be reused across multiple parts of the system, reducing duplication and improving design consistency

- **Abstraction via Component-Level Interface**
  Defining a component-level interface as an abstraction over its internal classes simplifies external interactions. Similar to the principle behind the *Facade* design pattern, this approach ensures that clients interact only with the interface, not with the internal complexity.

7.2.1 Task 1. Identify Data Components from Class Diagram

This task is to identify data components by clustering classes that are closely related. Data components can be systematically derived by analyzing and grouping classes based on the strength of their relationships.

Strengths of Inter-class Relationships
Among the five types of inter-class relationships defined in UML, the relative strength of each is illustrated in Fig. 7.12.

Fig. 7.12 Order of Relationship Strengths Between Classes

- **Relationship #1: Inheritance**
  Inheritance is the strongest form of relationship in UML, as it tightly couples subclasses with their superclass. This coupling is evident in several ways:
  When a subclass instance is created, the constructor of its superclass is automatically invoked. Thus, subclass construction depends on superclass construction.
  When a subclass instance is destroyed, the destructor of its superclass is also triggered, indicating lifecycle dependency.
  When a subclass receives a message invoking an inherited method, the method defined in the superclass is executed.
  These characteristics demonstrate that subclasses rely heavily on their superclass, making inheritance the strongest UML relationship type.
- **Relationship #2: Composition**
  Composition is the second strongest relationship in UML, characterized by the shared lifetime of a whole object and its parts. The creation of the whole object depends on the existence of its part objects—without them, it cannot be instantiated. Likewise, deleting the whole object automatically triggers the deletion of its parts, establishing strong lifecycle coupling.

- **Relationship #3: Aggregation**
  Aggregation is the third strongest relationship. A whole object depends on its parts for construction, but unlike composition, the part objects have independent lifecycles. They may exist separately from the whole, which weakens the coupling compared to composition.
- **Relationship #4: Association**
  Association is a weaker relationship, as associated classes are not inherently dependent on each other. The link supports message-based communication but does not enforce lifecycle constraints.
- **Relationship #5: Dependency**
  Dependency is the weakest UML relationship. It indicates a temporary and often unidirectional reliance, where one class uses another for a brief interaction. Dependencies are typically not persisted and are often omitted from class diagrams due to their transient nature.

Guidelines for Deriving Data Components Based on Relationship Strength
Data components can be systematically defined by identifying closely related classes based on the strength of inter-class relationships and grouping them into cohesive units. Apply the following procedure for defining data components:

[1] **Identify Classes with Inheritance Relationships**:
Group classes that are related through inheritance into the same data component.

[2] **Identify Classes with Composition Relationships**:
Group classes that share a composition relationship into the same data component, as their lifecycles are tightly coupled.

[3] **Identify Classes with Aggregation Relationships:**
Group the whole object class with its part object class(es) only if the part object class has no other relationships beyond the current aggregation.
If the part object class has additional relationships of aggregation, composition, or inheritance type, do not group it with the whole object class. Instead, assign them to separate data components.

[4] **Identify Classes with Association Relationships:**
Separate classes that are connected by association relationships into different data components, as their connection is relatively weak and does not require grouping.

[5] **Identify Classes with Dependency Relationships:**
Separate classes with dependency relationships into different data components, as these relationships are the weakest and typically transient.

Example
Following the provided guidelines, the data components for the Car Rental Management System are systematically derived from its class diagram, as shown in Fig. 7.13.

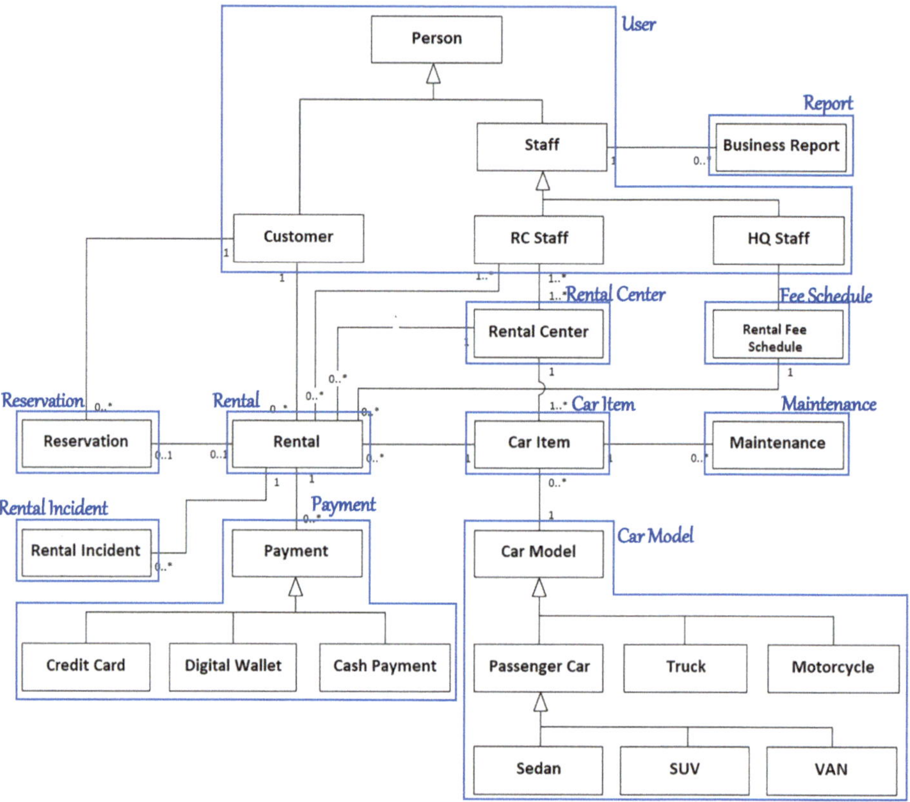

Fig. 7.13 Derivation of Data Components Based on Relationship Strengths

The 24 classes in the class diagram for the Car Rental Management System are organized into 11 data components, as shown in Fig. 7.14.

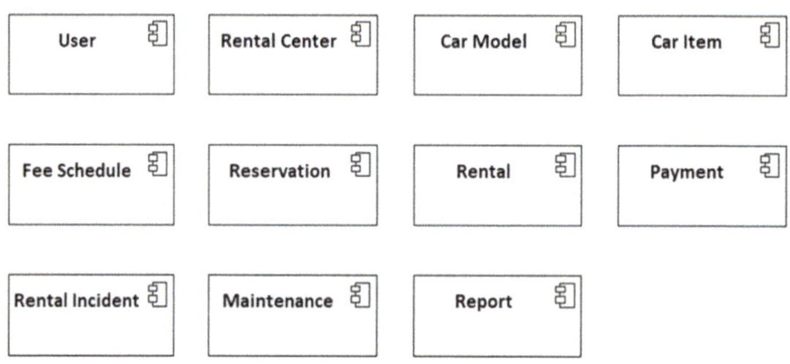

Fig. 7.14 Data Components in the Car Rental Management System

7.2.2 Task 2. Identify Data Components from Architecture Styles

This task is to define data components that represent persistent datasets manipulated by architecture-specific functional components. As outlined in the functional view design, certain architecture styles require the implementation of functional components to support their intended behavior. These components typically manipulate specific datasets, which may or may not be designated as persistent.

For example, the *Dispatcher* Architecture Style requires two functional components: the *QoS Evaluator* and the *Server Dispatcher*, which manipulate the *QoS Measurement Dataset* and the *Server Allocation Dataset*, respectively. If these datasets are designated as persistent, they should be mapped to data components, as illustrated in Fig. 7.15.

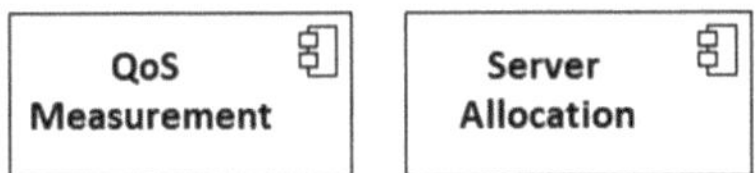

Fig. 7.15 Data Components Derived from Architecture Style

7.3 Step 3. Allocate Data Components

This step involves assigning data components to appropriate data placeholders within the schematic architecture. A *data placeholder* refers to a designated location in the architecture where components responsible for object persistence are deployed.

7.3.1 Task 1. Assign Data Components onto Tiers

This task involves assigning each data component to one or more tiers within the schematic architecture. This allocation determines where the responsibility for managing persistent data resides. The placement of data components can be represented using a table, as illustrated in Table 7.1.

Table 7.1 Data Component Allocation Table

Tiers / Components	Tier 1	Tier 2	Tier 3
Data component 1	✓		
Data component 2		✓	
Data component 3		✓	✓
Data component 4	✓		✓
...			

The table lists the tiers defined in the schematic architecture and maps each data component to at least one tier. Each tier is responsible for managing the persistence of the data components assigned to it.

To ensure efficiency and maintainability, data components should be allocated to the same tier as the functional components that manipulate them. This approach adheres to the design principle that data manipulated by a functional component should reside within the same tier, thereby minimizing cross-tier dependencies and enhancing overall system performance and maintainability.

Example

Consider the allocation of data components for the Car Rental Management System. The system's schematic architecture consists of four physical nodes. To ensure alignment with functional responsibilities, data components should be assigned to the appropriate tiers based on the functional components deployed in each tier. The resulting allocation is shown in Table 7.2.

Table 7.2 Data Component Allocation for Car Rental Management System

Data Components \ Tiers	Mobile Client	Rental Center Client	Dispatcher Server	Headquarters Server
User	✓	✓		✓
Rental center		✓		✓
Car model		✓		✓
Car item		✓		✓
Fee schedule		✓ **(Read)**		✓
Reservation	✓	✓ **(Read)**		✓ **(Read)**
Rental	✓ **(Read)**	✓		✓ **(Read)**
Payment		✓		✓
Rental incident		✓		✓
Maintenance		✓		✓ **(Read)**
Report		✓		✓

Each data component in the system is assigned to at least one tier. When a data component is distributed across multiple tiers, its access privileges may vary by tier. For example, the *Reservation* data component is allocated to three tiers: the *Mobile Client* tier supports full CRUD operations, whereas the *Rental Center Client* and *Headquarters Server* tiers are limited to read-only access.

Note that the *Dispatcher Server* tier is not assigned any data components, indicating that it does not manage or persist application data.

7.3.2 Task 2. Identify Data Placeholders

This task is to identify data placeholders defined in a schematic architecture. A *data placeholder* serves as a container for accommodating data components. These placeholders are typically represented as layers—or partitions within layers—dedicated to persistent data management.

To identify data placeholders, analyze the schematic architecture to determine where data components should logically reside. This involves reviewing the allocation of functional requirements and evaluating the dependencies between functional components and their associated data. Based on this analysis, data components can be appropriately assigned to corresponding placeholders.

Example

Consider the identification of data placeholders within the schematic architecture of the Car Rental Management System. Figure 7.16 shows the data placeholders of this system.

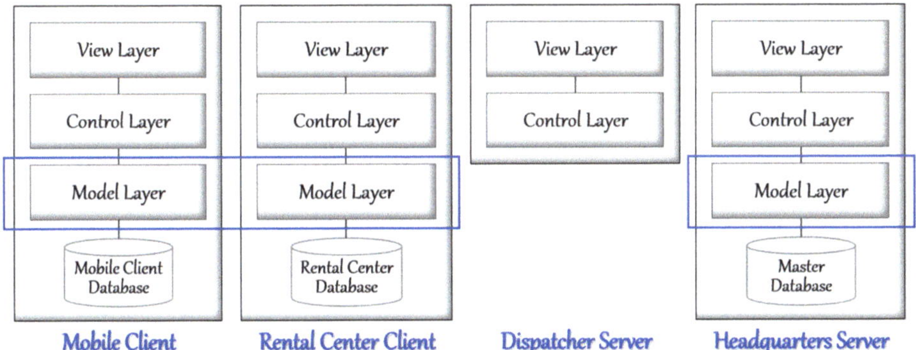

Fig. 7.16 Data Placeholders in Car Rental Management System

Three tiers of the architecture—*Mobile Client*, *Rental Center Client*, and *Headquarters Server*—include a *Model Layer*, which serves as a data placeholder for specific data components. The *Dispatcher Server* tier, however, does not include a data placeholder, as it does not manage or persist any datasets.

7.3.3 Task 3. Allocate Data Components onto Placeholders

This task involves assigning data components to their designated data placeholders. The allocation is performed by mapping each data component to the appropriate data placeholder within its corresponding tier, using the placement information summarized in Table 7.2.

Example

The data components for the Car Rental Management System are allocated according to their placement table, and the resulting allocation is illustrated in Fig. 7.17.

Data Components \ Tiers	Mobile Client	Rental Center Client	Dispatcher Server	Headquarters Server
User	✓	✓		✓
Rental Center		✓		✓
Car Model		✓		✓
Car Item		✓		✓
Fee Schedule		✓ (Read)		✓
Reservation	✓	✓ (Read)		✓ (Read)
Rental	✓ (Read)	✓		✓ (Read)
Payment		✓		✓
Rental Incident		✓		✓
Maintenance		✓		✓ (Read)
Report		✓		✓

Fig. 7.17 Allocation of Data Components to Data Placeholders

The data components for each tier, as specified in the table, are assigned to the corresponding data placeholders within that tier. With the allocation of both functional and data components, the schematic architecture is now more complete and structurally coherent.

Now, the schematic architecture of the system is further refined through the allocation of both functional and data components, as illustrated in Fig. 7.18.

In this figure, the *Control Layers* (shaded in gray) are populated with their respective functional components, while the *Model Layers* (shaded in black) are populated with the corresponding data components. This layered allocation enhances the schematic architecture by making it more complete, modular, and operationally representative.

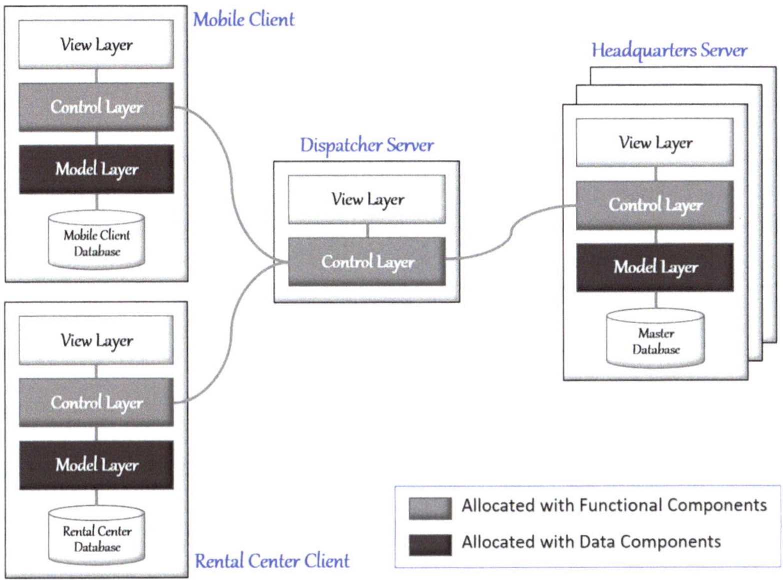

Fig. 7.18 Schematic Architecture with Functional and Data Components

7.4 Step 4. Define Data Component Interfaces

This step involves defining interfaces for data components. A *data component interface* serves as the public access point for interacting with the data managed by the component. It is typically specified as a set of method signatures accompanied by semantic descriptions.

Data component interfaces differ from those of functional components in both purpose and design. Whereas functional component interfaces expose services and behaviors, data component interfaces are primarily concerned with providing controlled access to underlying datasets. These interfaces support data encapsulation, enforce consistency, and apply access constraints—ensuring secure, maintainable, and efficient data management.

Methods in Data Component Interfaces

Data component interfaces typically provide methods that support CRUD-based operations, which encompass the following:

- **Create Methods**
  These methods add new data entries, such as *createRecord()* or *insertData()*. They often include validation logic to ensure data integrity during the creation process.
- **Read Methods**
  These methods retrieve data, such as *getDataById()* or *fetchAllRecords()*. They may include capabilities for filtering, sorting, and querying specific subsets of data to enhance retrieval efficiency.

- **Update Methods**
  These methods modify existing data, such as *updateRecord()* or *modifyData()*. They enforce validation rules and constraints to ensure consistent and correct updates.
- **Delete Methods**
  These methods remove data entries, such as *deleteRecord()* or *removeData()*. Safeguards are often included to prevent unintended data loss and maintain referential integrity.
  In addition to standard CRUD operations, data component interfaces may also include methods for managing transactional behavior and enforcing business constraints:
- **Data Transaction Methods**
  These methods, such as *commitTransaction()* and *rollbackTransaction()*, manage transactional boundaries. Advanced protocols like two-phase commit may also be applied to ensure atomicity, consistency, and recoverability in the event of failures.
- **Validation Methods**
  These methods, such as *validateData()*, enforce business rules and structural constraints before data is created or updated, helping maintain application-level integrity.

7.4.1 Task 1. Select Target Data Components

This task is to identify the data components that require a precise and well-defined interface specification. Architects focus on selecting components with the following characteristics and define their interfaces accordingly:

- **Components with High Complexity**
  These components often require a large set of interface methods due to their intricate functionality. As a result, their interfaces tend to be complex and demand careful definition. In such cases, architects typically assume responsibility for designing the interface themselves to ensure clarity, consistency, and alignment with system requirements.
- **Components Requiring Interface Standardization**
  Some components require standardized interfaces to support consistent access across multiple modules. For example, components responsible for managing shared data stores should expose stable and uniform interfaces to ensure consistent data retrieval and manipulation during runtime.

For example, in the Car Rental Management System, data components such as *Rental*, *Rental Incident*, and *Maintenance* exhibit high complexity and require interface standardization.

7.4.2 Task 2. Define Interfaces of Data Components

This task is to define the interfaces of the selected data components. Data components are derived from the class diagram by grouping related persistent object classes. Accordingly, the interface of a data component is defined by logically consolidating the methods of its constituent classes and ensuring that the resulting interface provides the required functionality.

The interfaces of data components can be systematically defined by applying the following procedure:

[1] **Define Methods for Classes with Inheritance**

When a data component includes classes with an inheritance hierarchy, the superclass or abstract class encapsulates common persistent attributes. Define methods in the superclass to manage these shared attributes, thereby avoiding redundancy and promoting consistency across subclasses.

Additionally, define subclass-specific methods to handle attributes unique to each subclass or concrete class. This ensures specialized functionality while preserving consistency with the superclass.

For example, the data component *Payment* includes four persistent object classes, as shown in Fig. 7.19.

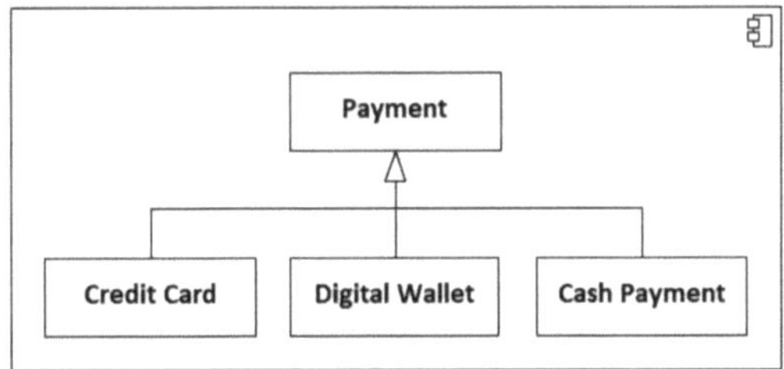

Fig. 7.19 Interface of Payment Data Component

- **Methods for Superclass, *Payment***

  Define methods to manipulate shared attributes such as *paymentId*, *amount*, *paymentDate*, and *status*, as shown below.

  + createPayment(paymentId: String, amount: double, paymentDate: String, status: String): void
  + getPaymentDetials(paymentId: String): Payment
  + updatePayment(payment: Payment): Boolean
  + deletePayment(): void

- **Methods for Subclasses**

  Subclasses extend the superclass by introducing attributes specific to each subclass. Accordingly, define methods to manipulate these subclass-specific attributes.

  In the example of *Payment* component, three subclasses extend the superclass by introducing additional attributes. Accordingly, define methods for manipulating these subclass-specific attributes.

[2] **Define Methods for Classes with Composition and Aggregation**
For data components that include persistent object classes with composition or aggregation, define methods in the data component interface to manage both class-specific data and inter-class relationships. This includes methods for handling CRUD operations on attributes specific to each class, as well as methods for managing the interactions and relationships between whole and part object classes, ensuring consistency and appropriate lifecycle management for composition and aggregation.

[3] **Define Methods for Supporting Data Transactions**
For data components that require transactional integrity, define methods that support both data transactions and validation. Data transaction methods are responsible for ensuring atomicity, consistency, isolation, and durability (ACID) of operations, allowing multi-step processes to either complete successfully or roll back entirely in the event of failure.
In parallel, validation methods ensure that data complies with business rules, constraints, and inter-object relationships before it is persisted or used. These methods prevent invalid data from being processed or stored.

7.5 Step 5. Design Object Persistence

This step is to design object persistence for data components, typically using database management systems (DBMS) or cloud storage solutions. Object persistence refers to the mechanisms used to store and retrieve objects so that their states are maintained beyond the execution of a program. This step is essential for systems requiring reliable, long-term data storage.

The key objectives of object persistence design are as follows:

- **State preservation**: Ensures that object states can be saved and restored after the application terminates or restarts
- **Data sharing and synchronization**: Support seamless sharing and synchronization of object states across multiple instances or distributed environments
- **System reliability**: Maintain data consistency and integrity during storage and retrieval, even in the event of system failures
- **Scalability**: Enable efficient handling of growing data volumes and concurrent access as the system scales

7.5.1 Task 1. Determine Object Persistence Medium

This task is to identify the most suitable medium for supporting object persistence. The *Object Persistence Medium* refers to the underlying storage mechanism or platform used to retain and retrieve objects in a manner that ensures their durability beyond the lifetime of program execution.

Object persistence can be achieved through various types of persistence media. The selection of an appropriate medium depends on factors such as the characteristics of the data model, performance and scalability requirements, and the programming language and framework employed.

Mapping to Relational Database

A relational database organizes and stores data in a tabular format consisting of tables, rows, and columns. Mapping persistent objects to a relational database involves a process called *Object-Relational Mapping* (*ORM*), a technique that bridges the gap between object-oriented programming and relational databases.

Although architects can manually define explicit mappings between classes and database tables, this approach is often tedious, time-consuming, and error-prone. To address these challenges, it is strongly recommended to utilize an ORM framework, which automates the majority of the mapping process, thereby improving efficiency, reliability, and reducing the risk of human error.

The typical steps for mapping objects to a relational database using an ORM framework are as follows:

[1] **Define Persistent Classes**
Identify the classes representing the domain objects to be persisted and annotate or configure them with metadata to define their mapping to database tables.

[2] **Configure ORM Metadata**
Specify mappings between class attributes and database table columns using annotations or configuration files.

[3] **Establish Relationships**
Define associations between classes (e.g., one-to-one, one-to-many, many-to-many), and map them to foreign key constraints in the database using ORM-specific constructs.

[4] **Generate Database Schema (Optional)**
Automatically generate the database schema based on class definitions and mapping configurations provided to the ORM framework.

[5] **Persist Objects**
Save class instances into the database by invoking persistence methods provided by the ORM framework.

[6] **Query and Retrieve Objects**
Execute queries using the ORM framework to retrieve data from the database, and map it back to objects.

[7] **Manage Transactions**
Wrap database operations in transactions using the ORM framework's transaction management capabilities to maintain data consistency and integrity.

ORM frameworks provide a high-level abstraction for interacting with relational databases using object-oriented constructs. They streamline development by automating SQL generation, schema mapping, and transaction management, making them especially effective for complex domain models aligned with object-oriented design. However, ORMs must bridge the *object-relational impedance mismatch*—the conceptual and structural differences between objects and relational tables—which can introduce complexity in certain mappings.

Mapping to Object Database

Mapping to an object database involves storing objects directly in their native form, eliminating the need for conversion to relational tables. Object databases are designed to integrate seamlessly with object-oriented programming paradigms, allowing objects—along with their attributes, relationships, and methods—to persist in the database. This approach eliminates the need for ORM frameworks and simplifies the persistence process.

Unlike relational databases, object databases natively support complex data structures, inheritance hierarchies, and associations. This enables more intuitive and efficient storage and retrieval of objects, closely aligning with object-oriented design principles.

The typical steps for mapping objects to an object database are as follows:

[1] **Define Persistent Classes**
Developers begin by defining classes in the application code that model the domain entities to be persisted. These classes encapsulate attributes, behaviors (methods), and relationships with other objects.

[2] **Annotate or Configure Persistence Properties (if required)**
Depending on the object database implementation, developers may need to annotate classes or apply configuration settings to indicate persistence behavior, inheritance mappings, and cascading rules.

[3] **Instantiate and Populate Objects**
Instances of the defined classes are created and populated with relevant data at runtime, including the establishment of object references that represent inter-object relationships.

[4] **Store Objects in the Database**
The object database persists the instantiated objects, preserving their attributes, relationships, and internal structure. The storage process is typically managed through the database's API or transaction interface.

[5] **Assign and Manage Object Identifiers (OIDs)**
Upon storage, each object is automatically assigned a unique Object Identifier (OID), which enables efficient retrieval, reference resolution, and version tracking.

[6] **Retrieve and Navigate Objects**
Objects are retrieved using their OIDs or query mechanisms provided by the object database. Relationships can be navigated directly via object references, supporting efficient traversal of complex object graphs.

Object databases provide seamless integration with object-oriented programming by allowing direct persistence of objects, including their attributes, relationships, and behaviors. This eliminates the need for object-relational mapping and reduces development complexity, especially for applications with rich domain models and deep inheritance hierarchies. They also support complex data types and provide efficient traversal of object graphs, making them well suited for domains such as engineering, scientific computing, and simulation. However, object databases face limitations such as limited standardization, lower adoption in industry, and reduced compatibility with widely-used query and reporting tools.

Mapping to NoSQL Database

Mapping objects to a NoSQL database involves designing data structures and relationships tailored to the specific type of NoSQL database, such as document stores, key-value stores, column-family stores, or graph databases. Unlike relational databases, NoSQL databases offer greater flexibility in schema design, enabling developers to efficiently manage unstructured or semi-structured data.

NoSQL databases are classified according to their underlying data model and the way they organize and store information. Each type of NoSQL database is characterized by distinct data modeling strategies, design principles, and typical use cases.

The primary types of NoSQL databases are summarized below:

- **Document Databases**
  Document databases store data in formats such as JSON, BSON, or XML-like documents, enabling hierarchical and flexible schemas in which each document encapsulates a complete entity. They are well suited for applications such as content management systems, e-commerce catalogs, and systems requiring frequently evolving schemas.
- **Key-Value Stores**
  Key-value stores manage data as simple key-value pairs, optimized for high-performance operations such as rapid lookups and writes. Typical use cases include session management, caching, and real-time analytics, such as leaderboard computations.
- **Column-Family Stores**
  Column-family stores organize data into rows and columns grouped into families, offering efficient handling of sparse datasets and high-volume writes. They are commonly used for time-series data, large-scale analytical processing, and workloads that demand high availability and write efficiency.
- **Graph Databases**
  Graph databases represent data as nodes, edges, and properties, allowing for the efficient traversal and querying of complex relationships. They are particularly effective in domains such as social networking, fraud detection, recommendation systems, and other applications involving interconnected data.

NoSQL data models offer significant advantages, including schema flexibility, horizontal scalability, and high performance for specific workloads such as real-time analytics, caching, and content management. They are particularly well suited for handling unstructured or semi-structured data and align closely with modern application requirements in distributed, cloud-native environments. However, these benefits come with trade-offs: NoSQL systems often sacrifice strong consistency for availability and partition tolerance, lack standardized query languages, and may require developers to manage more complex application-level data integrity. As a result, careful consideration is needed when choosing NoSQL over traditional relational models.

Mapping to Cloud Storage

Mapping objects to cloud storage involves persisting and retrieving application data using cloud-based, distributed storage infrastructures. In this approach, objects are typically serialized into formats such as JSON, XML, or binary and stored as files or binary large objects (blobs) in services such as Amazon Simple Storage Service (S3), Google Cloud Storage (GCS), or Microsoft Azure Blob Storage.

Unlike traditional file systems or relational databases, cloud object storage separates the physical storage layer from the compute layer, enabling independent and elastic scaling of both storage capacity and processing resources. This architectural decoupling supports flexible deployment models and aligns well with modern cloud-native design principles.

As a persistence medium, cloud object storage offers several key advantages: virtually unlimited scalability, high durability through built-in redundancy and geo-replication, and global accessibility via standardized APIs. It is particularly effective for managing unstructured or semi-structured data—such as multimedia content, log files, and backups—and supports advanced features like object versioning, lifecycle management, and fine-grained access control.

However, this approach also presents limitations: it typically incurs higher access latency compared to local or in-memory storage; it lacks native support for transactional guarantees; and it does not provide built-in mechanisms for complex querying. These limitations often require integration with complementary services such as cloud databases, data lakes, or search engines to support advanced data processing and analysis.

Mapping to File System

Mapping objects to a file system involves persisting and retrieving serialized objects using a file-based storage mechanism. It involves converting in-memory object instances into a serialized format—commonly JSON, XML, or binary—and writing the serialized data to files using the host language's file I/O facilities. Developers typically determine a file structure that reflects the application's data model, such as storing each object in a separate file or grouping related objects into a directory.

To retrieve persisted objects, the application reads the appropriate file, parses its contents, and reconstructs the object in memory through deserialization. This mapping process requires explicit implementation of serialization and deserialization logic, along with a file-naming convention and path management strategy to ensure consistency and traceability.

File system-based persistence offers simplicity, low overhead, and ease of implementation, making it suitable for small-scale applications, development prototypes, or environments with minimal resource requirements. It allows objects to be serialized into formats such as JSON, XML, or binary and stored directly as files, without the need for a database engine or network connectivity.

However, this approach has significant limitations: it lacks support for structured querying, transactional guarantees, concurrency control, and indexing. Moreover, as data volume grows, performance degrades, and maintainability becomes increasingly difficult. Due to these limitations, file system-based persistence is generally unsuitable for production-grade systems and is rarely adopted in modern, scalable, or multi-user applications.

7.5.2 Task 2. Apply Selected Object Persistence Medium

This task is to apply the selected object persistence medium to implement persistent storage for objects in accordance with the system's functional and non-functional requirements. It involves configuring the chosen medium and mapping application objects to the appropriate storage structures.

The implementation process is largely determined by the characteristics of the selected persistence medium. It typically includes defining data schemas or object mappings, implementing serialization and deserialization where applicable, and integrating the persistence medium with the application's data access layer. This task also ensures that the persistence layer provides essential capabilities such as transaction management, indexing, and data validation to maintain data consistency and integrity.

Through appropriate configuration, integration, and validation, this task establishes a reliable and efficient persistence mechanism that satisfies the system's performance, scalability, and reliability goals.

7.5.3 Task 3. Design for Data Resilience

Data Resilience refers to a system's ability to maintain data accessibility, consistency, and recoverability in the face of disruptions, failures, or unexpected events. This encompasses mechanisms to safeguard data against hardware malfunctions, software errors, cyberattacks, and natural disasters—while minimizing downtime and preventing data loss.

A resilient system incorporates strategies such as scheduled data backups, comprehensive recovery plans, redundancy, and fault-tolerant storage to preserve data integrity and availability.

Key guidelines for designing data resilience are outlined below:

- **Design Backup Policy and Schemes**
  This task involves designing mechanisms for regularly backing up persistent datasets to ensure data availability and integrity during system faults or failures. The backup policy should specify backup frequency, backup types (e.g., full, incremental, differential), and storage locations (e.g., local, remote, or cloud based). Redundancy and encryption should also be employed to enhance reliability and security.
- **Design Recovery Policy and Schemes**
  This task focuses on defining strategies for efficient data recovery in the event of data loss or corruption. Recovery policies should outline procedures for restoring backups, prioritizing critical datasets, and minimizing system downtime. Recovery point objectives (RPO) and recovery time objectives (RTO) must be established to satisfy business continuity requirements.
- **Design Archiving and Retention**
  This task defines policies for archiving datasets that are no longer actively used but must be retained for compliance, historical analysis, or auditing purposes. The design should include criteria for identifying archival data, specify retention periods based on regulatory or business needs, and adopt storage mechanisms that optimize cost, security, and long-term accessibility.

Together, these design activities establish a resilient data infrastructure that safeguards against loss, ensures timely recovery, and supports long-term accessibility.

7.6 Checklist for A4b: Information View Design

The following checklist items can be used to validate the design for information view.

7.6.1 Checklist for Step 1: Refine Persistent Object Model

Have all persistent datasets within the system been clearly identified?

Are persistent classes appropriately defined for all identified datasets, ensuring comprehensive coverage of the data domain?

Are logical classes—such as session-related or technology-dependent classes—properly represented in the model?

Are all associations between classes correctly defined, including those involving association classes with attributes?

Has the use of structural design patterns been considered and applied to enhance the organization and relationships among persistent object classes?

Are all persistent attributes within each class explicitly identified and clearly defined?

7.6.2 Checklist for Step 2: Define Data Components

Has the order and hierarchy of class relationships been analyzed to identify cohesive sets of related classes for grouping into data components?

Are the data components designed to ensure high cohesion and modularity, thereby facilitating maintainability and clarity?

Are dependencies and interactions between data components minimized to reduce coupling and increase independence?

Are part-object classes grouped with whole-object classes only when no other associations exist outside the current aggregation, ensuring exclusive and meaningful composition?

7.6.3 Checklist for Step 3: Allocate Data Components

Have all data components been correctly assigned to their respective tiers or layers within the schematic architecture?

Are data components co-located with the functional components that directly manipulate them to optimize access and interaction?

Are inter-tier dependencies minimized to reduce cross-tier communication overhead and preserve architectural clarity?

Have access privileges for each distributed data component been explicitly defined to ensure secure and appropriate access?

Are critical data components strategically replicated or distributed to achieve high availability, fault tolerance, and system resilience?

7.6.4 Checklist for Step 4: Define Data Component Interfaces

Are the public interfaces of data components clearly defined using CRUD operations to support core data manipulation tasks?

Are methods for managing transactions—such as commit, rollback, and validation—included where applicable?

Are method signatures fully specified, including visibility, parameters, return types, and relevant constraints?

Are common attribute operations for superclasses properly defined to promote consistency across all related data components?

Are subclass-specific methods carefully defined with appropriate visibility, ensuring public methods are exposed while internal logic remains encapsulated?

7.6.5 Checklist for Step 5: Design Object Persistence

Has the persistence medium (e.g., relational database, NoSQL database, or cloud storage) been selected appropriately to align with the system's functional and non-functional requirements?

Are the mapping techniques—such as Object-Relational Mapping (ORM) for relational databases or Object-Document Mapping (ODM) for NoSQL databases—correctly implemented to ensure seamless translation between objects and their persistent representations?

Are backup and recovery mechanisms comprehensively defined, properly implemented, and thoroughly tested to protect against data loss or corruption?

Have data sharing and synchronization strategies been designed to maintain consistency and availability across distributed system environments?

Have the persistence mechanisms been rigorously tested to validate fault tolerance, reliability, and resilience under failure conditions?

7.7 Exercise Problems

1. **Refinement of Context-Level Class Diagram**
   Refining the context-level class diagram is critical for clarifying the high-level structure of persistent entities and their relationships. What types of refinements can be applied to improve the accuracy and completeness of the information context?
2. **Essence of Association Class**
   An association class in a class diagram is a modeling construct that enables an association—particularly one involving a many-to-many cardinality—to encapsulate its own attributes and operations. Interpret and compare the two alternative approaches to modeling many-to-many relationships illustrated below.
3. **Identifying Session Classes for an eLearning System**
   A session class is a logical object class that records temporal or activity-specific information related to a transaction or user interaction. Identify appropriate session classes for an eLearning system in which students participate in online learning activities and instructors manage lecture materials and grading. Assign meaningful names to the session classes, and describe their respective roles within the system.
4. **Refining the Context-Level Class Diagram for a Food Delivery System**
   Refine the class diagram representing the information context of the Food Delivery System. Identify deficiencies in the initial diagram and revise it accordingly. Compare the context-level class diagram with the view-level class diagram by listing all changes made.
5. **Defining Data Components**
   Derive data components from the refined class diagram of the Food Delivery System, and represent them using a UML Component Diagram. Group related classes into data components by analyzing the strength of the relationships between class pairs.

6. **Strength of Inheritance Relationship Between Classes**
   Inheritance is considered the strongest type of relationship in a class diagram. Explain why inheritance represents the strongest relationship between a superclass and its subclass.
7. **Comparing the Strengths of Composition and Aggregation Relationships**
   Both composition and aggregation are used to model containment relationships in class diagrams. Explain why the relationship between two classes connected by composition is considered stronger than that between two classes connected by aggregation.
8. **Data Placeholders in Architecture Styles**
   A data placeholder is a designated element within an architectural schema intended to accommodate data components responsible for enabling object persistence. Accordingly, data placeholders are present in architecture styles that involve the management of persistent data. Identify architecture styles that incorporate data placeholders, as well as those that do not.
9. **Allocation of Data Components onto Multi-Tiered Architectures**
   In a multi-tier architecture, a data component may be distributed across multiple tiers under certain conditions. What scenarios necessitate the distribution of a data component across different tiers within a schematic architecture? Describe how the contents and responsibilities of such components vary when allocated to different tiers. Provide a specific example illustrating the distribution of a data component across multiple tiers.
10. **Consistency Between Functional Component and Data Component Allocations**
    Describe the design principle that emphasizes the co-location of a functional component and the data component(s) it accesses within the same architectural tier. Explain how this alignment promotes efficiency, maintainability, and architectural coherence.
11. **Comparing Data Component and Functional Component Interfaces**
    A data component interface defines a public protocol for accessing and manipulating the data managed by the component. Explain how the interface of a data component differs from that of a functional component. Use a specific example to illustrate this distinction.
12. **Identifying the Object Persistency Medium for a LLM Service Provider**
    A large language model (LLM) service provider system typically serves a high volume of concurrent users and maintains session data comprising user prompts and corresponding model responses. Identify an appropriate object persistency medium for this system. Justify your choice by analyzing the structure and volatility of the data (e.g., prompt-response pairs, user metadata), access characteristics (e.g., high write throughput, sequential or indexed retrieval), and system scalability requirements.

Activity A4c. Design for Behavior View

8

Objective of the Chapter

The objective of this chapter is to provide guidelines for designing the behavior view of a software system. It covers the refinement of the system's overall control flow to ensure cohesion across runtime operations, the identification of key behavioral elements with significant control logic or interaction complexity, and the specification of detailed control flows for these elements using appropriate behavioral modeling techniques. These guidelines enable architects to construct a precise and analyzable behavior architecture that accurately represents the system's dynamic behavior in alignment with functional requirements and architectural integrity.

Introducing Activity A4c. Design for Behavior View

This activity is to design the architecture for the behavior view of a target system. The behavior view of software architecture primarily addresses the system's runtime behavior and the detailed control flows of selected behavioral elements.

The functional and behavior views offer complementary yet distinct perspectives on system design. The functional view focuses on *what* the system does, encapsulating its services and features. In contrast, the behavior view focuses on *how* the system operates at runtime, detailing dynamic interactions, state transitions, and control flows that bring the functionalities to life.

The comparison between these two views is summarized in Table 8.1.

S. D. Kim, M. Kim, *Hands-on Software Architecture*,
https://doi.org/10.1007/978-3-032-01184-8_8

Table 8.1 Comparison Between Functional View and Behavior View Designs

Aspects	Functional View Design	Behavior View Design
Perspective	Static representation of system capabilities and features	Representation of system's dynamic behavior in terms of control flows and interactions
Focus	Addresses what the system does in terms of functionality	Describes how components operate and interact dynamically
Key Artifacts	Use Case Diagram, Component Diagram, Component Interface	Activity Diagram, Sequence Diagram, State Machine Diagram, Algorithm
Impactson Testing	Provides context for functional testing and validation	Defines paths for integration testing and system-level testing

Steps in A4c. Behavior View Design

The design for behavior view can be systematically achieved with a sequence of steps, as shown in Fig. 8.1.

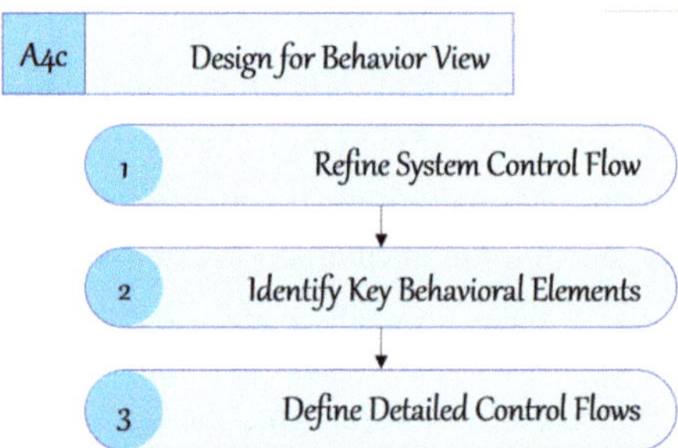

Fig. 8.1 Steps in A4c. Behavior View Design

- **Step 1. Refine Overall System Control Flow**
  This step is to refine the system's overall control flow by analyzing its runtime behavior and ensuring a well-defined and cohesive flow of control throughout the system.
- **Step 2. Identify Key Behavioral Elements**
  This step is to identify the key behavioral elements, prioritizing those with complex runtime interactions and control flows to focus the design effort on critical aspects of the system.
- **Step 3. Define Detailed Control Flow**
  This step is to define detailed control flows for the identified behavioral elements, leveraging appropriate modeling tools to capture and represent the system's runtime behavior with precision and clarity.

8.1 Step 1. Refine System Control Flow

This step is to refine the context-level system control flow by incorporating detailed observations of the system's runtime behavior. The system control flow refers to the structured sequence of interactions and transitions that govern how control is initiated, maintained, and transferred across various system components during execution.

The system control flow represents the structured patterns of runtime behavior that govern how control is initiated, maintained, and transferred across system components. It encompasses key behavioral mechanisms such as invocation methods, control transitions, synchronization, state management, and feedback loops. These elements collectively ensure coherent execution, responsiveness, and coordination throughout the system's operation.

Additionally, dynamic adaptation and error handling play critical roles in enabling the system to respond to changing conditions and recover from faults. Given the complexity and interplay of these mechanisms, the system control flow constitutes a highly intricate behavioral model, making its design both essential and inherently challenging in behavior view architecture.

Alignment Between Functional View Design and Behavior View Design

In defining the system control flow, the functional view design provides the foundation for deriving the core elements of behavioral specification represented in Activity Diagrams. This alignment ensures that the behavior view remains consistent with the system's functional requirements, promoting coherence between its structural and operational aspects.

This alignment between functional and behavioral models is illustrated in Fig. 8.2.

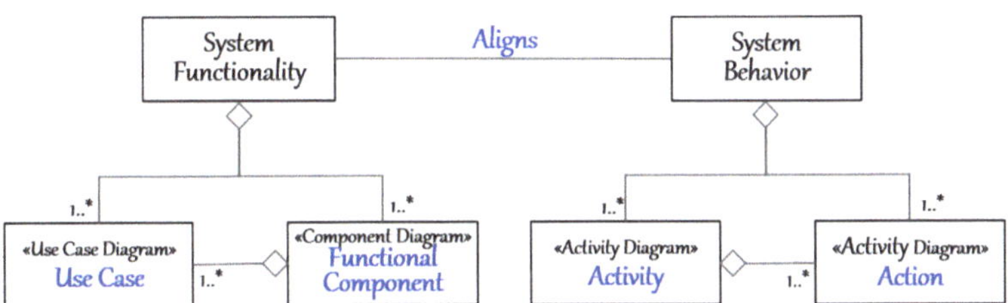

Fig. 8.2 Alignment Between Functional and Behavioral View Designs

System functionality is modeled through use cases and functional components, while system behavior is expressed through actions and activities, with each activity comprising a set of related actions. Consequently, alignment relationships exist between the elements of these two perspectives.

- **From the System Functionality Perspective**
  - A use case may correspond to a single action in the activity diagram.
  - A use case may correspond to a set of related actions in the activity diagram.
  - A use case may correspond to an activity in the activity diagram.
  - A functional component may correspond to a single action in the activity diagram.
  - A functional component may correspond to a set of related actions in the activity diagram.
  - A functional component may correspond to an activity in the activity diagram.

- **From the System Behavior Perspective**
  - An action in the activity diagram may correspond to a single use case.
  - An action in the activity diagram may correspond to a set of use cases.
  - An action in the activity diagram may correspond to a functional component.
  - An activity in the activity diagram may correspond to a set of use cases.
  - An activity in the activity diagram may correspond to a functional component.

By considering these bidirectional alignment relationships, architects can refine context-level activity diagrams to more accurately represent the system's behavior.

8.1.1 Task 1. Refine Invocation Patterns

This task is to refine the invocation patterns associated with functional components, as identified during behavior context analysis. Establishing effective invocation patterns is essential for designing a coherent and efficient system control flow.

An invocation pattern refers to a reusable control structure commonly observed in system behavior modeling. It is represented by a specific sequence of actions and activities in an Activity Diagram, each tailored to realize a particular form of control flow.

The common types of invocation patterns are revisited and further elaborated with additional details and clarifications.

Sequential Invocation

This invocation pattern is applied when a system requires actions or activities to be executed in a strict sequential order without involving loops or divergent branches. However, sequential invocation may include control flows that incorporate decision and merge nodes to support conditional progression within the linear sequence, as shown in Fig. 8.3.

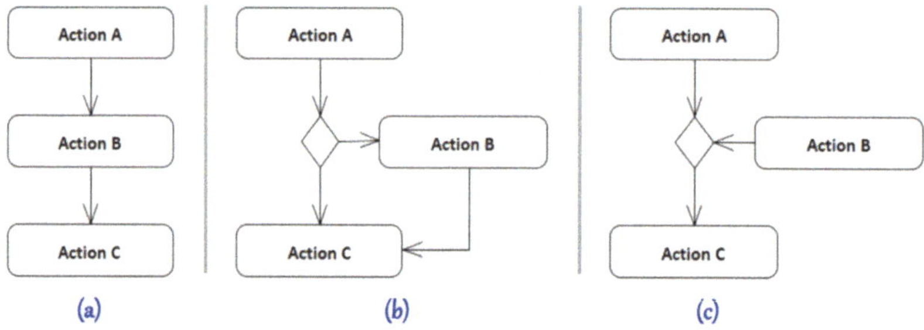

Fig. 8.3 Variations of Sequential Invocation Pattern

In the figure, diagram (a) shows a strict sequential flow in which actions are performed in a linear order without any conditional branches. Diagram (b) includes a decision node, enabling conditional execution where the control flow proceeds to either *Action B* or

Action C based on a specified condition. Diagram (c) incorporates a merge node that consolidates alternative incoming flows into a single outgoing path leading to *Action C*, thereby maintaining a sequential structure while supporting conditional entry points.

Explicit Invocation

The explicit invocation pattern is applied when a user selects an invocation option from a predefined set of choices. Typically, users interact with a main menu and, in some cases, additional submenus to make their selections. Some systems may also support multimodal input mechanisms, allowing users to invoke actions via voice commands, gesture recognition, or other input modalities.

Several variations of the explicit invocation pattern exist, each illustrating a different implementation approach. Despite these differences, all variants adhere to the core principle of user-driven selection, as shown in Fig. 8.4.

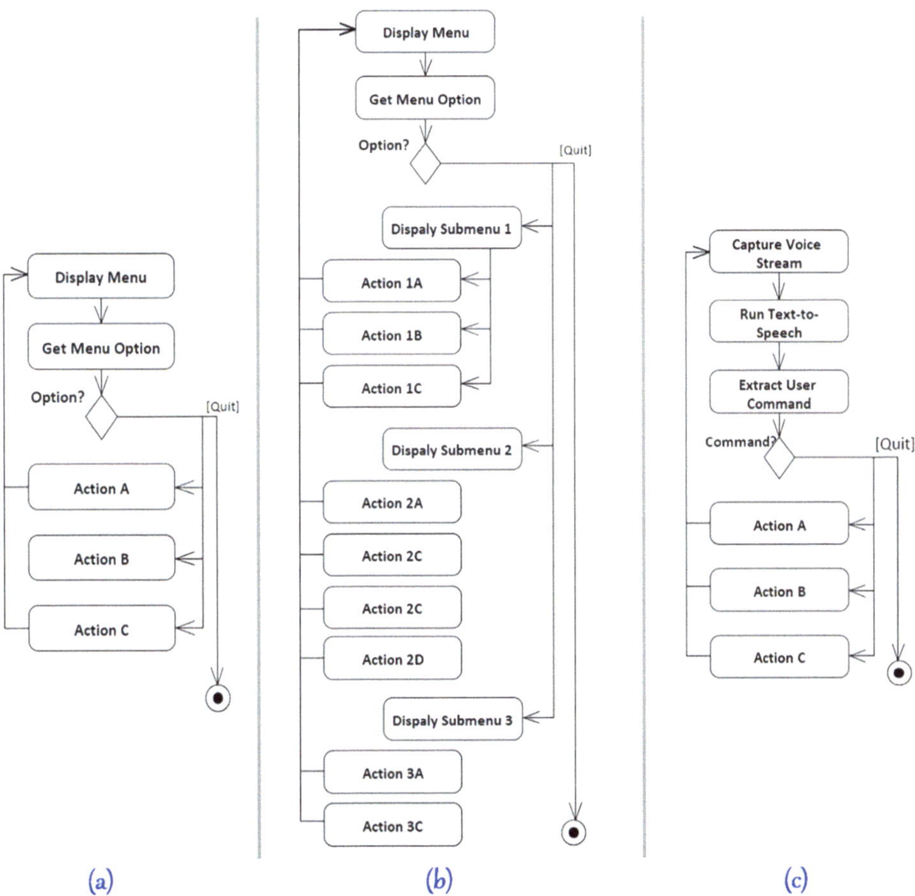

Fig. 8.4 Variations of Explicit Invocation Pattern

In the figure, diagram (a) depicts a simple menu-based structure in which users select from three direct options to invoke corresponding actions. Diagram (b) represents a hierarchical menu system that includes three submenus, each offering its own set of actions, thereby enabling more detailed user navigation. Diagram (c) demonstrates a multimodal interface in which user commands are explicitly invoked through voice input, utilizing speech processing and command extraction to support flexible, user-driven interactions.

Closed-Loop Invocation

The closed-loop invocation pattern is applied when a system requires uninterrupted, repetitive execution of a specific functionality. This pattern typically consists of a sequential control flow in which the final node is connected back to the initial node, enabling continuous and cyclic execution of the sequence.

This pattern can be extended to incorporate other invocation patterns within its loop, thereby creating structural variations. Representative examples are illustrated in Fig. 8.5.

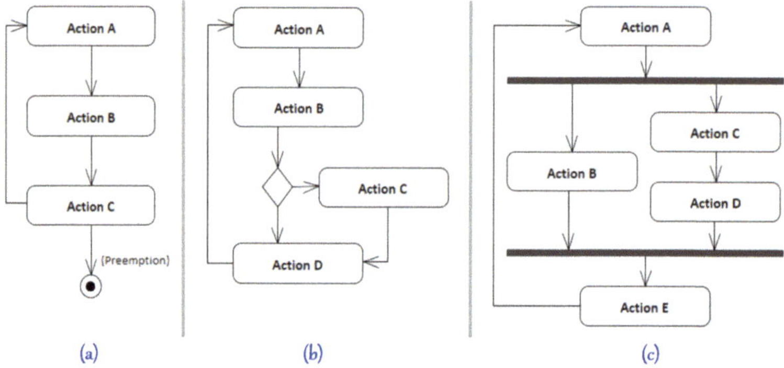

Fig. 8.5 Variations of Closed-Loop Invocation Pattern

In the figure, diagram (a) shows a simple closed loop in which actions A, B, and C are executed sequentially and then loop back to the start, with a preemption option allowing early termination. Diagram (b) introduces a decision node that enables conditional branching to either Action C or Action D before the flow returns to Action A. Diagram (c) demonstrates parallel execution in which one thread performs Action B, while the other thread executes Actions C followed by D. Both threads then synchronize before proceeding to Action E, after which the control loops back to Action A, supporting concurrent execution paths within the closed-loop structure.

The closed-loop invocation pattern is widely used to model automation and autonomous functionalities in advanced systems, as illustrated by the following examples:

- **Monitoring Systems**
  Closed-loop patterns enable continuous sensing and control. For instance, a thermostat monitors room temperature, compares it to a setpoint, and adjusts heating or cooling in a loop to maintain desired conditions.
- **Industrial Automation**
  Automation systems employ closed loops for repetitive operations. A robotic arm on an assembly line exemplifies this pattern by cyclically performing tasks such as picking, placing, or assembling components.
- **Control Systems**
  In systems like air traffic control, closed loops support uninterrupted monitoring and response. Radar systems continuously scan airspace, update aircraft positions, and adjust control parameters for safety.
- **Autonomous Systems**
  Autonomous vehicles use closed-loop control to adapt in real time. Sensor inputs are processed continuously to update perception and decision-making, and control commands are sent to actuators accordingly.
- **Real-Time Data Streaming**
  Streaming systems use closed loops for uninterrupted data capture and transmission. A video streaming app, for example, constantly captures, encodes, and transmits frames in repeating cycle.
- **Game Loops in Video Games**
  Games rely on closed loops to ensure responsiveness. The main loop updates the game state, processes user input, renders graphics, and handles events in real time.

Parallel Invocation

The parallel invocation pattern is applied when a system requires the execution of multiple threads of control concurrently. This pattern allows multiple actions or processes to run independently at the same time, enabling efficient utilization of system resources and improved performance for tasks that can be divided into smaller, independent units of work.

Parallel invocation is particularly beneficial in systems where tasks are computationally intensive or time sensitive, as it reduces overall execution time by distributing the workload.

The control flow of parallel invocation pattern is shown in Fig. 8.6.

In the figure, diagram (a) represents a parallel invocation pattern involving two concurrent threads, where each thread performs a separate sequence of actions before synchronizing at a common join point and proceeding to Action Y. Diagram (b) illustrates a parallel invocation pattern that incorporates nested parallel processing, where additional parallel branches are introduced within one of the initial threads to further divide the control flow into concurrent execution paths.

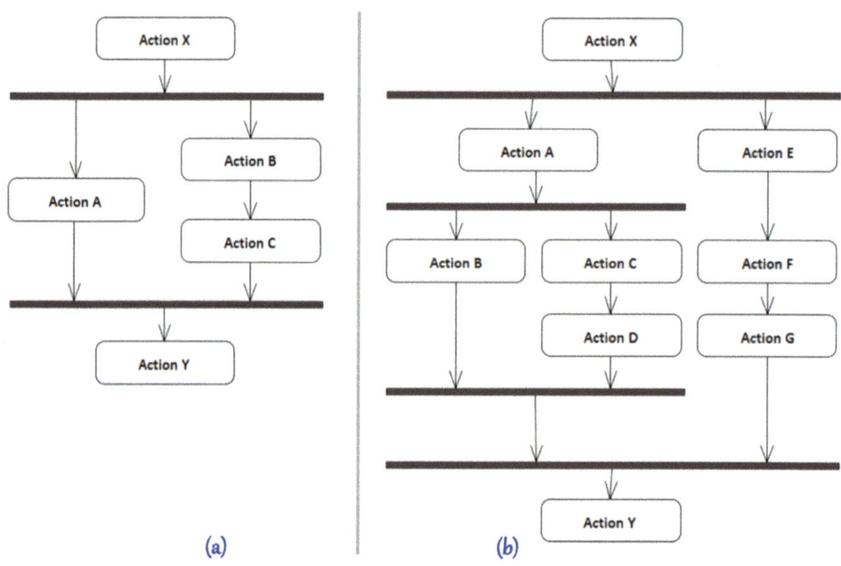

Fig. 8.6 Variations of Parallel Invocation Pattern

Event-Based Invocation

The event-based invocation pattern is applied when a system must execute functionality in response to incoming events. These events may originate from various sources, such as user interactions, environmental changes, or messages from other components. This pattern enables systems to be responsive and adaptive by executing actions only upon the occurrence of specific events, thereby optimizing resource utilization and minimizing unnecessary overhead.

This pattern is distinguished by its *asynchronous execution*, which facilitates non-blocking behavior and allows processes to proceed independently while awaiting events. It supports *dynamic adaptability*, enabling real-time responsiveness to diverse triggers. Furthermore, it fosters *loose coupling* between event producers and consumers, enhancing modularity and scalability.

Event exchanges may occur either within a single system tier or across multiple tiers, as illustrated in Fig. 8.7.

In the figure, diagram (a) illustrates an event-based invocation occurring within a single tier. *Action A* generates and sends an event labeled *E1*, which is asynchronously received by another thread within the same tier, triggering *Action C*. In parallel, *Action B* proceeds without being blocked by the event-handling sequence, while *Action D* is executed after *Action C* within the thread that processes the received event.

Diagram (b) depicts an event-based invocation across two distinct tiers. In *Tier 1*, *Action A* sends an event labeled *E1* to *Tier 2*. Upon receiving this event, *Tier 2* initiates *Action C*. Meanwhile, *Action B* in *Tier 1* proceeds independently without being blocked by the inter-tier event communication.

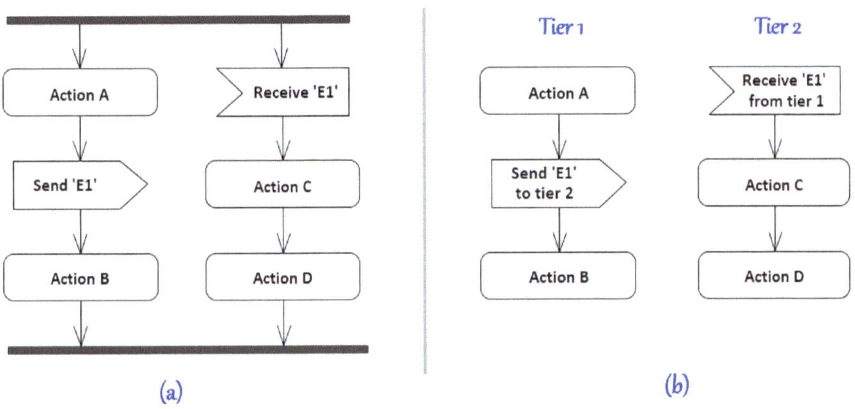

Fig. 8.7 Intra-Tier and Inter-Tier Event-Based Invocations

Timed Invocation

The timed invocation pattern is applied when a system requires the execution of functionality at specific time intervals or within predefined timing constraints. This pattern ensures that certain actions or processes are triggered according to a defined schedule or in response to temporal conditions, rather than external events or user inputs. It is commonly used in systems where precise timing or periodic execution is essential to achieving desired outcomes.

Timed invocation is often combined with a closed-loop pattern to support periodic task execution within a continuous and repetitive control flow, as illustrated in Fig. 8.8.

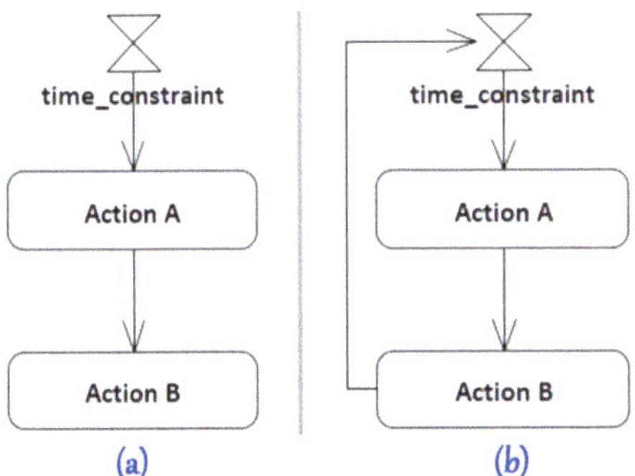

Fig. 8.8 Variations of Timed Invocation Pattern

In the figure, diagram (a) illustrates a timed control flow where actions are executed sequentially within a specified time constraint, without looping. In contrast, diagram (b) represents a timed behavior with a closed loop, where actions are repeatedly executed according to the defined timing constraint.

Invocation Patterns for Car Rental Management System

The invocation patterns for functional components in the Car Rental Management System are considered across multiple tiers. The initial context-level *Invocation Pattern Table* for this system has been further refined and is presented in Table 8.2.

Table 8.2 Refined Invocation Pattern Table for Car Rental Management System

Tiers / Functional Components	Mobile Client	Rental Center Client	Dispatcher Server	Headquarters Server
Customer Profile Manager	Explicit	Explicit (Read)		Explicit (Read)
Staff Profile Manager		Explicit		Explicit
Rental Center Profile Manager		Explicit		Explicit
Inventory Manager		Explicit		Explicit
Rental Rate Manager		Explicit (Read)		Explicit
Reservation Manager	Explicit	Explicit (Read)		Explicit (Read)
Checkout Manager	Explicit (Read)	Explicit, Event		Explicit (Read)
In-Rental Manager		Explicit, C-Loop, Event		Explicit (Read)
Return Manager	Explicit (Read)	Explicit, Event		Explicit (Read)
Payment Manager		Explicit		Explicit (Read)
Car Maintainer		Explicit		Explicit (Read)
Report Manager		Explicit, C-Loop, Timer		Explicit, C-Loop, Timer
QoS Evaluator			C-Loop, Timer	
Server Allocator			Explicit, Event	

Except for the Dispatcher Server, all tiers primarily operate using control flows based on the *explicit invocation* pattern. Many functional components in the system are distributed across multiple tiers, and the invocation pattern assigned to a given component often varies by tier. This variation reflects the distinct responsibilities and access privileges defined for each tier within the system architecture. For example, The Headquarters Server tier adopts the *Explicit Invocation* pattern for the *In-Rental Manager* component, whereas the Rental Center Client tier employs explicit and event-based invocation patterns, along with closed-loop control.

8.1.2 Task 2. Refine System Control Flows

This task is to refine the context-level activity diagrams based on the updated behavioral scope and the refined interaction patterns. The activity diagram for each tier is enhanced to align with the revised scope and associated invocation mechanisms, thereby reflecting the updated system control flows in a consistent and accurate manner.

Organization of Control Flows in Activity Diagrams

The activity diagram serves as a flexible modeling tool, offering a rich set of constructs for representing control flows across diverse software systems. Regardless of the specific application domain, activity diagrams often exhibit recurring behavioral structures that play a critical role in defining and organizing system-level control flows.

These common behavioral elements in an activity diagram are depicted in Fig. 8.9.

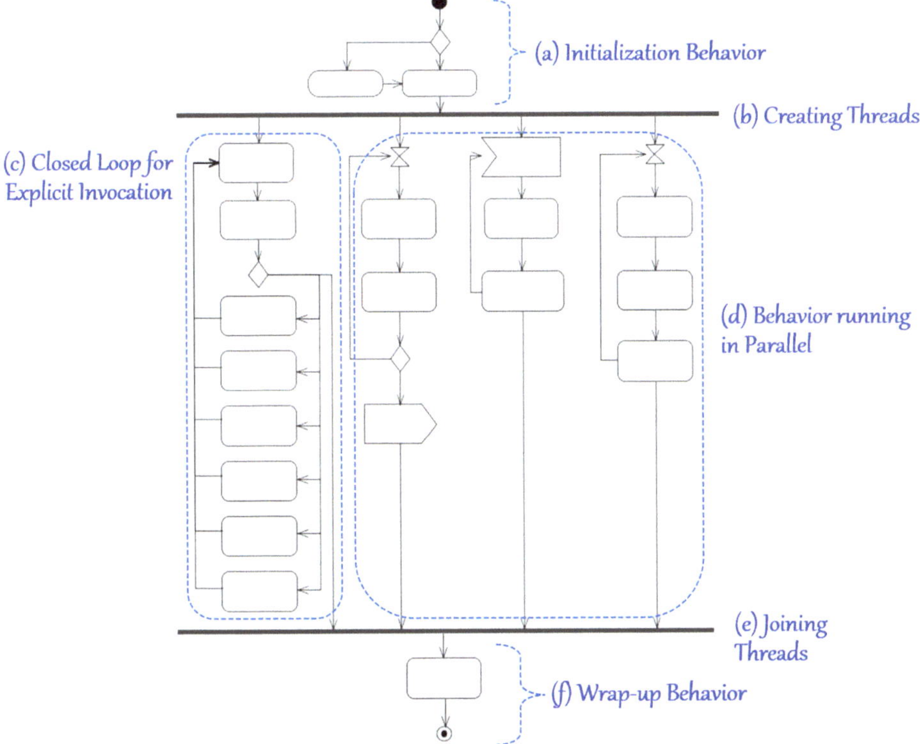

Fig. 8.9 Behavioral Elements in Activity Diagram

The figure illustrates several common behavioral elements that frequently appear in various activity diagrams, labeled (a) through (f).

(a) **Initialization Behavior**
This part defines an *Initial Node* followed by a sequence of initialization tasks that must be executed before the activation of the system's primary functional components. These tasks may include user authentication procedures such as logging in or signing up, displaying welcome messages on the startup screen, initializing connected hardware devices, and establishing network connections with external systems.

(b) **Creating Threads**
This part represents the initiation of multiple concurrent threads or execution flows to enable parallel processing. It involves identifying tasks that can execute independently and launching separate threads to handle them—*by referring to the identified invocation patterns*. This structure enhances system responsiveness and supports efficient utilization of processing resources.

(c) **Closed Loop for Explicit Invocation**
This part defines a closed-loop control flow for actions or activities triggered by *explicit invocation*. It typically consists of a sequential execution path with conditional branches embedded within the loop, enabling dynamic decision-making during iteration. The loop may also incorporate the capability to emit events that invoke other threads, thereby facilitating inter-thread coordination. This structure ensures that repeated actions are executed efficiently while maintaining synchronization with other concurrent activities as needed.

(d) **Behavior Running in Parallel**
This part represents the concurrent execution of multiple threads, where each thread independently performs its own sequence of actions or activities. It leverages parallel control flows to enhance system responsiveness and improve overall processing efficiency.
The parallel threads in this structure are typically associated with different invocation patterns, as described below:
   - **Thread with Closed-Loop Invocation**
     This thread executes a predefined sequence of actions repetitively. As a closed loop, it operates autonomously without external intervention, ensuring uninterrupted cyclic execution.
   - **Thread Triggered by Event-Based Invocation**
     This thread is activated upon receiving a specific event, which may be dispatched by another thread or system component. The asynchronous nature of event-based invocation supports loose coupling and flexible coordination.

- **Thread Triggered by Timed Invocation**
  This thread is executed periodically at specified intervals or within predefined timing constraints. Timed invocation ensures regular task execution based on scheduling requirements.
  Part (d) of the figure illustrates the control flows that combine closed-loop invocation with event-driven and timed invocation patterns.

(e) **Joining Threads**
This part consolidates multiple parallel threads into a single control flow. It ensures proper synchronization by pausing execution until all concurrent threads have completed. Once all parallel activities terminate, the unified control flow resumes, allowing subsequent tasks to be executed in a coordinated manner.

(f) **Wrap-Up Behavior**
This part defines the concluding tasks performed at the end of an activity flow. Typical actions include resource cleanup, session termination (e.g., logout), and the display of summary or farewell messages. The flow is finalized with a *Final Node*, which explicitly marks the completion of the activity.

Refined Control Flow of Rental Center Client Tier

The control flow of the Rental Center Client tier in the Car Rental Management System is refined based on its updated invocation patterns. These refinements reflect the distinct responsibilities and interaction mechanisms assigned to this tier. The resulting activity diagram, which incorporates the revised control structures and invocation types, is shown in Fig. 8.10.

After login, the Rental Center Client tier initiates four parallel threads, each corresponding to a distinct control flow based on specific invocation patterns:

- **Thread 1. Closed Loop for Explicit Invocation**
  This thread manages a menu-driven interface through which rental center staff explicitly invoke system functionalities, such as managing profiles, inventory, reservations, returns, and reports.
- **Thread 2. Closed Loop for Car Location Validation**
  This thread continuously monitors the locations of in-rental vehicles to ensure compliance with their assigned driving regions. If a vehicle is detected outside its permitted region, the thread sends an event labeled *Out of Region* to trigger appropriate system responses.
- **Thread 3. Event-Driven Notification for Driving Range Violations**
  This thread handles the *Out of Region* event by notifying the assigned driver and informing rental staff to take corrective action. It operates asynchronously in response to events dispatched from Thread 2.

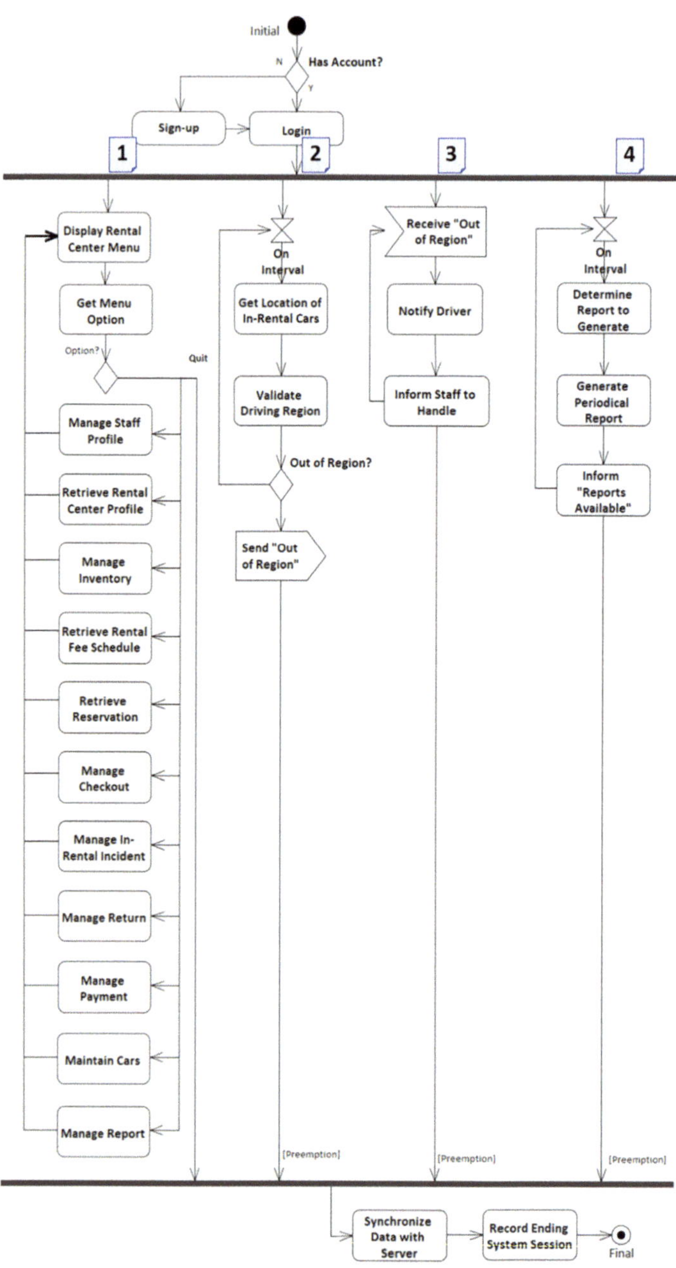

Fig. 8.10 Refined Control Flow of Rental Center Client Tier

- **Thread 4. Closed Loop for Generating Periodic Business Reports**
  This thread continuously evaluates reporting conditions, generates periodic business reports for the rental center, and notifies the system when reports become available.

After all parallel threads complete their execution, the system transitions to the wrap-up phase. During this phase, it synchronizes local session data with the Headquarters Server to ensure consistency across tiers. Finally, it logs the termination of the session, capturing essential details such as logout time, completed operations, and any unresolved issues for future resolution.

8.2 Step 2. Identify Key Behavioral Elements

This step is to identify key behavioral elements—such as actions, activities, or functional components—that exhibit complex runtime behavior and to specify appropriate behavior representation schemes for each selected element. That is, architects should design detailed control flows only for selected behavioral elements that are critical or complex, rather than modeling the behavior of every element in the system.

The selection of behavioral elements for detailed control flow modeling is based on the following criteria:

- **Element Representing Essential Functionality**
  Select an element that embodies a core functionality that is critical and indispensable to the operation of the target system.
- **Element Exhibiting High Complexity**
  Select an element that demonstrates intricate control logic or highly dynamic runtime behavior, warranting detailed behavioral modeling.
- **Element with Behavioral Ambiguity**
  Select an element whose behavior is not clearly defined, potentially subject to varying interpretations, or dependent on complex conditions. Such elements require explicit modeling to eliminate ambiguity and ensure consistent system behavior.

8.2.1 Task 1. Determine Target Behavioral Elements

This task is to identify behavioral elements that require detailed control flow design. A behavioral element refers to a functional unit that exhibits complex or intricate runtime interactions. Such elements are commonly identified in activity diagrams and may include the following:

- An Action or a Group of Actions
- An Activity
- A Thread
- A Partition

In addition, target behavioral elements may be identified within the functional view design. These elements may include:

- A Use Case or a Group of Use Cases
- A Functional Component
- Persistent Object Class
- This type of behavioral element represents its behavior through state transitions, typically triggered by method invocations or external events.

Note that target elements identified in the functional design often correspond to specific elements in an activity diagram. This correspondence arises from the mappings that exist among a group of use cases, a functional component, and an activity, as illustrated in Fig. 8.11.

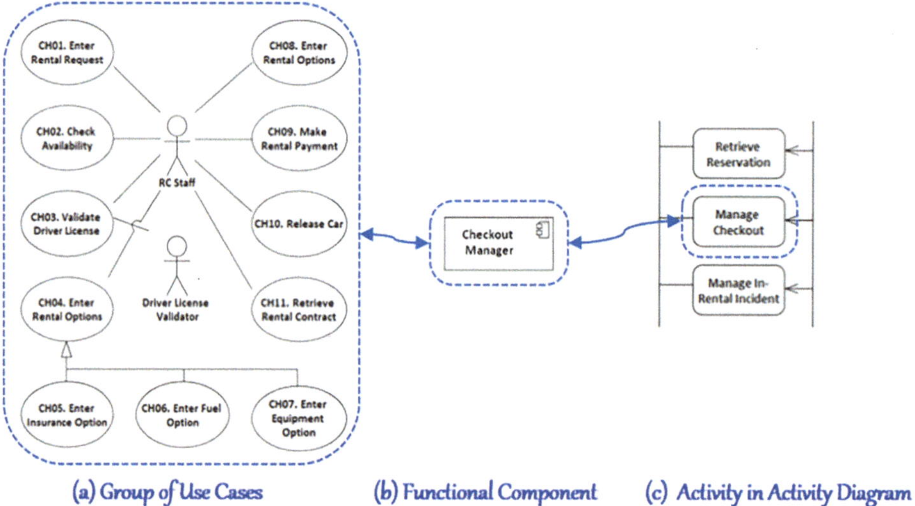

Fig. 8.11 Representation of Same Functionality Across Multiple Design Models

In the figure, the functionality of checking out rental cars is represented from three distinct modeling perspectives: as a group of use cases in (a), as a functional component in (b), and as an activity in (c). This approach offers architects the flexibility to select the most appropriate type of behavioral element for specifying detailed control flow.

Example

For the Car Rental Management System, some of the behavioral elements requiring detailed control flow are shown in Fig. 8.12.

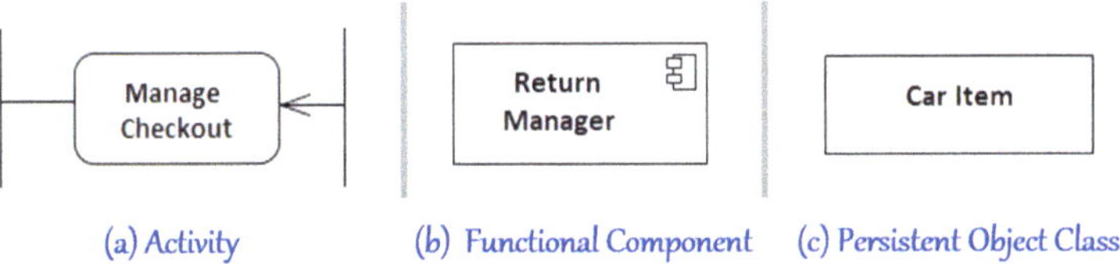

Fig. 8.12 Behavioral Elements Requiring Detailed Control Flow

The figure shows three behavioral elements selected as target elements for which detailed control flow design is required.

(a) **Activity**: Manage Checkout
This activity is selected because it represents an essential system functionality and entails a complex control flow that spans multiple use cases.
(b) **Functional Component**: Return Manager
This component is chosen because it encapsulates a set of use cases for managing rental car returns. It represents a critical functionality with relatively complex control flows across its use cases.
(c) **Persistent Object Class**: CarItem
This class represents rental cars, with behavior defined by methods originating from multiple components such as the Inventory Manager, Checkout Manager, and Return Manager. Its behavior involves cross-cutting concerns across several elements, leading to increased complexity.

8.2.2 Task 2. Determine Behavior Representing Schemes

This task is to identify the most appropriate scheme for representing the detailed control flow of each selected behavioral element. Various schemes are available, including UML Diagrams, non-UML visual models, and algorithmic representations.

Each scheme is defined by a distinct set of graphical notations and textual constructs that govern how control flows are specified. Since each scheme is best suited for particular modeling contexts, architects should assess the nature of the element, the complexity of its behavior, and the system requirements to determine the most effective representation scheme.

Behavior Representation with UML Diagrams

The following UML Diagrams are commonly employed to represent detailed control flows in software systems:

- **Sequence Diagram**
  A Sequence Diagram is ideal for modeling control flows by specifying the interacting objects within a behavioral element and detailing the temporal sequence of message exchanges among these objects. It provides a clear view of interactions in chronological order, making it particularly suitable for scenarios where the order of operations is critical. Constructing a Sequence Diagram requires a well-defined object model, including class structures and interface definitions.
- **Activity Diagram**
  An Activity Diagram is suitable for representing high-level control flows, especially when detailed, message-level interactions are not required. It provides a rich set of graphical constructs for modeling various control flow patterns, including event-driven interactions, loops, closed loops, timer-based behaviors, exception handling, and activity partitioning. This makes it well suited for visualizing workflows, business processes, and parallel or concurrent activities.
- **State Machine Diagram**
  A State Machine Diagram is effective for modeling control flows in systems characterized by discrete states and transitions. It represents behavior through a set of states connected by transitions triggered by events or conditions. This diagram defines valid behavioral sequences from an initial state to one or more final states. It is applicable only when the system exhibits clearly defined state-based behavior and is not appropriate for systems lacking such structure.
- **Timing Diagram**
  A Timing Diagram is specialized for illustrating control flows with a focus on timing constraints, object interactions, events, and synchronization. It is particularly useful for modeling real-time or time-sensitive behaviors and verifying compliance with temporal requirements. The explicit representation of time-based constraints and synchronization makes timing diagrams indispensable for systems where precise timing is a critical concern.

Behavior Representation with Non-UML Diagrams

The following non-UML diagrams are commonly employed to represent detailed control flows in software systems:

- **Flowchart**
  A flowchart is a traditional and versatile tool for visualizing sequential control flows, including decisions, loops, and actions in a process or algorithm. It provides a clear and intuitive depiction of procedural logic, making it particularly effective for simple to moderately complex systems where readability and ease of understanding are critical.

- **BPMN (Business Process Model and Notation)**
  BPMN is a standardized modeling language designed for representing complex business processes. It captures control flows through elements such as activities, events, gateways, and flows. BPMN is well suited for modeling detailed workflows in enterprise or service-oriented environments that require high precision, process clarity, and traceability.
- **Petri Net**
  A Petri Net is a formal graphical model well suited for representing concurrency, synchronization, and resource sharing. It models system states as places, events as transitions, and tokens as resources that move through the system. Petri Nets are particularly effective for modeling parallel and distributed systems with intricate control dependencies.
- **Data Flow Diagram (DFD)**
  A Data Flow Diagram emphasizes the movement and transformation of data within a system, using elements such as processes, data stores, external entities, and data flows. While not explicitly focused on control flow, DFDs can imply behavioral sequences based on data movement. They are most appropriate for systems where data flow is the primary focus and control flow emerges indirectly.

Behavior Representation with Algorithms

In software design, an algorithm is a textual, step-by-step procedure for solving a specific problem or performing a defined task. Unlike diagrams, algorithms provide a precise and unambiguous representation of control flow through explicitly defined instructions. This textual format enables detailed specification of logic, making algorithms particularly effective for capturing complex behaviors and handling edge cases.

Algorithms offer greater expressiveness than graphical representations, as they can incorporate nuanced control structures such as nested conditions, loops, recursion, and exception handling within a compact and structured format. Moreover, algorithms can often be translated directly into source code, thereby facilitating a seamless transition from design to implementation.

However, due to their textual nature, algorithms may be less intuitive and visually accessible than diagrammatic representations, particularly for communication with non-technical stakeholders. Consequently, algorithms are frequently used in combination with graphical models: while diagrams offer a high-level overview of behavior, algorithms capture the underlying procedural logic in detail. This complementary approach enhances both the comprehensibility and precision of behavioral design.

Example of Selecting Behavior Representing Schemes

Consider the selection of target behavioral elements for specifying detailed control flows and determining appropriate representation schemes in the Car Rental Management

System. Based on the complexity, behavioral characteristics, and required level of precision, the following representation schemes are chosen for the selected elements:

- **Sequence Diagram for *Manage Checkout***
  This activity is modeled using a sequence diagram to illustrate the detailed interactions between users and system components during the checkout process. The diagram emphasizes the order of operations and the flow of messages, providing a clear understanding of the dynamic interactions involved.
- **Algorithm for *Return Manager***
  This activity is described using an algorithm to define a precise, step-by-step procedure for handling car returns. This method enhances clarity in expressing complex logic, including conditional branching, iterations, and exception handling, which are essential to this process.
- **State Machine Diagram for *CarItem***
  The behavior of *CarItem* is driven by business methods associated with rental cars—i.e., instances of the *CarItem* class. A State Machine Diagram is appropriate for representing this control flow, as it captures the state-driven behavior of rental cars, allowing transitions between defined states to be explicitly modeled.

Behavior representation schemes for selected behavioral elements can be effectively specified using a tabular format. Table 8.3 outlines the representation schemes chosen for the behavioral elements in the Car Rental Management System.

Table 8.3 Representation Schemes for Target Behavioral Elements

Behavioral Elements	Type of Element	Representation Scheme
Manage Checkout	Activity	Sequence Diagram
Return Manager	Functional Component	Algorithm
CarItem	Persistent Object Class	State Machine Diagram

8.3 Step 3. Define Detailed Control Flows

This step is to represent the detailed control flows of the selected behavioral elements using the selected representation schemes in the previous step.

8.3.1 Task 1. Apply Selected Representation Schemes

This task is to define the detailed control flow of each behavioral element using its designated representation scheme. Each scheme is characterized by a specific set of notations, rules, and conventions that must be followed to ensure the accurate and effective representation of control flows.

Guidelines for Applying UML Diagrams

The following guidelines should be observed when applying UML Diagrams:

- **Proper Use of UML Notations**
  Apply UML notations correctly, adhering to the conventions of the selected diagram type—such as states and transitions in State Machine Diagrams or lifelines and messages in Sequence Diagrams.
- **Adherence to UML Syntax and Semantics**
  Ensure full compliance with standard UML syntax and semantics to maintain consistency, precision, and clarity, thereby supporting effective communication among stakeholders.
- **Utilization of Comprehensive Modeling Elements**
  Incorporate all relevant modeling elements where applicable to ensure that the detailed control flow is thoroughly captured and accurately reflects the system's intended behavior.
- **Use of Annotations for Clarity**
  Include annotations and supplementary details to clarify complex interactions or transitions, enhancing both the comprehensiveness and interpretability of the diagram.

Guidelines for Applying Non-UML Diagrams

The following guidelines should be observed when applying non-UML diagrams:

- **Adherence to Standard Notations**
  Apply standardized notations appropriate to the selected diagram type—for example, use correct symbols for processes, decisions, and flows in flowcharts or for tasks, events, and gateways in BPMN.
- **Clarity in Process Representation**
  Define all steps, actions, and decision points with clarity to ensure the control flow is accurately depicted and easily understood by stakeholders.
- **Consistency in Symbols and Conventions**
  Maintain consistent use of graphical symbols, layout conventions, and visual styles across the diagram to improve readability and minimize the risk of misinterpretation.
- **Emphasis on Completeness**
  Represent the control flow comprehensively, including all relevant paths, loops, and exception conditions, to ensure the diagram fully captures the intended behavior without ambiguity.

Guidelines for Applying Algorithms

The following guidelines should be observed when applying algorithms:

- **Clear and Structured Format**
  Present the algorithm using a well-organized format, such as pseudocode or step-by-step instructions, to enhance readability and precision.

- **Descriptive Naming**
  Use meaningful and descriptive names for variables, functions, and procedural steps to convey intent clearly and facilitate understanding.
- **Inclusion of Logical Constructs**
  Incorporate essential control structures—such as conditional branches, loops, and exception handling—to accurately represent all control flow scenarios.
- **Comprehensive Coverage**
  Address all relevant cases, including edge conditions and exceptional paths, to ensure the control flow is complete and robust.
- **Conciseness with Clarity**
  Strive for brevity without compromising clarity, avoiding unnecessary complexity while preserving the algorithm's comprehensibility and implementability.

Example: Applying Sequence Diagram to Manage Checkout

The *Manage Checkout* activity represents a core functionality of the Car Rental Management System, with its workflow detailed in the associated use case description. A sequence diagram provides a rich set of modeling constructs for effectively representing control flows among actors and participating objects through the exchange of messages.

The resulting sequence diagram for the *Manage Checkout* activity is shown in Fig. 8.13.

The sequence diagram for *Manage Checkout* illustrates the detailed interactions among the RC Staff, participating system components, and external actors throughout the car checkout process. The workflow begins with the RC Staff initiating the procedure through the *Checkout Controller*, which verifies the driver's license via the *Driver License Validator*. Conditional control flows are modeled using *opt* and *alt* constructs to capture scenarios such as invalid licenses, unmatched car models, and decisions to abort the rental process. Upon successful validation, the *CarModel* and *CarItem* components are queried to retrieve the data associated with the selected vehicle.

Once the vehicle is selected, the RC Staff specifies additional rental options, including insurance and rental duration. The system then calculates the rental fee and interacts with the *Payment Manager* to process the payment securely. Upon successful payment authorization, the car's status is updated to "Checked Out," completing the workflow.

This application of a sequence diagram enables precise modeling of the dynamic interactions involved in the *Manage Checkout* activity. It clarifies the temporal ordering of operations and facilitates both implementation and validation by making control dependencies and conditional flows explicitly visible.

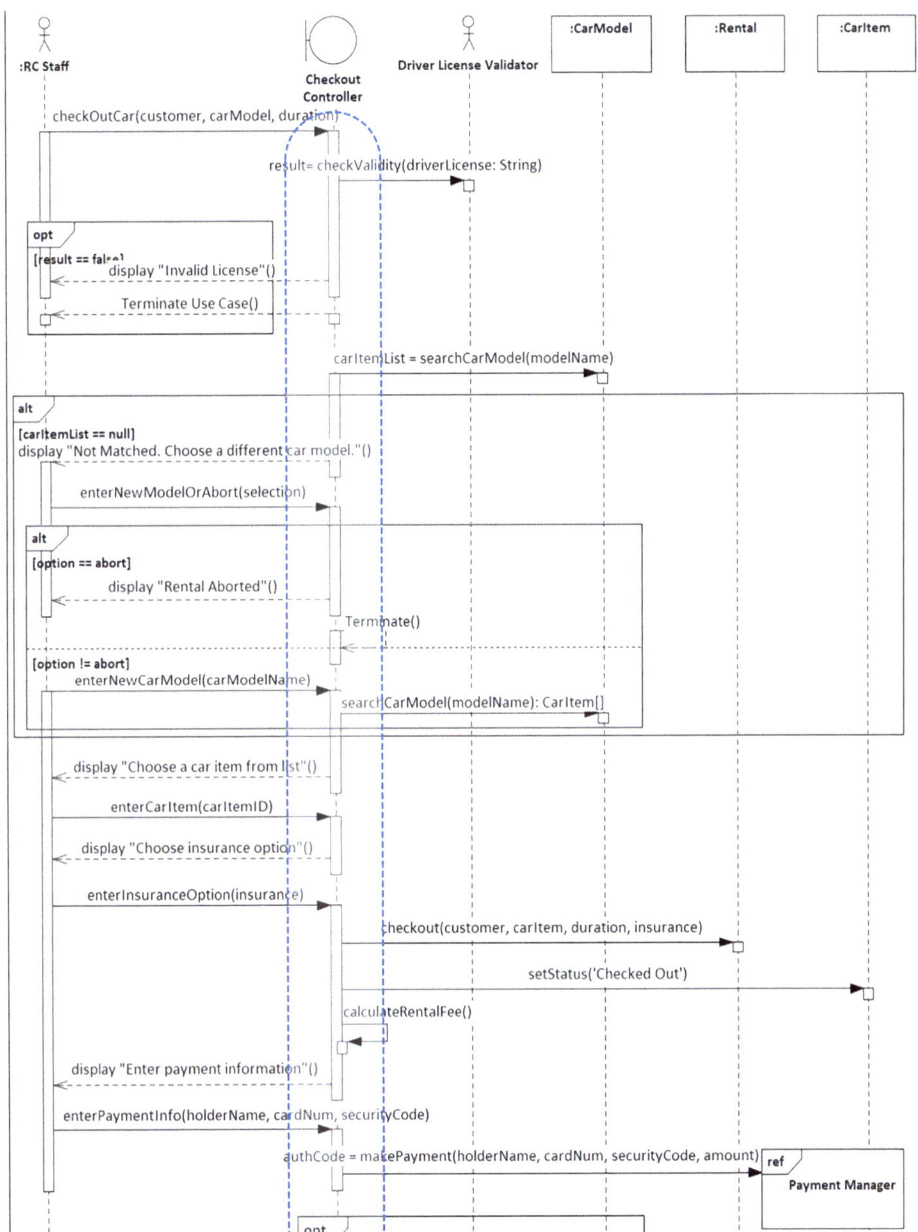

Fig. 8.13 Sequence Diagram for Manage Checkout Activity

Example: Applying State Machine Diagram to CarItem

Each rental car, represented as an instance of *CarItem*, undergoes state changes triggered by the invocation of various methods. These methods include *registerCar(), unregisterCar(), checkout(), return(), initiateRepair(), finishRepair()*, and *discard()*. In essence, the state transitions of a *CarItem* instance are governed by methods originating from multiple functional components.

The State Machine Diagram is an ideal representation scheme for this scenario, as it offers a robust set of modeling constructs for capturing the behavior associated with states, events, and transitions. It effectively visualizes the lifecycle of a *CarItem* instance, ensuring clarity in the representation of its dynamic behavior.

The resulting State Machine Diagram for the *CarItem* class is shown in Fig. 8.14.

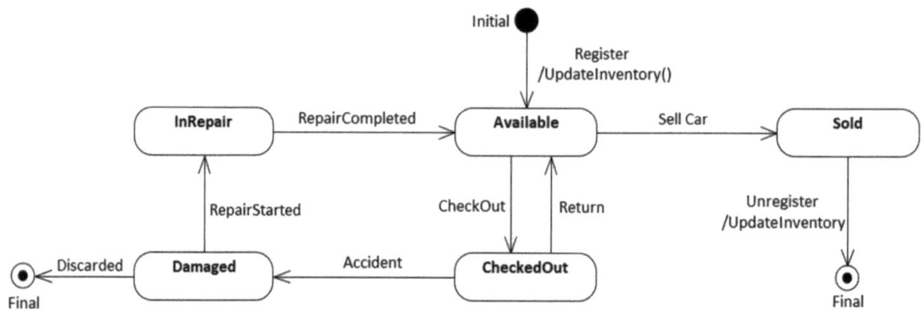

Fig. 8.14 State Machine Diagram for CarItem Class

The diagram illustrates the lifecycle of a rental car, depicting its key states and transitions. The control flow begins at the initial state, where the car is registered using the *registerCar()* method, transitioning it to the *Available* state. When rented, it moves to *CheckedOut* via the *checkout()* method and returns to *Available* upon execution of the *return()* method.

If maintenance is required, the car transitions from *Available* to *InRepair* using the *initiateRepair()* method and returns to *Available* after successful repair through the *finishRepair()* method. If the car is involved in an accident, it transitions to the *Damaged* state. From there, it may either proceed to *InRepair* for servicing or to the final *Discarded* state if deemed irreparable.

Additionally, a car in the *Available* state may be sold using the *sellCar()* method, moving it to the *Sold* state, or unregistered with the *unregisterCar()* method, transitioning it to the final state. This diagram effectively captures the key transitions and states that define the behavior of a rental car in the system.

This application of a State Machine Diagram enables a clear and structured representation of the *CarItem* lifecycle, supporting rigorous behavioral analysis and facilitating consistent implementation across components that interact with rental car objects.

Example: Applying Algorithm to Return Car

The control flow of the *Return Manager* is defined by the use cases within the component and can be effectively specified using an algorithm, as demonstrated below.

Algorithm: Processing Rental Car Return
Input : Rental Car ID, Current Mileage, Fuel Level, Condition, Return Location
Output : Rental Return Report, Total Charges (if applicable)
BEGIN

1. Collect the following information: Rental Car ID, Current Mileage, Fuel Level, and Car Condition.
2. *Actual_Rental_Duration* := difference (End Date – Start Date).
3. *Mileage_Driven* := Current mileage - Initial mileage
4. Calculate *Fuel_Charge* (if applicable) based on the difference in fuel level from the initial level.
5. Check the car's condition for any damage beyond normal wear and tear.
   Document any damage with photos or notes.
6. Calculate Additional_Charge by considering Actual_Rental_Duration, Cleaning Fee, or Damage Repair (if applicable).
7. Calculate *Total_Charge* by adding *Fuel_Charge* and *Additional_Charge* to the base rental fee.
8. Process a payment if *Total_Charge* is nonzero.
9. Update the rental car's status to "Returned".
10. Generate a Return Report including:
    Rental Car ID:
    Rental Period: (Start date, End date)
    Total Mileage Drive:
    Fuel Charges:
    Additional Charges:
    Car Condition:
11. Print or email a copy of the return report.
12. If necessary, coordinate any necessary maintenance or repairs for the rental car.

END

The algorithm for *Processing Rental Car Return* defines a structured sequence of operations executed by the *Return Manager* component. It begins by collecting key input data such as mileage, fuel level, and vehicle condition and proceeds to compute relevant charges—including fuel and additional fees—based on rental duration, usage, and any applicable penalties. The algorithm includes conditional logic to handle payments, status updates, and report generation, ensuring that all steps required for a comprehensive return process are addressed. This textual representation offers a precise and implementation-ready specification of the control flow, suitable for managing both standard and exceptional return scenarios.

8.3.2 Task 2. Align with Other Architectural Views

This task is to analyze the impact of detailed control flow designs on other architectural elements and to refine the system architecture accordingly to ensure consistency and alignment. The objective is to identify and resolve potential discrepancies where detailed control flows may necessitate updates to other architectural artifacts, thereby maintaining architectural cohesion and integrity across all views.

Analyzing Impacts on Other Architectural Design Elements
Evaluate how the refined control flows interact with existing architectural design elements, and identify necessary modifications to ensure seamless integration. This analysis should examine the relationships between control flows and architectural components, as well as assess any interdependencies that may affect overall system performance, scalability, or maintainability.

Note that not all detailed control flows will impact other architectural elements. Only those control flows that involve dependencies on other design components may require adjustments to maintain architectural consistency.

Examples of such impacts include the following:

- **Impact of the Algorithm for *Return Manager***
  The control flow defined in the algorithm outlines a sequence of return-related tasks that map directly to specific use cases within the *Return Manager* component. Consequently, the algorithm influences both the use cases and their interrelationships. To ensure consistency, the defined tasks in the algorithm must align with the corresponding use cases specified in the component's design.
- **Impact of the State Machine Diagram for *CarItem***
  The control flow specified in the State Machine Diagram defines valid sequences of state transitions, each governed by a combination of an event, guard condition, and action. In UML, each transition follows the pattern (*Event, Guard, Action*), where the event typically corresponds to a message received by the object—here, an instance of *CarItem*.
  Alignment is therefore required between the events in the state machine and the method invocations in related functional components such as *Inventory Manager*, *Checkout Manager*, and *Return Manager*. These method calls must be reflected consistently across corresponding control flow specifications to ensure proper system integration and behavioral correctness.

Aligning Architecture Design with Impact Assessment
This task is to ensure that any modifications or refinements introduced in the control flows are properly aligned with the overall system architecture. Such alignment is essential for maintaining consistency across architectural views and resolving dependencies or conflicts that may arise from changes.

The alignment process can be performed in the following sequence:

[1] **Identify Affected Components**
Determine which architectural elements or views are influenced by the refined control flows. These may include functional components, data components, component interfaces, behavioral design elements, deployment configurations, or system state definitions.

[2] **Update Architectural Artifacts**
Revise the identified architectural artifacts to incorporate the changes derived from the refined control flows. All updates should adhere to overarching architectural principles and maintain design integrity.

[3] **Verify Consistency Across Views**
Ensure coherence by cross-validating the refined control flows against other architectural views. For example, confirm that events defined in state transitions are consistent with corresponding data flows, use case scenarios, and inter-component dependencies across structural and behavioral models.

8.4 Checklist for A4c: Behavior View Design

The following checklist items can be used to validate the design for behavior view.

8.4.1 Checklist for Step 1: Refine System Control Flow

- Are the most appropriate invocation patterns correctly defined for each functional component in the system?
- Does every *Send-Event* action in the activity diagram have a corresponding *Receive-Event* action to ensure proper communication?
- Is each closed-loop thread explicitly associated with a termination mechanism, such as preemption or defined exit conditions?
- Are parallel threads within fork-join constructs designed to prevent unintended interactions or hidden interdependencies?
- Is there consistent alignment between use cases in the functional view and their corresponding actions and activities in the activity diagrams?

8.4.2 Checklist for Step 2: Identify Key Behavioral Elements

- Is the selection of target behavioral elements for detailed control flow design justified by their essential system functionality or behavioral complexity?

- Are the behavior representation schemes selected based on appropriate criteria, including intended usage, modeling formalisms, required level of detail, and clarity of interpretation?
- Are behavioral elements exhibiting ambiguity or adaptive behavior identified for explicit modeling to ensure clarity and system robustness?

8.4.3 Checklist for Step 3: Define Detailed Control Flows

- Are the selected behavior representation schemes applied in accordance with established standards and best-practice guidelines for modeling detailed control flows?
- When using UML or non-UML diagrams, are the notations, conventions, and modeling guidelines of the chosen diagram type correctly applied? Failure to adhere to diagram-specific conventions may result in misinterpretation, inconsistencies, or design flaws.
- Is there strict adherence to UML syntax and semantics to ensure precision, clarity, and consistency across diagrams?
- Are all relevant modeling elements—such as states, transitions, actions, events, or swimlanes—utilized to comprehensively represent the system's behavior?
- For non-UML diagrams (e.g., Flowcharts, BPMN), are standardized notations and conventions accurately followed to maintain clarity and correctness?
- When representing behavior as an algorithm, are control structures such as branches, loops, recursion, and exception handling explicitly specified to capture the complete control flow?
- Is the algorithm presented in a clear and structured format (e.g., pseudocode or step-by-step instructions) to ensure readability and ease of implementation?
- Does the algorithm provide complete coverage of the control flow, including edge cases and exceptional scenarios, with no logical gaps?

8.5 Exercise Problems

1. **Refinement of Context-Level Behavior Model**
   Refining the context-level activity diagram is a critical step in the design of the behavior view. This task enhances clarity in the overall control flow and establishes a solid foundation for specifying detailed control flows of individual activities. What specific refinement techniques can be applied to improve the accuracy and completeness of the context-level behavior model?
2. **Essence of Invocation Patterns**
   Describe the concept of an invocation pattern, and explain how it helps model common runtime control flows of a system. Give examples of sequential, explicit, closed-loop, timed, and event-based invocation patterns.

3. **Essence of Event-Based Invocation Pattern**
   Describe the significance of the event-based invocation pattern in modeling reactive and asynchronous interactions between event emitters and event handlers. Provide examples of both intra-tier and inter-tier event flows, and discuss how this pattern supports loose coupling in software systems.
4. **Consistency Between Functional View Design and Behavior View Design**
   Although functional and behavior views represent distinct architectural perspectives, consistency between them is essential for ensuring design integrity. Identify and elaborate on specific element pairs—such as use cases and activity flows—that should be aligned across the two views. Justify the importance of maintaining this alignment.
5. **Refine Context-Level Behavior Model for a Ride-Sharing System**
   Refine the context-level activity diagram for a Ride-Sharing System. Identify deficiencies in the initial model, and revise the diagram accordingly. Compare the revised view-level diagram with the original context-level model by listing all changes made and justifying the improvements.
6. **Refine Context-Level Behavior Model for a Hotel Reservation System**
   Refine the context-level activity diagram for a Hotel Reservation System. Identify deficiencies in the initial model, and revise the diagram accordingly. Provide a comparison between the initial and revised diagrams, listing all changes introduced and their architectural significance.
7. **Refine Context-Level Behavior Model for a Food Delivery System**
   Refine the context-level activity diagram for a Food Delivery System. Identify deficiencies in the original model, and revise the diagram accordingly. Compare the initial context-level and the refined view-level diagrams, documenting all changes and improvements made.
8. **Refine Context-Level Behavior Model for an Adaptive Cruise Control (ACC) System**
   Refine the context-level activity diagram for an Adaptive Cruise Control (ACC) System. Identify and correct deficiencies in the original model. Compare the revised view-level diagram with the original context-level model, and explain the rationale for each change.
9. **Selecting Appropriate Behavior Representation Schemes**
   For each of the following behavioral scenarios, identify the most appropriate behavior representation scheme—such as sequence diagrams, activity diagrams, state machine diagrams, timing diagrams, or algorithmic descriptions—and justify your selection:
   - Designing a detailed design showing object interactions
   - Modeling real-time constrains for a missile weapon system
   - Modeling collaborations among multiple generative AI models
   - Modeling shortest navigation paths in a relationship graph of participants

10. **Algorithm vs. Diagram-Based Behavior Representation Schemes**
    An algorithmic representation is a textual approach for specifying control flow, while diagrammatic representations use visual models. Compare these two approaches in terms of clarity, expressiveness, scalability, and suitability across different design contexts. Discuss their respective strengths and limitations.
11. **Using a State Machine Diagram for Treadmill Machine Behavior**
    A treadmill is an exercise device that enables a person to walk, jog, or run in place on a motor-powered moving belt. It features a control panel for managing power, adjusting speed and incline, selecting workout modes, and monitoring metrics such as time, distance, calories, and heart rate. Construct a state machine diagram that models the control flow of the treadmill software, incorporating events such as power on/off, start/stop, speed adjustment, incline modification, workout mode selection, and emergency stop.
12. **Using Alternative Representation Schemes for Treadmill Machine Behavior**
    Using a sequence or activity diagram, model the behavior of the treadmill machine and user interactions through its control panel. Analyze the limitations of the selected representation scheme in capturing the complete behavioral semantics of the treadmill, especially when compared to a state machine diagram.
13. **Using an Algorithm for Treadmill Machine Behavior**
    Develop a structured algorithm that models the behavior of the treadmill machine, including all relevant user interactions. Discuss the limitations of algorithmic representation in expressing the system's dynamic control states compared to a state machine diagram.

Activity A4d. Design for Deployment View

9

Objective of the Chapter
The objective of this chapter is to provide systematic guidelines for designing the deployment view of a software system. It covers the definition of computing device nodes that deliver processing capabilities, the specification of execution environments that support system-level services, the establishment of network connectivity to enable communication across distributed nodes, and the allocation of software artifacts to designated deployment targets. These guidelines enable architects to construct a deployment architecture that is clearly defined, operationally feasible, and aligned with the system's runtime and infrastructural requirements.

Introducing Activity A4d. Design for Deployment View
This activity is to design the architecture of the deployment view for the target system. The deployment view addresses the physical and logical configuration of the system's infrastructure, encompassing computing nodes, execution environments, network connections, and the mapping of software artifacts to deployment nodes. Designing the deployment view is essential, as it has a direct impact on critical runtime qualities such as scalability, performance, reliability, and system observability.

The deployment architecture is typically expressed using a UML Deployment Diagram, which provides a structured visualization of the system infrastructure, including nodes, communication paths, and the allocation of software components.

Deployment design must not be conducted in isolation. It should be systematically derived from the schematic architecture and closely integrated with the functional, information, and behavior views. This integrated approach ensures consistency across architectural perspectives and contributes to a cohesive, well-aligned system design.

S. D. Kim, M. Kim, *Hands-on Software Architecture*,
https://doi.org/10.1007/978-3-032-01184-8_9

Steps in A4D. Deployment View Design The Design for Deployment View can be systematically performed with a sequence of steps, as shown in Fig. 9.1.

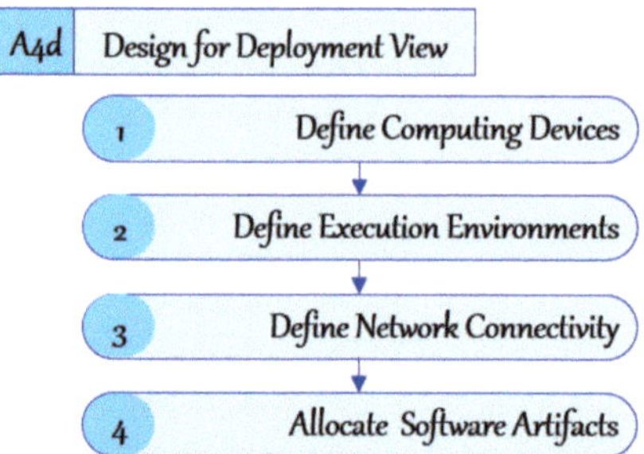

Fig. 9.1 Steps in A4d. Deployment View Design

- **Step 1. Define Computing Devices**
  This step is to define the computing devices required for the target system. A computing device is any hardware component capable of delivering the computing power necessary to execute software artifacts effectively.
- **Step 2. Define Execution Environments**
  This step is to specify the execution environments essential for the operation of the target system. An execution environment refers to the system software that provides essential services at the system level for deployed applications. These include operating systems, platforms, middleware, frameworks, and database management systems.
- **Step 3. Define Network Connectivity**
  This step is to establish network connectivity among computing device nodes. Modern software systems frequently comprise distributed nodes that rely on network connections to support seamless communication and coordination.
- **Step 4. Allocate Software Artifacts**
  This step is to allocate software artifacts onto the defined computing nodes and execution environments. Software artifacts include functional components, data components, control flow components, user interface artifacts, and database elements.

9.1 Step 1. Define Computing Device Nodes

This step is to specify the hardware configuration of computing device nodes for the target system. The schematic architecture defines one or more tiers, and each tier must be supported by dedicated computing resources provided by computing device nodes.

The UML Deployment Diagram defines two types of nodes.

- **Computing Device Node (Hardware)**
  This type of node represents physical hardware components such as servers, workstations, mobile devices, or embedded systems. These nodes provide the computing resources necessary to execute software artifacts.
- **Execution Environment Node (Software)**
  This type of node represents the software infrastructure hosted on device nodes. Examples include operating systems, virtual machines, containers, and application servers that deliver essential system-level services for software execution.

This distinction enables a clear separation between the physical infrastructure and the software execution environments within the system's deployment architecture.

9.1.1 Task 1. Determine Computing Device Nodes

This task is to identify the computing device nodes required for the system by analyzing its schematic architecture.

Identifying Computing Device Nodes
Computing device nodes are typically derived from the tiers defined in the schematic architecture, as each tier corresponds to a physical computing system in the target deployment. For example, the schematic architecture of the Car Rental Management System defines four distinct tiers: *Mobile Client*, *Rental Center Client*, *Dispatcher Server*, and *Headquarters Server*. Accordingly, the system is configured with four computing device nodes, each mapped to one of the four tiers specified in the schematic architecture.

However, there are exceptions and special cases that deviate from direct tier-to-node mapping, as outlined below.

- **Tier Consolidation for Deployment Efficiency**
  An exception to direct tier-to-node mapping arises in small-scale or resource-constrained systems, where multiple tiers are consolidated onto a single physical device to reduce cost, simplify infrastructure, or accelerate prototyping. In such scenarios, distinct functional tiers defined in the schematic architecture may share the same computing device node during deployment.
  For example, in a prototype or low-scale deployment of the Car Rental Management System, both the Dispatcher Server and Headquarters Server tiers may be hosted on the same machine. While this consolidation enhances deployment efficiency, it must be carefully considered to avoid potential performance bottlenecks and to ensure that non-functional requirements such as scalability and fault isolation are not compromised.

- **Tier Replication for Scalability or Availability**
  Tier replication is a common deployment strategy used to support scalability, fault tolerance, load balancing, or geographical distribution. In such cases, a single tier defined in the schematic architecture is mapped to multiple computing device nodes in the deployment view.
  For example, the schematic architecture of the Car Rental Management System applies the *Dispatcher Architecture Style* to the *Headquarters Server* tier. In UML Deployment Diagrams, such replication should be explicitly represented using stereotypes or constraints to indicate that multiple nodes host instances of the same tier, as shown below:

```
node «replicated» DispatcherServer
node Headquarters Server { {instances = 3} }
```

- **Modeling Cloud-Based Deployments in UML**
  A tier in the schematic architecture can be deployed in a cloud-based environment, where the underlying physical infrastructure is abstracted away and managed by a cloud provider. While UML Deployment Diagrams traditionally use the «device» stereotype to represent physical computing nodes, this notation can be extended to model cloud-based deployments by annotating the device node with appropriate constraints or tagged values. An example is shown below:

```
node «device» CloudNode
{
  {type = "virtual"}
  {provider = "AWS"}
  {service = "Lambda"}
}
```

Hardware Specification of Computing Device Nodes
Once computing device nodes are identified, their hardware capacities must be specified to ensure they can meet the system's operational requirements. This specification defines the necessary computing power and other critical hardware resources, such as memory, storage, and processing capabilities. The range of computing devices may vary significantly—from smartphones to high-performance mainframe servers. Therefore, defining hardware specifications requires careful consideration of each node's functional role and computational demands to ensure that performance, reliability, and availability targets are met.

The key attributes used to describe hardware specifications are as follows:

- **Core processing**
  - **Processor (CPU)**: Type, architecture, number of cores, clock speed, cache size, and bus width
  - **Memory (RAM)**: Type (e.g., DDR4, LPDDR5), size, and access speed

- **Secondary Storage**: Type (e.g., SSD, HDD, NVMe), capacity, and read/write performance
- **Networking**
  - **Network Interface**: Type (e.g., Ethernet, Wi-Fi, 5G)
  - **Bandwidth**: Supported network speed and throughput capacity
- **Graphics processing unit (GPU)**: Type, memory, compute capabilities, and compatibility with workloads (e.g., CUDA support)
- **I/O Interfaces**
  - **USB ports**: Version and number of ports
  - **Other ports**: HDMI, DisplayPort, Thunderbolt, and other peripheral interfaces
- **Additional hardware components**
- Sound card, cooling system, power supply unit (PSU), and any other specialized components required by the system

Examples

- **Headquarters Server Node in Car Rental Management System**
  The recommended hardware specification for this computing device node is outlined below.
  - **Processor/CPU**
    Type: Server-grade processor such as Intel Xeon or ARM-based processor
    Cores: 32 to 128 cores to support high concurrency and multitasking
    Clock Speed: 2.5 GHz to 3.5 GHz
    RAM: DDR4, minimum of 4 TB
  - **Secondary Storage**
    Type: NVMe SSDs for high-speed data access
    Configuration: RAID 10 for redundancy and performance
    Capacity: Scalable from several terabytes to petabytes
  - **GPU**
    High-end NVIDIA GPU with CUDA support for parallel processing workloads
  - **Networking**
    NIC: Dual 100 GbE Network Interface Cards
    Redundancy: Multiple NICs to support failover and maximize throughput
  - **Power Supply**
    Wattage: 2000 watts or higher to support power-intensive operations
    Redundancy: Dual or triple redundant power supplies for uninterrupted service
- **Training Server for Deep Learning Models**
  Consider defining the hardware specifications for the computing device node representing a server system used to train deep learning models on large-scale datasets, such as medical images from CT scans and MRIs. This server must possess robust computational capabilities, including high-performance CPUs, large memory capacity, powerful GPUs, and any specialized hardware required for deep learning workloads.

The recommended hardware specification for this computing device node is outlined below.

- **Processor/CPU**
  Type: Server-grade processor such as Intel Xeon or ARM-based processor
  Cores: 32 to 128 cores for high concurrency and multitasking
  Clock Speed: 2.5 GHz to 3.5 GHz
  RAM: DDR4, minimum of 4 TB
- **Secondary Storage**
  NVMe SSDs for high-speed data access
  Configuration: RAID 10 for data reliability and performance
  Capacity: Scalable from a few terabytes to petabytes
- **GPU**
  High-end NVIDIA GPU with CUDA support for parallel processing
  FLOPS (Floating Point Operations per Second): High throughput for compute-intensive training
  VRAM: Large memory capacity to support deep learning models and datasets
  Specialized Cores: Tensor cores or equivalent for deep learning acceleration
  CUDA Compatibility: Ensures efficient GPU computation
  Multi-GPU Scalability: Supports parallel training across multiple GPUs
- **Networking**
  NIC: Dual 100 GbE Network Interface Cards
  Redundancy: Multiple NICs for failover and throughput optimization
- **Power Supply**
  Wattage: 2000 watts or higher to support intensive GPU and CPU usage
  Redundancy: Dual or triple redundant power supplies for uninterrupted operation

9.1.2 Task 2. Representing Computing Device Nodes

This task is to visually represent the computing device nodes of the target system using UML notation. These device nodes serve as deployment targets for software artifacts and reflect the physical or virtual computing infrastructure that supports the system's execution environment.

Each node is depicted with the stereotype "device", as shown in Fig. 9.2.

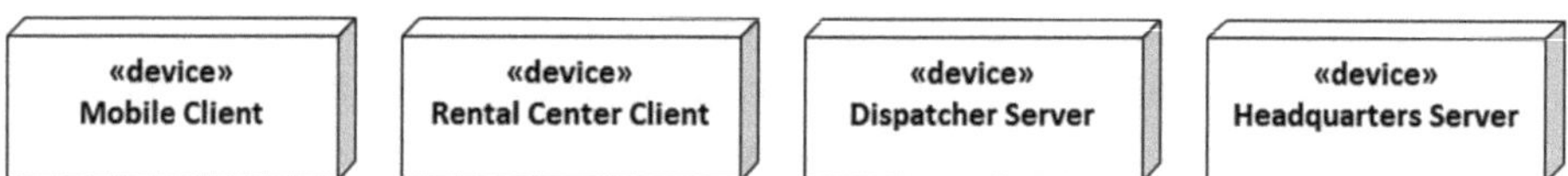

Fig. 9.2 Representing Computing Device Nodes in UML

The figure illustrates four computing device nodes, each corresponding to one of the four tiers defined in the schematic architecture of the Car Rental Management System. Each node is labeled with its specific device name, placed beneath the «device» stereotype.

9.2 Step 2. Define Execution Environments

This step is to specify the execution environment associated with each computing device node in the system. In UML Deployment Diagrams, an execution environment node represents a software infrastructure layer that provides the computational resources required to deploy and execute software artifacts within the system.

9.2.1 Task 1. Determine Execution Environments

This task is to identify the appropriate execution environments required for each computing device node. In UML, an execution environment node models a logical container or platform that offers system-level services essential for executing software components. These nodes are typically nested within «device» nodes in the deployment diagram and reflect the software stack or runtime layer responsible for managing software execution.

Types of Execution Environments
The common types of execution environments are the following:

- **Operating systems**: Linux-based OS, Windows, macOS, etc.
- **Virtual machines**: Java Virtual Machine (JVM), .NET Runtime, etc.
- **Containers**: Docker (for containerization), Kubernetes (for orchestration), etc.
- **Web servers**: Apache HTTP Server, Nginx, etc.
- **Application servers**: Apache Tomcat, Microsoft IIS, etc.
- **Database management systems**: MySQL, Microsoft SQL Server, MongoDB, etc.
- **Mobile environments**: Android Runtime, iOS Runtime, etc.

Specifying Specific Products
When defining execution environment nodes, architects may choose whether or not to specify particular product vendors, commercial offerings, or platform services. In general, it is considered best practice to avoid naming specific products in the deployment view, as doing so can create unnecessary dependencies and reduce flexibility.

However, in some cases, specifying a particular vendor or product may be appropriate—especially when the system's requirements tightly align with a specific platform or when only a limited number of viable options exist. This is often true for execution environments that provide specialized system-level services, such as cloud functions, GPU runtimes, or proprietary middleware.

While avoiding vendor lock-in is typically preferred, a deliberate and justified selection of a specific product may enhance clarity and support key system constraints when alternatives are limited.

Deriving Execution Environment Nodes

Execution environment nodes are derived from multiple sources, depending on the system requirements and the technology stack employed. These nodes can be systematically identified based on preceding architectural design artifacts, as illustrated in Fig. 9.3.

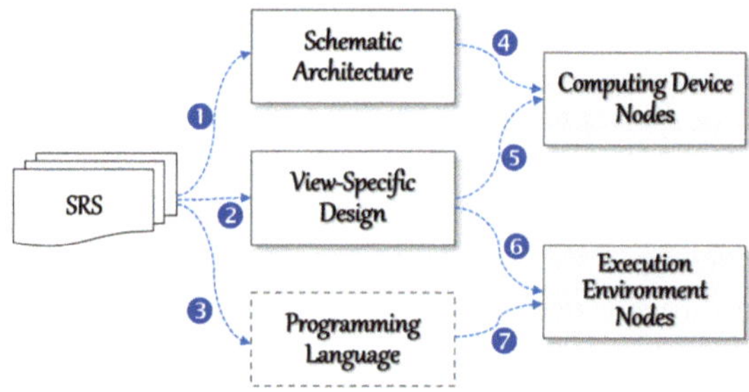

Fig. 9.3 Execution Environment Nodes Derived from Preceding Design Artifacts

The SRS serves as the foundational document for designing the schematic architecture and view-specific designs, as depicted in ❶ and ❷. Additionally, the SRS may explicitly specify the programming language to be used for implementing the system, as shown in ❸ . If the SRS does not specify the programming language, architects should propose one and seek consensus from stakeholders.

The schematic architecture guides the identification of computing device nodes as shown in ❹. The view-specific design serves as the foundation for identifying the hardware capabilities of computing device nodes and determining the configuration settings for execution environment nodes, as indicated in ❺ and ❻.

Each architectural view provides valuable insights that support the accurate specification of execution environment nodes, as outlined below:

- **Functional view design**: Provides information about the functionalities assigned to each tier and the computational complexity associated with their execution

- **Information view design**: Describes the structure and volume of persistent datasets, as well as the intensity of data manipulation operations
- **Behavior view design**: Offers insight into system workflows, the degree of parallelism, and overall behavioral complexity

In addition, the selected programming language defines the set of compatible execution environments that can be deployed, as indicated in ❼.

Example
If the Car Rental Management System is developed using the Python programming language, its execution environment nodes can be defined as follows:

- **Execution Environment of Rental Center Client**
  - Operating System: Ubuntu 22.04
  - Web Framework: Django (Python)
  - DBMS: MySQL
- **Execution Environment of Mobile Client**
  - Mobile Platform: Android or iOS runtime
  - DBMS: MySQL
- **Execution Environment of Dispatcher**
  - Operating System: Ubuntu 22.04
  - Web Framework: Django (Python)
- **Execution Environment of Headquarters Server**
  - Operating System: Ubuntu 22.04
  - Web Framework: Django (Python)
  - DBMS: MySQL

The Rental Center, Dispatcher, and Headquarters Server nodes all share the same operating system and Web framework. This architectural uniformity reflects a common industry practice aimed at improving cost efficiency, simplifying development and maintenance, and ensuring seamless interoperability across system tiers.

9.2.2 Task 2. Representing Execution Environment Nodes

This task is to define execution environment nodes in a UML Deployment Diagram. An execution environment node is represented using the stereotype «executionEnvironment» and typically resides within a computing device node, as illustrated in Fig. 9.4.

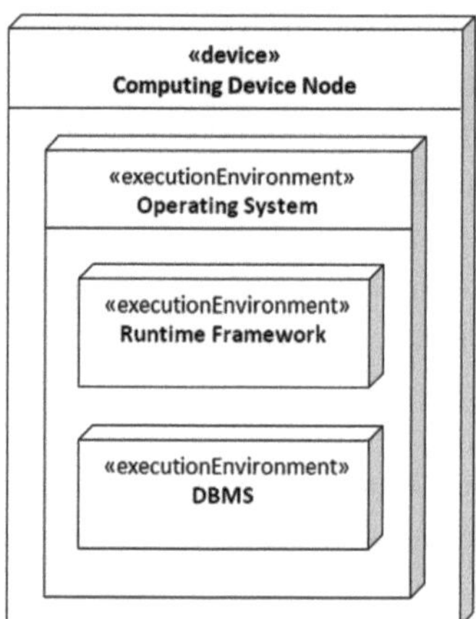

Fig. 9.4 Representing Execution Environment Nodes in UML

The diagram illustrates how execution environment nodes are provisioned and operate on designated hardware infrastructure. In this example, an Operating System node is deployed within a "device" node representing a computing device. Two additional execution environment nodes—Runtime Framework and DBMS—are nested within the operating system node, indicating that they are hosted and executed in the context of that particular OS.

This hierarchical relationship, where execution environments are contained within one another or within a device, is referred to as Containment in UML Deployment Diagrams. It denotes a hosting relationship, signifying which execution layer is responsible for managing the lifecycle and execution of other layers.

In deployment diagrams, the containment relationship indicates that one element exists or operates within another. It is represented visually by drawing the contained element entirely inside the containing element.

There are two main usages of the containment relationship in deployment diagrams.

- **Representing Nested Nodes**
  Containment is used to represent execution environments or other nodes nested within higher-level nodes. For example, an operating system may be nested within a computing device node, a virtual machine or runtime framework may be nested within the operating system, and a database management system may also be deployed within the operating system.
- **Representing Artifacts within Nodes**
  Containment is also used to indicate that software artifacts are deployed within execution environment nodes. For instance, functional components may be contained within an operating system node, while data components may be nested within a database management system node.

Example

The execution environment nodes for both the Mobile Client and Headquarters Server tiers of the Car Rental Management System are illustrated in Fig. 9.5.

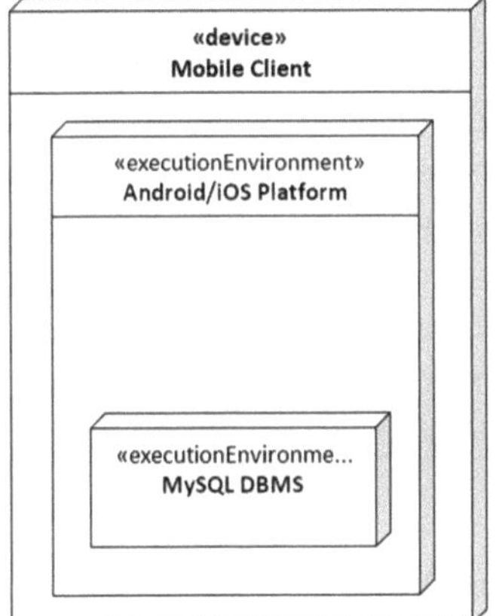

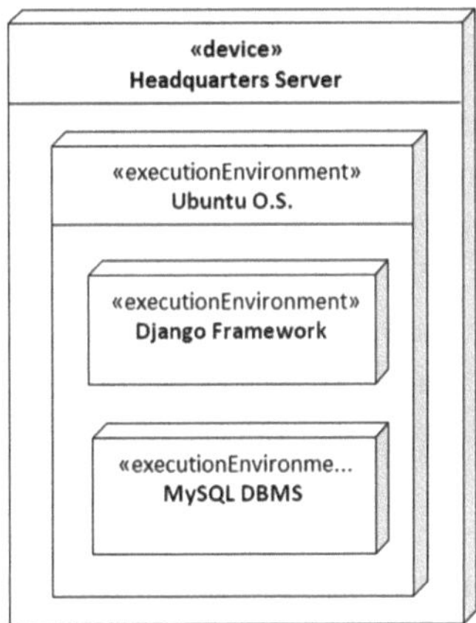

Fig. 9.5 Execution Environment Nodes for the Car Rental Management System

- **Mobile Client tier**
  This tier is represented as a computing device node hosting an execution environment node labeled *Android/iOS Platform*. This mobile platform, in turn, hosts another execution environment node for the *MySQL DBMS*, responsible for local data storage or caching on the client side.
- **Headquarters Server tier**
  This tier is modeled as a computing device node that hosts an execution environment node for the *Ubuntu* operating system. Within this environment, two additional execution layers are deployed: the *Django Framework*, which supports the Python-based Web application layer, and the *MySQL DBMS*, which manages the system's primary database.

9.3 Step 3. Define Network Connectivity

This step is to define the network connectivity among nodes, represented by communication paths in a deployment diagram. These paths are illustrated as lines connecting nodes, which may represent either physical computing devices or execution environments.

Network connectivity should be specified not only for physical device nodes but also for execution environment nodes. Environments such as virtual machines, containers, and cloud-based services often require explicit network configurations to enable communication with other components in the system.

- **Connectivity for Computing Device Nodes**
  This defines the physical network connections between hardware components such as servers, client machines, routers, switches, and other networked devices. These connections are typically established using wired Ethernet or wireless technologies and may involve IP-based addressing, port configurations, and routing setups.
- **Connectivity for Execution Environment**
  In modern cloud-native systems, execution environments communicate through various virtualized networking mechanisms. For example, virtual machines hosted on platforms like AWS, Azure, or Google Cloud typically connect via private virtual networks such as AWS VPC or Azure Virtual Network. Containers within Kubernetes clusters communicate through the platform's internal networking, which links pods using service endpoints. Microservices operating in service meshes rely on discovery protocols, load balancers, and sidecar proxies to interact efficiently.

9.3.1 Task 1. Determine Communication Paths

This task is to determine the communication paths among nodes in a deployment diagram. Communication paths define the capability of connected nodes to exchange messages, signals, or data and represent the system's network connectivity.

The schematic architecture outlines the interaction paths among the tiers within the system, which serve as the basis for inferring communication paths. That is, the communication paths between nodes in a deployment diagram should align with the interaction paths specified in the schematic architecture.

A communication path is specified using solid lines among nodes. For example, the communication paths in the architecture of the Car Rental Management System are shown in Fig. 9.6.

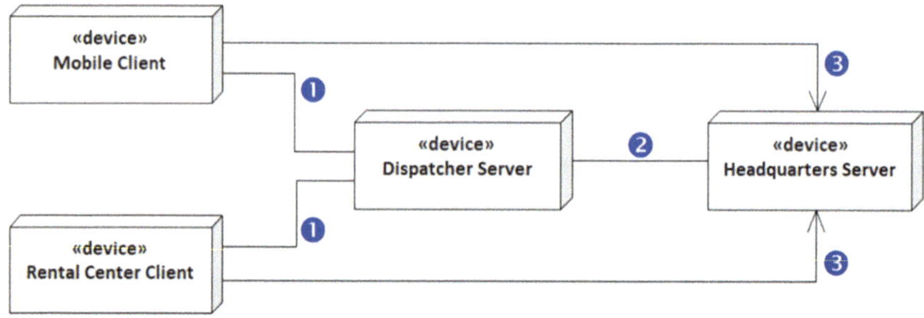

Fig. 9.6 Representing Communication Paths in UML

The deployment diagram in the figure defines the following communication paths:

- **Communication Path ❶**
  This path enables interactions between client applications and the Dispatcher Server. Its primary role is to facilitate the allocation of a Headquarters Server instance that meets high QoS requirements.
- **Communication Path ❷**
  This path enables communication between the Dispatcher Server and replicated Headquarters Server instances. It is used primarily to compute QoS metrics for the replicated instances.
- **Communication Path ❸**
  This path enables direct service invocations from client applications to their allocated Headquarters Server instance.

9.3.2 Task 2. Specify Network Configuration

This task is to specify the network configurations for the identified communication paths. Each communication path is specified with several descriptive attributes, including the following:

- **Protocol**
  A network protocol defines the set of rules and conventions that govern how data is transmitted, received, and processed between devices over a network. Specify the network protocols used for the communication paths, such as HTTP/HTTPS, FTP, TCP/IP, UDP, Bluetooth, and Zigbee.
- **Port Number**
  A port number is a numerical identifier used within a network to route data to specific processes in a computing system. Specify the port numbers assigned to each communication path, if applicable.
- **Bandwidth**
  Bandwidth denotes the maximum rate at which data can be transmitted across a network link. It serves as a key performance metric in network and communication systems. Specify the bandwidth requirements for each communication path, if necessary.
- **Network Latency**
  Network latency refers to the time required for a data packet to travel from the source to its destination across a network. Latency is a critical factor affecting the overall performance of communication paths. Specify latency expectations where relevant.
- **Other Characteristics**
  Include any additional network configuration details using UML's built-in extension mechanisms, such as stereotypes, constraints, and tagged values.

Representing Network Configuration

The network configuration for communication paths is represented in a deployment diagram by specifying configuration parameters and their corresponding values alongside the interaction paths. Alternatively, the network configuration may be described textually to complement the deployment diagram.

For example, the network configuration for the communication paths in the Car Rental Management System can be visualized in a deployment diagram, as shown in Fig. 9.7.

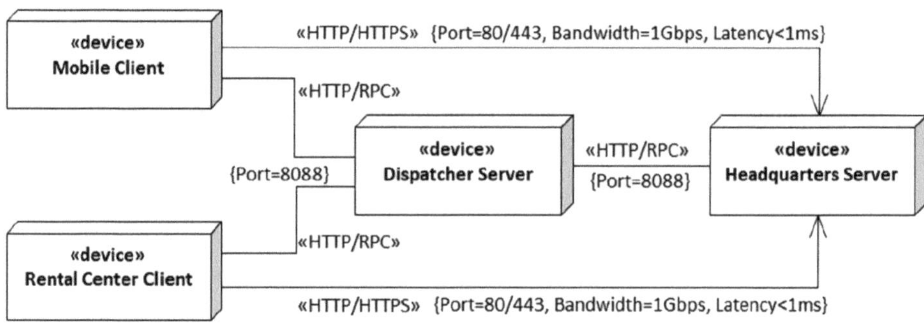

Fig. 9.7 Network Configuration for the Car Rental Management System

In this diagram, the communication paths between client applications and the Dispatcher Server are specified using the HTTP/RPC protocol. Each path is annotated with a protocol stereotype and port number using tagged values. Similarly, the communication paths between client applications and the Headquarters Server are defined using the HTTP/HTTPS protocols. These paths include additional configuration details such as port numbers, bandwidth, and latency.

Alternatively, the network configuration can be detailed in a separate textual description, as illustrated below.

- **Communication path between Mobile Client and Headquarters Server**
- **Protocol: HTTP/HTTPS**
- **Ports: 80/443**
- **Bandwidth: 1 Gbps**
- **Latency: <1 ms**

9.4 Step 4. Allocate Software Artifacts

This step is to allocate software artifacts onto the identified execution environment nodes.

9.4.1 Task 1. Identify Software Artifacts to Deploy

This task is to identify the software artifacts that will be deployed onto execution environment nodes. A software artifact is a tangible deliverable generated during the software development lifecycle and is regarded as a deployable unit.

A software artifact is represented as a rectangle and is often annotated with a stereotype, as illustrated in Fig. 9.8.

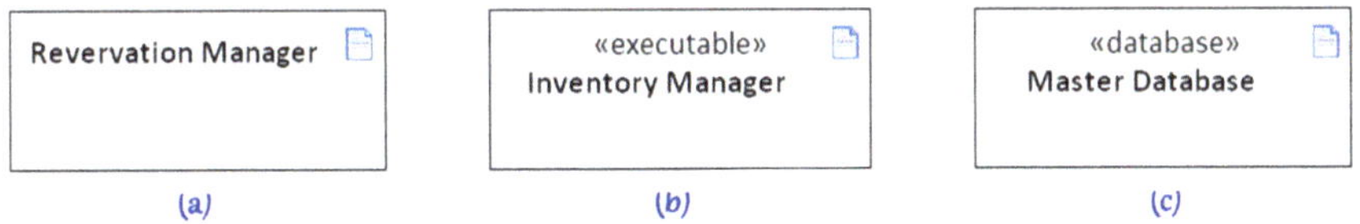

Fig. 9.8 UML Notations for Software Artifacts

In the figure, artifact (a) is represented by a rectangle labeled *Reservation Manager* without a stereotype. This form provides only the basic identification of the artifact, without specifying its type or role. In contrast, software artifacts can be annotated with stereotypes, such as «executable» or «database», along with their names. This approach, as illustrated in (b) with *Inventory Manager* and in (c) with *Master Database*, conveys additional semantic information about the artifact's nature or function within the system.

Identifying Software Artifacts to Deploy

Software artifacts are derived from various sources, including the designs for the functional view, information view, and behavior view. Apply the following guidelines to identify software artifacts for deployment:

- **Software Artifacts from Functional View Design**
  The functional view design specifies functional components and their logical placement within the system architecture. These functional components are identified as software artifacts to be deployed.
- **Software Artifacts from Information View Design**
  The information view design defines data components and their placements within the schematic architecture. These data components are treated as software artifacts for deployment.
- **Software Artifacts from Behavior View Design**
  The behavior view design specifies the system's overall control flow and the detailed execution sequences of selected elements. While these control flows themselves do not introduce new system functionality, *controller-type software artifacts* are still required to coordinate and manage these flows within the system.

For example, in the Car Rental Management System, such artifacts may include the *Mobile Client Controller*, which manages mobile client interactions, and the *Rental Center Client Controller*, which oversees rental center operations.

- **Software Artifacts from Presentation Layer**
  Although architects typically do not focus on user interface design, the architecture may include a blueprint for the presentation layer. When present, the user interface components defined in this view can be treated as software artifacts for deployment.
- **Software Artifacts of Files, Documents, Scripts, and Media Files**
  System design often includes files, documents, scripts, and media assets essential for supporting functionality. These elements are also recognized as software artifacts to be deployed.

Stereotypes for Software Artifacts

Software artifacts can be annotated with stereotypes to improve the clarity and specificity of the deployment model. Stereotypes serve as a secondary classification mechanism, offering additional semantic context about the nature and role of each artifact.

Common stereotypes for software artifacts—including the two UML-predefined stereotypes, "artifact" and "executable"—are summarized in Table 9.1.

Table 9.1 Stereotypes for Software Artifacts to Deploy

Stereotype	Usage
"executable"	Represents binary executable files
"library"	Represents static or dynamic library files
"script"	Represents script files, such as shell scripts, batch files, or files written in other scripting languages
"configuration"	Represents configuration files, such as XML or JSON files
"database"	Represents databases
"database-schema"	Represents database schema definitions
"document"	Represents documentation files, such as .pdf, .md, or .docx
"source"	Represents source code files, such as .java, .cpp, or .py
"resource"	Represents resource files, such as images, localization files, or asset bundles
"web"	Represents HTML, CSS, or JavaScript files that make up a Web page

In addition to these stereotypes, architects may define and apply custom stereotypes that are relevant to the specific roles and characteristics of the target software artifacts.

Example

The software artifacts to be deployed for the Car Rental Management System are identified as follows:

- **Software Artifacts from Functional View Design**
  - The complete set of identified functional components

- **Software Artifacts from Information View Design**
  - The complete set of identified data components
  - The complete set of identified databases, including the *Mobile Client Database*, *Rental Center Database*, and *Master Database*
- Software Artifacts from Behavior View Design
  - A collection of controllers responsible for coordinating control flows, including the Mobile Client Controller, Rental Center Controller, Dispatcher Server Controller, and Headquarters Server Controller

9.4.2 Task 2. Allocate Software Artifacts

This task is to allocate the identified software artifacts to the appropriate execution environment nodes. The architectural designs derived from the functional, information, and behavior views have already specified the distribution of components and behavioral elements across system tiers and layers. Specifically, the following distribution decisions for design elements have been previously established:

- Distribution of functional components
- Distribution of data components
- Distribution of behavioral elements
- Distribution of databases

Therefore, the allocation of software artifacts must align with these established distribution decisions in the view-based design to ensure consistency and coherence across the overall architecture.

Utilizing Software Artifact Packages

Software artifacts can be deployed either individually on execution environment nodes or grouped into packages for collective deployment. In complex systems with a large number of software artifacts, it is often more effective to organize related artifacts into packages and deploy them as cohesive units.

In UML, a package is represented either as a folder icon with the package name displayed inside the folder or as a rectangle with a tab at the top where the package name appears. Figure 9.9 shows examples of packages used to organize software artifacts.

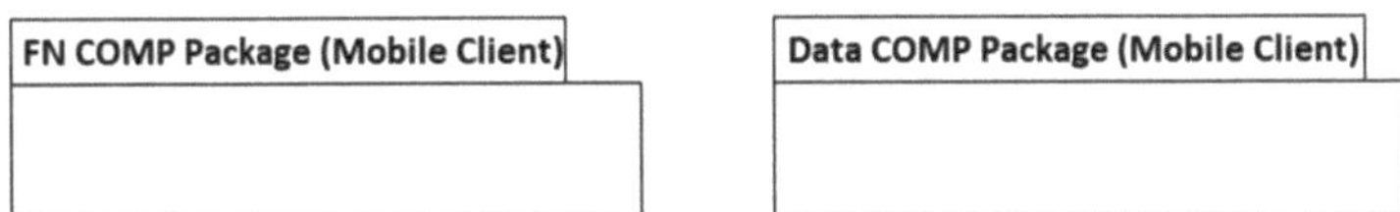

Fig. 9.9 Representing Package in UML

In the figure, the *FN COMP Package (Mobile Client)* is a package containing functional components allocated to the Mobile Client tier, whereas the *Data COMP Package (Mobile Client)* is a package containing data components assigned to the same tier.

The software artifacts contained within a package may be specified when necessary. These contents can be described either textually or illustrated using a UML diagram. For the two packages shown in Fig. 9.9, their internal contents are represented using a deployment diagram, as shown in Fig. 9.10.

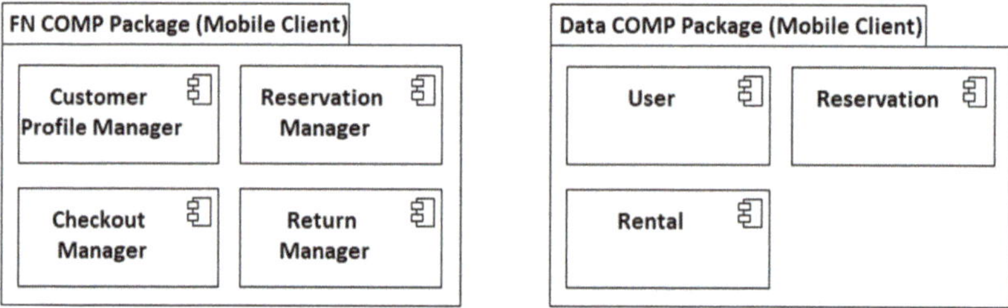

Fig. 9.10 Representing Software Artifacts Within Package

Accordingly, the deployment can be represented either by allocating software artifacts individually or by deploying them through their corresponding packages, as illustrated in Fig. 9.11

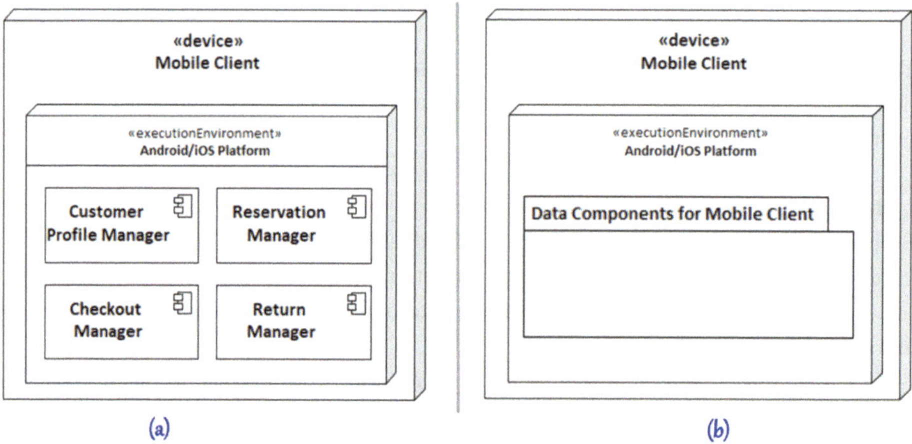

Fig. 9.11 Deployments Using Individual Artifacts and Packages

In Figure (a), four software artifacts—representing functional components—are deployed individually. In contrast, Figure (b) shows a single package that encapsulates the data components for deployment as a unified entity.

Representing Software Artifact Deployment

Software artifact deployment can be represented in two ways:

- **Nesting Software Artifacts within Nodes**

  The allocation of software artifacts to nodes can be visually represented by placing the artifacts directly within the corresponding node, as shown in Fig. 9.12a. Nesting artifacts within nodes provides clarity and precision, offering a straightforward depiction of the runtime context in which the artifacts operate.

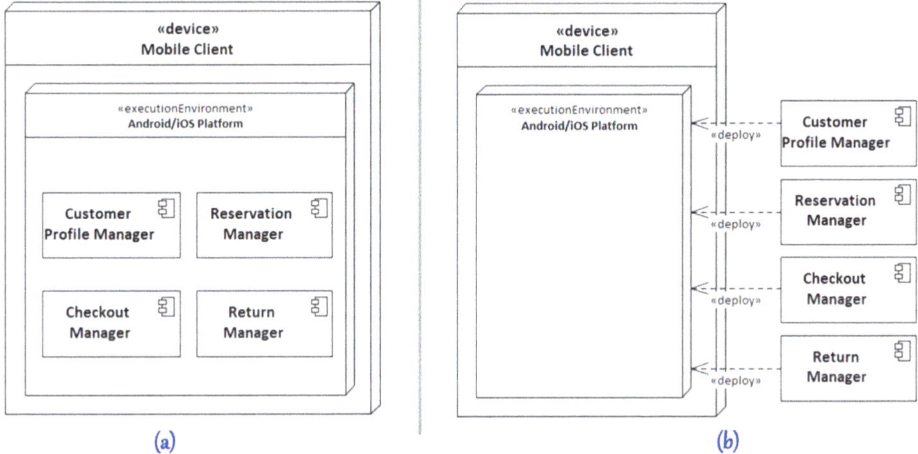

Fig. 9.12 Representing Deployment: Nesting vs. «deploy» Stereotype

- **Representing with the «deploy» Stereotype**

  The allocation of software artifacts to nodes can also be represented using dashed arrows with an open arrowhead. These arrows are typically annotated with the «deploy» stereotype to explicitly denote the deployment relationship, as illustrated in in Fig. 9.12b.

  In Figure(a), software artifacts are allocated directly within the *Mobile Client* node, which represents the runtime environment on the *Android/iOS Platform*. This method visually nests the artifacts within the node, providing clarity and a straightforward depiction of their runtime context.

In contrast, Figure(b) depicts the deployment relationship between the *Mobile Client* node and the software artifacts using dashed arrows annotated with the «deploy» stereotype. This representation maintains a separation between the artifacts and the node while clearly denoting the deployment relationship.

Example

Consider specifying the deployment architecture for the Car Rental Management System using a UML Deployment Diagram. This diagram should reflect the architectural decisions made in earlier design stages and incorporate the following elements:

- Set of computing device nodes
- Set of execution environment nodes
- Design of network connectivity
- Software artifacts or their packages

The resulting Deployment Diagram is presented in Fig. 9.13.

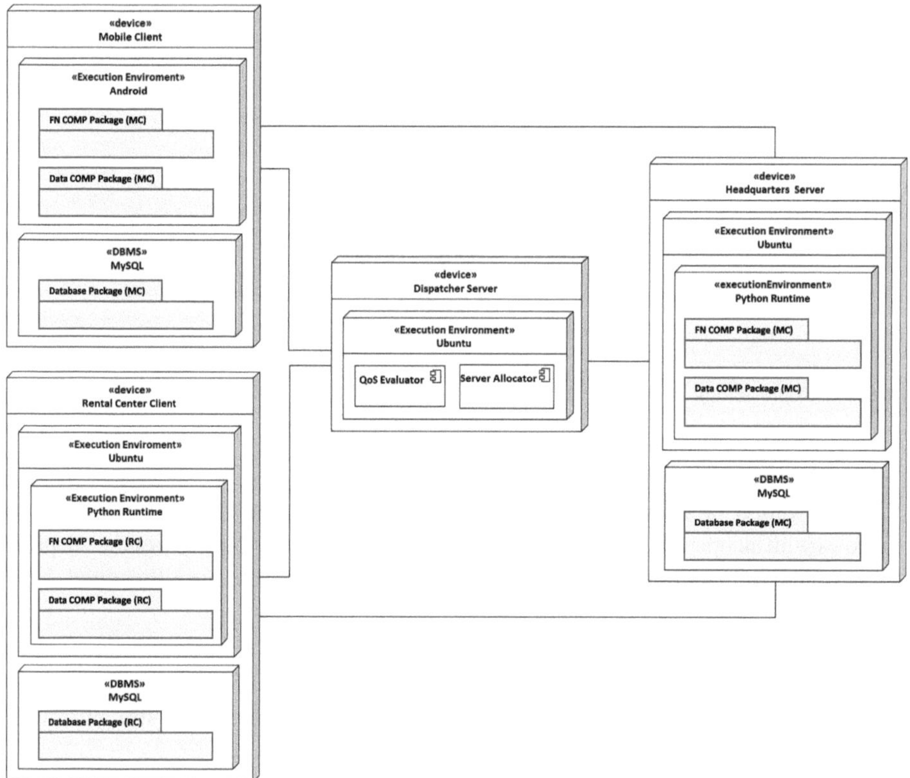

Fig. 9.13 Deployment Diagram for the Car Rental Management System

This deployment diagram specifies the deployment configuration of each tier in the system.

- **Mobile Client**: Operates on an Android execution environment. It hosts both functional and data component packages specific to the mobile tier, along with a MySQL database for local data storage and processing.
- **Rental Center Client**: Runs on an Ubuntu-based execution environment with an additional Python runtime. It includes its respective functional and data component packages and similarly integrates a MySQL database to support its operations.
- **Dispatcher Server**: Deployed on an Ubuntu environment, it encapsulates two functional components: one for evaluating the QoS of available servers and another for allocating servers based on that evaluation.
- **Headquarters Server**: Runs on Ubuntu with a Python runtime environment. It hosts its own functional and data component packages, along with a MySQL database, enabling centralized processing and coordination.

All nodes are interconnected through network communication paths, ensuring seamless interaction and service coordination across clients and servers in the system.

9.5 Checklist for A4D: Deployment View Design

The following checklist items can be used to validate the design for deployment view.

9.5.1 Checklist for Step 1: Define Computing Device Nodes

- Have the computing device nodes been clearly specified for each physical tier in the schematic architecture?
- Are hardware specifications for each computing device node provided, including all essential descriptive attributes?
- Do the specified hardware configurations satisfy the required performance and reliability criteria?
- Has the inclusion of specialized hardware (e.g., GPUs for computation-intensive tasks) been considered where appropriate?
- Are the computing device nodes designed to scale efficiently to accommodate potential future workloads?

9.5.2 Checklist for Step 2: Define Execution Environment Nodes

- Have the execution environments for each computing device node been identified based on the relevant design specifications?
- Has each computing device node been assigned an appropriate operating system to support its execution requirements and software components?
- Is a language-specific runtime platform or framework specified where required by the programming language in use?
- Has a database management system (DBMS) been designated for each computing device node that requires database support?
- Has compatibility and interoperability among all elements within the execution environments been thoroughly verified?

9.5.3 Checklist for Step 3: Define Network Connectivity

- Do the communication paths between device nodes align with the interaction patterns specified in the schematic architecture?
- Is the network connectivity between nodes defined with essential attributes, such as network protocols, port numbers, bandwidth, and latency?
- Have failover and redundancy mechanisms for network connections been specified where applicable?
- Is the network configuration designed to scale effectively to accommodate future growth and increased workload demands?

9.5.4 Checklist for Step 4: Allocate Software Artifacts

- Have all software artifacts intended for deployment been clearly identified?
- Are the identified software artifacts properly aligned with the functional and data components defined in the design?
- Have control flow components (e.g., controllers) been identified and included as deployable software artifacts?
- Are the software artifacts organized into deployment packages, where appropriate, to facilitate deployment and maintainability?
- Have all software artifacts and deployment packages been accurately allocated to the appropriate computing nodes?
- Are presentation layer artifacts (e.g., user interface components) deployed on the appropriate nodes to support user interaction?

- Have deployment relationships been explicitly represented using UML stereotypes (e.g., «deploy») to improve clarity and precision?
- Has a comprehensive deployment diagram been constructed that integrates all deployment-level design decisions?

9.6 Exercise Problems

1. **Purpose of Deployment View Design**
   Describe the purpose of the deployment view in software architecture. Explain how it contributes to achieving runtime qualities such as reliability, scalability, and performance. Discuss why deployment design must be aligned with other architectural views to ensure a consistent and effective system architecture.
2. **Distinguishing Computing Device Nodes from Execution Environment Nodes**
   Differentiate between computing device nodes and execution environment nodes in UML Deployment Diagrams. Provide representative examples of each. Explain how maintaining this distinction enhances the clarity, modularity, and scalability of deployment models.
3. **Defining Computing Device Nodes**
   Describe the guidelines for identifying computing device nodes in deployment design by analyzing the SRS and the schematic architecture. Explain how each architectural tier is mapped to a physical node, and specify the criteria used to determine the computing capacity required for each node.
4. **Defining Execution Environment Nodes**
   Describe the guidelines for identifying execution environment nodes in deployment design by analyzing the SRS, the defined computing device nodes, and relevant architectural views.
5. **Defining Network Connectivity**
   Describe the guidelines for specifying communication paths in deployment diagrams by referencing the interaction paths defined in the schematic architecture. Explain how to determine appropriate network configurations for these communication paths, including considerations such as protocol, port number, bandwidth, and latency.
6. **Defining Software Artifacts to Deploy**
   Describe the guidelines for identifying software artifacts to be deployed by referencing the designs from the functional, information, and behavior views. Explain how these artifacts represent deployable units of software and how their identification ensures consistency across architectural views.

7. **Specifying UML Stereotypes for Software Artifacts**
   Explain the use of UML stereotypes such as «executable», «database», and «script» for classifying software artifacts in deployment diagrams. Discuss how these stereotypes enhance semantic precision and improve the interpretability of deployment contexts.
8. **Identifying Software Artifacts and Stereotypes for a Food Delivery System**
   Identify the software artifacts to be deployed in a Food Delivery System by referencing the functional, information, and behavior views. For each identified artifact, assign an appropriate UML stereotype to clarify its role within the system architecture.
9. **Ensuring Consistency in Software Artifact Allocation**
   Explain how the allocation of software artifacts should align with the distribution decisions made in the functional, information, and behavior view designs. Discuss the importance of maintaining consistency across these views to ensure a coherent, maintainable, and scalable deployment architecture.
10. **Using Packages to Group Software Artifacts**
    Explain the scenarios in which packages should be used to group software artifacts in deployment design. Discuss the advantages of using packages in terms of modularity, manageability, and deployment efficiency.

Activity A5. Design for Non-Functional Requirements

10

Objective of the Chapter

The objective of this chapter is to provide guidelines for designing the non-functional aspects of a software system through the systematic selection and application of architectural tactics. It covers the identification of relevant facts and policies, the definition of tactic derivation criteria, the formulation and evaluation of candidate tactics, the integration of selected tactics into architectural views, and the validation of their conformance. These guidelines enable architects to construct an architecture that explicitly addresses non-functional requirements and ensures alignment with system-level quality objectives and architectural integrity.

Introducing Activity A5. Design for Non-Functional Requirements

This activity is to design the system architecture to address the non-functional requirements of the target system. Its objective is to enhance the view-based architectural design by incorporating architectural tactics that effectively respond to the specified non-functional concerns.

Architects begin by conducting a thorough analysis of each non-functional requirement to determine its architectural implications and constraints. Based on this analysis, they identify and define a set of architectural tactics tailored to address the requirements in question. These tactics are then systematically evaluated for feasibility, effectiveness, and compatibility with the overarching system goals. Finally, the selected tactics are integrated into the view-based architectural framework, ensuring that the resulting design achieves an appropriate balance between functional correctness and non-functional quality attributes.

S. D. Kim, M. Kim, *Hands-on Software Architecture*,
https://doi.org/10.1007/978-3-032-01184-8_10

Steps in A5. Design for Non-Functional Requirements

The design for non-functional requirements can be systematically performed with a sequence of steps, as shown in Fig. 10.1.

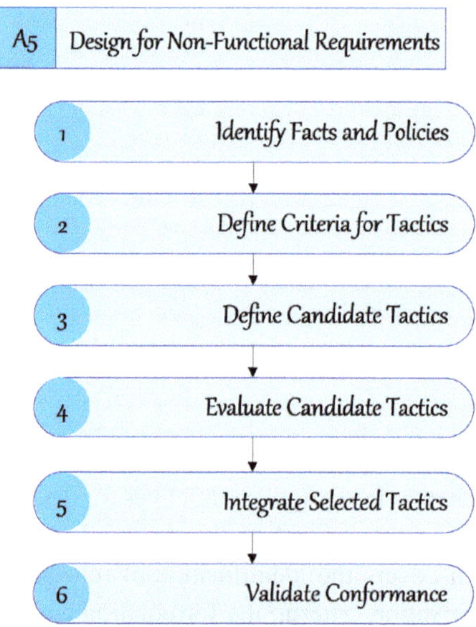

Fig. 10.1 Steps in A5. Design for Non-Functional Requirements

- **Step 1. Identify Facts and Policies**
  This step is to identify the underlying facts and organizational policies that influence each non-functional requirement of the target system. It involves applying requirement engineering practices to uncover the contextual drivers, constraints, and conditions that shape non-functional concerns, forming a foundational basis for tactic development.
- **Step 2. Define Criteria for Tactics**
  This step is to establish criteria for deriving architectural tactics that address the non-functional requirements. These criteria are systematically formulated from the identified facts and policies, offering a structured foundation for tactic definition.
- **Step 3. Define Candidate Tactics**
  This step is to propose candidate architectural tactics based on the defined criteria. Each tactic represents a technical or operational approach designed to fulfill one or more non-functional requirements. Candidate tactics should be described with sufficient technical detail to support evaluation.
- **Step 4. Evaluate Candidate Tactics**
  This step is to evaluate the effectiveness and feasibility of each candidate tactic and to select a subset of candidate tactics for implementation. The evaluation process applies

systematic methods, such as cost-benefit analysis (CBA) and trade-off assessment, to determine the most appropriate tactics for integration into the architecture.

- **Step 5. Apply Selected Tactics**
  This step is to assess the impact of the selected tactics on architectural views and incorporate them into the view-based architectural design. This integration ensures that the selected tactics are aligned with the design objectives and effectively address the system's non-functional requirements.
- **Step 6. Validate Conformance**
  This step is to ensure that the resulting architectural design satisfies both functional and non-functional requirements. Architecture validation serves as a final checkpoint to confirm that the design is complete, technically sound, and consistent with the project's objectives.

10.1 Step 1. Identify Facts and Policies

This step is to identify the facts and policies that underlie the non-functional requirements, serving as foundational elements for the design of architectural tactics. These identified elements provide a structured basis for developing tactics that effectively address non-functional concerns.

By applying principles and methods of requirements engineering, architects can identify underlying facts and policies effectively.

10.1.1 Task 1. Identify Underlying Facts

This task is to identify the facts associated with the given non-functional requirements. An underlying fact can represent any established knowledge, shared consensus, assumptions, or relevant de facto standards that are pertinent to the specific requirement.

More specifically, an underlying fact for a non-functional requirement can include, but is not limited to, the following:

- **Widespread Knowledge Relevant to the NFR**
  Refers to commonly accepted and well-documented information, practices, or principles that are broadly recognized within the domain and directly applicable to the specified non-functional requirement.
- **High-Agreement Consensus Regarding the NFR**
  Refers to areas where there is strong consensus among stakeholders or domain experts. These are cases in which opinions or decisions are closely aligned, offering a reliable foundation for architectural reasoning.

- **Logical Assumptions Deduced from the NFR**
  Refers to inferred conditions or expectations that logically arise from the non-functional requirement, even if not explicitly stated.
- **De Facto Standards Pertinent to the NFR**
  Refers to informal standards or widely adopted practices that are prevalent in addressing the type of non-functional requirement at hand. While these standards may not be formally issued by regulatory bodies, they have gained acceptance due to their effectiveness, maturity, and widespread use in industry.

Relevance of NFRs to Functional Requirements
NFRs are often inherently linked to specific system functionalities. Therefore, architects should first identify the relevant functionality associated with a given NFR and extract the underlying facts within the context of that functionality.

The relevance of NFRs to functionalities is demonstrated in the following examples:

- **For NFR of "Enhancing the Profitability of Car Rental Business"**
  This NFR refers to the system's ability to support generating high financial returns from its operations by optimizing pricing, reducing costs, and improving operational efficiency. The functionalities related to this NFR are as follows:
  - **Functionality of Dynamically Pricing Rental and Insurance Fees**
    The system must provide real-time pricing adjustments for rental and insurance fees based on factors such as demand, location, seasonality, and vehicle type, enabling competitive and profitable pricing strategies.
  - **Functionality of Assisting in Lowering Inventory Costs of Rental Cars**
    The system must support efficient inventory management by analyzing fleet utilization data, demand forecasts, and rental patterns to minimize idle vehicles and optimize the size and composition of the fleet
  - **Functionality of Assisting in Lowering Maintenance Costs of Rental Cars**
    The system must support predictive and preventive maintenance scheduling by leveraging vehicle usage data, maintenance history, and diagnostic reports to reduce unplanned repairs and extend vehicle lifespan, thereby reducing overall maintenance costs.
- **For NFR of "Providing High Safety of Smart Cruise Control"**
  This NFR is to ensure that the smart cruise control system operates with a high degree of safety, minimizing risks to passengers and other vehicles under all operating conditions. The functionalities related to this NFR are as follows:
  - **Functionality of Maintaining Safety Distance**
    The system must dynamically adjust its speed to maintain a safe distance from the vehicle ahead, ensuring collision prevention under varying traffic conditions.
  - **Functionality of Detecting Obstacles**
    The system must detect obstacles in the vehicle's path and perform appropriate maneuvers to safely avoid collisions.

- **Functionality of Assisting Lane-Keeping**
  The system must ensure that the vehicle stays within its designated lane, even when navigating curves or turns, by continuously monitoring lane boundaries and adjusting steering as necessary.
- **Functionality of Adaptive Speed Control**
  The system must regulate the vehicle's speed in real time, adapting to changing road conditions, traffic patterns, and speed limits to optimize safety and efficiency.

By analyzing the specific functionalities associated with each NFR, architects can more effectively uncover the underlying facts and organizational policies that influence architectural decisions. These functionalities provide contextual anchors that reveal operational constraints, expected behaviors, and domain practices—serving as practical entry points for identifying facts such as technical assumptions, consensus standards, or widely accepted practices, as well as relevant internal or regulatory policies.

Specifying Underlying Facts for NFRs
Each identified fact is assigned a unique identifier, prefixed with the letter "F," and followed by a sequential number to ensure clear differentiation. Each fact should be documented using the following structured format:

- **(Fact ID) <Title of the Fact>**
  <Description or the Fact>

This structured format promotes clarity, consistency, and ease of reference when managing and reviewing the defined facts.

Example: Underlying Facts for NFR #1. Profitability of Car Rental Business
This NFR focuses on designing the system to enhance the profitability of Car Rental Businesses. It is widely recognized that achieving high profitability requires both revenue augmentation and expense reduction.

The underlying facts relevant to this NFR can be identified as follows:

(F1) Enhanced Revenue Through Optimized Rental Fee Rates
Elevated profit margins achieved through strategically optimized rental fee rates are a primary driver of increased revenue, leading to overall improvements in net profit. Conducting a comprehensive market analysis is essential for ensuring competitive pricing.

(F2) High Profits on Insurance, Fuel, and Car Equipment
Higher profit margins on insurance, fuel, and car equipment contribute to increased revenue and, consequently, elevated net profit.

(F3) High Profits on Car Repair Charges
Car rental companies often pass on repair costs not covered by insurance to the customer. Higher profits from customer-paid repair charges lead to increased revenue and, in turn, greater net profit.

(F4) Use of Less Expensive Car Models
Procuring car models that meet minimum quality standards at lower cost helps reduce expenses, thereby increasing net profit.

(F5) Use of Low-Maintenance Car Models
Acquiring cars that require minimal maintenance reduces ongoing operational costs and supports profitability.

(F6) Use of Cars with Low Repair Costs
Car models with low repair costs reduce post-accident or damage-related expenses, thereby increasing overall profit margins.

(F7) Use of Low-Depreciation Car Models
Acquiring models with low depreciation supports higher resale value and reduced ownership cost, contributing to greater net profit.

(F8) Optimal Inventory Level
Maintaining an optimal inventory level prevents overcapacity and avoids vehicle unavailability. This balance minimizes costs while preserving service readiness and profitability.

Example: Underlying Facts for NFR #2. Wide Range of Applicability
This NFR focuses on designing the system to support broad applicability across diverse Car Rental Management scenarios. It is essential that the system accommodates variability in its components and external interactions to maximize its adaptability and relevance.

The underlying facts relevant to this NFR can be identified as follows:

(F1) Variability in Car Models Supported
A wide range of car models is available for rental. Designing the system to support diverse vehicle types enhances its applicability across different rental scenarios.

(F2) Variability in Installed GPS Devices
Rental vehicles may use GPS devices from various manufacturers. Supporting multiple GPS configurations improves the system's applicability in environments with diverse hardware standards.

(F3) Variability in Checkout Procedures
Rental companies may adopt different checkout workflows and periodically revise them. Designing the system to accommodate various checkout procedures enhances its flexibility and applicability.

(F4) Variability in Factors for Determining Rental Fees
Rental fee schedules are influenced by multiple factors such as location, vehicle type, and demand. Enabling dynamic configuration of these factors improves the system's adaptability and broadens its applicability.

(F5) Variability in Factors for Determining Discounts

Discount rates may vary across rental centers and depend on multiple factors. Supporting flexible discount calculation mechanisms enhances the system's applicability in diverse operational contexts.

(F6) Variability in Payment Methods

Rental payments can be made through various methods, including credit cards, digital wallets, or corporate accounts. Supporting a broad spectrum of payment types increases the system's compatibility with diverse user environments.

(F7) Variability in Interfaces with External Systems

The system must interact with external components such as driver's license validators and payment authorizers, which may differ across vendors. Accommodating multiple interface specifications improves integration and applicability in heterogeneous system environments.

10.1.2 Task 2. Identify Underlying Policies

This task is to identify the policies associated with the given non-functional requirements. An underlying policy may include legal mandates, regulatory obligations, organizational rules, de facto standards, constraints, or industry best practices that must be observed to fulfill the specified non-functional requirements.

More specifically, an underlying policy for a non-functional requirement can include, but is not limited to, the following:

- **Legal Requirements**
  Laws and regulations established by governmental or judicial authorities that the system must comply with to ensure lawful operation
- **Regulations**
  Formal directives issued by governing bodies or industry-specific organizations that must be followed to maintain regulatory compliance
- **Established Rules**
  Organization-specific or domain-specific guidelines defined to achieve desired outcomes in system design or operation
- **De Facto Standards**
  Widely adopted practices that, while not formally standardized, have become the accepted norm for addressing particular types of requirements
- **Constraints**
  Limiting conditions that define boundaries for system design or operation. These may include risk management requirements (e.g., redundancy for availability, disaster recovery protocols) or sustainability constraints (e.g., energy efficiency goals)
- **Industry Best Practices**
  Proven strategies and methodologies that have been widely recognized as effective through experience and demonstrated success in comparable scenarios.

Specifying Underlying Policies for NFRs
Each identified policy is assigned a unique identifier, prefixed with the letter "P," and followed by a sequential number to ensure clear differentiation. Each policy should be documented using the following structured format:

- **(Policy ID) <Title of the Fact>**
  <Description or the Policy>

This structured format promotes clarity, consistency, and ease of reference when managing and reviewing the defined policies.

Example: Underlying Policies for NFR #1. Profitability of Car Rental Business
The underlying policies relevant to this NFR can be identified as follows:

(P1) Budget Allocation for New Rental Car Procurement (Constraint)
A predefined budget is established for acquiring new rental vehicles. This financial constraint governs procurement decisions, ensuring that purchases remain within the allocated budget and support overall cost control.

(P2) Parking Lot Constraints for New Rental Car Procurement (Constraint)
Due to limited parking capacity at rental offices, a maximum number of rental vehicles is enforced. Accordingly, new car procurement must account for parking availability to prevent overcapacity and associated inefficiencies.

(P3) Incentivizing Advanced Reservations (Best Practice)
The company adopts a policy of offering discounts to customers who make advanced reservations. This best practice aligns with the principle that encouraging early bookings increases rental utilization, thereby enhancing profitability.

Limited Presence of Underlying Policies for Certain NFRs
Note that underlying policies for a given NFR are not always explicitly observable. This is particularly evident in NFRs related to system quality attributes such as performance, reliability, and maintainability.

For example, NFR #2 of the Car Rental Management System, "Providing a Wide Range of Applicability," does not yield any explicit underlying policies. This is because it is closely tied to the system's technical design, which requires variability modeling across the application family and mechanisms for both static and dynamic adaptability.

10.2 Step 2. Define Criteria for Tactics

This step is to define criteria for deriving architectural tactics that address the specified non-functional requirements. These criteria are systematically developed based on the identified facts and policies to ensure alignment with the system's requirements and constraints. Each criterion serves as an instructional or directive statement, providing a clear foundation for selecting and designing appropriate architectural tactics.

Mapping Between Facts/Policies and Criteria

The relationship between underlying facts and policies and the derived criteria is illustrated in Fig. 10.2.

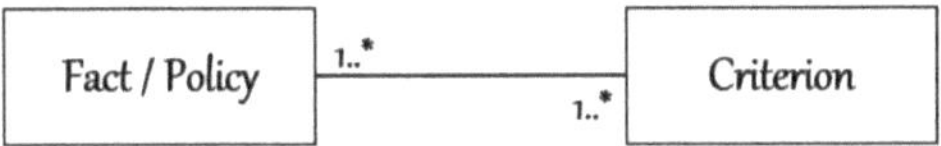

Fig. 10.2 Mapping Relationship Between Facts/Policies and Criteria

The mapping relationship is interpreted as follows:

- **Each criterion is grounded in one or more underlying facts or policies.** A criterion without such a foundation lacks justification and a logical basis for derivation, rendering it potentially invalid.
- **Each fact or policy contributes to the derivation of one or more criteria.** A fact or policy that does not inform any criterion is ineffective in supporting the architectural design process and may be considered irrelevant.
- **A one-to-one mapping often exists between facts/policies and criteria.** In many cases, a specific fact or policy directly informs the derivation of a single criterion, resulting in a clear and traceable relationship.

This mapping ensures traceability, logical coherence, and the validity of both the facts/policies and the criteria they support.

Specifying Criteria for Tactics

The criteria for deriving architectural tactics are typically expressed using consistent linguistic patterns to ensure clarity, traceability, and alignment with system objectives. Common phrasing patterns include:

- *The system should be designed to …*
- *There should be effective methods to …*
- *It is desirable to …*
- *The architecture must support …*

Each identified criterion is assigned a unique identifier, prefixed with the letter "C," and followed by a sequential number for clear differentiation. Each criterion should be documented using the following structured format:

- **(Criterion ID) <Title of the Criterion> (Relevant to <Fact #>)**
  <Description or the Criterion >

This structured format ensures clarity, consistency, and ease of reference when managing and validating the criteria derived from underlying facts and policies.

10.2.1 Task 1. Derive Criteria from Facts

This task is to derive criteria from the identified underlying facts in order to formulate effective architectural tactics. This process involves systematically analyzing each relevant fact and rephrasing it into clear, directive, and instructive language. The resulting criteria serve as actionable design guidelines that inform and guide the development of architectural tactics.

While underlying facts and their corresponding criteria are closely related, they differ in both purpose and form of expression. Underlying facts provide contextualized, detailed elaborations of non-functional requirements, whereas criteria are explicit, actionable directives that assist architects in selecting or designing suitable architectural tactics.

Example: Criteria From Underlying Facts

Consider the identified underlying facts for NFR #1, "Profitability of Car Rental Business." The following criteria are derived from these facts associated with this NFR:

(C1) Optimize and Propose Rental Fee Rates (Relevant to F1)
The system should be designed to analyze historical data and forecast future trends to identify high-demand car models. In addition, it should dynamically calculate and propose optimal rental fee rates. This optimization should balance customer appeal with profitability, ensuring the rates remain attractive while maximizing business revenue.

(C2) Maximize Profits from Insurance, Fuel, and Equipment Rentals (Relevant to F2)
The system should accurately compute and recommend optimal pricing for car insurance, pre-purchased fuel, and rental equipment fees. Pricing strategies must balance affordability with profitability, leveraging market trends, competitor analysis, and customer behavior to establish rates that encourage uptake while contributing positively to revenue.

(C3) Optimize Profits from Car Repairs (Relevant to F3)
The system should determine repair pricing by factoring in actual repair costs and applying an appropriate markup. Pricing should maintain a balance: excessive rates could reduce customer satisfaction, while overly low rates may impact net profit.

(C4) Select Cost-Effective Car Models (Relevant to F4)
The system should be designed to assist headquarters in identifying car models that provide the best value for money while meeting minimum quality standards. A highly effective decision-support mechanism should be utilized to evaluate models based on criteria such as purchase price, quality, reliability, and overall value.

(C5) Select Car Models with Low Maintenance Costs (Relevant to F5)
The system should be designed to assist headquarters choose car models that require minimal maintenance. A decision-support mechanism should be utilized to evaluate potential purchases based on historical maintenance records, durability, and total cost of ownership.

(C6) Select Car Models with Low Repair Costs (Relevant to F6)
The system should be designed to assist in selecting car models with lower associated repair costs. This involves integrating a decision-support mechanism that evaluates repair histories, assesses the cost-effectiveness of repairs, and analyzes overall vehicle reliability.

(C7) Select Car Models with Low Value Depreciation (Relevant to F7)
The system should support the selection of car models with low depreciation rates. It should incorporate a decision-support mechanism that analyzes and compares the depreciation trends of different models, ensuring investments retain value over time.

(C8) Maintain Dynamic Optimal Car Inventory Levels (Relevant to F8)
The system should facilitate dynamic management of car inventory levels, minimizing risks of overstocking or understocking. The design must account for seasonal fluctuations and demand variations from special events, ensuring the inventory remains aligned with optimal levels throughout the year.

As demonstrated in the example, criteria are systematically derived from underlying facts. To support traceability, each criterion is annotated with references to its corresponding underlying facts, indicated in parentheses (e.g., "Relevant to F1").

10.2.2 Task 2. Derive Criteria from Policies

This task is to derive criteria from underlying policies to formulate architecture tactics. This can be done systematically by analyzing the relevant policies and translating them into clear, instructive, and actionable language to ensure alignment with architectural goals.

Example: Criteria From Underlying Policies
Consider the identified underlying policies for NFR #1, "Profitability of Car Rental Business." The following criteria are derived from these policies associated with this NFR:

(C9) Procuring New Rental Cars by Considering Budget and Parking Lot Availability (Relevant to P1 and P2)
The system should be designed to generate optimal procedural plans that consider the allocated budget (as specified in policy P1) and the constraints of available parking space (as specified in policy P2).

(C10) Apply Tactics for Incentivizing Advanced Reservations (Relevant to P3)
The system should be designed to provide a range of incentives for customers who make reservations well in advance. This feature is intended to promote early bookings, thereby enhancing customer commitment and increasing predictability in rental demand.

At this stage, the total number of criteria for NFR #1 is 10—eight derived from underlying facts and two from underlying policies.

10.3 Step 3. Define Candidate Tactics

This step is to define candidate architecture tactics based on the identified criteria. The architecture tactics for the given NFR should be designed to align closely with and satisfy the specified criteria. The mapping relationship between criteria and their corresponding architecture tactics is illustrated in Fig. 10.3.

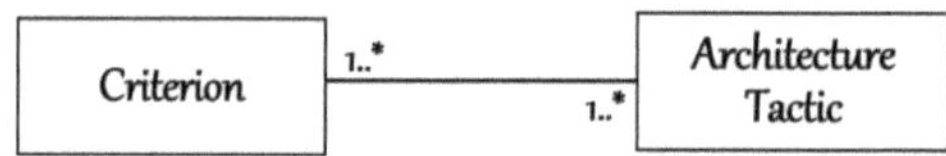

Fig. 10.3 Mapping Relationship Between Criteria and Architecture Tactics

This figure illustrates the many-to-many relationship between criteria and architecture tactics, characterized by two cardinalities. From criterion to architecture tactics, each criterion may influence one or more tactics. This means that a single criterion may require multiple tactics to address different aspects of the requirement or to offer alternative solutions. Conversely, from architecture tactics to criterion, each tactic may address one or more criteria. This implies that a single tactic can be designed to fulfill multiple criteria simultaneously, serving as a shared solution for related or overlapping requirements.

10.3.1 Task 1. Propose Candidate Architecture Tactics

This task is to propose candidate architecture tactics based on the identified criteria. An architecture tactic is a detailed method or strategy that realizes a specific non-functional requirement (NFR), either partially or fully. The relationship between architecture tactics and their associated NFRs is characterized by a *many-to-many cardinality*, as illustrated in Fig. 10.4.

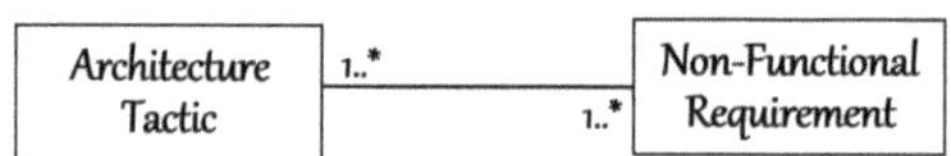

Fig. 10.4 Mapping Relationship Between Architecture Tactics and NFR Items

In the figure, the relationship is bidirectional. From architecture tactics to NFRs, each tactic may address one or more non-functional requirements (1..). While most tactics are designed to target a specific NFR, some may contribute to multiple requirements. Conversely, from NFRs to architecture tactics, each NFR is typically supported by a combination of multiple tactics (1..), as a single tactic is rarely sufficient to fully satisfy the complex and multifaceted characteristics of a given NFR.

Challenges in Defining Architecture Tactics

Deriving effective architecture tactics for NFRs is a highly technical and challenging design activity, particularly when addressing non-conventional or emerging NFRs. These challenges arise primarily due to the following factors:

- **Complexity of Non-Functional Requirements**
  NFRs are inherently complex and multi-dimensional, each being associated with various underlying factors, constraints, and policies. Many NFRs pertain to quality attributes such as performance, reliability, or security, which demand careful and systematic design strategies. Achieving high-quality attributes requires a deep understanding of the requirements, a rigorous evaluation of potential tactics, and innovative approaches.
- **Crosscutting Concerns of NFRs**
  The scope of an NFR often spans multiple components and processes within the system, complicating the design of effective tactics. These concerns impact various architectural views and design elements, increasing the complexity of coordination and the likelihood of unintended ripple effects.
- **Interdependencies among NFRs**
  NFRs often exhibit interdependencies, wherein fulfilling one may influence or constrain others. Although ideally independent, NFRs frequently conflict or overlap, making isolation difficult. Managing these interdependencies is essential to achieving balanced and coherent architectural solutions.
- **Conflicts among Applied Tactics**
  Architecture tactics intended for one NFR may conflict with those required for another. Resolving such conflicts demands prioritization, trade-off analysis, and coordination to avoid compromising overall system quality and integrity.
- **Context-Dependent Nature of Tactics**
  The effectiveness of a tactic depends on its fit with the system's technological, organizational, and operational context. "One-size-fits-all" approaches are rarely sufficient. Tailoring tactics to specific system environments is necessary to ensure successful implementation.
- **Impact of Resource Constraints on Tactics**
  Architecture tactics can be resource intensive, requiring time, expertise, and investment. Resource constraints may limit the ability to apply optimal tactics, forcing compromises in architectural decisions. Balancing resource availability with architectural quality is a critical aspect of NFR-oriented design.

Architecture Tactics for Conventional and Non-Conventional NFRs

NFRs can be categorized as conventional, non-conventional, or hybrid. Conventional NFRs are commonly found across various systems and often pertain to specific quality attributes. ISO/IEC 9126 is a representative international standard for defining a software quality model [33], extensively applied in industrial systems development.

The quality attributes specified in this standard are shown in Fig. 10.5.

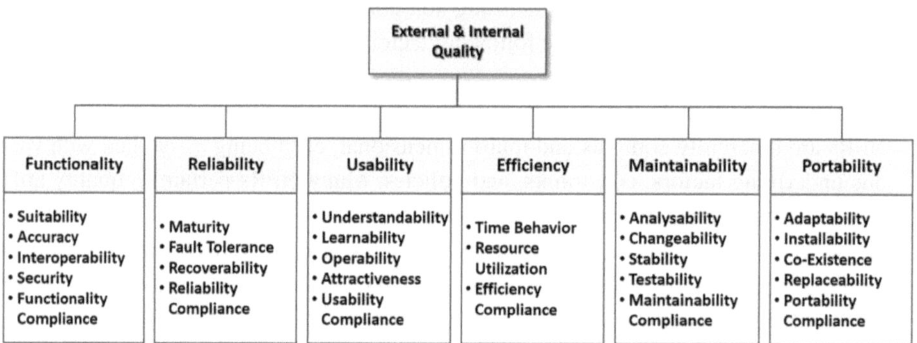

Fig. 10.5 Quality Attributes Defined in ISO 9126

This standard framework categorizes software quality into six characteristics, each further subdivided into corresponding sub-characteristics. For instance, the characteristic of *Reliability* is decomposed into sub-characteristics such as *Maturity*, *Fault Tolerance*, *Recoverability*, and *Reliability Compliance.*

Effective tactics for addressing conventional non-functional requirements (NFRs), including the quality attributes defined in ISO/IEC 9126, are widely available in books, academic literature, Web sites, and project reports. Consequently, architects are encouraged to prioritize leveraging existing resources to source proven tactics before developing new ones from scratch.

Non-conventional NFRs refer to requirements that are uniquely tailored to a specific software system and are not commonly encountered across a wide variety of systems. In contrast to conventional NFRs, which are broadly applicable to most software systems, non-conventional NFRs are typically customized to address specialized needs or constraints specific to a particular system or domain.

Examples of NFRs include enhancing the profitability of a car rental business and providing high performance in diagnosing liver cancers using CT scans. These NFRs are considered non-conventional because they are domain specific and do not directly align with traditional quality attributes. The first is specific to the car rental industry, emphasizing business-oriented objectives, while the second is tailored to the medical imaging domain, focusing on diagnostic efficiency and accuracy.

As illustrated by these examples, non-conventional NFRs often stem from niche user requirements, domain-specific constraints, or unique technical challenges. As a result, common solutions or best practices for addressing such NFRs are rarely available in existing literature or online resources. Instead, tailored methods, approaches, and strategies must be specifically developed to address the needs of the target system.

Taxonomy of Architecture Tactics

Addressing the challenges in defining architecture tactics raises two practical questions: how can architecture tactics be effectively formulated, and what qualifies as an architecture tactic that can be systematically identified? To address these questions, a taxonomy of architecture tactics can be employed. This taxonomy serves as a guiding framework for the systematic identification, classification, and application of tactics that are specifically tailored to satisfy non-functional requirements and align with the unique context of the system.

- **Tactics Based on Software Design Principles**
  These tactics apply foundational Software Design Principles—such as abstraction, encapsulation, modularity, separation of concerns, and the open-closed principle—to achieve NFRs like maintainability, scalability, and reusability.
- **Tactics Based on Object-Oriented Constructs**
  These tactics utilize object-oriented modeling constructs including inheritance, polymorphism, composition, and interfaces to satisfy NFRs by enhancing modularity, extensibility, and flexibility in design.
- **Tactics Based on Design Patterns**
  Design patterns are reusable solutions to recurring design problems. By applying patterns such as Singleton, Strategy, or Observer, architects can address NFRs including flexibility, performance, and maintainability through well-established, consistent strategies.
- **Tactics Based on Algorithms**
  Algorithmic tactics focus on the selection, design, and optimization of algorithms to fulfill specific NFRs. Since algorithms directly influence system behavior, response time, and resource utilization, these tactics are critical to performance, efficiency, and responsiveness.
- **Tactics Based on Machine Learning**
  These tactics integrate machine learning models to address NFRs in dynamic environments where systems must adapt, learn from data, and make data-driven decisions. Such tactics are particularly effective for enhancing adaptability, intelligence, and automation.
- **Tactics Based on Reusable Assets**
  These tactics promote the reuse of existing software components—such as libraries, modules, templates, or frameworks—to improve development efficiency, reduce cost, and ensure design consistency. They support standardization and faster development cycles.
- **Tactics for Utilizing Services**
  These tactics involve the integration of external services (e.g., APIs, microservices, cloud-based solutions) to offload functionality and meet NFRs such as scalability, modularity, and cost efficiency. Services provide specialized capabilities without duplicating effort.

- **Tactics for Utilizing Frameworks and Platforms**
  These tactics leverage established software frameworks (e.g., Spring, Django, Angular) and platforms (e.g., Kubernetes, AWS) to streamline development, enforce architectural consistency, and meet NFRs such as maintainability, scalability, and deployment efficiency.
- **Tactics Based on Operational Guidelines**
  Operational tactics define best practices and procedures for reliable system operation. These include protocols for monitoring, security, incident response, and backup. By enforcing operational discipline, such tactics help ensure system resilience, compliance, and predictability.

By systematically employing these categories of tactics, architects can more effectively address complex and multifaceted NFRs, ensuring alignment with system-level design objectives and constraints.

Example : Tactics for NFR #1. Profitability of Car Rental Business
Based on the defined criteria for this NFR, the following architecture tactics are proposed:

(T1) Support Vector Regression to Determine Optimal Rental Fee Rates (Relevant to C1)
(T2) Multi-Variable Multi-Class Classification Using Neural Network (Relevant to C2)
(T3) Dynamic Pricing: Balancing Supply-Demand and Competitor Pricing (Relevant to C2)
(T4) Customer Feedback Loop for Optimizing the Classification Model (Relevant to C2)
(T5) Customer Feedback Loop for Optimizing Repair Cost Rates (Relevant to C3)
(T6) Multi-variable Classification Using Neural Network (Relevant to C4, C5, C6, C7)
(T7) Simulated Annealing Algorithm for Rental Car Relocation Planning (Relevant to C8)
(T8) Cost-Benefit Analysis for Discarding High-Cost Incurring Rental Cars (Relevant to C8)
(T9) Loyalty Program for Advanced Reservations (Relevant to C9)

These tactics illustrate a many-to-many cardinality between the criteria and the proposed architecture tactics. For example, tactic *T6* is designed to address four criteria—*C4*, *C5*, *C6*, and *C7*—while some criteria, such as *C2* or *C8*, are addressed by multiple tactics.

Example : Tactics for NFR #2. Wide Range of Applicability
Based on the defined criteria for this NFR, the following architecture tactics are proposed:

(T1) Class Inheritance Hierarchy of *Car Model* (Relevant to C1)
(T2) GPS Gateway with Required Interfaces for Various GPS Models (Relevant to C2)
(T3) Template Method Pattern for Various Checkout Processes (Relevant to C3)
(T4) Decorator Patten to Dynamically Select Factors for Rental Fee Rates (Relevant to C4)
(T5) Decorator Pattern to Dynamically Select Discount Factors (Relevant to C5)
(T6) Strategy Pattern to Support Various Payment Methods (Relevant to C6)
(T7) Adaptor Pattern to Support Various Interfaces of External Systems (Relevant to C7)
(T8) Mediator Pattern to Support Various Interfaces of External Systems (Relevant to C7)

A total of eight architecture tactics were derived based on the identified set of seven criteria.

10.3.2 Task 2. Detail Candidate Architecture Tactics

This task is to comprehensively define the candidate architectural tactics, providing all necessary technical details. Each tactic should be described in a clear, precise, and concise manner to ensure that it is easily understood by other developers.

Architectural tactics are most effectively described using a combination of textual explanations, diagrams, figures, tables, examples, and pseudocode. Relying solely on simplified textual descriptions may introduce ambiguity, while presenting a tactic only through pseudocode without explanatory context can hinder comprehension. Therefore, a balanced and well-integrated approach to representation is essential for effective communication.

The level of technical detail required for describing tactics depends on several factors, including the following:

- **Complexity of the Tactic**
  Tactics that address highly complex or domain-specific requirements may necessitate more detailed and explicit descriptions.
- **Target Audience**
  The expertise and familiarity of the intended audience—such as developers, architects, or stakeholders—influence the required depth of technical elaboration.
- **Criticality of the Tactic**
  The significance of the tactic in achieving the system's objectives affects the level of detail needed. Tactics associated with critical NFRs often require in-depth technical elaboration to ensure correct and reliable implementation.
- **Availability of Supporting Resources**
  When complementary resources such as diagrams, examples, or related documentation are available, textual descriptions can be more concise and focused, leveraging those materials to enhance clarity and understanding.

Example: Description of Tactic T3 for NFR #1: Dynamic Pricing by Balancing Supply-Demand and Competitor Pricing
This tactic aims to determine optimal car rental fees by analyzing supply-demand dynamics and monitoring competitor pricing strategies, thereby enabling the formulation of pricing schemes that attract customers while ensuring profitability. This tactic is realized through the following tasks:

- **Constructing a Demand Forecasting Model**
  A demand forecasting model can be developed using time series analysis to predict future demand for rental cars. This model should incorporate historical demand patterns, market trends, holidays, and special events to improve accuracy.

- **Monitoring Competitor Pricing**
  Continuously collect and analyze pricing data from competing car rental services to identify pricing trends. The insights obtained can guide pricing adjustments to maintain competitiveness. This task may be conducted manually by centralized pricing teams.
- **Building Support Vector Regression (SVR) Model for Dynamic Price Adjustment**
  SVR is a supervised machine learning algorithm designed to predict continuous-valued target variables. It constructs a regression function that approximates the target outputs by fitting a hyperplane within an ε-insensitive margin (ε-tube), where deviations within ε are considered negligible. The model simultaneously aims to minimize the empirical prediction error and the complexity of the function, thereby achieving good generalization performance.
  To enhance the SVR model's responsiveness to market dynamics, the following contextual input features can be engineered and incorporated:
  - **Temporal features**: Encodings of seasonal patterns (e.g., month, week, holiday indicators), which account for recurring demand variations
  - **Event-based variables**: Binary or frequency indicators for local events (e.g., festivals, conventions, sporting events) that are known to cause temporary demand surges
  - **Competitor pricing metrics**: Time-aligned average or minimum prices from competing businesses, which serve as external benchmarks
  - **Demand proxies**: Real-time or historical indicators such as tourist arrival volumes, hotel occupancy rates, or Web search trends
    Select the Radial Basis Function (RBF) kernel to model nonlinear relationships inherent in pricing behavior. Evaluate the SVR model using time-series-aware cross-validation methods and appropriate performance metrics, such as Mean Absolute Error (MAE) and Root Mean Squared Error (RMSE), to ensure robust and accurate predictive performance.

Example: Description of Tactic T2 for NFR #2: GPS Gateway with Required Interfaces for Various GPS Models

This tactic defines a *GPS Gateway* that provides a device-independent interface for retrieving GPS location data. It serves the client component, *In-Rental Manager*, by abstracting the underlying GPS access mechanisms. As illustrated in Fig. 10.6, the gateway supports multiple retrieval schemes by defining three required interfaces.

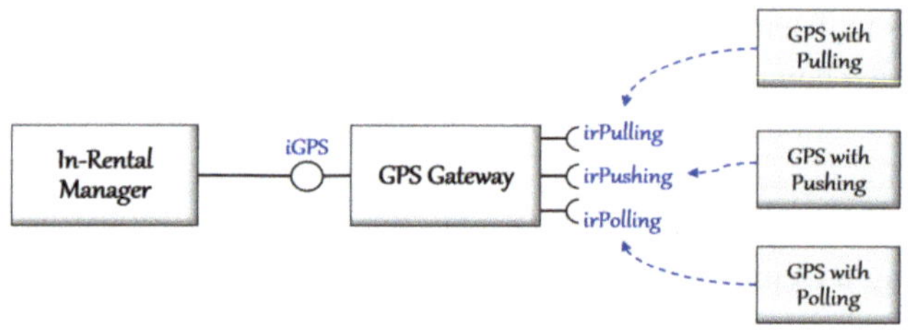

Fig. 10.6 GPS Gateway with Required Interfaces

- **Provided Interface of GPS Gateway**
  GPS devices support different location retrieval schemes, including pulling, pushing, and polling. The *GPS Gateway* functions as an intermediary between the *In-Rental Manager* component and the GPS devices installed in rental cars. It provides a standardized *Provided Interface*, denoted as *iGPS*, which abstracts the differences in retrieval methods. This interface standardization ensures consistent communication and neutralizes variability across heterogeneous GPS models.
- **Required Interface of GPS Gateway**
  GPS Gateway also specifies distinct *Required Interfaces* corresponding to each supported retrieval method. In UML, a required interface defines a set of methods that an external component must implement to achieve interoperability. Each GPS device model implements one of these interfaces based on its supported retrieval scheme. When a GPS device is integrated into the system, it connects to the *In-Rental Manager* through the *GPS Gateway*, ensuring seamless interoperability regardless of the retrieval mechanism employed.

By applying this tactic, the system achieves modularity and adaptability in handling diverse GPS device behaviors. It decouples the *In-Rental Manager* from device-specific logic, thereby facilitating integration of new GPS models with minimal impact on existing components and enhancing maintainability and scalability of the location retrieval subsystem.

10.4 Step 4. Evaluate Candidate Tactics

This step is to evaluate the candidate architectural tactics and select the most appropriate ones to be incorporated into the architectural design process. The evaluation ensures that the chosen tactics are aligned with the system's architectural objectives and constraints.

10.4.1 Task 1. Analyze Costs and Benefits

This task is to evaluate the costs and benefits associated with each candidate architectural tactic. Cost-benefit analysis in this context involves systematically assessing and comparing the implementation costs against the anticipated benefits of each tactic.

Cost Benefit Analysis (CBA)
CBA is a systematic process used to evaluate the financial and non-financial costs and benefits of a project, decision, or action. It is commonly used in decision-making across various domains to determine the best course of action by comparing the expected benefits to the associated costs.

CBA in the context of architecture design involves assessing the trade-offs associated with implementing specific architectural tactics. It helps architects determine which tactics provide the most value relative to their cost by considering factors such as development effort, resource allocation, operational efficiency, and alignment with system goals.

CBA for evaluating architectural tactics is conducted through the following steps:

- **Step 1. Estimate Benefits**
  Architectural tactics are designed to yield specific benefits by addressing targeted non-functional requirements (NFRs). This step involves summarizing the anticipated advantages of each tactic. These may include improvements in system quality attributes such as performance, reliability, or usability. Additionally, benefits may manifest as enhanced user satisfaction, reduced operational risks, or long-term cost savings achieved through increased efficiency and decreased maintenance demands.
- **Step 2. Estimate Costs**
  This step focuses on identifying and estimating the costs associated with implementing each tactic. These costs typically include the development time and effort required; expenditures for acquiring necessary hardware, software, or third-party services; and the ongoing maintenance and support throughout the system's lifecycle. An important consideration in this step is the potential for conflicts with other tactics, as the implementation of one tactic may interfere with or diminish the effectiveness of another within the architecture.
- **Step 3. Compare Costs and Benefits to Select Tactics**
  In this step, the cost-to-benefit ratio of each tactic is evaluated to identify those that provide the greatest value relative to their investment. The comparison involves assessing trade-offs between the costs and benefits and prioritizing tactics that maximize value while staying within project constraints. By carefully analyzing these factors, architects can select a set of tactics that best support the system's objectives and offer optimal returns in terms of quality and performance.

The CBA for evaluating architectural tactics can be effectively presented in a tabular format, as shown in Table 10.1.

Table 10.1 Tactic Evaluation Table

Tactics	Y/N	Justification
(T1) Title of Tactic	Y	**Benefits**: Describe the benefits of the tactic. **Costs**: Describe the associated costs, risks, and drawbacks. **Decision**: Explain the rationale behind the decision to adopt or reject the tactic.
(T2) Title of Tactic	N	**Benefits**: … **Costs**: … **Decision**: …

The *Tactic Evaluation Table* consists of three columns.

- **Column of Tactics**
  This column lists the architectural tactics under evaluation, each identified by a unique label and title.
- **Column of Y/N**
  This column indicates the selection status of each tactic: selected (Y) or rejected (N), based on the outcome of the evaluation process.
- **Column of Justification**
  This column summarizes the rationale for the decision to adopt or reject the tactic. It describes the anticipated benefits in addressing relevant non-functional requirements; outlines the associated costs, risks, and trade-offs; and presents the final decision logic. This ensures transparency and supports informed architectural decision-making.

10.4.2 Task 2. Determine the Applicability of Architecture Tactics

This task is to determine whether each candidate architectural tactic should be accepted or rejected based on a thorough analysis of its anticipated benefits and associated costs. A tactic should be selected if it offers substantial benefits and effectively contributes to satisfying the targeted NFR, provided that its implementation and operational costs are within acceptable limits. Conversely, a tactic should be discarded if its costs or risks outweigh the benefits, even when those benefits are potentially significant.

In cases where the trade-offs between benefits and costs are unclear—particularly when uncertainty exists regarding development effort, integration complexity, or long-term operational impact—the decision should be escalated to relevant stakeholders for further evaluation and resolution. For each tactic under consideration, indicate the decision in the *Tactic Evaluation Table* by marking "Y" (accepted) or "N" (rejected) in the corresponding column.

Example
Consider evaluating the candidate tactics for NFR #2, *Providing Wide Range of Applicability*, in the Car Rental Management System. The results of this evaluation are summarized in the tactic evaluation table, presented in Table 10.2.

The three tactics, T1, T2, and T3, were all accepted based on the results of their cost-benefit analysis (CBA). These tactics were selected because they offered substantial benefits in meeting the system's requirements while maintaining acceptable levels of cost and risk.

- **(T1) Class Inheritance Hierarchy of Car Model** was accepted due to its effectiveness in enhancing flexibility, modifiability, and extensibility for managing various car models, with minimal implementation costs.

Table 10.2 Tactic Evaluation Table for NFR #2 in Car Rental Management System

Tactics	Y/N	Justification
(T1) Class Inheritance Hierarchy of Car Model	**Y**	**Benefits:** Specializing the Car Model using a class inheritance hierarchy improves flexibility, modifiability, and extensibility, thereby facilitating the management of diverse car models **Costs:** The design and implementation of the class hierarchy incur minimal cost and complexity **Decision:** This tactic is essential for ensuring the system's high applicability, as it provides significant benefits with minimal development costs and no runtime overhead
(T2) GPS Gateway with Required Interfaces for Various GPS Models	**Y**	**Benefits:** The GPS Gateway provides a uniform provided interface for location retrieval, effectively neutralizing variability across different location retrieval schemes. It also defines distinct required interfaces for various location retrieval methods **Costs:** Implementing the GPS Gateway and the required interfaces for different GPS devices involves moderate costs **Decision:** This tactic efficiently manages the variability of GPS devices available in the market while offering a consistent interface to the In-Rental Manager component. It achieves this with moderate implementation costs and no significant risks
(T3) Template Method Pattern for Supporting Various Checkout Processes	**Y**	**Benefits:** The Template Method pattern defines the skeleton of the *checkoutRentalCar()* algorithm while allowing subclasses for different regions to customize specific steps of the algorithm **Costs:** Implementing the Template Method and defining four abstract methods for different regions incurs moderate costs **Decision:** This tactic improves the reusability of the template method and simplifies the implementation of invariant parts of the algorithm within the superclass, with no significant costs or risks
(T4) …		…

- **(T2) GPS Gateway with Required Interfaces** was also accepted, as it provides a standardized interface for location retrieval while efficiently handling variability across GPS devices. The associated costs are moderate, with no significant risks identified.
- **(T3) Template Method Pattern** was accepted for its ability to define a reusable algorithmic skeleton for the checkout process, enabling regional customization with moderate implementation effort and no apparent risks.

10.5 Step 5. Integrate Selected Tactics

This step is to assess the impacts of the selected architectural tactics and incorporate them into the view-based architectural design. The resulting architecture should be a comprehensive model that satisfies both functional and non-functional requirements.

Each architectural tactic influences one or more design elements to realize its intended effects. Therefore, it is essential to first conduct a thorough analysis of how each tactic affects relevant architectural components, connectors, interfaces, and configurations. Following this analysis, the selected tactics should be systematically integrated into the appropriate architectural views—such as structural, behavioral, or deployment views—ensuring that the architecture remains cohesive, traceable, and aligned with system objectives.

10.5.1 Task 1. Analyze Impacts of Architecture Tactics

This task is to evaluate the impact of each selected architectural tactic on various architectural views and, where applicable, on the schematic architecture. The influence on an architectural view may involve introducing new design elements or modifying existing ones. In the case of schematic architecture, the impact is typically more localized and may involve refining specific structural aspects of the system.

The architectural design elements influenced by a tactic are illustrated in Fig. 10.7.

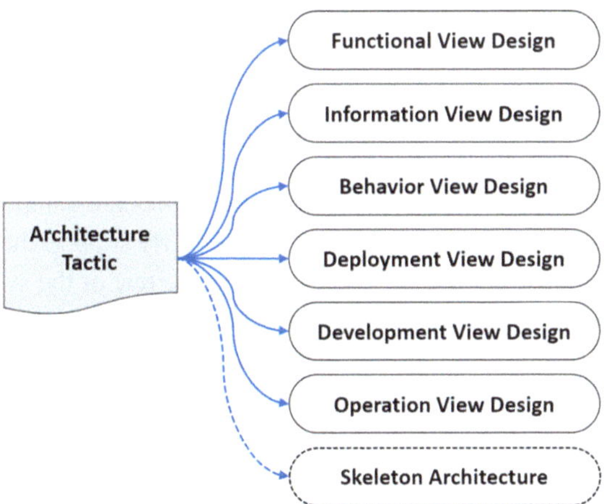

Fig. 10.7 Impacts of Architecture Tactics

As shown in the figure, architectural tactics can affect multiple architectural views. Occasionally, they may also influence the schematic architecture—though such impacts are typically rare and limited in scope.

The impacts of each tactic on various architectural design elements are elaborated as follows:

- **Impacts of Tactics on Functional View**
  Tactics can affect the functional view of a system in several ways. One effect is adding a new functional component, which is appropriate when the tactic introduces a new capability not supported by existing components. In this case, a new component should be added to provide the required functionality. Another effect is refining the functionality of a component, which involves adjusting the specific functions or features of an existing component to support the tactic.
  Tactics may also require modifying the allocation of functional components, especially when functionality needs to be redistributed across system tiers. This means reassigning components to better fit the new structure. Finally, if a tactic changes a component's functionality, it may also require modifying the component's interface. In such cases, the interface should be updated to reflect the new behavior and ensure proper integration.
- **Impacts of Tactics on Information View**
  Tactics can influence the information view of a system in various ways. One common impact is adding a new data component, which becomes necessary when a tactic introduces a new dataset not currently handled by existing components. In such cases, a new data component should be added to manage this persistent data. Another impact involves refining the persistence of a data component, which means updating the attributes of an existing component to reflect changes in how data is managed.
  Tactics may also require modifying the allocation of data components. This happens when the distribution of datasets across system tiers needs to change. To support this, data components should be reassigned to match the new structure. Finally, if a data component's attributes are modified, the interface of the data component may also need to change. This ensures that the component can properly support the updated data characteristics and continue to integrate correctly with the rest of the system.
  When a tactic requires changing the object persistence scheme, consider adapting the current object persistence design to support the new scheme. For example, this may involve transitioning from a relational database to a NoSQL database for object persistence. Such a change can result in significant modifications to both the functional and information views. Therefore, it is essential to provide a clear and well-justified rationale before proceeding with the change.
- **Impacts of Tactics on Behavior View**
  Tactics can influence the behavior view of a system in several important ways. One such effect is modifying the interaction patterns. Since invocation patterns among functional elements play a key role in shaping the system's overall control flow, any changes introduced by architectural tactics may require these patterns to be updated accordingly.

Another impact is modifying the overall control flow. When the functional view is changed due to tactics, and interaction patterns are adjusted, the control flow must be revised. This may involve updating threads, altering the sequence of actions, or adding new threads in activity diagrams to reflect the new system behavior.

Finally, modifying detailed control flows may also be necessary. These control flows describe the internal behavior of components using diagrams or pseudocode. If a tactic alters the way a component behaves, it is important to update the detailed control flow to match the new behavior.

- **Impacts of Tactics on Deployment View**

  Tactics can have several impacts on the deployment view of a system. One such impact is modifying device nodes, which occurs when changes to the hardware configuration are needed. In this case, the hardware specifications of the device nodes should be updated accordingly. Another impact is modifying execution environment nodes, where changes to the environment settings or configurations require revising the specifications of those environment nodes.

  Tactics may also lead to modifying network connectivity. When the network configuration between nodes is affected, it is necessary to update the network settings to reflect the new arrangement. Lastly, modifying the allocation of software artifacts may be required. If tactics affect how software components are deployed across nodes, the allocation of these artifacts should be revised to ensure they are properly distributed in the updated deployment configuration.

- **Impacts of Tactics on Development View**

  Although architects do not typically define the development view in detail, there are cases where specifying the ideal development process and technical guidelines becomes necessary—particularly for designing and implementing components, including the training of machine learning models. When a tactic impacts the development process, component design guidelines, or model training procedures, the development view should be updated accordingly to reflect these changes.

- **Impacts of Tactics on Operation View**

  Although architects do not typically define the operation view in detail, there are cases where specifying guidelines for system operations and maintenance becomes important. When a tactic affects operational procedures—such as backups, archival, system restoration, or version upgrades—the operation view should be updated to reflect these changes accordingly.

- **Impacts of Tactics on Schematic Architecture**

  The schematic architecture of a system is typically intended to remain stable throughout the development process, and architectural tactics generally do not directly affect it. However, in some cases, the initial schematic architecture may have been defined without fully accounting for critical structural characteristics, constraints, or key quality requirements.

For example, a schematic architecture based on a client-server model with a single server instance introduces the risk of a system-wide failure if the server becomes unavailable—commonly known as a Single Node Failure. To mitigate this risk and enhance system reliability, architects may apply tactics such as redundancy and load balancing. Applying these tactics may require adding new architectural elements or modifying the existing schematic architecture to improve fault tolerance.

Representing Impacts of Architecture Tactics

The impacts of architectural tactics can be systematically captured using a tabular format, as illustrated in Table 10.3.

Table 10.3 Impacts of Architecture Tactics

	Functional View	Information View	Behavior View	Deployment View	Development View	Operation View	Schematic Architecture
T1							
T2							
...							

This table provides a structured overview of how each architectural tactic influences various architectural views and the schematic architecture. Each row represents a specific tactic, while each column denotes a particular architectural view or the schematic architecture that may be affected by that tactic. Each cell in the table contains a brief description of the specific impact the tactic has on the corresponding architectural element, where applicable.

For example, consider the architectural tactics designed to address NFR #2, "Providing a Wide Range of Applicability," in the Car Rental Management System, as listed below.

(T1) Class Inheritance Hierarchy of *Car Model*
(T2) GPS Gateway with Required Interfaces for Various GPS Models
(T3) Template Method Pattern for Supporting Various Checkout Processes
(T4) Decorator Patten to Dynamically Select Factors for Rental Fee Rates
(T5) Decorator Pattern to Dynamically Select Discount Factors
(T6) Strategy Pattern to Support Various Payment Methods
(T7) Adaptor Pattern to Support Various Interfaces of External Systems
(T8) Mediator Pattern to Support Various Interfaces of External Systems

The impacts of these tactics are summarized in Table 10.4.

Table 10.4 Impacts of Architecture Tactics for NFR #2 in the Car Rental Management System

	Functional View	Information View	Behavior View	Deployment View
T1		Define an inheritance hierarchy of various car models	Define a subclass for a new model and specialize the methods	
T2	Define a provided interface and different required interfaces for GPS Gateway			Implement the required interface for new GPS device type, and bind it to *GPS Gateway* component
T3	Define a template method of checking out rental cars and subclasses for specializing varying steps		Bind an instance of an appropriate subclass, and invoke the template methods	
T4	Specialize classes of Decorator pattern to model the various rental fee factors		Choose concrete decorators for the applicable rental fee factors	
T5	Specialize classes of Decorator pattern to model the various discount factors		Choose concrete decorators for the applicable discount factors	
T6	Define an interface in the abstract strategy class and specialize the methods for various payment methods	Add attributes to store the payment methods used for the checkout transaction	Choose an appropriate concrete strategy class, and bind its instance to the superclass object	
T7	Implement adapter classes for accessing external systems		Invoke the adapter objects to access external systems	
T8	Implement mediator classes to enable collaboration with incompatible external systems		Invoke the mediator objects to access external systems	

As shown in the table, each architectural tactic is linked to specific impacts on relevant architectural views. For instance, Tactic T1 affects the information and behavior views, while Tactic T2 influences both the functional and deployment views.

10.5.2 Task 2. Apply Impacts of Architecture Tactics

This task is to integrate the selected architectural tactics into the existing architectural design, ensuring consistency with the impact analysis performed in the previous task. For each tactic, the corresponding impacts should be implemented across the relevant architecture views and, where applicable, the schematic architecture. This process may involve a range of updates, including revising textual descriptions, updating diagrams, and refining algorithms to reflect the applied tactics accurately.

Example

Consider applying Tactic T3 for NFR #2, which aims to support variability in checkout processes across car rental applications. This tactic allows specific steps of the checkout process to be customized by individual applications, both statically and dynamically.

This tactic impacts on both functional and behavior views, as specified in Table 10.4.

- **Applying the Tactic T3 on the Functional View**

  The impact of Tactic T3 on the functional view is to introduce a class inheritance hierarchy for the *CheckoutManager* by applying the *Template Method* design pattern. This pattern delineates the closed and open aspects in accordance with the Open-Closed Principle. The *template method* encapsulates the fixed procedure (closed part), while the *abstract methods*, implemented by subclasses, represent the customizable steps (open part).

  The resulting class diagram that reflects this impact is shown in Fig. 10.8.

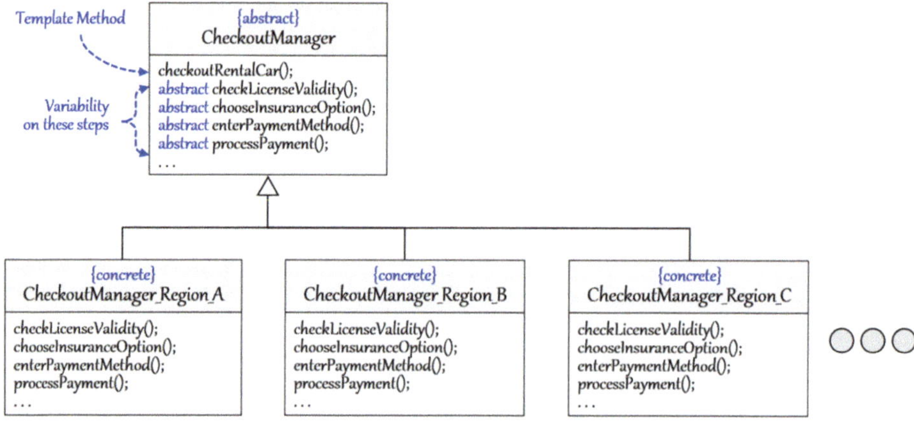

Fig. 10.8 Applying template method pattern on functional view design

The *CheckoutManager* serves as a central functional component within the Car Rental Management System. It is specialized into regional subclasses to accommodate region-specific checkout processes. A template method, *checkoutRentalCar()*, is defined to establish a common control flow.

It also declares four abstract methods to enable region-specific customization:

```
checkLicenseValidity()
chooseInsuranceOption()
enterPaymentMethod()
processPayment()
```

These methods are intentionally declared as abstract to support variability in implementation across different regions. Each subclass provides concrete definitions for these methods to meet the operational and regulatory requirements of its respective region.

- **Applying the Tactic T3 on Behavior View**

  The impact of Tactic T3 on the behavior view is to define a common control procedure for the *checkoutRentalCar()* method, as shown in Fig. 10.9.

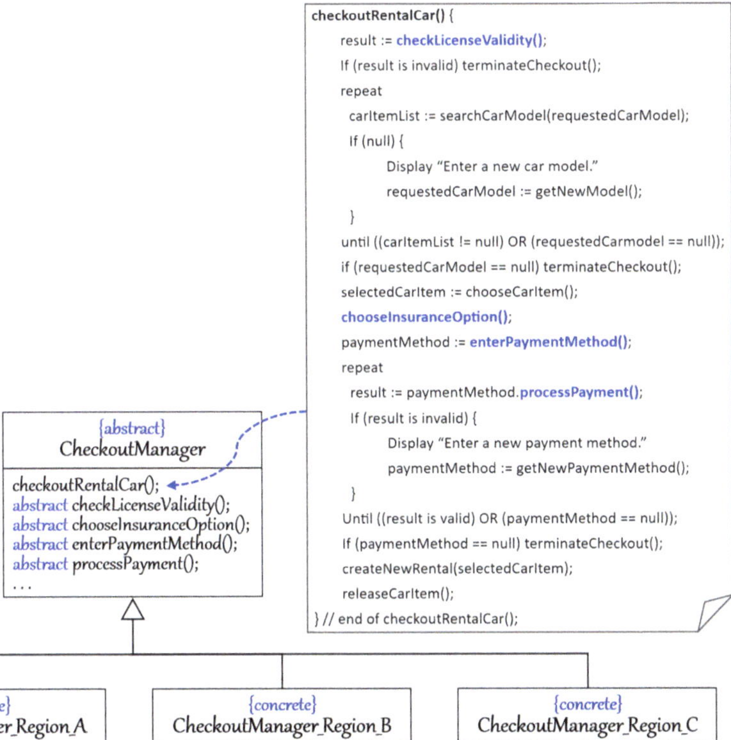

Fig. 10.9 Applying template method pattern on behavior view design

The figure illustrates the control flow of the checkoutRentalCar() template method in pseudocode format. This procedure is fixed and not subject to modification, comprising a sequence of method invocations, including four abstract methods: *checkLicenseValidity()*, *chooseInsuranceOption()*, *enterPaymentMethod()*, and *processPayment()*. These steps are highlighted in the diagram to indicate variability points. Each abstract method is implemented by a corresponding subclass. When the *checkoutRentalCar()* method is invoked, the runtime system dynamically binds to the subclass-specific implementations of these abstract methods. This behavior leverages object substitution and dynamic binding, enabling consistent execution of the overall procedure while supporting region-specific variations.

10.6 Step 6. Validate Conformance

This step aims to validate the conformance of intermediate design artifacts to their preceding artifacts, which were produced during earlier stages of the design process for NFRs. In software development, each artifact is typically derived from a foundational predecessor, and validating conformance ensures consistency and alignment with the intended design objectives [34].

More specifically, each step in the NFR-based design activity produces a corresponding set of design artifacts, as outlined below:

- **Step 1: Identify Facts and Policies** → Yields a documented set of relevant facts and system-level policies
- **Step 2: Define Criteria for Tactics** → Results in a well-defined set of selection criteria for evaluating architectural tactics
- **Step 3: Define Candidate Tactics** → Produces a list of potential tactics that address the targeted non-functional requirements
- **Step 4: Evaluate Candidate Tactics** → Results in a refined set of selected tactics based on the defined criteria
- **Step 5: Apply Selected Tactics** → Produces a set of architectural views refined through the integration of the selected tactics

The conformance relationships between artifacts produced in consecutive steps must be preserved to ensure the overall validity and traceability of the design process. Representative examples of these conformance relationships are provided below.

- Each criterion must be derived from one or more underlying facts or policies.
- Each candidate tactic must be formulated based on one or more defined criteria.
- Each selected tactic must be traceable to a corresponding candidate tactic.
- Each refinement in the view-based architectural design must explicitly reflect the impact of an applied tactic on the corresponding architectural view.

10.6.1 Task 1. Construct Conformance Map

This task is to construct a conformance map that illustrates the relationships between the artifacts produced in the current step and those produced in the preceding step. The conformance map ensures that artifacts align with and trace back to their foundational predecessors, thereby maintaining consistency and fidelity to the original design intent.

A conformance map is developed to represent these relationships by systematically visualizing how each artifact is derived. The construction of the map involves the following steps:

- **Organize Artifacts by Design Steps**
  Arrange the artifacts according to their production order across the design steps. Begin with underlying facts and policies in the first row, followed by design criteria in the second row, candidate tactics in the third row, selected tactics in the fourth row, and refined architectural views in the final row.
- **Define Conformance Relationships**
  Use directional arrows to represent the dependencies and derivation paths between artifacts across adjacent steps. These arrows indicate how each artifact is informed by and derived from one or more artifacts in the preceding step. This visual representation reinforces traceability and coherence throughout the design process.

Example
Consider constructing a conformance map for the design artifacts associated with NFR #2: *Ensuring a Wide Range of Applicability*. The design artifacts generated at each step are outlined below.

- **Underlying Facts Identified in Step 1**
  - (F1) Variability on Car Models to Carry
  - (F2) Variability on GPS Device Installed
  - (F3) Variability on Procedure of Checkout
  - (F4) Variability on Factors for Determining Rental Fee Rates
  - (F5) Variability on Factors for Determining Discounts
  - (F6) Variability on Payment Methods
  - (F7) Variability on Interfaces of External Systems
- **Criteria for Tactic Derivation Identified in Step 2**
  - (C1) Support for Variability in Car Models (Relevant to F1)
  - (C2) Support for Variability on GPS Models (Relevant to F2)
  - (C3) Support for Variability on Checkout Process (Relevant to F3)
  - (C4) Support for Variability on Factors for Determining Rental Fee Rates (Relevant to F4)
  - (C5) Support for Variability in Determining Rental Discounts (Relevant to F5)
  - (C6) Support for Variability on Payment Methods (Relevant to F6)
  - (C7) Variability for Variability on External System Interfaces (Relevant to F7)

- **Candidate Tactics Defined 2 in Step 3**
  - (T1) Class Inheritance Hierarchy of *Car Model* (Relevant to C1)
  - (T2) GPS Gateway with Required Interfaces for Various GPS Models (Relevant to C2)
  - (T3) Template Method Pattern for Supporting Various Checkout Processes (Relevant to C3)
  - (T4) Decorator Patten to Dynamically Select Factors for Rental Fee Rates (Relevant to C4)
  - (T5) Decorator Pattern to Dynamically Select Discount Factors (Relevant to C5)
  - (T6) Strategy Pattern to Support Various Payment Methods (Relevant to C6)
  - (T7) Adaptor Pattern to Support Various Interfaces of External Systems (Relevant to C7)
  - (T8) Mediator Pattern to Support Various Interfaces of External Systems (Relevant to C7)
- **Tactics Selected in Step 4**

  All candidate tactics were evaluated and selected through a cost-benefit analysis process.
- **Impacts of Selected Tactics**

  The impacts of the selected tactics on the architectural views are summarized in Table 10.4.

Based on the listed design artifacts, a conformance map is constructed by establishing traceable relationships among artifacts across design steps. The resulting conformance map for this NFR is shown in Fig. 10.10.

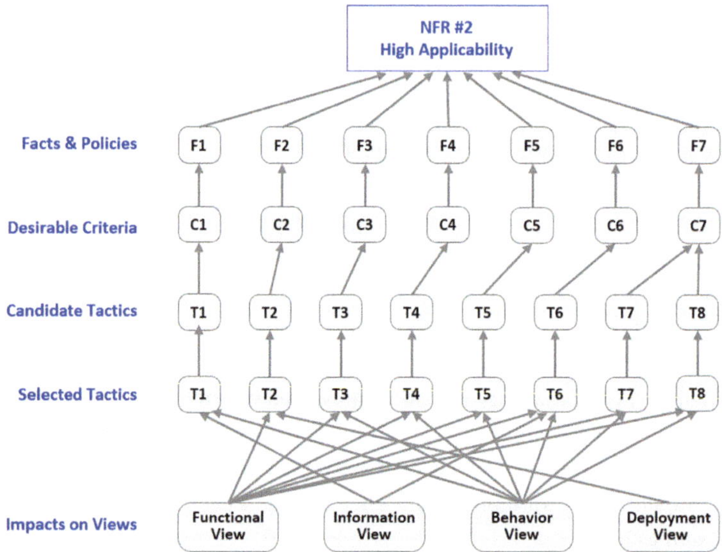

Fig. 10.10 Conformance Map for NFR #2 in the Car Rental Management System

In this example, all elements connected through *conforms-to* relationships ensure high traceability and consistency across the design artifacts. The impacts of selected tactics on architectural views vary in degree. Notably, the functional view, information view, and behavior view are substantially influenced by the selected tactics. In contrast, the deployment view exhibits only minimal impact from the selected tactics.

The successful construction and analysis of the conformance map in this example demonstrate effective conformance validation across design steps. Each artifact is shown to trace back to its foundational predecessor, ensuring alignment with the original intent of NFR #2. This validation confirms that the selected tactics are not only relevant and justifiable but also cohesively integrated into the architectural design, thereby enhancing design consistency, traceability, and overall quality.

10.6.2 Task 2. Remedy Missing Conformance

This task involves evaluating the conformance relationships depicted in the conformance map and resolving any missing conformance by revising the design as necessary to ensure proper alignment and consistency across all artifacts.

Missing conformance may arise in the following two scenarios:

- **Design Artifacts Not Defined for Preceding Artifacts**
  This scenario occurs when target design artifacts are not produced for earlier artifacts in the design flow. Examples include the absence of criteria for a defined fact or the absence of tactics corresponding to a given criterion.
- **Candidate Tactics Discarded During Cost-Benefit Analysis**
  This scenario arises when a candidate tactic associated with a criterion is excluded based on cost-benefit analysis results. As a result, the criterion lacks a corresponding tactic, creating a gap in the conformance chain.

Missing conformance disrupts traceability and alignment across design steps, requiring remediation to preserve the integrity and coherence of the overall design process.

Remedy Actions for Missing Conformance Relationships
To resolve missing conformance relationships, the following actions may be taken:

- **Define New Design Artifacts for Preceding Artifacts**
  Create new design artifacts to bridge existing gaps, ensuring that each artifact produced in an earlier step is properly supported by corresponding artifacts in subsequent steps. For example, criteria may be defined for facts or policies lacking them, or tactics may be added for criteria that are currently unaddressed.

- **Discard Preceding Design Artifacts with Careful Justification**
  In cases where introducing new artifacts is impractical or unnecessary, the preceding artifacts may be discarded. However, this should be done with thorough documentation and justification to ensure the decision aligns with overall design objectives and does not compromise architectural integrity.
- **Re-evaluate and Refine the Design Process**
  Investigate the root causes of missing conformance, and refine the design process to prevent recurrence. This may involve revisiting the criteria for selecting candidate tactics, adjusting the mapping methodology, or enhancing review checkpoints across design steps.

By taking these actions, architects can restore conformance, ensuring consistency and traceability throughout the design process.

10.7 Checklist for A5: NFR-Based Design

The following checklist items can be used to validate the design for non-functional requirements.

10.7.1 Checklist for Step 1: Identify Facts and Policies

- Have all specified non-functional requirements (NFRs) been thoroughly analyzed to extract the relevant underlying facts and policies?
- Are the identified facts and policies clearly documented, including references to applicable domain knowledge or standards where appropriate?
- Are the identified facts and policies directly aligned with the intent and scope of their corresponding NFRs?
- Are the identified facts and policies substantial and necessary for effectively addressing their respective NFRs?
- Are the identified facts mutually exclusive, ensuring no overlap in their scopes?
- Does the set of facts and policies for each NFR provide comprehensive coverage, ensuring that no critical aspects are omitted?

10.7.2 Checklist for Step 2: Define Criteria for Architecture Tactics

- Have all criteria been explicitly traced to their corresponding facts or policies to ensure traceability?
- Is each identified fact associated with at least one well-defined criterion?
- Is each identified policy addressed by at least one corresponding criterion?

- Does each criterion effectively respond to and support one or more relevant facts or policies?
- Are the criteria stated clearly using directive, actionable language to guide the formulation of architecture tactics?

10.7.3 Checklist for Step 3: Define Candidate Architecture Tactics

- Is each criterion associated with at least one architecture tactic to ensure end-to-end traceability?
- Does each architecture tactic effectively satisfy and operationalize at least one design criterion?
- Have the architecture tactics been evaluated to ensure they do not conflict with or interfere with one another?
- Are the architecture tactics accompanied by appropriate visual representations—such as figures, diagrams, tables, or algorithms—in addition to textual explanations?
- Are the tactics described with sufficient technical detail and specification to support accurate and efficient implementation?
- Are the architecture tactics feasible to implement given the available tools, technologies, human resources, and project constraints, including schedule and budget?

10.7.4 Checklist for Step 4: Evaluate Candidate Architecture Tactics

- Have the major costs and benefits of each candidate tactic been thoroughly analyzed as part of the cost-benefit analysis (CBA)?
- Have potential conflicts or trade-offs among candidate tactics been identified and adequately addressed during the CBA?
- Are the rejections of any candidate tactics clearly justified with objective reasoning and documented in the Tactic Evaluation Table?
- Does the final set of selected tactics align with the system's architectural goals, quality attributes, and design constraints?
- Has stakeholder input been appropriately considered in the evaluation process, especially for tactics involving cost, risk, or critical trade-offs?

10.7.5 Checklist for Step 5: Integrate Selected Architecture Tactics

- Have all architectural design elements affected by each selected tactic been clearly identified and documented?
- Have the impacts of each tactic on the corresponding design elements been thoroughly analyzed and evaluated?

- Are the selected tactics integrated into the architecture without introducing design inconsistencies, redundancies, or conflicts?
- Have all modifications required to accommodate the selected tactics been properly documented, reviewed, and validated for correctness?
- Has the integrated design—reflecting all selected tactics—been reviewed and formally approved by the appropriate stakeholders?

10.7.6 Checklist for Step 6: Validating Conformance

- Have all design artifacts produced during the architecture design process been considered and included in the construction of the Conformance Map?
- Are conformance relationships between artifacts from consecutive design steps clearly represented and properly denoted with arrows in the map?
- Have all instances of missing conformance been identified and analyzed to determine their root causes?
- Is there a clear, actionable plan for addressing each identified gap without introducing additional inconsistencies or conflicts?
- Have all remediation actions been validated, documented, and reviewed or approved by the relevant stakeholders?
- Has the outcome of the conformance validation been properly documented and effectively communicated to stakeholders?

10.8 Exercise Problems

1. **Significance of Designing for Non-Functional Requirements**
   Explain the significance of addressing non-functional requirements (NFRs) in software architecture. Describe how the incorporation of architecture tactics targeting these requirements contributes to building a system that meets stakeholder expectations.
2. **Identifying Facts and Policies as Requirements Engineering Efforts**
   Explain how the identification of relevant facts and policies for a given NFR reflects *Requirements Engineering* activity. Discuss how this enables precise specification and supports informed architectural decision-making.
3. **Guidelines for Validating Facts and Policies**
   Describe the guidelines for validating the identified underlying facts associated with a given NFR. Similarly, present the validation guidelines for the underlying policies to ensure their relevance, correctness, and completeness.

4. **Identifying Facts and Policies for an NFR in an Adaptive Cruise Control (ACC) System**
   Given the NFR of *ensuring high safety in cruise-based driving* for an Adaptive Cruise Control system, identify a set of essential underlying facts and a set of essential policies that support and constrain architectural decisions related to this requirement.
5. **Role of Criteria in Deriving Architecture Tactics**
   What is the specific role of defining criteria derived from underlying facts and policies in the process of architecture tactic selection? Discuss the potential challenges or risks that may arise if architecture tactics are derived without the guidance of well-defined criteria.
6. **Difference Between Conventional and Non-Conventional NFRs**
   Explain the distinction between conventional and non-conventional NFRs. Discuss how the design of architecture tactics varies across these categories, and identify the additional challenges involved in addressing non-conventional NFRs.
7. **Design Patterns as Architectural Tactics**
   Explain how design patterns can be effectively utilized as architectural tactics to satisfy specific NFRs. Select one design pattern, and describe which of its structural or behavioral features can be leveraged to address the target NFR.
8. **Open-Closed Principle (OCP) as Architecture Tactics**
   OCP is an effective design principle that applies closed design schemes to fixed features and open design schemes to variable features. Identify and characterize the types of non-functional requirements (NFRs) that can be effectively addressed using the OCP. Provide a specific example of one such NFR, and explain how applying the OCP facilitates its satisfaction.
9. **Machine Learning Models as Architectural Tactics**
   Discuss how machine learning models can be employed as architectural tactics to fulfill specific NFRs. Choose a representative model, and explain how its capabilities can be leveraged to satisfy a particular non-functional requirement.
10. **Types of Costs for Cost-Benefit Analysis**
    While architecture tactics often offer significant benefits in addressing NFRs, they may also introduce various costs. Identify and describe the types of costs typically considered in the cost-benefit analysis (CBA) of architectural tactics.
11. **Cost-Benefit Analysis for Tactic of Active Redundancy**
    Active Redundancy is an architectural tactic that enhances system availability and fault tolerance by operating multiple redundant components or subsystems concurrently. In the event of failure, the system seamlessly transitions to an active backup. Conduct a cost-benefit analysis of this tactic by evaluating the trade-offs between its reliability advantages and the architectural and operational costs it introduces.

12. **Impacts of Architecture Tactics on Views**
    The impact of an architectural tactic refers to the degree of enhancement or modification introduced into the architecture as a result of its application. Such impacts are typically more pronounced in the functional, information, and behavior views, while their influence on deployment, development, and operational views tends to be limited. Justify this observation using examples or reasoning based on architectural principles.
13. **Utilization of Conformance Map**
    What is the primary role of the conformance map in the design process for non-functional requirements? Discuss the consequences of insufficient traceability from facts and policies to architectural views, and describe the corrective actions that should be taken to restore conformance.

Activity A6. Architecture Evaluation 11

Objective of the Chapter
The objective of this chapter is to provide guidelines for evaluating the architecture design of a software system. It covers the identification of target elements for evaluation, the selection of appropriate evaluation approaches and methods, and the application of those methods to assess architectural soundness. These guidelines enable architects to systematically analyze architectural decisions, validate their alignment with system requirements, and refine the architecture based on evaluation outcomes.

Introducing Activity A6. Architecture Evaluation
This activity is to evaluate the architecture design for a target system. The goal of Architecture Evaluation is to identify potential risks, issues, drawbacks, and areas for improvement to ensure that the architecture aligns with the desired functional and non-functional requirements.

Architecture Evaluation is viewed as a process of transforming an assumed architecture design into a validated and proven architecture design, as illustrated in Fig. 11.1.

Fig. 11.1 Role of Architecture Evaluation

S. D. Kim, M. Kim, *Hands-on Software Architecture*,
https://doi.org/10.1007/978-3-032-01184-8_11

- **Assumed Architecture Design**
  Architects create an initial architecture design for the target system based on their expertise and experience. This design is assumed to work as intended, as depicted in the figure. However, the initial design often contains defects, risks, and significant deficiencies that may impact its effectiveness.
- **Proved Architecture Design**
  Through Architecture Evaluation, design deficiencies in the assumed architecture are identified and addressed. This process allows for the necessary refinements, resulting in a validated and proven architecture design that performs as expected.

Relevance to Software Verification and Validation (V&V)

Architectural Evaluation closely aligns with the objectives and methods of Software Verification and Validation. While often used together, they serve distinct purposes and involve different activities. *Software Verification* checks if the software is being built according to specifications through activities like code reviews, testing, and inspections. *Software Validation* determines if the software meets actual user needs and business requirements through real-world testing and evaluation.

Architecture Evaluation is a comprehensive process that incorporates both verification and validation activities to ensure the soundness of the architectural design. This process includes two critical elements, as illustrated in Fig. 11.2.

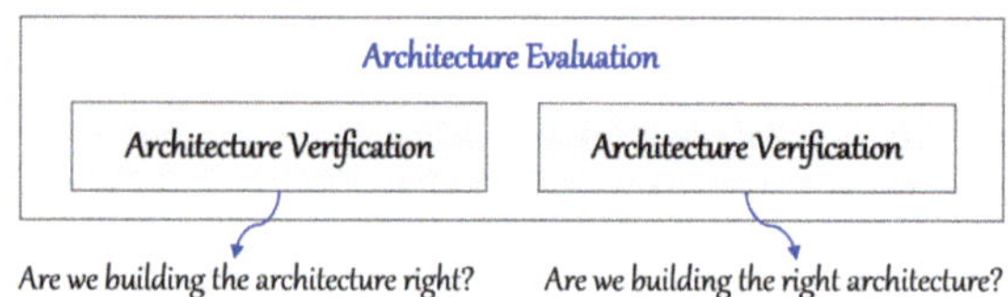

Fig. 11.2 Architecture Evaluation with Verification and Validation

These two aspects of evaluation work together to ensure that the architecture meets the specified requirements, design principles, and stakeholder expectations.

- **Architecture Verification**
  Architecture Verification ensures that the architecture complies with established specifications, standards, and best practices. It involves systematic analysis and testing to verify that the architecture has been correctly designed and documented. These activities aim to identify defects, inconsistencies, or deviations from the intended design.
- **Architecture Validation**
  Architecture Validation focuses on determining whether the architecture meets stakeholders' needs, goals, and expectations. It evaluates the architecture's suitability for fulfilling functional requirements and its ability to meet non-functional requirements.

Target Elements for Architecture Evaluation

What are the key elements of architectural design that should be evaluated? These elements encompass all design decisions articulated within the architectural description, as illustrated in Fig. 11.3.

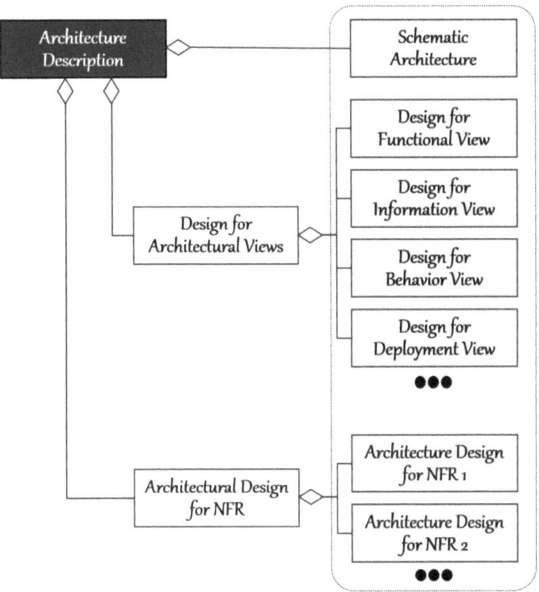

Fig. 11.3 Target Elements for Architecture Evaluation

An architecture description primarily consists of three key design elements: schematic architecture, architectural view designs, and non-functional requirement (NFR) designs. Architectural view designs are further refined into specific representations for individual views, while NFR designs are tailored to address distinct non-functional requirements.

Although all of these elements are valid candidates for architectural evaluation, architects often evaluate only a selected subset. This selection is influenced by factors such as the system's characteristics, the expected quality of the architecture, project constraints, and available resources.

Criteria for Architecture Evaluation

Architecture design is evaluated based on various criteria, which can differ depending on the specific characteristics of the target system. The common criteria for Architecture Evaluation are as follows:

- **Conformance to Functional Requirements**
  The evaluation should verify that the architectural design aligns with the specified functional requirements.

- **Addressing Non-Functional Requirements**
  The evaluation should assess how effectively the architecture addresses given non-functional requirements.
- **Feasibility and Practicality**
  The evaluation should assess the feasibility and practicality of implementing the architectural design within the given constraints, such as time, budget, technology, and resource availability.
- **Risk Identification**
  The evaluation should identify risks associated with the architectural design, including potential implementation issues or challenges related to scalability, maintainability, and adaptability.
- **Consistency and Correctness**
  The evaluation should ensure consistency among the design elements within the architecture and verify the correctness of the methods and strategies applied during the design process.
- **Compliance with Standards**
  The evaluation should confirm that the architectural design adheres to relevant industry standards and established best practices in software architecture.
- **Operational and Deployment Readiness**
  The evaluation should assess the ease of deployment, environmental compatibility, and robustness of the architecture in real-world operational settings.

Approaches to Architecture Evaluation

There are no universally accepted standards for categorizing architecture evaluation approaches across the industry. Architects must select evaluation approaches—that is, the methods, practices, and tools—that best align with the specific needs of their projects. Therefore, a comprehensive understanding of essential architecture evaluation approaches is critical for making informed and effective selection decisions.

The common approaches to Architecture Evaluation can be categorized as follows:

- **Scenario-Based Architecture Evaluation**
  This approach uses well-defined scenarios to assess how the architecture satisfies specific requirements or responds to potential challenges. Representative techniques include the Architecture Trade-off Analysis Method (ATAM) and the Cost-Benefit Analysis Method (CBAM).
- **Model-Based Architecture Evaluation**
  This approach involves constructing architectural models and analyzing them using techniques such as simulation, static analysis, or mathematical modeling to evaluate quality attributes like performance, reliability, or availability. Representative methods include the use of Architecture Description Languages (ADLs), UML, queuing models, statecharts, and network simulation models.

- **Formal Method-Based Architecture Evaluation**
  This approach applies mathematically rigorous techniques—such as model checking and theorem proving—to verify the architecture's correctness, internal consistency, and compliance with formal specifications. Representative methods include the Z Specification Language, OCL, Abstract State Machines, Petri Nets, and Temporal Logic.
- **Proof-of-Concept (PoC)-Based Architecture Evaluation**
  This approach validates critical aspects of the architectural design by implementing a small-scale version of the system. It is especially useful for demonstrating the feasibility of key design decisions, assessing the implementation of core functionalities, and uncovering risks early in the development process.
- **Prototype-Based Architecture Evaluation**
  This approach involves developing a functional prototype to examine the architecture's ability to meet specified requirements. It supports empirical evaluation of aspects such as usability, performance, and scalability and enables stakeholder feedback through interactive exploration of architectural behavior.

Each of these architecture evaluation approaches is defined by its specific application context, evaluation procedure, and associated strengths and limitations. They differ in terms of cost and effort, target evaluation focus, technical complexity, and the degree of analytical rigor.

A comprehensive overview of architecture evaluation methods is presented in Appendix A.

Steps in A6. Architecture Evaluation

The evaluation of architecture design can be systematically performed with a sequence of steps, as shown in Fig. 11.4.

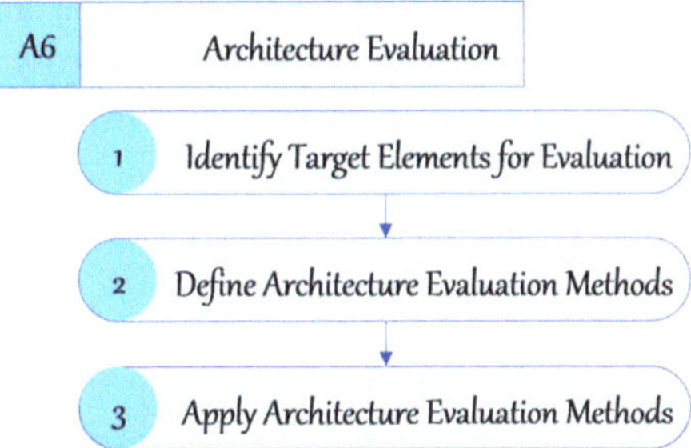

Fig. 11.4 Steps in A6. Architecture Validation

- **Step 1. Identify Target Elements for Evaluation**
  This step focuses on selecting the specific elements of the architecture design that require evaluation. An architecture description includes various design decisions, such as architecture styles, schematic architecture, view-specific designs, component allocation across tiers, and deployment designs. Architects often target a subset of these elements for evaluation based on project priorities or criticality.
- **Step 2. Define Architecture Evaluation Methods**
  This step is to determine the most suitable evaluation approach and specific methods within that approach for the selected architectural elements. Architects analyze the characteristics and content of each element to identify methods that ensure a thorough and effective evaluation.
- **Step 3. Apply Architecture Evaluation Methods**
  This step is to apply the determined evaluation methods for the selected elements. Architects proceed to follow the procedure and guidelines outlined by each evaluation method to assess and analyze the architecture design thoroughly. In addition, this step is to consolidate the results of evaluating target elements, analyze what refinements should be made, and subsequently refine the architecture based on these evaluation outcomes.

11.1 Step 1. Identify Target Elements for Evaluation

This step is to determine the specific architectural elements that are subject to evaluation.

11.1.1 Task 1. List Elements in Architecture Description

This task is to enumerate all design elements contained in the architecture description of the target system. As architecture descriptions may vary across systems, architects first construct a comprehensive list of design elements. This list serves as the foundation for identifying the specific elements to be evaluated.

Example
The design elements in the architecture for the Car Rental Management System are as follows:

- Design of Schematic Architecture
- Design for Architecture Views
  - Functional View Design
  - Information View Design
  - Behavior View Design
  - Deployment View Design
- Design for Non-Functional Requirements

Each of these elements typically have sub-elements. For example, the design for functional view includes a refined Use Case Diagram, defined functional components, allocation of functional components, interfaces of selected functional components, and design for functional variability.

The set of design elements in an architectural description can be effectively represented in a tabular format, as shown in Table 11.1.

Table 11.1 Architecture Evaluation Approach Table (Target Elements)

Elements	Sub-Elements	Select	Evaluation Approaches
Schematic Architecture			
	Selection of 3 Architecture Styles	✓	
	Integration of Selected Architecture Styles		
	Structural Integrity of Architecture		
	Scalability of Architecture	✓	
Design for Functional View			
	Use Case Diagram Capturing System Functionality	✓	
	Identification of 13 Functional Components		
Design for NFR #3 "High Availability of Headquarters Server"		✓	
	Architecture Tactics		
	Integrating Tactics into Architecture Design		
	Adherence to the given NFR		

The table presents the design elements of the architectural description in the first two columns, with the selected elements for evaluation indicated in the third column

11.1.2 Task 2. Select Target Elements for Evaluation

This task is to identify and select specific elements from the architectural description that require evaluation. Since evaluating all elements within an architecture design is typically impractical and unnecessary, a focused selection of critical elements is required.

The essential criteria for selecting target elements for architectural evaluation are as follows:

- **Criticality to System Requirements**
  Elements that directly impact the system's ability to meet functional or non-functional requirements, such as performance, scalability, or reliability
- **Stakeholder Prioritization**
  Design elements aligned with stakeholders' high-priority requirements, whether functional or non-functional
- **Architectural Risk**
  Elements that pose high technical or implementation risks, such as those involving novel technologies, complex integrations, or uncertain design decisions

- **Impact on System Quality Attributes**
  Elements that significantly influence quality attributes, including performance, security, modifiability, usability, and availability
- **Compliance and Regulatory Requirements**
  Elements critical for meeting compliance, legal, or regulatory standards
- **Technical Uncertainty**
  Features or modules where implementation details are unclear or existing knowledge gaps need addressing
- **Change Volatility**
  Components or areas within the architecture that are anticipated to undergo frequent modifications during the system's lifecycle

Example
Consider the selection of target elements for evaluation in the Car Rental Management System. The architectural design elements are listed, and those selected for evaluation are indicated with a checkmark, as shown Table 11.1.

11.2 Step 2. Define Architecture Evaluation Methods

This step is to determine and select appropriate methods for evaluating the target design elements of architecture description.

11.2.1 Task 1. Select Architecture Evaluation Approaches

This task is to select the most suitable evaluation approaches for the selected design elements. Not all architectural evaluation approaches are applicable to every design element; instead, each method is suited to a specific context for evaluation. Therefore, architects identify the most appropriate validation method for each selected element. The determined evaluation approaches can be specified in the fourth column of the same table, *Architecture Evaluation Approach Table*.

Consider the following comparison criteria when selecting appropriate architecture evaluation approaches:

- **Coverage Scope**
  Coverage scope refers to the extent to which an architecture evaluation approach comprehensively addresses various aspects of the system, including functional, non-functional, and operational requirements.
- **Rigorousness**
  Rigorousness refers to the degree to which an architecture evaluation approach employs systematic, detailed, and methodical analysis to evaluate the architecture. A high level of rigorousness reduces ambiguity and increases confidence in the evaluation outcomes.

- **Tangibleness**
  The tangibleness of an architecture evaluation approach is its ability to produce concrete, actionable results that can directly inform architectural decisions. Approaches with high tangibleness provide clear insights, practical recommendations, and measurable outcomes.
- **Objectivity**
  Objectivity refers to the ability of an architecture evaluation approach to provide unbiased, evidence-based assessments that are not influenced by subjective opinions or stakeholder biases. High objectivity enhances the credibility of the evaluation results and supports sound architectural decision-making.
- **Learning Curve**
  The learning curve of an architecture evaluation approach refers to the time and effort required for stakeholders to understand, adopt, and effectively apply the approach. Approaches with steep learning curves may necessitate substantial training and adaptation, whereas those with lower learning curves tend to be more accessible and easier to implement.
- **Cost-Effectiveness**
  Cost-effectiveness refers to the efficiency of resource utilization in performing the evaluation, considering both direct costs (e.g., tools and software) and indirect costs (e.g., personnel effort and operational disruptions).
- **Stakeholders Involvement**
  Stakeholder involvement in an architecture evaluation approach refers to the degree to which key stakeholders are actively engaged in the evaluation process. High involvement ensures that diverse perspectives are considered and fosters alignment with organizational objectives.

Applying these criteria, different architecture evaluation approaches are compared, as shown in Table 11.2.

Table 11.2 Comparing Architecture Evaluation Approaches

Approaches	Coverage Scope	Rigorousness	Tangibleness	Objectivity	Learning Curve	Cost-effective	Stakeholder Involvement
Scenario based	△	△	△	△	●	●	●
Model based	○	○	○	●	○	●	△
Formal method based	△	●	△	●	△	○	△
POC based	○	△	●	●	△	△	●
Prototype based	●	△	●	●	△	△	●

● for high, ○ for medium, △ for low

This table presents a concise comparison of various architecture evaluation approaches based on seven criteria. Each approach is rated as high (●), medium (○), or low (△). The analysis highlights that some methods are better suited for practical and dynamic environments, offering greater adaptability and stakeholder engagement, while others are more appropriate for theoretical or specialized contexts due to their rigor and objectivity.

Example

Consider selecting appropriate evaluation approaches for the architectural design elements identified in the Car Rental Management System. The complete list of design elements, the subset selected for evaluation, and the corresponding architecture evaluation approaches are presented in Table 11.3.

Table 11.3 Architecture Evaluation Approach Table (Completed)

Elements	Sub-Elements	Select	Evaluation Approaches
Schematic Architecture			
	Selection of 3 Architecture Styles	✓	Scenario based
	Integration of Selected Architecture Styles		
	Structural Integrity of Architecture		
	Scalability of architecture	✓	Model based
Design for Functional View			
	Use Case Diagram Capturing System Functionality	✓	Scenario based
	Identification of 13 Functional Components		
	Allocation of Functional Components		
	Interfaces of "Rental Manager"	✓	PoC based
	Interfaces of "Return Manager"	✓	PoC based
	Design for Functional Variability	✓	Model based
Design for Information View			
	Class Diagram Capturing Persistent Objects	✓	Model based
	Identification of 10 Data Components		
	Allocation of Data Components		
	Interfaces of Data Components		
	Design of Object Persistence	✓	Prototype based
Design for Behavior View			
	Activity Diagram Capturing System Behavior	✓	Scenario based
	Detailed Control Flow of "Checkout Car"	✓	PoC based
	Detailed Control Flow of "Return Car"	✓	PoC based
	Consistency to Functional View Design		
Design for Deployment View			
	Conformance to Schematic Architecture		
	Nodes of Devices and Execution Environments	✓	Model based
	Network Connectivity		

(continued)

Table 11.3 (continued)

Elements	Sub-Elements	Select	Evaluation Approaches
	Allocation of Software Artifacts		
Design for NFR #1. "Enhancing the Profitability"		✓	Scenario based
	Architecture Tactics		
	Integrating Tactics into Architecture Design		
	Adherence to the given NFR		
Design for NFR #2. "Wide Range of Applicability"			
	Architecture Tactics	✓	Model based
	Integrating Tactics into Architecture Design		
	Adherence to the given NFR		
Design for NFR #3. "High Availability of Headquarters Server"		✓	PoC based
	Architecture Tactics		
	Integrating Tactics into Architecture Design		
	Adherence to the given NFR		

The table presents the architectural design elements selected for evaluation in the third column, along with the corresponding evaluation approaches listed in the fourth column. The following provides a brief explanation of some design elements from the table

- **Evaluating *Architecture Styles*** Using Scenario-Based Evaluation
  The selection of three architecture styles for the system can be validated by defining scenarios of typical system use cases. These scenarios are used to assess how elements of each architecture style address and manage the requirements of these use cases.
- **Evaluating *Conformance to NFR #3*** Using PoC Evaluation
  The conformance of the schematic architecture to the "High Availability" NFR can be evaluated by developing a PoC system. This system implements only the relevant elements of the schematic architecture, such as the Dispatcher node and a few replicated servers, to demonstrate the system's availability characteristics.
- **Evaluating *Functional Variability Design*** Using Model-Based Evaluation
  The design for functional variability can be validated by defining a meta-model. This meta-model specifies variation points within each relevant functional component and includes a set of valid variants for each variation point. This approach ensures the design supports required variability effectively.
- **Evaluating *Object Persistence Design*** Using Prototype-Based Evaluation
  The design for object persistence in the system specifies the use of object-relational mapping with a relational DBMS. The effectiveness of this design in terms of runtime performance, stability, and scalability can be evaluated by implementing a prototype system using a relational DBMS product.

11.2.2 Task 2. Select Evaluation Methods Within Approach

This task is to identify the most appropriate evaluation methods within each selected architecture evaluation approach. An architecture evaluation method is a specific evaluation technique used within an architecture evaluation approach, providing a detailed, structured process and techniques for implementing the chosen approach.

The scenario-based evaluation approach includes the following evaluation methods:

- **Architecture Trade-off Analysis Method (ATAM)**
  This method is used to evaluate trade-offs among quality attributes □ by analyzing architectural decisions and their impact on these attributes.
- **Cost-Benefit Analysis Method (CBAM)**
  This method is used to assess the economic implications of architectural decisions, balancing quality attribute improvements against their associated costs.
- **SAAM (Software Architecture Analysis Method)**
  This method is used to analyze system functionality and determine how well quality attributes are satisfied in the architecture.
- **Performance Analysis Through Scenarios (PATS)**
  This method is used to evaluate the system's performance under predefined scenarios, identifying potential bottlenecks and ensuring scalability.

The model-based evaluation approach includes the following evaluation methods:

- **Unified Modeling Language (UML)**
  A standardized visual modeling language used to specify, visualize, construct, and document the structure and behavior of software systems
- **Systems Modeling Language (SysML)**
  A general-purpose modeling language designed to support system engineering activities such as specification, analysis, and design of complex systems
- **Business Process Model and Notation (BPMN)**
  A graphical representation method used to model and analyze business processes, enabling clear communication between stakeholders
- **Architecture Description Language (ADL)**
  Specialized languages, such as Acme, AADL, and SysADL, used to formally describe and analyze system architectures
- **Domain-Specific Language (DSL)**
  A customized modeling language tailored to address specific problems or domains with specialized syntax and semantics
- **Markov Model**
  A stochastic model used to represent systems that transition between states based on probabilities, useful for reliability and performance evaluation

- **Queueing Network**
  A mathematical model representing systems of queues, used to analyze system performance metrics such as response time and throughput

The formal method-based evaluation approach includes the following evaluation methods:

- **Z Specification Language**
  A formal specification language used for describing and modeling computing systems mathematically
- **Object Constraint Language (OCL)**
  A declarative language for describing rules that apply to UML models, ensuring that the models adhere to certain conditions
- **Abstract State Machine (ASM)**
  A methodology for modeling and analyzing complex computer algorithms and systems through abstract machines that change state with each step
- **Petri Net**
  A mathematical modeling tool used in computational fields to describe distributed systems graphically and analytically
- **Temporal Logic**
  A system of rules and symbols for representing and reasoning about propositions qualified in terms of time
- **Algebraic Specification**
  A method in computer science for formally specifying the data types of computer programs within a system

PoC-based and prototype-based evaluation approaches do not rely on specific named methods; instead, they are implementation driven and tailored to the system's context, focusing on validating key architectural decisions through executable PoC systems or prototypes.

A detailed description of essential architecture evaluation methods is provided in Chapter 1.

Example: Evaluation of Use Case Diagram
Consider evaluating the use case diagram that captures the system functionality of the Car Rental Management System. This design element can be effectively assessed using a scenario-based evaluation approach, specifically the Architecture Trade-off Analysis Method (ATAM). Stakeholder-defined scenarios—such as "Reserve Car," "Return Car," and "Manage Fleet"—can be used to examine system interactions and functional responsibilities. Each scenario is analyzed to identify architectural decisions involving system boundaries and the roles of actors and components.

Example: Evaluation of Scalability Design
Consider evaluating the scalability design within the architecture of the Car Rental Management System. This design element can be effectively assessed using a model-based evaluation approach, as it enables analytical modeling of performance-related aspects. More specifically, the Queueing Network Model would be selected within this approach, as it effectively captures resource contention, workload variability, and key performance metrics such as response time and throughput [35]. It facilitates detailed component analysis and simulates various load scenarios to identify bottlenecks and assess system behavior under increased demand.

Example: Evaluation of Functional Variability Design
Consider evaluating the functional variability design within the architecture of the Car Rental Management System. This design element can be effectively assessed using a model-based evaluation approach, specifically through the application of a feature model [36]. A feature model represents the features of a system or product line along with their hierarchical structure, constraints, and variability rules. It is well suited for modeling commonality and variability among features, enabling systematic analysis of configuration options. This approach supports the design of customizable systems and ensures alignment with variability requirements.

11.3 Step 3. Apply Architecture Evaluation Methods

This task is to apply selected architecture evaluation methods and refine the architecture design by incorporating feedback from the evaluation results.

11.3.1 Task 1. Evaluate Architecture Design with Selected Methods

This task is to evaluate the architecture design by systematically applying the selected evaluation methods to the target design elements. Architects must follow the procedures and guidelines specific to each method to thoroughly assess whether the design elements satisfy the system requirements.

Guidelines for Applying Scenario-Based Evaluation Methods
Scenario-based evaluation is most effectively performed by following the structured sequence of activities outlined below.

[1] **Identify Stakeholders**
Identify all stakeholders relevant to the system to ensure diverse perspectives are considered during the validation process. Architects may also recognize additional stakeholders who can provide valuable input beyond those identified during requirements refinement.

[2] **Develop Scenarios**
Create a set of scenarios illustrating the system's expected behavior under various conditions. Scenarios such as use case scenarios, growth scenarios, and exploratory scenarios are designed to evaluate how well the architecture meets functional and non-functional requirements, scalability, and robustness under stress.

[3] **Present Architectural Decisions**
Present the architectural design and decisions to stakeholders, explaining how they address identified requirements and scenarios. Transparency in rationale helps align stakeholder expectations, manage risks, and foster trust in the architectural choices.

[4] **Associate Scenarios with Architecture**
Map the developed scenarios to architectural components and configurations to analyze how the architecture supports each scenario. It identifies critical elements and interactions, highlighting potential weaknesses and guiding further architectural optimization.

[5] **Evaluate the Architecture**
Assess the architecture's performance against the mapped scenarios using established criteria and metrics. The evaluation identifies risks, weaknesses, and areas for improvement, providing actionable insights for refinement and validation of architectural design.

[6] **Analyze Evaluation Results**
Examine the analysis results to identify strengths, weaknesses, and potential issues in the architecture, and prepare an evaluation report summarizing findings, providing actionable recommendations to address issues, optimize the design, and enhance the system's ability to meet quality and performance objectives.

Guidelines for Applying Model-Based Evaluation Methods

Model-based evaluation is most effectively performed by following the structured sequence of activities outlined below.

[1] **Define Evaluation Objectives**
Clearly establish the objectives of the evaluation, such as modularity of design, system extensibility, and component interoperability, and ensure these align with stakeholder requirements.

[2] **Develop Architectural Models**
Develop architectural models that accurately and precisely represent the key properties and behaviors of the selected design elements, adhering to method-specific evaluation guidelines. Each method in the model-based evaluation approach provides specific representation schemes and conventions, which must be followed when developing the architectural models.

[3] **Define Metrics and Criteria**
Establish clear, measurable metrics reflecting key quality attributes like performance, reliability, scalability, and maintainability, and define criteria for each metric through thresholds or benchmarks aligned with stakeholder requirements. This ensures actionable insights for informed design optimization.

[4] **Perform Model-Specific Analysis**
Apply techniques and tools specific to the selected model-based evaluation methods to analyze the model and gather data on key performance indicators or quality attributes. If method-specific analysis techniques are not provided, architects should devise effective methods for evaluation.

[5] **Analyze Evaluation Results**
Examine the analysis results to identify strengths, weaknesses, and potential issues in the architecture, focusing on how the evaluation techniques reveal system behavior and performance under the defined metrics and criteria. Prepare an evaluation report summarizing findings, providing actionable recommendations to address issues, optimize the design, and enhance the system's ability to meet quality and performance objectives.

Guidelines for Applying Formal Method-Based Evaluation Methods

Formal method-based evaluation is most effectively performed by following the structured sequence of activities outlined below.

[1] **Define Evaluation Objectives**
Clearly define the objectives of the evaluation, such as verifying system correctness, ensuring compliance with requirements, or analyzing specific quality attributes like safety, reliability, or performance. These objectives should align with stakeholder priorities and system goals.

[2] **Develop Formal Specifications**
Create formal specifications of the system or architecture using mathematical notations or formal languages, such as Z, Alloy, or TLA+. These specifications precisely define the system's properties and constraints, forming the foundation for rigorous evaluation.
Each method in the formal method-based evaluation approach provides specific notations, semantic descriptions, and conventions, which must be adhered to when developing the architectural models.

[3] **Apply Formal Analysis Techniques**
Use formal analysis techniques, such as theorem proving, model checking, or equivalence checking, to evaluate the formal specifications. These methods systematically identify inconsistencies, errors, or non-conformances in the architecture and ensure its correctness against defined criteria.

[4] **Analyze Evaluation Results**
Examine the analysis results to identify strengths, weaknesses, and potential issues in the architecture, focusing on how the formal evaluation techniques reveal system behavior and performance under the defined metrics and criteria. Prepare a comprehensive evaluation report summarizing findings, highlighting actionable recommendations to address identified issues, optimize the design, and improve the system's ability to meet quality and performance objectives.

Guidelines for Applying PoC-Based Evaluation Method

PoC-based evaluation is most effectively performed by following the structured sequence of activities outlined below.

[1] **Define Objectives and PoC Implementation Scope**
Clearly define the objectives and scope of the PoC implementation, prioritizing key architectural aspects or design elements with potential risks or uncertainties that need validation. Ensure these objectives and the scope align with stakeholder requirements and overall system goals, providing a focused and relevant framework for evaluation.

[2] **Perform Detailed Design for PoC Implementation**
Create a detailed design for the selected elements, ensuring each is sufficiently developed and ready for the implementation phase. The design should remain minimal while effectively representing the core aspects of the selected elements, utilizing simplified components and interactions to enable accurate and efficient validation.

[3] **Implement the PoC System**
Select an appropriate implementation environment, including programming languages, tools, frameworks, and platforms that align with the PoC objectives and scope. Develop the PoC system by implementing the detailed design of the selected architectural components and design elements.
Focus on building a functional PoC system that accurately demonstrates critical system behaviors and interactions while adhering to the minimal yet representative design. Ensure that the implementation captures the essence of the design decisions without introducing unnecessary complexity, providing a foundation for effective evaluation.

[4] **Analyze Evaluation Results**
Examine the evaluation results to identify strengths, weaknesses, and potential issues in the architecture, emphasizing how the PoC system demonstrates behavior and performance under the defined metrics and criteria. Prepare an evaluation report summarizing findings, highlighting actionable recommendations to address identified issues, optimize the design, and enhance the system's ability to meet quality and performance objectives.

Guidelines for Applying Prototype-Based Evaluation Method

Prototype-based evaluation is most effectively performed by following the structured sequence of activities outlined below.

[1] **Define Objectives and Protype Implementation Scope**
Clearly define the goals and scope of the prototype implementation, focusing on critical architectural aspects or design elements with uncertainties or potential risks. Align these objectives with stakeholder requirements and overall system goals to provide a relevant and focused framework for evaluation.

[2] **Perform Detailed Design for Prototype Implementation**
Develop a detailed design for the prototype, concentrating on the selected design elements to be implemented. Ensure the design represents the critical aspects of the system while remaining minimal and focused, using simplified versions of components and interactions to facilitate validation and iteration.

[3] **Implement the Prototype System**
Choose an appropriate implementation environment, including programming languages, tools, frameworks, and platforms that align with the prototype objectives. Build the prototype based on the detailed design, focusing on accurately representing key system behaviors and interactions. Avoid unnecessary complexity while ensuring the implementation remains functional and effective for evaluation purposes.

[4] **Analyze Evaluation Results**
Examine the results obtained from the prototype to identify strengths, weaknesses, and potential issues in the architecture. Focus on how the prototype demonstrates system behavior under the defined metrics and criteria. Prepare an evaluation report summarizing findings, including actionable recommendations to refine the design, address identified gaps, and enhance the architecture's ability to meet quality and performance objectives.

11.3.2 Task 2. Incorporate Evaluation Results into Architecture

This task is to refine the architecture design by systematically integrating feedback from evaluation reports. Each evaluation report provides detailed analyses based on predefined metrics and criteria, along with actionable recommendations for architectural improvement. These reports are synthesized to guide targeted enhancements to the architecture design.

Incorporating evaluation results involves a range of refinements, such as adjusting structural decisions, redesigning components, optimizing algorithms, redefining deployment strategies, and revising tactics for addressing NFRs. These refinements ensure that the architecture more effectively addresses both functional and non-functional requirements, improving the system's overall quality and alignment with its objectives.

This task can systematically be conducted in the following order:

[1] **Synthesize Evaluation Results**
Gather and integrate the findings from all evaluation reports, identifying consistent patterns, key insights, and actionable recommendations. Analyze these results to determine specific areas of the architecture design requiring modification or enhancement, focusing on both functional and non-functional aspects.

[2] **Prioritize Architecture Refinements**
Rank the identified enhancements based on their impact on system functionality, non-functional requirements, and alignment with objectives. Consider dependencies among the change items to ensure that critical and foundational modifications are prioritized, enabling efficient implementation of subsequent refinements.

[3] **Modify Architecture Description**
Update the architecture description to incorporate the necessary enhancements, ensuring all modifications are accurately implemented and thoroughly documented. Clearly explain the rationale for each change, referencing evaluation findings to justify the enhancements. Ensure consistency across all architectural views and related documentation to comprehensively reflect the updated design.

[4] **Verify Refinements Against Requirements**
Reassess the refined architecture to ensure that the modifications address the identified issues and align with stakeholder requirements. Use validation techniques, such as walkthroughs or targeted evaluations, to confirm that the refinements improve the system's ability to meet its functional and non-functional objectives.

11.4 Checklist for A6: Architecture Evaluation

The following checklist items can be used to validate the architecture evaluation process.

11.4.1 Checklist for Step 1: Identify Target Elements for Evaluation

- Have all design elements in the architectural description been listed and evaluated for potential selection in the architecture evaluation?
- Have the design elements with high technical uncertainty or implementation risk been included in the selection?
- Have the design elements with significant impact on compliance, regulatory requirements, or system quality been included in the selection?
- Are the selected target elements aligned with stakeholder priorities and the project's objectives to ensure the evaluation addresses critical goals and expectations?

11.4.2 Checklist for Step 2: Define Architecture Evaluation Methods

- Have suitable evaluation approaches been identified for each selected design element?
- Are the chosen evaluation methods tailored to the system's characteristics and constraints?

- Do the selected methods comprehensively address all relevant metrics and criteria, to ensure a thorough and meaningful evaluation of the design elements?
- Are the selected evaluation methods compatible with the team's expertise and resources?
- Have the time and cost implications of the candidate evaluation methods been thoroughly analyzed to ensure feasibility and efficiency within project constraints?

11.4.3 Checklist for Step 3: Apply Architecture Evaluation Methods

- Have the selected evaluation methods been correctly prepared, including tools, frameworks, and necessary resources?
- Has the procedure for each evaluation method been applied rigorously and in strict accordance with its guidelines?
- Are the metrics and criteria clearly defined and tailored for each target design element to ensure accurate and meaningful evaluation?
- Are the evaluation results, including identified risks, deficiencies, and areas for improvement, sufficiently consolidated into a comprehensive analysis and detailed evaluation report?
- Have the findings made through architecture evaluation been communicated effectively to stakeholders, and is their feedback integrated into the evaluation process?
- Has the architecture design been refined and updated based on the findings and recommendations provided in the evaluation reports?

11.5 Exercise Problems

1. **Architecture Validation vs Architecture Verification**
   Define two related terms: *architecture validation* and *architecture verification.* The term *architecture validation* commonly appears in the literature, whereas *architecture verification* is used less frequently. Explain why validation is more emphasized than verification in architectural design.
2. **Architecture Evaluation as Integrated Approach**
   Architecture Evaluation integrates both architecture verification and validation. Explain why this integrated approach is more effective in ensuring that the architectural design both meets stakeholder requirements and maintains technical correctness and efficiency.
3. **Selecting Target Elements for Architecture Evaluation**
   Seven criteria—such as Criticality, Stakeholder Prioritization, and Architectural Risk—have been proposed to guide the selection of target elements for evaluation. Explain why each of these criteria provides a valuable basis for identifying which architectural elements should be prioritized for evaluation.

4. **Advantages of Scenario-Based Evaluation over Model-Based Evaluation**
   What are the advantages of scenario-based architecture evaluation compared to model-based architecture evaluation?
5. **Advantages of Model-Based Evaluation over Scenario-Based Evaluation**
   What are advantages of model-based architecture evaluation compared to scenario-based architecture evaluation?
6. **Advantages of Formal Method-Based Evaluation**
   What are the advantages of formal method-based architecture evaluation compared to the other four evaluation approaches?
7. **Advantages of PoC-Based and Prototype-Based Evaluation Approaches**
   What are the common advantages of PoC-based and prototype-based architecture evaluation approaches compared to the other three approaches?
8. **Comparing PoC-Based and Prototype-Based Architecture Evaluation Approaches**
   Compare the PoC-based and prototype-based architecture evaluation approaches by discussing their similarities, differences, and the situations in which each is most appropriately applied.
9. **Quantitative Analysis with Model-Based Architecture Evaluation Approach**
   The model-based architecture evaluation approach enables more quantitative analysis compared to the scenario-based approach. Explain how quantitative analysis is achieved in the model-based approach, and discuss the situations in which it is more appropriate than the scenario-based approach.
10. **Comparison of Scenario-Based Architecture Evaluation Methods**
    Four specific methods within the scenario-based evaluation approach were introduced earlier: ATAM, CBAM, SAAM, and PATS. What common features do these methods share? What are the key differences among them?
11. **Guidelines for Formulating Scenarios**
    Scenario-based architecture evaluation focuses on formulating and analyzing relevant scenarios to assess architectural decisions. Explain the guidelines for defining effective scenarios for representative methods in this category, such as ATAM, CBAM, and SAAM.
12. **Elements of Architecture Evaluation Report**
    An architecture evaluation report documents the procedures and outcomes of the architecture evaluation process. Describe the key elements that should be included in architecture evaluation reports.

Part III

Resources for Software Architecture Design

Catalog of Architecture Styles

12

Objective of the Chapter

The objective of this chapter is to present an essential overview of representative software architecture styles that serve as foundational design paradigms for structuring complex systems. Each style is systematically described in terms of its core structural elements, collaboration mechanisms, and associated strengths and limitations. This catalog serves as a reference framework for selecting appropriate architectural styles based on system requirements, quality attributes, and design constraints.

Introducing the Catalog of Architecture Styles

Architecture styles are essential in defining the schematic architecture of a target system. Like design patterns, these styles have been utilized in software engineering for decades, establishing themselves as valuable assets for reusable architecture design.

An effective approach to selecting suitable architecture styles for a target system is to first identify its inherent type. Once the inherent system type is determined, candidate architecture styles can then be systematically identified.

While there is no universally accepted taxonomy of system types, this catalog presents a practical classification derived from a comprehensive review of academic literature and real-world project experiences. Common types of software systems can be classified based

S. D. Kim, M. Kim, *Hands-on Software Architecture*,
https://doi.org/10.1007/978-3-032-01184-8_12

on their structural and behavioral characteristics. The corresponding architecture styles for each system type are presented as follows:

- **Data Flow Systems**
  A data flow system is characterized by a structural layout composed of multiple components that manipulate and transfer data in a sequential or parallel manner. These components perform specific processing tasks on the data and pass the transformed results to subsequent components.
- Applicable architecture styles include:
  - **Batch Sequential Architecture Style**
  - **Pipe-and-Filter Architecture Style**
- **Data Sharing Systems**
  A data sharing system is characterized by a structural layout designed to efficiently manage and store large volumes of data accessible by multiple applications. Data is written to and retrieved from a central repository, eliminating the need for direct data exchange between applications.
  Applicable architecture styles include:
  - **Shared Repository Architecture Style**
  - **Active Repository Architecture Style**
  - **Blackboard Architecture Style (for Sharing Data)**
- **Layered Systems**
  A layered system is characterized by a structural layout organized into a series of hierarchical layers, where each layer provides a well-defined set of functionalities and services to the layer directly above it. The topmost layer typically represents the user interface, while the bottom layer corresponds to the underlying infrastructure.
  Applicable architecture styles include:
  - **Layered Architecture Style**
  - **Model-View-Controller (MVC) Architecture Style**
  - **Variations of MVC Style**
- **Tiered Systems**
  A tiered system is characterized by a structural layout consisting of multiple tiers, each representing a distinct physical or logical computing environment. Each tier is responsible for a specific high-level functionality and interacts with other tiers to collectively fulfill the system's overall objectives.
  Applicable architecture styles include:
  - **N-Tier Architecture Style**
  - **Client-Server Architecture Style**
  - **Peer-to-Peer Architecture Style (as a Multi-Tier Architecture)**
- **Load-Balancing Systems**
  A load-balancing system is characterized by a structural layout comprising multiple servers and a load balancer that distributes computational workloads evenly across the servers. This configuration enhances overall system performance and reliability by preventing server overload and providing redundancy in the event of server failure.

Applicable architecture styles include:
- **Broker Architecture Style**
- **Dispatcher Architecture Style**
- **Master-Slave Architecture Style**
- **Edge Computing Architecture Style**
- **Peer-to-Peer Architecture Style (for Load Balancing)**

• **Event-Based Systems**
An event-based system is characterized by a structural layout in which the control flow is driven by the occurrence of events. These events may originate from various sources, including user interactions, hardware devices, software agents, or other system components.
Applicable architecture styles include:
- **Event-Driven Architecture Style**
- **Publisher-Subscriber Architecture Style**
- **Sensor Controller Actuator Architecture Style**

• **Service-Based Systems**
A service-based system is characterized by a structural layout in which the system leverages external services to fulfill specific aspects of its overall functionality. These external services may include cloud services, microservices, or other distributed service components.
Applicable architecture styles include:
- **Service-Oriented Architecture (SOA) Style**
- **Microservice Architecture Style**

• **Adaptive Systems**
An adaptive system is characterized by its ability to modify its behavior and configuration in response to changes in the environment or user needs. Its structural layout comprises both fixed elements, which represent stable, non-adaptable features, and variable elements, which enable dynamic reconfiguration to accommodate evolving conditions.
Applicable architecture styles include:
- **Microkernel Architecture Style**
- **Blackboard Architecture Style (for Sharing Components)**

• **Other System Types**
There can be software systems that do not fit neatly into one category.

12.1 Batch Sequential Architecture Style

The Batch Sequential Architecture Style is characterized by the ordered execution of data manipulation components, where each component processes a complete batch of input data and produces an output that serves as the input to the subsequent component in the sequence.

12.1.1 Structure

The structure of this architecture style follows the principle of decomposing the data processing workflow into discrete, sequential components. Each component is responsible for a specific stage of the workflow, with data flowing linearly from one component to the next until processing is complete.

The structure of this architecture style is shown in Fig. 12.1.

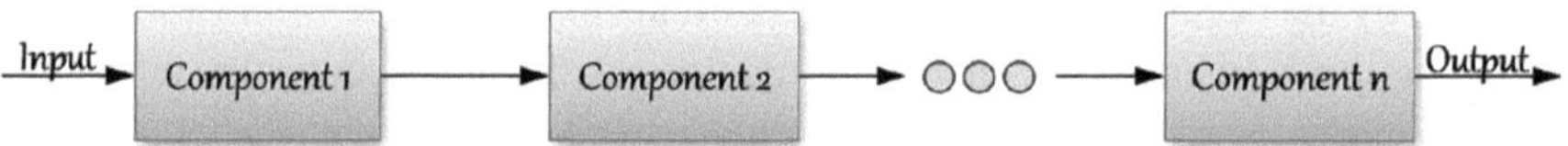

Fig. 12.1 Structure of Batch Sequential Architecture Style

Component 1 serves as the initial processing unit in the workflow. It receives the input data, applies a designated data manipulation operation, and generates an intermediate output.

Component 2 accepts this intermediate output, executes the subsequent processing step, and produces the next intermediate result. The architecture may include an arbitrary number of intermediate components, each responsible for a specific stage of the workflow. *Component n* functions as the final processing unit, and its output constitutes the final result of the entire data processing pipeline.

12.1.2 Collaboration Models

The collaboration model in this architecture style is defined by the linear and orderly flow of data through a sequence of discrete components, each responsible for a specific processing task.

- **Sequential Processing**
  Each component processes its input and passes the output to the next component in the sequence. The collaboration is strictly ordered—each component must complete its task before the next begins.
- **Batch Processing**
  Data is processed in discrete groups, or *batches*, with each batch flowing through the components as a single unit. Each component processes the entire batch before forwarding it to the next.
- **Non-interactivity**
  The sequential workflow in this architecture style is fully automated and does not involve user interaction during processing. Users do not intervene once the batch job has commenced; instead, the system executes each step in sequence until completion.

12.1.3 Strengths and Limitations

The Batch Sequential Architecture Style exhibits the following strengths:

- **Simplicity of interactions**
  The linear sequence of operations makes the Batch Sequential Architecture Style intuitive to understand and implement. Each step is clearly defined, and the flow of data through the system is easy to trace.
- **Modularity of Components**
  The system is composed of discrete components, each responsible for a specific data manipulation task. This modular structure enhances reusability across different systems and improves overall maintainability.

On the other hand, this architecture style exhibits the following limitations:

- **Processing Latency**
  The sequential and batch-oriented execution model introduces inherent delays between input and output. Consequently, batch sequential systems are unsuitable for applications that require real-time responsiveness or low-latency processing.
- **Structural Rigidity**
  The fixed order of operations and reliance on batch-based processing reduce the system's adaptability to evolving requirements or varying data characteristics. Structural modifications—such as inserting, removing, or reordering processing components—often necessitate significant architectural reconfiguration.
- **Lack of Interactivity**
  This style inherently lacks support for real-time user interaction during processing. Data is handled in complete batches, and processing must be completed for an entire batch before producing output.

12.2 Pipe-and-Filter Architecture Style

The Pipe-and-Filter Architecture Style is characterized by the streaming of data through a series of data manipulation components. The overall workflow is decomposed into independent units called *filters*, each responsible for a specific transformation or computation. These filters are connected by *pipes*, which serve as data channels that transmit the output of one filter as input to the next, enabling a continuous and orderly flow of data through the system.

12.2.1 Structure

The structure of this architecture style is founded on the principle of decomposing the data processing workflow into discrete components and organizing them in a pipeline. Accordingly, the architecture comprises a series of independent *filters* connected by *pipes*, which enable sequential or parallel flows of data between components.

The structure of this architecture style is shown in Fig. 12.2.

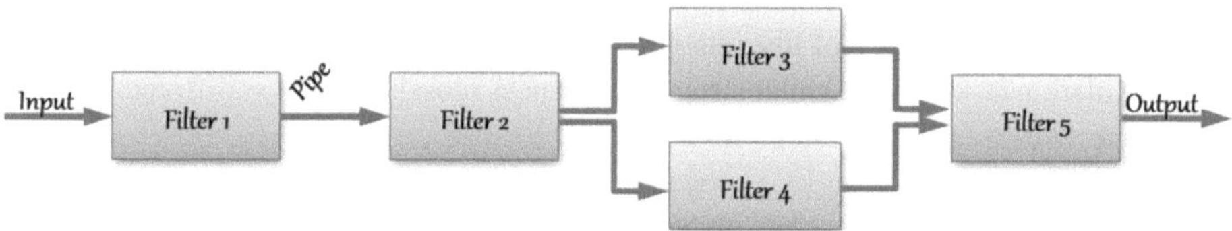

Fig. 12.2 Structure of Pipe-and-Filter Architecture Style

- **Filter**
  A *filter* performs a specific data manipulation task, such as transforming, processing, or generating data. Filters are designed to be modular and cohesive, with each encapsulating a well-defined, independent function.
- **Pipe**
  A *pipe* is responsible for transmitting data from one filter to the next in the processing chain using a streaming mode. Streaming refers to the continuous transmission and processing of data as it is produced or received, rather than processing it as a complete batch.

12.2.2 Collaboration Models

The collaboration model of this architecture style is defined by the topology of *filters* and their interconnections via *pipes*.

- **Data Streaming**
  Filters transmit data through pipes in a continuous stream, facilitating incremental and modular processing of data elements.
- **Sequential and Parallel Processing**
  Filters are typically arranged in a linear sequence. More complex configurations enable parallel or conditional processing through branching and merging structures.

- **Interactivity**
  Unlike the Batch Sequential Architecture Style, the Pipe-and-Filter Architecture Style can accommodate user interaction during processing if certain filters are designed to solicit or respond to user input.
- **Feedback Loops**
  Feedback loops may be introduced to support iterative processing, allowing the output of a filter to be routed back as input to an earlier stage.

12.2.3 Strengths and Limitations

The Pipe-and-Filter Architecture Style exhibits the following strengths:

- **Modularity**
  Each filter performs a specific transformation, promoting separation of concerns and simplifying the development, testing, and maintenance of individual components.
- **Reusability**
  Filters can be reused across different pipelines or applications, provided they adhere to compatible input/output formats.
- **Composability**
  Complex processing workflows can be constructed by composing simple filters, enabling flexible and scalable system design.
- **Ease of Parallelization**
  Independent filters can be executed concurrently on different processing units, making the architecture well suited for parallel and distributed execution environments.
- **Support for Feedback Loops**
  Though not inherent, the architecture allows for the introduction of feedback paths to support iterative or cyclic processing.

On the other hand, this architecture style exhibits the following limitations:

- **Runtime Performance Overhead**
  This architecture style may suffer from performance degradation due to data copying between filters and frequent context switching. Copying data through pipes increases memory usage and latency, while switching between numerous filter executions adds overhead from saving and restoring processor states.
- **Lack of Global Context and State Management**
  Filters operate independently, each with a localized view of the data, and do not maintain context beyond individual inputs. As a result, managing global state or performing operations that require awareness of historical or system-wide information is complex.

12.3 Shared Repository Architecture Style

The Shared Repository Architecture Style is characterized by a data-sharing paradigm in which multiple components or applications interact through a centralized data repository. This repository acts as a common access point, supporting both read and write operations across components.

12.3.1 Structure

The structure of this architecture style is defined by a central repository that is accessed and shared by multiple data accessors. The structure of this architecture style is shown in Fig. 12.3.

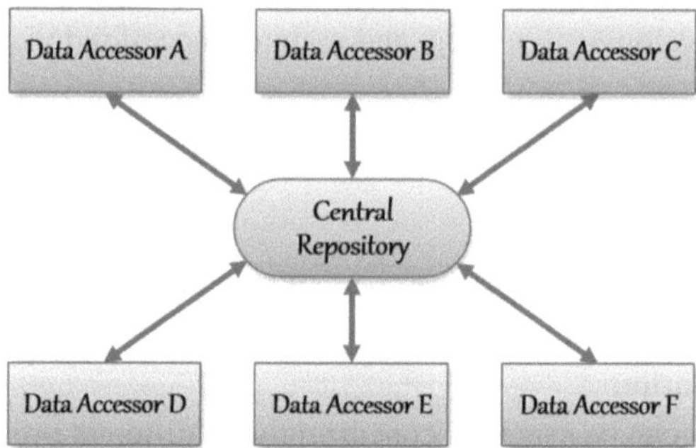

Fig. 12.3 Structure of Shared Repository Architecture Style

- **Central Repository**
  The *Central Repository* is a single, centralized storage system that maintains shared data accessible to multiple data accessors. It acts as the primary medium for indirect communication and coordination among components through shared data.
- **Data Accessor**
  A *Data Accessor* is any component, subsystem, or application that interacts with the central repository to perform read and/or write operations. These accessors encapsulate system functionality and depend on the repository to retrieve, update, and persist data.

12.3.2 Collaboration Models

The collaboration model in the Shared Repository Architecture Style is centered around data access patterns to the central repository. Data accessors can interact with the repository in two primary models: direct access to data and indirect access through a data access interface.

- **Direct Access to Data**
  In this model, data accessors interact directly with the central repository using native query languages (e.g., SQL) or repository-specific protocols. This approach is preferred in performance-critical scenarios where minimizing latency is essential and the overhead of an intermediary layer is undesirable.
- **Indirect Access Through Interface**
  In this model, data accessors interact with the repository through a standardized interface, referred to as the *Data Access Interface*. This interface abstracts the underlying data storage mechanisms and provides a consistent, controlled means of access. It facilitates better maintainability, security, and scalability by encapsulating the logic for data retrieval and updates.

12.3.3 Strengths and Limitations

The Shared Repository Architecture Style exhibits the following strengths:

- **Centralized Data Management**
  A single, centralized repository facilitates consistent data management, ensuring data integrity, synchronization, and a unified source of truth across the system.
- **Efficient Data Sharing**
  Data accessors exchange information by reading from and writing to the repository, enabling streamlined data sharing without requiring direct communication between components.
- **Decoupling of Data Accessors**
  Data accessors remain loosely coupled, as their interactions are mediated solely through the repository. This decoupling enhances modularity, maintainability, and component independence.

On the other hand, this architecture style exhibits the following limitations:

- **Difficulty in Managing Data Schema Evolution (with Direct Access)**
  When data accessors directly interact with the repository, they become tightly coupled to its data schema. As a result, any modifications to the schema may cause widespread disruptions and complicate maintenance and evolution of the system.
- **Performance Overhead (with Indirect Access through Interface)**
  The use of a Data Access Interface may introduce performance overhead. This limitation becomes evident when the volume of data operations exceeds the interface's processing capacity, leading to increased latency and degraded system responsiveness.

12.4 Active Repository Architecture Style

The Active Repository Architecture Style extends the Shared Repository model by enabling the central repository to proactively notify data accessors of changes in the data state. Unlike the Shared Repository style, the Active Repository Architecture Style introduces event-driven mechanisms that allow the repository to push notifications to accessors when relevant data is modified. This enhances responsiveness and synchronization among components, facilitating timely reactions to state changes within the system.

12.4.1 Structure

The structure of this architecture style comprises a central repository, multiple data subscribers, and a notification mechanism responsible for detecting changes and disseminating update notifications to subscribers.

The structure of this architecture style is shown in Fig. 12.4.

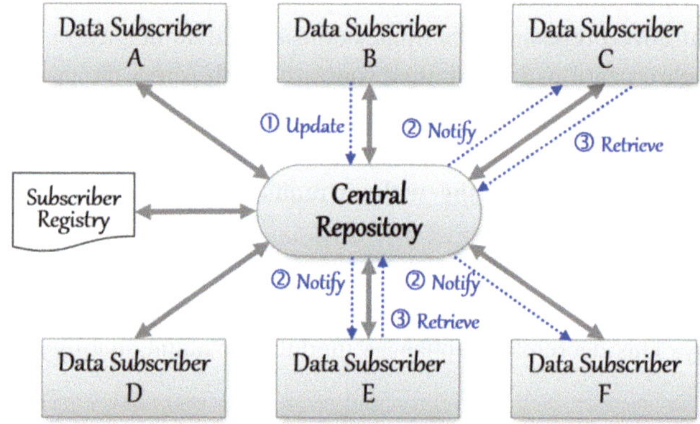

Fig. 12.4 Structure of Active Repository Architecture Style

- **Central Repository**
  The *Central Repository* serves as the authoritative data store for the system, maintaining all shared data and facilitating access and coordination among data subscribers.
- **Subscriber Registry**
  The *Subscriber Registry*, a component within the central repository, manages subscription metadata. It tracks which data subscribers have registered interest in specific data changes, enabling targeted notifications when those changes occur.
- **Data Subscribers**
  Data Subscribers function similarly to data accessors in the Shared Repository style, with the added capability of subscribing to specific data changes. Upon updates to the repository, they receive notifications and can promptly retrieve the modified data as needed.

12.4.2 Collaboration Models

The collaboration model in this architecture style is defined by an event-driven interaction pattern between the central repository and data subscribers. When a data update occurs, the repository—often in coordination with the Subscriber Registry—proactively notifies relevant subscribers based on their registered interests.

As illustrated in the figure, the collaboration sequence in this architecture style follows three key steps, indicated by the numbered arrows.

- **Step ①, Update, represents a data update operation initiated by a data subscriber.**
- **Step ②, Notify, denotes the repository's proactive notification to all subscribers who have registered interest in the modified data.**
- **Step ③, Retrieve, is optional and allows notified subscribers to retrieve the updated data as needed.**

In the example shown, Data Subscribers C and E respond to the notification by retrieving the updated data, while Data Subscriber F does not take further action.

12.4.3 Strengths and Limitations

The Active Repository Architecture Style offers the following strengths:

- **Real-Time Update Propagation**
  Subscribed data subscribers receive immediate notifications of data changes, enabling real-time synchronization and facilitating responsive system behavior.
- **Reduction in Network Traffic**
  The use of a notification mechanism eliminates the need for frequent polling by subscribers, thereby reducing unnecessary network traffic and lowering the system's communication overhead.
- **Improved System Responsiveness**
  By proactively alerting subscribers to relevant data changes, the system can support timely reactions, leading to faster decision-making and improved user experience, especially in time-sensitive applications.
- **Selective Data Awareness**
  Through the Subscriber Registry, notifications can be selectively targeted to only those subscribers interested in specific data changes, which enhances efficiency and reduces processing overhead for unrelated components.

On the other hand, this architecture style exhibits the following limitations:

- **Complexity of Event Management**
  The system must efficiently handle and route potentially high volumes of events, increasing the complexity of the central repository. Managing accurate subscription records and supporting dynamic registration and deregistration of subscribers add further operational overhead.
- **Notification Overhead and Scalability Concerns**
  If not properly managed, the cost of dispatching and processing notifications may outweigh the benefits of real-time updates. As the number of subscribers or the frequency of updates grows, maintaining system performance may require additional scaling mechanisms and architectural optimizations.

12.5 Blackboard Architecture Style

The Blackboard Architecture Style is characterized by a collaborative problem-solving framework in which independent *Knowledge Sources* (*KS*), each possessing specialized expertise, contribute incrementally toward solving complex problems. These modular components interact through a shared data structure known as the Blackboard, which serves as a central medium for communication and coordination.

Each knowledge source monitors the blackboard for relevant changes and activates when it can contribute toward progressing the solution. This architecture style is particularly well suited for problems that can be decomposed into sub-problems, each requiring distinct domain knowledge or heuristic strategies.

12.5.1 Structure

The structure of this architecture style is defined by three primary components: *Blackboard*, *Knowledge Sources*, and *Controller*. The structure of this architecture style is shown in Fig. 12.5.

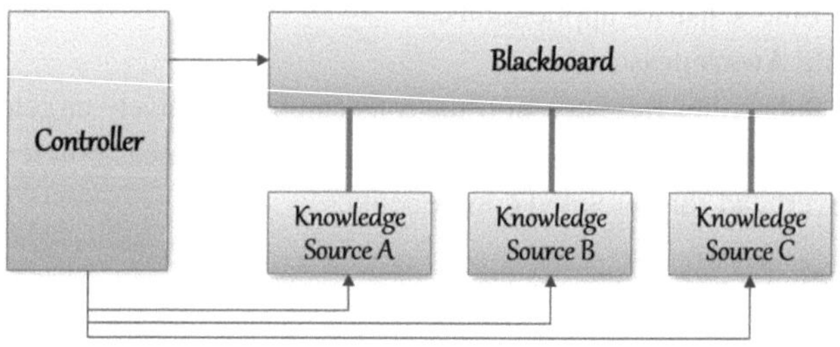

Fig. 12.5 Structure of Blackboard Architecture Style

- **Blackboard**
  A shared global data structure that represents the evolving state of the problem-solving process. It serves as the central communication medium through which knowledge sources exchange information and contribute to the solution.
- **Knowledge Sources (KS)**
  Independent, specialized modules that possess domain-specific expertise. They monitor the blackboard for relevant data patterns and activate opportunistically to contribute partial solutions or infer new knowledge.
- **Controller**
  A coordinating component responsible for managing the flow of control among knowledge sources. It determines which knowledge source to activate next, based on the current state of the blackboard and a defined control strategy (e.g., agenda based, priority based).

12.5.2 Collaboration Models

The collaboration model in this architecture style is driven by indirect, opportunistic interaction among knowledge sources through the blackboard. Knowledge sources do not communicate with each other directly; instead, they collaborate by observing changes on the blackboard and contributing their expertise when relevant data patterns appear. The controller orchestrates this interaction by monitoring the blackboard's state and determining which knowledge source should be activated next. This model supports dynamic, data-driven execution, where the order and timing of contributions are determined at runtime based on the evolving solution.

The collaboration model of this style is defined as a sequence of the following tasks:

- **Task 1. Post Initial Data to the Blackboard**
  The problem-solving process begins with the insertion of initial data or hypotheses into the blackboard, establishing the initial problem context.
- **Task 2. Monitor Blackboard for Activation Conditions**
  Each knowledge source observes the blackboard for specific data patterns or conditions that match its area of expertise. This passive monitoring enables knowledge sources to identify opportunities to contribute without direct invocation.
- **Task 3. Select an Applicable Knowledge Source**
  The controller evaluates the current state of the blackboard and, based on predefined control strategies (e.g., priority, readiness, or conflict resolution), selects the most appropriate knowledge source for activation.
- **Task 4. Activate the Selected Knowledge Source**
  The chosen knowledge source is invoked by the controller to perform its reasoning or transformation logic, contributing new insights or intermediate results.

- **Task 5. Update the Blackboard with Results**
  The activated knowledge source writes its output to the blackboard, altering the shared problem state and potentially triggering new activation opportunities.
- **Task 6. Iterate Until Solution is Reached**
  Steps 2 through 5 are repeated iteratively as the system incrementally refines the solution. The process continues until a termination condition is satisfied, such as reaching a complete solution or meeting a predefined goal criterion.

12.5.3 Strengths and Limitations

The Blackboard Architecture Style exhibits the following strengths:

- **Modularity and Reusability**
  Knowledge sources are designed as independent, self-contained modules, each contributing specific expertise. This modularity facilitates reusability, maintainability, and ease of integration or replacement.
- **Dynamic Problem-Solving**
  The architecture supports an opportunistic and data-driven approach to problem-solving. Knowledge sources are activated dynamically based on the evolving state of the blackboard, enabling flexible and adaptive execution paths.
- **Effective for Complex and Uncertain Problems**
  This style is well suited for domains where problems cannot be solved through a single algorithm and require diverse, specialized reasoning—such as language understanding, image interpretation, or medical diagnosis.
- **Incremental Solution Development**
  The solution evolves progressively as knowledge sources contribute partial results over time. This incremental refinement allows the system to converge toward a solution even in uncertain or evolving problem spaces.

On the other hand, this architecture style exhibits the following limitations:

- **Control Complexity**
  Managing the activation and coordination of multiple independent knowledge sources requires a sophisticated control mechanism. Designing an effective control strategy can be challenging, especially in systems with a large number of components and dynamic interactions.
- **Potential for Non-Optimal Solutions**
  Due to its opportunistic and heuristic nature, the blackboard architecture may converge on acceptable but suboptimal solutions. Without a global optimization mechanism, the quality of results may depend heavily on the control strategy and the order of knowledge source activation.

- **Difficulties in Debugging and Testing**
  The non-deterministic execution order of knowledge sources makes it difficult to reproduce and trace system behavior, complicating debugging, validation, and performance tuning.

12.6 Layered Architecture Style

The Layered Architecture Style organizes a system into a hierarchical set of layers, each responsible for a specific group of functionalities. Each layer typically offers services to the layer directly above it while receiving services from the layer below. This separation promotes modularity and abstraction. The idea of each layer acting as a "virtual machine" for the layer above encapsulates this principle, enabling clear and controlled interactions between adjacent layers.

12.6.1 Structure

The structure of this architecture style is defined by a hierarchical arrangement of layers, where each layer encapsulates a distinct set of responsibilities and exposes a well-defined interface to the layer above. Lower layers provide foundational services, while higher layers build upon them, ensuring unidirectional dependencies and minimizing coupling across non-adjacent layers.

The structure of this architecture style is shown in Fig. 12.6.

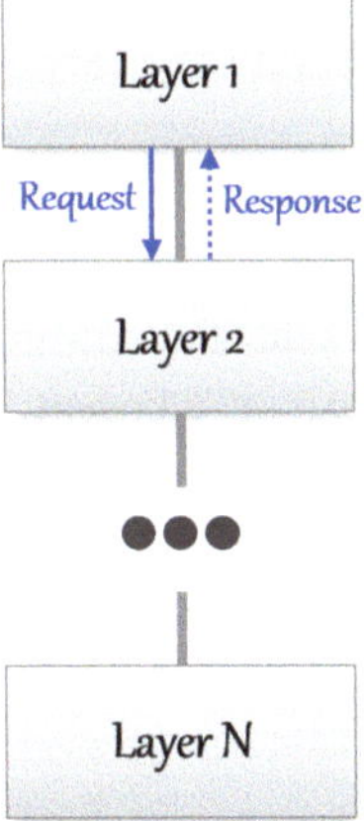

Fig. 12.6 Structure of Layered Architecture Style

- **Layers**
  A *layer* refers to a logical grouping of components that share similar responsibilities within the system. Each layer abstracts a specific concern, such as presentation, business logic, or data access, and encapsulates its internal implementation details.
- **Connections**
  The system is structured as a hierarchy of layers, where each layer provides services to the layer directly above and consumes services from the layer directly below.
  - Layer 1 is the topmost layer, typically the *Presentation Layer*, which handles user interaction. It initiates a request to Layer 2 and expects a response.
  - Layer 2 processes the request from Layer 1, potentially delegating tasks to lower layers. After processing, it composes a response and passes it back to Layer 1.
  - Layer N at the bottom is usually the *Data Access Layer*. It interacts with data storage systems and provides raw data or persistent service results to its upper layer.

12.6.2 Collaboration Models

The collaboration model in this architecture style is defined by the directional flow of requests and responses between adjacent layers. Upper layers initiate requests to lower layers to perform specific services or retrieve data. In response, the lower layers execute the requested operations and return responses back up the stack.

- Communication occurs only between neighboring layers, preserving encapsulation.
- Each layer serves as a virtual machine for the layer above, abstracting implementation details.
- The flow follows a strict order, discouraging backward or cross-layer interactions, which enhances system maintainability and testability.

In Fig. 12.6, the solid blue arrow labeled "Request" represents the downward flow of a service invocation. For instance, Layer 1 sends a service request to Layer 2. The dashed blue arrow labeled "Response" represents the upward flow of the result and returning the outcome to the upper layer. Each pair of adjacent layers follows this request-response cycle, which cascades through the hierarchy when necessary, and the final response bubbles back up the chain.

The collaboration model in the Layered Architecture Style is depicted in Fig. 12.7.

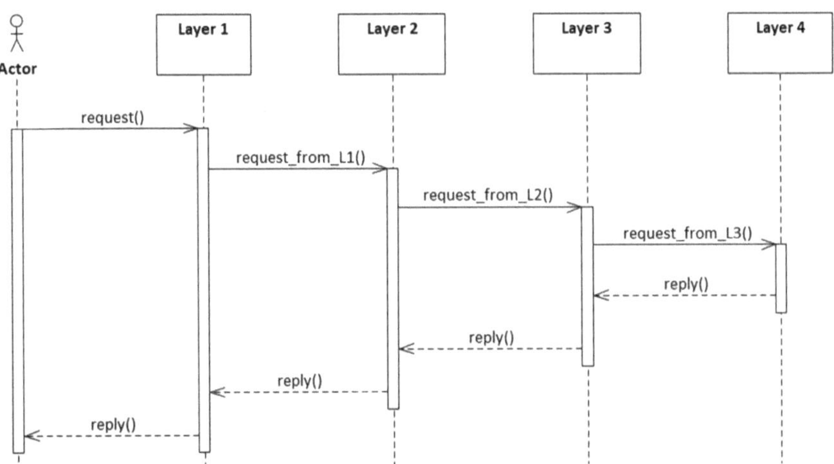

Fig. 12.7 Collaboration in Layered Architecture Style

In the figure, Layer 1 receives the initial request() from the external Actor. It performs initial processing, such as input validation or request transformation, and then delegates the refined request (request_from_L1()) to Layer 2. Layer 2 continues the processing based on its responsibilities—often related to business logic—and passes the request further down to Layer 3 via request_from_L2(). This chain continues as Layer 3 processes the request and forwards it to Layer 4 using request_from_L3().

Layer 4, typically the lowest and most foundational layer, executes the requested operation, such as retrieving or updating data, and produces a result in the form of a reply(). This reply then propagates back through the layers in reverse order: from Layer 4 to Layer 3, then to Layer 2, and finally to Layer 1. Each layer may optionally process or wrap the reply before forwarding it upward. Ultimately, Layer 1 sends the final reply() back to the Actor.

12.6.3 Strengths and Limitations

The Layered Architecture Style exhibits the following strengths:

- **Separation of Concerns**
  Each layer is responsible for a specific concern, ensuring that no two layers overlap in functionality. This clear delineation allows developers to focus on a single aspect of the system at a time, promoting better organization, ease of understanding, and improved maintainability.

- **Modularity**
  By structuring the system into distinct, self-contained layers, this style enhances modularity. Each layer can be developed, tested, and maintained independently, allowing changes to be made in one layer with minimal impact on others. This modular structure simplifies debugging, supports parallel development, and improves system manageability.
- **Reusability of Layers**
  The clear separation between layers enables the reuse of common functionalities—such as business logic or data access—in other systems or components. This promotes consistency, reduces duplication, and accelerates development across multiple projects.
- **Scalability Support**
  The architecture supports scalability by allowing individual layers to be scaled independently. Depending on the system's needs, horizontal or vertical scaling strategies can be applied to specific layers without requiring significant architectural changes across the system.

On the other hand, this architecture style exhibits the following limitations:

- **Performance Overhead**
  Layered architecture may introduce performance overhead due to the cumulative processing time required by each layer and the communication costs between them. This can be particularly problematic in systems requiring real-time responsiveness or low-latency interactions.
  To mitigate this issue, shortcut paths can be introduced as shown in Fig. 12.8.

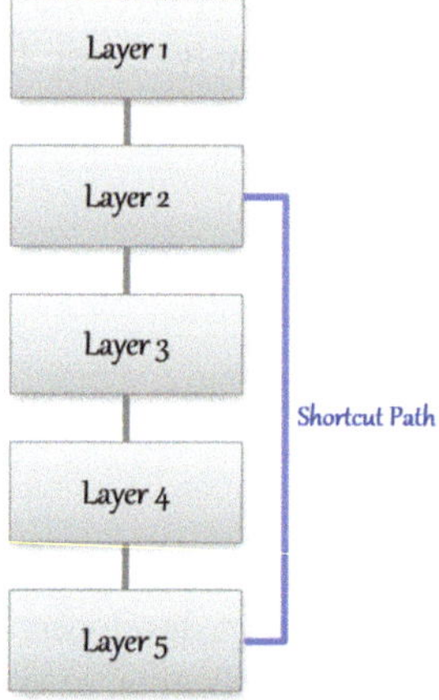

Fig. 12.8 Layered Architecture Style with Shortcut Path

A shortcut path refers to a direct interaction between non-adjacent layers, allowing a higher layer to bypass one or more intermediate layers and directly access a lower layer. This mechanism can reduce communication latency and improve system performance. However, such shortcuts should be used judiciously; excessive or unregulated use can erode the benefits of modularity and separation of concerns that the layered architecture is designed to preserve.

- **Complexity of Layer Management**
  As the system grows, maintaining strict separation and disciplined interaction between layers can become increasingly complex. Ensuring that each layer communicates only with its immediate neighbors requires rigorous architectural governance. Without careful design and adherence to layering principles, the architecture may degrade into a tangled structure that is difficult to understand, modify, or scale.

12.7 Model-View-Controller Architecture Style

The Model-View-Controller (MVC) Architecture Style, as a specialized form of the Layered Architecture Style, structures a system into three distinct layers: Model, View, and Controller. This separation of concerns simplifies the development of complex applications, enhances maintainability, and supports scalability.

12.7.1 Structure

The structure of this architecture style is defined by three interconnected layers—Model, View, and Controller—each responsible for a specific aspect of the application's functionality.

The structure of this architecture style is shown in Fig. 12.9.

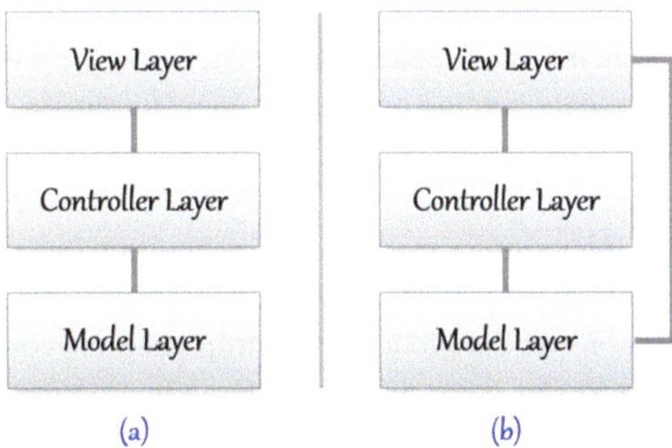

Fig. 12.9 Structure of MVC Architecture Style

- **Model Layer**
  The Model layer is responsible for managing the system's persistent data and encapsulating the associated business logic.
  - **Managing Persistent Data**
    This layer interfaces with the system's database or other storage mechanisms to perform CRUD operations. It maintains the system state and acts as the data access layer, exposing well-defined interfaces through which the Controller layer can interact with the underlying data repositories.
  - **Handling Business Logic**
    The Model layer handles the business logic of the system, which refers to the rules, constraints, and procedures that define how a system should behave and process data from a business perspective. More specifically, it handles domain rules, data processing, validation, and data integrity.
- **View Layer**
  The View layer is responsible for presenting information to the user and managing the visual representation of the system's data.
  - **Interacting with the Controller**
    The View also interacts with the Controller layer to delegate user actions. When users perform actions such as clicking a button, entering data, or navigating between views, the View captures these inputs and forwards them to the Controller for processing. This separation allows the View to remain free of business logic while still supporting user interaction.
  - **Presenting Data from the Model**
    The View layer may explicitly query the Model to retrieve the current state of data for presentation. This typically occurs in response to user actions or initialization events. The retrieved data is rendered using appropriate user interface elements.
  - **Observing Model State Changes (Optional)**
    In loosely coupled implementations, the View may subscribe to the Model's state changes using an observer mechanism. When the Model updates, it notifies the View, which can then refresh the display automatically.
    This feature is explicitly supported in the Model-View-ViewModel (MVVM) architecture style, where data binding enables the View to remain synchronized with the underlying Model through the ViewModel.
- **Controller Layer**
  The Controller layer functions as an intermediary between the View and the Model. It receives and processes user inputs from the View, interprets these inputs, and invokes corresponding operations on the Model. By coordinating the control flow between the user interface and the Model layer, the Controller defines the application's behavioral responses to user interactions.

Note on Control Flow and Business Logic

In the MVC Architecture, the Controller layer is responsible for managing the system's control flow, while the Model layer handles the business logic. Although closely related, control flow and business logic are distinct modeling elements that serve different purposes within a software system.

The control flow refers to the order and conditions under which different components of the system are executed. In contrast, business logic encompasses the rules, constraints, and domain-specific operations that govern how the system behaves and processes data. Business logic is typically executed in accordance with the control flow, which determines when and under what conditions various parts of the business logic are invoked.

12.7.2 Collaboration Models

The collaboration model in this architecture style is defined by the interaction among the three core layers: Model, View, and Controller.

- The View receives user interactions and delegates them to the Controller.
- The Controller interprets the user inputs, performs application-specific processing, and invokes the appropriate operations on the Model.
- The Model updates its internal state and business logic based on the Controller's requests and, if applicable, notifies the View of state changes.
- The View then queries the Model to retrieve the updated data and refreshes the presentation accordingly.

This collaborative interaction ensures a clean separation of concerns: the Controller governs control flow, the Model encapsulates business logic and state, and the View manages user interface rendering.

Interaction Between the View and Model Layers

Interaction between the View and the Model layers is permitted in the MVC architecture to facilitate efficient communication and user interface responsiveness. As shown in Fig. 12.9b, direct interaction between the View and the Model allows flexible updates without routing all communication through the Controller. This is especially beneficial when the View needs to remain synchronized with the Model's state.

More specifically, Figure 12.10 illustrates three representative interaction patterns between the View and the Model layers.

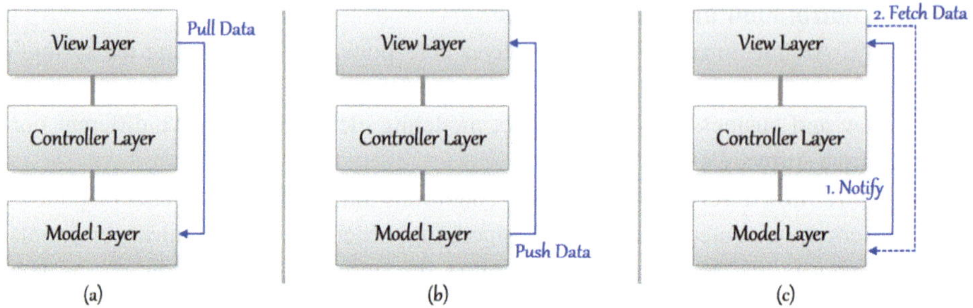

Fig. 12.10 Direct Interactions Between View and Model Layers

(a) **Pull Model**
The View layer explicitly pulls data from the Model as needed. This approach gives the View control over when and what data to retrieve.

(b) **Push Model**
The Model actively pushes updated data to the View when changes occur. This reduces the need for the View to query the Model and is often used in reactive systems.

(c) **Observer Pattern**
The Model notifies the View of state changes (1. Notify), and the View subsequently fetches the updated data from the Model (2. Fetch Data). This pattern supports a decoupled and event-driven architecture, commonly used in systems requiring dynamic UI updates.

12.7.3 Strengths and Limitations

The MVC Architecture Style exhibits the following strengths:

- **Separation of Concerns**
  The architecture divides the system into three distinct layers, each with clearly defined responsibilities. This separation enhances modularity, making the system easier to develop, test, maintain, and evolve, as modifications to one layer typically do not impact the others.
- **Parallel Development**
  The modular structure enables different team members to work on the Model, View, and Controller layers concurrently. This parallelism accelerates the development process and promotes more efficient collaboration.
- **Reusability**
  The separation of concerns facilitates the reuse of the Model and Controller layers across multiple View implementations. This improves consistency in business logic and behavior while supporting diverse user interfaces tailored to different platforms or contexts.

- **Improved Maintainability**
  The modular organization of MVC allows for localized changes. For example, modifications to the user interface can typically be made within the View layer without impacting the business logic or control flow, which simplifies bug fixing and system enhancement over time.
- **Flexibility in User Interface Design**
  Multiple Views can be created for the same Model to support different types of users, devices, or display formats. This enables the development of rich, adaptive, and accessible user interfaces.

On the other hand, this architecture style exhibits the following limitations:

- **Increased Complexity for Small Applications**
  The structural overhead of separating the system into three distinct components may introduce unnecessary complexity for simple or small-scale applications, where such modularity may not provide tangible benefits.
- **Difficulty in Synchronizing Views**
  When multiple Views depend on the same Model, ensuring consistent updates across all Views can be complex, particularly in the absence of a robust observer or data-binding mechanism.

12.8 Variations of MVC Architecture Style

The Model-View-Controller (MVC) Architecture Style has been widely adopted in the design of software system architectures across various domains. Over time, several variations have emerged to address specific requirements of target systems and to overcome limitations associated with the traditional MVC approach.

12.8.1 Model-View-Presenter (MVP)

The Model-View-Presenter (MVP) Architecture Style separates the application into three layers: the Model for data and business logic, the View for the user interface, and the Presenter for the user interface logic and mediation between the Model and the View. The Presenter acts as a mediator between the Model and the View as shown in Fig. 12.11.

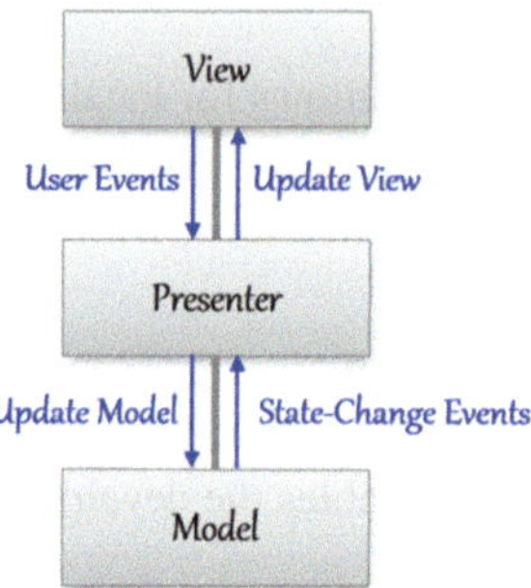

Fig. 12.11 MVP Architecture Style

- **Model**
  In MVP, the Model layer embodies the application's data and business logic. Upon any state change within the Model, it notifies the Presenter through "State-Change Events." Subsequently, the Presenter updates the View to reflect these changes.
- **(Passive) View**
  The View layer is responsible for the user interface of the application. It defines the layout, controls, and visual elements that the user interacts with. The View is passive and only receives updates from the Presenter, making it easier to test the UI logic independently.
- **Presenter**
  The Presenter layer contains the user interface logic and acts as a mediator between the Model and the View. It receives user events from the View, interacts with the Model to retrieve or modify data, and updates the View based on the state-changes. That is, the Presenter actively prepares the data and provides it to the View.
  The Presenter can be viewed as a more tightly integrated and proactive variant of the Controller in MVC. While both mediate between the View and the Model, the Presenter assumes greater responsibility for orchestrating the application's presentation logic and enforces a unidirectional flow, ensuring the View is completely passive.

The MVP architecture offers several benefits, including enhanced separation of concerns, improved testability, and greater flexibility in managing user interface logic. By decoupling the View from the Model and delegating all presentation logic to the Presenter, the MVP pattern facilitates easier unit testing, supports multiple UI implementations, and promotes maintainable and modular code.

12.8.2 Model-View-ViewModel (MVVM)

The Model-View-ViewModel (MVVM) Architecture Style is characterized by the separation of the user interface from business logic and data management through an intermediary component known as the ViewModel. The ViewModel encapsulates presentation logic and exposes data and commands to the View, enabling the View to reflect changes automatically via data binding.

While both MVP and MVVM focus on separating concerns, their main difference is how the View interacts with the middle layer. In MVP, the Presenter directly controls updates to both the Model and the View. In MVVM, the ViewModel uses data binding to expose data and behavior, and the View automatically updates in response.

The structure and the collaboration model of this architecture are shown in Fig. 12.12.

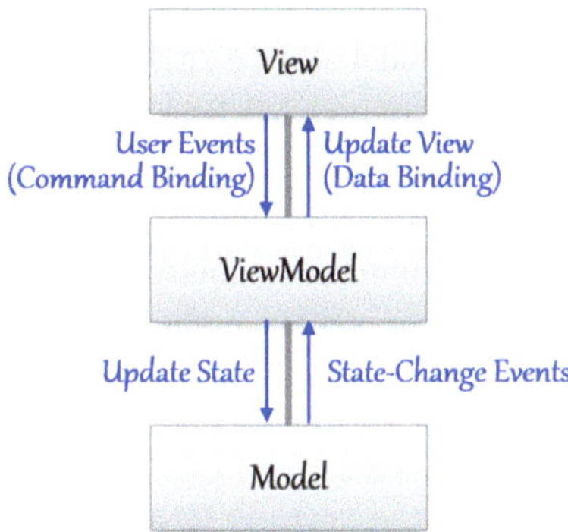

Fig. 12.12 MVVM Architecture Style

- **View**
  The View handles the user interface and collects user input. It stays passive, meaning it doesn't contain logic for business rules or app behavior. Instead, it uses command binding to send user actions to the ViewModel and data binding to automatically update the UI when the ViewModel's data changes. This keeps the UI in sync without needing manual updates.
- **ViewModel**
  The ViewModel sits between the View and the Model. It holds the presentation logic and provides data and commands that the View can bind to. When a user does something in the UI, the ViewModel handles it and may update the Model. It also listens for changes from the Model and updates itself, so the View stays current through data binding. The ViewModel doesn't know about the View, which keeps things separate and easier to test.
- **Model**
  The Model contains the main business logic and handles the app's data, usually things that are saved or specific to the domain. It provides methods that the ViewModel uses to get or change data. When the data changes, the Model notifies the ViewModel. The Model doesn't deal with the user interface, so it can be reused with different UIs.

The MVVM architecture has several advantages, such as clear separation of parts, easier testing, and better maintenance. It separates the user interface from the logic and data, making the system more modular and reusable. Data binding lets the View automatically update when the ViewModel changes, so less code is needed. Also, because the ViewModel doesn't depend on the View, it can be tested on its own, which is helpful for apps with complex UIs or used on different platforms.

12.8.3 Model-View-Presenter-ViewModel (MVPVM)

The Model-View-Presenter-ViewModel (MVPVM) Architecture Style is a hybrid approach that combines the strengths of both MVP and MVVM. In this style, the Presenter manages business logic and coordinates updates between the Model and the View, while the ViewModel enables data binding to streamline UI updates and simplify presentation logic. This integration supports both imperative control and declarative binding, offering a flexible and maintainable solution for complex applications.

The structure and the collaboration model of this architecture are shown in Fig. 12.13.

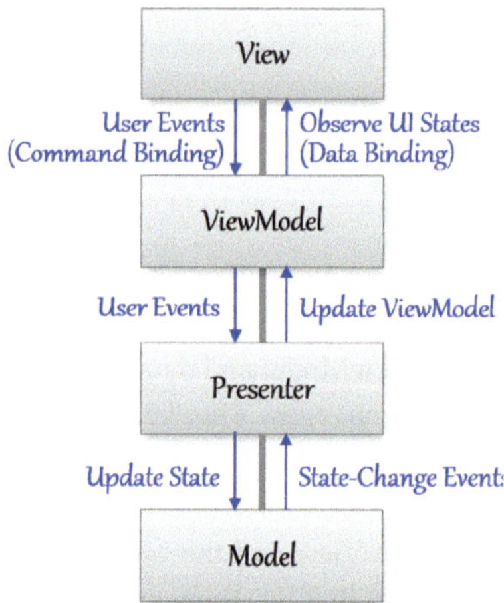

Fig. 12.13 MVPVM Architecture Style

- **View**
  The View is responsible for rendering the user interface and capturing user input. It remains passive, relying on **command binding** to delegate user actions to the ViewModel and **data binding** to observe and reflect UI state changes. By avoiding embedded logic, the View enhances maintainability and promotes separation of concerns, allowing the presentation logic to reside outside of the UI layer.

- **ViewModel**
  The ViewModel serves as a binding layer between the View and the Presenter. It exposes data and commands to the View, enabling two-way interaction through declarative bindings. It receives user events from the View and forwards them to the Presenter for processing. Once the Presenter updates the ViewModel, it automatically notifies the View of state changes, ensuring responsive and consistent UI updates without direct UI manipulation.
- **Presenter**
  The Presenter manages the core presentation logic and orchestrates interactions between the ViewModel and the Model. It processes user events received via the ViewModel, applies business rules, and updates the application state by communicating with the Model. The Presenter also receives state-change events from the Model and reflects the results back to the ViewModel, enabling a clean separation between business logic and UI behavior.
- **Model**
  In canonical MVPVM architecture, the Model primarily connects to the Presenter, not directly to the ViewModel. The Model layer represents the persistent data and handles the business logic of the system.

The MVPVM architecture has several advantages, combining the strengths of both MVP and MVVM styles to achieve a balanced separation of concerns, enhanced flexibility, and improved testability. By incorporating a Presenter to manage business logic and a ViewModel to enable data binding, MVPVM supports both imperative and declarative programming paradigms. This hybrid approach simplifies UI updates, reduces boilerplate code, and allows for modular, maintainable components.

12.8.4 Hierarchical-Model-View-Controller (HMVC)

The Hierarchical-Model-View-Controller (HMVC) Architecture Style structures the target system as a hierarchy of multiple MVC triads, where each triad represents an independent module or subsystem implementing the standard MVC pattern.

The structure of the MHVC architecture is shown in Fig. 12.14.

- **MVC Triad**
  Each rectangle in the figure represents an MVC triad, which serves as a modular unit within the overall system. A MVC triad consists of its own Model, View, and Controller layers and provides a specific functionality of the system.
  Inside each triad, the Controller is positioned at the top and is responsible for handling user input and coordinating communication between the Model and the View. The View presents data to the user and updates the user interface in response to changes in the Model. The Model encapsulates the business logic and maintains the application's state.

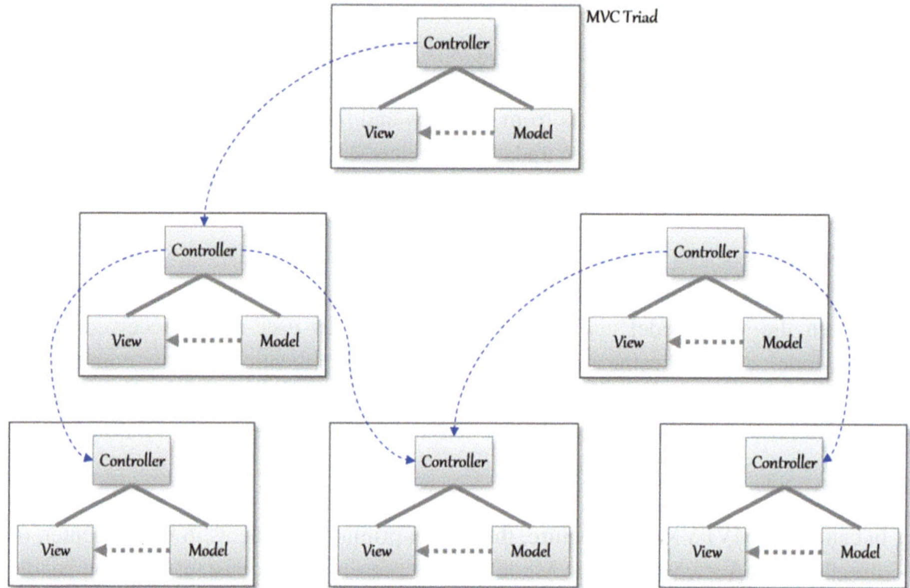

Fig. 12.14 Structure of HMVC Architecture Style

The gray arrows in the diagram represent the direction of control and data flow within the triad: the Controller sends commands to both the View and the Model, while the dotted arrow from the Model to the View indicates that the View is updated automatically when the Model's state changes.

- **Hierarchical Interaction Among Triads**
  The dashed blue arrows between Controllers in the architecture represent inter-controller communication across MVC triads, illustrating the hierarchical nature of the HMVC architecture. A parent Controller can invoke or delegate responsibilities to child Controllers, enabling coordination across modular units. This hierarchical communication supports the modular decomposition of complex systems, where each triad operates independently yet participates in a larger, organized structure.

The HMVC architecture offers several benefits, including improved modularity, reusability, and maintainability. By organizing the system into independent MVC triads, it enables easier testing, parallel development, and simplified integration of new features. This structure also supports better scalability and clearer separation of concerns, making it well suited for complex and evolving software systems.

12.8.5 Model-View-Adapter (MVA)

The Model-View-Adapter (MVA) Architecture Style is a variation of the MVC and MVP architectures, designed to address the challenges of integrating with environments where the View and Model layers are not easily separable. This architecture style introduces an

Adapter component to mediate between the View and the Model, promoting better separation of concerns and enabling more flexible system integration.

The structure of the MVA architecture is shown in Fig. 12.15.

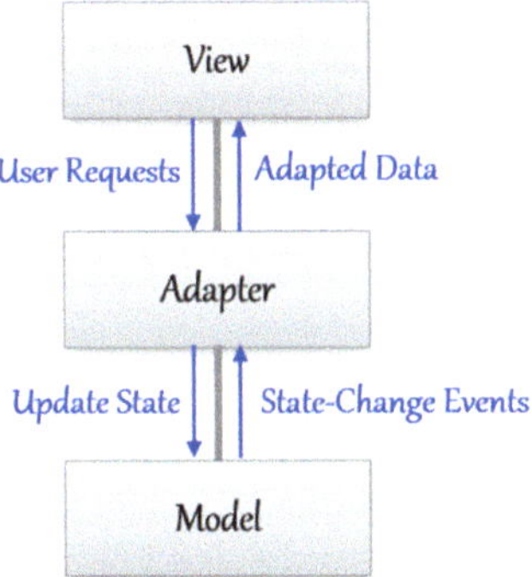

Fig. 12.15 Structure of MVA Architecture Style

- **View**
  The View handles the user interface and collects user input. It doesn't talk directly to the Model. Instead, it sends user requests to the Adapter and receives adapted data to display. This keeps the View focused only on showing information and getting input, without dealing with how the data is handled or stored.
- **Adapter**
  The Adapter takes user requests from the View and tells the Model what to do. When the Model changes, the Adapter listens for updates, adjusts the data format if needed, and sends it back to the View. This helps keep the View and Model separate, especially when they can't easily be split apart.
- **Model**
  The Model stores the app's data and handles business logic. It changes its state when asked by the Adapter and sends state-change updates back. It doesn't know about the View or the Adapter, so it stays focused only on managing the data and logic.

The MVA architecture offers several benefits, including better separation of concerns, improved modularity, and easier integration with systems where the View and Model are tightly coupled. The Adapter enables flexible data transformation, simplifies UI logic, and enhances maintainability and testability by decoupling the View from the Model.

12.9 N-Tier Architecture Style

The N-Tier Architecture Style, or multi-tier architecture, divides a system into separate tiers deployed on different physical machines. Each tier handles a specific functionality and communicates with others over a network. While layers represent the logical organization of responsibilities within the application, tiers refer to their physical deployment across computing nodes.

12.9.1 Structure

The structure of this architecture style is defined by a set of physically separated tiers, each responsible for a distinct functional role within the system. The structure of this architecture style is shown in Fig. 12.16.

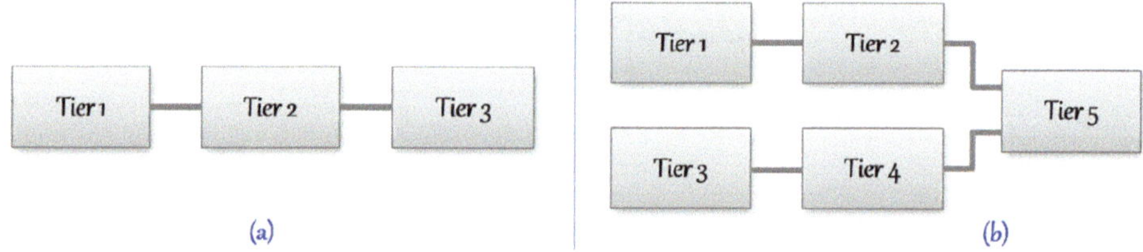

Fig. 12.16 Structure of N-Tier Architecture Style

The figure illustrates two structural variations of the N-Tier Architecture Style.

(a) **Linear Sequence Connection**
The tiers are organized in a linear sequence, representing a traditional deployment where each tier communicates strictly with its adjacent tier.

(b) **Branched N-Tier Connection**
This connection model features multiple parallel tier paths that converge at a common backend, supporting modular processing and centralized integration.

12.9.2 Collaboration Models

The collaboration model in this architecture style defines how different tiers within a system interact to process requests and deliver responses in a coordinated manner. This model is primarily influenced by the structural organization of the tiers.

Since inter-tier communication over a network can introduce significant performance overhead, the organization of tiers should carefully balance the cohesiveness and independence of each tier with the runtime efficiency of their interactions.

12.9.3 Strengths and Limitations

The N-Tier Architecture Style exhibits the following strengths:

- **Scalability**
  Each tier can be scaled independently based on resource demands and usage patterns. For example, the presentation tier may be expanded to support increased user traffic, while the data tier can be scaled to accommodate larger volumes of storage or higher query throughput.
- **Load Balancing**
  Client requests can be distributed across multiple servers within a tier, reducing the load on individual components and improving overall responsiveness and system availability.
- **Parallel Deployment**
  Development teams can work on different tiers concurrently, enabling faster development cycles and facilitating specialization across functional areas.
- **Flexibility and Maintainability**
  Tiers can be modified, updated, or replaced independently, minimizing the impact on the overall system. This modularity simplifies maintenance, debugging, and future enhancements.

On the other hand, this architecture style exhibits the following limitations:

- **Performance Overhead**
  In an N-Tier system, communication between tiers occurs over network connections, introducing latency and overhead. This is generally more costly than intra-process communication in layered architectures, where components share the same memory space.
- **Resource Consumption**
  Deploying multiple tiers on separate servers or instances increases resource usage, including hardware, memory, and network bandwidth, which can lead to higher infrastructure and operational costs.
- **Complexity**
  N-Tier architectures are inherently more complex to design, implement, and maintain. Coordinating interactions across distributed tiers requires careful interface management, monitoring, and error handling, especially in large-scale systems.

12.10 Client-Server Architecture Style

The *Client-Server Architecture Style* is primarily characterized by a two-tier structure that partitions system functionality between two distinct roles: the *server*, which provides services or resources, and the *client*, which requests them. This separation of responsibilities promotes a clear delineation of concerns, thereby facilitating systematic design while enhancing scalability and maintainability. As a result, the optimal allocation of system functionality between client-side and server-side operations becomes a critical design activity within this architecture style.

12.10.1 Structure

The structure of this architecture style is defined by a logical separation between two primary tiers: the *client* and *the server*. The structure of this architecture style is shown in Fig. 12.17.

Fig. 12.17 Structure of Client-Server Architecture Style

- **Client Tier**
  The *Client Tier* represents the set of components responsible for initiating communication with the server. These components primarily manage the user interface, capture user inputs, and issue service requests to the server. In addition to user interaction, the client may implement client-specific functionality such as local data validation, caching, or session management to improve performance and user experience. The client tier typically resides on the user's device—such as a Web browser, mobile app, or desktop application—and delegates core business logic and data management responsibilities to the server tier.
- **Server Tier**
  The *Server Tier* represents the set of components that provide services or resources requested by clients. These components are responsible for handling incoming requests, executing business logic, accessing and managing persistent data, and ensuring secure and reliable service delivery. Typically hosted on centralized or distributed server infrastructure, the server tier supports scalability, maintains data integrity, and enables centralized control over system operations.

12.10.2 Collaboration Models

The collaboration model in this architecture style is defined by a *request-response* interaction between clients and servers, in which clients initiate service requests and servers respond by processing those requests and returning the results. This loosely coupled communication enables the independent evolution of client and server components.

To support this interaction, various patterns can be employed, including *Request-Response*, *Remote Procedure Call* (*RPC*), and *Publish-Subscribe*, selected based on the system's communication requirements, scalability demands, and responsiveness.

12.10.3 Strengths and Limitations

The Client-Server Architecture Style exhibits the following strengths:

- **Modularity and Separation of Concerns**
  The clear division between client-side and server-side responsibilities promotes modularity, making the system easier to develop, maintain, and extend.
- **Centralized Control and Management**
  Since core and common functionalities and data management reside on the server, system behavior can be centrally managed, enabling better control over security, consistency, and resource allocation.
- **Scalability**
  The architecture supports horizontal scalability by allowing multiple clients to interact with the same server or distributed servers through load balancing mechanisms.
- **Interoperability**
  Clients and servers can be implemented on different platforms and using different technologies, as long as they adhere to common communication protocols.
- **Ease of Maintenance and Updates**
  Updates and maintenance to core logic or data storage can be performed at the server side without requiring changes to the client applications, streamlining deployment and reducing client-side disruptions.

On the other hand, this architecture style exhibits the following limitations:

- **Single Point of Failure**
  If the server becomes unavailable due to hardware failure, network issues, or software errors, all client operations depending on the server are disrupted, leading to system-wide downtime.

- **Limited Client Autonomy**
  Clients are often dependent on the server for critical functionality. This tight dependency can reduce fault tolerance and limit offline or standalone operation capabilities.
- **Potential Scalability Bottlenecks**
  As the number of clients increases, the server may become a performance bottleneck unless load balancing, replication, or server clustering techniques are employed.

12.11 Peer-to-Peer Architecture Style

In the Peer-to-Peer (P2P) Architecture Style, there is no central coordination or control over participating nodes. Each node operates autonomously and can both request and provide services or resources. A peer functions simultaneously as both a client and a server, enabling decentralized collaboration and resource sharing among nodes in the network.

12.11.1 Structure

The structure of this architecture style is defined by a decentralized network composed of peer nodes, each capable of acting as both a client and a server without relying on a central authority. The structure of this architecture style is shown in Fig. 12.18.

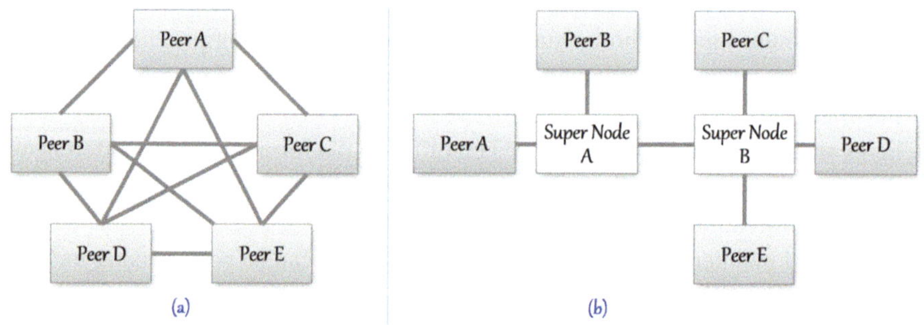

Fig. 12.18 Structure of Peer-to-Peer Architecture Style

- **Peer Node**
  A *peer node* is the fundamental unit of the P2P architecture. Each peer operates autonomously and simultaneously functions as both a client and a server, enabling the mutual sharing of resources and services among participating nodes.

- **Decentralized Network**
  The P2P architecture is characterized by a *decentralized network* in which control, data, and service provision are distributed across multiple peer nodes. This decentralized structure eliminates reliance on a central server.
- **Super Node (Optional)**
  A *super node* refers to a peer node endowed with additional responsibilities to improve overall network efficiency and scalability. Super nodes may be optionally introduced, as illustrated in Fig. 12.18b. These nodes typically manage routing, indexing, and coordination tasks for a group of connected peers.
  They are often selected based on specific criteria such as high availability, bandwidth, processing power, or stability. While super nodes enhance performance and reduce communication overhead, they also introduce a degree of centralization and potential points of failure within the otherwise decentralized architecture.

Figure 12.18 illustrates two structural variations of the P2P Architecture Style:

(a) **Pure Peer-to-Peer Structure**
In this configuration, all nodes—Peer A through Peer E—operate as equal participants in a fully decentralized network. Each peer can initiate and respond to communication requests, effectively acting as both a client and a server. The network topology is non-hierarchical, and each peer maintains direct or indirect communication paths with other peers.

(b) **Hybrid Peer-to-Peer Structure with Super Nodes**
This configuration introduces hierarchical elements into the P2P architecture by incorporating *super nodes* (e.g., Super Node A and Super Node B). Super nodes serve as intermediaries that manage and coordinate communication among associated peers, such as Peer A and Peer B under Super Node A and Peer C, D, and E under Super Node B.
This hybrid structure improves efficiency in resource discovery and reduces the communication overhead associated with fully decentralized networks, albeit at the cost of partial centralization and potential vulnerability in the super nodes.

12.11.2 Collaboration Models

The collaboration model in this architecture style is based on decentralized peer interactions, where each peer can initiate and respond to service requests without relying on a central coordinator. In a pure P2P model, peers directly discover and communicate with one another, forming dynamic and adaptive topologies. In contrast, hybrid P2P models introduce super nodes that facilitate collaboration by indexing resources, routing requests, or managing peer clusters.

In cases where a contacted peer cannot provide the requested service or resource, it may forward the request to other peers in the network, effectively acting as a relay. This forwarding process continues until a peer capable of fulfilling the request is found or a predefined search threshold—such as a maximum number of hops or a time-to-live (TTL) limit—is reached.

12.11.3 Strengths and Limitations

The Peer-to-Peer Architecture Style exhibits the following strengths:

- **Scalability**
  The ability to scale seamlessly with the addition of new nodes is one of the most critical advantages, especially for systems with dynamic and growing user bases.
- **Fault Tolerance**
  The decentralized nature enhances robustness, allowing the system to remain operational despite node failures—essential for high-availability systems.
- **Load Distribution**
  Distributing workload across multiple peers mitigates bottlenecks and improves system responsiveness, which is especially valuable in high-traffic scenarios.
- **Resource Sharing**
  Leveraging distributed storage, processing, or data across peers increases overall system capacity without requiring central resources.
- **Autonomy and Decentralized Control**
  The absence of centralized coordination simplifies deployment and management, particularly in open or ad hoc networks.

On the other hand, this architecture style exhibits the following limitations:

- **Complexity in Resource Discovery and Coordination**
  Without centralized control, locating resources and coordinating interactions among peers can be inefficient and require complex algorithms, especially in large-scale or unstructured networks.
- **Network Overhead and Performance Variability**
  The decentralized communication required for dynamic service discovery and peer collaboration introduces additional network traffic. Combined with the heterogeneous capabilities of peers, this can result in inconsistent quality of service and degraded performance.
- **Security and Trust Issues**
  Ensuring secure communication, verifying peer authenticity, and protecting against malicious behavior are challenging due to the open and decentralized nature of the system.

12.12 Broker Architecture Style

The *Broker Architecture Style* is characterized by the use of middleware that facilitates communication and coordination between clients and registered service providers through a central component known as the *broker*. This style promotes load balancing by distributing client requests across multiple service providers.

12.12.1 Structure

The structure of this architecture style is defined by three core elements: the Client, the Broker, and the Servers. The structure of this architecture style is shown in Fig. 12.19.

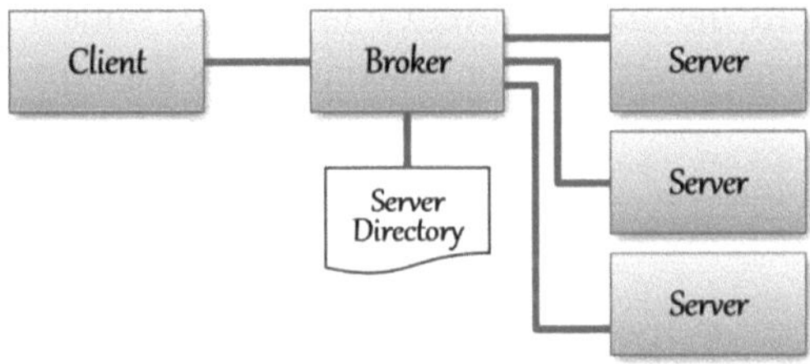

Fig. 12.19 Structure of Broker Architecture Style

- **Server**
  Servers are typically deployed as multiple instances to support scalability and reliability. This replication enables the Broker to distribute client requests based on criteria such as load balancing, fault tolerance, or geographic proximity.
- **Broker**
  The Broker functions as a central intermediary that manages communication between clients and servers. It receives requests from clients, consults the *Server Directory* to identify suitable service providers, and routes the requests accordingly—often selecting servers based on QoS requirements.
- **Client**
  The Client component is responsible for initiating service requests and receiving responses. It communicates exclusively with the Broker, remaining unaware of the underlying server infrastructure.

12.12.2 Collaboration Models

The collaboration model in this architecture style is centered on indirect communication between clients and servers, coordinated by the Broker. The interaction typically follows these steps:

(1) **Service Registration**
Servers register their capabilities and metadata (e.g., service types, availability, QoS parameters) with the Broker, which maintains this information in a *Server Directory*.
(2) **Service Request**
A client issues a service request to the Broker, specifying the required service functionality and possibly additional constraints (e.g., latency, reliability).
(3) **Service Lookup and Selection**
The Broker consults the Server Directory to identify suitable service providers. It selects an appropriate server based on criteria such as load distribution, proximity, or QoS preferences.
(4) **Request Dispatching**
The Broker forwards the client request to the selected server instance. The server processes the request and sends the response back to the Broker.
(5) **Response Delivery**
The Broker relays the server's response to the client, completing the interaction.

12.12.3 Strengths and Limitations

The Broker Architecture Style exhibits the following strengths:

- **Load Balancing**
The Broker distributes client requests across multiple server instances based on load or performance metrics, promoting efficient resource utilization and enhancing system responsiveness.
- **Fault Tolerance, Availability, and Reliability**
The Broker maintains a registry of multiple server instances, enabling it to reroute client requests to alternative servers in the event of failure or unavailability. This redundancy enhances overall system reliability and ensures high availability of services.
- **Loose Coupling**
Clients are decoupled from servers by interacting solely with the Broker. This separation simplifies system maintenance and allows independent evolution of clients and servers.
- **Centralized Control and Monitoring**
The Broker acts as a control point for managing service registration, monitoring performance, and enforcing global policies such as security and access control.

- **Location Transparency through Decompiling**
  Clients can request services without knowing the physical or network locations of the servers. This location transparency simplifies the system development and maintenance.

On the other hand, this architecture style exhibits the following limitations:

- **Single Point of Failure**
  The Broker is a central component and may become a single point of failure. If the Broker becomes unavailable or overloaded, the entire system's operation can be disrupted unless redundancy or replication mechanisms are in place.
- **Increased Latency**
  The additional communication layer introduced by the Broker may increase response time, as all interactions between clients and servers must pass through this intermediary.
- **Resource Overhead**
  Supporting replication requires maintaining multiple server instances, which increases the consumption of computational resources such as memory, processing power, and network bandwidth.

12.13 Dispatcher Architecture Style

The Dispatcher Architecture Style is characterized by a middleware structure in which a central component, known as the Dispatcher, manages the distribution of client requests to registered servers. Upon receiving a request, the Dispatcher selects an appropriate server based on QoS criteria, returns the server reference to the client, and enables the client to invoke the selected server directly.

This architecture style is similar to the Broker Architecture Style in that both rely on a central coordinator to manage service discovery and selection. However, unlike the Broker style, the Dispatcher does not remain involved in subsequent client-server communication, thereby reducing runtime overhead.

12.13.1 Structure

The structure of this architecture style is defined by three core elements: the Client, the Dispatcher, and the Servers. The Dispatcher acts as a central coordinator that maintains a registry of available servers along with associated metadata such as service types and QoS attributes. The Client sends a request to the Dispatcher, which selects an appropriate Server and returns its reference. The Client then communicates directly with the selected Server, enabling efficient service invocation with minimal middleware involvement.

The structure of this architecture style is shown in Fig. 12.20.

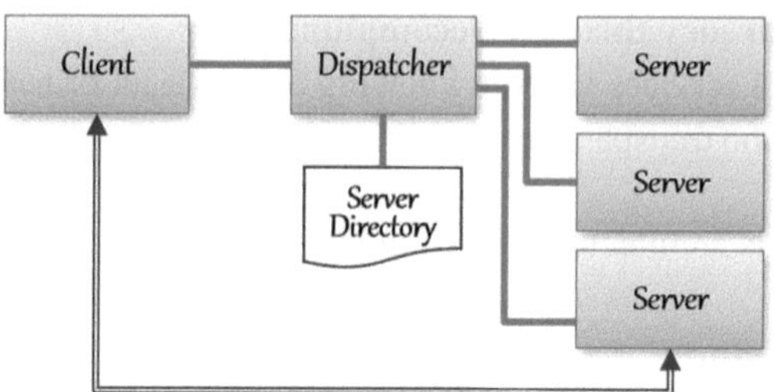

Fig. 12.20 Structure of Dispatcher Architecture Style

- **Server**
  Servers are typically replicated, similar to the Broker Architecture Style, to support scalability, load balancing, and fault tolerance. These server instances register their services with the Dispatcher.
- **Dispatcher**
  The Dispatcher functions as a central coordinator that manages service registration and request distribution. Upon receiving a client request, it identifies an appropriate server based on QoS attributes and returns the selected server's reference to the client. The Dispatcher maintains a *Server Directory* for registering and locating available services.
- **Client**
  The Client represents the consumer component that initiates service requests. It interacts solely with the Dispatcher to obtain a server reference and subsequently communicates directly with the designated server to complete the service interaction.

12.13.2 Collaboration Models

The collaboration model in this architecture style is centered on mediated service discovery followed by direct client-server communication, coordinated by the Dispatcher. The interaction typically follows these steps:

(1) **Service Registration**
Servers register their service capabilities and associated metadata (e.g., service types, availability, QoS attributes) with the Dispatcher, which maintains this information in a *Server Directory*.

(2) **Service Request**
A client sends a service request to the Dispatcher, indicating the desired functionality and any relevant constraints (e.g., performance or availability requirements).

(3) **Service Lookup and Selection**
The Dispatcher consults the Server Directory to identify suitable server instances. It selects a server based on QoS or other selection criteria and returns the server's reference to the client.

(4) **Direct Invocation**
The client uses the provided reference to directly invoke the selected server. Unlike the Broker style, the Dispatcher does not participate in this communication path.

(5) **Response Delivery**
The server processes the client request and returns the response directly to the client, completing the interaction without further involvement from the Dispatcher.

12.13.3 Strengths and Limitations

The Dispatcher Architecture Style exhibits the following strengths:

- **Load Balancing**
Similar to the Broker Architecture Style, the Dispatcher can distribute client requests across multiple replicated server instances based on QoS criteria or current load, promoting efficient use of system resources and improved responsiveness.
- **Loose Coupling**
Clients do not need to know the specific details of available servers. By interacting only with the Dispatcher during service discovery, they remain decoupled from the service infrastructure, supporting modularity and independent evolution of components.
- **Direct Client-Server Communication**
Unlike the Broker Architecture Style, where the broker remains in the communication loop, the Dispatcher enables clients to invoke servers directly after dispatching. This design decouples request execution from the middleware once the server reference is provided.
- **High Efficiency of Interaction**
By eliminating the need for intermediary mediation during service execution, the Dispatcher Architecture Style significantly reduces communication overhead. This direct interaction improves runtime performance and responsiveness, particularly in latency-sensitive systems.
- **Centralized Service Discovery**
The Dispatcher maintains a centralized registry of service metadata, simplifying the discovery and selection of appropriate services based on client requirements and QoS constraints.

On the other hand, this architecture style exhibits the following limitations:

- **Single Point of Failure**
The Dispatcher serves as a central coordinator and may become a single point of failure. If the Dispatcher is unavailable or becomes a bottleneck, clients cannot locate or connect to servers. Redundancy or failover mechanisms are required to mitigate this risk.

- **Resource Overhead**
  As in the Broker Architecture Style, supporting fault tolerance and load balancing requires replicating servers, which increases demands on memory, processing power, and network bandwidth.

12.14 Master-Slave Architecture Style

The Master-Slave Architecture Style is characterized by centralized workflow control managed by a coordinating component, known as the Master, and a set of subordinate components, referred to as Slaves. The Master is responsible for orchestrating the overall workflow by decomposing tasks, distributing them to the Slave nodes, and aggregating their results to produce the final output.

12.14.1 Structure

The structure of this architecture style is defined by two primary component roles: the *Master* and the *Slaves*. The structure of this architecture style is shown in Fig. 12.21.

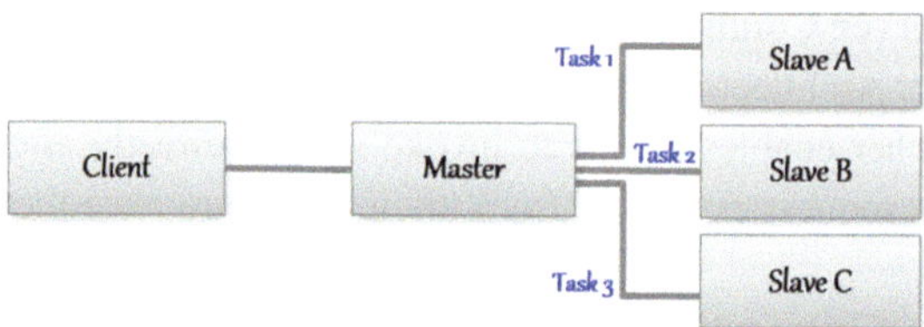

Fig. 12.21 Structure of Master-Slave Architecture Style

- **Client**
  The Client initiates a request for a specific workflow or computational task. It interacts only with the Master and remains unaware of the internal distribution of tasks or the presence of individual Slave nodes.
- **Master**
  The Master acts as the central controller responsible for orchestrating the execution of workflows. Upon receiving a request from the Client, the Master decomposes the task into subtasks—such as Task 1, Task 2, and Task 3—and assigns each to an appropriate Slave node. It then collects and aggregates the results produced by the Slaves to form a cohesive response.
- **Slave**
  Each Slave is responsible for executing a specific subtask delegated by the Master. Unlike the replicated servers in the Broker or Dispatcher Architecture Styles, Slaves are typically specialized and non-redundant, each providing distinct functionality required by the overall workflow.

Deployment Variants of the Master-Slave Architecture Style

This architecture style can be configured in two primary deployment models, depending on the scale and complexity of the target system:

- **As a Tiered Architecture**
  This style can be deployed as a tiered architecture in large-scale systems, where the Master and Slaves reside in separate tiers. This configuration is common in distributed computing platforms or cloud-based batch processing environments. The Master tier is responsible for global coordination, task decomposition, and result aggregation, while the Slave tier consists of parallel worker nodes that perform specialized tasks.
- **As a Component-Level Architecture**
  Alternatively, the style can be implemented as a component-level architecture in smaller-scale or embedded systems. In this configuration, the Master and Slaves are realized as software components operating within the same execution environment, such as a single device or tightly coupled system.

This architectural flexibility makes the Master-Slave style applicable to a wide spectrum of deployment scenarios, from lightweight embedded systems to high-throughput distributed platforms.

12.14.2 Collaboration Models

The collaboration model in this architecture style is based on centralized coordination and parallel task execution, managed by the Master. The interaction typically follows these steps:

(1) **Request Submission**
The Client submits a request to the Master to initiate a workflow or computational task.

(2) **Task Decomposition**
The Master decomposes the overall task into a set of subtasks, each of which can be processed independently or in parallel.

(3) **Task Assignment**
The Master assigns the subtasks to appropriate Slaves based on their functional roles or processing capabilities.

(4) **Parallel Execution**
Each Slave executes its assigned subtask under the supervision of the Master. The Slaves do not communicate with each other and operate independently.

(5) **Result Aggregation**
Upon completion, each Slave returns its result to the Master. The Master collects and aggregates these results to form the final output.

(6) **Response Delivery**
The Master returns the aggregated result to the Client, completing the workflow.

This collaboration model emphasizes *centralized control*, *specialized task execution*, and *parallel processing*, making it suitable for systems that require coordination of heterogeneous tasks with a clear control hierarchy.

12.14.3 Strengths and Limitations

The Master-Slave Architecture Style exhibits the following strengths:

- **Centralized Workflow Control**
  The Master centrally manages task distribution and result aggregation, simplifying orchestration and enabling consistent control over the execution process.
- **Parallel Task Execution**
  Subtasks can be executed concurrently by multiple Slaves, significantly improving performance and throughput for compute-intensive or large-scale workflows.
- **Task Specialization**
  Each Slave can be designed to perform a specific function, allowing for modularity and the integration of heterogeneous processing capabilities within the system.
- **Scalability**
  The architecture supports horizontal scaling by adding more Slave components, which can enhance processing capacity and reduce overall execution time.
- **Separation of Concerns**
  The clear division between coordination (Master) and execution (Slaves) promotes modularity, making the system easier to understand, develop, and maintain.

On the other hand, this architecture style exhibits the following limitations:

- **Single Point of Failure and Master Bottleneck**
  The Master serves as the central coordinator; its failure can disrupt the entire system. Moreover, as the number of Slaves increases, the Master may become a performance bottleneck due to coordination overhead.
- **Limited Flexibility and Slave Autonomy**
  The centralized control model restricts runtime adaptability and prevents Slaves from acting independently or collaborating. All decision-making is handled by the Master, which can limit responsiveness to dynamic conditions.
- **Complexity and Resource Imbalance**
  The Master must manage task decomposition, scheduling, and result aggregation, increasing system complexity. Additionally, uneven task distribution may lead to inefficient resource utilization across Slave components.

12.15 Edge Computing Architecture Style

The Edge Computing Architecture Style is characterized by a distributed computing paradigm that places computation and data storage resources closer to data sources, such as IoT devices and sensors. By processing data near its point of origin, this architecture reduces the distance over which data must travel to centralized servers. As a result, it achieves lower latency, improved bandwidth efficiency, enhanced system responsiveness, and stronger data privacy through localized processing.

Comparison to Peer-to-Peer (P2) Architecture Style

Edge Computing and P2P Architecture Styles both reduce reliance on centralized servers by distributing computation across multiple nodes. However, they differ in purpose and structure. Edge Computing places processing near data sources to reduce latency and improve efficiency, often in a hierarchical setup. In contrast, P2P systems consist of equal nodes that share resources directly with each other, without central coordination. While both are decentralized, Edge Computing is infrastructure based, and P2P is more collaborative and symmetric.

12.15.1 Structure

The structure of this architecture style is defined by a three-layer hierarchy: the Cloud layer, the Edge layer, and the Device layer. Each layer plays a distinct role in the distribution of computation and data management, collectively enabling efficient, scalable, and low-latency processing across the system.

The structure of this architecture style is shown in Fig. 12.22.

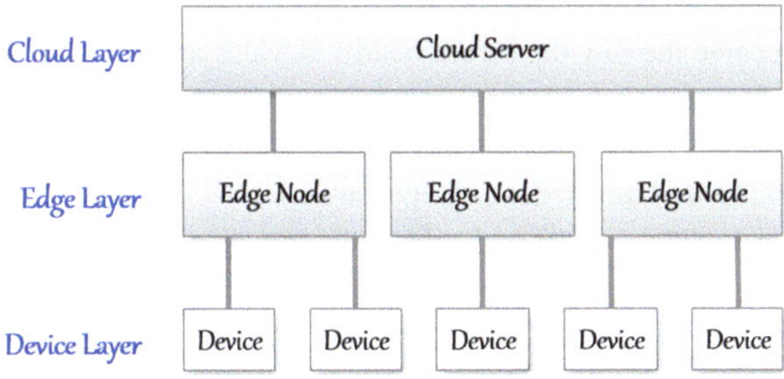

Fig. 12.22 Structure of Edge Computing Architecture Style

- **Cloud Layer**
  This layer consists of centralized cloud servers responsible for performing resource-intensive tasks such as large-scale data analytics, model training, global coordination, and long-term storage. It provides high computational power and global accessibility but typically incurs higher latency due to network distance from data sources.
- **Edge Layer**
  This layer includes intermediate nodes located near data sources, such as gateways, edge servers, or local microdata centers. These nodes handle time-sensitive processing, data filtering, aggregation, and localized decision-making. By reducing the volume of data sent to the cloud and responding quickly to events, this layer helps minimize latency and bandwidth consumption.
- **Device Layer**
  This layer comprises end devices such as sensors, actuators, smartphones, and IoT-enabled equipment. These devices generate raw data and may perform minimal processing. They rely on the Edge and Cloud layers for complex analysis, decision support, and coordination.

12.15.2 Collaboration Models

The collaboration model in this architecture style is characterized by a sequence of tasks distributed across three layers to enable efficient, scalable, and low-latency processing. The interaction typically follows these steps:

(1) **Data Generation (Device Layer)**
Devices such as sensors, actuators, or mobile clients generate raw data from the physical environment or user interactions.
(2) **Local Preprocessing (Edge Layer)**
Edge nodes receive the raw data from nearby devices and perform preliminary tasks such as filtering, aggregation, transformation, or event detection. This reduces the volume of data and ensures rapid local responsiveness.
(3) **Decision-Making or Forwarding (Edge Layer)**
Based on local logic or predefined rules, edge nodes either make decisions autonomously (e.g., triggering alerts or actions) or determine that further analysis is needed and forward the processed data to the cloud.
(4) **Advanced Processing and Analytics (Cloud Layer)**
The cloud layer performs more computationally intensive tasks such as historical trend analysis, machine learning model training, and cross-regional coordination. It may return high-level insights, updated models, or system-wide directives back to the edge.
(5) **Action Execution and Feedback (Device and Edge Layers)**
Based on the decisions made at the edge or cloud, appropriate actions are executed by devices or edge nodes. Feedback may be logged, reported, or used to refine subsequent data processing.

This collaboration model emphasizes hierarchical processing, bandwidth optimization, reduced latency, and localized intelligence, aligning well with the requirements of real-time, distributed, and resource-constrained systems.

12.15.3 Strengths and Limitations

The Edge Computing Architecture Style exhibits the following strengths:

- **Low Latency**
  By processing data close to its source, this style significantly reduces the time required to respond to events, making it ideal for real-time applications such as autonomous vehicles, industrial automation, and smart healthcare.
- **Bandwidth Efficiency**
  Local preprocessing at the edge reduces the volume of data transmitted to the cloud, conserving network bandwidth and lowering communication costs.
- **Improved Scalability**
  Distributing computational workloads across edge nodes reduces pressure on centralized infrastructure and allows the system to scale horizontally as more devices and edge nodes are added.
- **Enhanced Data Privacy and Security**
  Sensitive data can be processed locally without transmitting it to centralized servers, reducing exposure and supporting compliance with privacy regulations such as GDPR.
- **Increased System Resilience**
  Edge nodes can continue functioning independently even if connectivity to the cloud is temporarily lost, enhancing fault tolerance and system availability.

  On the other hand, this architecture style exhibits the following limitations:

- **Resource Constraints**
  Edge nodes often have limited processing power, memory, and storage compared to cloud servers. These constraints can limit the complexity and scale of local data processing tasks.
- **System Complexity and Maintenance Overhead**
  Coordinating computation across the device, edge, and cloud layers introduces architectural and operational complexity. Maintaining, updating, and securing a large number of distributed edge nodes—often located in remote or unmanaged environments—adds to system overhead.
- **Data Fragmentation and Consistency Challenges**
  Processing data at multiple edge locations can lead to fragmented datasets, making it difficult to maintain a consistent and unified system-wide view for analytics or decision-making.

- **Security and Scalability Limitations**
  The increased number of distributed endpoints broadens the attack surface, requiring robust security mechanisms. Additionally, scaling the physical edge infrastructure across geographically dispersed locations can involve significant cost and logistical challenges.

12.16 Event-Driven Architecture Style

The Event-Driven Architecture (EDA) Style is characterized by the decoupled orchestration of event production, publication, detection, and consumption. An event signifies a noteworthy change in system state or the occurrence of an action that is recognized and communicated across system components. Events serve as the primary mechanism for triggering communication and coordination among distributed components.

12.16.1 Structure

The structure of this architecture style is defined by four key elements: Event, Event Producer, Event Channel, and Event Consumer. The structure of this architecture style is shown in Fig. 12.23.

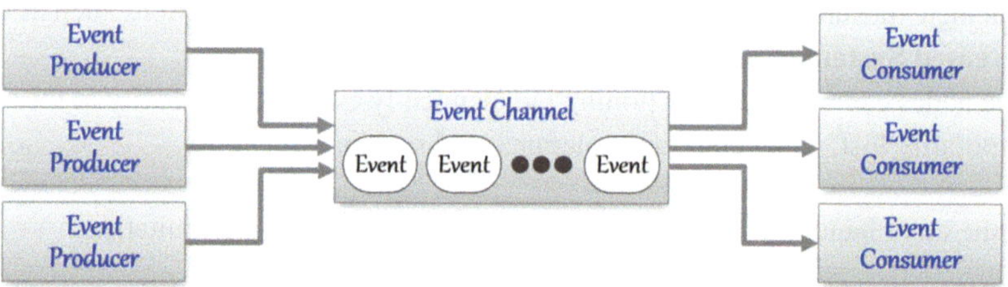

Fig. 12.23 Structure of Event-Driven Architecture Style

- **Event Producer**
  An *Event Producer* is a component or subsystem responsible for detecting significant changes in system state and generating corresponding events. It initiates the communication process by publishing these events to an *Event Channel*, without any direct knowledge of the components that may consume them. This decoupling promotes modularity and flexibility in system design.

- **Event Channel**
  The *Event Channel*, also referred to as an *Event Bus* or *Message Broker*, serves as the communication backbone between producers and consumers. It acts as a central conduit for transporting events from their origin (producers) to their destinations (consumers). Advanced event channels may support features such as event filtering, content-based routing, prioritization, and persistence. This component plays a critical role in enabling asynchronous, scalable, and loosely coupled interactions within the system.
- **Event Consumer**
  An *Event Consumer* is a component or subsystem that subscribes to and processes events received through the *Event Channel*. It performs actions or triggers functionality in response to the arrival of specific event types. *Event Consumers* are reactive in nature, allowing for dynamic and context-sensitive behavior that is driven by system events rather than direct invocation.

12.16.2 Collaboration Models

The collaboration model in this architecture style is characterized by asynchronous interactions among independent components that communicate through events. The interaction typically follows these steps:

(1) **Event Detection and Generation (Event Producer)**
Components such as services, sensors, or application modules detect changes in system state or external input conditions. These components generate events representing significant occurrences (e.g., a transaction completion or a threshold being crossed).

(2) **Event Publication (Event Producer)**
Once generated, the event is published to the event channel. The producer does not require knowledge of which components will receive or act on the event, supporting loose coupling and modular design.

(3) **Event Distribution and Routing (Event Channel)**
The event channel serves as the intermediary responsible for distributing events to the appropriate consumers. It may support filtering, transformation, prioritization, or routing of events based on event type, content, or consumer subscriptions.

(4) **Event Processing and Reaction (Event Consumer)**
Subscribed consumers receive the relevant events and execute associated logic, which may include state updates, service invocations, alert generation, or downstream event emissions. Consumers process events independently, allowing parallelism and responsiveness.

12.16.3 Strengths and Limitations

The Event-Driven Architecture Style exhibits the following strengths:

- **Loose Coupling**
  Event producers and consumers are decoupled in both time and space. Producers do not need to know which consumers will handle the events, enabling independent development, deployment, and scaling of components.
- **Asynchronous Communication**
  Events are communicated asynchronously, allowing producers and consumers to operate independently. This enhances system responsiveness and supports non-blocking interactions.
- **Scalability and Flexibility**
  Components can be scaled horizontally to handle increased workloads. New consumers can be added or removed dynamically without impacting existing producers or the event channel.
- **Extensibility and Modularity**
  New functionality can be integrated into the system by adding new event consumers that subscribe to existing events, without modifying the producers or other consumers.
- **Resilience and Fault Isolation**
  Failures in one component (e.g., a consumer) do not directly affect other components. This isolation improves fault tolerance and system reliability.

On the other hand, this architecture style exhibits the following limitations:

- **Latency and Delivery Uncertainty**
  While asynchronous messaging promotes responsiveness, it may introduce variability in message delivery times. Ensuring timely delivery, especially under high load, often requires tuning and advanced queuing strategies.
- **Event Traceability and Debugging Difficulties**
  Tracking the flow of events across multiple producers, channels, and consumers can be difficult, making debugging, auditing, and root cause analysis more complex compared to synchronous architectures.
- **Event Management Overhead**
  As the number of events and consumers grows, managing event schemas, subscriptions, filtering rules, and versioning can introduce significant overhead in design and maintenance.

12.17 Publisher-Subscriber Architecture Style

The Publisher-Subscriber Architecture Style, commonly referred to as Pub/Sub, is characterized by a decoupled communication paradigm in which publishers and subscribers interact indirectly through a messaging infrastructure. In this model, subscribers explicitly express interest in specific topics, while publishers send messages to those predefined topics without knowledge of the recipients. A Message Broker is responsible for managing subscriptions and delivering messages only to those subscribers who have registered interest in the corresponding topics.

12.17.1 Structure

The structure of this architecture style is defined by three principal elements: Publishers, Subscribers, and a Message Broker. The structure of this architecture style is shown in Fig. 12.24.

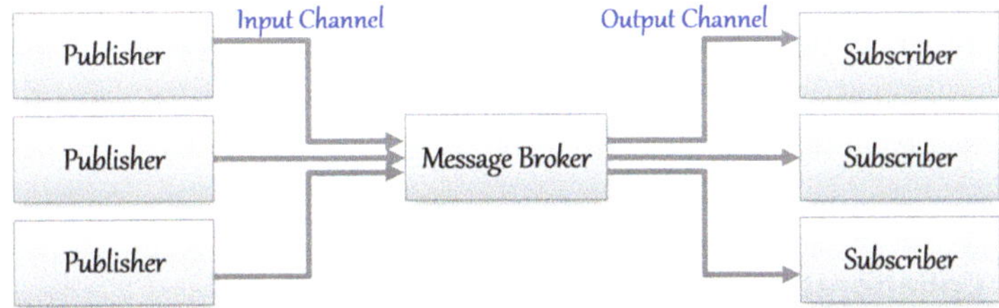

Fig. 12.24 Structure of Publisher-Subscriber Architecture Style

- **Publisher**
  A *Publisher* is a component responsible for generating messages that encapsulate relevant information, such as system events, state changes, or data updates. These messages are sent to a *Message Broker* without requiring knowledge of which components will receive them.
- **Subscriber**
  A *Subscriber* is a component that registers interest in specific topics or channels managed by the message broker. Upon subscription, it automatically receives messages related to those topics. Subscribers process incoming messages by executing domain-specific logic in response to the received content, enabling event-driven behavior.

- **Message Broker**
  The *Message Broker* acts as an intermediary that facilitates communication between publishers and subscribers. It manages the lifecycle of topics or channels, handles incoming messages from publishers, and ensures their delivery only to those subscribers that have explicitly registered for the relevant topics.

Variations of Publisher-Subscriber Architecture Style
Notable variations of this architecture style include the following:

- **Brokerless Publisher-Subscriber Architecture (Multicast-Based Model)**
  In this variation, message distribution occurs without a centralized broker. Publishers multicast messages directly to subscribers using mechanisms such as peer-to-peer overlay networks, distributed hash tables, or multicast groups. Subscribers express interest in specific topics or content patterns and receive only those messages that match their subscriptions.
- **Cloud-Native Publisher-Subscriber Architecture (Managed Broker Model)**
  In this variation, managed messaging services such as Google Cloud Pub/Sub, AWS SNS/SQS, or Azure Service Bus are used to handle message delivery, topic management, and scaling. Publishers send messages to a cloud-hosted broker, while subscribers receive them asynchronously through push or pull mechanisms, supporting reliable and scalable event-driven systems.

12.17.2 Collaboration Models

The collaboration model in this architecture style is characterized by a decoupled, asynchronous message exchange facilitated by a message broker and proceeds through the following steps:

(1) **Message Generation (Publisher)**
Publishers create messages containing data, event notifications, or updates relevant to subscribers.

(2) **Message Publication (Publisher → Message Broker)**
Publishers send these messages to a message broker via an input channel, without knowing the identity or number of subscribers.

(3) **Subscription Registration (Subscriber → Message Broker)**
Subscribers register their interest in specific topics or channels maintained by the message broker.

(4) **Message Routing (Message Broker)**
The message broker filters and routes incoming messages to the appropriate subscribers based on their registered topics.

(5) **Message Delivery (Message Broker → Subscriber)**
The Message Broker delivers messages asynchronously to all subscribers that have registered interest in the relevant topics, using the output channel.

(6) **Message Processing (Subscriber)**
Subscribers receive the messages and execute application-specific logic in response to the message content.

12.17.3 Strengths and Limitations

The Publisher-Subscriber Architecture Style exhibits the following strengths:

- **Loose Coupling**
  Publishers and subscribers are decoupled in both time and space. Publishers are not aware of the number or identity of subscribers, which promotes modularity and independent component evolution.
- **Asynchronous Communication**
  Messages are exchanged asynchronously, allowing publishers and subscribers to operate independently without blocking or waiting, thus improving system responsiveness and throughput.
- **Scalability**
  The architecture supports horizontal scaling of both publishers and subscribers. Multiple components can be added or removed without disrupting the overall system behavior.
- **Flexibility and Extensibility**
  New subscribers can be added dynamically without modifying existing publishers. This makes the architecture adaptable to changing requirements and simplifies system evolution.

On the other hand, this architecture style exhibits the following limitations:

- **Dependency on Message Broker**
  In broker-based implementations, the message broker can become a bottleneck or single point of failure if not properly replicated or scaled.
- **Latency in Message Delivery**
  Asynchronous processing, broker overhead, and network transmission can introduce latency, which may be unacceptable in real-time or time-sensitive applications.
- **Difficulties in Tracing and Debugging**
  The decoupled nature of publishers and subscribers makes it challenging to trace message flows, hindering debugging, monitoring, and auditing.

12.18 Sensor-Controller-Actuator (SCA) Architecture Style

The Sensor-Controller-Actuator (SCA) Architecture Style is characterized by a control-oriented design in which sensors collect data from the environment, a controller processes the sensor input and computes control signals, and actuators execute these signals to influence the environment. This architecture forms a closed-loop feedback system, enabling the system to continuously adjust its behavior based on the effects of prior actions.

The SCA architecture is particularly well suited for embedded systems, robotics, automotive control, and industrial process automation, where timely and precise responses to dynamic environmental changes are essential.

12.18.1 Structure

The structure of this architecture style is defined by three principal elements, sensors, controllers, and actuators, all interacting with a shared environment. The structure of this architecture style is shown in Fig. 12.25.

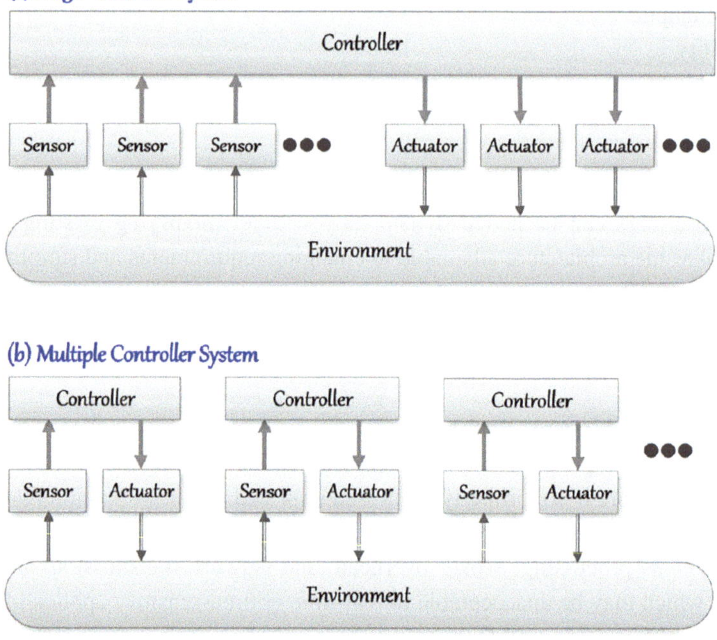

Fig. 12.25 Structure of Sensor-Controller-Actuator Architecture Style

- **Sensor**
  A sensor is responsible for collecting data from the environment, such as temperature, position, or speed. It serves as the system's interface with the physical world and provides the input signals needed for control decisions.
- **Controller**
  The controller receives input from one or more sensors, processes the data, and determines appropriate control actions. It generates control signals based on predefined logic, algorithms, or feedback rules.
- **Actuator**
  An actuator receives control signals from the controller and executes the corresponding actions to modify the state of the environment—such as moving a motor, adjusting a valve, or activating a mechanism.
- **Environment**
  The environment represents the physical domain in which sensors observe changes and actuators exert control. It completes the feedback loop by continuously responding to the system's outputs.

Variations of SCA Architecture
This figure illustrates two structural variations of the SCA architecture commonly used in control-oriented systems.

- **Single Controller System**
  As shown in Fig. 12.25a, a centralized controller manages interactions with multiple sensors and actuators. Sensors gather data from the environment and transmit it to the controller, which processes the inputs and generates corresponding control signals for the actuators. While this configuration simplifies global decision-making, it may become a performance bottleneck or single point of failure in large or complex systems.
- **Multiple Controller System**
  As shown in Fig. 12.25b, this variation adopts a distributed architecture in which each controller operates independently with its own set of sensors and actuators. Controllers process local sensor data and issue control commands in isolated control loops. This approach improves modularity, scalability, and fault tolerance, making it well suited for systems that require localized, real-time responsiveness—such as autonomous robotics, intelligent vehicles, and industrial automation systems.

12.18.2 Collaboration Models

The collaboration model in this architecture style is characterized by a closed-loop interaction among sensors, controllers, and actuators, enabling continuous monitoring and adaptive control of the environment.

- **Collaboration in Single Controller System**
  In this configuration, multiple sensors send data to a centralized controller, which processes the inputs and generates control signals for all actuators. The actuators update the environment, and the resulting changes are sensed again, forming a closed feedback loop. This model centralizes control logic but may introduce latency and become a performance bottleneck in large systems.
- **Collaboration in Multiple Controller System**
  In this configuration, each controller operates independently with its own sensors and actuators. Local sensor data is processed by the corresponding controller, which issues control signals to its actuator. Each loop functions autonomously, enabling parallel control, modularity, and fault isolation—ideal for systems requiring localized, real-time responsiveness.

12.18.3 Strengths and Limitations

The SCA Architecture Style exhibits the following strengths:

- **Closed-Loop Feedback Control**
  The architecture enables continuous monitoring and adjustment through closed-loop feedback, allowing the system to dynamically respond to changes in the environment.
- **Modularity and Separation of Concerns**
  The clear separation between sensing, decision-making, and actuation supports modular design, making systems easier to develop, maintain, and extend.
- **Real-Time Responsiveness**
  The architecture supports timely processing and reaction to environmental inputs, which is essential in domains such as robotics, automotive systems, and industrial automation.
- **Scalability Across Configurations**
  The architecture can be implemented using a single controller for centralized decision-making or multiple distributed controllers for parallel, localized control—offering design flexibility based on system complexity and performance needs.
- **Applicability to Physical Systems**
  The SCA pattern naturally fits systems that interact with the physical world, making it a foundational structure in embedded and cyber-physical system design.

On the other hand, this architecture style exhibits the following limitations:

- **Single Point of Failure in Centralized Systems**
  In single-controller configurations, the entire system becomes vulnerable if the controller fails, reducing overall system reliability.

- **Scalability Constraints in Centralized Control**
  As the number of sensors and actuators increases, a centralized controller may encounter performance bottlenecks, limiting scalability and responsiveness.
- **Complexity in Distributed Coordination**
  In multi-controller systems, coordinating actions across independently operating controllers can be complex, particularly when control loops are interdependent or require synchronization.

12.19 Service-Oriented Architecture (SOA) Style

The Service-Oriented Architecture (SOA) Style organizes software into loosely coupled services with well-defined interfaces and standard protocols. Each service encapsulates a specific business function and can be independently developed, deployed, and maintained. Services communicate over a network using message-based interactions.

SOA is underpinned by a range of standards that enable interoperability, secure communication, and service coordination, including the Web Services Description Language (WSDL) for defining service interfaces; the Simple Object Access Protocol (SOAP) and Representational State Transfer (REST) for message exchange; Universal Description, Discovery, and Integration (UDDI) for service registry and discovery; and the Business Process Execution Language (BPEL) for orchestrating service workflows.

12.19.1 Structure

The structure of this architecture style is defined by a collection of loosely coupled services that interact through a centralized middleware component known as the Enterprise Service Bus (ESB). The structure of this architecture style is shown in Fig. 12.26.

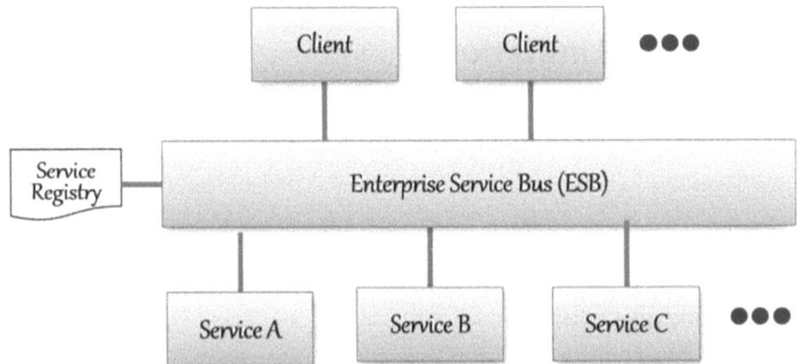

Fig. 12.26 Structure of Service-Oriented Architecture Style

- **Client**
  A client is a service consumer—any software entity that requests and utilizes the functionality exposed by one or more services.
- **Service**
  A service is a self-contained, modular software component that encapsulates a specific business capability. Services are loosely coupled and expose standardized interfaces using specifications such as WSDL or OpenAPI, promoting reuse and interoperability.
- **Service Registry**
  The Service Registry is a centralized directory that stores service descriptions and metadata. It enables service providers to publish their offerings and allows clients to discover and bind to appropriate services dynamically.
- **Enterprise Service Bus**
  The Enterprise Service Bus is a middleware infrastructure that manages communication and integration among services. It supports message routing, transformation, protocol mediation, and orchestration, enabling seamless interaction between heterogeneous and distributed components.

12.19.2 Collaboration Models

The collaboration model in this architecture style involves message-based communication between clients and services, coordinated by the Enterprise Service Bus (ESB). When a client invokes a service, the request is marshalled—converted into a standardized, platform-independent message format for network transmission. The ESB then performs message routing, protocol mediation, and, if necessary, data transformation to ensure compatibility between the communicating parties. Upon reaching the target service, the message is unmarshalled into a native format that the service can process. This process ensures seamless interoperability and decoupling across heterogeneous and distributed systems.

12.19.3 Strengths and Limitations

The SOA Architecture Style presents several advantages and disadvantages.

- **Loose Coupling**
  Services are designed to operate independently, allowing changes to be made to one service without impacting others.
- **Reusability of Services**
  Services encapsulate specific business capabilities and can be reused across multiple applications and domains.

- **Interoperability**
  Standardized communication protocols (e.g., SOAP, REST) and interface descriptions (e.g., WSDL, OpenAPI) enable integration across heterogeneous platforms and technologies.
- **Scalability and Flexibility**
  New services can be added or existing ones modified with minimal disruption, supporting the dynamic needs of evolving systems.
- **Maintainability**
  Independent deployment and versioning of services facilitate easier maintenance and continuous delivery.

On the other hand, this architecture style exhibits the following limitations:

- **Performance Overhead**
  The use of XML or JSON for message formatting, along with the involvement of middleware such as the ESB, can introduce latency and increase resource consumption during service invocation.
- **Increased Complexity**
  Designing, deploying, and maintaining a distributed system composed of loosely coupled services introduces significant architectural complexity. Effective adoption of SOA requires mastering a wide range of standards—such as WSDL, SOAP, REST, UDDI, and BPEL—as well as implementing robust mechanisms for service orchestration, monitoring, versioning, and governance.
- **Network Dependency**
  The architecture relies heavily on network communication, making it vulnerable to network latency, bandwidth limitations, and connectivity issues.
- **Testing and Debugging Challenges**
  Testing distributed and asynchronous service interactions can be complex, requiring specialized tools and environments to simulate service behavior and dependencies.

12.20 Microservices Architecture Style

Evolving from the principles of SOA, the Microservices Architecture Style adopts the core concept of decomposing systems into modular services but avoids the heavy reliance on complex standards that characterize traditional SOA. A system as a collection of small, loosely coupled services, each of which is independently developed, deployed, and maintained. Every microservice is self-contained, encapsulating a specific business capability and operating as an autonomous unit within the broader system.

12.20.1 Structure

The structure of this architecture style is defined by a collection of independently deployable microservices and a central API Gateway, which serves as the unified entry point for client requests and routes them to the appropriate microservices.

The structure of this architecture style is shown in Fig. 12.27.

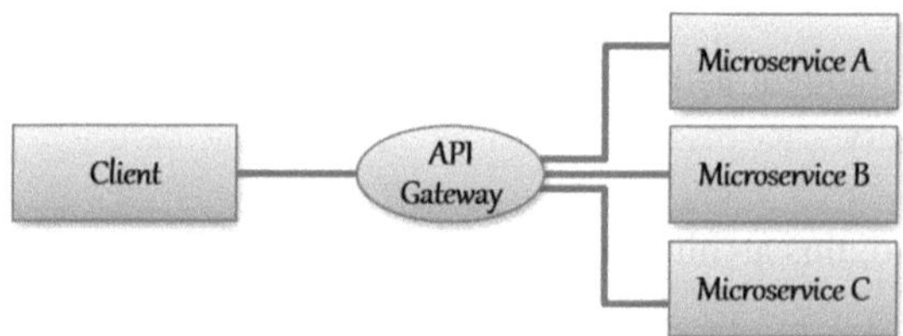

Fig. 12.27 Structure of Microservice Architecture Style

- **Client**
  The client represents any service consumer, such as a Web application, mobile app, native desktop application, or even another microservice. Rather than communicating with individual services directly, the client interacts with the system by sending requests to the API Gateway, which then routes those requests to the appropriate microservices.
- **Microservice**
  A microservice is a small, autonomous unit that encapsulates a specific business function. Each microservice is independently developed, deployed, and scaled, allowing for modular system evolution. Microservices may be hosted on separate physical devices, virtual machines, or containerized environments, depending on infrastructure needs. They can be developed in-house, offering full control over design and implementation, or sourced from third-party providers, enabling faster integration and leveraging specialized functionality in a cost-effective manner.
- **API Gateway**
  The API Gateway acts as the centralized access point through which all client requests are funneled. It abstracts the complexity and heterogeneity of the underlying microservices—differences in programming languages, platforms, databases, and communication protocols—from the client. Beyond request routing, the API Gateway can handle cross-cutting concerns such as authentication, rate limiting, load balancing, and response aggregation, thus simplifying client interaction and promoting architectural consistency.

12.20.2 Collaboration Models

The collaboration model in this architecture style is centered around a central API Gateway, which acts as the single entry point for all client requests. Instead of calling microservices directly, the client sends requests to the API Gateway. The gateway then routes each request to the appropriate microservice based on the requested functionality. Microservices may also communicate with each other when needed, either through lightweight HTTP calls or asynchronous messaging systems. This approach ensures that microservices remain loosely coupled and independent, while the API Gateway manages common tasks such as authentication, logging, rate limiting, and combining responses when necessary.

12.20.3 Strengths and Limitations

The Microservices Architecture Style exhibits the following strengths:

- **Independent Deployment**
  Each microservice can be developed, tested, deployed, and scaled independently, enabling faster release cycles and continuous delivery.
- **Modularity and Maintainability**
  The separation of business capabilities into discrete services simplifies codebases, making systems easier to understand, maintain, and evolve over time.
- **Technology Heterogeneity**
  Different microservices can be built using different programming languages, databases, and frameworks, allowing teams to choose the most suitable technology for each service.
- **Scalability**
  Microservices can be scaled individually based on their resource demands, resulting in more efficient use of infrastructure compared to monolithic systems.
- **Team Autonomy**
  Small, cross-functional teams can own and manage individual microservices, improving development efficiency and accountability.

On the other hand, this architecture style exhibits the following limitations:

- **Runtime Overhead of Invoking Services over Network**
  Although inter-service communication may be limited, client-to-service interactions through the API Gateway still incur serialization, deserialization, and network-related overhead, which can affect latency and system performance under high load.
- **Distributed Data Management**
  When microservices manage their own data stores, maintaining data consistency across services can be challenging—especially for operations that require coordination or aggregate queries. Although not all services handle session or contextual data, those that do must address additional complexity in managing state and ensuring coherence across distributed components.

- **Operational Complexity**
  Managing a large number of independently deployed services introduces complexity in deployment pipelines, monitoring, fault detection, and configuration management.

12.21 Microkernel Architecture Style

The Microkernel Architecture Style is characterized by the separation of system responsibilities into a minimal core and a set of plug-in components, also known as user-space services. The core system provides only the essential services and mechanisms required for basic operation, while additional and more complex functionalities are implemented as external plug-ins that extend or tailor the system's behavior.

12.21.1 Structure

The structure of this architecture style consists of two parts: Core System and the set of

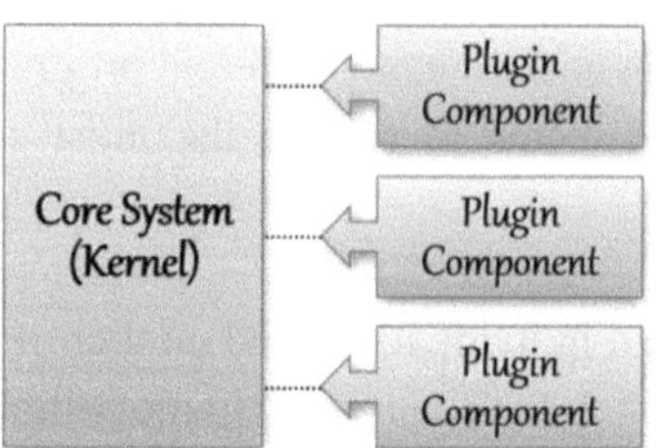

Fig. 12.28 Structure of Microkernel Architecture Style

plugin components. The structure of this architecture style is shown in Fig. 12.28.

- **Core System (Kernel)**
  This is the central, minimal part of the system responsible for providing the essential services and runtime environment. It includes fundamental mechanisms such as communication, plugin registration, and lifecycle management. The kernel remains stable and independent from any specific functionality added by plugins.
- **Plug-In Components**
  Each Plug-In Component represents an independently developed and deployable module that extends or customizes the system's behavior. These components implement specific functionality and depend on the services provided by the core. Plug-ins can be loaded either statically at start-up or dynamically at runtime, depending on system requirements.

12.21.2 Collaboration Models

The collaboration model in this architecture style is centered around the interaction between a minimal core system and a set of plug-in components. The core system begins by initializing the essential runtime environment necessary for basic system operations. It serves as the central coordinator, receiving user service requests and routing them to the appropriate plug-in components. The core system functions as an intermediary between the user interface and the plug-in modules, managing communication and ensuring seamless integration.

Dynamic Adaptability Through Plug-In Substitution
A key feature of this model is its support for dynamic adaptability: at runtime, a plug-in component can be replaced or updated with a different implementation without altering the core system. In such cases, the core continues to handle service requests using the same workflow, while the specific functionality can evolve dynamically.

12.21.3 Strengths and Limitations

The Microkernel Architecture Style exhibits the following strengths:

- **Modularity and Extensibility**
  The architecture facilitates modular design by separating the minimal core from plug-in components. This separation enables the system to be easily extended with new features or functionalities without modifying the core.
- **Runtime Adaptability**
  Plug-in components can be loaded, replaced, or updated dynamically at runtime. This allows the system to adapt to changing requirements or operational contexts without requiring downtime or system restarts.
- **Fault Isolation**
  Since plug-in components are decoupled from the core, failures in one plug-in are less likely to propagate and affect the entire system, thereby improving fault tolerance and system stability.
- **Portability and Reusability**
  The core system provides only essential services, making it lightweight and portable across different hardware platforms or operating systems. Plug-ins can be reused or customized across various deployments.

On the other hand, this architecture style exhibits the following limitations:

- **Performance Overhead**
  The additional layer of indirection introduced by the core system—through which all service requests must pass—can result in performance overhead, especially in systems with frequent inter-component communication.
- **Increased System Complexity**
  Designing and managing the interactions between the core and multiple plug-in components introduces architectural complexity. Ensuring consistency, compatibility, and correct behavior across dynamic plug-in updates can be challenging.
- **Difficult Debugging and Testing**
  Since plug-in components may be loaded and updated at runtime, testing the system in all possible configurations and states becomes more difficult. Debugging runtime issues in dynamically evolving systems can also be more complex.

12.22 Other Architecture Styles

In addition to the commonly adopted architecture styles discussed above, various other architecture styles exist, each characterized by its own set of strengths and limitations.

12.22.1 Monolithic Architecture Style

The Monolithic Architecture Style is characterized as a traditional software design approach in which the entire system is developed as a single, cohesive unit. All system functionalities are tightly coupled and operate within a unified codebase that encapsulates the complete application logic. The system is deployed as a single executable on a single computing environment. As a result, any modification to one part of the system typically requires rebuilding and redeploying the entire application, which can impede agility and scalability.

12.22.2 Plug-In Architecture Style

The Plug-In Architecture Style is structured around a host application that defines well-specified extension points. Functionality is extended through independent plug-in modules that are discovered and invoked by the host at runtime or start-up, allowing the system to be customized or enhanced without modifying its main codebase.

In contrast, the Microkernel Architecture Style incorporates a core system that not only supports plug-in integration but also takes an active role in managing service coordination, enforcing system policies, and enabling runtime adaptability.

12.22.3 Serverless Architecture Style

The Serverless Architecture Style is a cloud-native design approach in which application components are deployed as discrete functions or services that are automatically managed by a cloud provider. In this style, developers delegate infrastructure concerns—such as server provisioning, scaling, and maintenance—to the cloud platform and instead focus solely on writing and deploying functional units of application logic, typically using a Function-as-a-Service (FaaS) model.

Serverless computing is primarily associated with public cloud platforms such as AWS, Microsoft Azure, and Google Cloud; however, it can also be implemented in private cloud environments or on-premises infrastructures using serverless frameworks and container orchestration technologies.

12.22.4 Representational State Transfer (REST) Architecture Style

The Representational State Transfer (REST) Architecture Style defines a set of architectural constraints—such as stateless communication, a uniform interface, and layered system structure—for designing scalable and loosely coupled distributed systems. RESTful systems identify resources using URIs and manipulate them through standard HTTP methods like GET, POST, PUT, and DELETE. Each client-server interaction is self-contained, enhancing simplicity and scalability.

Widely adopted for Web services, REST offers lightweight implementation, compatibility with Web standards, and ease of integration. While its uniform interface and statelessness improve scalability, they may introduce limitations for session-based or transactional operations. Nonetheless, REST remains a dominant architecture style for APIs and cloud-native applications due to its simplicity and interoperability.

12.22.5 Presentation-Abstraction-Control Architecture Style

The Presentation-Abstraction-Control (PAC) Architecture Style structures interactive systems as a hierarchy of cooperating agents, each composed of three interconnected components: Presentation (user interface), Abstraction (data and logic), and Control (coordination and communication). This style promotes modularity by separating concerns within each agent and enabling communication between agents through their control components.

PAC is particularly effective for complex interactive systems, such as multi-user applications or those involving multiple input/output modalities, where decentralized control and scalability are essential.

12.22.6 Reflective Architecture Style

The Reflective Architecture Style, also known as Meta-Level Architecture, is based on the principle of reflection, which allows a system to maintain metadata about its own structure and behavior and to use this information to dynamically modify itself at runtime. Systems designed with this style are capable of inspecting, analyzing, and adapting their own execution structure and behavior while the system is running, thereby enabling a high degree of flexibility and adaptability in response to changing conditions or requirements.

The term Meta-Level Architecture refers to a structural organization in which the system is divided into two distinct levels:

- **Base level**: represents the functional layer of the system that performs domain-specific operations.
- **Meta level**: Maintains representations and policies that describe or govern the behavior of the base level. It has the capability to observe, interpret, and dynamically modify the base level during execution.

12.22.7 Space-Based Architecture Style

The Space-Based Architecture Style addresses scalability and high-concurrency challenges by removing centralized bottlenecks. It relies on a distributed memory space—often called a *tuple space* or *data grid*—as the core medium for communication among components. Instead of direct interaction, components exchange data by writing, reading, or taking entries from this shared space, enabling decoupling in time, space, and execution.

SBA is well suited for systems with dynamic workloads. It supports elastic scalability and fault tolerance by allowing processing units to scale independently.

Architecture Evaluation Methods 13

Objective of the Chapter
The objective of this chapter is to provide a comprehensive foundation for understanding and applying architecture evaluation methods. It elaborates five distinct evaluation approaches—scenario based, model based, formal method based, proof-of-concept (PoC) based, and prototype based—by presenting their overviews, key features, evaluation procedures, representative methods, advantages, and disadvantages. In addition, the chapter provides a detailed exposition of representative evaluation methods under each approach, delineating their fundamental components and analysis techniques to facilitate their effective application across a range of architectural contexts.

Architecture Evaluation Approaches
An architecture evaluation approach refers to a high-level classification of methods used to assess the quality and effectiveness of software architecture designs. It delineates the fundamental paradigms that shape how architecture evaluation is conducted and provides a conceptual framework for selecting appropriate methods aligned with specific evaluation objectives.

The commonly adopted architecture evaluation approaches include:

- **Scenario-based Architecture Evaluation**
- **Model-based Architecture Evaluation**
- **Formal Method-based Architecture Evaluation**
- **Proof-of-Concept (PoC)-based Architecture Evaluation**
- **Prototype-based Architecture Evaluation**

S. D. Kim, M. Kim, *Hands-on Software Architecture*,
https://doi.org/10.1007/978-3-032-01184-8_13

Architecture Evaluation Methods
An architecture evaluation method is a specific, structured technique used within the framework of an architecture evaluation approach. It defines a systematic process and set of guidelines for assessing the quality and suitability of an architecture design.

For example, architecture evaluation methods under the scenario-based architecture evaluation approach include:

- **Architecture Trade-off Analysis Method (ATAM)**
- **Cost-Benefit Analysis Method (CBAM)**
- **Software Architecture Analysis Method (SAAM)**
- **Performance Analysis Through Scenarios (PATS)**

This chapter presents a comprehensive overview of representative methods corresponding to each architecture evaluation approach.

13.1 Scenario-Based Architecture Evaluation

Scenario-based architecture evaluation is a systematic approach to assessing the quality of software architecture by analyzing its behavior in response to predefined scenarios. This approach emphasizes the use of carefully constructed scenarios to evaluate how the architecture supports specific quality attributes.

The key features of this evaluation approach include scenario-driven analysis that examines how the architecture responds to well-defined use cases and quality attribute scenarios. It emphasizes active stakeholder involvement to ensure that the selected scenarios align with real-world concerns and system priorities.

Scenario-based architecture evaluation offers practical benefits by focusing on specific use cases and quality attribute scenarios to assess how well an architecture meets stakeholder concerns. It enables early detection of risks, supports communication among stakeholders, and guides design trade-offs through concrete, context-driven analysis. However, its effectiveness depends heavily on the completeness and relevance of the selected scenarios. If scenarios are poorly defined or fail to capture critical concerns, the evaluation may overlook key risks or provide an incomplete assessment of architectural quality.

13.1.1 Applicable Situations

Scenario-based architecture evaluation is particularly well suited for situations where stakeholders seek to understand how architectural decisions influence the system's ability to meet quality requirements under realistic operational conditions. This approach is most effective during the early to mid-stages of the software development lifecycle, when architectural decisions are still malleable and their impact can be meaningfully assessed and improved.

13.1.2 Procedure of Scenario-Based Architecture Evaluation

The scenario-based architecture evaluation follows a structured process comprising the following steps:

(1) **Identify Stakeholders**
Identify all relevant stakeholders to ensure that diverse perspectives are incorporated into the evaluation process.

(2) **Develop Scenarios**
Define concrete scenarios that illustrate expected system behavior under various conditions. These scenarios serve as the foundation for evaluation by revealing how well the architecture addresses functional and quality requirements.
Scenarios should include:
- **Use case scenarios**: Represent typical user interactions derived from functional requirements; used to evaluate support for normal, exception, and error-handling workflows
- **Growth scenarios**: Represent future changes such as increased load or feature extensions; used to assess scalability and adaptability
- **Exploratory scenarios**: Represent fault, stress, or abnormal conditions; used to uncover system limitations, failure points, and robustness under extreme situations

(3) **Present Architectural Decisions**
Present key architectural decisions and their rationale, including selected styles, patterns, tactics, and deployment strategies. This promotes transparency, facilitates stakeholder alignment, and supports informed evaluation.

(4) **Associate Scenarios with Architecture**
Map each scenario to the relevant architectural components and interactions. Analyze how architectural elements fulfill scenario requirements and identify critical paths or risk areas.
Example: For the scenario "Handling High Traffic During a Sale Event" in an eCommerce system, relevant elements include load balancers, scalable servers, and caching layers.

(5) **Evaluate the Architecture**
Systematically assess how the architecture responds to each scenario. Identify risks, weaknesses, or limitations using predefined criteria and quality attribute metrics.

(6) **Analyze Evaluation Results**
Summarize evaluation findings to highlight architectural strengths, weaknesses, and areas for improvement. Prepare a structured report with observations, evidence, and actionable recommendations to guide design refinement and ensure alignment with quality objectives.

13.1.3 Representative Methods

13.1.3.1 Architecture Trade-off Analysis Method (ATAM)

ATAM is a scenario-based architecture evaluation method to assess the quality attributes of a software architecture [37]. This method focuses on identifying architectural risks, trade-offs, sensitivity points, and non-functional property interactions by analyzing how the architecture responds to carefully defined scenarios.

ATAM involves active participation from stakeholders, including architects, developers, and end users, to ensure that diverse concerns are addressed. The method systematically examines the impact of architectural decisions on quality attributes such as performance, modifiability, and availability, providing early insight into potential issues and guiding design improvements before implementation.

Formulating Scenarios for ATAM

In ATAM, scenarios are the primary instruments for evaluating how well an architecture supports specific quality attributes. They are developed collaboratively with stakeholders to ensure that the evaluation reflects real-world operational needs and concerns. Each scenario is composed of a *stimulus* (an event or condition that affects the system), the *stimulus source* (the origin of the event), and the *response* (the desired behavior of the system).

Scenarios in ATAM are typically categorized into three types:

- **Use Case Scenarios**
  These scenarios describe normal system usage and are derived from functional requirements. They are used to assess how effectively the architecture supports typical workflows.
  Example: When an authenticated user (stimulus source) requests to view their account balance (stimulus), the system retrieves and displays the information within 2 s (response).
- **Growth Scenarios**
  These scenarios anticipate future changes such as increased workload, expanded user base, or added functionality. They are used to evaluate the architecture's scalability and adaptability over time.
  Example: As the user base (stimulus source) increases threefold over the next year (stimulus), the system scales horizontally to handle the increased load without performance degradation (response).
- **Exploratory Scenarios**
  These scenarios examine the system's behavior under exceptional or adverse conditions, such as faults, failures, or security breaches. They help identify architectural risks, limitations, and potential failure points.
  Example: If the network infrastructure (stimulus source) causes the database server to become unavailable unexpectedly (stimulus), the system fails over to a replicated server and resumes operation within 10 s (response).

Together, these scenario types enable a comprehensive evaluation of the architecture's responsiveness, robustness, and ability to meet quality attribute goals.

13.1.3.2 Cost-Benefit Analysis Method (CBAM)

CBAM is a scenario-based architecture evaluation method that incorporates economic analysis into architectural decision-making [38]. It focuses on assessing the relative value of architectural strategies by analyzing their expected impact on quality attributes alongside their implementation cost and technical risk. Like other scenario-based methods, CBAM uses quality attribute scenarios to guide evaluation but distinguishes itself by explicitly quantifying trade-offs to support economically rational design choices.

CBAM involves identifying architectural strategies (e.g., replication, caching, or service decomposition), estimating their impact on system quality attributes, and assigning utility scores and cost estimates to each. Stakeholders assess these factors collaboratively to produce cost-benefit curves that inform the prioritization of architectural investments.

Formulating Scenarios for CBAM

In CBAM, scenarios serve as the foundation for evaluating the utility of architectural strategies. These scenarios should reflect critical quality attributes—such as performance, availability, or modifiability—and describe realistic operational contexts where architectural decisions have measurable impact. Each scenario is typically structured using the standard format: stimulus source, stimulus, and response. Additionally, CBAM extends the role of scenarios by associating them with utility values, which represent stakeholder-perceived benefits when the scenario is effectively addressed.

Example: When a marketing campaign manager (stimulus source) initiates a push notification to all mobile users during a flash sale event (stimulus), the system delivers notifications to 95% of recipients within 30 s (response). In the CBAM process, stakeholders begin by identifying a scenario that captures a critical quality concern. In this case, the scenario involves sending push notifications to mobile users during a flash sale, with the goal of delivering 95% of messages within 30 s—targeting performance and scalability attributes.

Next, a set of architectural strategies is proposed to address the scenario, such as using a cloud-based notification service, introducing message queues, or deploying regional edge servers. For each strategy, stakeholders estimate the utility (benefit to the business or system) and the cost (including effort, risk, and resource requirements). These values are used to compute benefit-to-cost ratios, which facilitate the comparison of strategies.

By analyzing these trade-offs, stakeholders can prioritize architectural decisions that offer the highest value for the lowest cost. For example, choosing a cloud-based service may yield high utility at moderate cost, making it a cost-effective solution to meet the performance goals of the scenario.

13.1.3.3 Software Architecture Analysis Method (SAAM)

SAAM is a scenario-based architecture evaluation method used to assess software architectures, with a primary focus on modifiability and other quality attributes such as maintainability and extensibility [39]. It offers a structured process for eliciting scenarios from stakeholders, mapping them to architectural elements, and analyzing the impact of potential changes.

The method involves defining use case and change scenarios, assessing their effects on the architecture, and identifying conflicts or weaknesses. Scenarios are categorized as direct (requiring no architectural change), indirect (requiring modifications), or non-supportable.

The process of SAAM consists of several structured steps: identifying stakeholders, eliciting and prioritizing scenarios, describing the proposed architecture, mapping scenarios to architectural elements, and analyzing the impact of each scenario. This impact analysis includes classifying scenarios as direct, indirect, or non-supportable and examining the effort required to accommodate each change. The process concludes with a synthesis of findings, including identification of architectural risks, sensitivity points, and areas requiring further refinement or redesign.

SAAM is particularly effective in the early stages of architectural design, where the cost of change is low and architectural decisions are still flexible. Its emphasis on modifiability makes it highly applicable in systems expected to evolve over time. The use of stakeholder-driven scenarios promotes shared understanding and helps uncover quality attribute concerns that may not be evident in static models.

13.1.3.4 Scenario-Based Architecture Reengineering (SBAR)

SBAR is a scenario-driven evaluation method designed to support the analysis, transformation, and improvement of existing software architectures [40]. It is particularly useful in legacy system modernization projects, where the goal is to align an outdated architecture with evolving functional and quality requirements. SBAR combines scenario-based analysis with reengineering practices to identify architectural deficiencies and guide systematic refactoring. Through stakeholder-defined scenarios, SBAR evaluates how well the current architecture supports desired system behaviors and provides insights for targeted architectural changes.

This method emphasizes the use of quality attribute scenarios to enhance architectural understanding and inform decision-making during reengineering. It combines analysis of both static structures (e.g., components and module dependencies) and dynamic behaviors (e.g., runtime interactions) to evaluate architectural conformance and detect discrepancies between intended and actual implementations. Unlike forward-looking methods such as ATAM, SBAR focuses on retrospective analysis, making it well suited for brownfield systems. It enables incremental architectural improvement by prioritizing refactoring efforts based on scenario relevance and system criticality.

The SBAR process generally includes identifying and prioritizing quality attribute scenarios, analyzing existing architectural representations, mapping scenarios to relevant components, and evaluating the system's ability to support those scenarios. Based on the analysis, architectural weaknesses are identified, and targeted refactoring plans are developed to improve alignment with quality requirements.

13.2 Model-Based Architecture Evaluation

Model-based architecture evaluation is a systematic approach to assessing software architectures by using abstract models to represent and analyze structural and behavioral aspects of the system. This method emphasizes the construction of simplified yet accurate architectural representations that facilitate the evaluation of both functional and non-functional requirements. These models serve as analytical tools that support early design reasoning, enabling architects to detect potential issues, explore alternatives, and make informed architectural decisions before implementation.

A variety of model types may be employed in model-based architecture evaluation, each addressing specific architectural concerns.

- **Structural Models**
  These models represent the static organization of the system, including components and their interconnections. They help visualize architectural layout, identify modularity issues, and evaluate design scalability.
- **Behavioral Models**
  These models capture the dynamic interactions among components, illustrating how the system fulfills its functional responsibilities. These models aid in identifying runtime bottlenecks and validating coordination logic.
- **Quality Models**
  These models focus on non-functional attributes, providing a basis for quantifying and analyzing quality concerns such as performance, reliability, and security.

Model-based architecture evaluation offers a systematic approach using structural, behavioral, or parametric models to assess system properties, enabling early validation, change impact analysis, and architectural consistency. However, it could be time-consuming and requires expertise and quality tools to create accurate models.

13.2.1 Applicable Situations

Model-based architecture evaluation is beneficial in various situations including the following:

- **Quantitative Evaluation of Non-Functional Properties**
  Analytical models—such as queuing networks for performance and Markov chains for reliability—enable early prediction of system behavior. These models provide quantitative estimates for key quality attributes like response time, availability, and risk exposure, supporting informed architectural decisions before implementation.

- **Model-Driven Evaluation of Architectural Alternatives**
  Model-based evaluation facilitates comparison of design options by constructing analyzable models for each alternative. By varying parameters such as workload intensity, deployment configurations, or communication delays, architects can simulate and analyze the predicted outcomes.
- **Model-Based Analysis of Architectural Evolution and Change Impact**
  Structural models—such as component-and-connector diagrams and dependency graphs—show how components are connected and help analyze the impact of changes, interface dependencies, and modularity. Parametric models represent variables like input load or processing rate, allowing simulation of system behavior as conditions change. Together, these models support effective impact analysis and help keep the architecture robust, scalable, and adaptable over time.

13.2.2 Procedure of Model-Based Architecture Evaluation

The procedure for model-based architecture evaluation typically comprises the following steps:

(1) **Define Evaluation Objectives**
This step is to clearly establish the objectives of the evaluation—such as modularity, extensibility, and component interoperability—and ensure they align with stakeholder requirements and system-level goals.

(2) **Develop Architectural Models**
This step is to construct architectural models that accurately represent the system's structure and behavior, in accordance with the modeling conventions of the selected evaluation method. Each model-based evaluation approach provides specific representation schemes, which must be followed.
For example, when using a Markov Model to evaluate rental car operations, a state-transition model should be built to represent valid car states, transitions, and probabilities based on the Markov property. This model can then be analyzed using techniques such as steady-state and transient analysis.

(3) **Define Metrics and Criteria**
This step is to define clear, quantifiable metrics that reflect quality attributes of interest—such as performance, reliability, scalability, or maintainability. For instance, in a Markov model, relevant metrics may include state probabilities, transition rates, expected time to absorption, or accumulated rewards.
Additionally, evaluation criteria should be established by setting thresholds or benchmark values for each metric. These criteria provide the basis for interpretation and ensure the evaluation results are actionable and aligned with stakeholder expectations.

(4) **Perform Model-Specific Analysis**
This step is to apply analytical techniques and tools specific to the selected modeling approach to derive insights from the model. If the method does not prescribe formal analysis techniques, evaluators should adopt appropriate analytical strategies to interpret the model.

(5) **Analyze Results**
This step is to interpret model analysis results to identify strengths, limitations, and improvement areas. Findings are evaluated against predefined criteria, and a summary report with recommendations is prepared to guide design refinement and ensure alignment with system goals.

13.2.3 Representative Methods

13.2.3.1 Architecture Description Language (ADL)

ADL is a formal language used to specify the structure and behavior of software architectures [4]. It provides a precise and standardized framework for defining architectural elements, including components, connectors, configurations, and interfaces. ADLs enable rigorous analysis through techniques such as consistency checking, behavioral modeling, performance prediction, formal verification, and dependency analysis. ADLs are commonly supported by modeling tools that offer both textual and graphical views of the architecture.

The common elements of ADLs are the following:

- **Components**
  Represent the primary computational units or data stores of the system. Each component encapsulates a specific functionality and defines interfaces for interaction with other architectural elements.
- **Connectors**
  Define the interaction mechanisms between components, such as data exchange, control flow, or protocol coordination. Connectors abstract communication semantics and may include roles, glue code, and interaction rules.
- **Configurations**
  Describe the overall topology of the system by specifying how components and connectors are composed. Configurations define system structure, specifying how architectural elements are instantiated and connected.
- **Interfaces**
  Specify the points of interaction between components and connectors. Interfaces define the types of services provided and required, including method signatures, data types, and interaction constraints.

- **Properties and Constraints**
  Capture non-functional attributes and architectural constraints, enabling analysis and validation of quality attributes.
- **Behavioral Specifications**
  Define how components and connectors behave over time, often using models. These specifications enable dynamic analysis and verification of behavioral properties.

The common analysis methods supported by ADLs include the following:

- **Consistency Checking**
  This method ensures that the architectural description is internally consistent, with no conflicting definitions or incompatible interactions. It verifies that all components, connectors, configurations, and interfaces are properly defined and used in accordance with the architectural rules.
- **Behavioral Analysis**
  This method evaluates the dynamic behavior of the system by analyzing interactions among components as defined by connectors and interfaces. It examines system responses under various operational scenarios, such as differing workloads, input patterns, or environmental conditions.
- **Performance Analysis**
  This method uses the architectural model to predict performance metrics such as latency, throughput, and resource utilization. It involves constructing analytical or simulation models derived from the architecture to assess system behavior under anticipated load conditions.
- **Dependency Analysis**
  This method identifies and evaluates dependencies among architectural elements to assess their implications for system robustness and maintainability. It supports the detection of tightly coupled components that may hinder modularity, adaptability, or fault isolation.

Representative Architecture Description Languages
Representative ADLs include the following:

- **ACME**
  ACME is an influential ADL designed as a generic framework to unify and standardize architectural descriptions across diverse domains [41]. It provides foundational constructs for modeling architectural components, connectors, and configurations.
- **Architecture Analysis and Design Language (AADL)**
  AADL is a widely adopted ADL, particularly suited for the design and analysis of embedded and real-time systems [42]. Its ability to describe both software and hardware components makes it especially valuable in safety-critical domains such as

aerospace and automotive. AADL is supported by comprehensive tools for performance, reliability, and safety analysis.

- **C2 Software Architecture Description Language (C2 SADL)**
  C2 SADL provides both textual and graphical notations for specifying software architectures based on the C2 architectural style [43]. This style structures systems as hierarchical networks of concurrent components that communicate through asynchronous message passing via connectors.
- **Wright**
  Wright is a formal ADL that specifies both the structural and behavioral aspects of software architectures using notations based on Communicating Sequential Processes (CSP) [44]. It supports the precise definition of component interfaces, connector protocols, architectural styles, and behavioral constraints. Wright enables rigorous analysis of properties such as deadlock freedom and protocol compatibility through automated tools.
- **xADL**
  xADL is an extensible, XML-based ADL designed for modeling dynamic and evolving software architectures [45]. Its flexibility allows for the representation of systems with changing structures and behaviors at runtime. xADL is notable for its compatibility with XML tools and its support for customization in research and dynamic system modeling.
- **Darwin**
  Darwin is an ADL developed for specifying distributed and dynamically configurable systems, especially in telecommunications [46]. It enables the modeling of component configurations and runtime interactions within distributed environments.
- **Rapide**
  Rapide is an event-driven ADL focused on modeling and analyzing the timing and ordering of events in software architectures [47]. It supports simulation and verification of component interactions in event-based systems.
- **Koala**
  Koala is an ADL specifically developed for the consumer electronics domain, with a focus on component-based software architectures [48]. It facilitates the specification of reusable and composable components, supporting efficient development and integration for products such as televisions and home appliances.

13.2.3.2 Unified Modeling Language (UML)

The Unified Modeling Language (UML) is a standardized visual modeling language used to represent the object-oriented design of software systems. It provides a comprehensive set of graphical notations for constructing visual models that capture structural and behavioral aspects of a system. Software architects use UML diagrams to visualize, analyze, and document architectural designs, thereby enhancing communication, alignment, and understanding among development stakeholders.

UML Diagrams

The Unified Modeling Language (UML) defines 14 types of diagrams for modeling various structural and behavioral aspects of a software system. Software architects can select the most appropriate diagrams to represent specific architectural elements, facilitating design validation and effective communication among stakeholders.

The Structural Diagrams defined in UML and their respective purposes are summarized in Table 13.1.

Table 13.1 Structural Diagrams in UML

Structural Diagrams	Usage
Class Diagram	To represent persistent object classes and their static relationships
Object Diagram	To depict specific instances of classes and the links between them at a given moment
Component Diagram	To represent software components, their interfaces, and inter-component dependencies
Composite Structure Diagram	To show the internal structure of a classifier and the collaborations among its parts
Package Diagram	To represent packages as white-box containers grouping related elements
Deployment Diagram	To describe the physical deployment of nodes, artifacts, and communication paths
Profile Diagram	To extend UML using stereotypes, tagged values, and constraints for domain-specific modeling

The Behavioral Diagrams defined in UML and their respective purposes are summarized in Table 13.2.

Table 13.2 Behavioral Diagrams in UML

Structural Diagrams	Usage
Use Case Diagram	To depict the functionality provided by a system in terms of use cases and the roles (actors) that interact with them
Activity Diagram	To represent the control flow of actions or activities within a system
Sequence Diagram	To show the sequence of messages exchanged among objects to accomplish specific functions
Communication Diagram	To depict object interactions in terms of sequenced messages and their relationships
Interaction Overview Diagram	To provide an overview of complex control flows by combining elements of activity and sequence diagrams
State Machine Diagram	To illustrate the states of an object or component and the transitions between those states
Timing Diagram	To represent state changes of objects over time with a focus on event timing and duration

Architects can select appropriate UML Diagrams to represent specific elements of the software architecture.

UML-Specific Analysis Methods

The analysis methods applicable to UML Diagrams used in architectural modeling are outlined in Table 13.3.

Table 13.3 Analysis methods using UML Diagrams

UML Diagram	Analysis Methods
Class Diagram	To validate the identification of persistent object classes and the correctness of their relationships
Object Diagram	To validate the correctness of class relationships and cardinalities by analyzing specific object instances
Component Diagram	To validate the cohesiveness of component design and the consistency of provided and required interfaces
Composite Structure Diagram	To validate internal part relationships, structural cohesion, and interaction quality among collaborating parts
Package Diagram	To validate package-level cohesion by examining interdependencies among internal elements
Deployment Diagram	To validate the system's infrastructure, including artifact allocation, node configuration, and communication paths
Profile Diagram	To validate the correctness of domain-specific customizations using UML extension constructs
Use Case Diagram	To validate the completeness, consistency, and alignment of functional requirements with system objectives
Activity Diagram	To validate the correctness of control flows within a system, subsystem, or component
Sequence Diagram	To validate the temporal ordering of message exchanges and their consistency with class definitions
Communication Diagram	To validate that object interactions are consistent, efficient, and aligned with intended system behavior
Interaction Overview Diagram	To validate the logical structure, completeness, and consistency of combined interaction flows
State Machine Diagram	To validate state definitions, transitions, and conformance with behavioral requirements
Timing Diagram	To validate that temporal constraints and state transitions occur as expected over time

These analysis methods aim to validate the structural, behavioral, and temporal aspects of UML models to ensure their consistency, accuracy, and alignment with system requirements and architectural design objectives.

13.2.3.3 Queueing Model

The Queueing Model is a mathematical representation of a queue, which consists of a sequence of waiting entities—such as customers, tasks, or data packets—requiring service from a service mechanism, such as a server, processor, or other service facilities. These models employ mathematical techniques to analyze and evaluate key performance metrics, including arrival rates, service rates, queue lengths, waiting times, and system utilization.

The key elements of Queueing Models are as follows:

- **Queue**
  A queue represents a waiting line where entities—such as customers, tasks, or requests—await service. The default queue discipline is First-In-First-Out (FIFO), also known as First-Come-First-Served (FCFS), where entities are processed in the order of their arrival.
- **Server**
  A server is a resource responsible for delivering service to entities in the queue. A queuing system may consist of one or more servers, forming a single-server or multi-server configuration.
- **Arrival Rate**
  The arrival rate, denoted by λ, is the average number of entities entering the queue per unit time.
- **Service Rate**
  The service rate, denoted by μ, is the average number of entities a server can process per unit time.

The analysis methods supported by the Queueing Model include the following:

- **Average Queue Length**
  The expected number of entities in the queue at a given time
- **Average Waiting Time**
  The average time an entity spends waiting in the queue before receiving service
- **System Utilization**
  The proportion of time the server(s) is actively engaged in servicing entities
- **Throughput**
  The rate at which entities are processed by the system
- **Probability Distributions**
  The likelihood of specific queue states, such as the system being idle or fully utilized

13.2.3.4 Statecharts

Statecharts extend traditional finite state machines by incorporating hierarchy, concurrency, and communication, offering a more expressive and scalable approach to specifying complex system behaviors [49]. While both Statecharts and UML State Machine Diagrams capture state-dependent behavior, Statecharts introduce key enhancements. They support hierarchy through nested states and substates, enabling a structured and modular representation of system behavior. Concurrency is modeled using orthogonal regions, which allow parallel execution of state machines within the system. Communication is facilitated through event broadcasting, enabling coordinated interactions between states and components across different regions of the model.

Statecharts are particularly well suited for modeling systems with complex, state-dependent behaviors that require precise control and clear visualization. They are especially effective in representing systems characterized by hierarchical state structures, concurrent processes, and event-driven interactions, making them a powerful tool for accurately capturing dynamic system behavior.

The key elements of Statecharts are as follows:

- **States**
  Represent distinct modes of operation within the system. States may be simple (atomic) or composite, containing nested substates to support hierarchy.
- **Transitions**
  Define the conditions under which the system moves from one state to another. Transitions are typically triggered by events and may include guards (conditions) and actions.
- **Events**
  External or internal occurrences that trigger transitions. Events can be generated by user inputs, system signals, or other components.
- **Hierarchy**
  Allows states to be nested within other states, supporting abstraction and reducing diagram complexity by encapsulating related behaviors.
- **Concurrency (Orthogonal Regions)**
  Enables the modeling of simultaneous activities by allowing multiple state machines to operate in parallel within different regions of a composite state.
- **Actions**
  Actions are operations executed in response to state transitions or while a state is active. These include entry actions, which are performed upon entering a state; exit actions, executed when leaving a state; transition actions, triggered during the transition between states; and internal actions, which are performed within a state in response to internal events. Together, these actions provide precise control over system behavior and enhance the expressiveness of state-based modeling.
- **History States**
  Preserve the last active substate of a composite state, enabling the system to resume prior behavior upon re-entering the composite state.

The analysis methods supported by Statecharts include the following:

- **Reachability Analysis**
  Determines whether a particular state or configuration can be reached from the initial state, helping verify completeness and detect unreachable or dead states
- **Consistency Checking**
  Ensures that there are no conflicting transitions, ambiguous behaviors, or undefined states, supporting the correctness and determinism of the model
- **Deadlock Detection**
  Identifies situations where the system could enter a state from which no further progress is possible, which is critical for ensuring reliability
- **Liveness and Safety Analysis**
  Verifies that desired system behaviors eventually occur (liveness) and that undesirable conditions are avoided (safety)
- **Scenario-Based Simulation**
  Allows the execution of event sequences to simulate system behavior, enabling stakeholders to validate interactions and dynamic responses early in the design process

13.2.3.5 Network Simulation Model

The Network Simulation Model represents a real or hypothetical computer network to simulate its behavior and performance under varying conditions. It enables the evaluation of different configurations, such as network topologies, traffic patterns, and communication protocols, without requiring physical deployment.

Network simulation tools are essential for managing the complexity of modern networks, which involve diverse devices, protocols, and interactions. These tools facilitate the assessment of key performance metrics such as throughput, latency, and packet loss while also supporting the configuration and analysis of intricate setups.

The primary types of network simulation models are as follows:

- **Packet-Level Simulation**
  This approach models the behavior of individual packets as they traverse the network. It provides a highly detailed and accurate representation of network activity, capturing the complexities of packet handling, routing, and queuing. However, it is computationally intensive and may be impractical for simulating large or complex networks due to high resource demands.
- **Flow-Level Simulation**
  Flow-level simulation abstracts away individual packet details and focuses on modeling aggregated flows. While this reduces granularity, it significantly improves simulation speed and scalability, making it well suited for large-scale network evaluations where fine-grained precision is not essential.

- **Hybrid Simulation**
  Hybrid simulation integrates both packet-level and flow-level techniques to balance detail and efficiency. It enables fine-grained modeling in critical areas while maintaining overall simulation performance. This flexibility makes it particularly effective for analyzing complex networks that require both precision and scalability.

The key elements of network simulation models are as follows:

- **Node**
  A node represents a network device, such as a computer, router, switch, or other hardware component. Each node may have multiple interfaces to establish connections with other nodes.
- **Link**
  A link denotes the physical or logical connection between nodes. It is characterized by attributes such as bandwidth, latency, error rate, and packet loss, which influence overall network performance.
- **Protocol**
  A protocol defines the set of rules governing communication between network entities. Examples include transport protocols (e.g., TCP, UDP), application protocols (e.g., HTTP), wireless protocols (e.g., Wi-Fi, Bluetooth, Zigbee), and routing protocols (e.g., OSPF, BGP).
- **Traffic Model**
  A traffic model specifies data transmission patterns within the network. It encompasses factors such as packet size, arrival rate, and traffic types (e.g., voice, video, or data), forming the basis for simulating realistic network behavior.
- **Network Topology**
  Network topology refers to the physical or logical arrangement of nodes and links. Common topologies include star, ring, mesh, tree, bus, hybrid, point-to-point, point-to-multipoint, and daisy chain, each offering distinct structural and performance characteristics.

The analysis methods supported by network simulation models include the following:

- **Network Performance Analysis**
  Evaluates critical metrics such as throughput, latency, packet loss, and jitter to assess overall network efficiency and reliability
- **Network Scalability Testing**
  Assesses the network's capacity to support increased numbers of nodes, traffic volume, or users without significant performance degradation
- **Traffic Analysis**
  Examines data flow patterns to optimize routing strategies, manage congestion, and ensure effective load balancing

- **Failure Analysis**
  Simulates node or link failures to evaluate the network's fault tolerance and recovery capabilities under adverse or unexpected conditions
- **Topology Optimization**
  Analyzes different network configurations to identify designs that improve performance, reduce operational costs, and enhance fault tolerance

13.3 Formal Method-Based Architecture Evaluation

Formal method-based architecture evaluation is a systematic and rigorous approach that employs mathematical formalisms to validate software architecture designs. By enforcing strict adherence to predefined specifications, constraints, and system properties, this method provides a robust foundation for assessing the correctness and reliability of architectural decisions. It eliminates ambiguity in architectural specifications, enabling a precise and unambiguous interpretation of system behavior.

Formal methods are particularly valuable in the design of safety- or mission-critical systems, where failure can have severe consequences. By offering a high level of assurance regarding correctness, consistency, and compliance with system requirements, formal method-based evaluation ensures that architectural designs perform as intended under defined operational conditions.

Formal method-based architecture evaluation ensures precision through mathematically defined specifications, eliminating inconsistencies and enabling shared understanding. It supports rigorous analysis and facilitates formal verification techniques such as model checking to validate critical properties. Despite their strengths, formal method-based architecture validation faces challenges such as a steep learning curve, limited tool support, and integration difficulties. These methods are often resource-intensive and struggle to scale for complex systems, limiting their practical applicability.

13.3.1 Applicable Situations

Formal method-based architecture evaluation is particularly effective in scenarios that demand rigorous analysis to satisfy strict requirements and compliance standards. Examples of such systems include the following:

- **Safety-Critical Systems**
  Safety-critical systems are those where failures can result in severe consequences, such as loss of life, environmental damage, or destruction of property. For example, aviation control systems manage flight safety and navigation, automotive safety mechanisms like anti-lock braking systems ensure safe vehicle operation, and nuclear plant monitoring systems prevent hazardous events.

- **Security-Sensitive Systems**
  Security-sensitive systems require robust defenses to protect sensitive data, ensure system integrity, and prevent unauthorized access or malicious attacks. For example, military communication systems protect classified information, and cybersecurity frameworks counter evolving threats.
- **Performance-Critical Systems**
  Performance-critical systems are those with stringent requirements for real-time responsiveness, low latency, or high throughput, where delays or performance bottlenecks can compromise system effectiveness. For example, telecommunication networks handle large-scale data transmissions with minimal latency.
- **Compliance-Critical Systems**
  Compliance-critical systems must meet stringent regulatory and industry standards to ensure legality, safety, and operational reliability. For example, automotive software must satisfy ISO 26262 requirements to ensure functional safety in critical driving systems.
- **High-Assurance Systems**
  High-assurance systems are characterized by their requirement for near-perfect reliability, as failures in such systems can lead to catastrophic or costly consequences. For example, space exploration software, defense systems, and mission-critical applications for unmanned vehicles must operate with high precision and reliability to avoid failures and ensure success without human intervention.

13.3.2 Procedure of Formal Method-Based Architecture Evaluation

The procedure for formal method-based architecture evaluation typically comprises the following steps:

[1] **Define Evaluation Objectives**
This step is to clearly establish the objectives of the evaluation using formal methods. The evaluation objectives should be precise, measurable, and aligned with the system's critical properties, guiding the application of formal techniques throughout the assessment process.
Typical system properties evaluated using formal methods include:
- **Correctness**
  Correctness refers to the degree to which the architectural design conforms to its specified requirements, ensuring that all intended functions and constraints are properly addressed.
- **Consistency**
  Consistency ensures that the architectural design is free from internal contradictions. It verifies that there are no conflicting constraints, definitions, or behaviors among the architectural design elements, thereby supporting coherent interpretation and analysis.

- **Completeness**
  Completeness ensures that the architectural design comprehensively addresses all relevant functional and non-functional requirements, leaving no critical aspects unrepresented or unspecified.
- **Accuracy**
  Accuracy refers to the extent to which the architectural design faithfully reflects the intended real-world conditions, behaviors, or operational context it is meant to represent or respond to. It ensures that the system's structure and behavior are aligned with domain expectations and practical usage scenarios.

[2] **Develop Formal Specifications**
Develop formal specifications to model selected architectural design decisions using appropriate formal methods. These specifications emphasize critical elements—such as component behavior, constraints, and interconnections—rather than modeling the system in its entirety. The selection of formal methods should align with the evaluation objectives.

[3] **Apply Formal Analysis Techniques**
This step is to rigorously evaluate the developed specifications using the analysis techniques provided by the selected formal methods, with respect to the defined evaluation objectives. Each method offers specialized techniques to assess critical aspects of the architecture, ensuring that it conforms to the specified functional behaviors and system constraints.

[4] **Analyze Evaluation Results**
Analyze the evaluation outcomes to assess the architecture's strengths, weaknesses, and areas for improvement. This involves interpreting artifacts such as formal proofs, counterexamples, or mismatches uncovered during equivalence checking. The analysis should produce a report summarizing the applied formal methods, key findings, quality-related issues, and recommendations for design improvement.

13.3.3 Representative Methods

A wide range of formal methods is available for evaluating software architecture, each providing rigorous techniques for specifying, verifying, and analyzing architectural design decisions. The selection of an appropriate method is typically guided by the characteristics of the system, the defined design elements under evaluation, and the evaluation objectives.

13.3.3.1 *Z* Specification Language

Z Specification Language is a comprehensive formal method for system modeling and verification, characterized by well-defined syntax and semantics grounded in set theory and predicate logic [50]. *Z* is particularly well suited for applications where correctness and reliability are critical, offering a robust framework for modeling complex system behaviors with mathematical precision.

The key elements of Z Specification are the following:

- **Schemas**
  Schemas are the fundamental construct in Z, serving to group the state—comprising variables and their associated types—and the predicates, which define the constraints on these variables.
- **Types and Sets**
  Z uses basic types and user-defined types, often represented as sets. Set theory is a core aspect of Z, used to model data structures, relationships, and constraints. For example, `S= {1, 2, 3}` defines a finite set, and `[Person]` declares an abstract set of entities.
- **Predicate Logic**
  Predicate logic provides the formal foundation for defining constraints and relationships within schemas. It ensures precision and unambiguity in specifying system properties. For example, $(x > 0) \wedge (y = x + 1)$ expresses that x must be positive and y is derived from x.
- **Schema Calculus**
  Schema calculus allows schemas to be combined and reused. Operations like conjunction ($\wedge$) combine constraints, while schema inclusion enables embedding one schema within another. This promotes modular design and simplifies the specification of large systems.
- **State and Operations**
  Z models systems through state schemas, which represent the current condition of the system, and operation schemas, which describe state transitions. Operation schemas define input/output variables and preconditions/postconditions, capturing how the system evolves over time.
- **Δ (Delta) and Ξ (Xi) Operators**
  These operators are used in operation schemas to specify state changes. The Δ operator (`ΔState`) indicates a state update, while the Ξ operator (`ΞState`) signifies that the state remains unchanged during an operation.

The analysis methods supported by *Z* Specification include the following:

- **Type Checking**
  Verifies that all variables and expressions conform to their declared types, identifying mismatches, undeclared elements, and incorrect usage
- **Proof Obligations**
  Ensures that specified properties (e.g., preconditions, postconditions, invariants) hold under given constraints, typically using theorem provers
- **Schema Consistency Checking**
  Validates that constraints within a schema are logically consistent and can represent valid system states

- **State Space Analysis**
  Explores all possible states and transitions to verify properties such as reachability, liveness, and deadlock freedom
- **Model Validation**
  Assesses whether the specification aligns with intended requirements through test cases and scenario-based evaluations

13.3.3.2 Object Constraint Language (OCL)

Object Constraint Language (OCL) is a formal language used to define precise expressions, constraints, and rules within UML models, complementing UML's graphical notation with a text-based specification method. It enables the formal specification of invariants, preconditions, postconditions, and derived properties that are difficult to express visually. OCL is particularly effective in systems that require rigorous definition of business rules and consistency conditions, making it well suited for enhancing the precision and analyzability of UML-based system models.

The key elements of OCL are the following:

- **Context**
  OCL context is the model element—such as a class, operation, or attribute—within which an OCL expression is defined and evaluated. It establishes the scope and reference point for the expression, determining which elements of the UML model are accessible and how the expression is interpreted in relation to the model structure.
- **Expressions**
  An OCL expression is a well-formed, declarative, and side-effect-free construct used to evaluate values, enforce constraints, or derive properties within a UML model. It can be used to specify invariants for classes, preconditions and postconditions for operations, and conditions for derived attributes or associations.
- **OCL Constraints**
  Constraints in OCL are Boolean expressions that evaluate to either true or false, ensuring that specified conditions within the model are satisfied. They can be classified as follows:
  - **Invariants**: Conditions that must always hold true for instances of a class throughout their lifetime
  - **Preconditions**: Conditions that must be true before the execution of an operation
  - **Postconditions**: Conditions that must be true after the execution of an operation
  - **Guards**: Conditions that control the flow of state transitions in state machines
  - **Derive expressions**: Conditions that define the value of a derived attribute or association end based on other model elements
- **Data Types**
  OCL provides a set of basic data types, including `Boolean`, `Integer`, `Real`, and `String`, along with support for user-defined types and enumerations.

- **Collection Types**
  OCL supports collection types such as *Set*, *Bag*, *Sequence*, and OrderedSet. These collections offer rich operations such as *select*, *collect*, *forAll*, and *exists*.
- **Standard Library**
  OCL includes a standard library of predefined operations for all supported types, including arithmetic operations for numeric types, string manipulation functions, logical operators, and collection-based operations to facilitate expressive and concise model constraints.

The analysis methods supported by OCL include the following:

- **Syntax Checking**
  Ensures that OCL expressions conform to the language's formal syntax rules by verifying the correct use of constructs such as operators, functions, and type declarations.
- **Type Checking**
  Verifies that OCL expressions operate on compatible data types as defined in the UML model. This process helps detect type mismatches early in the modeling phase, preventing errors during execution or model transformation.
- **Constraint Validation**
  Ensures that OCL constraints, including invariants, preconditions, and postconditions, are logically sound and aligned with the semantics of the UML model. It checks that constraints are satisfiable, non-redundant, and free of internal contradictions.
- **Model Consistency Checking**
  Evaluates whether the integration of OCL constraints preserves the internal consistency of the UML model. It verifies that constraints do not conflict with each other or with structural and behavioral elements, thereby maintaining overall model coherence.

13.3.3.3 Abstract State Machine (ASM)

Abstract State Machine (ASM) is a formal method used to specify and verify the behavior of computational systems—systems that manipulate information through defined operations and state transitions [51]. Such systems are typically modeled as a set of states representing specific configurations, along with transition rules that define how the system evolves from one state to another. ASMs capture system behavior through logical, deterministic, or probabilistic processes, making them well suited for rigorous formal analysis and verification.

The key elements of ASM are the following:

- **States**
  A state represents a snapshot of the system at a specific point in time. It is defined by the values of a collection of variables or functions that characterize the system's configuration.

- **Functions**
  Functions define relationships among elements within the state. They may be static (unchanging across states) or dynamic (subject to change during transitions).
- **Transition Rules**
  Transition rules define how the system evolves from one state to another. They are expressed in an abstract, high-level syntax that specifies updates to state variables or functions. ASMs support both deterministic and non-deterministic transitions, enabling the modeling of systems with multiple possible behaviors.
- **Guards**
  Guards are logical conditions associated with transition rules. A rule is executed only when its guard evaluates to true.
- **Updates**
  Updates describe changes made to the state during a transition. They are executed atomically and deterministically to ensure consistency in state transformations.
- **Abstraction Levels**
  ASMs support modeling at varying levels of abstraction, from conceptual system designs to implementation-level details. This facilitates stepwise refinement from abstract specifications to executable systems.
- **Universes**
  Universes are sets that define domains of discourse, such as objects, data types, or values used in the model. They determine the allowable elements that functions and variables may reference.

The analysis methods supported by ASM include the following:

- **Syntax Checking**
  Ensures that ASM specifications conform to the defined syntax and semantics of the formalism. This includes verifying the correct definition of rules, functions, and states within the model.
- **State Consistency Checking**
  Validates that transitions between states, as defined by ASM rules, maintain the internal consistency of the model. This involves ensuring that state updates do not violate constraints or lead to invalid configurations, thereby supporting coherent system behavior.
- **Rule Validation**
  Analyzes transition rules to ensure they produce the intended effects on the system state. This includes verifying associated preconditions and postconditions, and checking that rules do not introduce contradictions or unintended side effects.
- **State Space Exploration**
  Examines all possible states and transitions in the ASM model to identify issues such as deadlocks, unreachable states, or infinite loops. This analysis helps confirm that the specification robustly captures all expected system behaviors.

- **Refinement Checking**
  Ensures that a more detailed ASM specification preserves the properties and behaviors of a corresponding abstract specification. This supports stepwise refinement, enabling a reliable transition from high-level models to concrete implementations.

13.3.3.4 Petri Net

Petri Net is a formal modeling technique used to specify and analyze the behavior of concurrent systems, particularly in the context of distributed and parallel computing [52]. It is represented as a directed bipartite graph composed of two types of nodes—places and transitions—connected by arcs that define the flow between them. Petri Nets are especially effective for modeling systems where concurrency, synchronization, and resource sharing are critical, providing a precise framework for visualizing and analyzing dynamic behaviors such as parallel execution, conflict resolution, and deadlock detection.

The key elements of Petri Net are the following:

- **Places (*P*)**
  Places represent conditions, states, or resources in the system and are visually depicted as circles. Formally, P is a finite set of places. Each place $p \in P$ can hold zero or more tokens, which collectively represent the system's current state.
- **Transitions (*T*)**
  Transitions represent actions or events that may cause a change in the system state and are typically depicted as rectangles or bars. A transition is enabled when the required number of tokens is available in its input places, and it fires by consuming and producing tokens according to the arc definitions. Formally, transitions form a finite set T, where each transition $t \in T$ represents a discrete event that causes state changes.
- **Arcs (*F*)**
  Arcs define the flow of control by connecting places to transitions and transitions to places. They are directed and determine how tokens move within the Petri Net. Formally, F is a finite set of directed arcs where $F \subseteq (P \times T) \cup (T \times P)$. Each arc $f \in F$ is associated with a weight $W(f)$, which is a positive integer indicating the number of tokens to be consumed or produced when a transition fires.
- **Tokens and Marking (*M*)**
  Tokens are depicted as small filled circles residing in places and dynamically represent the system's current configuration. The number of tokens in a place $p \in P$ at a given marking M is denoted by $M(p)$, reflecting the marking-dependent nature of the token count.

The analysis methods supported by Petri Net include the following:

- **Reachability Analysis**
  Determines whether a particular marking (distribution of tokens) can be reached from the initial marking. This helps assess whether desired or undesired states, such as goal states or deadlocks, are attainable.

- **Liveness Analysis**
  Evaluates whether transitions in the Petri Net can eventually fire, ensuring that the system does not enter a deadlock or livelock. A live Petri Net guarantees that the system can continue operating indefinitely without halting.
- **Boundedness Analysis**
  Checks whether the number of tokens in each place remains within a finite bound across all reachable markings. Boundedness ensures that the system does not encounter resource overflow or unmanageable growth.
- **Deadlock Detection**
  Identifies states in which no transitions are enabled, indicating that the system cannot proceed further. Detecting such markings helps ensure operational continuity and robustness.
- **Invariant Analysis**
  Examines place and transition invariants to identify conserved properties in the system. *Place invariants* confirm that specific token combinations remain constant, while *transition invariants* validate balanced firing sequences that preserve system behavior.

13.3.3.5 Temporal Logic

Temporal logic is a formal framework for representing and reasoning about time-dependent statements and properties. It extends classical logic by introducing temporal operators such as "always," "eventually," "until," and "next," which capture the evolution of truth values over time. Temporal logic is particularly valuable for analyzing concurrent systems, verifying software correctness, and specifying behavioral requirements in real-time and reactive systems.

The two primary types of temporal logic are Linear Temporal Logic (LTL) and Computational Tree Logic (CTL).

- **Linear Temporal Logic (LTL)**
  LTL is a formalism used to describe the behavior of a system over linear time. In LTL, time is modeled as a single sequence of states (or events), and temporal operators like *always*, *eventually*, *next*, and *until* are used to specify how propositions change over this linear timeline. LTL is particularly useful for specifying and verifying properties of systems such as sequential workflows, where each execution path is analyzed as a sequence of states.
- **Computational Tree Logic (CTL)**
  CTL is a temporal logic used to describe system behavior in branching-time models. Time is modeled as a tree of possible execution paths, allowing reasoning about multiple potential future scenarios. CTL combines path quantifiers ("for all paths" and "there exists a path") with temporal operators to specify properties across different paths. It is particularly useful in verifying systems with concurrency or nondeterministic behavior, such as distributed systems and communication protocols.

The key elements of Temporal Logic are the following:

- **Propositions**
  Propositions are fundamental statements in temporal logic that evaluate to either true or false. They represent conditions or properties of the system under analysis.
- **Temporal Operators**
- Temporal logic extends classical logic by introducing temporal operators that express time-dependent behaviors and constraints:
  - **Always** (□): Specifies that a condition is true in all future states
  - **Eventually** (◇): Specifies that a condition will be true at some point in the future
  - **Next (X)**: Specifies that a condition is true in the immediate next state
  - **Until (U)**: Specifies that a condition will hold true until another condition becomes true
- **Path Quantifiers (in CTL)**
  Path quantifiers are used in branching temporal logics like CTL to reason about multiple possible execution paths:
  - **For All Paths** (A): Specifies that a property holds true for all possible paths
  - **There Exists a Path** (E): Specifies that a property holds true for at least one path
- **Time Representation**
  Time is modeled either as a linear sequence of states, as in LTL, or as a branching tree of states, as in CTL, each capturing different perspectives of system behavior.
- **Models and States**
  Temporal logic operates on models composed of states and transitions. States represent discrete snapshots of the system, while transitions define how the system evolves from one state to another over time.
- **Syntax and Semantics**
  Temporal logic defines a formal syntax for constructing valid expressions and a corresponding semantics that interprets these expressions in relation to system behavior over time.

The analysis methods supported by Temporal Logic include the following:

- **Syntax Validation**
  Syntax validation checks whether Temporal Logic formulas conform to the formal syntactic rules. This includes verifying the correct use of temporal operators, logical connectors, and structural constructs.
- **Semantic Validation**
  Semantic validation verifies that temporal expressions accurately capture the intended system behavior. It ensures that specified properties, such as safety and liveness, are both meaningful and aligned with the system's functional and non-functional requirements.

- **Model Checking**
  Model checking evaluates whether a system model satisfies a set of temporal logic specifications. Using automated tools, this method systematically verifies each property. If a specification is violated, the tool generates a counterexample that demonstrates the violation path within the model.
- **Property Validation**
  Property validation confirms that specific system properties—such as deadlock freedom, mutual exclusion, or responsiveness—hold under all possible executions. Each property is encoded as a temporal formula and checked against the system model.
- **State Space Exploration**
  State space exploration examines all reachable states and transitions in the system model to detect violations of specified temporal properties. This approach ensures compliance with constraints related to event ordering, timing, and behavioral correctness.

13.4 PoC-Based Architecture Evaluation

Proof-of-Concept (PoC)-based architecture evaluation is an approach for assessing the viability and quality of a software architecture by implementing selected critical and high-risk design elements. This partial implementation allows architects and stakeholders to validate key architectural decisions, explore the feasibility of novel technologies or integration strategies, and identify potential issues early in the development lifecycle.

The key features of the PoC-based evaluation approach include the following:

- **Validation Through Implementation**
  This approach validates the functionality and feasibility of selected critical architectural components through concrete implementation, demonstrating that the proposed design is both practical and technically feasible.
- **Focused Scope for Evaluation**
  The evaluation concentrates on specific, high-priority aspects of the architecture—such as innovative components, critical integration points, or complex algorithms—rather than attempting to assess the system as a whole.
- **Assessment of Resource Feasibility**
  The approach examines the architecture's ability to function within available resource constraints, including processing capacity, memory, storage, and network bandwidth. This ensures the design's viability in the target deployment environment.

PoC-based architecture evaluation offers clear evidence that critical parts of the system are feasible and functional. It helps confirm key design decisions, reveal integration challenges, and test new technologies in realistic environments. However, creating a PoC can be time-consuming and resource intensive. Since it only covers selected parts of the system, the evaluation may be incomplete, and the findings might not fully apply to the entire system.

13.4.1 Applicable Situations

PoC-based architecture evaluation is particularly well suited for scenarios in which the functionality and the quality of a proposed architecture must be validated before committing to full-scale implementation. This approach is especially beneficial in the following contexts:

- **Adoption of Emerging Technologies**
  When introducing new or unfamiliar technologies, PoC helps assess their integration feasibility and performance in the target environment.
- **Evaluation of High-Risk Architectural Decisions**
  For design elements that involve significant uncertainty or complexity, a PoC allows early validation and risk mitigation.
- **Complex System Integration**—In systems that require the interaction of diverse components or external systems, PoC helps verify interoperability and identify potential integration issues.
- **Demonstration for Stakeholders**
  A functional prototype can serve as a tangible artifact to communicate architectural choices, gain stakeholder buy-in, and justify investment decisions.

13.4.2 Procedure of PoC-Based Architecture Evaluation

PoC-based architecture evaluation is most effectively applied through the following steps:

[1] **Define Objectives and Scope**
Clearly define the objectives of the PoC, ensuring alignment with business needs or technical goals. Specify what the PoC is intended to validate, focusing on measurable outcomes. Identify the critical architectural components or design elements—such as high-risk or innovative features—that require evaluation, and define the PoC scope accordingly.

[2] **Design the PoC Implementation**
Develop a focused and detailed design for the selected architectural elements targeted for implementation. The design should effectively capture the essential structure and behavior required for validation while remaining minimal and purpose-driven. Consider the following design criteria:

- **Simplicity and relevance**: Focus on core components and interactions directly tied to the PoC objectives. Avoid unnecessary features or complexity.
- **Modularity**: Design components to be self-contained and loosely coupled, enabling easy modification, testing, and reuse.
- **Minimal dependencies**: Limit inter-component dependencies to reduce integration complexity and promote flexibility.

- **Standardized interfaces**: Define clear, consistent interfaces to support interoperability and ease of integration.
- **Testability and observability**: Incorporate mechanisms for logging, monitoring, and metrics collection to enable effective validation and performance assessment.

[3] **Implement the PoC System**

Choose an implementation environment that aligns with the PoC objectives and scope, selecting appropriate programming languages, tools, and frameworks to support development. Implement the PoC system by the established implementation guidelines including the following:

- **Adhere to design specifications**: Ensure that the implementation aligns closely with the detailed design to preserve architectural intent and validation objectives.
- **Focus on core functionality**: Develop only the essential components and interactions necessary to meet the PoC's validation goals; avoid adding features beyond the defined scope.
- **Use simplified constructs**: Employ mock components, stubs, or placeholders for non-critical elements to streamline development and reduce complexity.
- **Support testing and monitoring**: Integrate logging, debugging tools, and performance metrics to enable thorough evaluation and observability of system behavior.
- **Ensure readiness for evaluation**: Validate that the implemented system is functional and demonstrable and that it supports evaluation against the predefined success criteria.

[4] **Analyze Evaluation Results**

Conduct thorough testing to validate the PoC against defined objectives. Apply functional, performance, stress, and integration tests to assess the design's effectiveness. Summarize the results in an evaluation report, highlighting strengths, limitations, and improvement areas. Use the insights to guide architectural refinements and inform decisions for further development.

13.5 Prototype-Based Architecture Evaluation

Prototype-based architecture evaluation is an approach in which a functional prototype of the system is developed to validate architectural decisions and assess their feasibility in a realistic context. Unlike PoC-based evaluation, which targets a minimal implementation of selected critical components, prototype-based evaluation offers a more comprehensive and production-like representation of the overall architecture.

The prototype is typically refined through iterative development cycles, gradually evolving into a fully executable system. Consequently, this approach not only facilitates architectural validation but also serves as a practical implementation strategy, effectively bridging the gap between architectural evaluation and full system development.

The key features of the prototype-based evaluation approach include the following:

- **Functional Representation of the Architecture**
  The prototype provides a working model of the system, capturing key functionalities and interactions that mimic the final architecture. It allows for a practical assessment of how the system behaves under realistic conditions.
- **Broader Scope Compared to PoC**
  Unlike PoC-based evaluation, prototypes cover a more extensive range of architectural elements, including additional functionalities and non-functional requirements (NFRs) such as scalability, performance, and usability.
- **Validation of Non-Functional Requirements (NFRs)**
  Prototypes enable a detailed assessment of NFRs like reliability, scalability, and security in a near-production environment, ensuring the architecture meets critical quality attributes.
- **Stakeholder Engagement**
  By providing a tangible and interactive model, prototypes facilitate clear communication with stakeholders. This enhances feedback collection, aligns expectations, and builds confidence in the architecture.
- **Support for User-Centric Design**
  The prototype allows for direct user interaction, enabling the collection of feedback on user experience, interface design, and overall usability. This fosters a user-centered approach to system development.
- **Realistic Testing Environment**
  Prototypes are tested in environments that simulate real-world conditions, providing more accurate insights into how the system will perform under production-like scenarios.
- **Bridge Between Design and Implementation**
  Prototypes act as an intermediate step between conceptual design and full-scale implementation, providing a practical framework for transitioning to a complete system.

Prototype-based architecture evaluation enables early validation of architectural decisions by building a partial implementation that simulates key functionalities or system behaviors. It supports user feedback, uncovers design flaws, and facilitates iterative refinement. However, developing prototypes can be costly and time-consuming, especially if not reused in the final system. Moreover, prototypes may oversimplify complex behaviors, leading to inaccurate conclusions if their limitations are not properly considered.

13.5.1 Applicable Situations

Prototype-based architecture evaluation is suited for scenarios where a more comprehensive and detailed implementation is needed to evaluate the architecture. Unlike PoC-based evaluation, which validates specific aspects or technologies in a controlled, limited environment, prototype-based evaluation involves developing a more complete version of the system.

Prototype-based architecture evaluation is particularly advantageous in the following contexts:

- **Validation Through Implementation**
  This approach validates the functionality, feasibility, and performance of architectural decisions through concrete implementation, demonstrating that the design is both practical and technically sound in a working system.
- **Comprehensive Architectural Representation**
  The prototype captures a broad range of architectural elements, offering a more complete and realistic view of the system than a PoC. This enables the evaluation of both functional and non-functional aspects under near-operational conditions.
- **Early Detection of Design Issues**
  Executing substantial portions of the architecture helps identify design flaws, integration challenges, and performance constraints early in the development process.
- **Stakeholder Engagement**
  A working prototype serves as a tangible artifact for demonstration and review, facilitating communication with stakeholders and enabling early feedback to refine requirements and design.
- **Foundation for Full System Development**
  As the prototype closely mirrors the target system, it can often be incrementally evolved into the final implementation, reducing duplication of effort and accelerating development.

13.5.2 Procedure of Prototype-Based Architecture Evaluation

Prototype-based architecture evaluation is most effectively conducted through the following sequence of steps:

[1] **Define Objectives and Prototype Scope**
Establish clear objectives that align with business needs and technical requirements. Define what the prototype aims to demonstrate, focusing on measurable outcomes. The scope should cover core functionalities and representative workflows, enabling evaluation of usability, performance, and integration without modeling the entire system.

[2] **Perform Detailed Design**

Develop a design that reflects the broader scope of the prototype while remaining practical.

- **Address Core System Scope**: Include major workflows and functionalities, simplifying non-essential parts.
- **Balance Detail and Efficiency**: Use realistic interactions and data while simplifying peripheral components.
- **Ensure Modularity**: Design self-contained modules with minimal dependencies and clear interfaces.
- **Replicate Real-World Interactions**: Capture essential interactions without introducing unnecessary complexity.
- **Enable Validation and Feedback**: Integrate test hooks, monitoring tools, and performance metrics.
- **Simulate Near-Realistic Behavior**: Model workflows, interfaces, and data structures close to the final system.

[3] **Implement the Prototype System**

Choose an implementation environment that aligns with the protype objectives and scope.

Implement the prototype system by the established implementation guidelines including the following:

- **Follow design specifications**: Ensure alignment with planned architecture and objectives.
- **Use simplified constructs**: Employ stubs or placeholders to reduce complexity.
- **Maintain modularity**: Enable independent testing, updates, and scalability.
- **Integrate testing and monitoring**: Support evaluation through logging, debugging, and performance tracking.
- **Adhere to best practices**: Apply coding standards and provide clear documentation.
- **Prepare for demonstration**: Ensure readiness for stakeholder review with a focus on critical workflows.

[4] **Analyze Evaluation Results**

Conduct comprehensive testing to validate the prototype against its defined objectives, focusing on functionality, performance, integration, and usability. Apply various test methods—such as functional, stress, and user experience testing—to assess how well the prototype reflects the intended architecture and supports key workflows. Summarize the evaluation results in a report that highlights strengths, limitations, and areas for improvement. Use the findings to refine architectural decisions, address design issues, and guide the transition toward full-scale system development.

Appendix A. Quick Reference for Unified Architecture Process

This appendix provides a concise overview of the Unified Architecture Process. It summarizes the key activities, outlines the steps within each activity, and highlights the tasks associated with each step. The descriptions are intentionally brief to serve as a quick and accessible reference.

The Unified Architecture Process consists of six primary activities as shown in Fig. A.1.

Software architecture is designed from multiple system views, as explained in Sect. 1.2.2. Accordingly, Activity A4—Design for Architectural Views—is further subdivided into design activities specific to each architectural view.

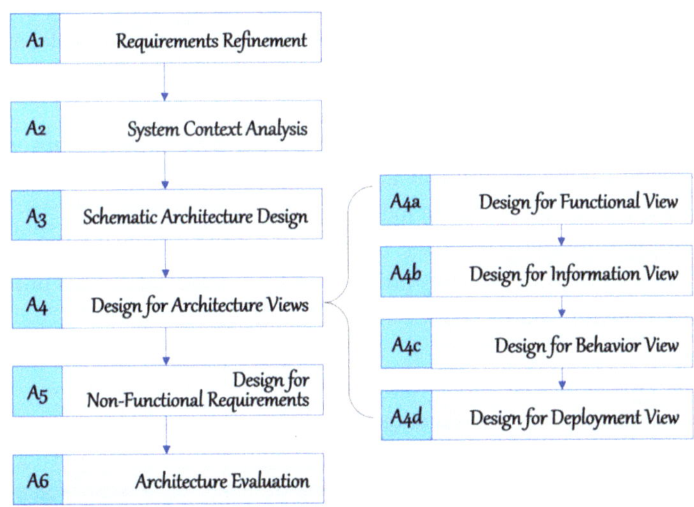

Fig. A.1 Activities in the Unified Architecture Process

S. D. Kim, M. Kim, *Hands-on Software Architecture*,
https://doi.org/10.1007/978-3-032-01184-8

A.1. Activity A1. Requirements Refinement

The purpose of this activity is to refine the initial requirements provided by stakeholders to ensure clarity and completeness for subsequent design stages. The activity is structured into three steps, each comprising a set of specific tasks, as outlined below.

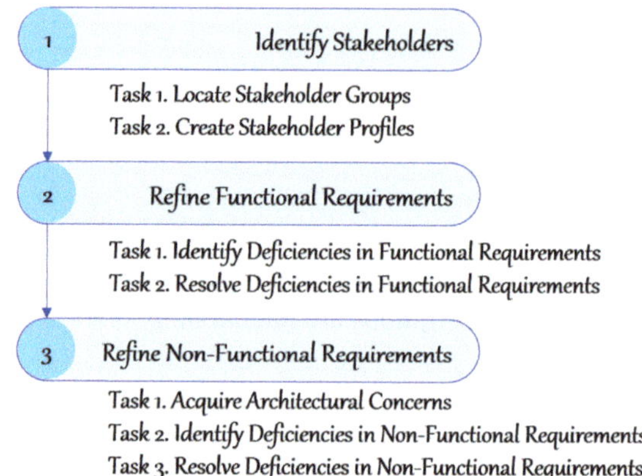

Step 1. Identify Stakeholders

This step is to identify the stakeholders of the target system. Engaging relevant stakeholders enables architects to make more informed and comprehensive design decisions, ensuring that the architecture aligns with stakeholder expectations. This step is carried out through the following tasks:

- Task 1, Locate Stakeholder Groups, is to identify key stakeholder groups for the target system, ensuring their involvement in providing insights, expressing concerns, and specifying requirements relevant to the system.
- Task 2, Create Stakeholder Profiles, involves identifying specific individuals within each stakeholder group and creating profiles for them. Each stakeholder profile includes details such as identification, contact information, and availability.

Step 2. Refine Functional Requirements

This step is to refine the system's functional requirements by applying the principles and techniques of requirement engineering. It is carried out through the following tasks:

- Task 1, Identify Deficiencies in Functional Requirements, is to identify gaps and weaknesses in the functional requirements by thoroughly reviewing each requirement in the initial SRS.
- Task 2, Resolve Deficiencies in Functional Requirements, is to address identified issues by clarifying ambiguities with stakeholders, gathering additional insights, and refining the updated functional requirements.

Step 3. Refine Non-Functional Requirements

This step is to refine the non-functional requirements of the system by applying principles and techniques of requirement engineering. It is carried out through the following tasks:

- Task 1, Acquire Architectural Concerns, is to gather architectural concerns from stakeholders and derive corresponding non-functional requirements (NFRs) based on those concerns.
- Task 2, Identify Deficiencies in Non-Functional Requirements, is to detect shortcomings in the NFRs by thoroughly reviewing each requirement in the initial Software Requirements Specification (SRS), using methods similar to those applied for functional requirements.
- Task 3, Resolve Deficiencies in Non-Functional Requirements, is to address and resolve identified NFR deficiencies by analyzing each issue, consulting stakeholders for clarification, and revising the requirements accordingly.

A.2. Activity A2. System Context Analysis

The purpose of this activity is to develop a context model for the system by analyzing the refined requirements, where the context model represents a high-level abstraction of the system's boundaries, functionality, datasets, and behavior. The activity is structured into four steps, each comprising a set of specific tasks, as outlined below.

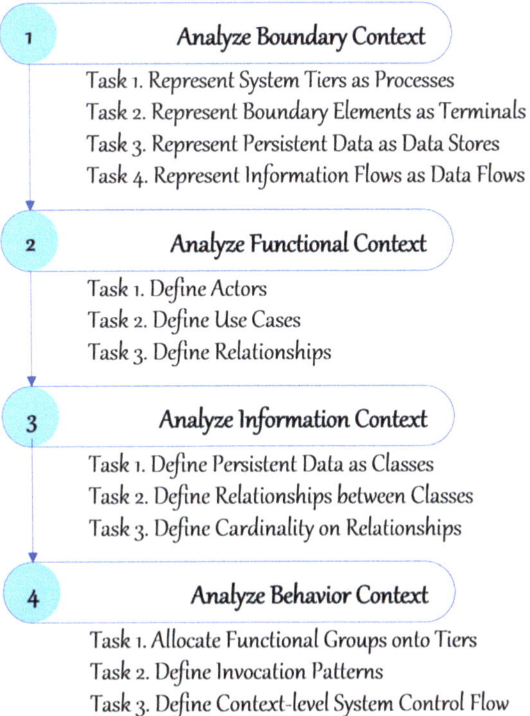

Step 1. Analyze Boundary Context

This step is to analyze the boundary context of the target system, which can be effectively represented using a DFD. It is carried out through the following tasks:

- Task 1, Represent System Tiers as Processes, is to identify the system tiers of the target system and represent them as processes. In a Level 0 DFD, each process symbolizes a physical system tier, which may correspond to the entire computer system or a specific subsystem.
- Task 2, Represent Boundary Elements as Terminals, is to model the boundary elements of the system and represent them as terminals. In a DFD, a terminal represents a boundary element that interacts with the system by providing input or receiving output.
- Task 3, Represent Persistent Data as Data Stores, is to identify the persistent datasets managed by the target system and represent them as data stores.
- Task 4, Represent Information Flows as Data Flows, is to identify the data flows among processes, terminals, and data stores within the context of the system.

Step 2. Analyze Functional Context

This step is to analyze the functional context of the target system and represent it using a use case diagram. It is carried out through the following tasks:

- Task 1, Define Actors, is to identify the actors that interact with the target system, where each actor represents a distinct role assumed by an entity engaging with the system.
- Task 2, Define Use Cases, is to analyze the system's functionality and represent it through use cases, each capturing a specific and cohesive functional behavior.
- Task 3, Define Relationships, is to define the relationships depicted in the use case diagram, including those between actors, between actors and use cases, and among use cases.

Step 3. Analyze Information Context

This step is to analyze the informational context of the target system and represent it using a class diagram. It is carried out through the following tasks:

- Task 1, Define Persistent Data as Classes, is to identify the persistent datasets managed by the system and represent them as persistent object classes.
- Task 2, Define Relationships between Classes, is to establish relationships among the identified classes using the five standard relationship types in a class diagram: Dependency, Association, Aggregation, Composition, and Inheritance.
- Task 3, Define Cardinality on Relationships, is to specify the cardinalities of relationships, indicating the number of instances of one class that can be associated with instances of another class.

Step 4. Analyze Behavior Context

This step aims to analyze the behavioral context of the target system and represent it using an activity diagram. It is carried out through the following tasks:

- Task 1, Allocate Functional Groups onto Tiers, is to assign the functional groups of the system across multiple tiers, aiming to optimally distribute functional components so that each tier is responsible for specific aspects of the system's overall functionality.
- Task 2, Define Invocation Patterns, is to identify the most appropriate invocation patterns for each functional group within its designated tier.
- Task 3, Define Context-level System Control Flow, is to establish the context-level control flow of the system by creating an activity diagram for each tier, utilizing the invocation patterns associated with the functional groups.

A.3. Activity A3. Schematic Architecture Design

The purpose of this activity is to design the schematic architecture of the target system by integrating appropriate architecture styles. The schematic architecture represents the system's stable and enduring structural layout, serving as the foundation for subsequent architectural decisions. The activity is structured into four steps, each comprising a set of specific tasks, as outlined below.

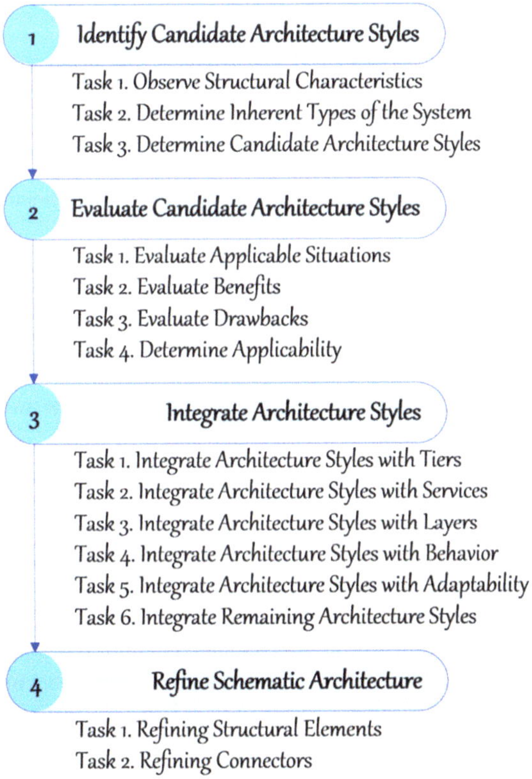

1 Identify Candidate Architecture Styles

Task 1. Observe Structural Characteristics
Task 2. Determine Inherent Types of the System
Task 3. Determine Candidate Architecture Styles

2 Evaluate Candidate Architecture Styles

Task 1. Evaluate Applicable Situations
Task 2. Evaluate Benefits
Task 3. Evaluate Drawbacks
Task 4. Determine Applicability

3 Integrate Architecture Styles

Task 1. Integrate Architecture Styles with Tiers
Task 2. Integrate Architecture Styles with Services
Task 3. Integrate Architecture Styles with Layers
Task 4. Integrate Architecture Styles with Behavior
Task 5. Integrate Architecture Styles with Adaptability
Task 6. Integrate Remaining Architecture Styles

4 Refine Schematic Architecture

Task 1. Refining Structural Elements
Task 2. Refining Connectors

Step 1. Identify Candidate Architecture styles

This step is to identify architecture styles suitable for designing the schematic architecture. It is carried out through the following tasks:

- Task 1, Observe Structural Characteristics, is to identify the structural properties and constraints of the target system that are relevant to informing its architectural design.
- Task 2, Determine Inherent Types of the System, is to identify the inherent types of the target system in order to narrow down and guide the selection of appropriate architecture styles.
- Task 3, Determine Candidate Architecture Styles, is to identify the most suitable architecture styles based on the system's inherent types and structural characteristics.

Step 2. Evaluate Candidate Architecture Styles

This step is to evaluate candidate architecture styles to determine their suitability for the target system. It is carried out through the following tasks:

- Task 1, Evaluate Applicable Situations, is to assess whether the target system aligns with the applicable conditions and assumptions defined for each candidate architecture style.
- Task 2, Evaluate Benefits, is to evaluate the extent to which the target system can leverage the benefits offered by each candidate architecture style.
- Task 3, Evaluate Drawbacks, is to analyze whether the target system can effectively manage or mitigate the potential drawbacks associated with each candidate architecture style.
- Task 4, Determine Applicability, is to determine the overall suitability of each candidate architecture style by synthesizing the evaluations of applicability, benefits, and drawbacks.

Step 3. Integrate Architecture Styles

This step is to incorporate the selected architecture styles into the schematic architecture of a target system. It is carried out through the following tasks:

- Task 1, Integrate Architecture Styles with Tiers, is to incorporate architecture styles that define structural organization in terms of system tiers.
- Task 2, Integrate Architecture Styles with Services, is to incorporate architecture styles that utilize external services delivered over a network.
- Task 3, Integrate Architecture Styles with Layers, is to incorporate architecture styles that follow a layered architectural approach.
- Task 4, Integrate Architecture Styles with Behavior, is to incorporate architecture styles that specify behavioral structures, such as invocation or interaction paradigms.
- Task 5, Integrate Architecture Styles with Adaptability, is to incorporate architecture styles that enhance the adaptability and flexibility of the target system.

- Task 6, Integrate Remaining Architecture Styles, is to incorporate any remaining architecture styles that have not yet been addressed in the preceding integration tasks.

Step 4. Refine Schematic Architecture

This step is to refine the schematic architecture by making additions and modifications to ensure it fully meets the requirements of the target system. It is carried out through the following tasks:

- Task 1, Refine Structural Elements, is to further develop and clarify the structural elements of the schematic architecture to ensure completeness and coherence.
- Task 2, Refine Connectors, is to refine the connectors within the schematic architecture, detailing the interaction mechanisms and communication paths among components.

A.4. Activity A4A. Design for Functional View

The purpose of this activity is to design the architecture for the functional view, which focuses on modeling system functionality, identifying functional components, defining their interfaces, and designing the components while accounting for functional variability. This activity consists of five steps, each consisting of specific tasks, as shown below.

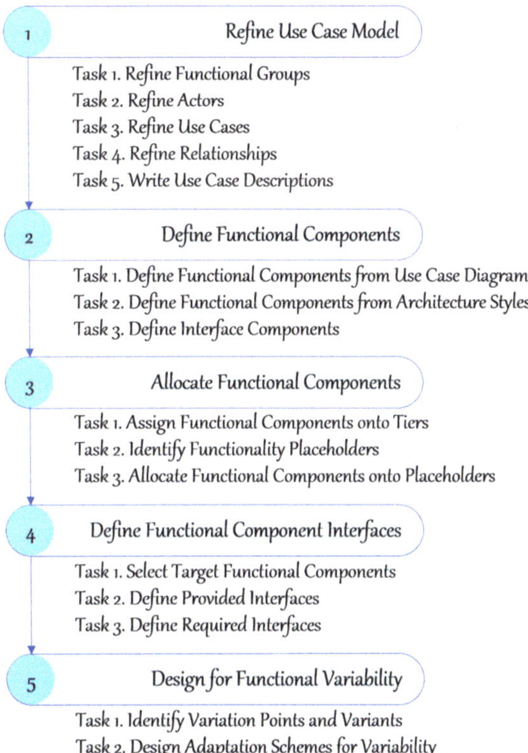

Step 1. Refine Use Case Model

This step is to refine the context-level use case diagram and provide detailed descriptions for use cases with complex functionality. It is carried out through the following tasks:

- Task 1, Refine Functional Groups, is to refine the functional groups initially identified in the context model to enhance their clarity and alignment with system functionality.
- Task 2, Refine Actors, is to refine the actors represented in the context-level use case diagram, ensuring accurate depiction of their roles and interactions with the system.
- Task 3, Refine Use Cases, is to refine the use cases in the context-level use case diagram to better capture the system's functional behavior.
- Task 4, Refine Relationships, is to refine the relationships in the context-level use case diagram, including associations between actors and use cases as well as dependencies among use cases.
- Task 5, Write Use Case Descriptions, is to select use cases that exhibit high complexity, critical functionality, or user-centered behavior and to document detailed descriptions for each selected use case.

Step 2. Define Functional Components

This step is to define the functional components of the target system based on the use case diagram, by considering the cohesiveness of functionality. It is carried out through the following tasks:

- Task 1, Define Functional Components from Use Case Diagram, is to identify functional components by grouping related use cases into cohesive units that represent distinct functionalities of the system.
- Task 2, Define Functional Components from Architecture Styles, is to define functional components based on the structural and organizational principles of the selected architecture style.
- Task 3, Define Interface Components, is to identify the interface components of the target system, where each interface component specifies the protocols and mechanisms for external or inter-component interactions.

Step 3. Allocate Functional Components

This step is to allocate the function components to their respective functionality placeholders within a schematic architecture. It is carried out through the following tasks:

- Task 1, Assign Functional Components onto Tiers, is to allocate each functional component to one or more tiers within the schematic architecture, based on its role and functional scope.

- Task 2, Identify Functionality Placeholders, is to identify functionality placeholders within the schematic architecture that represent designated locations for hosting functional components.
- Task 3, Allocate Functional Components onto Placeholders, is to assign the functional components to their corresponding functionality placeholders, ensuring consistency with the architectural structure and design intent.

Step 4. Define Functional Component Interfaces

This step is to specify the interfaces of selected functional components. It is carried out through the following tasks:

- Task 1, Select Target Functional Components, is to identify the functional components that require a precise and rigorous definition of their interfaces.
- Task 2, Define Provided Interface, is to define the provided interface of black-box functional components, where the provided interface specifies the set of services offered to other components.
- Task 3, Define Required Interface, is to define the required interface for functional components that rely on services offered by other components, specifying the methods and interactions needed for integration.

Step 5. Design for Functional Variability

This step is to model the variability inherent in functional components and design them to support flexible configurations that accommodate diverse static and dynamic functional demands while maintaining system consistency and integrity. It is carried out through the following tasks:

- Task 1, Identify Variation Points and Variants, is to identify inherent variability within functional components and explicitly define it through well-specified variation points and their corresponding variants.
- Task 2, Design Adaptation Schemes for Variability, is to design appropriate adaptation schemes that effectively manage the identified variability within each functional component.

A.5. Activity A4B. Design for Information View

The purpose of this activity is to design the architecture for the information view of the target system, which involves identifying persistent datasets, defining their relationships, and mapping them to persistent storage. This activity consists of five steps, each consisting of specific tasks, as shown below.

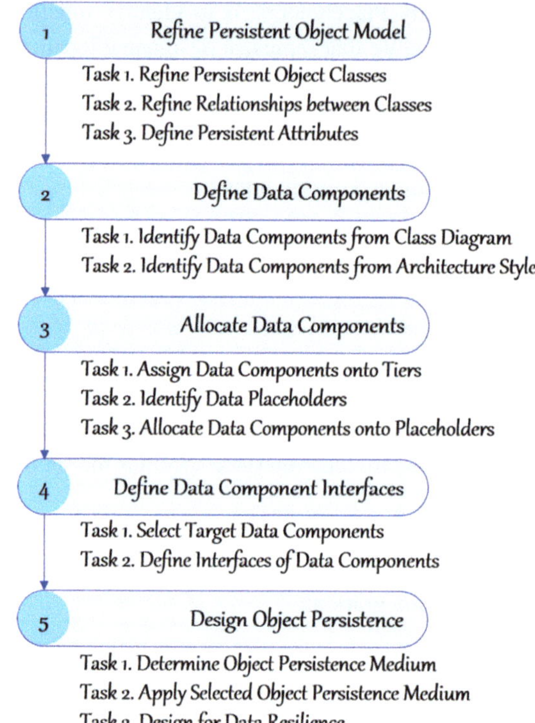

Step 1. Refine Persistent Object Model

This step is to produce a well-defined persistent object model by refining and enhancing the context-level object model. It is carried out through the following tasks:

- Task 1, Refine Persistent Object Classes, is to refine the persistent object classes defined in the context-level class diagram to ensure they accurately represent the system's data structures.
- Task 2, Refine Relationships between Classes, is to refine the relationships among classes, including the specification of cardinalities to indicate instance-level associations.
- Task 3, Define Persistent Attributes, is to define the essential persistent attributes for each class in the class diagram, ensuring completeness and alignment with the system's data requirements.

Step 2. Define Data Components

This step is to derive data components from the refined class diagram where a data component is a cohesive unit that consists of closely related classes. It is carried out through the following tasks:

- Task 1, Identify Data Components from Class Diagram, is to identify data components by grouping closely related classes based on their structural and semantic relationships.
- Task 2, Identify Data Components from Architecture Styles, is to define data components that represent persistent datasets manipulated by functional components according to the selected architecture styles.

Step 3. Allocate Data Components

This step is to assign the data components to their respective data placeholders within a schematic architecture. It is carried out through the following tasks:

- Task 1, Assign Data Components onto Tiers, is to allocate each data component to one or more tiers within the schematic architecture, based on its storage and access characteristics.
- Task 2, Identify Data Placeholders, is to identify data placeholders represented in the schematic architecture, which serve as designated locations for data component deployment.
- Task 3, Allocate Data Components onto Placeholders, is to assign the data components to their corresponding data placeholders, ensuring alignment with the architectural structure and data access requirements.

Step 4. Define Data Component Interfaces

This step is to define the interfaces for selected data components. It is carried out through the following tasks:

- Task 1, Select Target Data Components, is to identify the data components that require a precise and well-defined specification of their interfaces.
- Task 2, Define Interfaces of Data Components, is to define the interfaces of the selected data components, specifying the operations for accessing and manipulating the underlying persistent data.

Step 5. Design Object Persistence

This step is to design object persistence for the data components. It is carried out through the following tasks:

- Task 1, Determine Object Persistence Medium, is to identify the most appropriate medium for supporting object persistence based on the system's storage and access requirements.
- Task 2, Apply Selected Object Persistence Medium, is to apply the chosen persistence medium to provide reliable storage for persistent objects in accordance with the system's design.
- Task 3, Design for Data Resilience, is to design the object persistence mechanism to ensure that data remains accessible, consistent, and recoverable in the event of disruptions or failures.

A.6. Activity A4c. Design for Behavior View

The purpose of this activity is to design the architecture for the behavior view of the target system, which focuses on the system's runtime behavior and the detailed control flows of selected behavioral elements. This activity consists of three steps, each consisting of specific tasks, as shown below.

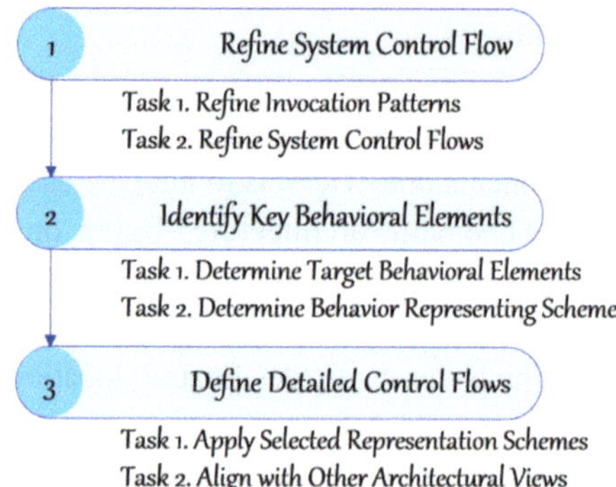

Step 1. Refine System Control Flow

This step is to refine the context-level system control flow with detailed observations on the systems' runtime behavior. It is carried out through the following tasks:

- Task 1, Refine Invocation Patterns, is to refine the invocation patterns of functional components identified during the behavior context analysis, ensuring they accurately represent component interactions.
- Task 2, Refine System Control Flows, is to refine the context-level activity diagrams by incorporating the updated behavioral scope and the refined interaction patterns among components.

Step 2. Identify Key Behavioral Elements

This step is to identify key behavioral elements and to specify the most appropriate behavior representation schemes for these selected elements. It is carried out through the following tasks:

- Task 1, Determine Target Behavioral Elements, is to identify the behavioral elements that require detailed control flow modeling based on their complexity, criticality, or interaction characteristics.
- Task 2, Determine Behavior Representation Schemes, is to identify the most appropriate representation scheme for modeling the detailed control flow of each selected behavioral element.

Step 3. Define Detailed Control Flows

This step is to represent the detailed control flows for the selected behavioral elements by adhering to the representation schemes. It is carried out through the following tasks:

- Task 1, Apply Selected Representation Schemes, is to define the detailed control flow of each behavioral element using its designated behavior representation scheme.
- Task 2, Align with Other Architectural Views, is to analyze the impact of the detailed control flow designs on other architectural views and refine the overall architecture to ensure consistency and alignment across views.

A.7. Activity A4d. Design for Deployment View

The purpose of this activity is to design the architecture for the deployment view of the target system, which focuses on the physical and logical configuration of the system's infrastructure. This activity consists of four steps, each consisting of specific tasks, as shown below.

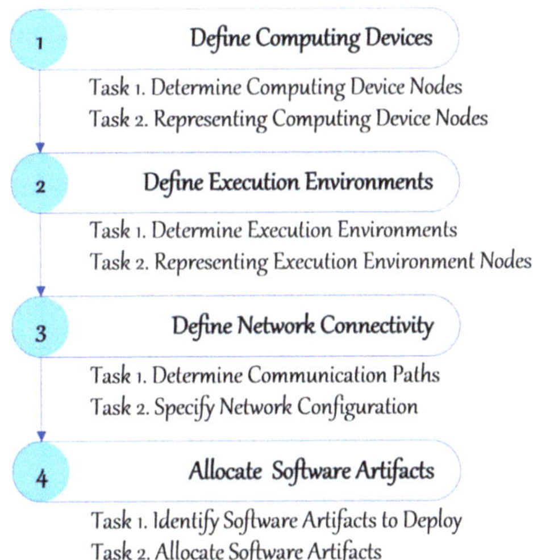

Step 1. Define Computing Device Nodes

This step is to specify the hardware configuration of computing device nodes for the target system. It is carried out through the following tasks:

- Task 1, Determine Computing Device Nodes, is to identify the computing device nodes required by the system through analysis of its schematic architecture.

- Task 2, Represent Computing Device Nodes, is to visually represent the identified computing device nodes using UML notation, applying the stereotype «device» to denote their role in the system.

Step 2. Define Execution Environments
This step is to specify the execution environment of each computing device node in the system. It is carried out through the following tasks:
- Task 1, Determine Execution Environments, is to identify the execution environments required for each computing device node, based on the system's deployment requirements.
- Task 2, Represent Execution Environment Nodes, is to define and visually represent the execution environment nodes in the deployment diagram, applying the UML stereotype «executionEnvironment».

Step 3. Define Network Connectivity
This step is to define the network connectivity among nodes, represented by communication paths. It is carried out through the following tasks:
- Task 1, Determine Communication Paths, is to identify the communication paths among nodes in the deployment diagram, reflecting the system's required interactions across distributed components.
- Task 2, Specify Network Configuration, is to define the network configurations for the identified communication paths, including parameters such as protocols, port numbers, bandwidth, and latency.

Step 4. Allocate Software Artifacts
This step is to allocate software artifacts onto the identified execution environment nodes. It is carried out through the following tasks:
- Task 1, Identify Software Artifacts to Deploy, is to determine the software artifacts that need to be deployed onto execution environment nodes based on the system's architectural design.
- Task 2, Allocate Software Artifacts, is to assign the identified software artifacts to the appropriate execution environment nodes within the deployment diagram.

A.8. Activity A5. Design for Non-Functional Requirements

The purpose of this activity is to design the architecture to address the non-functional requirements of the target system by augmenting the view-based architectural design with architectural tactics that effectively fulfill the identified non-functional requirements. This activity consists of six steps, each consisting of specific tasks, as shown below.

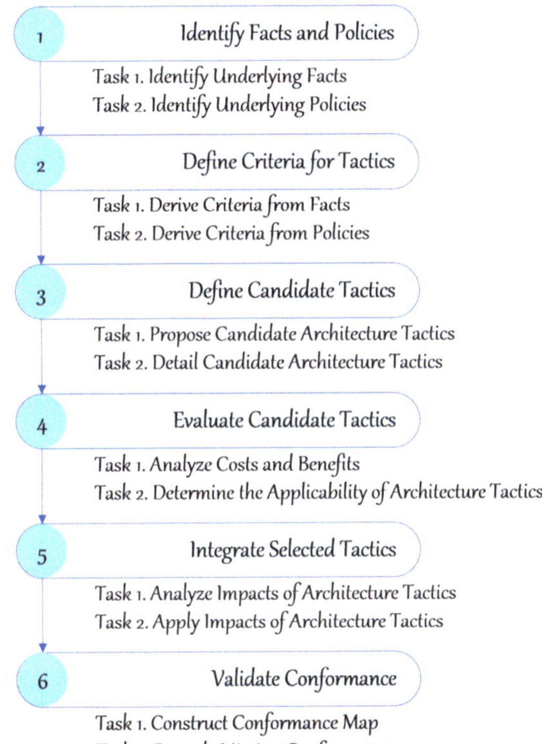

Step 1. Identify Facts and Policies

This step is to identify facts and policies that underline the non-functional requirements, serving as the foundational elements for designing architectural tactics. It is carried out through the following tasks:

- Task 1, Identify Underlying Facts, is to identify the system-specific facts that are associated with the given non-functional requirements and may influence architectural decisions.
- Task 2, Identify Underlying Policies, is to identify the organizational or regulatory policies related to the given non-functional requirements that must be considered in the architectural design.

Step 2. Define Criteria for Tactics

This step is to define the criteria for deriving architectural tactics that address the given non-functional requirement. It is carried out through the following tasks:

- Task 1, Derive Criteria from Facts, is to systematically derive criteria from underlying facts by rephrasing them into clear, instructive, and directive statements that support the formulation of effective architecture tactics.

- Task 2, Derive Criteria from Policies, is to derive criteria from underlying policies by translating them into clear, instructive, and actionable statements that guide the development of architecture tactics aligned with architectural objectives.

Step 3. Define Candidate Tactics

This step is to define candidate architecture tactics based on the identified criteria. It is carried out through the following tasks:

- Task 1, Propose Candidate Architecture Tactics, is to propose candidate architectural tactics derived from the previously identified criteria, ensuring alignment with the targeted non-functional requirements.
- Task 2, Detail Candidate Architecture Tactics, is to comprehensively define each candidate architectural tactic by specifying its structure, behavior, and technical implementation details.

Step 4. Evaluate Candidate Tactics

This step is to evaluate the candidate architectural tactics and select the most appropriate ones to be incorporated into the architectural design process. It is carried out through the following tasks:

- Task 1, Analyze Costs and Benefits, is to assess the costs and benefits associated with each candidate architectural tactic, considering factors such as implementation effort, resource consumption, and impact on system quality.
- Task 2, Determine the Applicability of Architecture Tactics, is to evaluate the suitability of each candidate architectural tactic by determining whether it should be adopted or discarded based on the results of the cost-benefit analysis.

Step 5. Integrate Selected Tactics

This step is to evaluate the impacts of the selected architectural tactics and integrate them into the view-based architectural design. It is carried out through the following tasks:

- Task 1, Analyze Impacts of Architecture Tactics, is to evaluate the influence of each selected architectural tactic on the various architectural views and, where applicable, on the schematic architecture.
- Task 2, Apply Impacts of Architecture Tactics, is to incorporate the selected architectural tactics into the existing architectural design, ensuring consistency with the outcomes of the preceding impact analysis.

Step 6. Validate Conformance

This step is to validate the conformance of intermediate artifacts to their preceding artifacts using a conformance map. It is carried out through the following tasks:

- Task 1, Construct Conformance Map, is to create a conformance map that illustrates the relationships between the artifacts produced in the current step and those generated in the preceding step, highlighting how they align with one another.

- Task 2, Remedy Missing Conformance, is to evaluate the conformance relationships represented in the conformance map and address any identified gaps by revising the design to ensure proper alignment and consistency across all related artifacts.

A.9. Activity A6. Architecture Evaluation

The purpose of this activity is to evaluate the architecture design of the target system, with the goal of identifying potential risks, issues, drawbacks, and areas for improvement to ensure alignment with the given functional and non-functional requirements. This activity consists of three steps, each consisting of specific tasks, as shown below.

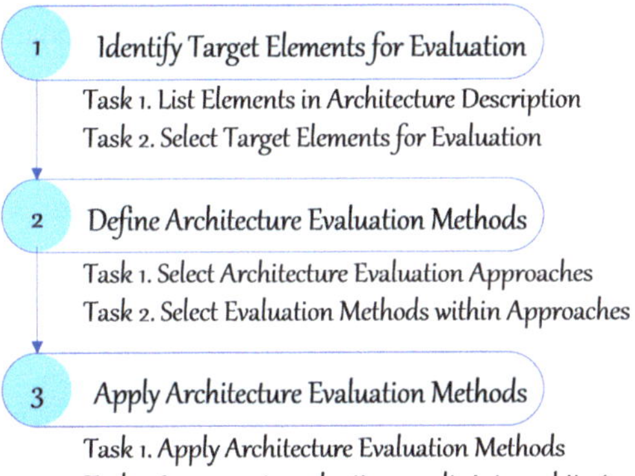

Step 1. Identify Target Elements for Evaluation
This step is to identify the specific elements in the architecture design that require evaluation. It is carried out through the following tasks:

- Task 1, List Elements in Architecture Description, is to enumerate all design elements included in the architectural description of the target system.
- Task 2, Select Target Elements for Evaluation, is to identify and select specific elements within the architectural description that require focused evaluation based on their importance, complexity, or potential risk.

Step 2. Define Architecture Evaluation Methods
This step is to determine and select appropriate methods for evaluating the design elements of architecture description. It is carried out through the following tasks:

- Task 1, Select Architecture Evaluation Approaches, is to choose the most appropriate evaluation approaches for assessing the selected design elements, considering the nature and criticality of each element.

- Task 2, Select Evaluation Methods within Approaches, is to identify the most suitable evaluation methods for each chosen architecture evaluation approach, ensuring that they are well aligned with the characteristics of the selected design elements.

Step 3. Apply Architecture Evaluation Methods

This task is to apply selected architecture evaluation methods and enhance the architecture design by incorporating feedback from the evaluation results. It is carried out through the following tasks:

- Task 1, Evaluate Architecture Design with Selected Methods, is to assess the architecture design by systematically applying the selected evaluation methods to the targeted design elements.
- Task 2, Incorporate Evaluation Results into Architecture, is to refine the architecture design by systematically integrating feedback and recommendations derived from the evaluation results.

Appendix B. SRS for Case Study System

This book presents the Unified Architecture Process through a case study, providing numerous examples throughout the methodology. The case study centers around a *Car Rental Management System*, which is consistently used to illustrate various architectural design principles and methods.

B.1. System Overview

The *Car Rental Management System* is a software application designed to provide a comprehensive set of functions for managing car rental operations. It supports essential functionalities such as customer and staff profile management, vehicle inventory management, reservation processing, checkout and return operations, and business analytics.

The system is deployed with a centralized server and multiple client applications, as depicted in Fig. B.1.

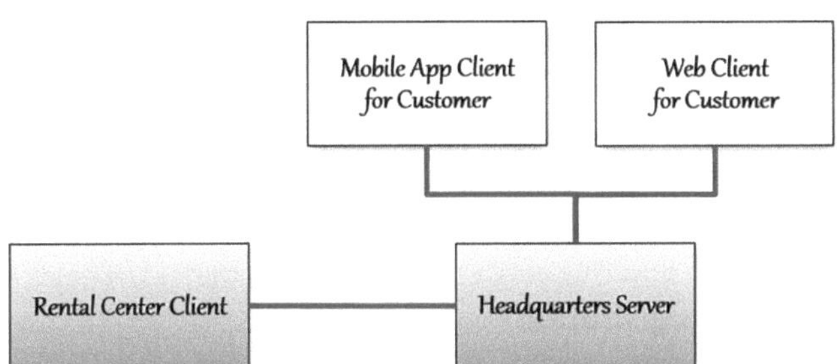

Fig. B.1 Configuration of the Car Rental Management System

- **Headquarters Server**
  This tier delivers server-side functionalities to all connected client applications. It supports centralized car inventory management, oversight of service quality across rental centers, business analytics, and maintenance of a master database.

S. D. Kim, M. Kim, *Hands-on Software Architecture*,
https://doi.org/10.1007/978-3-032-01184-8

- **Rental Center Client**
  This tier is used by staff at rental centers to perform day-to-day operations such as managing vehicle inventory, processing checkouts and returns, handling payments, and generating reports. It interacts directly with the Headquarters Server.
- **Mobile App Client**
  This mobile app offers customers essential functionalities, including making reservations and retrieving rental contracts. It communicates with the Headquarters Server to fulfill these requests.
- **Web Client**
  This tier provides the same functionalities as the Mobile App Client through a Web-based interface.

B.2. Functional Requirements

Functional requirements are grouped by the core functionalities offered by the system.

B.2.1. Customer Profile Management

This functionality manages customer profiles and oversees authentication processes, including login and logout operations. Each customer profile contains key information such as personal identification, contact details, payment methods, loyalty program status, and authentication credentials. The system periodically analyzes rental history to identify high-volume customers and automatically upgrades them to VIP membership. VIP members receive benefits such as expedited checkout and access to exclusive rental discounts.

B.2.2. Staff Profile Management

This functionality manages staff profiles and oversees authentication activities, including login and logout operations. Each staff profile contains essential information such as identification, contact details, department affiliation, and authentication credentials. Profiles are maintained for employees assigned to either rental centers or the headquarters office.

B.2.3. Rental Center Registration

This functionality manages the profiles of the company's rental centers. These centers are strategically located—often near airports or in city centers—to serve areas with high customer demand. Each rental center profile includes key attributes such as location details, operating hours, service capabilities, and current inventory information.

B.2.4. Inventory Management

This functionality manages the rental car inventory to ensure accuracy and availability for customer use. Two distinct types of vehicle profiles are maintained:

- **Car Model Profile**: Contains information such as manufacturer, model name, model year, available trims, and technical specifications

- **Car Item Profile**: Contains details of individual vehicles, including model association, VIN, color, equipment options, purchase date, and condition history
  Key operations include:
- **Maintaining a Portfolio of Car Models**
  The rental company establishes an optimal portfolio of car models by balancing market appeal with cost-efficiency in procurement and maintenance. This portfolio typically comprises a diverse selection of vehicle types (e.g., sedans, SUVs, vans) and powertrain configurations (e.g., gasoline, hybrid, electric). Priority is assigned to models that demonstrate mechanical reliability, low maintenance costs, and high customer preference.
- **Procuring New Vehicles Based on Projected Demand**
  The company acquires new vehicles in response to rental demand, ensuring that each rental center maintains an adequate supply to meet customer requirements. This demand-driven procurement strategy enables flexible adaptation to demand fluctuations while minimizing costs associated with inventory shortages and overstock.
- **Relocating Vehicles Among Rental Centers to Optimize Regional Availability**
  Vehicles are redistributed among rental centers as necessary to optimize availability across locations. Relocation decisions are guided by current rental activity, future reservations, and demand forecasts, ensuring that the fleet is strategically positioned to effectively accommodate anticipated demand.
- **Retiring Vehicles**
- Rental vehicles are periodically assessed and retired from the fleet when they no longer satisfy the company's operational standards. The decision to retire a vehicle is determined based on several key factors:
  - **Age**: Vehicles are retired when they reach a certain age or mileage, as older cars often need more maintenance and may not meet customer expectations.
  - **Mechanical integrity**: Vehicles with frequent mechanical problems or reduced performance are retired to ensure safety, reduce maintenance costs, and maintain customer satisfaction.
  - **Accident history**: Vehicles involved in major accidents or with significant damage may be retired early due to safety concerns, high repair costs, or lower resale value.

B.2.5. Rental Fee Pricing

This functionality determines optimal rental rates, which play a critical role in influencing customer demand and overall profitability. Rental fees are strategically adjusted to balance competitive pricing with revenue maximization, ensuring both market responsiveness and financial efficiency.

Rental fees are periodically adjusted based on several key factors to align with market dynamics and optimize profitability:

- **Popularity of Car Models**
  Rates may be increased for high-demand models that are favored by customers due to brand appeal or desirable features.

- **Demand for Specific Car Models**
  Prices are dynamically adjusted according to current demand levels. High-demand models may incur rate increases, while underutilized models may be discounted to improve fleet utilization.
- **Seasonal Demand Fluctuations**
  Rates are modified to reflect predictable seasonal trends, such as holidays or vacation periods, during which rental activity typically increases. Higher pricing during these peaks helps optimize revenue.
- **Special Events**
  During large-scale events (e.g., exhibitions, conferences, concerts, or sporting events), rental rates are elevated to capture increased demand and ensure vehicle availability for premium-paying customers.

Conversely, in the absence of major events, rental rates may revert to standard or discounted levels to attract customers and maintain consistent rental volume. By strategically aligning pricing with the timing and location of special events, the company can enhance fleet utilization, respond effectively to short-term demand surges, and improve overall profitability.

B.2.6. Reservation Management

This functionality supports the end-to-end management of rental car reservations. It enables customers to create, view, modify, and cancel reservations as needed. Upon receiving a reservation request, the system checks the projected inventory for the specified check-out date to assess the availability of the requested car model. If projected availability is insufficient, the system restricts the reservation to prevent overbooking.

B.2.7. Checkout Management

This functionality supports the vehicle checkout process by guiding staff members through each step of the procedure, as outlined in Fig. B.2.

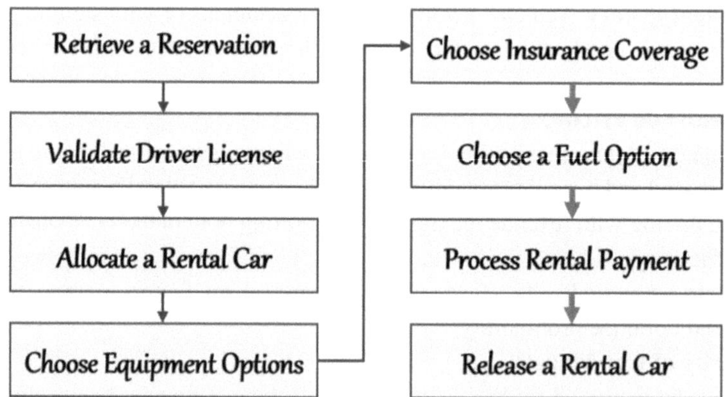

Fig. B.2 Procedure of rental car checkout process

- **Step 1. Retrieve a Reservation**
  A staff member retrieves reservation details for customers with existing bookings. For walk-in customers without a reservation, service is provided based on current vehicle availability.
- **Step 2. Validate Driver's License**
  The customer's driver's license is verified using an external validation system. If the license is invalid, the checkout process is terminated.
- **Step 3. Allocate a Rental Car**
  A staff member confirms the rental details and assigns a vehicle that matches the customer's specified preferences.
- **Step 4. Choose Equipment Options**
  The customer may select optional equipment such as a GPS device, tollway pass, or child car seat.
- **Step 5. Choose Insurance Coverage**
  The customer selects an insurance option, which may include no coverage, a damage waiver, or full coverage. If no coverage is selected, the staff verifies that the customer's personal insurance includes rental vehicles.
- **Step 6. Choose a Fuel Option**
  The customer chooses a fuel policy (e.g., pre-purchase or refill upon return). This option applies only to fuel-powered vehicles.
- **Step 7. Process Rental Payment**
  The system calculates the total rental cost, including charges for insurance, equipment, and fuel. A staff member then processes the payment using the customer's preferred method, such as credit card, digital wallet, or cash.
- **Step 8. Release a Rental Car**
  Upon completion of the rental agreement, the vehicle is released to the customer, and the car key is provided.

B.2.8. In-Rental Management

This functionality supports operations related to active rentals while the vehicle is in the customer's possession. It ensures service continuity, safety, and compliance throughout the rental period through the following activities:

- **Replacing Rental Vehicles**
  If a rental vehicle becomes inoperable due to mechanical failure or other issues, a replacement vehicle is promptly provided to minimize disruption to the customer.
- **Handling Vehicle Accidents**
  In the event of an accident involving a rental vehicle, the company offers necessary assistance to help the customer manage the incident and resolve related matters effectively.
- **Tracking Vehicle Location**
  Customers intending to travel abroad with a rental vehicle must notify staff in advance. The staff arranges appropriate insurance coverage for international use, subject to

company policies. Since cross-border travel is often restricted, GPS-enabled vehicles are used to track real-time locations. If a vehicle crosses a national border without authorization, the system automatically issues an alert, prompting staff to take necessary action.

B.2.9. Return Management

This functionality supports the processing of vehicle returns, which are categorized based on their timeliness:

- **Return by Due Date/Time**
  A staff member inspects the returned vehicle's mileage, fuel level, and overall condition. Any additional charges—such as those for excess mileage or insufficient fuel—are calculated and applied accordingly.
- **Return after Due Date/Time**
  For late returns, the system assesses additional fees based on the number of days or hours exceeding the original return deadline.

B.2.10. Car Maintenance

This functionality supports the monitoring and documentation of vehicle maintenance activities to ensure the operational reliability and safety of the rental fleet. Typical maintenance tasks include:

- **Refueling Vehicles**
  Refilling fuel tanks of gasoline or diesel-powered vehicles to ensure they are ready for the next rental
- **Charging Electric Vehicles**
  Recharging the batteries of electric vehicles to maintain sufficient charge levels for upcoming rentals
- **Reconditioning Vehicles**
  Performing cosmetic and minor functional enhancements to restore the vehicle's appearance and usability
- **Performing Repairs**
  Addressing mechanical or electrical issues to restore the vehicle to operational condition and ensure safety
- **Conducting Preventive Maintenance**
  Carrying out scheduled maintenance tasks, such as oil changes and brake inspections, to prevent future failures and extend vehicle lifespan

B.2.11. Business Analytics

This functionality performs comprehensive analysis of rental operations to support data-driven decision-making and strategic planning. It generates both scheduled and on-demand reports that offer insights into key aspects of the business. Areas of analysis include inventory utilization, rental performance, reservation trends, maintenance and repair activities, and profitability metrics. These analytics provide actionable intelligence to optimize operations and enhance overall business outcomes.

B.3. Non-Functional Requirements

A range of NFRs can be derived from stakeholder needs. However, since this is a case study system, the focus is limited to the following representative NFRs.

B.3.1. NFR #1. Enhancing the Profitability of Car Rental Business

Profitability reflects the company's ability to generate a positive financial return from its operations. It indicates how effectively the organization manages pricing, expenses, and revenue to ensure that income from rentals exceeds the costs of acquiring, maintaining, and operating the fleet, along with other operational expenditures.

- **Maximizing Net Profits**
  The system should be designed to support revenue-generating operations that enhance net profit. This includes enabling features such as reservation promotions, dynamic rental fee pricing, and the sale of supplementary services (e.g., insurance and equipment options). Among these, rental pricing is a particularly critical strategy, requiring a multifactorial approach based on customer demand, vehicle popularity, seasonality, and special events.
- **Minimizing Expenses**
  The system should also facilitate cost-saving operations, such as optimizing vehicle acquisition strategies, automating routine rental processes, and efficiently managing inventory levels. These capabilities contribute to reducing operational costs and improving overall profitability through increased cost-effectiveness and process efficiency.

B.3.2. NFR #2. Providing a Wide Range of Applicability

Applicability refers to the system's capacity to serve diverse use cases within the car rental domain. The system should be designed to accommodate varying operational needs across different car rental businesses by addressing the following concerns:

- **Support for Commonalities**
  The system must model core functionalities shared across all car rental operations. Failing to incorporate these may result in missing essential features, reducing the system's utility and generalizability.
- **Support for Variability**
  Since operational practices differ among rental companies, the system must be capable of addressing company-specific variations. Neglecting variability limits customization and hinders the system's adaptability.
- **Stakeholder Inquiry for Completeness**
  Architectural inquiries should be conducted to identify and clarify missing or ambiguous requirements, ensuring that the system accurately captures both common and variable aspects of rental operations.
- **Customizability of Variable Features**
  The system should support the efficient customization of variable elements such as pricing models, maintenance schedules, and loyalty program configurations. These customizations should be achievable without extensive effort or code modification.

By incorporating these design considerations, the system can offer broad applicability and adaptability across a range of business contexts.

B.3.3. NFR #3. Ensuring High Availability of Headquarters Server

High availability refers to the extent to which a system remains operational and accessible when needed. It is commonly measured as a percentage of uptime over a defined period. For the *Car Rental Management System*, ensuring the availability of the Headquarters Server is critical due to its central role in supporting all client applications.

To achieve high availability, the system must address the following considerations:

- **Continuous Operational Support**
  The Headquarters Server must provide 24/7 availability to ensure uninterrupted service for all connected client applications, including rental center clients, mobile apps, and Web clients.
- **Centralized Resource Dependency**
  Since the Master Repository is hosted on the Headquarters Server, any downtime directly affects access to essential data and system services, underscoring the need for robust availability measures.
- **Failure Resilience and Recovery**
  The system should be capable of withstanding hardware failures, software faults, or network disruptions. It must either prevent these issues or recover from them quickly to minimize downtime.
- **Quantifiable Reliability**
  Availability should be supported by measurable reliability metrics, often expressed as a percentage of operational time (e.g., 99.9% uptime), to ensure service-level expectations are met.

By meeting these criteria, the system can deliver dependable, continuous service across all its operational components.

Glossary

A

Action (in UML) A fundamental unit of executable behavior in an activity diagram, representing a single, fine-grained operation performed within the system's control flow.

Active Repository Architecture Style Architecture style characterized by extending the *Shared Repository style* with the capability for the central repository to actively notify data accessors about changes in data state, enabling timely updates and retrieval.

Activity (in UML) A unit of behavior represented in an activity diagram, typically comprising a collection of logically related actions that collectively achieve a specific objective within a workflow.

Activity (in UAP) A high-level unit of work in the *Unified Architecture Process*, focused on accomplishing a main design objective. UAP defines six core activities for systematically designing system architecture.

Activity Diagram A graphical representation in UML that depicts the dynamic behavior of a system, illustrating the flow of control or data between activities.

Actor An entity that interacts with a system to achieve a specific goal such as a user, external system, or device. An *activity actor* initiates interactions with the system by providing inputs or triggering events, whereas a *passive actor* responds to system-initiated actions without actively initiating interaction.

Adaptive System A system that dynamically modifies its behavior or configuration in response to changes in the environment or user requirements to maintain flexibility and optimize performance.

Aggregation A *part-of* relationship where one class represents the "whole" and contains instances of other classes as its "parts," depicted as a hollow diamond on the association line in a class diagram.

Architecture Description A structured representation of a system's architecture, documenting its components, relationships, and design decisions to address stakeholder concerns and guide development.

S. D. Kim, M. Kim, *Hands-on Software Architecture*,
https://doi.org/10.1007/978-3-032-01184-8

Architecture Evaluation A systematic and structured activity for assessing the quality, effectiveness, and overall suitability of a system's architectural design with respect to its intended requirements and constraints.

Architecture Evaluation Approach A high-level classification of strategies for assessing the quality and effectiveness of software architecture designs, encompassing qualitative, quantitative, or hybrid techniques to guide the evaluation process.

Architecture Evaluation Method A specific evaluation technique used within an architecture evaluation approach, providing a structured process for assessing design elements; multiple methods may be applicable to each evaluation criterion, requiring careful selection to align with design objectives and ensure effective analysis.

Architecture Style A high-level, reusable design abstraction that defines the structural organization, interaction patterns among components, and design constraints of a software system, providing a foundational guideline for its overall behavior and systematic development.

Architecture Tactic A design decision, strategy, or technique used to effectively address and realize a specific non-functional requirement.

Architecture Validation A process focused on determining whether the architecture meets stakeholders' needs, goals, and expectations, evaluating its suitability for fulfilling the given requirements.

Architecture Verification A process that ensures the architecture complies with established specifications, standards, and best practices, involving systematic analysis and testing to detect defects, inconsistencies, or deviations from the intended design, enabling timely corrections.

Architecture View A structured representation of a system's architecture from a specific perspective, tailored to address particular stakeholder concerns and highlight relevant aspects of the system.

Association Class A specialized class in a class diagram that represents an association relationship between two or more classes, used when the association requires its own attributes and methods.

B

Batch Sequential Architecture Style Architecture style characterized by the sequential execution of data manipulation components, where each component processes a batch of input data, produces an output, and passes it as input to the next component in the sequence.

Behavior Context A high-level description of the system's dynamic aspects, focusing on runtime behavior, control flows, and interactions between components.

Behavior View A representation of the dynamic behavior of a system, emphasizing the control flow and interactions within the system as a whole or among selected behavioral components.

Blackboard Architecture Style Architecture style characterized by a framework where independent knowledge sources, each with specialized expertise, collaborate to solve complex problems by interacting through a shared data structure called the *Blackboard*, enabling incremental problem-solving.

Boundary Context A description of the external environment of a system, defining its scope, interactions with external systems, and interfaces with external entities.

Broker Architecture Style Architecture style characterized by a middleware component, known as the broker, that coordinates interactions between clients and servers, facilitating communication and service requests in a decoupled, distributed system.

C

Candidate Architecture Style An architecture style identified as a potential fit for the schematic architecture, selected based on the intrinsic characteristics and requirements of the target system.

Candidate Architecture Tactic A potential architectural solution designed to address a specific non-functional requirement, developed in alignment with the identified criteria to ensure adherence to system requirements and constraints.

Class Diagram A graphical representation in UML that depicts classes, their attributes, methods, and relationships, often used to model the structure of persistent objects within a system.

Client-Server Architecture Style Architecture style characterized by a two-tier structure that partitions system functionality between service providers (servers) and service requesters (clients), enabling clear separation of concerns and enhancing scalability and maintainability.

Closed Loop Invocation An invocation pattern designed for continuous and uninterrupted execution of specific functionality, commonly used in self-managing systems like autonomous vehicles, with termination or pausing achieved through preemption or interruption mechanisms.

Component Diagram A diagram in UML that represents the structural organization of components, emphasizing their interfaces and interactions, effectively modeling blackbox components.

Composition A strong form of aggregation where the part objects' lifetimes are tied to the whole object, such that destroying the whole object also destroys its parts, represented by a filled diamond on the side of the whole class in a class diagram.

Computing Device Node A hardware configuration that provides dedicated computing power for a specific tier in a system's schematic architecture.

Conformance Map A graphical representation that illustrates the conformance relationships between artifacts produced in the current step and those in the preceding step, ensuring alignment with foundational predecessors and maintaining consistency with the design intent.

Context View A representation of the high-level understanding of the system's boundary, functionalities, datasets, and runtime behavior.

Cost Benefit Analysis A process used to evaluate the trade-offs of implementing specific architectural tactics by comparing the expected benefits to the associated costs, considering factors such as development effort, resource allocation, operational efficiency, and alignment with system goals.

D

Data Component A cohesive unit derived from the refined class diagram, consisting of closely related classes grouped together based on their interrelationships.

Data Flow Diagram (DFD) A graphical representation of a system that illustrates the flow of data between processes, external entities (terminals), and data stores within the system.

Data Flow System A system characterized by an architectural configuration of components dedicated to data manipulation, where large volumes of data flow between components, each performing specific operations and passing the modified data to subsequent components.

Data Placeholder A container within a schematic architecture designated for accommodating data components, often identified within layers and partitions of a layer.

Dependency A relationship between two classes where one class temporarily depends on or uses the other, represented by a dashed arrow pointing from the dependent class to the supplier class.

Deployment Diagram A graphical representation in UML that depicts the physical deployment of software artifacts onto nodes, illustrating the system's hardware configuration, execution environments, and network connectivity.

Deployment View A representation of the system's physical deployment, showing the mapping of software artifacts to hardware resources and their configurations.

Design Pattern A generalized, reusable solution to a recurring design problem within a given context, formulated using established best practices. Design patterns are categorized into three major types: *Creational*, *Structural*, and *Behavioral* patterns.

Development View A representation of the system's implementation structure, detailing the organization of software modules, components, and their dependencies.

Dispatcher Architecture Style Architecture style characterized by a middleware component, known as the dispatcher, that distributes client requests to registered servers by identifying an appropriate server with high Quality of Service and providing the server's reference to the client, enabling direct client-server interaction without intermediary intervention.

E

Edge Computing Architecture Style Architecture style characterized by a distributed computing framework that places computing resources and data storage near data sources, such as IoT devices, to reduce latency, improve bandwidth efficiency, enhance system performance, and increase data privacy through localized processing.

Event-Based Invocation An invocation pattern for triggering specific functionality in response to events, with event emitters and handlers operating asynchronously across the same or different tiers for distributed event-driven processing.

Event-Based System A system structured around a control flow driven by events, which can originate from sources such as user interactions, hardware devices, software agents, or other software components.

Event-Driven Architecture Style Architecture style characterized by orchestrating the production, detection, and consumption of events, where an event signifies a significant change in state or an occurrence identified within a system.

Execution Environment Node A logical container in a Deployment Diagram representing a software execution context—such as a virtual machine, application server, or operating system—within which components or artifacts are deployed and executed.

F

Formal Method An evaluation approach that employs mathematically rigorous techniques—such as model checking, theorem proving, and formal specification—to verify the correctness, consistency, and compliance of a software architecture with its defined requirements and specifications.

Functional Component A software module defined according to the selected architecture style, characterized by a set of specific functions, relationships, and interactions essential to support the style's core features and behaviors.

Functional Context A high-level description of the system's functional aspects, including core functionalities, functional components, and their interactions required to fulfill user and system-level requirements.

Functional Group A distinct category of system functionality, enabling the system's overall functionality to be organized and understood as a collection of cohesive functional groups

Functional Requirement A specification of the system's functionality or behavior, detailing the operations or services it must perform to meet stakeholder needs.

Functional Variability The capability of functional components to support flexible configurations that address diverse static and dynamic functional demands while maintaining system consistency and integrity.

Functional View A representation of the system's functionalities, functional components, and their interfaces to meet stakeholder needs.

Functionality Placeholder A container within a schematic architecture, typically located in layers or partitions, designated to accommodate functional components and support specific functionalities.

H

Hardware Abstraction Layer (HAL) A software layer that defines standardized interfaces to abstract and mediate interactions between application-level software and underlying hardware components, promoting portability, modularity, and hardware-independence in system design.

Hierarchical Model-View-Controller (HMVC) Architecture Style Architecture style characterized by organizing a system as a hierarchy of multiple MVC triads, where each triad functions as a module or subsystem, with controllers interacting to promote modularity, reusability, and scalability in large-scale, complex systems.

I

Impacts of Architecture Tactics The effects of selected architectural tactics on various architectural views and the schematic architecture, which may include additions or modifications to design elements in the views and refinements to specific aspects of the architecture, ensuring alignment with both functional and non-functional requirements.

Include Relationship A relationship in a use case diagram where an *Included* use case is always invoked as a mandatory part of the functionality of a *Base* use case.

Information Context A high-level description of the system's data-related aspects, including datasets, data flows, and the relationships between data components.

Information View A representation of the system's persistent datasets, relationships, and persistence.

Inheritance A generalization relationship between a superclass and a subclass, where the subclass inherits attributes, methods, and relationships from the superclass, enabling reusability and hierarchical class organization.

Inter-tier Event An event generated in one tier and processed in another, facilitated by inter-tier messaging schemes for communication and coordination across system layers or components.

Interface A defined set of methods or protocols that specify how components interact with each other, allowing communication and data exchange between different parts of a system.

Interface Component A component that specifies a set of public methods to define interactions and data exchanges with other system components or external entities, ensuring standardized communication without implementing the underlying functionality.

Intra-tier Event An event generated and processed within the same tier, typically using message broadcasting schemes for local event handling among components in the tier.

Invocation Pattern A reusable control flow in system behavior modeling, defined by a specific sequence of actions to achieve a distinct type of system behavior.

L

Layered Architecture Style Architecture style characterized by structuring a system into a hierarchy of layers, where each layer handles specific responsibilities and provides services to the layer above, creating a virtual machine-like abstraction for the upper layer.

Layered System A system structured as a series of hierarchical layers, where each layer provides specific functionalities and services to the layer above it while relying on the layer below for support.

Load-Balancing System A system with a structural layout that includes multiple servers and a load balancer, designed to distribute workloads evenly across servers, improving performance, reliability, and redundancy while preventing server overloads.

Logical Object Class A class that represents abstract concepts or system constructs, such as those managing transactions, sessions, or configuration settings, which are essential for system functionality but do not correspond to physical entities.

M

Mapping to Relational Database The process of organizing and storing data in a tabular format using relational databases, facilitated by Object-Relational Mapping to bridge the gap between object-oriented programming and relational databases.

Master-Slave Architecture Style Architecture style characterized by centralized workflow control orchestrated by a coordinating component, referred to as the Master, which distributes tasks to service components known as Slaves and aggregates their results.

Microkernel Architecture Style Architecture style characterized by dividing system responsibilities between a minimal core that provides essential services and a set of user-space services, or plug-in components, that extend system functionality, promoting modularity and flexibility.

Microservices Architecture Style Architecture style characterized by organizing a system as a collection of small, independently developed, deployed, and maintained services, each providing a specific business capability, enabling greater agility and scalability.

Method Signature A definition that specifies a method's name, visibility, input parameters, return type, and any exceptions it may throw.

Model-Based Architecture Evaluation An evaluation approach that involves creating architectural models and analyzing them using tools such as simulation, static analysis, or mathematical modeling to evaluate the performance, reliability, and other qualities of the architecture.

Model-View-Controller (MVC) Architecture Style Architecture style characterized by structuring a system into three layers—Model, View, and Controller—as a specialized form of Layered Architecture, aimed at simplifying complex application development, ensuring maintainability, and facilitating scalability.

Monolithic Architecture Architecture style characterized by developing an entire system as a single, unified unit, where all functionalities are tightly coupled and operate as a single service.

N

Network Configuration A specification within a UML Deployment Diagram that defines the configuration of communication paths between nodes, including descriptive attributes such as protocol, bandwidth, latency, and security properties.

Non-Functional Requirement (NFR) The quality attributes or operational constraints that a system must satisfy to ensure it performs effectively under specified conditions.

N-Tier Architecture Style Architecture style characterized by organizing a system into distinct, physically separated tiers, each running on separate computer systems, to handle specific responsibilities and interact over a network to deliver the system's functionality.

O

Object Persistence The design of mechanisms to ensure the long-term storage and retrieval of data components, typically implemented using relational or NoSQL database systems, or cloud-based storage services.

Object-Oriented Analysis and Design (OOAD) A structured and disciplined design methodology in which a target system is analyzed and designed based on the principles of the object-oriented paradigm.

Open-Closed Principle (OCP) A fundamental design principle in software engineering asserting that software entities, such as classes, modules, and functions, should be open for extension but closed for modification.

Operation View A representation of the system's operational aspects, focusing on activities such as backups, archiving, upgrades, and monitoring to ensure effective and reliable operation.

P

Package Diagram A diagram in UML that represents the hierarchical organization of packages and their dependencies, effectively modeling whitebox components with detailed structural visibility.

Parallel Invocation An invocation pattern for executing multiple threads of control simultaneously, where each thread operates independently until they converge at a synchronization point to ensure process integrity.

Peer-to-Peer (P2P) Architecture Style Architecture style characterized by a decentralized computing paradigm where each node, or peer, functions simultaneously as both client and server, sharing resources directly with other peers without the need for a central authority.

Persistent Attribute A data element in a class whose value is stored in permanent storage, representing essential information to be retained across sessions or system restarts.

Persistent Object An object that encapsulates specific persistent data, maintaining its state across sessions and application restarts.

Physical Object Class A class that represents tangible entities in the real world, such as Customer, Vehicle, or Product, modeling their attributes and behaviors within the system.

Pipe-and-Filter Architecture Style Architecture style characterized by managing data streams among data manipulation components within a system, where data processing is decomposed into independent components called filters. Filters are interconnected by data channels, or pipes, which facilitate the streaming of data between components in sequence.

Plug-In Architecture Style Architecture style characterized by a design approach that promotes extending an existing system with new functionalities without altering its core structure, allowing plug-in components to be developed, discovered, and dynamically loaded at runtime.

PoC-Based Architecture Evaluation An evaluation approach that develops a Proof-of-Concept (PoC) implementation to validate key aspects of the architecture, particularly useful for demonstrating the feasibility of critical design decisions and identifying potential risks early in development.

Presentation-Abstraction-Control (PAC) Architecture Style Architecture style characterized by structuring interactive systems into a hierarchy of cooperating agents, each comprising three components—Presentation, Abstraction, and Control—to manage user interactions and system data processing.

Prototype-Based Architecture Evaluation An evaluation approach that involves creating a prototype to assess the architecture's suitability in meeting requirements, enabling stakeholders to explore architectural aspects such as usability, performance, and scalability while identifying strengths and weaknesses through hands-on interaction.

Provided Interface An interface that defines the set of services a component offers to other components, enabling interaction and access to its functionalities.

Publisher-Subscriber Architecture Style Architecture style characterized by a decoupled communication mechanism where subscribers register interest in specific channels, publishers broadcast messages to these channels, and a message broker distributes messages only to subscribers of the relevant topics.

R

Reflective Architecture Style Architecture style characterized by a system's ability to maintain information about its own structure and behavior, enabling it to inspect and modify itself dynamically at runtime to adapt to changing requirements or environments.

Required Interface An interface that specifies the services a component depends on from other components, defining the interactions necessary for the component to function correctly.

Requirements Engineering The area of study and practice focused on understanding, documenting, and managing the functional and non-functional requirements of a software system.

Representational State Transfer (REST) Architecture Architecture style characterized by a set of constraints—such as stateless communication, client-server separation, cacheability, a uniform interface, and layered system design—that guide the behavior of distributed, hypermedia systems like the World Wide Web.

S

Scenario-Based Architecture Evaluation An evaluation approach that uses well-defined scenarios to assess how the architecture meets specific requirements or addresses potential challenges, employing techniques like ATAM and CBAM.

Schematic Architecture A structured and visual representation of a system's stable and enduring layout, serving as a foundation for making further architectural decisions.

Sensor-Controller-Actuator (SCA) Architecture Style Architecture style characterized by a control system design in which sensors gather data, controllers process this data to generate control signals, and actuators execute these signals to modify the environment, forming a closed-loop feedback system that enables dynamic adjustments based on the outcomes of previous actions.

Serverless Architecture Architecture style characterized by deploying applications on third-party managed infrastructure, allowing developers to focus on code without managing server hardware or software, as the cloud provider handles provisioning, scaling, and maintenance.

Service-Oriented Architecture (SOA) Style Architecture style characterized by the availability of loosely coupled, self-contained services that perform specific functions and can be invoked over a network through well-defined interfaces and protocols, enabling effective integration and interoperability across diverse applications and platforms.

Sequence Diagram A graphical representation in UML that depicts the control flows among actors and participating objects through the exchange of messages in a structured and sequential manner.

Sequential Invocation An invocation pattern used for executing actions or activities in a strict sequence without branching, often appearing within other patterns like closed loop or parallel invocation.

Service-Based System A system structured to utilize external services, such as cloud services, microservices, or stand-alone services, to fulfill specific parts of its overall functionality, with each service contributing a defined role.

Session A comprehensive record of system usage or user activities, capturing essential data for analysis, auditing, or reporting. Sessions may include system sessions, user sessions, or business transaction sessions, depending on the context and purpose.

Session Class A class designed to manage and represent session information, encapsulating the attributes and behaviors required to log, store, and retrieve data about specific types of sessions, such as system, user, or business transaction sessions.

Shared Repository Architecture Style Architecture style characterized by a data-sharing paradigm where multiple components or applications interact through a common data repository, which serves as a central point for both reading and writing.

Software Architect A senior-level technical expert responsible for designing and overseeing the software architecture, ensuring it meets both functional and non-functional requirements.

Software Architecture The design of a system, encompassing a schematic layout, the definition of architectural views, and the application of architectural tactics to fulfill both functional and non-functional requirements.

Space-Based Architecture Style Architecture style characterized by utilizing a distributed, in-memory data grid, referred to as *space*, to store and share data across multiple nodes in a cluster, enabling communication and coordination between different nodes of a distributed system.

State Machine Diagram A graphical representation in UML that depicts the states of an object and the transitions between those states, triggered by events or conditions during its lifecycle.

Stereotype for Software Artifacts A secondary classification used to specify software artifacts, enhancing clarity and precision in the deployment model by providing additional context and details about the artifacts.

System Control Flow A structured representation of the sequence and interaction of processes or activities that govern the operation of a system or subsystem, often depicted using an Activity Diagram.

System Context Analysis An activity of building a context model for the system, encompassing the boundary context, functional context, information context, and behavioral context.

T

Taxonomy of Architecture Tactics A structured framework that categorizes architecture tactics into types such as software design principles, object-oriented constructs, design patterns, algorithms, machine learning, reusable assets, external services, frameworks and platforms, and operation guidelines to address specific non-functional requirements.

Tier A distinct physical computer system or subsystem within a system architecture, analogous to a device node in a Deployment Diagram.

Tiered System A system with a structural layout consisting of multiple tiers, where each tier represents a distinct physical computer system responsible for specific large-scale functionality and interacts with other tiers to achieve the system's overall objectives.

Timed Invocation An invocation pattern for executing functionality at predefined time intervals or within specific time constraints, ensuring adherence to temporal requirements in system operations.

U

Underlying Fact An established piece of knowledge, shared consensus, assumption, or relevant de facto standard associated with a given non-functional requirement, serving as a basis for its design considerations.

Underlying Policy A set of legal requirements, regulations, established rules, de facto standards, constraints, or industry best practices that must be adhered to when addressing specific non-functional requirements.

Unified Architecture Process A full-blown software methodology specifically designed to facilitate the development of high-quality software architecture in a cost-effective manner.

Use Case Description A structured narrative detailing the control flow of a use case, including its preconditions, postconditions, main scenario, alternative scenarios, and error scenarios.

Use Case Diagram A graphical representation in UML that depicts the relationships between actors and use cases, illustrating the system's functional requirements and interactions.

V

Variability A fundamental concept observed across various aspects of life and products, enabling flexibility, adaptability, and improved efficiency in meeting diverse needs and contexts. In software systems, variability refers to the capacity of a software system to be customized, extended, or configured efficiently to meet specific contexts or requirements.

Variability Adaptation Scheme A structured strategy or design approach enabling functional components to accommodate valid variants of their variation points, either statically at compile time or dynamically at runtime.

Variation Point A specific location within a functional component where variability is introduced, affecting elements such as control flow, logic, interfaces, persistent datasets, or external services.

Variant A valid value or object that can be bound to a corresponding variation point, defining the variability through a set of options that may range from binary choices to open-ended possibilities.

Verification and Validation (V&V) A set of critical processes aimed at ensuring the quality, correctness, and compliance of a software system with its specified requirements, where verification ensures the system is built correctly according to specifications and validation ensures the system meets the intended purpose and user needs.

W

Whitebox Component A component whose internal structure, design, and implementation details are fully visible and accessible to the user or developer, enabling inspection and understanding of its workings.

References

1. F. D. K. Ching, *Architecture: Form, Space, and Order*, 4th ed. Hoboken, NJ: Wiley, 2014.
2. N. Leach, *Cambridge Introduction to Modern Architecture*. Cambridge, UK: Cambridge University Press, 2006.
3. M. Sarkisian, *Designing Tall Buildings: Structure as Architecture*, 2nd ed. Abingdon, UK: Routledge, 2016.
4. M. Shaw and D. Garlan, *Software Architecture: Perspectives on an Emerging Discipline*, Prentice Hall, 1996.
5. L. Bass, P. Clements, and R. Kazman, *Software Architecture in Practice*, 3rd ed. Upper Saddle River, NJ: Addison-Wesley, 2012.
6. R. N. Taylor, N. Medvidovic, and E. M. Dashofy, *Software Architecture: Foundations, Theory, and Practice*. Hoboken, NJ: Wiley, 2009.
7. M. Fowler, Patterns of Enterprise Application Architecture. Boston, MA: Addison-Wesley, 2002.
8. M. Richards, *Software Architecture Patterns*. Sebastopol, CA: O'Reilly Media, 2015.
9. G. Hohpe and B. Woolf, Enterprise Integration Patterns: Designing, Building, and Deploying Messaging Solutions. Boston, MA: Addison-Wesley, 2003.
10. P. Kruchten, *The Rational Unified Process: An Introduction*, 3rd ed. Boston, MA: Addison-Wesley, 2004.
11. N. Rozanski and E. Woods, Software Systems Architecture: Working with Stakeholders Using Viewpoints and Perspectives, 2nd ed. Boston, MA: Addison-Wesley, 2012.
12. G. Booch, J. Rumbaugh, and I. Jacobson, *The Unified Modeling Language User Guide*, 2nd ed. Boston, MA: Addison-Wesley, 2005.
13. ISO/IEC/IEEE, *Systems and Software Engineering — Architecture Description*, ISO/IEC/IEEE 42010:2011, Geneva, Switzerland: International Organization for Standardization, 2011.
14. ISO/IEC/IEEE, Systems and Software Engineering — Software Life Cycle Processes, ISO/IEC/IEEE 12207:2008, Geneva, Switzerland: International Organization for Standardization, 2008.
15. The Open Group, *The Open Group Architecture Framework (TOGAF), Version 9.2*. San Francisco, CA, USA: The Open Group, 2018.
16. ISO/IEC, *Unified Modeling Language (UML)*, ISO/IEC 19505-1:2012, Geneva, Switzerland: International Organization for Standardization, 2012.
17. J. F. S. de Sousa and C. A. D. Barbosa, "Applying MVC Architecture in Web-based Applications," *IEEE Software*, vol. 19, no. 2, pp. 50-57, Mar.-Apr. 2002, doi: https://doi.org/10.1109/52.991331.
18. M. Richards and N. Ford, *Fundamentals of Software Architecture: An Engineering Approach*. Sebastopol, CA, USA: O'Reilly Media, 2020.

S. D. Kim, M. Kim, *Hands-on Software Architecture*,
https://doi.org/10.1007/978-3-032-01184-8

19. G. Hohpe, *The Software Architect Elevator: Redefining the Architect's Role in the Digital Enterprise*. Sebastopol, CA, USA: O'Reilly Media, 2020.
20. N. Ford, M. Richards, P. Avgeriou, and O. Zimmermann, "Architectural Decisions as Code," *IEEE Software*, vol. 38, no. 6, pp. 70–77, Nov./Dec. 2021.
21. P. Clements, F. Bachmann, L. Bass, D. Garlan, J. Ivers, R. Little, R. Nord, and J. Stafford, *Documenting Software Architectures: Views and Beyond.* Boston, MA, USA: Addison-Wesley, 2002.
22. P. Kruchten, "The 4+1 View Model of Architecture," *IEEE Software*, vol. 12, no. 6, pp. 42–50, 1995.
23. E. Gamma, R. Helm, R. Johnson, and J. Vlissides, *Design Patterns: Elements of Reusable Object-Oriented Software*. Boston, MA, USA: Addison-Wesley, 1994.
24. IEEE, "IEEE Recommended Practice for Software Requirements Specifications," IEEE Std 830-1998, 1998.
25. F. A. Cifuentes, D. M. Berry, and N. Juristo, "Classification of Defect Types in Requirements Specifications," in Proc. IEEE Int. Conf. Requirements Eng., 2010, pp. 205–214.
26. P. A. Laplante and M. H. Kassab, *Requirements Engineering for Software and Systems,* 4th ed. Boca Raton, FL, USA: CRC Press, 2022.
27. R. R. Young, *The Requirements Engineering Handbook.* Norwood, MA, USA: Artech House, 2020.
28. Zowghi, D. and Coulin, C., "Requirements Elicitation: A Survey of Techniques, Approaches, and Tools," in *Engineering and Managing Software Requirements,* A. Aurum and C. Wohlin, Eds. Berlin, Germany: Springer, 2005, pp. 19–46.
29. S. Kim, J. Her, and S. Chang, "A theoretical foundation of variability in component-based development," *Information and Software Technology*, Vol.47, No. 10, July 2005.
30. E. Cho, S. Kim, and S. Rhew, "A Domain Analysis and Modeling Methodology for Component Development," *International Journal of Software Engineering and Knowledge Engineering,* Vol. 14, No. 2, March 2004.
31. B. Meyer, *Object-Oriented Software Construction*, 2nd ed. Upper Saddle River, NJ, USA: Prentice Hall, 1997.
32. R. C. Martin, Agile Software Development, Principles, Patterns, and Practices. Upper Saddle River, NJ, USA: Prentice Hall, 2003.
33. ISO/IEC, *Software Engineering – Product Quality – Part 1: Quality Model, ISO/IEC 9126-1:2001,* Geneva, Switzerland: International Organization for Standardization, 2001.
34. J. S. Her, H. Yuan, and S. D. Kim, "Traceability-Centric Model-Driven Object-Oriented Engineering," *Information and Software Technology*, vol. 52, no. 8, pp. 845–870, Aug. 2010.
35. G. Bolch, S. Greiner, H. de Meer, and K. S. Trivedi, Queueing Networks and Markov Chains: Modeling and Performance Evaluation with Computer Science Applications, 2nd ed. Hoboken, NJ, USA: Wiley, 2006.
36. K. C. Kang, S. G. Cohen, J. A. Hess, W. E. Novak, and A. S. Peterson, "Feature-Oriented Domain Analysis (FODA) Feasibility Study," Software Engineering Institute, Carnegie Mellon University, Pittsburgh, PA, USA, Tech. Rep. CMU/SEI-90-TR-021, Nov. 1990.
37. Clements, P., Kazman, R., & Klein, M. *Evaluating Software Architectures: Methods and Case Studies.* Boston, MA, USA: Addison-Wesley Professional, 2002.
38. R. Kazman, J. Asundi, and M. Klein, *The Cost Benefit Analysis Method (CBAM)*, CMU/SEI-2002-TR-035, Pittsburgh, PA, USA: Software Engineering Institute, Carnegie Mellon University, 2002.
39. R. Kazman, L. Bass, G. Abowd, and M. Webb, "SAAM: A Method for Analyzing the Properties of Software Architectures," *Proceedings of the 16th International Conference on Software Engineering (ICSE)*, Sorrento, Italy, 1994, pp. 81–90.

40. Kazman, R., Clements, P., & Klein, M. "Evaluating Software Architectures to Support Reengineering." *Proceedings of the IEEE Working Conference on Reverse Engineering (WCRE)*, pp. 219–228, 1999.
41. D. Garlan, R. Monroe, and D. Wile, "Acme: Architectural Description of Component-Based Systems," in Foundations of Component-Based Systems, Cambridge University Press, 2000, pp. 47–67.
42. SAE International, "Architecture Analysis and Design Language (AADL)," SAE AS5506, Rev. C, Jan. 2017.
43. N. Medvidovic, P. Oreizy, J. E. Robbins, and R. N. Taylor, "Using object-oriented typing to support architectural design in the C2 style," in Proceedings of the ACM SIGSOFT Symposium on Foundations of Software Engineering, 1996, pp. 24–32.
44. R. Allen and D. Garlan, "A formal basis for architectural connection," ACM Transactions on Software Engineering and Methodology (TOSEM), vol. 6, no. 3, pp. 213–249, July 1997.
45. E. Dashofy, A. van der Hoek, and R. N. Taylor, "An infrastructure for the rapid development of XML-based architecture description languages," in Proceedings of the International Conference on Software Engineering (ICSE), 2002, pp. 266–276.
46. J. Magee and J. Kramer, "Dynamic structure in software architectures," in Proceedings of the ACM SIGSOFT Symposium on Foundations of Software Engineering (FSE), 1996, pp. 3–14.
47. D. Luckham and J. Vera, "An event-based architecture definition language," IEEE Transactions on Software Engineering, vol. 21, no. 9, pp. 717–734, Sept. 1995.
48. R. van Ommering, F. van der Linden, J. Kramer, and J. Magee, "The Koala component model for consumer electronics software," *IEEE Computer*, vol. 33, no. 3, pp. 78–85, Mar. 2000.
49. Harel, D., "Statecharts: A Visual Formalism for Complex Systems," *Science of Computer Programming*, vol. 8, no. 3, pp. 231–274, 1987.
50. J. M. Spivey, *The Z Notation: A Reference Manual*, 2nd ed., New York, NY, USA: Prentice Hall, 1992.
51. E. Börger and R. F. Stärk, Abstract State Machines: A Method for High-Level System Design and Analysis, Springer, 2003.
52. Murata, T., "Petri Nets: Properties, Analysis and Applications," *Proceedings of the IEEE*, vol. 77, no. 4, pp. 541–580, Apr. 1989.

Index

S. D. Kim, M. Kim, *Hands-on Software Architecture*,
https://doi.org/10.1007/978-3-032-01184-8

MIX
Papier aus verantwortungsvollen Quellen
Paper from responsible sources
FSC® C105338

If you have any concerns about our products,
you can contact us on
ProductSafety@springernature.com

In case Publisher is established outside the EU,
the EU authorized representative is:
Springer Nature Customer Service Center GmbH
Europaplatz 3, 69115 Heidelberg, Germany

Printed by Libri Plureos GmbH
in Hamburg, Germany